C0-ASJ-536

# .NET Game Programming with DirectX 9.0

ALEXANDRE SANTOS LOBÃO
AND
ELLEN HATTON

.NET Game Programming with DirectX 9.0

Copyright ©2003 by Alexandre Sántos Lobão and Ellen Hatton

All rights reserved. No part of this work may be reproduced or transmitted in any form or by any means, electronic or mechanical, including photocopying, recording, or by any information storage or retrieval system, without the prior written permission of the copyright owner and the publisher.

ISBN (pbk): 1-59059-051-1

Printed and bound in the United States of America 12345678910

Trademarked names may appear in this book. Rather than use a trademark symbol with every occurrence of a trademarked name, we use the names only in an editorial fashion and to the benefit of the trademark owner, with no intention of infringement of the trademark.

Technical Reviewer: David Jung

Editorial Directors: Dan Appleman, Gary Cornell, Simon Hayes, Karen Watterson, John Zukowski

Managing Editor: Grace Wong

Project Manager: Sofia Marchant

Copy Editor: Ami Knox

Production Manager: Kari Brooks

Compositor: Diana Van Winkle, Van Winkle Design Group

Artist and Cover Designer: Kurt Krames

Indexer: Lynn Armstrong

Manufacturing Manager: Tom Debolski

Distributed to the book trade in the United States by Springer-Verlag New York, Inc., 175 Fifth Avenue, New York, NY, 10010 and outside the United States by Springer-Verlag GmbH & Co. KG, Tiergartenstr. 17, 69112 Heidelberg, Germany.

In the United States, phone 1-800-SPRINGER, email orders@springer-ny.com, or visit http://www.springer-ny.com.

Outside the United States, fax +49 6221 345229, email orders@springer.de, or visit http://www.springer.de.

For information on translations, please contact Apress directly at 2560 9th Street, Suite 219, Berkeley, CA 94710.

Phone 510-549-5930, fax: 510-549-5939, email info@apress.com, or visit http://www.apress.com.

The information in this book is distributed on an "as is" basis, without warranty. Although every precaution has been taken in the preparation of this work, neither the author nor Apress shall have any liability to any person or entity with respect to any loss or damage caused or alleged to be caused directly or indirectly by the information contained in this work.

*To the funniest game of all: Real Life*
*And to its Great and Omnipotent Designer*

# Contents at a Glance

# Contents

# Foreword

Ever since I built my first S100 Z80 PC kit, I was hooked. That was 1975. Twenty-eight years later, I still have very little life away from my "babies"—my array of systems. I use them to work, to write, to explore the outside world, and to play. I've written games and reviewed games, but mostly I've played games of all kinds. I've played Adventure, Hammurabi, and air traffic control simulators on the Z80—with 48KB of RAM. More recently, I've had to attend 12-step meetings to get over my addiction to Ages. Age of Mythology is my latest obsession. I only wish I had the source. It seems to have a pretty nasty memory/resource leak.

When I heard that Alexandre and Ellen were writing a book on gaming, I jumped at the chance to take an early look. When I heard that the book focused on Visual Basic, I was convinced that I wanted to read it (and got cajoled into writing this foreword). It's been a long road for BASIC. I used (the other) Bill's BASIC on my Z80 system and even wrote CP/M systems software using the BASIC-80 compiler in the early 1980s. BASIC has always been seen as a fun little language to write simple "toy" applications—something like the "Easy-Bake Oven" language with a small lightbulb for heat. Visual Basic 1.0 changed a lot of minds, but Visual Basic 5.0 and its "real" compiler changed a lot more. Visual Basic .NET (which I fondly call "Visual Fred" due to its lack of similarity to any previous version of Visual Basic) is a deadly serious full-featured development tool. It's suitable for authoring virtually anything. No, I would not write a device driver with Visual Basic .NET, but I'll bet *you* could. It's a great choice for serious developers because it's so easy to learn and use. For MBASIC-80 developers, it will be somewhat of a challenge to learn, but for Visual Basic folks, it will take no time at all to come back up to speed (so to speak).

DirectX (in my opinion) is the new de facto "Windows" interface of the gaming industry. In the early days, no computer would sell (no matter how technically superior it was) if it didn't run Lotus 1-2-3. That's because the application software was so closely tied to the hardware. When an application shipped in the DOS world, it had to have drivers for your printer or you couldn't print and drivers for your video card or you couldn't run the application at all. In those days, game companies got in bed with the video card companies and wrote straight to their newest hardware. There was only a slim chance a game would work with some other card. Windows changed some of that. It standardized video management, printing, memory management, and more to help application developers write just applications and leave all of the hardware worries to Microsoft and device driver developers. The game folks found that Windows simply got in the way; it wasn't nearly fast enough for anything except solitaire—and that was sluggish. When DirectX arrived, a new dawn appeared for the game developers. Now they had a much faster and generic way to write to the hardware and not worry (so much) about performance. Now (nine versions later) DirectX games are pervasive. They're fast, fun, easy to install (and uninstall), and easy to write, maintain, and support.

As far as the technical content of the book, in case you're wondering, I took an extra close look at Chapter 6 where Alexandre and Ellen touch on ADO.NET. I think their approach to data access is fine. It's not that tough when you don't have to worry about more than a single user and more than a few thousand rows, but they don't lead you astray.

Okay. I don't make a living writing games. I'm not that smart, and I couldn't talk my spouse into doing something that's challenging *and* fun but would not return me enough to buy groceries. My focus is Visual Basic, data access, and SQL Server. I like playing games, but I would like so much more to be able to write my own. I expect the easy-to-read tutorial style that Alexandre and Ellen use will make that very easy for both of us—amateur and pro alike.

Enjoy.

*William R. Vaughn*
*Microsoft MVP and author of* ADO.NET and ADO
Examples and Best Practices for VB Programmers, Second Edition
*President, Beta V Corporation* (http://www.betav.com)
*Redmond, Washington*

# About the Authors

**Alexandre Santos Lobão** got his first computer in 1981, when he was 12, and immediately started to create simple games in Basic. Since then, computers have evolved massively, and so has he. Graduating with a bachelor's degree in computer science in 1991, he founded that same year with six friends a company that came to be known as a synonym for high-quality services in Brasilia, Brazil: Hepta Informática.

Besides his excellent work in many software development areas, from financial to telecommunication, he never forgot his first passion, and has always worked as a nonprofessional game programmer. From 1997 to 1999 he also worked at Virtually Real (`http://www.vrealware.com`), a virtual Australian amateur game programming company founded by Craig Jardine.

At the end of 2000, Alexandre started searching for new horizons and, leaving the company he helped to create, entered Microsoft as a consultant. Looking at the new and extremely interesting possibilities offered by the .NET Framework, he decided to take everything he's learned over the last decade and apply it to this new development platform.

**Ellen Hatton** is a computer science undergraduate at Edinburgh University. She was exposed to computers at a very early age and has been fascinated with them ever since. Her first experience of computer games was playing Dread Dragon Doom, at which she quickly excelled at the age of 5. She's been hooked on games ever since.

Ellen is not only interested in computers. She skis frequently, amongst other sports, and enjoys general student life in the bustling Scottish capital, Edinburgh.

As her choice of degree suggests, Ellen still finds computers very interesting and is constantly looking for new challenges. This book is the latest.

# About the
# Technical Reviewer

**David Jung** has over ten years' programming experience with leading organizations such as Mullin Consulting, Johnson & Johnson, City of Hope National Medical Center, Moss Software, ARCO Products, and Ernst & Young. He has specialized in distributed application and data warehousing solutions over the Internet and intranets using Visual Basic, C#, and other Internet technology.

Mr. Jung has coauthored an extensive array of books and articles on programming and debugging Visual Basic, Microsoft Outlook, Java, and other Internet solutions that have been published internationally. He frequently is a speaker at seminars and user groups discussing how Visual Basic, Java, C#, and Internet technology can be integrated into business solutions. He has published several Microsoft Windows utility programs that help track down and eliminate system crashes as well as help prevent script-based viruses from spreading on Windows-based computers. Two of his programs, DLL Checker and VBS Defender, were reviewed by PC World and were given an Editor's Choice award, and have been sold to users all over the world.

# Acknowledgments

## Alexandre Lobão

To Kentaro Takahashi, the guy who helped me take my first steps in the computer graphics world, back at university about 15 years ago, and helped me with all my previously published works in this area. I think this is a late acknowledgement, but better late than never!

To Homero Picollo, the best teacher at my university, who guided me through these first steps.

To Craig Jardine, Jonty Bell, and all the guys from Virtually Real, who believed in my work even before they had seen it!

To Evali Gamarra and Keniston Rodrigues, who helped me take my first steps with DirectX.

To Peter Blackburn, who believed in my dream, and to all the Apress guys who helped me to make it come true.

To Tom Miller, the development leader from the Microsoft's Managed DirectX team, who always had the right answer for me, and great patience.

To Phillip Taylor, the managed DirectX program manager, and to all members of the Managed DirectX SIG, who always supported me when I needed.

To Igor Ripoll, who gave me invaluable logistics help, which made this book possible.

To Igor Sinkovec and Waldivar Cesar, who helped me with their great graphics skills.

To Bruce Shelley, Paul Sullivan, Geoff Howland, and Sarbasst Hassanpour, who kindly gave me permission to publish their own vision about game creation as appendices in the book.

To Ellen Hatton, who helped me by translating my barely legible drafts to real chapters, and to David Jung, who reviewed all the code and increased the book's quality as much as possible.

To everyone who helped me in any way to create this book (so if you are not mentioned before, feel free to include your name here!).

And, most of all, to my family, who supported me even when I was stealing time from them to write this book.

Thanks to all of you.

Or, in good and loud Portuguese, "Muito Obrigado!!"

## Ellen Hatton

I also have a few acknowledgements to make:

To Alexandre for being the most understanding and talented person I've ever had the pleasure to work with. It was your ideas that made this book—not anyone else's. It's been fun working with you.

To Peter Blackburn, you've been a constant source of support. You were the person who introduced me to this project, for which I am eternally grateful.

There are too many people to thank you all individually, but you know who you are so thanks for everything. From a cup of tea to a friendly chat—it all helped.

Also thanks to my family for getting me here in the first place and always encouraging me and my crazy ideas.

Thanks again.

# Credits

Figure 4-5, page 217: Sid Meier's Civilization®, Civilization®, and Civ® are U.S. registered trademarks. Sid Meier's Civilization® courtesy of Infogrames Interactive © 2002 Infogrames Interactive, Inc. All Rights Reserved. Used With Permission.

Figure 6-2, page 350: Leisure Suit Larry is a trademark of Sierra Entertainment, Inc., and is used with permission.

Figures 6-3, 6-4, and 6-5, pages 351–352: Sam & Max Hit the Road® and The Secret of Monkey Island® © 2003 LucasArts Entertainment Company LLC & ™ or ® as indicated. All rights reserved. Used under authorization. LucasArts and the LucasArts logo are registered trademarks of Lucasfilm Ltd.

Figures A-1 and A-2, page 597: American McGee's Alice™ Software © 2000 Electronic Arts Inc. All rights reserved. Portions © 2000 Rogue Entertainment, Inc. All rights reserved. This product contains software technology licensed from Id Software, Inc. Id Technology © 2000 Id Software, Inc. All rights reserved. Electronic Arts, the Electronic Arts logo and American McGee's Alice are trademarks or registered trademarks of Electronic Arts Inc. in the U.S. and/or other countries. The Rogue Entertainment logo is a trademark of Rogue Entertainment, Inc.

Figure A-3, page 600: Quake® is a trademark of Id Software.

Figure A-4, page 600: Unreal Tournament ©1999–2001 Epic Games Inc. Created by Epic Games, Inc. in collaboration with Digital Extremes. Unreal and the Unreal logos are trademarks of Epic Games, Inc. All rights reserved. All other trademarks are the property of their respective companies.

Figures A-5 and A-6, pages 602–603: Clive Barker's Undying™ © 2000 Electronic Arts Inc. Undying, EA GAMES and the EA GAMES logo are trademarks or registered of Electronic Arts Inc. in the U.S. and/or other countries. All rights reserved. EA GAMES is an Electronic Arts™ brand.

Figure C-1, page 617: Quake® is a trademark of Id Software.

Figure C-3, page 621: PAC-MAN® ©1980 Namco Ltd., All Rights Reserved. Courtesy of Namco Holding Corp.

Figure C-4, page 623: GALAGA® ©1980 Namco Ltd., All Rights Reserved. Courtesy of Namco Holding Corp.

Figure C-5, page 624: GAUNTLET® DARK LEGACY™ © 1998–2000 Midway Games West Inc. GAUNTLET DARK LEGACY is a trademark of Midway Games West Inc.

# Preface

THIS BOOK IS intended to fill a gap that exists in books about game programming: Some are too basic, and some are too advanced, so intermediate programmers who want to create something new can't find anything to meet their needs.

The main idea of this book is this: If you can do it the easy way, do it the easy way. Of course, we explore some very advanced concepts, like voice generation and recognition, multiplayer games, and the basics of 3-D game creation. However, we always look for the simplest way to do something. And if there's no easy way, then we just create some basic classes that do the dirty work, and create everything else over these classes.

The whole book is designed to be read in a continuous way. In Chapter 1, we start by creating a very simple game while presenting the basics of collision detection. Chapter 2 shows how to build a new game, using the concepts presented in Chapter 1 and adding new explanations and examples about artificial intelligence in games.

In the following chapters, we continue to build new games and explore new topics relating to game programming, such as the basics of sprite creation, scrolling games, adventure games, multiplayer features, voice generation, porting a game to Pocket PC, and much more. We start with the basics and increase the complexity as we go along, so that by the time you come to the advanced topics, you have all the background you need to gain the most from them.

But there's one more thing that makes this book unique: our discussion about several nonprogramming topics related to game creation—for example, how to design good character movement, the history of adventure games, and how to create an adventure game from a basic storyline.

We don't restrict ourselves to showing only advanced game programming techniques, like DirectX and the Speech API. We teach you some simple tricks that don't require a lot of expertise, like how to control simple dialog in adventure games, using data from a Microsoft Access database, or how to create a nonrectangular window to add some extra spice to a game's screens.

Although we don't explore all the details about managed DirectX 9.0, this book is a very good starting point for Managed DirectX 9.0 programming because we delve into the basics of every DirectX component—Direct3D, DirectSound, Direct-Music, DirectPlay, DirectInput, and DirectShow—creating reusable classes that will make it easier to use each of these components.

We also discuss other programming topics apart from DirectX, including ADO.NET, Speech API for voice generation, GDI+ for creating simple games, programming for Pocket PCs with the .NET Compact Framework, and creating multithreading games. Since we show you how to create a set of reusable classes throughout the book, after finishing the book you'll be able to create your own games much more easily by simply sticking these classes together.

This book is also a good starting point for those who want to understand the basics of .NET programming, but it is NOT intended to teach .NET programming on its own. Of course, we talk about many important .NET concepts, and every new concept in Visual Basic .NET programming is explained, but it's not our aim to write an exhaustive explanation of all that VB .NET has to offer.

Nor is this book intended to provide a route to the professional game programming world, since we do not go deep enough into some essential aspects professional game developers need to know. However, you can think of this book as a first step into this world, since we do provide insights into important concepts such as the need to create a good game project and organizing the game's team, as well as appendixes written by professionals from the game industry that serve as guides to game creation.

# Introduction

## .NET—A Whole New Game Horizon

FOR THOSE WHO have been inside a cave for the last 2 years, .NET is Microsoft's new paradigm for creating the next generation of Internet programs, allowing any site on the Web to offer and use services, and joining the efforts from programmers around the world to make things better.

But .NET is much more. You can create stand-alone programs with it (as we'll see in this book), and you can create programs targeted at many different platforms. For example, if your program runs in a browser, it'll appear using the full functionality offered by the browser. If instead it is running on a mobile device, such as a handheld computer, it'll use only the functionality offered by that device. We can expect to see .NET support for many new devices using different user interfaces (like voice recognition) to show up in the next few years.

In short, we can say that .NET is the next big step in home computing. First, the PC became a standard for home and office computers. Then we saw Windows offering the new standard for programmers and users, with a graphical interface and the mouse as a new input device. Now, we have an open door to many new devices and user interfaces, and, most importantly, interaction between programs, allowing programmers to build over previously created services and give the end user more sophisticated services every time, with less programming and higher quality.

Of course, the .NET Framework is still taking its first steps, but it's already worth a closer look for anyone seriously interested in programming in general, particularly game programming.

## Why Use .NET?

Certainly there are many good reasons to use .NET besides the fact that it's a new programming paradigm that will probably take on the world in the next few years. Let's just review some of them:

- **.NET is multiplatform:** Although Java had promised this before, and sadly didn't make it, .NET had a bigger industrial commitment, not only by Microsoft and its partners, even before the launch of the final version of Visual Studio. One example: There are many initiatives to make a .NET JIT (just-in-time) compiler in Linux and other operating systems. Oh, yes, and there's another advantage over Java when running on a Web site: The .NET programs are just-in-time compiled before they run, and that means that they run in machine-native code (not interpreted), which makes for better performance. Another interesting point is that the compiled program is stored in memory, so the next executions don't have to pass to the compiler unless the computer is turned off or needs to free the memory used by the program.

- **.NET is NOT just a new programming environment:** It's a whole new framework of applications and services, many of them already released by Microsoft, and many others to come from Microsoft and other companies.

- **.NET is service based:** There are many servers that expose special features that we can use, and there are a huge collection of services coming from Microsoft and many other companies. What does this mean for game developers? For example, do you want to make your game speak, or understand what the player says? Do you need to add multiplayer features? Do you want to create a 3-D texture-mapped environment? Well, some services already do all of this and more. Why code again and again if someone has already done it?

- **.NET is multilingual:** You can write your .NET program in any language supported by the Visual Studio environment—right now, that means Visual Basic, Visual C#, Visual C++, FORTRAN, Visual J#, and COBOL, among others. Microsoft created a single and open environment to run it all, so you can write your programs in any language in the same programming console. Other languages are already being developed by other companies: APL, Pascal, Eiffel, Haskell, ML, Oberon, Perl, Python, Scheme, Smalltalk. Just choose the one you like best, or create your own!

Of course, many other reasons exist for using .NET, like the extensive XML support or the enhanced data access features. When you start coding with Visual Studio, you'll see a lot more: The environment is even cleverer than previous versions, and helps the programmer a lot. It makes game creation a real pleasure, because you can concentrate on what you want your game to do, not how to make it.

## Why Use Visual Basic?

Until Visual Basic 4.0, the code generated by the compiler was in fact a pseudo-code, interpreted by a special DLL at execution time. The performance for some tasks was very poor, but we could already make some simple games on it, if the graphics weren't very demanding.

In Visual Basic 5.0, Microsoft brought in part of the Visual C++ development team to create a native-code compiler. The performance increase was astonishing: We could see some benchmarks for floating-point calculations where the VB code performance was almost the same as VC++, but the graphical operations were still much slower than in C++.

In Visual Basic 6.0, all the internal routines for drawing controls on screen and many of the features were refactored to aim for better performance. With this version, we could already create somewhat sophisticated games using COM inter-faces to access DirectX features.

Now, we have Visual Studio .NET. As we saw before, Visual Studio .NET is a multilanguage environment, which means, besides other things, that all languages share the same compiler. Therefore, there'll be a little difference, if any at all, in the performance of this compiler for each language.

It's interesting to consider an interview with one of the Doom creators that appeared in a games magazine some years ago. When it was released, Doom was simply the best game ever from the technical point of view of creating a 3-D texture-mapped environment. And this guy basically said that Doom was proof to all assembly "pin-heads" that everything didn't have to be coded in assembly in order to achieve the best performance, because the game had just two assembly routines: one that drew a point on screen, and one that drew a line. Everything else was written in C.

Time has passed. When the first reviewers looked at this book, they told me, "Game programming in Visual Basic? Using .NET Framework? Are you sure?" They thought Visual Basic performance could be a real problem, and that .NET Framework was designed only to create Web services. But they were wrong.

Just look at games like the X-COM series, or the SIMCity series. We don't see anything that we can't do in Visual Basic. They aren't graphically intensive games. For fast-action shooters like Quake, we confess that Visual Basic won't be the best choice for programming for a while. But for other sophisticated games, if you can do them with a simple language like VB, why use assembly or C? Just think about the simplicity of coding and debugging, and you'll see there's no other choice. Even some hardcore C++ programmers gave us very good feedback about this book, telling us how they were astonished with the ease of creating games in Visual Basic that still have acceptable performance.

But you don't have to just take our word for it. Just read the rest of the book, and you'll see for yourself.

## A Game Starts with a Good Idea

Although the games released nowadays are more and more graphics intensive, the main point in a game is sometimes forgotten: the playability.

We see games with breathtaking graphics, amazing cut-scenes, and 3-D worlds to make your eyes pop out, but many of them are really annoying to play. Even when a game's responsiveness is okay, sometimes the gameplay isn't clear or isn't fair.

What about playing an old Pac-Man? With all these gorgeous games around, Pac-Man and the earlier versions of Mario Brothers on Nintendo are still successes with kids.

We aren't here to tell you to forget everything and get back to basics. Instead, remember that a good game always starts with a good idea, and sometimes that's enough.

One of the most cloned games ever, Tetris, was designed by a single man, a Russian programmer. It's still interesting to play after all these years, and, of course, we have a Tetris clone here too—our version of a "Hello World" program in the first chapter.

You could say that Tetris is one in a million, and we'd agree. But if you were to say that creating a good game by yourself is only possible if it's as simple as Tetris, then we'd have to disagree. Older guys will remember Another World, a game that has a sequel called FlashBack. The game had very good graphics and sound for its time, with very nice character animation and various cut-scenes that completed the game story by showing the characters and a fantastic world from many different points of view. Well, a single person, a French programmer, designed this game.

Today we can see many sites on the Web with games from amateur game programmers. Some of them are really good, with high-quality graphics and sound; and, most important of all, almost all are very playable too, maybe because they were designed by people who love to create and play games but don't have the urge to make money.

In this book, we'll see many tips and tricks that will help anyone to design his or her own games alone. However, if you can count on someone to help you, do.

After all, there's more to a game than just a good idea. . . .

## A Game Is More Than Just a Good Idea

Although a game must start with a good idea, there is a lot more to the game programming world than our humble minds can imagine. Let's look at some points we must keep in mind when we start our game project:

- **Music:** Although we can always make a game using only bleeps and bloops, good background music and nice sound effects for game actions (shooting, dying, earning bonus points, etc.) do make our games better. Even if we don't plan to have a music expert on our staff, we can't forget that it'll take a lot of time to look for music with the correct ambiance and the best sound effects among the millions we'll find on the Internet or in CD libraries.

- **Drawing:** It's not good practice to use graphics ripped off from someone else's game, because our game will lack originality and we can also be prosecuted. Since not everyone can draw anything better than a square house and a smiley sun, we'll want a good artist (or several of them) on our game team.

- **Colors:** Coloring things on the computer is very different from coloring it on paper. If our artists can't color using a graphics tool, we'll need someone who can.

- **Animation:** Creating animated graphics is slightly different from creating static ones. Almost everyone can draw a nice tree, for example, but to draw a walking man or a flying bird demands someone with animation experience. Even when our games don't use animated sprites, don't forget that we may need an animated introduction or cut-scenes.

- **Code:** Well, without this one we would be reading a board game book.

- **Level design:** The level designers are the ones who'll always be working to ensure optimum gameplay and the most enjoyable playing experience for players.

- **Quality assurance:** If we can't afford to have a very good quality assurance team, we're better off not bothering to make games. A buggy game is by far the worst thing that can happen in a game company's profile.

- **Project management:** Working with many people with different skills and personalities requires an organized way to get the best from each of them. Even when we are working alone, we mustn't underestimate the importance of a good project: If we don't set some milestones to control our project, we may work on it forever and never see any good results. It's far beyond the scope of this book to teach you how to manage a project, but we strongly suggest you take a look at some stuff on this topic, if you've never had the opportunity of working with an organized team.

- **Etc.:** There'll be lots more too, but in general we must be ready to deal with any new and unexpected problems.

The task of creating a commercial game nowadays is anything but simple. The time when the "lone wolf" programmer could create a new hit and even get rich with it is most certainly over. Nevertheless, let's keep one thing in mind: This book is for those who love game design, who will be happy with making games just to have the pleasure of seeing people enjoy their ideas. If you want to make professional games, or if you want to learn DirectX or .NET, this book is a really good starting point, but there's a lot more you need to study before entering the game industry.

As we have seen, it takes a lot of hard work and coordinated effort to make a blockbuster game nowadays, but don't be scared off by the size of the mountain we are about to climb. Remember: Maybe your game will be the next Pac-Man, Tetris, or Flight Simulator.

Just keep in mind one thing: A game *starts* with a good idea!

## How to Read This Book

This book aims to be a practical guide for game programming, and to get the most out of it, we suggest that you start each chapter by running the chapter's sample game from the CD-ROM that comes with this book. Open the project in Visual Studio .NET, and compile and run it. Play for a while, looking at the details of the game, so that when you start reading each chapter you'll know what the chapter is about.

To make it easier to understand the main concepts in each chapter, we have divided the chapters into five main sections. Next we'll describe the parts of each chapter.

## Introduction and Technical Background

At the beginning of each chapter, we have a little introduction that presents the chapter's sample game and the ideas we'll explore in the chapter, and one or more sections presenting specific information about the technical background needed for the chapter's sample game.

For example, in Chapter 4, we introduce DirectInput and create a scrolling game, so we have sections describing what DirectInput is and how to create reusable classes to include DirectInput features, plus sections describing the ideas behind creating a scrolling game, and technical tips to follow when creating such a game.

## The Game Proposal

In a commercial game, the game proposal is the document we'll show to everyone, even discuss with our kids, to achieve a clear understanding about what the game will really be. If everyone agrees that it'll be a great game, then we advance to the next step. If not, then we'll improve it until we reach the desired result.

In this book, we are working with very simplified game proposals that deal with the minimum amount of information needed for a clear understanding of the sample game. A real game proposal follows the basic rules of creating ordinary projects, showing the details gathered in the early analysis and user interviews.

## The Game Project

While the game proposal tells us how the game will work, including artificial intelligence, user interaction, and graphical styling, in a language that anyone can understand (especially the sponsor who is paying the game development team), the game project document includes the technical mumbo-jumbo that will guide the developing team through the code phase. Again, in this book we'll deal with *very* simplified game projects, because even with the simplest games we must have a project.

## The Coding Phase

This is where we'll show the main parts of the code, including highlights of what is new in the .NET world. Instead of showing pages and pages of code, we'll show only the essential parts that are instrumental in the understanding of the game mechanics, along with explanations about each code listing. The full code is on the accompanying CD-ROM.

### Final Touches

When a game is being developed, lots of people have ideas. Some of these ideas are very practical and easy to implement, and others are not so. The team must decide if an idea will be implemented in a future version of the game or if implementation of that idea is worth a delay in the schedule in order to achieve a better game.

In each chapter, we have included some of these ideas in the "Adding the Final Touches" section; and like in real-life games, some of the ideas are implemented, and others are just suggestions for you to try and further improve the game on your own.

### Summary

In the last part of each chapter, we'll look back at what we have discussed to help you check if you have understood the chapter's main concepts, or if you need to go back and reread something.

In the next section, we'll preview the sample games and the main ideas covered in each of the chapters.

## Book and CD-ROM Contents

In this book, we'll create five different games spanning nine chapters and a bonus chapter at the end.

Each game will have two versions, developed in two different chapters. For example, the first version of our little adventure game, Magic KindergarteN., will be created in Chapter 6, which will explore DirectShow and ADO.NET. A second version of this game is featured in Chapter 7, where we'll include voice generation by using the Speech API.

There are a couple exceptions. In Chapter 9, we'll create a very simple game without including a second version in this book. Chapter 3 is dedicated to introducing DirectX and Direct3D, presenting some uncomplicated samples to make the explanations clearer.

As for the book's CD-ROM, it is organized in a manner that matches the book's organization: It has one directory per chapter that contains the chapter sample game. In the Chapter 8 directory we have two samples, so there is a separate subdirectory for each of them. The CD-ROM programs were created and tested with DirectX 9.0 and Visual Studio 2003 (code-named Everett) Beta 1. There are some known issues when running the games with Everett on reference rasterizers of laptops that will probably be fixed in the final versions. Any updates on the code will be available for download at the Apress site (http://www.apress.com). The complete DirectX 9.0 is also available in the CD-ROM, under the DirectX directory.

In the next sections, we give a brief description of the contents of each chapter.

## Chapter 1–.Nettrix: GDI+ and Collision Detection

In the first chapter, we introduce the concept of collision detection in games, present simple algorithms to manage the detection of collision between objects in a game, and introduce basic concepts about the GDI+, the new graphical library used by the .NET Framework to perform simple graphical operations.

In this chapter, we create a Tetris clone called .Nettrix to illustrate the use of these concepts.

## Chapter 2–.Netterpillars: Artificial Intelligence and Sprites

Here we examine the concept of object-oriented programming, along with a glossary of related terms. We also explain the idea of creating a library of game classes, which can be used in further game developments to improve the game quality and the game project schedule.

In this chapter, we also provide a brief introduction to artificial intelligence in games, presenting some classical problems we need to deal with in our games along with some suggestions about how to solve them.

The chapter's sample game, .Netterpillars, is a Snakes clone that explores the concepts presented in the chapter. Here we create the first reusable class of this book—a GDI+-based sprite.

## Chapter 3–Managed DirectX First Steps: Direct3D Basics and DirectX vs. GDI+

Chapter 3 presents Managed DirectX 9.0, exploring the Direct3D basics such as the use of matrix transformations, transparent texturing, and colored lights. Here we also discuss how to decide which graphics library (DirectX or GDI+) to use depending on the game type.

In this chapter, we have no game, just a simple application in which we'll exercise each of this chapter's concepts.

### Chapter 4—River Pla.Net: Tiled Game Fields, Scrolling, and DirectAudio

In Chapter 4, we discuss the creation of scrolling games, exploring the possibilities of scrolling effects and presenting some technical tips on how to create such games. We also discuss the use of tiled game fields in games and demonstrate some tricks to help you create better tiles.

Using the Direct3D concepts presented in Chapter 3, we create two new classes for our game library that will be used in almost all of the later chapters: a Direct3D-based Sprite class and a Direct3D-based GameEngine class.

We also explore the basics of DirectSound and DirectMusic, creating two extra classes that will help us to add sound effects and background music to our games.

Using the classes and concepts discussed in this chapter, we create a River Raid clone called River Pla.Net.

### Chapter 5—River Pla.Net II: DirectInput and Writing Text to Screen

Here we look at the basics of DirectInput, the DirectX library used to manage input devices, including how to use joystick force-feedback features and creating three simple classes for our library that control mice, keyboards, and joysticks. We also introduce the use of fonts in our games by creating a new class that will help us to write on screen.

With the newly created game classes, we improve the River Pla.Net game to include a status line and joystick control and add new river obstacles that trigger the force-feedback features.

### Chapter 6—Magic KindergarteN.: Adventure Games, ADO.NET, and DirectShow

In Chapter 6 we briefly trace the evolution of adventure games and provide tips for you to follow when creating games of this genre.

We present the managed libraries that give us access to basic DirectShow features, which allow us to play streaming media, like videos and MP3 files, and we create a class to help us play videos in our games.

We also give a very simple introduction to data access using ADO.NET—just enough to help you read the chapter's sample game data.

In this chapter, we illustrate the concepts learned by creating a very simple adventure game with five screens, some action verbs, and a basic inventory control.

## Chapter 7—Magic KindergarteN. II: Animation Techniques and Speech API

Here we discuss animation techniques while presenting some samples and simple tricks that can help improve a game's animation.

We also introduce the Speech API, the application programming interface used for speech recognition and generation, and create a simple game class that will allow us to include voice generation in our games.

Using the concepts presented in this chapter, we create a second version of the Magic KindergarteN. game, including dialogs between game characters and voice generation, with associated mouth animations that are dynamically generated according to the sounds of speech.

## Chapter 8—.Netterpillars II: Multiplayer Games and DirectPlay

In Chapter 8, we discuss the challenges associated with creating a multiplayer game, and present a list of tips compiled from various game development teams. We look at DirectPlay, the DirectX library used to add network support to our games, and include a new class in our library that can be used to add multiplayer features to our games in an easy way.

Using the class we just created, we implement a second version of .Netterpillars, the game created in Chapter 2.

## Chapter 9—D-iNfEcT: Multithreading, Nonrectangular Windows, and Access to Nonmanaged Code

Chapter 9 explores various concepts that can help add some extra spice to our games: the use of multithreading, the creation of nonrectangular windows, and access to nonmanaged code, like the old Windows' APIs.

With these concepts, we create a very simple multithreaded game, called D-iNfEcT, which generates lots of germs on your screen that must be caught before time is up. This chapter illustrates how to create addictive games that can be easy and fun.

## Bonus Chapter: Porting .Nettrix to Pocket PC

In this bonus chapter, we discuss the problems we face when porting games to different devices, and present the .NET Compact Framework.

Using these concepts, we create a second version of our Tetris clone by porting the sample game created in Chapter 1 to run on a Pocket PC.

## Appendixes

In order to give you a sense of what professional gamers think about game creation, we have included as appendixes articles from four professionals who already work in the game industry:

- "The State of PC Gaming," by Paul Sullivan

- "Motivations in Games," by Sarbasst Hassanpour

- "How Do I Make Games?—A Path to Game Development," by Geoff Howland

- "Guidelines for Developing Successful Games," by Bruce Shelley

These guys kindly let us republish their articles, and we hope you enjoy them as much as we did.

# CHAPTER 1

# .Nettrix: GDI+ and Collision Detection

IN THIS CHAPTER we examine the basic concepts of GDI+, the extended library for native graphic operations on Windows systems, and discuss one of the most important aspects of game development: the collision detection algorithms. Although game developers use GDI+ functions to draw images on screen, collision detection algorithms are responsible for making the drawings interact with each other, allowing a program to know when an image is over another one and to take the appropriate action, such as bouncing a ball when it hits a wall.

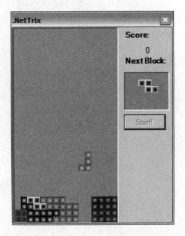

*Figure 1-1.*
*.Nettrix, this chapter's*
*sample game*

To accomplish these goals and illustrate these concepts, we'll be creating a game called .Nettrix. "Hello World" is always the first program that's written when learning a new programming language. When learning to program games, Tetris is considered to be the best game to try first. In this simple game we can see many basic concepts at work—for example, basic graphic routines, collision detection, and handling user input.

To begin, we'll look at the basic GDI+ concepts and examine the idea of collision detection algorithms, so you'll have the necessary technical background to code the sample game for this chapter.

## Basic GDI+ Concepts

GDI+ is the new .NET SDK class-based application programming interface (API) for 2-D graphics, imaging, and typography.

With some substantial improvements over the old GDI, including better performance and the capacity to run even on a 64-bit system, GDI+ is worth a look. The new features in GDI+ are discussed in the following sections.

### Path Gradients

Path gradients allow programs to fill 2-D shapes with gradients, with great flexibility, as shown in Figure 1-2.

*Figure 1-2. Using path gradients*

### Alpha Blending

GDI+ works with ARGB colors, which means that each color is defined by a combination of red, green, and blue values, plus an alpha value relating to its degree of transparency. We can assign a transparency value from 0 (totally transparent) to 255 (opaque). Values between these two make the colors partially transparent to different degrees, showing the background graphics, if any are present.

In Figure 1-3 we have a rectangle with different degrees of transparency; if we had an image below it, we could see it, just like looking though glass.

*Figure 1-3. Changing the alpha from 0 to 255 in a solid color bitmap*

## Cardinal Splines

Cardinal splines allow the creation of smooth lines joining a given set of points, as shown in Figure 1-4.

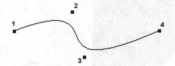

*Figure 1-4. Creating a smooth curve that joins points with a spline*

As we can see, the spline curve has fixed starting and ending points (in Figure 1-4, the points marked 1 and 4), and two extra points that will "attract" the curve, but won't pass through them (points 2 and 3).

## Applying Transformations to Objects Using a 3×3 Matrix

Applying transformations (rotation, translation, or scale) is especially useful when dealing with a sequence of transformations, as they speed up performance. A sample of some transformations is shown in Figure 1-5.

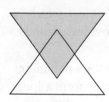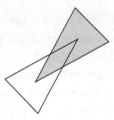

*Figure 1-5. Applying a rotation and scale transformation over a figure*

## *Antialiasing*

Antialiasing is the smoothing of graphics, avoiding a stepped look when, for example, a bitmap is enlarged. An image exemplifying this is shown in Figure 1-6.

Nonzoomed Image

Zoomed Image,
Not Antialiased

Zoomed Image,
Antialiased

*Figure 1-6. Applying antialiasing to an image*

**NOTE** *In this book, we'll show examples of the first two new GDI+ features: path gradients in this chapter and alpha blending in the next. There are many code examples for the other GDI+ features in the .NET Framework SDK.*

## Performing Graphic Operations with a Graphics Object

When using GDI+, the very first step always is to create a Graphics object, which will help us to perform graphics operations. The Graphics class provides methods for drawing in a specific device context.

There are four ways to attain the correct graphics object: with the e parameter received in the Paint event, from a window handle, from an image, or from a specified handle to a device context. There's no real difference among these different approaches; we'll use each one depending on our program needs. For example, if we are coding our drawing functions on the Paint event of the form, we'll use the e parameter; but if we are coding a class to draw on a form, we'll probably want to use a window handle to create the graphics object. We discuss each method in the sections that follow.

## Creating a Graphics Object with the e Parameter

In this case, all drawing code must be associated with the Paint event of the destination image object. The following code shows how to draw a simple red rectangle at the 10, 20 position (in pixels) on the screen, 7 pixels high and 13 pixels long:

```
Private Sub PicSource_Paint(sender As Object, e As PaintEventArgs)_
                    Handles PicSource.Paint
    e.Graphics.FillRectangle(New SolidBrush(color.red), 10, 20, 13, 7)
End Sub
```

**NEW IN .NET**

*In these first few lines of code we can see many new features of .NET, as described here:*

*Every event handler in Visual Basic .NET receives at least one parameter, the* sender *object, which is the object that generates the event.*

*The event handler procedure is now associated with the object by the keyword* Handles. *There's no more implicit association using the procedure name, as occurred in the later versions of Visual Basic.*

*The* e *parameter is of the type* Windows.Forms.PaintEventArgs. *Those with Visual Basic experience will understand that we are dealing with an object hierarchy. In fact, everything in .NET languages is organized into managed units of code, called* namespaces. *In this case, we are using the* System.Windows.Forms *namespace, which contains classes for creating Windows-based applications using the features of the Windows operating system. Inside this namespace, we are using the* PaintEventArgs *class, which basically gives the* Paint *event access to the rectangle structure that needs to be updated (*ClipRectangle *property), and the* Graphics *object used to update it.*

*The* Graphics *and* SolidBrush *classes are defined in the* System.Drawing *namespace. This namespace has several classes that provide all the functionality we need to work with 2-D drawings, imaging control, and typography. In the code sample, we create a* SolidBrush *object with red color (using the* color *structure), to draw a filled rectangle using the* FillRectangle *method of the* Graphics *object.*

*In the .NET architecture, all objects are organized into hierarchies called namespaces.*

## Creating Graphics Objects from a Window Handle

In the code shown here, `Graphics.FromHwnd` is a shortcut for the `System.Drawing.Graphics.FromHwnd` method, which creates a `Graphics` object used to draw in a specific window or control, given its handle. This code references a `pictureBox` control named `picSource`:

```
Dim graph as Graphics
graph = Graphics.FromHwnd(picSource.Handle)
graph.FillRectangle(New SolidBrush(color.red), 10, 20, 13, 7)
```

**NEW IN .NET**

*In .NET, there's no need to use the* Set *keyword when setting an object variable. If we write the second line as*

```
Set  graph = Graphics.FromHwnd(picSource.Handle)
```

*the Visual Studio environment just erases the* Set *part for us. Pretty smart!*

## Creating Graphics Objects from an Image

The `FromImage` method shown here creates a graphics object from the specified image:

```
Dim graph as Graphics
graph = Graphics.FromImage(picSource.image)
graph.FillRectangle(New SolidBrush(color.red), 10, 20, 13, 7)
```

Note that the previous code sample will work only if we have a valid bitmap image loaded on the `pictureBox` control. If we try to execute it against an empty picture box or using a picture box with an indexed pixel format image loaded (such as a JPEG image), we'll get an error and the graphics object won't be created.

## Creating a Graphics Object from a Specified Handle to a Device Context

Similar to the previously mentioned methods, the `Graphics.FromHDC` method creates a `Graphics` object that allows the program to draw over a specific device context, given its handle. We can acquire the device handle from another `Graphics` object, using the `GetHdc` method, as shown in the next code snippet:

```
Public Sub FromHdc(e As PaintEventArgs)
    ' Get handle to device context.
    Dim hdc As IntPtr = e.Graphics.GetHdc()
    ' Create new graphics object using handle to device context.
    Dim newGraphics As Graphics = Graphics.FromHdc(hdc)
    newGraphics. FillRectangle(New SolidBrush(color.red), 10, 20, 13, 7)
    ' Release handle to device context.
    e.Graphics.ReleaseHdc(hdc)
End Sub
```

## Creating Gradients

In the previous section, we saw some code samples used to create solid red rectangles via a SolidBrush object. GDI+ allows the programmer to go beyond flat colors and create linear and path gradients, using special gradient brushes that provide very interesting effects.

GDI+ has features to create horizontal, vertical, and diagonal *linear gradients*. We can create linear gradients in which the colors change uniformly (the default behavior), or in a nonuniform way by using the Blend property of the gradient brush.

The sample code here shows how to create a uniform gradient brush and draw a rectangle with color changing from red to blue from the upper-left to the lower-right vertex:

```
Dim graph as Graphics
Dim linGrBrush as Drawing2-D.LinearGradientBrush

graph = Graphics.FromHwnd(picSource.Handle)

linGrBrush = new Drawing2-D.LinearGradientBrush( _
    new Point(10, 20),                 ' start gradient point
    new Point(23, 27),                 ' end gradient point
    Color.FromArgb(255, 255, 0, 0),  ' Red
    Color.FromArgb(255, 0, 0, 255))  ' Blue
graph.FillRectangle(linGrBrush, 10, 20, 13, 7)
```

**NEW IN .NET**

*The most important part of this sample code is the color definition using the* FromArgb *method of the* Color *object. As we can see, each color in GDI+ is always defined by four values: the red, green, blue (RGB) values used by the classic GDI functions, plus the alpha (A) value, which defines the* transparency *of the color. In the preceding example, we use an alpha value of 255 for both colors, so they will be totally opaque. Using a value of 128, we create a 50 percent transparent color, so any graphics below are shown through the rectangle. Setting alpha to zero means that the color will be 100 percent transparent, or totally invisible. The in-between values allow different degrees of transparency.*

*Path gradients* allow us to fill a shape using a color pattern defined by a specified path. The path can be composed of points, ellipses, and rectangles, and we can specify one color for the center of the path and a different color for each of the points in the path, allowing the creation of many different effects.

To draw an image using gradient paths, we must create a PathGradientBrush object, based on a GraphicsPath object that is defined by a sequence of lines, curves, and shapes. The code here shows how to draw the same rectangle from the previous examples, using a gradient that starts with a green color in the center of the rectangle and finishes with a blue color at the edges:

```
Dim Graph As Graphics
Dim rectSquare As Rectangle
Dim graphPath As Drawing2-D.GraphicsPath
Dim brushSquare As Drawing2-D.PathGradientBrush

Graph = Graphics.FromHwnd(picSource.Handle)

' Create a path consisting of one rectangle
graphPath = New Drawing2-D.GraphicsPath()
rectSquare = New Rectangle(10, 20, 23, 27)
graphPath.AddRectangle(rectSquare)
brushSquare = New Drawing2-D.PathGradientBrush(graphPath)
brushSquare.CenterColor = Color.FromArgb(255, 0, 255, 0)
brushSquare.SurroundColors = New Color() {Color.FromArgb(255, 0, 0, 255)}

' Create the rectangle from the path
Graph.FillPath(brushSquare, graphPath)
```

**NOTE** *We won't go into much detail here about brushes and paths. Refer to the .NET SDK documentation for some extra examples about how to use these features. For a complete overview about this topic, look for "System.Drawing.Drawing2-D Hierarchy" in the online help.*

In the next section we'll discuss collision detection, after which we'll have an understanding of all the basic concepts we need to implement our first game.

## Collision Detection

As we said at the start of the chapter, one of the most important concepts in game development is the collision detection algorithm. Some commercial games have gathered significant market shares just because their collision detection routines are faster, leaving more time for the graphics routines and allowing more responsive game play.

Just try to imagine some games without collision detection: a pinball game where the ball won't bounce; a 3-D labyrinth where players go through the walls and the bullets don't hit the enemy; an adventure game where the cursor doesn't know if it's over a specific object on screen. No, it's simply not possible!

Our main goal here is to examine some basic concepts, so we can use them within the scope of the book and create a stepping stone to provide us with the basic tools and terms used in collision detection.

**NOTE** *For those who want to look into this topic in more detail, a simple search on the Internet will show many improved algorithms for advanced collision detection in 2-D and, mostly, in 3-D environments.*

In the next sections we'll see some common collision detection algorithms.

### Bounding Boxes

One of the most common collision detection algorithms, the *bounding boxes algorithm*, uses the idea of creating boxes around objects in order to test a collision with minimum overhead and, depending on the object, an acceptable degree of precision. In Figure 1-7 we see some objects that we want to test for collisions, along with their bounding boxes.

*Figure 1-7. Bounding boxes for an archer and a monster*

In the game code, we must test if there's any overlap between the boxes to test for collision, instead of testing every single pixel of the images. In Figure 1-7, for example, if the box surrounding the arrow touches the box surrounding the monster, it's a hit.

Using bounding boxes on the sample in Figure 1-7 will probably lead to good results, although as a rule it's better to use smaller boxes for the player. If a monster blows up when a bullet (or arrow) just misses it by a pixel, the player won't complain; but if the situation is reversed, the player will feel cheated by the game. It's better to create a narrower box for the archer to give the player a little more satisfaction.

We can now redefine the boxes as shown in Figure 1-8.

*Figure 1-8. Revised bounding boxes for an archer and a monster*

An easy way to implement the bounding box test is simply to check if the x,y position of the upper bound corner of the first box is inside the second box. In other words, check whether x and y of the box being tested are less than or equal to the corresponding x and y of the other box, plus the width of the other box.

## Calculating Collision with Boxes

Here's a possible approach to calculating collision with boxes:

```
If rectangle1.x <= rectangle2.x + rectangle2.width and _
   rectangle1.y <= rectangle2.y + rectangle2.height) or
   (rectangle2.x <= rectangle1.x + rectangle1.width and _
   rectangle2.y <= rectangle1.y + rectangle1.height) then
      => The boxes are overlapping
Else
      => The boxes don't collide!!!
end if
```

Check the code against the graphic example from Figure 1-9 to be sure you understand the algorithm.

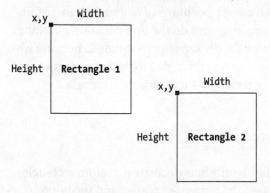

*Figure 1-9. Two nonoverlapping boxes*

According to the code sample, the two boxes will only overlap if both x and y coordinates of rectangle 2 are within range (x to x + width, y to y + height) of rectangle 1. Looking at the diagram, we see that the y coordinate for rectangle 2 is *not* greater than the y coordinate plus the height of rectangle 1. This means that our boxes *may* be colliding. But when checking the x coordinate of rectangle 2, we see that it's greater than the x coordinate plus the width of rectangle 1, which means that no collision is possible.

In Figure 1-10, we do have a collision.

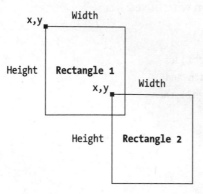

*Figure 1-10. Two overlapping boxes*

In this case, we can check that both x and y positions of rectangle 2 are within the range of rectangle 1. In the code sample we also do the opposite test, checking if the x,y coordinates of rectangle 1 are within the range of rectangle 2, because we are checking just one point, and it's possible for rectangle 2's top-left corner to be outside of rectangle 1, but the top left of rectangle 1 to be inside rectangle 2.

## Creating Custom Rectangle Objects

A simple improvement we can do in the algorithm is to create a custom rectangle object, which stores two points of the box, the upper-left corner and the bottom-right one, so we can do the tests directly on the variables without having to perform a sum operation.

This method can be easily extended to nonrectangular objects, creating for each object a set of rectangles instead of a single rectangle. For example, for a plane, instead of using a single box (Figure 1-11), we can achieve much better precision using two overlapping boxes (Figure 1-12).

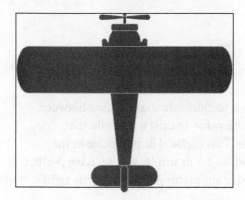

*Figure 1-11. Approximating a plane shape with one box*

*Figure 1-12. Approximating a plane shape with two boxes*

The drawback of this approach is that if we use too many boxes, the calculations will take longer, so we need to find a balance between precision and speed for each game or object.

## Proximity Algorithms

Another type of algorithm commonly used to calculate object overlapping is the *proximity algorithm*. Proxy algorithms are somewhat similar to the bounding boxes algorithm, depending on the formula used.

The basic idea behind such algorithms is to calculate the distance between the centers of two objects, and then check the value against a formula that describes approximately the objects' shapes. This method is as precise as the formula used to approximate the object shape—for example, we can have perfect collision detection between balls, in a snooker simulator game, using the right formula.

Some of the most common formulas calculate the distances between squares, circles, and diamonds. Figure 1-13 shows a graphical representation for a square-based proximity test.

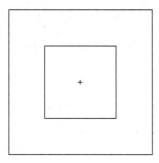

*Figure 1-13. Square proximity*

## Calculating Collision for Square or Circle Objects

To calculate collision for objects with a shape that can be approximated to a square, the basic formula is

> Distance between centers = Maximum value between the distances in the x axis and the y axis

To calculate the distance in a specific axis, all we need to do is to subtract the x values of the center coordinates from each object, picking the absolute value of the result, so we don't need to worry about which object is the furthest to the left or the nearest to the top of the screen. The code for calculating square collisions, considering that we have objects with CenterX and CenterY properties, would be as follows:

```
Distance = math.max( math.abs(Object1.CenterX - Object2.CenterX), _
             math.abs(Object1.CenterY - Object2.CenterY))

If Distance < Object1.width + Object2.width then
    ' => The square objects are overlapping
Else
    ' => The squares don't collide!!!
end if
```

Figure 1-14 illustrates the next proximity algorithm for figures that can be approximated by circles.

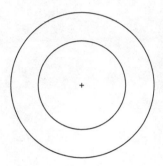

*Figure 1-14. Circle proximity*

When dealing with circular objects, we achieve a perfect calculation using the Pythagorean theorem, which allows us to calculate the distance between the centers (hypotenuse) using the square root of the sum of the squares of the other sides:

```
Cathetus1 = math.abs(Object1.CenterX - Object2.CenterX)
Cathetus2 = math.abs(Object1.CenterY - Object2.CenterY)
Distance = math.sqrt(Cathetus1^2 + Cathetus2^2)

If Distance < Object1.width + Object2.width then
    ' => The circle objects are overlapping
Else
    ' => The circles don't collide!!!
end if
```

If we just want to check the distance against a constant value, we don't need to calculate the square root, making operations faster.

### Calculating Collision of Diamond-Shaped Objects

The next approximation algorithm uses much simpler calculations, and gives a good degree of precision when dealing with objects of a diamond shape, as depicted in Figure 1-15.

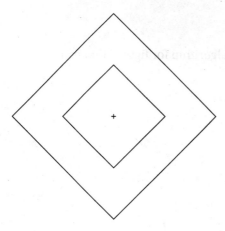

*Figure 1-15. Diamond proximity*

To use this approach, all we need to do is calculate the sum of the distances:

```
Distance = math.abs(Object1.CenterX - Object2.CenterX) + _
    math.abs(Object1.CenterY - Object2.CenterY)

If Distance < Object1.width + Object2.width then
    ' => The diamond objects are overlapping
Else
    ' => The diamonds don't collide!!!
end if
```

## Optimizing the Number of Calculations

As the number of objects in the game grows, it becomes increasingly difficult to perform all the necessary calculations, so we'll need to find a way to speed things up. Because there's a limit to how far we can simplify the calculations, we need to keep the number of calculations low.

The first method to consider is to only perform calculations for the objects that are currently on screen. If we really need to do calculations for off-screen objects, we'll perform them less frequently than those for on-screen objects.

The next logical step is to attempt to determine which objects are near, and then to calculate the collisions only for those. This can be done using a zoning method. If most of our objects are fixed on the screen and have the same size, we can calculate the collisions using tiled game fields; if we have many objects but need to test only one against all others (such as a bullet that may hit enemies or obstacles), we can simply divide the screen in zones and control them with single-bit information for each zone; and if we need to test a limited number of objects against all others, we'll have to store extra information about each zone, using arrays of bits.

We'll discuss each of these approaches in the following sections.

### Tiled Game Field

The tiled game field approach is the zone method taken to the limit; there's only one object per area in the zone, and we use a bidimensional array where each position on the array refers to a tile on the screen. When moving objects, all we have to do is to check the array in the given position to know if there'll be a collision. In this chapter, we do a simple variation of this method, using a bit array where each bit maps to a tile on the screen. This approach is possible because we only want to store one piece of information—whether the tile is empty or not. If we need to store any extra data about the object (for example, an identifier about the object type), we have to create an integer array to store numbers, and create a mapping table in which each number represents a specific type of object (as we do in the next chapter). Figure 1-16 shows a tiled game where each screen object is held in an array.

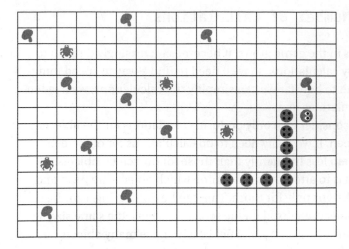

*Figure 1-16. In a tiled game field, we have an array that maps to screen objects.*

## Zoning with Bits

If we have a game with many objects but infrequent collisions, we can minimize the number of calculations dividing our screen in zones, and only calculate collisions for objects that are on the same zone (this is what's known as *zoning*). To divide a screen in zones, we'll create an array to store information about each zone's y and x axis. So, if we divide our screen into 64 zones (8 × 8), we'll need one array with 8 elements to store information about the y axis of each zone, and another array with 8 elements to store information about the x axis of each zone. Figure 1-17 shows an example of such zoning.

If all we want to know is whether a certain zone contains an object (disregarding which one), we can use bytes (instead of arrays) to store the zone information, where each bit will represent a zone on screen; this is called *zoning with bits*. We can divide our screen in zones according to the number of bits on each variable used: 64 (8 × 8) zones with a byte, 256 (16 × 16) zones in an int16, 1024 (32 × 32) zones in an int32, and so on.

Using the zoning with bits method, at each game loop we reset the variables and, for each object, we process any movement. We then calculate the zone of each object (multiply the current position of the object by the number of zones on each axis and divide by the width or height of the screen), and set the bit corresponding to the result at the x-axis variable and at the y-axis variable, accordingly. We have to set a second bit if the sum of the position and the size of the object (width for x axis, height for y axis) lies in another zone.

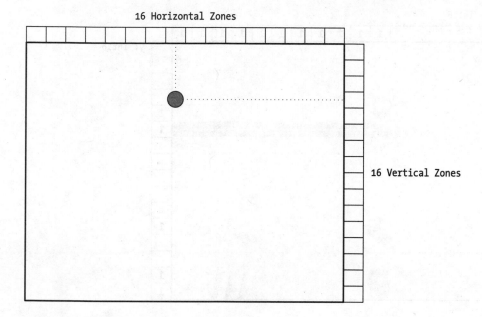

*Figure 1-17. Dividing a screen into 64 zones*

If when checking the variables we see that the bit in both variables is already set, then there's an object in our zone, so we check all the objects to find out which one it is. Using this method, if we have 15 objects on the screen, and only one collision, we'll have to do only one check against a given number of objects (14 in the worst case of this scenario), instead of 15 tests with 14 objects. This method has some drawbacks:

- We don't know which object set the bit, so we have to test all the objects looking for the collision.

- Some "ghost objects" are created when crossing the bit set for the x zone by one object with the bit set for the y zones by another object, as depicted by Figure 1-18.

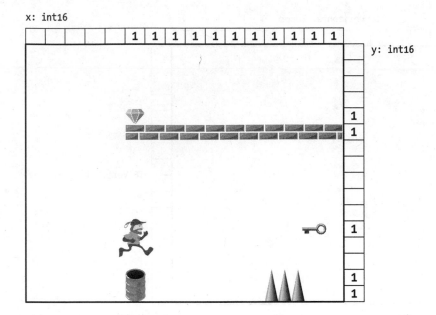

*Figure 1-18. Using zone bits, if we have big objects (like the bricks), there'll be lots of "ghost objects."*

This method is most useful when we want to test a group of objects against other objects (for example, bullets against enemies on screen); if we need to test all the objects against each of the others, we'd better use zoning with arrays of bits, as described in the next section.

## Zoning with Arrays of Bits

If we have a limited number of objects on screen, we can use two arrays, instead of variables, to define our zones. Each object will correspond to a specific bit in the array elements, so we'll use byte arrays to control 8 objects, int16 arrays to control 16 objects, and so on, and create a mapping table linking each bit with a specific object. The size of each array will define the number of pixels in a zone for each dimension. For example, creating two arrays each with 10 positions in a 640×480 resolution, we'll have zones measuring 64 pixels wide by 48 pixels high.

We use the same idea as the previous method to define the zone (or zones) in which each object may be, and then check to see if both x and y array elements aren't empty. If they aren't zero, and the bits set in both arrays are the same, then we know for sure that there's another object near us (not a ghost object), and only check for collision with the one that corresponds to the bit set. An example of this is shown in Figure 1-19.

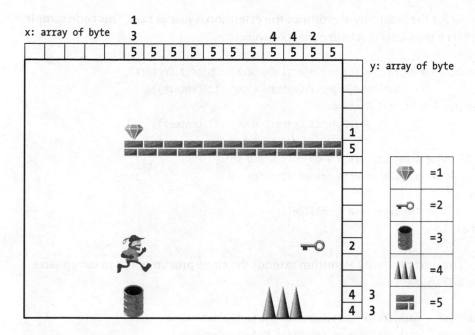

*Figure 1-19. Using zone arrays, we can keep track of which objects are in each zone.
The legend shows the bit set in each array element, for each object.*

## Extending the Algorithms to Add a Third Dimension

There are many advanced algorithms for 3-D collisions described on game-related
sites all over the Internet. We'll not stress the many implications on including a z
axis in the collision detection algorithms; instead we'll just add some simple
extensions to the preceding algorithms.

Extending the bounding box algorithm is very straightforward, as shown here:

```
If object1.x <= object2.x + object2.width and _
   object1.y <= object2.y + object2.height and _
   object1.z <= object2.z + object2.depth) or
   (object2.x <= object1.x + object1.width and _
   object2.y <= object1.y + object1.height and_
   object2.z <= object1.z + object1.depth) then
      ' => The 3-D boxes are overlapping
Else
      ' => The 3-D boxes don't collide!!!
end if
```

As for the proximity algorithms, the extension is just as easy. This code sample depicts a proximity test with cube-like objects:

```
Distance = math.max( math.abs(Object1.CenterX - Object2.CenterX), _
              math.abs(Object1.CenterY - Object2.CenterY))
Distance = math.max( Distance,
              math.abs(Object1.CenterX - Object2.CenterX))

If Distance < Object1.width + Object2.width then
      ' => The cube objects are overlapping
Else
      ' => The cubes don't collide!!!
end if
```

The next proximity algorithm extends the circle proximity test to use spheres in a 3-D space:

```
Cathetus1 = math.abs(Object1.CenterX - Object2.CenterX)
Cathetus2 = math.abs(Object1.CenterY - Object2.CenterY)
Cathetus3 = math.abs(Object1.CenterZ - Object2.CenterZ)
Distance = math.sqrt(Cathetus1^2 + Cathetus2^2 + Cathetus3^2)

If Distance < Object1.width + Object2.width then
      ' => The sphere objects are overlapping
Else
      ' => The spheres don't collide!!!
end if
```

The last proximity test is used for 3-D diamond-shaped objects:

```
Distance = math.abs(Object1.CenterX - Object2.CenterX) + _
      math.abs(Object1.CenterY - Object2.CenterY) + _
      math.abs(Object1.CenterZ - Object2.CenterZ)

If Distance < Object1.width + Object2.width then
        => The 3-D diamond objects are overlapping
Else
        => The 3-D diamonds don't collide!!!
end if
```

In the next sections we'll see how to apply these theoretical ideas in a real game project.

# The Game Proposal

The first step in developing any project is to establish the project's scope and features.

 **NOTE** *The main purpose for creating a game proposal is to have clear objectives stated; and everyone involved in the game creation must agree on every point.*

For our project we can summarize the scope in a list of desired features, as shown here:

- Our game will be a puzzle game, and it'll be called .Nettrix.

- The main objective of the game is to control falling blocks and try to create full horizontal lines, while not allowing the block pile to reach the top of the game field.

- The blocks will be made out of four squares (in every possible arrangement) that fall down in the game field, until they reach the bottom of the field or a previously fallen block.

- When the blocks are falling, the player can move the blocks horizontally and rotate them.

- When a block stops falling, we'll check to see if there are continuous horizontal lines of squares in the game field. Every continuous line must be removed.

- The player gets 100 points per removed line, multiplied by the current level. After every couple of minutes, the blocks must start falling faster, and the level number should be increased.

- If the stack of blocks grows until it's touching the top of the game field, the game ends.

This list contains many definitions that are important for any game proposal:

- The game genre (puzzle)

- The main objective of the game

- The actions the player can perform (e.g., to shoot and to get objects)

- Details about how the player interacts with the game and vice-versa: keyboard, intuitive interface, force-feedback joystick, etc.

- How the player is rewarded for his or her efforts (points, extra lives, etc.)

- How the player gets promoted from one level to the next (in this case, just a time frame)

- The criteria for ending the game

---

 **NOTE** *In more sophisticated games, there may be other considerations, such as the storyline, the game flow, details about the level design or level of detail for the maps or textured surfaces, the difficulty levels for the game, or even details on how the artificial intelligence (AI) of the game should work.*

---

## The Game Project

In a commercial game project, the game project starts with a complete game proposal (not just some simple phrases like ours) and continues with a project or functional specification. Although the proposal is written in natural language—so anyone can understand and approve it (including the Big Boss, who will approve or reject the budget for the project)—the project includes programming details that will guide the development team through the coding phase.

It's not our objective here to explain what must appear in the project documents (it depends largely on the development methodology used by the team), and we won't create any complete projects since this isn't the focus of the book. But since it's not advisable to start any coding without a project, we'll take a quick look at projects just to make some implementation details clearer.

**TIP** *Of course you can start coding without a project, but even when working alone, a project is the best place to start, since it lets you organize your ideas and discover details that were not clear before you put pen to paper. Even if the project is just some draft annotations, you'll see that the average quality of your code will improve with its use. The more detailed the project is, the better your code will be, since they'll help you see the traps and pitfalls along the way before you fall into them.*

Object-oriented (OO) techniques are the best to use in game projects, because usually games deal with some representation (sometimes a very twisted one) of the real world, as OO techniques do. For example, in Street Fighter, we don't have real fighters on the screen, we have some moving drawings, controlled by the player or the computer, that create the illusion of a fight. Using an OO approach to project creation is roughly the same thing: We decide the important characteristics from the real-world objects that we want to represent in our program, and write them down. We aren't going to go any deeper into this topic at this stage, but you can find some very good books on this topic.

Since this is our first program, we'll go through the process of making it step by step, in order to demonstrate how we evolve from the game proposal to the final code; in later chapters we'll take a more direct approach. In the next sections we'll see a first version of a class diagram, then pseudo-code for the game main program, and after that we'll go back to the class diagram and add some refinements.

## The Class Diagram: First Draft

Let's start with a simple class diagram (shown in Figure 1-20) illustrating the basic structures of the objects for our game, and then we can add the details and go on refining until we have a complete version. Almost all of the object-oriented analysis methodologies suggest this cyclic approach, and it's ideal to show how the game idea evolves from draft to a fully featured project.

From our game proposal we can see the first two classes: Block, which will represent each game piece, and Square, the basic component of the blocks.

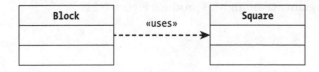

*Figure 1-20. The class diagram—first draft*

Reviewing our game proposal, we can think about some methods (functions) and properties (variables) for the Block class, as described in Table 1-1.

*Table 1-1. The Block Class Members*

| TYPE | NAME | DESCRIPTION |
| --- | --- | --- |
| Method | Down | Makes the block go down on the screen |
| Method | Right | Moves the block right |
| Method | Left | Moves the block left |
| Method | Rotate | Rotates the block clockwise |
| Property | Square 1 | One of the squares that compose the block |
| Property | Square 2 | One of the squares that compose the block |
| Property | Square 3 | One of the squares that compose the block |
| Property | Square 4 | One of the squares that compose the block |

Each block is composed of fours objects from the Square class, described in Table 1-2.

*Table 1-2. The Square Class Members*

| TYPE | NAME | DESCRIPTION |
| --- | --- | --- |
| Method | Show | Draws the square on the screen at its coordinates (Location property) and with its size (Size property), colored with a specific color (ForeColor property) and filled with BackColor |
| Method | Hide | Erases the square from the screen |
| Property | ForeColor | The square border color |
| Property | BackColor | The square inside color (fill color) |
| Property | Location | The x,y position of the square on the screen |
| Property | Size | The height and width of the square |

Comparing the two tables, we can see that there are methods to show and hide the square. Because the squares will be drawn from the Block object, we must have corresponding methods in the Block class, and the corresponding properties too. We can adjust the first diagram accordingly to produce Figure 1-21.

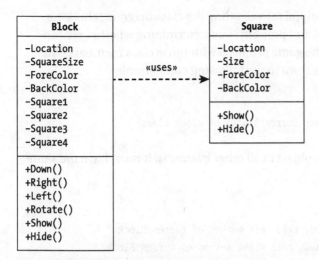

*Figure 1-21. The class diagram—second draft*

We use SquareSize as the size property for the block, since it's not important to know the block size, but the block must know the size of the squares so that it can create them.

We can return to this diagram later and adjust it if necessary. Let's think now about the game engine, described in the next section.

## The Game Engine

Using the Visual Basic events jargon, we can think about coding three main events to implement the behaviors described at the game proposal:

1.  When the form loads, we can create the first block.

2.  At the form KeyPress event, we can handle the keyboard input from the user.

3.  With a timer we can call the Down method at each clock tick, producing the desired falling effect for the blocks. As we'll see later, using a timer isn't a recommended practice when creating games that need to run at full speed, but that's not the case here.

Writing pseudo-code is helpful for validating the class diagram, checking whether we use every method and property, and determining whether we can achieve the results stated in the game proposal with those class members. The pseudo-code for our game is shown in the following code sample:

```
Form_Load
        Creates an object (named currentBlock) of block class
```

We'll use the currentBlock object in all other events, so it must have the same scope as the form:

```
Form_KeyPress
        If Left Arrow was pressed, call Left method of currentBlock
        If Right Arrow was pressed, call Right method of currentBlock
        If Up Arrow was pressed, call Rotate method of currentBlock
        If Down Arrow was pressed, call Down method of currentBlock
```

In the previous pseudo-code, we are using the up arrow key to rotate the block and the down arrow key to force the block to go down faster, while the right arrow key and left arrow key move the block in the horizontal direction.

The game engine core will be the timer event. Reviewing the game proposal, we see what we must do here: Make the block fall, stop it according to the game rules, check to see if there are any full horizontal lines, and check for the game being over. Possible pseudo-code to do this is shown in the following sample:

```
If there is no block below currentBlock,
    and the currentBlock didn't reach the bottom of the screen then
        Call the Down method of currentBlock
Else
        Stop the block
        If it's at the top of the screen then
        The game is over
        If we filled any horizontal lines then
        Increase the game score
        Erase the line
        Create a new block at the top of the screen
```

Analyzing this code, we can see some features our current class diagram doesn't take into account. For instance, how can we check if there is no block below the current block? How can we erase the horizontal line we just managed to fill? We'll discuss these points in the next section.

## The Class Diagram: Final Version

In order to check the previous block positions to see if there are any blocks below the current block or if there are any filled lines, we must have a way to store and check each of the squares of the block, independently of the original blocks (remember, when we erase a line, we can erase just a square or two from a given block). We can do this by creating a new class representing the game field, which will store the information of all squares and have some methods that allow line erasing, among other features. With a quick brainstorm, we can add this class to our model, which will evolve into the diagram shown in Figure 1-22.

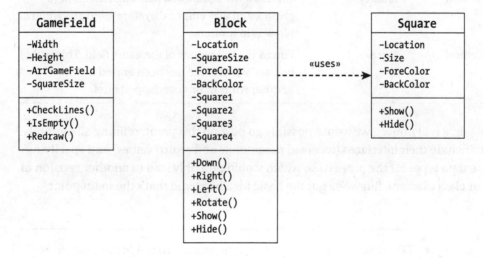

*Figure 1-22. The final class diagram*

Table 1-3 lists the methods and properties of the new class, along with a short description for each one.

*Table 1-3. The Game Field Class Members*

| TYPE | NAME | DESCRIPTION |
|------|------|-------------|
| Properties | Width and Height | Represents the width and height of the game field, measured in squares. |
| Property | SquareSize | Indicates the size of each square, so we can translate pixels to squares. |
| Property | ArrGameField | Constitutes an array to store all the squares from all the blocks that stopped falling. |
| Method | CheckLines | Checks if there are any complete horizontal lines, erasing them if so, and returns the number of erased lines so the main program can increase the player's score. |
| Method | IsEmpty | Checks if the square at a particular location (a given x and y) is empty, therefore telling us when a block is in motion. |
| Method | Redraw | Forces the full redraw of the game field. This will be used when a line has been erased or when another window has overlapped ours. |

In a real project, we would possibly go beyond this point, refining all methods to include their interfaces (received parameters and return values) and specifying the data types for the properties, which would probably lead to another revision of our class diagram. But we've got the basic idea here, and that's the main point.

 **TIP** *Those interested in looking into project creation in more depth can find more detailed explanations in books covering object-oriented analysis.*

## The Coding Phase

When coding any project, it's always useful to create drivers and stubs to allow us to test each component separately. *Drivers* are programs that control other lower-level programs, and *stubs* are programs that mimic low-level programs' behavior, allowing the testing of higher level code. To provide a vision of a real coding phase, we'll sometimes use such techniques to validate the code written, step by step.

We'll go through three versions, from our first draft to the final code:

1. First draft: Code the Square class.

2. Second draft: Code the Block class.

3. Final version: Code the GameField class and the game engine.

We start coding from the lowest level class, Square, in the next section.

## First Draft: Coding the Square Class

Reviewing the game project, we find the basic structure of the class and create the class interface:

```
Public Class ClsSquare
    Public location As Point
    Public size As size
    Public forecolor As Color
    Public backcolor As Color

    Public Sub Show(WinHandle As System.IntPtr)
    Public Sub Hide(WinHandle As System.IntPtr)
End Class
```

There's nothing here that we couldn't do in the previous version of Visual Basic. In later chapters we'll see some improvements brought about by .NET lconcerning object orientation. The class methods are shown in the next section.

## The New and Hide Methods

In the Show method all we need to do is to adapt the code for creating a path gradient rectangle we saw in the previous section. For the Hide method, we can hide the rectangle in an easier way: Since we'll be working with a one-color background (no textures or bitmaps yet), we can simply draw the rectangle again, this time using a solid color, the same as the background.

To create a generic code that can be updated later by any programmer, it's always a good idea to not use fixed values inside our program. In our example, we'd better read the game field background color from some variable, so that if it's updated later to another color, our Hide method will still work. This color value should be a property of the GameField class, but since this property doesn't appear in our game project, we'll need to update it with this new property. In a real project it's common for some details (like this one) to only become visible at the coding phase, since it's not possible for the project to predict all possible details.

The code for the Square class is shown here:

```
Public Class ClsSquare
    Public location As Point
    Public size As size
    Public forecolor As Color
    Public backcolor As Color

    ' Draws a rectangle with gradient path using the properties above
    Public Sub Show(WinHandle As System.IntPtr)
        Dim rectSquare As Rectangle
        Dim graphPath As Drawing2-D.GraphicsPath
        Dim brushSquare As Drawing2-D.PathGradientBrush
        Dim surroundColor() As Color
        Dim GameGraphics As Graphics

        ' Gets the Graphics object of the background picture
        GameGraphics = Graphics.FromHwnd(WinHandle)
```

```
        ' Creates a path consisting of one rectangle
        graphPath = New Drawing2-D.GraphicsPath()
        rectSquare = New Rectangle(location.X, location.Y, _
                                   size.Width, size.Height)
        graphPath.AddRectangle(rectSquare)

        ' Creates the gradient brush which will draw the square
        ' Note: There's one center color and an array of border colors
        brushSquare = New Drawing2-D.PathGradientBrush(graphPath)
        brushSquare.CenterColor = forecolor
        surroundColor = New Color() {backcolor}
        brushSquare.SurroundColors = surroundColor

        ' Finally draws the square
        GameGraphics.FillPath(brushSquare, graphPath)
    End Sub

    Public Sub Hide(WinHandle As System.IntPtr)
        Dim GameGraphics As Graphics
        Dim rectSquare As Rectangle

        ' Gets the Graphics object of the background picture
        GameGraphics = Graphics.FromHwnd(WinHandle)

        ' Draws the square
        rectSquare = New Rectangle(location.X, location.Y, _
                                   size.Width, size.Height)
        GameGraphics.FillRectangle( _
            New SolidBrush(ClsGameField.BackColor), rectSquare)
    End Sub
End Class
```

*Visual Basic comes fully packed with new data types. For example, for integer values we have the type* integer, *as in the previous versions, plus the types* int16, int32, int64, *representing integers of different sizes, and* intPtr, *which is a special integer type that will use the size of the pointers (such as window handles) specific to the destination machine.*

*In Visual Basic .NET we can set the initial values of variables when defining them. A common example is*

```
Dim x as integer = 10
```

*The variable* x *is created and then the value 10 is assigned to it. When setting initial values to arrays, the values may appear separated with commas and delimited by* {}. *That's what we see in the code for the* Square *class in the line*

```
surroundColor = New Color() {backcolor}
```

surroundColor *is an array of colors with a single element. The following code has the same effect as the previous line:*

```
Redim surroundColor(1)
surroundColor(1) = backcolor
```

*This new feature becomes more interesting when dealing with larger arrays. Compare the following code samples:*

```
Dim myArray () as integer = {1, 2, 3, 4, 5}
```

*The corresponding code in the previous versions is as follows:*

```
Dim myArray() as integer
Redim myArray(5)
myArray(1) = 1
myArray(1) = 2
myArray(1) = 3
myArray(1) = 4
myArray(1) = 5
```

*In .NET all the arrays must be defined without boundaries, which are later assigned in the code. So we must always use* Redim *before assigning values to an array.*

**NEW IN .NET**

*In the Hide method shown previously, we can see an unusual use of the backcolor property: We are using the property directly from the class definition, instead of from a previously created object in this class. In this case, we are using a new feature of .NET: the shared properties or methods. Defining a method or a property as Public Shared makes it available for any part of the program directly from the class name, without the need for explicitly creating an object. An important point is that the property or method is shared by all the instances of the objects created from the class. For example, we can have a shared counter property that each object increments when it's created and decrements when it's destroyed, and any object can read this counter at any time in order to see how many objects are available at any given time.*

## Testing the Square Class

Now we are ready to test our program. To do this, we'll need to create a driver to call the class (a window with a button and a pictureBox will suffice), and a stub for the GameField class, since our Square class uses the backcolor property of this class.

The stub is very simple, just a new file composed of the code lines shown in the next sample:

```
Public Class ClsGameField
    Public Shared backcolor As Color
End Class
```

The driver will be replaced by the main program in the final version, so we can implement it as code on the form that will be used as the game user interface. In this case, we can create a simple form with a picture (picBackground) and a button (cmdStart), with the code to create the objects and set the properties of the clsSquare class, then call the Draw method:

```
Sub CmdStart_Click(sender As System.Object, e As System.EventArgs) _
                              Handles CmdStart.Click

    Dim objSquare as clsSquare

    objSquare = new clsSquare

    ' Set the Properties
    objSquare.location = new Point (40,20)
    objSquare.Size = new Size (10,10)
    objSquare.Forecolor = color.blue
```

```
        objSquare.BackColor = color.green
        ' Set the backcolor property of clsGameField class
        clsGameField.backcolor = picBackground.BackColor

        ' Draws the square
        objSquare.Draw(picBackground.Handle)
End Sub
```

Running the code, we can see the fruits of our labor: a nice, path gradient–colored square is drawn on screen as shown in Figure 1-23.

*Figure 1-23. Our first results with GDI+*

Because in our game the squares won't change color or size, we can assign these values when creating the objects, creating a New method in the class to do this, as illustrated in the next code sample:

```
Public Sub New(InitialSize As size, _
   InitialBackcolor As Color, InitialForecolor As Color)
     size = InitialSize
     backcolor = InitialBackcolor
     forecolor = InitialForecolor
   End Sub
```

So the code for our Start button will be as follows:

```
Sub CmdStart_Click( sender As System.Object, e As System.EventArgs) _
                                Handles CmdStart.Click
    Dim objSquare as clsSquare

    objSquare = new clsSquare (new Size (10,10), color.blue, color.green)

    ' Set the Location of the square
    objSquare.location = new Point (40,20)
    ' Set the backcolor property of clsGameField class
    clsGameField.backcolor = picBackground.BackColor

    ' Draws the square
    objSquare.Draw(picBackground)
End Sub
```

*In Visual Basic .NET, the* New *method is called when an object is created, and receives the parameters used in the object's creation. In the previous versions, the corresponding method was called* Initialize, *and could receive no arguments.*

**NEW IN .NET**

Now that everything is working correctly, let's continue with the coding by looking at the Block class.

## Second Draft: Coding the Block Class

We can map the Block class, defined in the class diagram created for our game project, to the final class interface including the data types for the properties and parameters for the methods. The proposed class interface is shown in the next code listing:

```
Public Class clsBlock
    Public Location as Point
    Public SquareSize as integer = 10
    Private ForeColor As Color
    Private BackColor As Color
    ' The 4 squares that compose the block
    Public square1 As ClsSquare
    Public square2 As ClsSquare
    Public square3 As ClsSquare
    Public square4 As ClsSquare
```

```
      Public Function Down() As Boolean
      Public Function Right() As Boolean
      Public Function Left() As Boolean
      Public Sub Rotate()
      Public Sub Show(WinHandle As System.IntPtr)
      Public Sub Hide(WinHandle As System.IntPtr)
End Class
```

In the game proposal, we said that the blocks will be composed of four squares (in every possible arrangement). We can start the coding by thinking about the possible combinations, and give each of them a name, as shown in Figure 1-24.

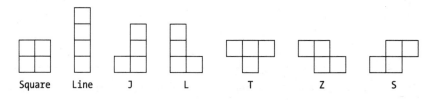

Square    Line    J    L    T    Z    S

*Figure 1-24. The square arrangements to form each block*

Because each block will have a specific square combination, we can think of three new elements for our class: a `BlockType` property, an enumeration for the block types, and a `New` method that creates the squares in the desired positions and the color of each square. To give a visual clue to the player, the colors must be fixed for each block type, so it's a good idea to create arrays to hold the forecolor and backcolor for each type. The extra definitions for the class are shown in the next code listing:

```
Public Enum enBlockType
      UNDEFINED = 0
      SQUARE = 1
      LINE = 2
      J = 3
      L = 4
      T = 5
      Z = 6
      S = 7
End Enum

Public BlockType As enBlockType
```

```
Private backColors() As Color = _
            {Nothing, Color.Red, Color.Blue, Color.Red, Color.Yellow, _
             Color.Green, Color.White, Color.Black}
Private foreColors() As Color = _
        {Nothing, Color.Purple, Color.LightBlue, Color.Yellow, _
         Color.Red, Color.LightGreen, Color.Black, Color.White}
```

## The New Method

The New method will receive two parameters: the block type and the location
where the block will be created. Since we need random block types, we can make
the block type parameter optional, and choose a new block type inside the New
procedure when this isn't given. The default value for the optional parameter must
be the UNDEFINED member of the block type enumeration, so we know when the
block type isn't given by the caller function.

We won't use the optional parameter immediately, but it's a good idea to
create code following this pattern, so we'll be able to test a specific block type
easily. For example, if the Rotate procedure doesn't work well for the T block type,
we can call the New function with the corresponding parameter to allow us to do
the testing. Code to do this is shown in the following listing:

```
Public Sub New(location As Point, _
    Optional newBlockType As enBlockType = enBlockType.UNDEFINED)

        ' Create the new block, chooses a type if not informed
        If newBlockType = enBlockType.UNDEFINED Then
            Randomize()
            BlockType = Int(Rnd(7) * 7) + 1
        Else
            BlockType = newBlockType
        End If

        ' Create each of the squares of the block
        ' and set the square colors, based on the block type
        square1 = New ClsSquare(New Size(squareSize, squareSize), _
                backColors(BlockType), foreColors(BlockType))
        square2 = New ClsSquare(New Size(squareSize, squareSize), _
                backColors(BlockType), foreColors(BlockType))
        square3 = New ClsSquare(New Size(squareSize, squareSize), _
                backColors(BlockType), foreColors(BlockType))
        square4 = New ClsSquare(New Size(squareSize, squareSize), _
                backColors(BlockType), foreColors(BlockType))
```

```
' Set the squares' positions based on the block type
Select Case BlockType
    Case enBlockType.SQUARE
            ' Creates a Square block
    Case enBlockType.LINE
            ' Creates a Line block
    Case enBlockType.J
            ' Creates a J block
    Case enBlockType.L
            ' Creates an L block
    Case enBlockType.T
            ' Creates a T block
    Case enBlockType.Z
            ' Creates a Z block
    Case enBlockType.S
            ' Creates an S block
End Select
End Sub
```

In this sample, the code inside each case statement must set the square positions, based on each block type, according to Figure 1-24. For example, let's analyze the Square block type, depicted in Figure 1-25.

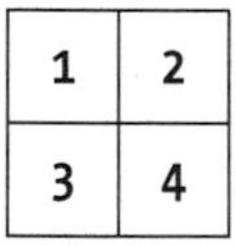

| 1 | 2 |
|---|---|
| 3 | 4 |

*Figure 1-25. The squares for the Square block type*

The code for creating the Square block type is shown here:

```
Case enBlockType.SQUARE
    square1.location = New Point(location.X, location.Y)
    square2.location = New Point(location.X + SquareSize, location.Y)
    square3.location = New Point(location.X, location.Y + SquareSize)
    square4.location = New Point(location.X + SquareSize, _
                            location.Y + SquareSize)
```

As for the Line block type, the squares that compose it are shown in Figure 1-26.

| |
|---|
| 1 |
| 2 |
| 3 |
| 4 |

*Figure 1-26. The squares for the Line block type*

The code for the Line block type is as follows:

```
Case enBlockType.LINE
    square1.location = New Point(location.X, location.Y)
    square2.location = New Point(location.X, location.Y + SquareSize)
    square3.location = New Point(location.X, location.Y + 2 * SquareSize)
    square4.location = New Point(location.X, location.Y + 3*SquareSize)
```

The code for the other blocks follows the same idea. For the full code of the New method, check the samples on the accompanying CD-ROM.

Once the blocks are created, we can start coding the moving operations over them, as described in the next section.

## The Down, Right, and Left Methods

The next methods, following the class diagram order, are Down, Right, and Left. These methods are fairly simple, since all we need to do is to update the block position in the defined direction, regardless of the block type. The basic code for the Down procedure could be as simple as this:

```
Public Function Down() As Boolean
    Down = true
    ' Hide the block (in the previous position)
    Hide(ClsGameField.WinHandle)
    ' Update the block position
    square1.location=New Point(square1.location.X, _
                               square1.location.Y + SquareSize)
    square2.location=New Point(square2.location.X, _
                               square2.location.Y + SquareSize)
    square3.location=New Point(square3.location.X, _
                               square3.location.Y + SquareSize)
```

```
    square4.location=New Point(square4.location.X, _
                              square4.location.Y + SquareSize)
    ' Draw the block in the new position
    Show(ClsGameField.WinHandle)
End Function
```

Because we'll need to hide and redraw the block every time these methods are called, we can reduce the calling overhead by creating a new shared property on the GameField class, the WinHandle used in the preceding code, and the handle of the pictureBox used as the game field on the form. With this approach, we can set this property in the New method and use it for every drawing operation, instead of passing the handle as a parameter to the drawing methods every time it's called.

The Right and Left methods will be similar to this one, except this time the horizontal block position is changed—incrementing it to move the block to the right and decrementing it to move the block to the left. We are moving the blocks using the default value of the SquareSize property, assigned to 10 in the class definition. This means that the blocks will always move a square down, left, or right, so we don't have to take worry about the squares' alignment.

There's one more detail to include in this procedures: the test for collision detection. The block can't move down, left, or right if there are any squares (or screen limits) in the way. Since the block itself can't know if other blocks are in the way, it must ask the GameField class if it can move this way. We already thought about this in the game project: The IsEmpty method of the GameField class will check if a specified square in the game field is empty.

In the Down method, we must check if there are any blocks in the way and stop falling if we hit an obstacle. When the block stops falling, we must inform the Game-Field class of this, so it can update its internal controls to allow the proper function of the IsEmpty method. We can do this by creating a new method, named StopSquare, which will inform the GameField that a specific square is now not empty, and pass the square object and its coordinates as parameters. After that, each square will be treated separately from each other (no more blocks) by the GameField class, because when a line is removed, some squares of the block can be removed while others remain.

Since the IsEmpty and StopSquare methods are based on an array of Squares, ArrGameField (as defined in our game project), the logical approach is for these methods to receive the array coordinates to be used. We can translate screen coordinates to array positions by simply dividing the x and y position of each square by the square size.

The final code for the down procedure will now be as follows:

```
Public Function Down() As Boolean
    Down = True
    ' If there's no block below the current one, go down
    If ClsGameField.IsEmpty(square1.location.X / SquareSize,
                            square1.location.Y / SquareSize + 1) _
        And ClsGameField.IsEmpty(square2.location.X / SquareSize, _
                            square2.location.Y / SquareSize + 1) _
        And ClsGameField.IsEmpty(square3.location.X / SquareSize, _
                            square3.location.Y / SquareSize + 1) _
        And ClsGameField.IsEmpty(square4.location.X / SquareSize, _
                            square4.location.Y / SquareSize + 1)    Then
        ' Hide the block (in the previous position)
        Hide(ClsGameField.picGameField)
        ' Update the block position
        square1.location = New Point(square1.location.X, _
                                    square1.location.Y + SquareSize)
        square2.location = New Point(square2.location.X, _
                                    square2.location.Y + SquareSize)
        square3.location = New Point(square3.location.X, _
                                    square3.location.Y + SquareSize)
        square4.location = New Point(square4.location.X, _
                                    square4.location.Y + SquareSize)
        ' Draw the block in the new position
        Show(ClsGameField.picGameField)
    Else
        ' If there's a block below the current one, don't go down
        ' -> put it on the array that controls the game and return FALSE
        Down = False
        ClsGameField.StopSquare(square1, _
            square1.location.X / SquareSize, square1.location.Y / SquareSize)
        ClsGameField.StopSquare(square2, _
            square2.location.X / SquareSize, square2.location.Y / SquareSize)
        ClsGameField.StopSquare(square3, _
            square3.location.X / SquareSize, square3.location.Y / SquareSize)
        ClsGameField.StopSquare(square4, _
            square4.location.X / SquareSize, square4.location.Y / SquareSize)
    End If
End Function
```

In this code sample, we are using the GameField class again with shared methods (no objects created). The concepts of shared properties and methods were explained earlier in this chapter.

The Right and Left methods are very similar to this one, with the slight difference that we don't stop the block if it can't go right or left. The code for the Right method is shown next. The Left method is built upon the same basic structure.

```
Public Function Right() As Boolean
    Right = True
    ' If there's no block to the right of the current one, go right
    If ClsGameField.IsEmpty(square1.location.X / SquareSize + 1, _
                    square1.location.Y / SquareSize) _
        And ClsGameField.IsEmpty(square2.location.X / SquareSize + 1, _
                    square2.location.Y / SquareSize) _
        And ClsGameField.IsEmpty(square3.location.X / SquareSize + 1, _
                    square3.location.Y / SquareSize) _
        And ClsGameField.IsEmpty(square4.location.X / SquareSize + 1, _
                    square4.location.Y / SquareSize) Then
        ' Hide the block (in the previous position)
        Hide(ClsGameField.picGameField)
        ' Update the block position
        square1.location = New Point(square1.location.X + SquareSize, _
                                    square1.location.Y)
        square2.location = New Point(square2.location.X + SquareSize, _
                                    square2.location.Y)
        square3.location = New Point(square3.location.X + SquareSize, _
                                    square3.location.Y)
        square4.location = New Point(square4.location.X + SquareSize, _
                                    square4.location.Y)
        ' Draw the block in the new position
        Show(ClsGameField.picGameField)
    Else
    ' If there's a block to the right of the current one,
    ' doesn't go right and return FALSE
        Right = False
    End If
End Function
```

The next method for the Block class, Rotate, is a little more complicated, so we'll take a closer look at it in the next section.

## The Rotate Method

While in the previously discussed methods all we needed to do was to change a single coordinate for all the squares of the block (incrementing y to go down, and modifying x to go right or left), in this case we need to change the squares' positions, one by one, to achieve the effect of rotation. The rotation movement must be based on the block type and on the current orientation of the block.

To track the current rotation applied to the block, we'll need a new property. Creating a new enumeration for the possible rotation status will make our code more readable:

```
Public Enum enStatusRotation
    NORTH = 1
    EAST = 2
    SOUTH = 3
    WEST = 4
End Enum


Public StatusRotation As enStatusRotation = enStatusRotation.NORTH
```

In order to make the method simpler, and to avoid calculating the rotation twice—once to test for empty squares and again to rotate the block—we'll store the current position, rotate the block, and then test to see if the squares of the new block position are empty. If so, we just draw the block in the new position. If not, we restore the previous position.

The basic structure for the method (without the rotation code for each block type) is shown next:

```
Public Sub Rotate()
    ' Store the current block position
    Dim OldPosition1 As Point = square1.location
    Dim OldPosition2 As Point = square2.location
    Dim OldPosition3 As Point = square3.location
    Dim OldPosition4 As Point = square4.location
    Dim OldStatusRotation as enStatusRotation = StatusRotation
    Hide(ClsGameField.picGameField)

    ' Rotate the blocks
    Select Case BlockType
        Case enBlockType.SQUARE
            ' Here will go the code for rotate this block type
        Case enBlockType.LINE
            ' Here will go the code for rotate this block type
```

```
      Case enBlockType.J
          ' Here will go the code for rotate this block type
      Case enBlockType.L
          ' Here will go the code for rotate this block type
      Case enBlockType.T
          ' Here will go the code for rotate this block type
      Case enBlockType.Z
          ' Here will go the code for rotate this block type
      Case enBlockType.S
          ' Here will go the code for rotate this block type
  End Select

  ' After rotating the squares, test if they overlap other squares.
  '  If so, return to original position
  If Not (ClsGameField.IsEmpty(square1.location.X / SquareSize, _
                            square1.location.Y / SquareSize) _
      And ClsGameField.IsEmpty(square2.location.X / SquareSize, _
                        square2.location.Y / SquareSize) _
      And ClsGameField.IsEmpty(square3.location.X / SquareSize, _
                            square3.location.Y / SquareSize) _
      And ClsGameField.IsEmpty(square4.location.X / SquareSize, _
                        square4.location.Y / SquareSize)) Then
      StatusRotation = OldStatusRotation
      square1.location = OldPosition1
      square2.location = OldPosition2
      square3.location = OldPosition3
      square4.location = OldPosition4
  End If
  ' Draws the square at the correct position
  Show(ClsGameField.picGameField)
End Sub
```

Based on each block type and its current status, we can calculate the rotations. There will be three types of rotation:

- **Square blocks:** These do nothing. Squares don't need to rotate since they look the same when rotated.

- **Line, S, and Z blocks:** These will have only two possible directions for rotation, north and east.

- **T, J, and L blocks:** These will have four different positions, north, east, south, and west.

In any case, we must choose a specific square to stay fixed while the others rotate around it. In the examples that follow, we show what must be in each case statement of the Rotate method, starting with the rotation for a Line block type, represented in Figure 1-27.

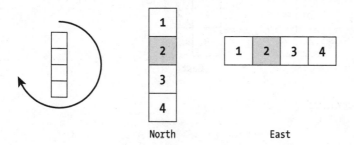

North                    East

*Figure 1-27. Line block: rotation around the second square*

The code to implement the rotation of the Line block is shown in the next code listing:

```
Select Case StatusRotation
    Case enStatusRotation.NORTH
        StatusRotation = enStatusRotation.EAST
        square1.location = New Point( _
                square2.location.X - SquareSize, square2.location.Y)
        square3.location = New Point( _
                square2.location.X + SquareSize, square2.location.Y)
        square4.location = New Point( _
                square2.location.X + 2 * SquareSize, square2.location.Y)
    Case enStatusRotation.EAST
        StatusRotation = enStatusRotation.NORTH
        square1.location = New Point( _
                square2.location.X, square2.location.Y - SquareSize)
        square3.location = New Point( _
                square2.location.X, square2.location.Y + SquareSize)
        square4.location = New Point( _
                square2.location.X, square2.location.Y + 2 * SquareSize)
End Select
```

Notice that the new square positions are all based on the position of the second square of the block; we just add or subtract the square sizes to move the square up and down (y coordinate) or right and left (x coordinate). In each case, we set the new status of the rotation.

Figure 1-28 illustrates the rotation for the Z block type. The S and Z block types rotate in a very similar way.

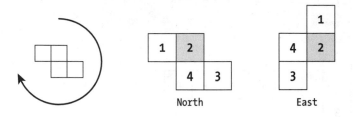

*Figure 1-28. The Z block rotation*

Following is the code for the Z block type; the S block follows the same logic.

```
Select Case StatusRotation
    Case enStatusRotation.NORTH
        StatusRotation = enStatusRotation.EAST
        square1.location = New Point(square2.location.X, _
                                    square2.location.Y - SquareSize)
        square3.location = New Point(square2.location.X - SquareSize, _
                                    square2.location.Y)
        square4.location = New Point(square2.location.X - SquareSize, _
                                    square2.location.Y + SquareSize)
    Case enStatusRotation.EAST
        StatusRotation = enStatusRotation.NORTH
        square1.location = New Point(square2.location.X - SquareSize, _
                                    square2.location.Y)
        square3.location = New Point(square2.location.X, _
                                    square2.location.Y + SquareSize)
        square4.location = New Point(square2.location.X + SquareSize, _
                                    square2.location.Y + SquareSize)
End Select
```

As for the T, J, and L block types, the procedure will be a little longer, since we have four directions, but the basic idea remains the same: All squares run around a fixed one. Let's see some examples, starting with the T block type rotation, portrayed in Figure 1-29.

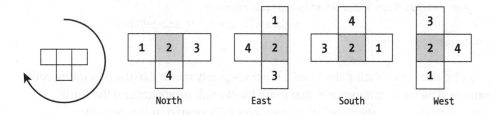

*Figure 1-29. Rotation of the T block*

The next code listing implements the rotation illustrated in Figure 1-29:

```
Select Case StatusRotation
Case enStatusRotation.NORTH
    StatusRotation = enStatusRotation.EAST
    square1.location = New Point(square2.location.X, _
                            square2.location.Y - SquareSize)
    square3.location = New Point(square2.location.X, _
                            square2.location.Y + SquareSize)
    square4.location = New Point(square2.location.X - SquareSize, _
                            square2.location.Y)
Case enStatusRotation.EAST
    StatusRotation = enStatusRotation.SOUTH
    square1.location = New Point(square2.location.X + SquareSize, _
                            square2.location.Y)
    square3.location = New Point(square2.location.X - SquareSize, _
                            square2.location.Y)
    square4.location = New Point(square2.location.X, _
                            square2.location.Y - SquareSize)
Case enStatusRotation.SOUTH
    StatusRotation = enStatusRotation.WEST
    square1.location = New Point(square2.location.X, _
                            square2.location.Y + SquareSize)
    square3.location = New Point(square2.location.X, _
                            square2.location.Y - SquareSize)
    square4.location = New Point(square2.location.X + SquareSize, _
                            square2.location.Y)
Case enStatusRotation.WEST
    StatusRotation = enStatusRotation.NORTH
    square1.location = New Point(square2.location.X - SquareSize, _
                            square2.location.Y)
    square3.location = New Point(square2.location.X + SquareSize, _
                            square2.location.Y)
```

```
        square4.location = New Point(square2.location.X, _
                                square2.location.Y + SquareSize)
End Select
```

The code for rotating the J and L blocks is pretty much like the preceding code sample. The main difference is that these blocks will rotate around the third square, as shown in the rotation for the J block illustrated in Figure 1-30.

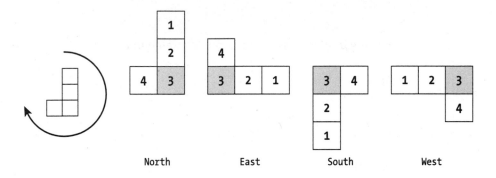

North          East          South          West

*Figure 1-30. Rotation for the J block*

The last two methods for the Block class are discussed in the next section.

## *The Show and Hide Methods*

The implementation of the Show and Hide methods is very straightforward: the Show and Hide methods are called for each of the block squares, as shown here:

```
Public Sub Show(WinHandle As System.IntPtr)
    ' Draws each square of the block on the game field
    square1.Show(WinHandle)
    square2.Show(WinHandle)
    square3.Show(WinHandle)
    square4.Show(WinHandle)
End Sub

Public Sub Hide(WinHandle As System.IntPtr)
    ' Hides each square of the block on the game field
    square1.Hide(WinHandle)
    square2.Hide(WinHandle)
    square3.Hide(WinHandle)
    square4.Hide(WinHandle)
End Sub
```

To see the full code for the Block class, refer to the samples on the accompanying CD-ROM.

To test our new class, we'll have to create a new stub for the GameField class and update our main program, as shown in the next section.

## Testing the Block Class

The new stub for the GameField class must include the properties and methods accessed by the Block class, as shown in the next code listing:

```
Public Class ClsGameField
    Public Shared backcolor As Color
    Public Shared WinHandle As System.IntPtr

    Public Shared Function IsEmpty(x As Integer, y As Integer) As Boolean
            IsEmpty = True
    End Function
    Public Shared Function StopSquare(Square As ClsSquare, _
                            x As Integer, y As Integer) As Boolean
        StopSquare = True
    End Function
End Class
```

The IsEmpty and StopSquare methods always return True; we'll add code for these methods in the final version of the program.

The next code listing shows the logic for testing the Block class, and must be included in the game field form:

```
Private CurrentBlock as clsBlock

Sub Form_Load(sender As System.Object, e As System.EventArgs) _
                    Handles MyBase.Load
    ' Set the properties of clsGameField class
    clsGameField.backcolor = picBackground.BackColor
    clsGameField.picGameField = PicBackground
End Sub

Sub CmdStart_Click( sender As System.Object, e As System.EventArgs) _
                    Handles CmdStart.Click
    CurrentBlock = new clsBlock(new Point (40,20))
    CurrentBlock.Show(PicBackground)
End Sub
```

```
Private Sub Form1_KeyDown(sender As Object, _
    e As System.Windows.Forms.KeyEventArgs) Handles MyBase.KeyDown
        Select Case e.KeyCode
            Case Keys.Right
                CurrentBlock.Right()
            Case Keys.Left
                CurrentBlock.Left()
            Case Keys.Up
                CurrentBlock.Rotate()
            Case Keys.Down
                CurrentBlock.Down()
        End Select
    End Sub
```

**NEW IN .NET**

*All the constants in the .NET Framework are organized within enumerations. This approach allows a more intuitive organization, so it's easier to find exactly what you need in the help feature. The intelligence of Visual Studio was also improved, giving more hints and softening the learning curve. In the preceding sample code, we are using the* Keys *enumeration to get the key code (Left, Down, Up, and Right). There are also modifiers to test if Shift, Ctrl, and Alt keys are pressed. The namespace for the* Keys *enumeration is* SYSTEM.Windows.Forms.

To test the program, just run it, click the Start button, and press the various keys to move the blocks: the down arrow key makes the block go down, the up arrow key rotates the block, and the right arrow and left arrow keys move the block horizontally. Clicking the Start button again will create a new block, so we can test the random creation of different block types. A sample screen is shown in Figure 1-31.

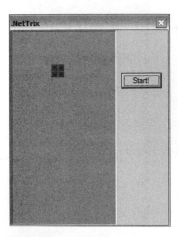

*Figure 1-31. Testing the Block class*

In the next section we'll implement the collision detection and the main program logic, finishing our game.

## Final Version: Coding the GameField Class and the Game Engine

To finish our program, we'll have to complete the code for the game engine and the GameField class, as shown in the next sections.

## GameField Class

Let's examine the code to implement the interface for the GameField class, as defined in our game project.

```
Public Class ClsGameField
    Public Const Width As Integer = 16
    Public Const Height As Integer = 30
    Public Const SquareSize As Integer = 10
    Public Shared WinHandle As System.IntPtr
    Public Shared backcolor As Color
    Private Shared arrGameField(Width, Height) As ClsSquare

    Public Shared Function IsEmpty(x As Integer, y As Integer) As Boolean
    Public Shared Function CheckLines() As Int16
    Public Shared Function StopSquare(Square As ClsSquare, _
                    x As Integer, y As Integer) As Boolean
    Public Shared Function Redraw() As Boolean
End Class
```

The GameField interface shown in the preceding code has its members (properties and methods) defined in the class diagram proposed in the game project, plus the new properties and methods defined in the stubs we created previously. Then again, although it isn't unusual that such changes really happen in a real-life project, it's one of our goals to define a clear and comprehensive project before starting to code. Remember, changing a project is far easier (and cheaper) than changing and adapting code; and that if there are many unpredictable changes to code, the project tends to be more prone to errors and more difficult to maintain. (We refer to this as the "Frankenstein syndrome": the project will be no longer a single and organized piece of code, but many not so well-sewed-on parts.)

One interesting point about this class is that every member is declared as shared! In other words, we can access any method or property of the class without creating any objects. This isn't the suggested use of shared properties or methods; we usually create shared class members when we need to create many objects in the class, and have some information—such as a counter for the number of objects created, or properties that, once set, affect all the objects created.

The next sections discuss the GameField class methods, starting with the IsEmpty method.

## The IsEmpty Method

The first class method, IsEmpty, must check if a given x,y position of the game array (arrGameField) is empty. The next method, CheckLines, has to check each of the lines of the array to see if any one of them is full of squares, and remove any such lines.

Since the arrGameField is an array of Square objects, we can check if any position is assigned to a square with a simple test:

```
Public Shared Function IsEmpty(x As Integer, y As Integer) _
                                        As Boolean

    If arrGameField(x,y) is nothing
        IsEmpty = True
    Else
        IsEmpty = False
    End if
End Function
```

Some extra tests should be done to see if the x or the y position is above (or below) the array boundaries.

Although in this game we don't need high-speed calculations, we can use an improved algorithm for collision detection, so that we can see a practical example of using these algorithms.

We can improve the performance of the IsEmpty and CheckLines functions using an array of bits to calculate the collisions. Since our game field is 16 squares wide, we can create a new array of integers, where each bit must be set if there's a square associated with it. We still must maintain the arrGameField array, because it will be used to redraw the squares when a line is erased or the entire game field must be redrawn (for example, when the window gets the focus after being below other window).

The array that holds the bits for each line must have the same Height as the arrGameField, and will have just one dimension, since the Width will be given for the bits in each integer (16 bits per element). The array definition is shown in the next code line:

```
Private Shared arrBitGameField(Height) As Integer
```

And the `IsEmpty` function is as follows:

```
Public Shared Function IsEmpty(x As Integer, y As Integer) _
                    As Boolean
    IsEmpty = True
    ' If the Y or X is beyond the game field, return false
    If (y < 0 Or y >= Height) Or (x < 0 Or x >= Width) Then
        IsEmpty = False
    ' Test the Xth bit of the Yth line of the game field
    ElseIf arrBitGameField(y) And (2 ^ x) Then
        IsEmpty = False
    End If
End Function
```

In this sample code, the first `if` statement checks whether the x and y parameters are inside the game field range. The second `if` deserves a closer look: What is `arrBitGameField(y) And (2 ^ x)` supposed to test? In simple words, it just checks the xth bit of the `arrBitGameField(y)` byte.

This piece of code works well because the comparison operators of Visual Basic, since earlier versions, work in a binary way. The `AND` operator then performs a bit-to-bit comparison, and returns a combination of both operands. If the same bit is set in both operands, this bit will be set in the result; if only one or none of the operators have the bit set, the result won't have the bit set. In Table 1-4 we show the operands' bits for some `AND` comparisons.

*Table 1-4. Bits and Results for Some AND Operations*

| NUMBERS | BITS |
| --- | --- |
| 1 AND 2 = 0 | 01 AND 10 = 0 (false) |
| 3 AND 12 = 0 | 0011 AND 1100 = 0000 (false) |
| 3 AND 11 = 3 | 0011 AND 1011 = 0011 (true) |

In our code, if we want to check, for example, the 7th bit, the first operand must be the array element we want to check, `arrBitGameField(Y)`, and the second operand must have the bits 00000000 01000000 (16 bits total, with the 7th one checked).

If we did our binary homework well, we'd remember that setting the bits one by one results in powers of 2: 1, 2, 4, 8, 16, and so on, for 00001, 00010, 00100, 01000, 10000, etc. The easiest way to calculate powers of 2 is just to shift the bits to the left; but since we have no bit shift operators in Visual Basic, we need to use the power operator (^).

Looking again at the second `if` statement, everything should make sense now:

- `arrBitGameField(y)`: The 16 bits of the yth line of the game field.

- `2 ^ x`: Calculates a number with **only one** bit set—the xth one.

- `arrBitGameField(y) And (2 ^ x)`: If the xth bit of the array element is set, then the test will return a nonzero number; any other bit set won't affect the result, since the second operand has only the xth bit set.

The `CheckLines` method will use this same bit array to more easily check if a line is filled with squares, as we'll discuss next.

### The `CheckLines` method

In the next `GameField` method, `CheckLines`, we need to check if a line is totally filled (all bits set) and, if so, erase this line and move down all the lines above it. We don't need to copy the empty lines (all bits reset) one on top of another, but we must return the number of cleared lines. To improve the readability of our code, we'll define some private constants for the class:

```
Private Const bitEmpty As Integer = &H0&      '00000000 0000000
Private Const bitFull As Integer = &HFFFF&     '11111111 1111111
```

See the comments in the code and the following explanation to understand the function:

```
Public Shared Function CheckLines() As Integer
    Dim y As Integer, x As Integer
    Dim i As Integer
    CheckLines = 0
    y = Height - 1
    Do While y >= 0
        ' stops the loop when the blank lines are reached
        If arrBitGameField(y) = bitEmpty Then y = 0
```

```
    ' If all the bits of the line are set, then increment the
    '     counter to clear the line and move all above lines down
    If arrBitGameField(y) = bitFull Then
        ' Same as: If (arrBitGameField(y) Xor bitFull) = 0 Then
        CheckLines += 1

        ' Move all next lines down
        For i = y To 0 Step -1
            ' if the current line is NOT the first of the game field,
            '   copy the line above
            If i > 0 Then
                ' Copy the bits from the line above
                arrBitGameField(i) = arrBitGameField(i - 1)

                ' Copy each of the squares from the line above
                For x = 0 To Width - 1
                    ' Copy the square
                    arrGameField(x, i) = arrGameField(x, i - 1)
                    ' update the Location property of the square
                    Try
                        With arrGameField(x, i)
                            .location = New Point(.location.X, _
                                                .location.Y + SquareSize)
                        End With
                    Catch
                        ' Ignore the error if arrGameField(x, y) is Nothing
                    End Try
                Next
            Else
                ' if the current line is the first of the game field
                '   just clear the line
                arrBitGameField(i) = bitEmpty
                For x = 0 To Width - 1
                    arrGameField(x, i) = Nothing
                Next
            End If
        Next
    Else
        y -= 1
    End If
Loop
End Function
```

In the preceding code sample, two points need more explanation: the structured error handling and the bit checking logic.

---

**NEW IN .NET**

*.NET introduced in Visual Basic structured error handling, an old item on the wish list of programmers. Structured error handling is composed of three blocks—Try, Catch, and Finally—as shown in the code sample that follows. The Catch block receives a variable that is filled with information about the exception, and could be used to do proper error handling.*

```
Try
    '  Statements that could cause an error
Catch e As Exception
    ' Code to be executed only if an error occurred in the Try block
Finally
    ' Code to de executed in any situation, after the Try block
End Try
```

---

In the CheckLines method, we use structured error handling in order to avoid an extra test when copying squares. Since we can copy a square or an empty variable, we should test to see if the Square variable is set before setting the Location property, to avoid errors. Using error handling, the error is just ignored, with no collateral effects. The test we avoid is this one:

```
If arrBitGameField(y - 1) And (2 ^ x) Then
' Same as: If arrGameField(x, y - 1) = Nothing then
    With arrGameField(x, y)
        .location = New Point(.location.X,.location.Y + squaresize)
    end with
end if
```

In the CheckLines method we can see the real benefits of creating arrBitGameField for collision detection: We can check if a line is completely filled or empty with only one test, with the use of bitFull and bitEmpty constants we previously created, avoiding the 16 tests we would have had to create for each of the ArrGameField members in a line. The next code listing highlights these tests:

```
If arrBitGameField(y) = bitFull Then    '  The line is full
If arrBitGameField(y) = bitEmpty Then   '  The line is empty
```

The next section discusses the last two methods for the GameField class.

## The StopSquare and Redraw Methods

The last two methods, StopSquare (which sets the arrays when a block stops falling) and Redraw (which redraws the entire game field), have no surprises. The code implementing these methods is shown in the next listing:

```
Public Shared Function StopSquare(Square As ClsSquare, _
                    x As Integer, y As Integer) As Boolean
    arrBitGameField(y) = arrBitGameField(y) Or (2 ^ x)
    arrGameField(x, y) = Square
End Function

Public Shared Function Redraw() As Boolean
    Dim x As Integer, y As Integer
    ' at first, clear the game field
    picGameField.Invalidate()
    Application.DoEvents()

    ' Draws all the squares until reaching the empty lines
    y = Height - 1
    Do While y >= 0 And arrBitGameField(y) <> bitEmpty
        For x = Width - 1 To 0 Step -1
            Try
                arrGameField(x, y).Show(picGameField)
            Catch
                ' there's no square do draw... do nothing
            End Try
        Next
    Loop
End Function
```

**NEW IN .NET**

*In Visual Basic .NET, the graphic routines went through a major transformation, making them much closer to the underlying graphics API , the DLLs for graphics operations. One example is shown in the preceding code: The previous* CLS *method is now called* Invalidate, *and can be used to invalidate the whole* Image *object (and then force it to be redrawn) or receive a specific rectangular structure, which tells us exactly which part of the image must be redrawn. Those who worked with graphics manipulation in the C language will be comfortable with this new notation as it's the same in both languages.*

*Another interesting point is that many functions from the earlier versions of Visual Basic are organized into objects and methods. We can see the math functions compiled as methods into the* Math *object, or, in the preceding sample, system functions like* DoEvents *organized as methods of the* Application *object. This is another useful group of functions that are organized as methods from the* System *object.*

The next section shows the code for the final version of the main program, finishing our game code.

## The Game Engine

Now that all the base classes are coded, let's finish the main procedures.

In the first drafts for the game engine, we used the form procedures to call methods in our base classes, so we could see if they were working well. Now, the game engine must be coded to implement the features defined in the game proposal, stated earlier in this chapter. Let's remind ourselves of the pseudo-code defined in the game project:

```
Form_Load
     Creates an object (named currentBlock) of block class
Form_KeyPress
     If Left Arrow was pressed, call Left method of currentBlock
     If Right Arrow was pressed, call Right method of currentBlock
     If Up Arrow was pressed, call Rotate method of currentBlock
     If Down Arrow was pressed, call Down method of currentBlock
Timer_Tick
     If there is no block below currentBlock,
          and the currentBlock didn't reach the bottom of the screen then
          Call the Down method of currentBlock
     Else
          Stop the block
```

```
        If it's at the top of the screen then
                The game is over
        If we filled any horizontal lines then
                Increase the game score
                Erase the line
        Create a new block at the top of the screen
```

Before starting to translate this pseudo-code to actual Visual Basic code, it's important to stress two points:

- It's not common to use timer objects to control games. The timer object doesn't have the necessary precision or accuracy (we can't trust it entirely when dealing with time frames less than 10 milliseconds). But for games like .Nettrix, the levels of accuracy and precision available with the timer are adequate (remember that we are trying to make the production of this game as simple as possible). In the next chapter, we'll see a GDI+ application that runs at full speed, without using a timer.

- It's not common in game programming to put the game engine code in a form. Usually we create a GameEngine class that deals with all the game physics and rules (as we'll see in the next chapter).

Looking back at the pseudo-code, we see the following instruction:

```
        If it's at the top of the screen then
```

This tests if the block is at the top of the screen. Reviewing our Block class, we see that we have no direct way to retrieve the block Top position, so we would have to test each of the Top positions of the block's composing squares. To solve this, let's make a final adjustment to the Block class, including a new method, as depicted in the next code listing:

```
Public Function Top() As Integer
    Top = Math.Min(square1.location.Y, _
    Math.Min(square2.location.Y, _
    Math.Min(square3.location.Y, square4.location.Y)))
End Function
```

Now we are ready to finish our program. Based on the preceding pseudo-code and on some minor changes made in the game coding phase, the code for the form will be as follows:

```
Dim CurrentBlock As clsBlock
Dim blnRedraw As Boolean

Private Sub tmrGameClock_Tick(sender As System.Object, e As System.EventArgs) _
                            Handles tmrGameClock.Tick
    Static stillProcessing As Boolean = False
Dim ErasedLines As Integer
    ' Prevents the code from running if the previous tick
    '    is still being processed
    If stillProcessing Then Exit Sub
    stillProcessing = True

    ' Controls the block falling
    If Not CurrentBlock.Down() Then
        ' Test for game over
        If CurrentBlock.Top = 0 Then
            tmrGameClock.Enabled = False
            CmdStart.Enabled = True
            MessageBox.Show("GAME OVER", ".Nettrix", _
                    MessageBoxButtons.OK, MessageBoxIcon.Stop)
            Exit Sub
        End If
        ' increase the score using the number of deleted lines, if any
            ErasedLines = ClsGameField.CheckLines()
            lblScoreValue.Text += 100 * ErasedLines
            ' Clear the game field
            If ErasedLines > 0 Then
                PicBackground.Invalidate()
                Application.DoEvents()
                ClsGameField.Redraw()
            End If
        ' Releases the current block from memory
        CurrentBlock = Nothing
        ' Creates the new current block
        CurrentBlock = New clsBlock( _
                        New Point(ClsGameField.SquareSize * 6, 0))
        CurrentBlock.Show(PicBackground)
    End If
```

```
        stillProcessing = False
End Sub
```

Compare the preceding code listing with the previous pseudo-code to make sure each line of code has been understood.

The Load event for the form, and the KeyDown event and the code for the Start button remain unchanged. The final version of .Nettrix has now been coded. When the game is run, it looks like the screen shown in Figure 1-32.

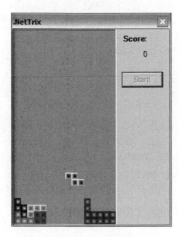

*Figure 1-32. The final version of .Nettrix*

We can now play our own homemade clone of Tetris, and are ready to improve it, with the changes discussed in the next section.

## Adding the Final Touches

After playing the first version of .Nettrix for a few minutes, every player will miss two important features present in almost every Tetris type of game: a feature to show the next block that will appear, and some way to pause the game, for emergency situations (like your boss crossing the office and heading in your direction). Now that we have all base classes already finished, this is easily done. The next sections discuss these and some other features to improve our first game.

## Coding the Next Block Feature

To show the next block, we can create a new `pictureBox` on the form, to hold the next block image, and adjust the click of the Start button and the `timer_tick` event. We can use the optional parameter we created on the `Block` constructor (the `New` method) to create the new blocks following the block type of the next block.

To implement this feature, we'll create a variable to hold the next block in the general section of the form:

```
Dim NextBlock As clsBlock
```

At the end of the `cmdStart_click` event, we'll add two lines to create the next block:

```
NextBlock = New clsBlock(New Point(20, 10))
NextBlock.Show(PicNextBlock.Handle)
```

And finally we'll adjust the `Tick` event of the timer, to create a new block every time the current block stops falling, and to force the `CurrentBlock` type to be the same as the `NextBlock` type.

```
' Releases the current block from memory
CurrentBlock = Nothing
' Creates the new current block
CurrentBlock = New clsBlock(New Point(ClsGameField.SquareSize * 6, 0),_
                               NextBlock.BlockType)
CurrentBlock.Show(PicBackground.Handle)

' Releases the next block from memory
NextBlock.Hide(PicNextBlock.Handle)
NextBlock = Nothing
' Creates the new next block
NextBlock = New clsBlock(New Point(20, 10))
NextBlock.Show(PicNextBlock.Handle)
```

We can now run the game, and see the next block being displayed in the picture box we've just created, as shown in Figure 1-33.

*Figure 1-33. Showing the next block*

The next section shows another improvement, the game pause feature.

## Coding the Game Pause Feature

To create a pause function, all we need to do is to stop the timer when a specific key is pressed—usually, the Esc key is used for such features. A simple adjustment in the KeyDown event, including an extra case clause for the Keys.Escape value, will do the trick:

```
Private Sub Form1_KeyDown(sender As Object, e As KeyEventArgs)
                    Handles MyBase.KeyDown
    Select Case e.KeyCode
        Case Keys.Right
            CurrentBlock.Right()
        Case Keys.Left
            CurrentBlock.Left()
        Case Keys.Up
            CurrentBlock.Rotate()
        Case Keys.Down
            CurrentBlock.Down()
        Case Keys.Escape
            tmrGameClock.Enabled = Not tmrGameClock.Enabled
            If tmrGameClock.Enabled Then
                Me.Text = ".Nettrix"
            Else
```

```
                    Me.Text = ".Nettrix - Press ESC to continue"
                End If
        End Select
End Sub
```

In the next section we'll discuss an improvement to the graphical part of our game.

## Coding the Window Redraw

A little problem with our game is that, when the .Nettrix window is covered by other windows, the game field isn't redrawn. We can adjust this by including a call to the GameField's Redraw method, at the Activate event of the form (the Activate event occurs every time the form gets the focus again, after losing it to another window):

```
Private Sub FrmNetTrix_Activated(sender As Object, e As System.EventArgs)
                    Handles MyBase.Activated
    ' This event occurs when the window receives back the focus after
    '        losing it to another window
    '   So, we redraw the whole game field
    ClsGameField.Redraw()
End Sub
```

Even using this approach there'll be some situations when the windows won't be redrawn properly. To achieve the best results, we should include the call to the Redraw method in the Tick event of the timer, but since it could compromise the speed of our game, we'll keep the code as shown.

The next section discusses some suggestions for future enhancements to our game.

## Further Improvements

Two last improvements we could make are creating levels for the game and producing a configurations screen, but these we'll leave for you to do by yourself.

To create levels for the game, we could use a basic rule like this one: Every 3 minutes the blocks falling speed is increased by 10 percent, the game level is incremented by one, and the points earned for each block gets multiplied by the level number. We can just adjust the timer tick procedure to include the logic for this rule.

In the case of a configurations screen, we could choose to see or not to see the next block image (setting the Visible property of the picNextBlock accordingly) and adjust the block size on the screen, so the visually impaired can play with big blocks, and those who like to play pixel hunt can do so with single-pixel square blocks.

Since the whole game is based on the GameField.SquareSize constant, implementing this feature is just a matter of creating the configuration window and adjusting the screen size according to the chosen square size. The next code listing is provided to underscore this last point; just add the following code to the procedure to be able to adjust the screen size after the configuration:

```
' Adjusts the size and controls position based on the class constants
' On the window height, sums the size of the window title bar
Me.Height = ClsGameField.Height * ClsGameField.SquareSize + _
        (Me.Height - Me.ClientSize.Height) + 3 ' 3=border width
Me.Width = ClsGameField.Width * ClsGameField.SquareSize + 92
Me.PicBackground.Height = ClsGameField.Height * ClsGameField.SquareSize + 4
Me.PicBackground.Width = ClsGameField.Width * ClsGameField.SquareSize + 4
Me.PicNextBlock.Left = ClsGameField.Width * ClsGameField.SquareSize + 12
Me.LblNextBlock.Left = ClsGameField.Width * ClsGameField.SquareSize + 12
Me.lblScore.Left = ClsGameField.Width * ClsGameField.SquareSize + 12
Me.lblScoreValue.Left = ClsGameField.Width * ClsGameField.SquareSize + 12
Me.CmdStart.Left = ClsGameField.Width * ClsGameField.SquareSize + 12
```

We are adjusting neither the font size nor the button sizes, so to work with smaller sizes, some updating of the code will be necessary.

In the samples CD-ROM, the code is on the Load event of the form, so you can play with different sizes by simply adjusting the SquareSize constant and recompiling the code.

## Summary

In this chapter we created our first game, .Nettrix, and explored some important concepts that will be used even in sophisticated games, including the following:

- Basic concepts about GDI+ and the new graphics objects used on Visual Basic .NET

- Basic concepts about collision detection and some suggestions on how to implement fast collision algorithms in our games

- Creation of simple classes and structured error handling in Visual Basic .NET

- Basic game engine creation, based on a game proposal and with the support of a game project

In the next chapter, we'll look at the concept of artificial intelligence, how to create a game with computer-controlled characters, and how to create faster graphics routines with GDI+. We'll also examine some additional concepts concerning object-oriented programming.

# CHAPTER 2

# .Netterpillars: Artificial Intelligence and Sprites

IN THIS CHAPTER we'll explore the concepts of artificial intelligence (AI) and sprites. We'll also extend our knowledge of GDI+ functions, including some tips intended to give us a boost in performance. To accomplish these goals and illustrate these concepts, we'll create a game called .Netterpillars.

.Netterpillars is an arcade game in which each player controls a caterpillar (in fact, a "netterpillar") that takes part in a mushroom-eating race with other netterpillars. The objective of the game is to be the last surviving netterpillar, or the longest one (they grow when they eat) when every mushroom has been eaten. We'll describe the game in more detail in the section "The Game Proposal" later in this chapter.

.Netterpillars is a more complex game than the one we saw in the last chapter because it involves the following components:

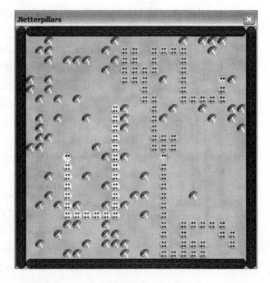

*Figure 2-1.*
*.Netterpillars, this chapter's sample game*

- **AI:** Creating a game with opponents will make us exercise our ability to create a computer-controlled character that challenges players, while giving them a fair chance of winning.

- **Sprites:** Using nonblocky game objects will force us to find a way to draw nonrectangular moving objects on screen. Including a background image in our game screen will help us to check if our moving code is working (remember, in the last chapter we simply painted the objects with the flat background color).

- **GDI+:** Creating an interface where many objects (one to four caterpillars, wooden branches, and a lot of mushrooms) will be drawn and interact with each other will challenge us to find a faster way to update the screen.

While covering these topics, we'll also look at new concepts related to object-oriented programming so we can create easily reuseable classes to improve the productivity when coding our games. For example, a "sprite" class is something that almost any game will need; so we can code it once and use it forever. We'll discuss all these points in the next sections, starting with some object-oriented concepts.

## Object-Oriented Programming

There are many technical books that explain the academic details of object-oriented analysis (OOA) and object-oriented programming (OOP). It's not our goal to enter into such particulars, but instead loosely define a few terms and demonstrate some practical uses of these techniques.

The main idea behind creating objects is to make our code simpler to write and easier to maintain. By creating high-level objects to take care of specific tasks, we can build our games using these objects without needing to remember every tiny detail about a new game.

A good analogy to consider is jigsaw puzzles: How many blue skies have you seen in different puzzles? And, for each one, you always have to put the pieces together one by one, regardless of the skies you have assembled before. If we could use OO concepts on puzzles, we would assemble the sky once, and for every new puzzle we could use this ready-made sky as a starting point, and build only the different parts around it.

Even considering a single puzzle, the analogy is still relevant: It's far easier to assemble the puzzle if we put similar pieces in different groups, assemble the groups, and then glue them together to see the final picture. That's pure OOP: Group related functions and data inside objects, code and test the objects, and then code the interface between them.

Table 2-1 lists some common terms used when talking about object-oriented programming and analysis, along with a definition of each.

*Table 2-1. Common Object-Oriented Terminology*

| TERM | DEFINITION |
| --- | --- |
| Class | The code we write that is used as a blueprint to create objects. It can have methods, properties, and events. |
| Object | An instance of a class, or, in other words, a variable of a specific class, after the object has been created. |
| Methods | Functions defined inside a class. |
| Properties or attributes | Variables defined inside a class. |
| Events | Procedures in the call triggered by the object called. May be associated to a user action (such as clicking a button) or to a system action (such as a specific time slice elapsed). |
| Constructor | Special method called when creating an object—in Visual Basic .NET, this is any function with the New name. |
| Destructor | Special method called when the object is being destroyed. In Visual Basic, to code the destructor we have to override (see the Overriding entry) the Dispose method of the base class. |
| Inheritance | Object-oriented concept which defines that one class can be derived from another class or classes (called *base* or *mother* classes), and inherit their interface and code (called the *derived* or *child* class). |
| Overriding | Object-oriented concept which defines that a derived class can create a different implementation of a base class method, to deal with specific needs of the derived class. |
| Interface | The set of public methods, properties, and events of one class. Public elements are visible to any program that creates an object from a class. When applied to a method, this means its parameters and return values. |
| Encapsulation | Concept related to the puzzle analogy: All details are embedded in the class, so the program that creates the object doesn't need to care about them. |
| Overloading | Object-oriented concept which states that one method can have many different interfaces, while keeping the same name. |
| Polymorphism | Object-oriented concept which says that different objects can have different implementations of the same function. An Add method, for example, can sum integers and concatenate strings. |

**NOTE** *We'll refer to these concepts and terms throughout the rest of the book, reinforcing their meanings as we go along.*

Continuing with the introductory concepts of this chapter, let's talk about artificial intelligence, giving a real-life application of this concept born in science fiction books.

## Artificial Intelligence

AI, for our purposes, is the code in a program that determines the behavior of an object—in other words, how each game object will act upon and react to the game environment in each specific time frame.

The game's AI is often confused with the game physics, or the "simulation" as some gamers prefer to call it. While the AI decides what to do, the physics sets the constraints and limits of the AI and your game play. Some examples will make this distinction clearer:

- Classic pinball games have no AI, only physics.

- In the SimCity game series, when players can't build a new residential block over a river, it's the game physics acting. When the Sims start creating their houses, it's the game AI's turn.

- In the 3-D maze fever started long ago by Castle Wolfenstein, the game physics tells players that they can't go through walls, and that their bullets will lower the enemy's energy until death. The game AI tells the enemy to turn around and fire at players if they shoot him, or if he "hears" them shooting.

A good game project usually has the physics and the AI very well defined and separated, and most times the AI acts just like a player over the game physics. For example, in a multiplayer race game, the players control some cars, and the AI will drive all cars with no pilots, ideally with the same difficulties that the human players have.

## AI Categories

We can divide the AI into three categories:

- **Environmental AI:** The kind of AI found in games like SimCity, where the environment (in this example, the city) acts as a lifelike environment, reacting to the player input and including some unexpected behavior of its own.

- **Opposing player AI:** Used in games where the AI will act like a player playing against the human. For example, in chess and other board games, we usually have a very sophisticated AI to play the part of an opponent.

- **Nonplayer characters (NPCs):** Many games have computer-controlled characters that could be friendly (for example, the warriors that join players in a quest on role-playing games, or RPGs, like Diablo), unfriendly (the monsters and enemies in 3D mazes), or neutral (the characters are there just to add color to the environment, such as the cooker at the Scumm bar in LucasArts' The Secret of Monkey Island).

Of course this division exists only for teaching purposes; sometimes there's no distinct barrier between the categories.

## General AI Considerations

Without entering into specific details, there are some things we have to remember when writing AI code:

- Don't let users find out that the AI has access to their internal data. For example, in games like Microsoft's Age of Empires, players only see part of the map. Even though the AI can access the full map, the computer-controlled tribes don't act as if they know all the players' characters positions.

- Create different levels of difficulty. Having a game with different levels lets players decide how tough they want their opponents to be. In some chess games, for example, players can choose how many future moves the computer will analyze, making the game easier or harder.

- Let the AI fail sometimes. If there's anything computers do well, it's executing code exactly the same way over and over. If you are coding a shooter game where the computer can shoot the player, don't forget to make the computer miss sometimes; and don't forget that an opponent that never misses is as bad as an opponent that always misses. Players play the game to win, but if they don't find it challenging, they'll never play your game again.

- Don't forget to take into account the environment variables. If players can't see through the walls, the NPCs must act as if they can't either. If the computer-controlled adversary has low energy, but is very well protected by walls, he or she won't run away. If players can hear sounds when someone is approaching or when someone shoots, the NPCs must act like they hear it too.

- Always add some random behavior. The correct balance of randomness will challenge players more, without making the game so unpredictable that it becomes unplayable. If the game has no element of chance, players can find a "golden path" that will allow them to always win when using a specific strategy.

- Let the AI "predict" players' moves. In some games, it's possible to predict players' moves by analyzing the possibilities based on the current situation, like in a checkers game. But in other games the AI can "cheat" a little, pretending that it predicted the moves of a good human player. For example, if the AI discovers that a player is sending soldiers through a narrow passage in the direction of its headquarters, it can put a sentinel in the passage and pretend that it "had considered" that someone could use that passage. And never forget to give players a chance (they can kill the sentinel, for example)!

## Common AI Techniques

When talking about AI, it's usual to hear about neural networks, genetic algorithms, fuzzy logic, and other technical terms. It's beyond the scope of this book to explain each of these approaches, but those who want to get deeper on the AI topic can search for these terms on the Internet to discover lots of interesting sites and relevant discussion groups.

These terms, when applied to games, have the main goals of adding unpredictability to the game actions and helping to create a game that seems to learn players' tricks and adapt to them to be more challenging. To take a more practical approach, we can obtain these results by applying some simple tricks that will require a lot less effort. In the next sections we discuss some of these tricks.

## Adaptable Percentage Tables

A neural network can be simplified as a table with adaptable results, represented by percentages. For example, when coding a war game, we can create a table to help the AI choose the tactics with which to attack the other players. The AI will use each tactic a set percentage of the time depending on the success rate that is represented by the percentage. The greater the success rate, the more often this tactic will be used. The table can be filled with some initial values, as shown in Table 2-2, and can evolve according to the results of each turn in the game.

*Table 2-2. Starting Values for an Adaptable Percentage Table*

| ATTACK TYPE | PERCENTAGE |
| --- | --- |
| Attack with "V" formation | 20 percent |
| Divide the soldiers in small groups and attack in waves | 20 percent |
| Guerrilla attack—surprise attack with a few soldiers, shoot and run away | 20 percent |
| Attack with full force, in a big group | 20 percent |
| Surround the player and attack from every direction | 20 percent |

After each attack, we'll change the table values according to the results. For example, if the attack is successful, we can add 10 percent to its corresponding percentage column on the table; if not, subtract 10 percent, distributing the difference to the other attack types. After some attacks, the program will "learn" which kind of attack is most efficient against the current player. For example, if the AI uses the first kind of attack (in "V" formation) and it was successful, the table would be updated to the values shown in Table 2-3.

*Table 2-3. Adaptable Percentage Table Values After a Successful "V" Formation Attack*

| ATTACK TYPE | PERCENTAGE |
| --- | --- |
| Attack with "V" formation | 30 percent |
| Divide the soldiers into small groups and attack in waves | 17.5 percent |
| Guerrilla attack—surprise attack with a few soldiers, shoot and run away | 17.5 percent |
| Attack with full force, in a big group | 17.5 percent |
| Surround the player and attack from every direction | 17.5 percent |

In the next turn, if the AI tries an attack using the guerrilla tactic and it fails, the table will be updated again, to the values shown in Table 2-4.

*Table 2-4. Adaptable Percentage Table Values After a Failed Guerrilla Attack*

| ATTACK TYPE | PERCENTAGE |
| --- | --- |
| Attack with "V" formation | 32.5 percent |
| Divide the soldiers in small groups and attack in waves | 20 percent |
| Guerrilla attack—surprise attack with a few soldiers, shoot and run away | 7.75 percent |
| Attack with full force, in a big group | 20 percent |
| Surround the player and attack from every direction | 20 percent |

And so on . . .

Of course in a real game it's better to add many interacting factors. For example, we can choose the best attack for each type of terrain or climatic condition. The more factors we take into account, the better results we'll have. In games like SimCity, there are dozens (sometimes even hundreds) of factors that contribute to generating the desired result.

## Line of Sight

For games that use NPCs, a classical problem is how to discover if the computer character can see the player or not. There are many different solutions to this problem, but possibly the simplest one is the *line of sight algorithm*. We can implement this in a few steps:

1. Consider an NPC's eyes as a point just in front of it. It will be "looking" in this direction.

2. Using the techniques for calculating the distance between two points, which we saw in the previous chapter, calculate the distance between the NPC and the player's character. If distance to the player is greater than a certain value (the "seeing distance"), the NPC can't see the player, as shown in Figure 2-2.

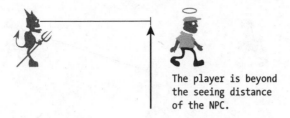

The player is beyond
the seeing distance
of the NPC.

*Figure 2-2. The player (good guy) is outside the seeing distance of the NPC (devil).*

3. If the distance is less than the seeing distance of the NPC, create an (invisible) object having the player character center and the NPC's "eyes" as vertices.

4. Use one of the collision detection algorithms we saw in the previous chapter to calculate if there's a collision between this object and the NPC's head. If so, it's because the line of sight goes through the NPC's head. The player is NOT in front of the NPC, so the NPC can't see the player. Figure 2-3 illustrates this situation.

The line object hits
the NPC's head.
It doesn't see the player.

*Figure 2-3. The player is behind the NPC, so it can't see the player.*

5. If there's no collision with the NPC's head, calculate the collision among the created object and other game objects. If there's no collision, there are no obstacles between the player and the NPC, so the NPC can see the player. See Figure 2-4 for a graphical view of this last calculation.

The line object hits an obstacle.        No hits.
The NPC doesn't see the player.          The NPC sees the player.

*Figure 2-4. The NPC tries to see the player.*

## Making NPCs "Hear" the Player

There's a simple solution to making NPCs aware of player sounds: Every time the player makes a sound, the program must compute the distance (using the Pythagorean theorem, discussed in Chapter 1) from the player to the NPCs. Any NPC whose distance is less than a constant value (the "hearing distance") would turn to look for the sound origin. After a while, if there are no further sounds and the NPC has not seen the player, the NPC returns to its previous activity (patrol, stand still, walk erratically, etc.).

It's a common practice to have different hearing distances for different kinds of sounds: A gun shooting can be heard from a distance, while the player must be really near to the NPC for it to hear his or her footsteps.

## Path Finding

Like the line of sight problem, there are also many different algorithms to solve the problem of path finding. If we don't know in advance how the game field will take shape, we could employ some of the following methods:

- Mark some "milestones" along the path the character is walking. If it hits an obstacle, return to the last milestone and try another way. This algorithm is useful when we have labyrinths or tiled game fields.

- Use invisible "bumpers" around the game characters: The program checks for any collision with these invisible objects, and chooses a way according to the noncolliding paths. The game can create bumpers following the NPCs from different distances, in order to allow them to see remote obstacles.

- Create a line of sight between the current position and the destination position. If there are obstacles on the way, move the line of sight to one side until there's no obstacle. Mark this point as a way point, and repeat the process between this point and the desired destination point.

If we know the game field, such as a fixed screen in an adventure game, some common approaches are as follows:

- Define fixed paths, so the player and the NPCs always walk over these paths.

- Define *path boxes*, where each part of the screen is defined as a box with some characteristics, including a list of reachable boxes from that area. When walking inside a box, the player and the NPCs have full freedom; when going to a place on screen that's inside another box, have the player and NPCs walk to the junction point between the two boxes, and then to the desired point in the next box. This method provides a more flexible look and feel for the game, but the boxes must be well planned to avoid strange behaviors (like the NPC running in circles if all the boxes are connected). This is the approach used by LucasArts in the first three games of the Monkey Island series.

## Use Your Imagination

Although a lot of different techniques exist for solving problems relating to a game's AI, there's always room for new ideas. Learn from other people's experience; see how the games behave and try to figure out how to mimic such behaviors in your game. There are a lot of good game developers' sites where you can learn directly from the masters; a simple Web search using the keywords "artificial intelligence" and "games" will uncover the most interesting ones.

## Keep Libraries of Reusable Graphics and Objects

Our final piece of advice is to always have your graphical routines and objects well polished and ready to use, so you can spend more time on the game's physics and AI, the most important parts. To this effect, let's start our library with a Sprite class, described in the next section.

# Sprites and Performance Boosting Tricks

We'll now start to create a set of generic classes that can be used in our future game projects, such as the Sprite class.

*Sprite* is a common term used by game programmers to specify any active object on the screen—for example, the player character, bullets, bonus objects, etc. We can also define *sprite* as any element on a game screen that is neither background nor information (such as menus or tips on the screen).

For our purposes in this chapter, we'll create a simple Sprite class, which can be enhanced later to include additional features. With a fast brainstorm, we can list some of the basic attributes we may need, and these are shown in Table 2-5.

*Table 2-5. Suggested Properties for a Simple Sprite Class*

| PROPERTY NAME | DESCRIPTION |
| --- | --- |
| Bitmap | Holds a simple image for the sprite. In advanced sprite objects, we can have multiple arrays of images to deal with different animations (such as walking, jumping, dying, etc.). |
| Position | The actual x,y position of the sprite. Following the .NET property names, we can call this property Location. |
| Scale | The scale to be used for the position coordinates: pixel or the sprite's size. |
| Direction | If the object is moving to (or "looking at") a new position, we must have a direction property to hold this information. |

As for the methods, three basic routines are obviously needed, and these are shown in Table 2-6.

*Table 2-6. Suggested Methods for a Simple Sprite Class*

| METHOD NAME | DESCRIPTION |
| --- | --- |
| New | We can create overloaded New methods that will receive different parameters: the sprite bitmap, the bitmap and the position, these two plus the direction, and so on. We will use Visual Basic .NET method overloading to implement these different initialization methods. |
| Draw | This one is a must: All sprites must be drawn. |
| Undraw | Erases the sprite, restoring the background picture, if it exists. To erase the sprite, this method must have access to the background bitmap, in order to copy the background over the previously drawn sprite. |

Figure 2-5 shows a graphical representation of the `Sprite` class.

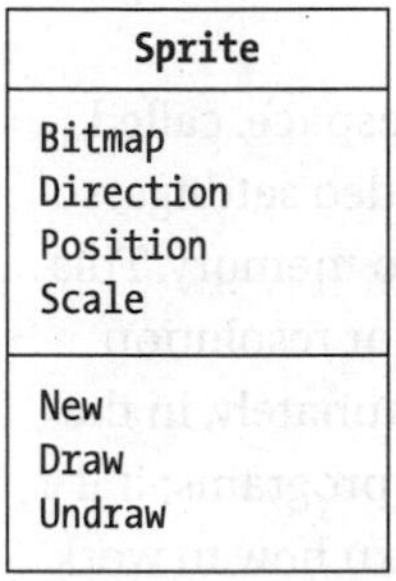

| Sprite |
| --- |
| Bitmap<br>Direction<br>Position<br>Scale |
| New<br>Draw<br>Undraw |

*Figure 2-5. The* `Sprite` *class*

Of course, we can come up with many other attributes and methods, such as velocity and acceleration attributes and a move method (which, using the direction, velocity, and acceleration, erases the sprite from the previous position and draws it on the new one). But let's keep it simple for now! This kind of approach—defining the basic structure of a class or program, and then redefining it to produce many interactions (if needed)—is recognized as a good approach by the latest object-oriented software processes, such as Rational Unified Process (RUP). We'll not enter into any details here, but we'll use some simplified concepts from this software development philosophy.

## Sprite: Fast and Transparent

Before we start coding the `Sprite` class, there are two things we must know:

- How to draw the sprite as fast as possible.

- How to draw nonrectangular sprites: Since most of our game objects won't be rectangles or squares (like in the .Nettrix example), and all the functions draw rectangular images, we have to learn how to draw an image with a transparent color, in order to achieve the illusion of nonrectangular sprites.

As for the first point, the GDI+ `Graphics` object has a method called `DrawImage` that draws an image at a given position in our work area. This method is very flexible, but it incurs a lot of overhead since it includes an internal method to scale the image, even when we don't use the scaling parameters.

Fortunately, we have a second method, DrawImageUnscaled, that just *blits* (copies a memory block directly to video memory) the source image, as is, to the destination position, with very low overhead. We'll use this function, since it gives us all the speed we need.

There's also a third, even faster function on the Graphics namespace, called DrawCachedBitmap, that maps the bitmap to the current memory video settings, so the drawing is just a matter of copying a memory position to video memory. This approach has only one drawback: If the player changes the monitor resolution when the game is playing, we'll have unpredictable results. Unfortunately, in the first release of Visual Studio, this function is only available to C++ programs; it'll probably be available in Visual Basic's next version. Since we'll learn how to work with high-speed graphics through DirectX in the next chapters, this limitation won't be a problem if we want to create fast-paced action games.

As for the transparent color, we have two possible approaches. We can set a so-called color key to be transparent, after loading the image, with the MakeTransparent Graphics method, or we can create a color-mapping array, which is much more flexible because we can set different degrees of transparency to different colors. We'll be using the first approach here, because it's simpler and all we need for now is a single transparent color, but we'll show you how to use a color map array, which can be used in other situations.

The Sprite class is the base class for all active game objects, and since it must have access to some of the properties of the class that will manage the game (such as the background image used in erasing), some programmers like to derive it from that class. We'll use this approach here, deriving the Sprite class from the GameEngine class (discussed later in the section "The Game Proposal").

## Coding the Sprite Attributes

We'll start coding the attributes. Because attributes don't require special treatment for now, we'll create them as public variables and some helper enumerations.

```
Public Class clsSprite
    Inherits clsGameEngine

    ' Image size, to be used by the child classes
    Public Const IMAGE_SIZE As Integer = 15

    Protected BmpSource As Bitmap
    Public Direction As enDirection
    Public Location As Point
    Public Scale As enScale = enScale.Sprite
```

```
Public Enum enScale
    Pixel = 1
    Sprite = IMAGE_SIZE
End Enum

Public Enum enDirection
    North = 1
    NorthEast = 2
    East = 3
    SouthEast = 4
    South = 5
    SouthWest = 6
    West = 7
    NorthWest = 8
End Enum
```

## The Sprite's New Method

As for the constructor of the class, we can define many different overloaded functions for it: a method that receives no parameters (to be implemented by the derived classes, if needed), a method that receives the sprite image name, and two others that receive the initial position of the sprite and the color code to be used as a transparent color. If we need more overloads, we can create them as the project evolves. Observe that, in order to simplify the New code, we create a private Load method, which can be called with one or more parameters, according to the constructor used when creating the object.

```
Sub New()
    ' this empty constructor is to be used by the child classes
    ' when they want to implement everything from the ground up
End Sub

Sub New(strImageName As String)
    BmpSource = Load(strImageName)
End Sub

Sub New(strImageNamem As String, keycolor As Color)
    Load(strImageNamem, keycolor)
End Sub

Sub New(strImageName As String, ponLocation As Point)
    BmpSource = Load(strImageName)
```

```
            Location = ponLocation
        End Sub


        Function Load(strImageName As String) As Bitmap
            Dim BackColor As Color

            Try
                Load = Bitmap.FromFile(strImageName)
                ' The transparent color (keycolor) was not informed,
                '  then we will use the color of the first pixel
                BackColor = Load.GetPixel(0, 0)
                Load.MakeTransparent(BackColor)
            Catch
                MessageBox.Show("An image file was not found." & Keys.Enter & _
                "Please make sure that the file " & strImageName & " exists.", _
                ".Netterpillars", MessageBoxButtons.OK, MessageBoxIcon.Stop)
                Load = Nothing
            End Try
        End Function


        Function Load(strImageName As String, keycolor As Color) As Bitmap
            Try
                Load = Bitmap.FromFile(strImageName)
                Load.MakeTransparent(keycolor)
            Catch
                MessageBox.Show("An image file was not found." & Keys.Enter & _
                "Please make sure that the file " & strImageName & " exists.", _
                ".Netterpillars", MessageBoxButtons.OK, MessageBoxIcon.Stop)
                Load = Nothing
            End Try
        End Function
```

**NEW IN .NET**

*In Visual Basic .NET, we can create methods with the same name and different parameters, in order to implement different behaviors. As we saw in the "Object-Oriented Programming" section, this is called method overload, and it's not a new idea; many object-oriented languages already have this feature. In Visual Basic we only have to use the* overload *keyword when creating an overloaded method on a derived (child) class; to overload methods within a class, as in the previous code listing, we simply create many functions with the same name.*

*The main purpose for creating various methods with the same name and different parameters is to give the programmers that will use our class enough flexibility to use only the parameters they need in a given case. For example, if we are creating a sprite that will be fixed throughout the game, we'll probably want to pass this fixed position when creating the sprite; if the sprite moves every time, it's better to pass only the image name, and so on.*

## Drawing and Erasing Sprite Code

The last two methods of a basic Sprite class must be, as we said before, the Draw and Erase methods. Since Erase is a keyword in Visual Basic, we called the erasing method Undraw.

```
Sub Draw(WinHandle As System.IntPtr)
        Dim graphBack As Graphics
        graphBack = Graphics.FromHwnd(WinHandle)
        graphBack.DrawImageUnscaled(BmpSource, Location.X * Scale, _
                                    Location.Y * Scale)
        graphBack.Dispose()
End Sub


Sub UnDraw(WinHandle As System.IntPtr)
        Dim graphBack As Graphics
        graphBack = Graphics.FromHwnd(WinHandle)
        graphBack.DrawImage(BackgroundImage, New Rectangle_
    (Location.X * Scale, _
        Location.Y * Scale, IMAGE_SIZE, IMAGE_SIZE), _
        New Rectangle(Location.X * Scale, Location.Y * Scale, _
        IMAGE_SIZE, IMAGE_SIZE), GraphicsUnit.Pixel)
        graphBack.Dispose()
End Sub
```

In the Undraw method we are using a background image property that will be shared by all the sprites, and that stores the background image of the game field, which must be drawn over the sprite image to create an illusion of erasing it. Since we need a little more flexibility than the DrawImageUnscaled offers, we'll use the DrawImage function to copy a specific rectangle of the background image over the sprite image.

If we want to extend the class to deal with multiple transparent colors or different degrees of transparency, we can adjust the New procedure to use a color map table, as shown in the following code. The color alpha values range from 255 (opaque) to 0 (totally transparent).

```
Sub New(strImageName As String, ColorKey as Color)
    Dim ImgAttributes As System.Drawing.Imaging.ImageAttributes
    Dim ImgColorMap As System.Drawing.Imaging.ColorMap()
    Dim BackColor As Color
    Dim width As Integer
    Dim height As Integer

    BmpSource.FromFile(Application.StartupPath & "\" & strImageName)
    width = BmpSource.Width
    height = BmpSource.Height

    ImgColorMap(0).OldColor = ColorKey
    ImgColorMap(0).NewColor = New Color()
    ImgColorMap(0).NewColor.FromArgb(0, ColorKey.R, ColorKey.G, _
                        ColorKey.B)   ' Set alpha to 0 = transparent
    ' Set here all other colors with an alpha value <> 255
    ImgAttributes.SetRemapTable(ImgColorMap, _
                    System.Drawing.Imaging.ColorAdjustType.Bitmap)

    graph.DrawImage(BmpSource, _
        New Rectangle(150, 10, width, height), _
        0, 0, width, height, _
        System.Drawing.GraphicsUnit.Pixel, _
        ImgAttributes)
End Sub
```

Using the Dispose() method of the Graphics object ensures that the memory used by the graphics object will be released as soon as possible, which is very important since we'll be calling the Draw and Undraw methods many times a second.

This completes the explanation of the technical concepts we'll use in our game. We'll define some details of this chapter's sample game, .Netterpillars, in the next section, "The Game Proposal."

# The Game Proposal

When creating games, remember that the very first step is to write a clearly defined game proposal. This ensures that everyone involved in the game creation process can understand and agree with the game objectives. Even very sophisticated games must start with a simple proposal, so the programmers can build the project upon a previously established goal.

As mentioned in the introduction to this chapter, we'll create a fast-action arcade game called .Netterpillars. Here are some details about the game:

- The game objective is to control a caterpillar-like character around the game field, trying not to collide with other caterpillars or any obstacles. If you collide, you are dead.

- The game field must be filled with mushrooms and every time a netterpillar eats a mushroom, he gets bigger.

- The game is over when all the players die (computer or human ones), or when the last mushroom is eaten.

- There must be a configuration screen where the player can choose the field size, how many mushrooms there'll be in the game, and the number of computer-controlled opponents (from 0 to 3).

- The game must allow the smooth inclusion of multiplayer routines in future versions, so all the project and coding must be done with this goal in mind.

The basic idea in creating different configurations for a game is to add endurance to the game. That means that the game will interest the player for a longer time. It's a common approach to add many different ways of playing in order to keep the player's attention. A good example of this approach is Microsoft's Age of Empires: Players can start a new game and go on building from the ground up, or players can choose a quest, where a previously created status quo is presented and they must solve some specific problems to win the game.

In our sample, the player can choose, for example, a small and mushroom-crowded game field, and try to eat them all without getting trapped by his or her own tail; or choose a big field with fewer mushrooms and more opponents, in order to try to be the longest one, eating as many mushrooms as possible while trying to kill the enemies, trapping them with his or her tail. Many intermediary combinations would be possible, making the game more interesting to play.

With the basic game plan set, it's time to start thinking about the technical details: creating a project for the game.

## The Game Project

Once all the team members share the project vision, it's time to create our project. This can be as simple as a feature list and a scratch class diagram on paper. And even if you are working solo, as you will see, organizing and planning work before actually doing it is highly beneficial!

Our game project will include a simple class diagram, showing the class, properties and methods, a main program workflow definition, and the drafts for each game screen (as discussed in the next sections).

## *Defining the Game Classes and the Game Engine*

The game characters are the first natural candidates for game objects, based on our library's Sprite class. So we can take the nouns on the list of topics from the game proposal and create a first draft of our class diagram, as shown in Figure 2-6.

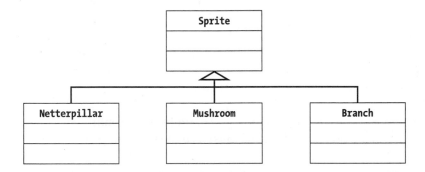

*Figure 2-6. The class diagram—first draft*

This looks fine for a first draft. We see here an extra class, not mentioned in the game proposal: the Branch class. We include it just for fun, in order to improve the look of the game with branches at the screen limits.

Following what we learned in the previous chapter, there must be a class for controlling the game field and physics. Since this class will have more features than the GameField class from Chapter 1, we'll use a more appropriate name for it: GameEngine.

Before putting this class in our diagram, it must be clear what the game engine should and should not do. It follows that the game engine is solely responsible for creating and maintaining the entire environment where the game characters will act. Usually, the game engine works according to the physical laws (gravity, action-reaction, etc.) in the real world, with more or less realism depending on the game goals.

The game engine doesn't include the AI control. Instead, it just puts constraints over the game's characters, regardless of whether they are computer or human controlled. Hence we'll need another class to control the AI of our computer-controlled netterpillars. Since this class must have a high integration with the game engine (to collect information that will allow it to make decisions—for example choosing the direction to go), we'll create this class as a child of the GameEngine class.

Since the sprite must have access to the game field background in order to erase itself, we'll also include the Sprite class as a derived class from the game engine in the class diagram.

Our final class diagram (without the attributes and methods) is shown in Figure 2-7. Notice that it's not the *right* diagram, or the only approach. It's just an idea, and if you don't agree with it—great! You understand our subject so well that you already have your own opinion about it.

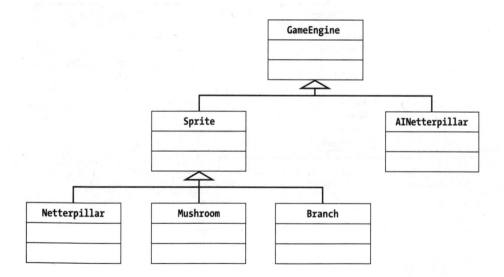

*Figure 2-7. The class diagram—second draft*

As for the properties (attributes) and methods, we can use what we learned before as a starting point, and build on it.

After more brainstorming, we select a set of attributes and methods for each class, as shown in Figure 2-8. We don't expect any surprises with the classes that deal with the game objects, and the other ones, such as the AI class, are created based on our previous experience of similar projects.

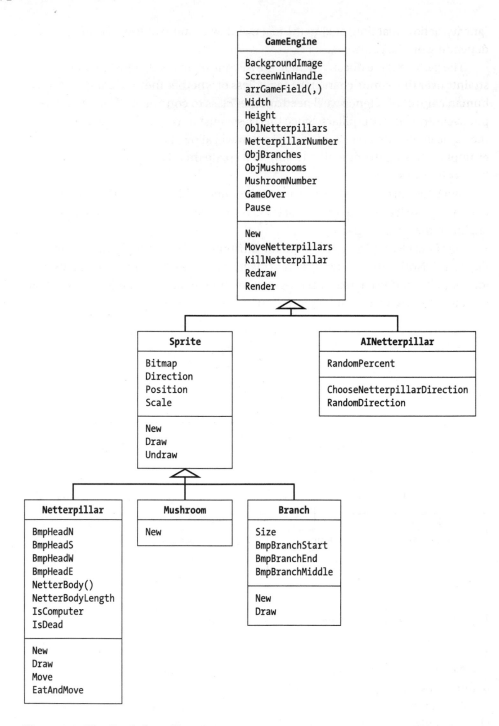

*Figure 2-8. The final class diagram*

We don't need to have a totally finished diagram by now, just a guide for our coding. We can return to this diagram later, at the game-coding phase, and adjust it if necessary, when new ideas and problems arise. Even the most detailed projects aren't steady; modifications always occur after the coding starts. There is a quote from a famous general that fits perfectly in this situation: "No battle is won according to the battle plans, but no battle was ever won without a plan."

In the next sections we discuss each of the classes shown in the diagram from Figure 2-8, including brief explanations of their properties and methods.

## The Sprite Class

We'll use this class, defined in the "Sprites and Performance Boosting Tips" section, as the base class for all other game objects. Remember that all the members (properties and methods) of this class become members of the derived classes too.

## The Netterpillar Class

The Netterpillar class will control the drawing of the netterpillar characters on screen, both for human-controlled and computer-controlled ones. It'll have some methods for making the netterpillar bigger (when it eats a mushroom) and to store the bitmaps and current status for the character. Table 2-7 lists the initial suggestion for the members of this class, along with a short description.

*Table 2-7. The Members of the Netterpillar Class*

| TYPE | NAME | DESCRIPTION |
| --- | --- | --- |
| Method | New | We'll have an overloaded New method, which will load with the multiple images of a netterpillar: the head (looking at different directions) and the body parts. |
| Method | Draw | The overloaded function that draws all the parts of the netterpillar. |
| Method | Move | Instead of Undraw, Move is more appropriate here: Move the head and every body part according to the current direction, erasing the field only after the last body part. |

*Table 2-7. The Members of the Netterpillar Class (Continued)*

| TYPE | NAME | DESCRIPTION |
|------|------|-------------|
| Method | EatAndMove | If the netterpillar eats a mushroom, the last part doesn't get erase, because the body length is increased. |
| Properties | BmpNetterHeadN, BmpNetterHeadS, BmpNetterHeadE, BmpNetterHeadW | We'll need one image for the head for each direction that the netterpillar is looking at/moving to. |
| Property | NetterBody() | We'll need an array to store all the body parts |
| Property | NetterBodyLength | The current size of the netterpillar, which will be used to keep track of the body parts array. |
| Property | IsComputer | We have to have a way of knowing which players are human controlled and which are computer controlled; this will help with the future evolution of a multiplayer game. |
| Property | IsDead | Instead of actually destroying the netterpillar, we'll just set a flag saying that it's dead, thus avoiding internal tests to see if a given netterpillar object exists. |

## The Mushroom Class

Since a mushroom does nothing except for standing and waiting to be eaten, all we need is an overloaded New method that will load the appropriate image file, so we won't need to pass the filename when creating a new mushroom. The Mushroom class will then have all the members from the Sprite class, plus the overloaded New method that loads the mushroom image file in a given position

## The Branch Class

A branch will be composed of three different images: one for each branch edge, and a middle one that can be repeated many times to create bigger branches. Since the Sprite base class only stores a single image, we'll have to create three properties to store these images, and create new overloaded functions for the New and Draw methods. Since the branch doesn't move, we won't need to create an Undraw method. The list of members for the branch class is shown in Table 2-8.

*Table 2-8. The Members of the Branch Class*

| TYPE | NAME | DESCRIPTION |
|------|------|-------------|
| Method | New | This overloaded version of the New method will receive the size and orientation (north-south or east-west) of the branch. |
| Method | Draw | This method draws the branch, according to its size, position, and orientation. |
| Property | Size | The size of the branch. |
| Properties | BmpBranchTop, BmpBranchBottom | The images of the branch extremities. |
| Property | BmpbranchMiddle | The image for the middle part of the branch that will be repeated over and over by the Draw method, until the branch reaches the desired size. |

## The AINetterpillar Class

To define a basic set of members for the class that will handle the netterpillar artificial intelligence requires a little more thinking. The first question that arises is, How smart is our computer-controlled character meant to be? Even in this simple game we can think about some very difficult AI routines. For example, will a computer-controlled netterpillar do any of the following?

- Chase the player (or one another) and try to surround the player with its tail, in order to kill him or her.

- Analyze its tail positions on every move, in order to avoid getting trapped by its own tail.

- Analyze the whole game field to look for places where there are more mushrooms or fewer netterpillars.

Since all we need here is a simple example, our netterpillar won't be that smart, at least for the first version of the game. All we want to do is

- Avoid getting killed by hitting a wall, while eating everything that is near to the head.

- Add some random behavior to make the movement of the computer-controlled netterpillars more unpredictable to the player.

Table 2-9 shows the first suggested methods and properties we'll create to address these goals.

*Table 2-9. The Members of the AINetterpillar Class*

| TYPE | NAME | DESCRIPTION |
|---|---|---|
| Method | ChooseNetterpillarDirection | This method will analyze the netterpillar position and direction and choose the best direction to move to, based on the immediate surroundings of the netterpillar's head. |
| Method | RandomDirection | This method will add the random behavior, based on the RandomPercent property, and taking care not to lead the netterpillar straight to collision and death. |
| Property | RandomPercent | This property will control how random the behavior of our netterpillar will be. Remember that a new direction will be chosen many times each second, so any number greater than 10 may make the netterpillar's movements too random to seem intelligent. |

Of course, these members could also be part of our Netterpillar class, but we decided to create a new class for them in order to have the artificial intelligence code isolated from the drawing code, making it easier to maintain and improve.

The last game class, which deals with the game engine, is discussed next.

## The GameEngine Class

For the GameEngine class, we can pick some ideas from the .Nettrix sample we saw in the last chapter:

- It's important to have a method to redraw the game field.

- We'll also need a direct reference to the game field (such as a handle) to be used in the drawing operations.

- Since we'll have a dedicated class to control the game, we'll need a property to control if the game is running or paused, just like the variable on the form in the previous chapter. A property to control whether the game is over is a good idea too.

- According to the idea of having an array to control collisions (which seems to be the right choice in our case, since our game will be a tile-based one), we'll need a property to store the game field array.

- Since the game engine will need to do all the physics of the game, it'll need to have access to all game objects. The best way to allow this is to let the GameEngine class create and handle them, so we'll need properties to store the branch objects; the netterpillar objects and the netterpillars quantity; and the mushroom objects and the mushroom quantity.

- We'll have a configuration screen to set some game properties, and we'll need corresponding properties to store the configurable parameters: width and height properties, since our game field can have different sizes; a property to hold the desired mushroom quantity; and another one to hold how many netterpillars will be present.

- Since we'll control only one netterpillar, we'll need some property to define, for each netterpillar, if it's computer controlled or human controlled. Having such a property will help in another game objective: to code a game ready to be turned into a multiplayer version in the future. In this case, in the next version we can add information to tell if the netterpillar is a local gamer, a remote gamer, or a computer.

- Since the sprites will need to erase themselves, we'll need a property to store the initial background image of the game field.

---

 **NOTE** *That's a lot of things to be thinking about, and we haven't covered the methods yet. But don't expect to remember everything in the first brainstorm. It's usual to create a first draft, and then refine it. When we think about the game logic and create some pseudo-code for the most important parts of the game, new properties and methods arise. When refining the new set, other new details arise. This process is repeated over and over until we have a stable set of classes, properties, and methods. In (very) few words, that's the basis of what is suggested in most of the books covering object-oriented analysis currently.*

---

We can list a basic set of methods based on the features coded in the previous chapter—for example, a method to initialize the game field, a method to redraw it, a method to render (which will basically do the physics, update the object states, and then redraw the game field), and some methods to move the game objects and to change their states (such as setting a netterpillar as dead, and asking the netterpillar object to remove its drawing from the screen).

Based on the previously discussed points, our class will have the interface shown in Table 2-10.

*Table 2-10. The Members of the GameEngine Class*

| TYPE | NAME | DESCRIPTION |
|------|------|-------------|
| Method | New | This method creates the game field and initializes all properties |
| Method | MoveNetterpillars | A method for moving the netterpillars, according to the current direction of each one. Also checks for collisions. |
| Method | KillNetterpillar | This method removes the netterpillar from the game field, if it collides with some wall or other netterpillar. |
| Method | Redraw | This method redraws the game field. |
| Method | Render | A method for calling all other methods; in other words, it moves everyone, kills anyone who must be killed, checks for game over, and calls the Redraw method. |
| Property | ScreenWinHandle | The handle of the game field window, used for drawing the game objects. |
| Properties | Width, Height | The game field dimensions, which will be configured by the user. |
| Properties | ObjNetterpillars(), NetterpillarNumber | The netterpillar objects array and the total number of netterpillars. |
| Property | ObjBranches() | The branch objects array. |
| Properties | ObjMushrooms(), MushroomNumber | The mushroom objects array and its total number. |
| Property | GameOver | If true, the game is over. |
| Property | Paused | If true, the Render procedure won't move any netterpillar. |
| Property | ArrGameField() | The array with the game objects, used for implementing the collision detection. |
| Property | BackGroundImage | The initial background image, which will be used by the sprites to erase themselves (drawing a portion of the background image over them). |

Since our class diagram now is stable, it's time to define how the main program will call the classes. In the next topic we discuss the structure of the game's main program.

## The Main Program Structure

Now let's think about how the game will work. We need to define a starting place, from which the game engine object and the game window will be created, and from which the Render procedure of the game engine will be called repeatedly.

Since we'll need a configuration screen, too, it's better to first have an introductory screen, in which players can choose if they want to start the game or to change the game configuration.

Although it's common in some OOA techniques to suggest the creation of new classes for the forms (sometimes called *interface classes*), it'll be easier not to mix user interface with the game logic for now. Instead, we'll use common window forms, and create a simple workflow diagram, as shown in Figure 2-9, in order to clarify how the game flow will be.

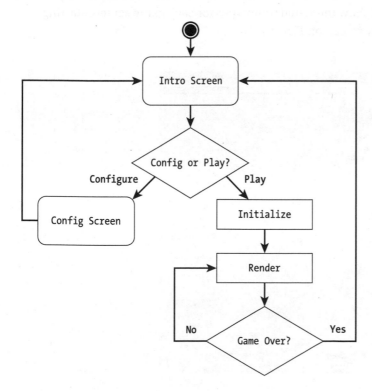

*Figure 2-9. The game main workflow*

We could give details of the Render procedure, including in the loop shown on the diagram in Figure 2-9 boxes for such processes as gathering user input, updating game objects, redrawing, etc. (and in a real project we strongly suggest that you do). However, the goal for this diagram is only to make it easier to understand the basic game flow across the many screens and the basic game loop, and it does this effectively.

In the next topic we'll create a draft of each game screen, thus finishing our game project.

## Defining the Game Screens

Although the windows implementation will be done in the code phase, it's good practice to create at least a draft of the screens in the project phase, because when drawing the screen we usually remember more details that can be added to the class diagram. If we can imagine how the previously discussed classes will work in each screen, then there's a good chance we haven't missed any important details.

Since Visual Basic allows us to create screens quickly, the best sketches are the ones done directly in Visual Basic. Let's call our first screens "visual prototypes." The next images will show the visual prototypes for each game screen, starting with the introductory screen on Figure 2-10.

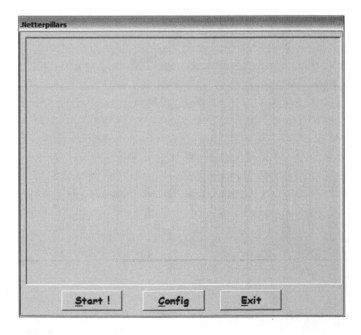

*Figure 2-10. The intro screen*

The intro screen will only show an intro image (or *splash screen*) for the game, along with buttons to allow the player to end the game, start a new game, or change the game configuration. According to the workflow shown in the last topic, after a game ends, players will be redirected to this screen.

Figure 2-11 shows the second draft: the game configuration screen.

*Figure 2-11. The game configuration screen*

On the configuration screen, we can set the number of netterpillars and mushrooms and the size of the game field. Since it's not up to the user to decide the exact number of pixels in a game or the exact number of mushrooms on screen, we can use domain up-down controls to make the configuration more user friendly: Few/Just Right/Many selections for mushrooms and Small/Medium/Big selections for the game field size.

As we said before, as the game project evolves, we uncover new details that may require new properties and methods. Looking at the screen shown in Figure 2-11, we need only two enumerations for the GameEngine class, which will lead to simpler and cleaner code: enMushrooms for the number of mushrooms, and enSize for the possible field sizes. We'll also include two new properties that will receive the values of these enumerations directly from the configuration screen—Mushrooms and Size.

In the code phase we'll see how to code *property procedures* in Visual Basic .NET: a pair of procedures in the class that correspond to an object property, allowing us to do some processing—such as setting the Width and Height properties when the Size property is set, and setting the MushroomNumber property when the Mushrooms property is set.

The draft for next game screen is shown in Figure 2-12.

.Netterpillars

*Figure 2-12. The game field screen is just a form with an image control.*

We can set the `Picture` property of the image control in the game field window with any bitmap we want to use as background, since we write a generic code in the `Sprite` class to do the drawing and erasing. In this case, we set it to a simple sand pattern.

## Refining the Game Project

You've learned about making progressive refinements in the game project, until you reach the point to start the coding phase. But how do you know when to stop making refinements?

If, after you've drawn the class diagram and the workflow diagram, and also created the visual prototypes for all game screens, you still don't have a clear idea about how any part of the game will work, it's important to write pseudo-code for this part and check the workflow, the classes, and the screen drafts again until everything seems to fit. Only start the code phase after you have a clear idea about how things will work, but take care not to get stuck on the project, creating an excessive level of details (except, maybe, for big projects where the lack of detail can cost a lot).

Just remember: It's much easier and faster to correct a class diagram or a screen prototype than to redo a lot of code because you forgot something important!

With these points in mind, let's get into the next phase: the code.

## The Coding Phase

As we did in the previous chapter, let's start coding the basic objects for the game (simplest first), and then tackle the more difficult code of the game engine and the netterpillar AI classes.

To allow us to test every new method created, we'll do our code in five steps:

1.   First draft: Code the static objects.

2.   Second draft: Code the player character.

3.   Third draft: Code the game engine and collision detection.

4.   Fourth draft: Code the configuration screen and game over.

5.   Final version: Code the netterpillars AI.

The details of each of these versions are shown in the next sections.

## First Draft: Coding the Static Objects

In the next sections we show the code and discuss the details of the classes for the static objects, mushrooms, and branches, and create an early version of the main program and the GameEngine class, so we can test these classes.

### The Sprite Class

We'll only add a new property in this class, the IMAGE_PATH constant, which will be used by all the child classes to compose the full path from where the images should be loaded.

### The Mushroom Class

There's not much to say about the Mushroom class. It just has an overloaded New method that creates a sprite with the mushroom drawing, to be used instead of the original sprite New method with a parameter. This will allow cleaner code when creating mushrooms.

```
Public Class clsMushroom
    Inherits clsSprite
    Sub New()
End Class
```

**NEW IN .NET**

*Visual Basic .NET is a fully object-oriented language, which differs from the previous version. All basic OO concepts are included, such as method overload and inheritance between classes, including multiple inheritances. The inheritance is implemented using the* Inherits *keyword, as in the preceding sample code.*

The code for the New method will be as follows:

```
Sub New()
    MyBase.New(Application.StartupPath & "\" & IMAGE_PATH & "\Mushroom.gif")
End Sub
```

Note that all we did is call the base class New event, passing the appropriate parameters.

**NEW IN .NET**

*When a child class defines a method that already exists in the base class, any object created from the child class will call the code in the method of this class, unless we explicitly call the base class method, as in the code sample above (using* MyBase.<method name>*).*

## The Branch Class

The Branch class will also be derived from the Sprite base class, but since a branch can have different sizes, we'll have to add extra variables to hold the branch bitmaps, and create new Draw and New methods that will do the branch creation and drawing. The next code sample presents the Branch class interface:

```
Public Class clsBranch
    Inherits clsSprite
    Private bmpBranchStart As Bitmap
    Private bmpBranchMiddle() As Bitmap
    Private bmpBranchEnd As Bitmap
    Public Size As Integer
    Sub New(branchDirection As enDirection, intSize As Integer)
    Shadows Sub Draw(winHandle As System.IntPtr, x As Integer, y As Integer)
End Class
```

**NEW IN .NET**

*The keyword Shadows helps the developer to extend base classes in a more flexible way, allowing the child class to block any methods with the same name defined in the base class, even if they have different parameters. In the preceding sample, if we had defined the method Draw without the Shadows keyword, we'll have two different Draw methods in the Branch class: one that would receive only a window handle (inherited from the base class Sprite), and another (overloaded) one that would receive the parameters as we need in the branch class.*

As noted before, our Branch class will be used to improve the visual interface by placing branches around the game field. This class will have only two methods: the New method, which will load the bitmaps from disk, and the Draw method, which will draw the branch on screen. Since the branches don't move or disappear during the game, we won't need to code an Undraw method.

Each branch will be composed by a set of at least three images: a "branch start," a "branch end," and one or more "branch middles." Since we'll need horizontal and vertical branches, we'll need six different images, created with a specific naming convention to help us, as shown in Figure 2-13.

*Figure 2-13. The branch images*

The New method will use the concepts explained in the Load method of the Sprite class, extending the code to store the images in the specific properties of the Branch Class—branchStart, branchMiddle array, and branchEnd:

```
Sub New(branchDirection As enDirection, intSize As Integer)
    ReDim bmpBranchMiddle(intSize - 3)
    Dim i As Integer
    Dim strImagePrefix As String

    Size = intSize
    Direction = branchDirection
    ' Picks the prefix for the branch - horizontal or vertical?
    strImagePrefix = "Hor" ' Default direction is east-west (Horizontal)
    If Direction = clsSprite.enDirection.North Or Direction = _
        clsSprite.enDirection.South Then
        strImagePrefix = "Vert"
    End If

    ' Load the top, the middle parts and the end of the branch
    '  Magenta is the colorkey (which will be transparent) for_
    '   the Load Method
    bmpBranchTop = Load(Application.StartupPath & "\" & IMAGE_PATH & "\" & _
      strImagePrefix & "BranchStart.gif", Color.FromArgb(255, 255, 0, 204))
    For i = 0 To Size - 3
        bmpBranchMiddle(i) = Load(Application.StartupPath & _
            "\" & IMAGE_PATH & "\" & strImagePrefix &_
            "BranchMiddle.gif", Color.FromArgb(255, 255, 0, 204))
    Next
    bmpBranchBack = Load(Application.StartupPath & "\" & IMAGE_PATH & "\" & _
        strImagePrefix & "BranchEnd.gif", Color.FromArgb(255, 255, 0, 204))
End Sub
```

Here are some points to note about the preceding code:

- We use the naming conventions stated before to load the appropriate images, including the prefix "Hor" for the horizontal images and "Vert" for the vertical ones. We are using the branchDirection parameter of the enDirection enumeration (defined in the base class Sprite) to choose if the branch will be vertical (north and south directions) or horizontal (west and east directions).

- The image files were drawn using the magenta color where we need to create transparency, that's why we use Color.fromARGB(255, 255, 0, 204) as the parameter for the keycolor of the Load function (defined in the Sprite base class).

- The dimension of the BranchMiddle array is defined as intSize-3 because the size of the branch will take into account the start and the end of the branch, so we need an array with the defined size minus two. Since all arrays in Visual Basic .NET are zero based, we have intSize-2 elements when defining an array that goes from 0 to intSize-3. A little tricky, isn't it?

The Draw method will be very similar to the method with the same name on the base class. In fact, we'll be calling the base class method in order to draw each of the parts of the branch, so we won't have any real drawing code in this method.

```
Shadows Sub Draw(winHandle As System.IntPtr, x As Integer, y As Integer)
    Dim i As Integer
    ' Sets the location and draws the start of the branch
    Location = New Point(x, y)
    MyBase.Draw(bmpBranchTop, winHandle)
    ' Sets the location and draws each of the branch middle parts
    If Direction = clsSprite.enDirection.North Or _
        Direction = clsSprite.enDirection.South Then
        ' it's a horizontal branch
        For i = 0 To Size - 3
            y += 1
            Location = New Point(x, y)
            MyBase.Draw(bmpBranchMiddle(i), winHandle)
        Next
        y += 1
```

```
      Else
          ' it's a vertical branch
          For i = 0 To Size - 3
              x += 1
              Location = New Point(x, y)
              MyBase.Draw(bmpBranchMiddle(i), winHandle)
          Next
          x += 1
      End If
      ' Sets the location and draws the end of the branch

      Location = New Point(x, y)
      MyBase.Draw(bmpBranchBack, winHandle)
  End Sub
```

## Main Program and GameEngine Class

Since we already have two of the base classes, it's time to do some tests to check if everything is okay so far. Instead of doing a simple test program, let's go one step ahead and start implementing the game Main procedure and the GameEngine class, so we can start to understand the game logic, and add to them when new features become available.

Looking at the class diagram, we can pick some properties and methods that will help us to create a subset of the final clsGameEngine class, which will allow us to test the classes we created. We'll need to code the properties associated with mushrooms and branches, the New method (to initialize the objects), the Redraw method (to draw the objects), and a Render object, the method which will do all the game physics (for now, only calling the Redraw method). Our stub class will be as follows:

```
Public Class clsGameEngine
    Public Width As Integer = 25
    Public Height As Integer = 25
    Public Shared BackgroundImage As Image
    Private ScreenWinHandle As System.IntPtr

    ' Game objects
    Private objBranchs() As clsBranch

    Private objMushrooms() As clsMushroom
    Private MushroomNumber As Integer = 75

    ' Controls the game end
    Public GameOver As Boolean
```

```
    Sub New (WinHandle As System.IntPtr)
    Sub Render()
    Sub Redraw()
End Class
```

In the New procedure, all we do is redimension the object arrays and create each of the objects. We'll also store the window handle received in the function to be used by the Redraw procedure:

```
Sub New(WinHandle As System.IntPtr)
    Dim i As Integer
    Dim x As Integer, y As Integer
    ReDim objBranchs(4)
    ReDim objMushrooms(MushroomNumber)

    ScreenWinHandle = WinHandle
    ' Initialize the random number generator (for the mushroom positions)
    Randomize()

    ' Create the branches
    objBranchs(0) = New clsBranch(clsSprite.enDirection.North, Me.Height)
    objBranchs(1) = New clsBranch(clsSprite.enDirection.North, Me.Height)
    objBranchs(2) = New clsBranch(clsSprite.enDirection.East, Me.Width - 2)
    objBranchs(3) = New clsBranch(clsSprite.enDirection.East, Me.Width - 2)

    ' Create the mushrooms
    For i = 0 To MushroomNumber - 1
        objMushrooms = New clsMushroom()
        x = Int(Rnd(1) * (Me.Width - 2)) + 1
        y = Int(Rnd(1) * (Me.Height - 2)) + 1
        objMushrooms(i).location = new point (x,y)
    Next
End Sub
```

For now, the Render method just calls the Redraw method; in future versions it will call the functions to implement the game physics.

```
Sub Render()
    Redraw()
End Sub
```

As for our `Redraw` method, all we need is to call the `Draw` method of each game object.

```
Sub Redraw()
    Dim i As Integer
    For i = 0 To MushroomNumber - 1
        objMushrooms(i).Draw(ScreenWinHandle)
    Next

    objBranchs(0).Draw(ScreenWinHandle, 0, 0)
    objBranchs(1).Draw(ScreenWinHandle, (Me.Width - 1), 0)
    objBranchs(2).Draw(ScreenWinHandle, 1, 0)
    objBranchs(3).Draw(ScreenWinHandle, 1, (Me.Height - 1))
End Sub
```

Now, with the `clsGameEngine` class stub done, all we need to do is to create a `Main` procedure that will generate the game engine object and call the `Render` method until the game is over (in this case when the Esc key is pressed). To do this, add a module to the solution and include the following code:

```
Public objGameEngine As clsGameEngine

Sub main()
    ' Create the game field form (as defined in the game project)
    Dim WinGameField As frmGameField
    ' Create the game engine object
    objGameEngine = New clsGameEngine(WinGameField.PicGameField.Handle)

    WinGameField = New frmGameField()
    WinGameField.Show()

    ' Creates a copy of the background image to allow
    '    erasing the sprites
    objGameEngine.BackgroundImage=WinGameField.PicGameField.Image.Clone
    Do While Not objGameEngine.GameOver
            objGameEngine.Render()
            Application.DoEvents()
    Loop
    MsgBox("Game Over", MsgBoxStyle.Exclamation, ".Netterpillars")

    WinGameField.Dispose()
    objGameEngine = Nothing
End Sub
```

**NEW IN .NET**

*As everyone who worked with previous versions of Visual Basic can see in the preceding code, there are a lot of modifications in the way Visual Basic works with forms. Now, every form we create is just a class (in the previous versions, we could work with them as classes or as objects); so we always have to create a new object of the form class in order to have a workable window. There's no more* Unload *command. We now dispose of a window by calling the* Dispose *method of the object previously created. The members of the form object are also somewhat different: There are new methods, properties, and events, and some of the old ones have disappeared. The Visual Basic help has a comprehensive list of all changes, including the* Unload/QueryUnload *events, which don't exist anymore and are replaced by a* Closing *event; and the changes to each event depending on the parameters received.*

All we need to finish this first draft is to capture the Esc key to end the game. This can be done using the KeyDown event of frmGameField:

```
Private Sub frmGameField_KeyDown(sender As Object, e As KeyEventArgs) _
                                        Handles MyBase.KeyDown
    ' We are dealing with just one key for now, but all the game
    ' control will be here in the finished game
    Select Case e.KeyCode
        Case Keys.Escape
            objGameEngine.GameOver = true
    End Select
End Sub
```

Running our program now, we can see a basic game field filled with mushrooms, as shown in Figure 2-14.

*Figure 2-14. Testing the first basic classes*

## Second Draft: Coding the Player Character

The next step in our code phase is to code the Netterpillar class and make all adjustments needed to our first draft for the main program and the game engine to allow the player character to be drawn on screen and be controlled by the player, using the keyboard navigation (arrow) keys. The next sections show and discuss the code to do this.

### The Netterpillar Class

We'll now look at the Netterpillar class and begin to code it. The main body of this class is shown here. We'll look at the methods belonging to it in the subsequent code samples.

```
Public Class clsNetterpillar
    Inherits clsSprite
    Private bmpNetterHeadN As Bitmap
    Private bmpNetterHeadS As Bitmap
    Private bmpNetterHeadE As Bitmap
    Private bmpNetterHeadW As Bitmap
    Public NetterBody() As clsNetterBody
    Public NetterBodyLength As Integer = 4
```

```
    Public IsComputer As Boolean = True
    Public IsDead As Boolean = False
    Sub New(x As Integer, y As Integer, _
            InitialDirection As clsSprite.enDirection, bIsComputer As Boolean)
    Sub EatAndMove(x As Integer, y As Integer, WinHandle As System.IntPtr)
    Sub Move(x As Integer, y As Integer, WinHandle As System.IntPtr
    Public Sub Draw(WinHandle As System.IntPtr)
End Class
```

When deriving the code interface from the class diagram, if we don't have a detailed project we usually start with few or even no parameters in the methods. The rich interface just shown, with many parameters in some methods, was created step by step when coding each of the methods. For example, the parameter bIsComputer in the New method is included later on in the coding process, when we discover that after each call to the New method, we are setting the IsComputer property of the class, a clear indication that we should include this property as a parameter in the New method.

Another surprise here is the NetterBody() array. When doing the class diagram, we thought about having an array of "body parts" of the netterpillar. But what exactly is a body part in this case? It might be an array of Point objects, which would store the position to which the body bitmap must be drawn, for example. But then we would need to create a complex logic in the Netterpillar class to deal with the drawing of body parts. So we opt to create a new class, NetterBody, that will be as simple as the Mushroom class (except that a different bitmap is used), so we can use the Location property and Draw method of the Sprite base class.

Is this the best choice for the implementation? There's no right answer. The best option is the one that will be simpler for us to create and, most importantly, to debug and update.

As for the images of the netterpillar, besides four different bitmaps for the head (each one heading to a different direction) and one for the body, we'll need two different sets of images to allow a visual contrast between the player-controlled netterpillar and the computer-controlled ones. Using the prefix "player" for the player bitmaps, we'll follow the naming conventions shown in the Figure 2-15.

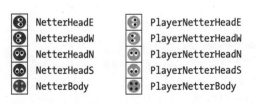

*Figure 2-15. The names for the netterpillar images*

With these names in mind, we can create the NetterBody class and the New method of the Netterpillar class.

```
Public Class clsNetterBody
    Inherits clsSprite
    Sub New(IsComputer As Boolean)
        MyBase.new(Application.StartupPath & "\" & IMAGE_PATH & "\" _
        & IIf(IsComputer, "", "Player") & "NetterBody.gif")
    End Sub
End Class
```

As we defined in the class properties, the default length of the body of the netterpillar (NetterBodyLength property) is four, so the netterpillar starts with a minimum size. Since the New procedure will receive the initial direction for the netterpillar, we'll use this direction to position the body parts behind the head (for example, if the netterpillar is heading east, the body parts will appear to the west of the head (lower values on the x axis). This code sample works out the position of the body relative to the head:

```
Sub New(x As Integer, y As Integer, InitialDirection _
        As clsSprite.enDirection, bIsComputer As Boolean)
    ' Start with a bigger length so we needn't redim it so soon
    ReDim NetterBody(25)
    Dim i As Integer
    Dim incX as integer = 0, incY as integer = 0

    IsComputer = bIsComputer
    bmpNetterHeadN = Load(Application.StartupPath & "\" & IMAGE_PATH & "\" & _
                              IIf(IsComputer, "", "Player") & "NetterHeadN.gif")
    bmpNetterHeadS = Load(Application.StartupPath & "\" & IMAGE_PATH & "\" & _
                              IIf(IsComputer, "", "Player") & "NetterHeadS.gif")
    bmpNetterHeadE = Load(Application.StartupPath & "\" & IMAGE_PATH & "\" & _
                              IIf(IsComputer, "", "Player") & "NetterHeadE.gif")
    bmpNetterHeadW = Load(Application.StartupPath & "\" & IMAGE_PATH & "\" & _
                              IIf(IsComputer, "", "Player") & "NetterHeadW.gif")

    For i = 0 To NetterBodyLength - 1
        NetterBody(i) = New clsNetterBody(IsComputer)
    Next

    ' Position the Netterpillar on the given point
    Direction = InitialDirection
    Location.X = x
    Location.Y = y
```

```
    ' Position each of the body parts
    Select Case Direction
        Case clsSprite.enDirection.East
            incX = -1
        Case clsSprite.enDirection.South
      incY = -1
        Case clsSprite.enDirection.West
            IncX = 1
        Case clsSprite.enDirection.North
            incY = 1
    End Select
    For i = 0 To NetterBodyLength - 1
        x += incX
        y += incY
        NetterBody(i).Location.X = x
        NetterBody(i).Location.Y = y
    Next
End Sub
```

Observe that we simply set the location of the netterpillar (the head) and the location of each of the body parts, but there's no drawing yet. The drawing is done in the Draw procedure (shown in the next code listing), which considers the direction in which the netterpillar is heading in order to choose which bitmap will be used for the head, and then runs through the NetterBody array to draw the body parts.

```
Public Overloads Sub Draw(WinHandle As System.IntPtr)
    Dim i As Integer
    Select Case Direction
        Case clsSprite.enDirection.East
            MyBase.Draw(bmpNetterHeadE, WinHandle)
        Case clsSprite.enDirection.South
            MyBase.Draw(bmpNetterHeadS, WinHandle)
        Case clsSprite.enDirection.West
            MyBase.Draw(bmpNetterHeadW, WinHandle)
        Case clsSprite.enDirection.North
            MyBase.Draw(bmpNetterHeadN, WinHandle)
    End Select

    For i = 0 To NetterBodyLength - 1
        NetterBody(i).Draw(WinHandle)
    Next
End Sub
```

The last two methods of the Netterpillar class are very similar: Move and EatAndMove. The Move method will update the head location according to the new X and Y values passed as parameters from the game engine, and then update all the body parts to move one step ahead. We could erase and draw everything, but since all the body parts look the same, we can just erase the last body part, copy the first body part over the head, and draw the head in the new position, which will be much quicker than redrawing the whole body.

```
Sub Move(x As Integer, y As Integer, WinHandle As System.IntPtr)
    Dim i As Integer
    ' Erase the last part of the body
    NetterBody(NetterBodyLength - 1).UnDraw(WinHandle)

    ' Updates the whole body's position and then the head position
    For i = NetterBodyLength - 1 To 1 Step -1
        NetterBody(i).Location = NetterBody(i - 1).Location
    Next
    NetterBody(0).Location = Location
    Location = New Point(x, y)

    ' Redraws only the first part of the body and the head
    NetterBody(0).Draw(WinHandle)

    'We don't need to erase the netterpillar head, since the body will cover it
    Draw(WinHandle)
End Sub
```

The main difference between the EatAndMove method and the Move method is that in the first method the netterpillar is eating a mushroom and is getting bigger; so we'll need to create a new body part (redimensioning the NetterBody array), set its position to the position of the last body part, and then reposition all other body parts, redrawing only the first one and the head; while in the second method the netterpillar will only move, following a similar approach.

```
Sub EatAndMove(x As Integer, y As Integer, WinHandle As System.IntPtr)
    Dim i As Integer

    ' Try to create a new body after the last body of the Netterpillar,
    '  if there's an error, then we must extend our body array
    Try
        NetterBody(NetterBodyLength) = New clsNetterBody(IsComputer)
    Catch
        ReDim Preserve NetterBody(NetterBodyLength + 25)
```

```
        NetterBody(NetterBodyLength) = New clsNetterBody(IsComputer)
    End Try
    NetterBody(NetterBodyLength).Location = _
            NetterBody(NetterBodyLength - 1).Location

    ' Updates the whole body's position and then the head position
    For i = NetterBodyLength - 1 To 1 Step -1
        NetterBody(i).Location = NetterBody(i - 1).Location
    Next

    NetterBody(0).Location = Location
    NetterBody(0).Draw(WinHandle)

    NetterBodyLength += 1
    ' Updates the Netterpillar head position
    Location = New Point(x, y)

    'Clear the mushroom
    UnDraw(WinHandle)

    ' Draw the Netterpillar head
    Draw(WinHandle)
End Sub
```

One extra detail here is that we need to erase the mushroom as we are eating it. We can do that by simply calling the Undraw method before we call the Draw method of the Netterpillar class.

## Main Program and GameEngine Class

To test our Netterpillar class, we can add the MoveNetterpillars procedure to the clsGameEngine, and improve the keypress code of the frmGameField to update the direction of our netterpillar.

In order to make the code more readable, we'll add a Player1 property, which will point to the netterpillar that the player controls. Our netterpillar won't be eating anything for now; we'll test the EatAndMove method after we code the collision detection in the GameEngine class, in the final version of the game.

```
Public objNetterpillars(4) As clsNetterpillar
Public Player1 As clsNetterpillar
```

We can update the `New` method of the `clsGameEngine` class to add four new net-terpillars, and point the `Player1` property to the first one, adding the following lines of code:

```
objNetterpillars(0) = New clsNetterpillar(Int(Me.Width / 3),_
        Int(Me.Height) / 3, clsSprite.enDirection.South, False)
objNetterpillars(1) = New clsNetterpillar(Int(Me.Width / 3),_
        Int(Me.Height) / 3 * 2, clsSprite.enDirection.East, True)
objNetterpillars(2) = New clsNetterpillar(Int(Me.Width / 3) * 2,_
        Int(Me.Height) / 3 * 2, clsSprite.enDirection.North, True)
objNetterpillars(3) = New clsNetterpillar(Int(Me.Width / 3) * 2,_
        Int(Me.Height) / 3, clsSprite.enDirection.West, True)
Player1 = objNetterpillars(0)
```

**NOTE** *Notice that we have put the netterpillars a distance apart from each other, and set their initial direction to be different, so they won't hit each other just after the game starts.*

Our `Move` method is ready to move the netterpillar using the direction dictated by the game engine, so we'll create a simple `MoveNetterpillars` method in the `clsGameEngine` class that will update the x or y position of each of the netterpillars, based on their current direction.

```
Sub MoveNetterpillars()
    Dim i As Integer
    Dim incX As Integer = 0, incY As Integer = 0

    For i = 0 To NetterpillarNumber - 1
            ' Moves all the Netterpillars
            Select Case objNetterpillars(i).Direction
                Case clsSprite.enDirection.East
                    incX = 1
                    incY = 0
                Case clsSprite.enDirection.West
                    incX = -1
                    incY = 0
                Case clsSprite.enDirection.North
                    incX = 0
                    incY = -1
```

```
            Case clsSprite.enDirection.South
                incX = 0
                incY = 1
        End Select


    objNetterpillars(i).Move( _
            objNetterpillars(i).Location.X + incX, _
            objNetterpillars(i).Location.Y + incY, ScreenWinHandle)
    Next
End Sub
```

To finish the second draft of the GameField class, we need to call the MoveNetterpillars method from the Render procedure, as follows:

```
Sub Render()
    MoveNetterpillars()
    Redraw()
End Sub
```

and update the Redraw method to include the lines that will draw the netterpillars:

```
For i = 0 To 3
    objNetterpillars(i).Draw(ScreenWinHandle)
Next
```

Our Main program won't need any updates, but if we want to test the Move method, we'll have to add some new lines in the keyboard handler, to update the direction of the player's character depending on which key is pressed:

```
Private Sub frmGameField_KeyDown(sender As Object, e As KeyEventArgs) _
                                        Handles MyBase.KeyDown
    ' Set the next direction for the player.
    '  We will not let the player go backwards from the current direction,
    '    because he would die if he does so.
    Select Case e.KeyCode
        Case Keys.Right
            If objGameEngine.Player1.Direction <> clsSprite.enDirection.West Then
                objGameEngine.Player1.Direction = clsSprite.enDirection.East
            End If
        Case Keys.Left
            If objGameEngine.Player1.Direction <> clsSprite.enDirection.East Then
                objGameEngine.Player1.Direction = clsSprite.enDirection.West
            End If
```

```
        Case Keys.Up
            If objGameEngine.Player1.Direction <> clsSprite.enDirection.South Then
                objGameEngine.Player1.Direction = clsSprite.enDirection.North
            End If
        Case Keys.Down
            If objGameEngine.Player1.Direction <> clsSprite.enDirection.North Then
                objGameEngine.Player1.Direction = clsSprite.enDirection.South
            End If
        Case Keys.Escape
            objGameEngine.GameOver = true
    End Select
End Sub
```

In the keyboard handler in the preceding code, note the conditional statements: These test the current player's direction and stop it from running backwards, which will lead to the immediate death of the netterpillar when we include collision detection.

Figure 2-16 presents the test of this code draft.

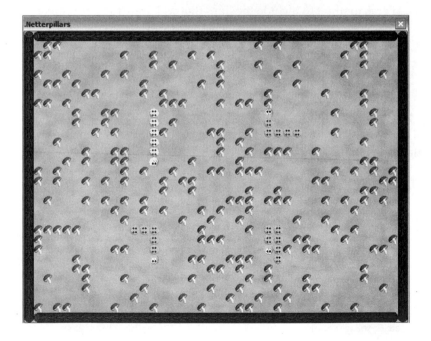

*Figure 2-16. Testing the netterpillars*

This test will be a really quick one: Since we aren't implementing collision detection yet, nor the AI, the computer-controlled netterpillars will go straight through the field and disappear off the edge of the screen. The game will crash a few seconds after that.

# Third Draft: Coding the Game Engine and Collision Detection

In this last part of our coding, we'll finish the GameEngine class and code the AI for the computer-controlled netterpillars. We'll also add the code to allow the configuration screen to function properly.

## The GameEngine Class

To code the interface of the GameEngine class, we must refer to the class diagram we created in the game project phase and include the implementation details. The GameEngine class interface is presented in the following code listing:

```
Public Class clsGameEngine
    Public Width As Integer = 25
    Public Height As Integer = 25
    Public Shared BackgroundImage As Image

    ' This array and enum controls the object collision
    Protected Shared arrGameField(,) As enGameObjects
    Protected Enum enGameObjects
        Mushroom = 0
        Empty = 1
        Branch = 2
        Netterpillar = 3
    End Enum

    Private ScreenWinHandle As System.IntPtr

    ' Game objects
    Private objBranchs() As clsBranch

    Private objMushrooms As clsMushroom
    Private MushroomNumber As Integer = 75
```

```
        Public objNetterpillars(4) As clsNetterpillar
        Public NetterpillarNumber As Integer = 1
        Public Player1 As clsNetterpillar

        'Controls the game end
        Public GameOver As Boolean
        Public Paused As Boolean

        ' This properties will be defined as property procedures, and
        '  they'll use the enumerations below as property types
        Property Size() As enSize
        Property Mushrooms() As enMushrooms

        Sub MoveNetterpillars()
        Sub KillNetterPillar(Netterpillar As clsNetterpillar)
        Sub Render()
        Sub New (WinHandle As System.IntPtr)
        Sub Redraw()
    End Class
```

Let's start coding the collision detection, which is accomplished by making the arrGameField array hold all the game objects and, before moving the netterpillars (the only moving objects), checking to see if there's any collision.

We fill the array in the New method, including some lines to set the array just after creating the objects. At this point, we can make a simple improvement in our New and Draw procedures: Instead of creating dozens of mushroom objects, we could create a single object and move it as needed to draw all the mushrooms on the game field. This will have no effect on our collision detection algorithms, since we'll use arrGameField instead of the Mushroom object to test the collision.

We'll just include the following lines in the New procedure we coded previously, starting with an initialization loop that will set all the objects in the array to Empty:

```
    ' Initialize the game array (for collision detection)
    For x = 0 To Width - 1
        For y = 0 To Height - 1
            arrGameField(x, y) = enGameObjects.Empty
        Next
    Next
```

After creating the netterpillars, we insert the code for setting all the positions in the array (head and bodies) for each netterpillar to the Netterpillar enGameObjects enumeration member:

```
' Populates the array with the netterpillars
For i = 0 To NetterpillarNumber - 1
    arrGameField(objNetterpillars(i).Location.X, _
                objNetterpillars(i).Location.Y) = enGameObjects.Netterpillar
    For j = 0 To objNetterpillars(i).NetterBodyLength - 1
        arrGameField(objNetterpillars(i).NetterBody(j).Location.X, _
                    objNetterpillars(i).NetterBody(j).Location.Y) = _
                    enGameObjects.Netterpillar
    Next
Next
```

Since the branches are just limiting our game field, we can simply do some loops that will set all the borders (the array elements with x = 0, y = 0, x = Width – 1 or y = Height – 1) to the Branch enGameObjects enumeration member:

```
For x = 0 To Width - 1
    arrGameField(x, 0) = enGameObjects.Branch
    arrGameField(x, Height - 1) = enGameObjects.Branch
Next
For y = 0 To Height
    arrGameField(0, y) = enGameObjects.Branch
    arrGameField(Width - 1, y) = enGameObjects.Branch
Next
```

And as for the mushrooms, we just need to set the array position to the enumeration element Mushroom for each new mushroom added. We also need to make two more improvements to the code we used previously as a stub: First, let's check if the random array position chosen has no objects in it, and if it does, choose another position, until we find an Empty array slot. Second, as planned before, let's save some memory by creating just one mushroom, and simply moving it from place to place when we need to draw the game field. The final code for the mushroom creation will be as follows:

```
objMushrooms = New clsMushroom()
For i = 0 To MushroomNumber - 1
    ' Check to seek if we are not creating the mushrooms over other objects
    Do
        x = Int(Rnd(1) * (Me.Width - 2)) + 1
        y = Int(Rnd(1) * (Me.Height - 2)) + 1
    Loop While arrGameField(x, y) <> enGameObjects.Empty
    arrGameField(x, y) = enGameObjects.Mushroom
Next
```

Note that we have to change the `objMushrooms` property definition to a variable, instead of an array. The code for drawing the mushrooms in the `Draw` method will be as follows:

```
For x = 0 To Width - 1
    For y = 0 To Height - 1
        If arrGameField(x, y) = enGameObjects.Mushroom Then
            objMushrooms.Location = New Point(x, y)
            objMushrooms.Draw(ScreenWinHandle)
        End If
    Next
Next
```

With these modifications, our `New` and `Draw` methods are filling the array that will help us with collision detection. We now need to change the `MoveNetterpillars` method to check for any collisions when the netterpillars move, and take the appropriate action:

- Kill the netterpillar if it hits an obstacle.

- Make the netterpillar bigger when it collides with a mushroom, calling the `EatAndMove` method of the `clsNetterpillar` class; at this point we should decrement the mushroom number counter in order to know when all the mushrooms have been eaten.

- Move the netterpillar when there's no collision.

In each case, we'll have to remember to empty the array in every position the netterpillar has visited previously to avoid ghost collisions. We'll have to change the call of the `Move` method in `MoveNetterpillars` to a selection that takes into account the actions just mentioned. Remember, this code goes immediately after the code that will set the `incX` and `incY` variables; to point to the next position the netterpillar will occupy, we have to test the current position added to these increment variables:

```
Select Case arrGameField(objNetterpillars(i).Location.X + incX, _
                    objNetterpillars(i).Location.Y + incY)
    Case enGameObjects.Empty
            objNetterpillars(i).Move(objNetterpillars(i).Location.X + incX,_
                objNetterpillars(i).Location.Y + incY, ScreenWinHandle)
            ' Update the Game Field - Empty the field after the Netterpillar
            arrGameField(objNetterpillars(i).NetterBody(_
                    objNetterpillars(i).NetterBodyLength - 1).Location.X, _
```

```
                    objNetterpillars(i).NetterBody(_
                        objNetterpillars(i).NetterBodyLength - 1).Location.Y) = _
                    enGameObjects.Empty
            ' Update the Game Field - Sets the Netterpillar Head
            arrGameField(objNetterpillars(i).Location.X, _
                    objNetterpillars(i).Location.Y) = enGameObjects.Netterpillar
        Case enGameObjects.Mushroom
            ' Decrement the number of Mushrooms
            MushroomNumber -= 1
            objNetterpillars(i).EatAndMove(objNetterpillars(i).Location.X + incX, _
                    objNetterpillars(i).Location.Y + incY, ScreenWinHandle)
            ' Update the Game Field - Sets the Netterpillar Head
            arrGameField(objNetterpillars(i).Location.X, _
                        objNetterpillars(i).Location.Y) = enGameObjects.Netterpillar
        Case Else
                KillNetterPillar(objNetterpillars(i))
End Select
```

All we need to do now to test our program is to code the `KillNetterpillar` method, which will erase the netterpillar from the game field and do the updates on the `Netterpillar` object and the array field:

```
Sub KillNetterPillar(Netterpillar As clsNetterpillar)
    Dim i As Integer

    Netterpillar.IsDead = True
    ' Clears the game field
    arrGameField(Netterpillar.Location.X, Netterpillar.Location.Y) = _
                enGameObjects.Empty
    Netterpillar.UnDraw(ScreenWinHandle)

    For i = 0 To Netterpillar.NetterBodyLength - 1
        arrGameField(Netterpillar.NetterBody(i).Location.X, _
                Netterpillar.NetterBody(i).Location.Y) = enGameObjects.Empty
        Netterpillar.NetterBody(i).UnDraw(ScreenWinHandle)
    Next
End Sub
```

In the previous code we reset the array elements for the head and the bodies; then we call the `Undraw` method of the `Netterpillar` class to remove it from the sight; and finally we set the `IsDead` property of the netterpillar to true.

At this point, after coding the KillNetterpillar method, you may have noticed that we forgot to do something on the methods we had already coded: We forgot to test if the netterpillar is alive when moving it at the MoveNetterpillars method and when drawing it in the Redraw method! Okay, don't panic, let's just add an If statement to solve this. The MoveNetterpillar method will become as follows:

```
Sub MoveNetterpillars()
...
    For i = 0 To NetterpillarNumber - 1
        If Not objNetterpillars(i).IsDead Then
...     <Moving code here>
        End if
    Next
End Sub
```

And here's how the Redraw procedure will look:

```
...
    For i = 0 To NetterpillarNumber - 1
        If Not objNetterpillars(i).IsDead Then
            objNetterpillars(i).Draw(ScreenWinHandle)
        End If
    Next
...
```

This will prevent the dead netterpillar from moving and being drawn again.

We can test our program now. The interface will be the same as in the second draft, but now we can effectively eat the mushrooms and get bigger, and die when we hit an obstacle.

# Fourth Draft: Coding the Config Screen and Game Over

Before starting the AI code, let's include some details to our game, adding the code for the configuration screen and the test for ending the game.

## Coding for the Configuration Screen

Looking at the visual prototype of the configuration screen, we can see that we have two properties that don't map directly to numbers: the game field size and the quantity of mushrooms on the screen. In order to create a more direct mapping from the screen to the game field properties, let's add two property procedures: Size (which will set the width and height properties) and Mushrooms (which will set the MushroomNumber property, according to the current size of the game field), as shown in the following code.

Here's the Size property:

```
Public Enum enSize
    Small = 2
    Medium = 1
    Big = 0
End Enum
Private pSize As enSize = enSize.Medium

Property Size() As enSize
    Get
        Size = pSize
    End Get
    Set(Value As enSize)
        pSize = Value
        Select Case Value
            Case enSize.Small
                Width = 15
                Height = 15
            Case enSize.Medium
                Width = 25
                Height = 25
            Case enSize.Big
                Width = 40
                Height = 30
        End Select
    End Set
End Property
```

And now the Mushroom property:

```
Public Enum enMushrooms
    Few = 2
    JustRight = 1
    Many = 0
End Enum
Private pMushrooms As enMushrooms = enMushrooms.JustRight
```

```
Property Mushrooms() As enMushrooms
    Get
        Mushrooms = pMushrooms
    End Get
    Set(Value As enMushrooms)
        pMushrooms = Value
        Select Case Value
            Case enMushrooms.Few
                MushroomNumber = 25
            Case enMushrooms.JustRight
                MushroomNumber = 75
            Case enMushrooms.Many
                MushroomNumber = 125
        End Select

        If Size = enSize.Medium Then
            MushroomNumber *= 2
        ElseIf Size = enSize.Big Then
            MushroomNumber *= 3
        End If
    End Set
End Property
```

**NEW IN .NET**

*The property procedure definition differs a lot from the previous version of Visual Basic. Instead of two procedures,* Property Let *and* Property Get, *we have a new statement, named* Property, *where we can add two blocks:* Get/End Get *for the code that will be called when the property is read, and* Set/End Set *for the code that will be called when a value is set to the property. If we want to create a read-only property, we use the modifier* ReadOnly *before the* Property *keyword, and simply don't provide a* Set *block; we can also define a write-only property using the modifier* WriteOnly *and not coding the* Get *block.*

We must adjust the New method too, since we are always creating four netter-pillars. Instead of using a fixed number, we should use the NetterpillarNumber property, which will be set in the configuration window.

Since we'll be creating one to four netterpillars, let's define where each of them will be created:

- If we have one netterpillar, create it in the center of the screen.

- If we have two netterpillars, create them in the center of the y axis (vertical), and at 1/3 and 2/3 along the x axis (horizontal), so we'll have a constant distance from the borders to the netterpillars and between the two netterpillars. It's better to initialize them running in different directions; so one will head north and another south.

- If we have three netterpillars, we'll put them at 1/4, 2/4, and 3/4 along the x axis, and in the middle of the y axis, heading south, north, and south again.

- If we have four netterpillars, we'll put them in a square, each heading in the direction of the next vertex. The vertices will be at 1/3 vertical, 1/3 horizontal; 1/3 vertical, 2/3 horizontal; 2/3 vertical, 2/3 horizontal; and 2/3 vertical, 1/3 horizontal.

The code for this logic is show here:

```
' Create the netterpillars
Select Case NetterpillarNumber
    Case 1
        objNetterpillars(0) = New clsNetterpillar(Int(Me.Width / 2), _
                    Int(Me.Height) / 2, clsSprite.enDirection.South, False)
    Case 2
        objNetterpillars(0) = New clsNetterpillar(Int(Me.Width / 3), _
                    Int(Me.Height) / 2, clsSprite.enDirection.South, False)
        objNetterpillars(1) = New clsNetterpillar(Int(Me.Width / 3) * 2,_
                    Int(Me.Height) / 2, clsSprite.enDirection.North, True)
    Case 3
        objNetterpillars(0) = New clsNetterpillar(Int(Me.Width / 4), _
                    Int(Me.Height) / 2, clsSprite.enDirection.South, False)
        objNetterpillars(1) = New clsNetterpillar(Int(Me.Width / 4) * 2, _
                    Int(Me.Height) / 2, clsSprite.enDirection.North, True)
        objNetterpillars(2) = New clsNetterpillar(Int(Me.Width / 4) * 3, _
                    Int(Me.Height) / 2, clsSprite.enDirection.South, True)
    Case 4
        objNetterpillars(0) = New clsNetterpillar(Int(Me.Width / 3), _
                    Int(Me.Height) / 3, clsSprite.enDirection.South, False)
        objNetterpillars(1) = New clsNetterpillar(Int(Me.Width / 3), _
                    Int(Me.Height) / 3 * 2, clsSprite.enDirection.East, True)
```

```
                objNetterpillars(2) = New clsNetterpillar(Int(Me.Width / 3) * 2, _
                        Int(Me.Height) / 3 * 2, clsSprite.enDirection.North, True)
                objNetterpillars(3) = New clsNetterpillar(Int(Me.Width / 3) * 2, _
                        Int(Me.Height) / 3, clsSprite.enDirection.West, True)
        End Select
```

To allow us to test the configuration code, we need to add some lines to the Load event and the OK button of the configuration screen.

When loading the form, we must set the controls to the current value of each of the objGameEngine configuration properties:

```
Private Sub frmConfig_Load(sender As Object, e As System.EventArgs) _
                    Handles MyBase.Load
    updGameField.SelectedIndex = objGameEngine.Size
    updNetterpillars.Value = objGameEngine.NetterpillarNumber
    updMushrooms.SelectedIndex = objGameEngine.Mushrooms
End Sub
```

In the OK click procedure, we'll do the opposite, setting the objGameEngine properties to the values set on the form:

```
Sub cmdOK_Click(sender As System.Object, e As System.EventArgs) _
                Handles cmdOK.Click
    objGameEngine.Size = updGameField.SelectedIndex
    objGameEngine.NetterpillarNumber = updNetterpillars.Value
    objGameEngine.Mushrooms = updMushrooms.SelectedIndex
End Sub
```

Everything is now correctly positioned, but we need to show the configuration dialog box at some point in the program, else we won't be able to change the configuration settings. It's time to go back to our Main procedure, and include in it the main window, through which we can change the configuration, start a new game, or exit the game. The window will be the one that was shown as a visual prototype in the project phase, including some lines of code in the Config button to show the configuration screen, as demonstrated in the code that follows. Some code to close the window must also be included on the click event of the Exit button.

```
Sub cmdConfig_Click(sender As System.Object, e As System.EventArgs) _
            Handles cmdConfig.Click
    Dim WinConfig As frmConfig
    WinConfig = New frmConfig()
    WinConfig.ShowDialog()
    WinConfig.Dispose()
End Sub
```

**NEW IN .NET**

*In Visual Basic .NET, we don't have a parameter of the form* Show *method anymore to say if it should be shown modally (the form is shown and execution continues after the form is closed) or modeless (the form is shown and the code continues executing); instead we have a* ShowDialog *method that should be used when we wish to show a form modally. In the preceding sample code, the* WinConfig.Dispose() *line is only executed after the form is closed by the user.*

## Coding for the Introduction Screen

Now is a good time to create an intro screen for our game. Our suggestion is shown in the Figure 2-17, but feel free to use your artistic talent to improve it.

*Figure 2-17. The .Netterpillars splash screen*

The `Main` procedure must be changed to reflect the workflow diagram created in the project phase:

```
Sub main()
    Dim WinSplash As frmSplash
    Dim WinGameField As frmGameField

    ' Create the game engine object
    objGameEngine = New clsGameEngine(WinGameField.PicGameField.Handle)
    WinSplash = New frmSplash()

    Do While WinSplash.ShowDialog() = DialogResult.OK
        WinGameField = New frmGameField()
        WinGameField.Show()
        Application.DoEvents()  ' Shows the window immediately
    objGameEngine.BackgroundImage=WinGameField.PicGameField.Image.Clone
        Do While Not objGameEngine.GameOver
            objGameEngine.Render()
            Application.DoEvents()
        Loop
        MsgBox("Game Over ", MsgBoxStyle.Exclamation, ".Netterpillars")
        WinGameField.Dispose()
    Loop
    objGameEngine = Nothing
    WinSplash.Dispose()
End Sub
```

That's it. We can now play with different field sizes, number of mushrooms, and netterpillars. But after playing a couple of times, we'll soon discover that when we run our game a second time without making any configuration changes, our properties don't get reset; so, among other things, we'll start with the last quantity of mushrooms (that is, without the ones that were eaten). And worst of all: If the game field screen is being created for each game, our handle (passed to the `objGameEngine New` method) becomes invalid.

Since we can't simply move the `objGameEngine` creation to inside the loop (we'll need it in the configuration screen, and if we re-create the object, the previous configuration will be lost), a solution is to create a new method to reset the game variables, which can be called just after the program Game Over loop. We can call this method `CreateGameField`, and move all the code from the `New` procedure to it, including the parameter that receives the window handle.

We have shown these details to clarify a point: A game project, as any other project, will have problems en route. The better the project, the less unexpected the behavior in the coding phase. Nevertheless, there's no way to guarantee immediate success. Don't be ashamed to go back and correct everything if you think that it'll make your game faster, more stable, or easier to update with new features.

Another detail that requires extra care is the code for setting the game field size: When we resize the game field, the game field window must be resized accordingly. We must do that in the Load event of the frmGameField window:

```
Sub frmGameField_Load(sender As System.Object, e As System.EventArgs)_
                Handles MyBase.Load
    PicGameField.Location = New Point(0, 0)
    PicGameField.Size = New Size(objGameEngine.Width * clsSprite.IMAGE_SIZE, _
            objGameEngine.Height * clsSprite.IMAGE_SIZE)
    Me.ClientSize = PicGameField.Size
End Sub
```

With this last little adjustment, our code will work. But we don't have code for the game over yet. We'll show that next.

## Coding for Game Over

Looking back at our game proposal, we stated that "the game is over when all the players die (computer or human ones), or when the last mushroom is eaten."

Since we have a property stating whether a player is dead or not, and a property that stores the number of mushrooms (that is already reduced every time a mushroom is eaten), all we need to do is include the code in the Render procedure to test the preceding conditions and set the GameOver property to True if one of the requirements is met.

```
Sub Render()
    Dim i As Integer
    ' Move the Netterpillars
    MoveNetterpillars()

    ' If all Netterpillars die - GameOver
    GameOver = True
    For i = 0 To NetterpillarNumber - 1
        If Not objNetterpillars(i).IsDead Then
            GameOver = False
        End If
    Next
```

```
      ' If all mushrooms got eaten - Game Over
     If MushroomNumber = 0 Then
         GameOver = True
     End If
End Sub
```

We mustn't forget to remove the code for forcing the game to finish when the Esc key is pressed, on the keyboard event handler for the frmGameField, unless we need this behavior in our finished game.

Although the code for the "game over" works fine, it can be improved if we include a screen with game statistics—such as the netterpillar's size—so players can have clearer information about how well they played. Such a screen is added in the "Adding the Final Touches" section; for now, let's alter our code to include a real computer-controlled competitor.

# Final Version: Coding the Netterpillars AI

To finish our game, we need to code the NetterpillarAI class and make the final adjustments in the Main procedure, as shown in the next sections.

## The Netterpillar AI Class

As we decided in the game proposal and in the game project, we only need to use a simple form of artificial intelligence. Just avoid walls and eat mushrooms if they are near, that's all.

```
Public Class clsAINetterpillar
    Inherits clsGameEngine

    Private RandomPercent As Integer = 5
    Function ChooseNetterpillarDirection(CurrentLocation As Point, _
CurrentDirection As clsSprite.enDirection) As clsSprite.enDirection
    Function RandomDirection(CurrentLocation As Point, _
ChoosenDirection As clsSprite.enDirection) As clsSprite.enDirection
End Class
```

Let's review what the game objects are:

```
Protected Enum enGameObjects
    Mushroom = 0
    Empty = 1
    Branch = 2
    Netterpillar = 3
End Enum
```

Not by accident, when we defined this enumeration, did we put the game objects in ascending order of collision preference. When we check the objects around us, the lowest value is the preferred one: A mushroom is better than empty space, and both are preferable to a collision resulting in death. We can use this to our advantage, to ease the choice of the best object by checking the lowest value (with the min function) from the positions around the current position of the netterpillar's head:

```
BestObject = Math.Min(Math.Min(Math.Min( _
    arrGameField(CurrentLocation.X + 1, CurrentLocation.Y), _
    arrGameField(CurrentLocation.X - 1, CurrentLocation.Y)), _
    arrGameField(CurrentLocation.X, CurrentLocation.Y + 1)), _
    arrGameField(CurrentLocation.X, CurrentLocation.Y - 1))
```

Once the best object has been chosen, we can check it against the next object in the current direction; and if they are the same (there can be two or more optimal objects), we choose to stay in the current direction, to make the netterpillar's movement less erratic.

One last step is to add some random behavior to make the movement less predictable and less prone to getting stuck in an infinite loop; for example, the netterpillar could move in circles around the game field forever if there's no aleatory component. In our tests, anything greater than 10 percent randomness can lead to erratic behavior (remember, we choose a new direction many times a second); a value between 0 and 5 generates good results.

```
Function ChooseNetterpillarDirection(CurrentLocation As Point, _
        CurrentDirection As clsSprite.enDirection) As clsSprite.enDirection
    Dim BestObject As enGameObjects
    Dim NextObject As enGameObjects

    Select Case CurrentDirection
        Case clsSprite.enDirection.East
            NextObject = arrGameField(CurrentLocation.X + 1, CurrentLocation.Y)
```

```
        Case clsSprite.enDirection.West
            NextObject = arrGameField(CurrentLocation.X - 1, CurrentLocation.Y)
        Case clsSprite.enDirection.South
            NextObject = arrGameField(CurrentLocation.X, CurrentLocation.Y + 1)
        Case clsSprite.enDirection.North
            NextObject = arrGameField(CurrentLocation.X, CurrentLocation.Y - 1)
    End Select


    ' Pick the lowest value - Mushroom or empty
    BestObject = Math.Min(Math.Min(Math.Min( _
        arrGameField(CurrentLocation.X + 1, CurrentLocation.Y), _
        arrGameField(CurrentLocation.X - 1, CurrentLocation.Y)), _
        arrGameField(CurrentLocation.X, CurrentLocation.Y + 1)), _
        arrGameField(CurrentLocation.X, CurrentLocation.Y - 1))


    ' If the current direction is equal the best direction,
    '    stay in current direction
    If NextObject = BestObject Then
        ChooseNetterpillarDirection = CurrentDirection
    Else
        ' Select the direction of the best object
        Select Case BestObject
            Case arrGameField(CurrentLocation.X + 1, CurrentLocation.Y)
                    ChooseNetterpillarDirection = clsSprite.enDirection.East
            Case arrGameField(CurrentLocation.X - 1, CurrentLocation.Y)
                    ChooseNetterpillarDirection = clsSprite.enDirection.West
            Case arrGameField(CurrentLocation.X, CurrentLocation.Y + 1)
                    ChooseNetterpillarDirection = clsSprite.enDirection.South
            Case arrGameField(CurrentLocation.X, CurrentLocation.Y - 1)
                    ChooseNetterpillarDirection = clsSprite.enDirection.North
        End Select
    End If


    ChooseNetterpillarDirection = RandomDirection(CurrentLocation, _
                        ChooseNetterpillarDirection)
End Function
```

To code the `RandomDirection` method, called in the last line of the preceding code, we'll simply pick a random number from 0 to 100, and if it's less than the `RandomPercent` property, choose a new movement direction for the netterpillar. The next code sample presents the full code for this method:

```
Function RandomDirection(CurrentLocation As Point, ChoosenDirection _
     As clsSprite.enDirection) As clsSprite.enDirection
  Dim x As Integer = Rnd(1) * 100

  RandomDirection = ChoosenDirection
  If x < RandomPercent Then
     Select Case ChoosenDirection
        Case clsSprite.enDirection.East
           ' Try the other directions
           If arrGameField(CurrentLocation.X, CurrentLocation.Y + 1) <= _
                                          enGameObjects.Empty Then
              RandomDirection = clsSprite.enDirection.South
           ElseIf arrGameField(CurrentLocation.X, CurrentLocation.Y - 1) <= _
                                          enGameObjects.Empty Then
              RandomDirection = clsSprite.enDirection.North
           ElseIf arrGameField(CurrentLocation.X - 1, CurrentLocation.Y) <= _
                                          enGameObjects.Empty Then
              RandomDirection = clsSprite.enDirection.West
           End If
        Case clsSprite.enDirection.West
           ' Try the other directions
           If arrGameField(CurrentLocation.X, CurrentLocation.Y + 1) <= _
                                          enGameObjects.Empty Then
              RandomDirection = clsSprite.enDirection.South
           ElseIf arrGameField(CurrentLocation.X, CurrentLocation.Y - 1) <= _
                                          enGameObjects.Empty Then
              RandomDirection = clsSprite.enDirection.North
           ElseIf arrGameField(CurrentLocation.X + 1, CurrentLocation.Y) <= _
                                          enGameObjects.Empty Then
              RandomDirection = clsSprite.enDirection.East
           End If
        Case clsSprite.enDirection.North
           ' Try the other directions
           If arrGameField(CurrentLocation.X, CurrentLocation.Y + 1) <=_
                                          enGameObjects.Empty Then
              RandomDirection = clsSprite.enDirection.South
           ElseIf arrGameField(CurrentLocation.X + 1, CurrentLocation.Y) <= _
                                          enGameObjects.Empty Then
```

```
                RandomDirection = clsSprite.enDirection.East
        ElseIf arrGameField(CurrentLocation.X - 1, CurrentLocation.Y) <=_
                                            enGameObjects.Empty Then
                RandomDirection = clsSprite.enDirection.West
        End If
    Case clsSprite.enDirection.South
        ' Try the other directions
        If arrGameField(CurrentLocation.X, CurrentLocation.Y - 1) <= _
                                            enGameObjects.Empty Then
                RandomDirection = clsSprite.enDirection.North
        ElseIf arrGameField(CurrentLocation.X + 1, CurrentLocation.Y) <= _
                                            enGameObjects.Empty Then
                RandomDirection = clsSprite.enDirection.East
        ElseIf arrGameField(CurrentLocation.X - 1, CurrentLocation.Y) <= _
                                            enGameObjects.Empty Then
                RandomDirection = clsSprite.enDirection.West
        End If
    End Select
    End If
End Function
```

Since the code in the clsGameEngine is intended to take care of the game's physics (for example, it moves the netterpillars, regardless of whether one is changing direction), we'll have to put the code for moving the netterpillars based on the AI outside the game engine object; our Main procedure is the best option.

Another valid approach would be to include the AI code inside the Netterpillar object—it's just a matter of choice: a small number of bigger classes or many smaller ones.

## The Main Program: Final Version

In order to call the AI code, we create a new procedure, which will be called from the game main loop. The procedure, shown in the following code, just loops through the Netterpillars objects and, if they aren't dead and if they are computer controlled, sets the current direction to the result of the ChooseNetterpillarDirection method.

```
Private objAINetterpillar As New clsAINetterpillar()
Sub MoveComputerCharacters()
    Dim i As Integer

    ' Move the Netterpillars
    For i = 0 To objGameEngine.NetterpillarNumber - 1
        If Not objGameEngine.objNetterpillars(i).IsDead Then
            ' A.I. for the computer-controled Netterpillars
            If objGameEngine.objNetterpillars(i).IsComputer Then
                objGameEngine.objNetterpillars(i).Direction = _
                    objAINetterpillar.ChooseNetterpillarDirection( _
                    objGameEngine.objNetterpillars(i).Location, _
                    objGameEngine.objNetterpillars(i).Direction)
            End If
        End If
    Next
End Sub
```

The main program loop should include one more section to call the MoveComputerCharacters procedure.

```
        Do While Not objGameEngine.GameOver
            MoveComputerCharacters()
            objGameEngine.Render()
            Application.DoEvents()
        Loop
```

This finishes our coding phase; some code to add polish to the final product is suggested in the next section.

# Adding the Final Touches

In this section we add some extra features to our game. These final touches, although simple, are important and need to be considered.

## Coding the Pause Game Feature

As in the .Nettrix game, we could insert code to pause (and restart) the game when the Esc key is pressed. This basic improvement is shown here:

```
Private Sub frmGameField_KeyDown(sender As Object, _

                e As System.Windows.Forms.KeyEventArgs) Handles MyBase.KeyDown
        . . .
        Case Keys.Escape
            objGameEngine.Paused = Not objGameEngine.Paused
            If objGameEngine.Paused Then
                Me.Text = ".Netterpillars - Press ESC to continue"
            Else
                Me.Text = ".Netterpillars"
            End If
    End Select
End Sub
```

## Improving the Game Over Screen

Our game over routine also needs an improvement. A good game programmer should not forget that a good game ending is far more important that a nice intro screen. Players must be rewarded for all their efforts in completing the game; it's very frustrating for players to spend days and days finishing a game and not getting anything in return to give them a feeling of accomplishment. In our game, the "Game Over" message box is one of these frustrations. Although a high scores table would be better, let's at least give players some feedback about the results of the game and how well they played.

We can do this by creating a new Game Over window, where we can display some game statistics, as shown in Figure 2-18.

*Figure 2-18. A Game Over screen*

This screen can access the objGameEngine, which is a public variable, and gather information about players and how long their netterpillars were when the game finished.

To load the label with the statistics, we must access each of the objNetterpillars objects, checking the IsComputer property and the NetterBodyLength property. We'll need to avoid unset objects (remember, the player could be playing with any number of opponents, from 0 to 3).

The IIF commands in the next code sample (which must be placed on the Load event of the window) aren't new to .NET, although they aren't commonly used because sometimes they can lead to more complex code. The IIF command tests the first parameter (an expression) and, if true, returns the second parameter; otherwise it returns the last parameter.

```
LblPlayer1Length.Text= _
        objGameEngine.objNetterpillars(0).NetterBodyLength
LblPlayer1Is.Text= _
        IIf(objGameEngine.objNetterpillars(0).IsComputer, "Computer", "Human")

If Not objGameEngine.objNetterpillars(1) Is Nothing Then
    LblPlayer2Length.Text = _
        objGameEngine.objNetterpillars(1).NetterBodyLength
    LblPlayer2Is.Text = _
        IIf(objGameEngine.objNetterpillars(1).IsComputer, "Computer", "Human")
Else
    LblPlayer2Length.Text = "-"
    LblPlayer2Is.Text = "-"
End If
```

```
If Not objGameEngine.objNetterpillars(2) Is Nothing Then
    LblPlayer3Length.Text = _
        objGameEngine.objNetterpillars(2).NetterBodyLength
    LblPlayer3Is.Text = _
        IIf(objGameEngine.objNetterpillars(2).IsComputer, "Computer", "Human")
Else
    LblPlayer3Length.Text = "-"
    LblPlayer3Is.Text = "-"
End If

If Not objGameEngine.objNetterpillars(3) Is Nothing Then
    LblPlayer4Length.Text=_
        objGameEngine.objNetterpillars(3).NetterBodyLength
    LblPlayer4Is.Text= _
        IIf(objGameEngine.objNetterpillars(3).IsComputer, "Computer", "Human")
Else
    LblPlayer4Length.Text = "-"
    LblPlayer4Is.Text = "-"
End If
```

In final version of the main program, we must replace the "Game Over" message box by a call to the ShowDialog method of the game over form.

## Coding for the Garbage Collection

A technical enhancement is to improve the speed of the garbage collection calling the Collect method of the System.GC object, in the end of the Render method, as shown:

```
Sub Render()
    ...
    System.GC.Collect()
End Sub
```

**NEW IN .NET**

*The .NET Framework provides an advanced garbage collector that frees the memory from all objects left behind by the program. The garbage collection takes place in idle system time, but we can force it to run by calling the* Collect *method, which is good practice if we are dealing with lots of memory allocations and reallocations—which we do, for example, with the* Graphics *object in each* Draw *method in the game objects.*

## Further Improvements

We saved the best for last: What about creating new intelligent characters for our game, maybe some opposition—like a spider who eats the netterpillars?

In the code for this chapter on the samples CD-ROM, you will find an almost fully working spider character. We already did all the dirty work: the `Spider` and `AISpider` class interfaces, the call to the moving functions at the `MoveComputerCharacters` routine and at the `Render` and `Redraw` method of the `objGameEngine`—almost everything is there. The code for `ChooseDirection` method of the `AISpider` class is empty, so our spiders aren't going anywhere. This gives you the opportunity to create the AI from scratch, without worrying about the details. Will the spider attack the netterpillars heads and kill them? Or will they just eat part of their tails? Or, maybe make new mushrooms grow? Start making your proposal for the second version of the game, and enjoy!

## Summary

In this chapter, via the .Netterpillars game sample, we explored some additional concepts related to game programming, including

- Basic concepts about object-oriented programming and analysis

- Basic concepts about artificial intelligence, and ideas about how to implement it to solve different challenges when programming games

- The difference between game AI and game physics

- How to create a basic objects library and use its derived classes in games

- How to produce high-performance drawings with GDI+, when we need to draw images with transparent colors

- How to create computer-controlled characters that interact with the game engine like player-controlled characters, with the same physics restrictions

In the next chapter, we'll introduce the use of DirectX graphics with a sample program that will test many of the basic features of Direct3D, so we can in later chapters use these concepts in our games.

CHAPTER 3

# Managed DirectX First Steps: Direct3D Basics and DirectX vs. GDI+

IN THIS CHAPTER we'll
follow a different
approach from all
the other ones:
There'll be no sample
game, and we'll
instead concentrate
on understanding
the basic features of

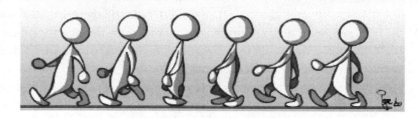

*Figure 3-1. The walking man, presented as this chapter's sample*

DirectX (particularly Direct3D) and how to go through its initialization routines,
creating a sample application that will exemplify each of these features.

Our sample application, as we'll see in the section "The Application Proposal,"
will comprise a main window, which will display our 3-D board capabilities, and a
set of separate windows that will test a specific feature each, like use of lights, 3-D
transformations, and full-screen drawings. In each of these test windows we'll
present sequentially the drawings of a walking man, shown in Figure 3-1, providing the illusion of movement.

DirectX is a set of libraries and components that allow the programmer to
access hardware features (such as 3-D acceleration boards and advanced sound
systems) using the same interface, disregarding the device details, while still
taking advantage of each hardware-specific feature to enhance the multimedia
operation speed.

The latest version of DirectX can be downloaded from http://www.microsoft.com/
directx; this download includes the DirectX APIs, the managed DirectX interfaces
(used to provide access to DirectX from .NET languages), the DirectX Software
Development Kit (SDK), a comprehensive set of samples, and detailed documentation about all DirectX features.

In the next section we'll present an overview of DirectX, which will give us
enough information to go on exploring Direct3D features in the later sections.

## DirectX Overview

In this section we'll discuss some common terms used in the DirectX world and see how they fit together to provide us a framework for building great games.

First of all, those who already know previous versions (7 or earlier) of DirectX need to be aware that since DirectX 8 we no longer have direct support for 2-D games. That means there is no capability for screen flipping and no bitmap blitting directly on video memory. We don't have the DirectDraw interface anymore, which was very comfortable to those who programmed DOS games, because it used much of a familiar, basic philosophy: Create one or more screen back buffers, draw in a back buffer, move the back buffer to video memory—in other words, make it visible to the player—and then start drawing in the next buffer (usually, we simply "flip" the buffers, moving memory pointers).

In fact, the DirectDraw interface is still there, but it's for now just a backward-compatibility feature, so the old programs that use this library will still work. It's better for us not to rely on the older interface because no one knows if it will be present in the next versions.

The good news is that, while we need to expend a little more effort in Direct3D than in DirectDraw, we can rely on the hardware acceleration capabilities to do most of the dirty work for us, reaching incredible speeds that would not be possible with DirectDraw.

Using hardware acceleration is a wonderful thing, because we can go from dozens of frames to hundreds of frames drawn per second. In our tests in this chapter, the basic samples easily reach three hundred frames per second, and can go to almost a thousand depending on the hardware capabilities.

Of course, there's a price to pay. Even the simplest games must go through some complex routines, and we'll have to learn some new concepts, even if we don't want to take full advantage of the hardware acceleration features.

When we manage to understand these initialization routines and the basic concepts, we can use the Direct3D interface to create our 2-D games without even worrying about depth buffers or vertex blending.

Let's start with an overview of the main concepts used by DirectX and how they are related.

## *Presenting the DirectX Top-Level Objects*

When programming DirectX 9.0 or earlier with nonmanaged (pre-.NET) languages, we have to create a master object of type DirectX*n* (where *n* is the main number of the DirectX version, for instance, DirectX8 for the 8.1 version), and everything can be created from this object.

In the managed version of DirectX 9.0, we can directly create the second-level objects, as listed here:

- **Direct3D** for access to the 3-D acceleration layer.

- **Direct3DX** for access to utility functions to make coding easier (such as matrix multiplication functions).

- **DirectDraw** for compatibility with older programs, although there are no new features for this component. It's mainly used to create 2-D games, because it allows access to a hardware *blittler* (hardware acceleration to allow fast transfer of large memory blocks) and creation on drawing surfaces easily.

- **DirectInput** for controlling any input devices, including newer ones, like joysticks with force feedback.

- **DirectPlay** for creating multiplayer games, creating fast and reliable data transmission across computers. It's based mainly in TCP sockets, but has some game-related extra features.

- **DirectAudio** for manipulating and playing all kinds of sounds. It includes the **DirectSound** and **DirectMusic** interfaces from previous releases, and, in fact, it's not a new interface, just a new way to call the other two when used together. Although both DirectSound and DirectMusic are present in DirectX 9.0, only DirectSound has a managed interface.

- **DirectShow** for video and audio playback or capture. In DirectX 9.0, we have only a simple playback feature in DirectShow; if we need to use advanced streaming manipulation features, we have to use the nonmanaged version.

- **DirectSetup** for access to the setup API of DirectX, which can help with creating distribution packages for DirectX-based applications.

In this chapter we'll concentrate in the first object listed, Direct3D, and learn some helper functions from Direct3DX. In upcoming chapters, we'll examine the other objects one by one, with the exception of the outdated DirectDraw and the Direct-Setup interface.

## Understanding Adapters

This section relates directly to video hardware. DirectX provides some functions that allow us to list all display adapters and gather some information about them.

We don't do any direct operations over an adapter; the functions are here just for informational purposes, or to allow us to choose between adapters when we have more than one acceleration board.

Usually we'll have only one adapter (the default), but with machines with secondary adapters (such as 3-D-only boards), we can use the adapter identifier (a sequential number) to switch from one adapter to another.

To gather the adapter information, we can use the following code sample:

```
Dim AdapterInfo As AdapterDetail
Dim i As Integer

For i = 0 To Manager.Adapters.Count - 1
        AdapterInfo = Manager.Adapters(i).Information
      messageBox.show (AdapterInfo.Description, "Current Adapters")
Next i
```

In managed DirectX, many of the methods were reengineered to provide a more intuitive interface. For example, many Get methods were replaced by properties, such as the Adapters.Count property in the preceding code, which replaced the previous GetAdapterCount property. Some functions that return values as parameters were also rewritten to return values as the result of the function. There's also a new object, the Manager, presented in the previous code sample, that handle basic interactions with Direct3D. This kind of modifications made the code cleaner for the managed version of DirectX.

The code listing uses the Adapters.Count property to run across the adapters and gather the description of each one. Although Description can vary for the same device and driver when dealing with different vendors, it's the only human-readable information, along with the DriverName property of the AdapterDetail structure. The other members of this structure are numeric values that identify the driver version, revision, and other internal control numbers, and won't be of interest to us (refer to DirectX SDK help for further information).

## Understanding Devices

DirectX offers a special object type, Device, which allows us to have access to the 3-D acceleration layer. We can choose up to three types of devices for each adapter:

- Hardware (Hardware Abstraction Layer): When creating HAL devices, we have direct access to the hardware acceleration features (and increased speed). If we try to create a device of this type but have no 3-D acceleration board, DirectX will raise an error and won't create the device.

- Reference (Reference Rasterizer): This type of device, included in the DirectX SDK, provides most of the features available for the DirectX functions, and doesn't depend on any hardware support—everything is made by software. Although this type of device is very flexible, it's very slow, and must only be used for debugging purposes, because it allows us to test many features not supported by our hardware. Don't even think about creating a game with it, as the frame rate is very low—between 1 and 5 frames per second, usually.

- Software (Software Device): Not used, unless you need plug-in support for creating a custom renderer.

When creating a device, we must specify the adapter being used (usually the default, defined as "0" [zero]), the type of the device as described in the preceding list, the handle of the window that will be used as a viewport, and two other parameters that will define the details about the device creation, the behavior flags and the presentation parameters, as shown in the next code sample:

```
objDirect3DDevice = New Device(Manager.Adapters.Default.Adapter, _
    DeviceType.hardware, WinHandle, CreateFlags.SoftwareVertexProcessing, _
    objDirect3Dpp)
```

The behavior flags must be one of the following flags defined by the CreateFlags enumeration:

- SoftwareVertexProcessing: The most common option, it tells DirectX that all vertex calculations will be made by software. This option is the slowest, but is always available.

- HardwareVertexProcessing: This option forces DirectX to rely on hardware capabilities to make all the vertex-processing operations, leaving extended operations (like shading and lighting) for the software layer. If the hardware is not able to perform the vertices calculation, the creation of the device will fail.

- MixedVertexProcessing: As the constant name states, this uses a mix of available hardware features and software-implemented ones to achieve the best results. If the hardware offers no vertex-processing features, this call will fail, too.

These flags are mutually exclusive, but they can be combined with the following flags to pass additional information to DirectX when creating a device:

- `FPU_Preserve`: This flag informs DirectX to perform all the calculations using double-precision floating points, which can lead to slower performance.

- `MultiThreaded`: Use this flag to inform DirectX that you need a multithread safe environment. In order to control the critical sections, DirectX can lose performance, so you must use this flag only when needed.

- `PureDevice`: This flag is used only in combination with the `HardwareVertex-Processing` flag, and specifies that the hardware can do rasterization, matrix transformations, and lighting and shading calculations. It's the best choice for any application, but few boards offer these features.

The last parameter for creating a device, the Presentation Parameters, is a complex structure whereby the programmer can define many low-level details about the device being created. We'll present here the most commonly used attributes. For a full list refer to the DirectX SDK help feature.

- `EnableAutoDepthStencil` and `AutoDepthStencilFormat`: These structure members tell DirectX that you want to use a depth buffer, and which is the format to be used in such buffer (according to the Format enumeration), respectively. The depth buffer helps with defining the relative distance of the object in relation to the screen, which is used to draw nearby objects in front of far ones. Although this seems to be a concept exclusive to the 3-D gaming world, it's not entirely true: Even some very basic 2-D games have so-called layers—usually the background and any objects that must appear behind the player (such as trees or bushes) stay in a back layer, and the player and other objects stay in the front layers. After creating the device, the program must set the `ZBufferEnable` member of the device's `RenderState` component to enable the depth buffering.

- `BackBufferCount`, `BackBufferFormat`, `BackBufferWidth`, and `BackBufferHeight`: These members define the number of back buffers (from 1 to 3), the format of such buffers (defined by the Format enumeration), and their width and height. The back buffer format (as with the depth stencil buffer) must be valid, one that can be checked by the `CheckDeviceType` method of the `Direct3D` object. If the buffer cannot be created (at least one is required), the creation of the `Device` will fail. The back buffers are used to render the scene being draw in the background automatically, in order to allow a smooth transition between frames drawn (no partial drawing is shown to the player). This parameter is closely related to the SwapEffect attribute, which will tell DirectX how to swap the back buffers to the screen, and to the Windowed attribute, which will force some limitations to the possible values.

- SwapEffect: A constant of the SwapEffect enumeration that defines the behavior of the buffers swap operation. This enumeration includes the following options:

    - SwapEffect.Discard: The back buffers content isn't preserved in the swap operation, allowing the application to choose the best performing technique, sometimes leading to big performance gains in the swapping operation. However, the scene must be completely redrawn for each frame.

    - SwapEffect.Flip: Creates a circular list of buffers to be swapped to screen (called a *swap chain*), allowing synchronization with the video refresh rate in a smooth way when running full screen. The "flip" term means that we have no copy of the memory block—DirectX just repositions the video memory start pointer to the next buffer. When running in windowed mode, there's no real flip; the video memory gets copied to the window, which is an operation with slower performance. In this operation, the front buffer becomes one of the back buffers, so the game can rely on this to redraw only part of the scene.

    - SwapEffect.Copy: This setting preserves the contents of the back buffer, just copying it over the front buffer (the screen). This setting forces BackBufferCount to be set to 1, since there's no need to more buffers. This is the most simple of the buffer swap operations, although it's the one with the worst performance. The most important gain for the programmer is that the application is not forced to perform complex control operations over multiple back buffers.

- Windowed: When set to True, indicates that the application will run in a window; a setting of False indicates the application will run full screen. When running in windowed mode, BackBufferFormat must match the current display resolution, and BackBufferWidth and BackBufferHeight may not be specified, assuming the window client area dimensions. When running in full screen, the width and height of the back buffer must match one of the possible display modes (explained in the next section) for the device.

- `DeviceWindowHandle`: The handle of the window to be used by DirectX. If it's set to `Nothing`, DirectX will use the active window.

## Understanding Display Modes

While the term *adapter* refers to the hardware and its driver and the term *device* refers to the main object used to access a specific window and draw over it, we use the term *display modes* to define the objects (the `DisplayMode` class) that store basic information about the screen status, including width, height, refresh rate, and a format flag that returns extra information about how colors are controlled by the display. The formats for rendering displays are as follows:

- `A8R8G8B8`: Color format in which each pixel on screen is defined using a 32-bit ARGB value—255 possible values for each red, green, and blue (RGB) color component, and an extra alpha (A) value that defines the transparency of each pixel (255 is fully opaque and is 0 is totally transparent).

- `X8R8G8B8`: Color format with 32-bit RGB values, and an extra byte (indicated by the "X") for color definition, not used. As with the previous setting, this color format allows up to 16 million colors.

- `R5G6B5`: Color format using 16 bits, where each RGB color component can assume 32 different values; an extra bit for green make this show 64 possible values, reaching a total of about 64 thousand colors.

- `X1R5G5B5`: 16-bit color format in which each color component takes 5 bits (32 possible values), making a total of a little more than 32 thousand colors.

When choosing the display mode for games, it's important to balance the number of desired colors against the memory used to display them. The 32-bit format spends almost twice as much time to display the same number of pixels when using the copy swap modes than do the 16-bit formats. However, the 32-bit format enables a huge number colors, which may be needed with games that have more sophisticated artwork. The rule of thumb is always use 16-bit format, unless you need more colors, so you'll get the best performance.

---

**NOTE**  *When running in windowed mode, we must use the computer's current resolution and color depth, so this discussion does apply only to full-screen modes.*

---

## Creating a Simple Direct3D Program

Now that we understand the basic concepts involved in a DirectX (specifically Direct3D) program, let's put it all together and see the basic structure for a Direct3D program. This basic structure will always be the same, even for the most sophisticated programs.

All the drawing operations on Direct3D are made with the use of a Device object, and must occur between the calls of the BeginScene and EndScene methods. These methods internally lock the back buffer we use while rendering and unlock it when we finish. Calling the Present method of the Device object, after ending the scene, will display the contents of the back buffer to the screen (front buffer), according to the behavior parameters set when creating the device.

The basic structure for a Direct3D program is shown in the following pseudo-code:

```
Set the presentation parameters for the device to be created
Create the Device object
Repeat in a loop, until Game Over
        Clear the Device
        Begin the Scene
        Draw the Scene (render)
        End the Scene
        Present the Scene to the user
Dispose the Device object
```

This will map to the following code:

```
Dim ObjDirect3DDevice As Device
Dim DispMode As DisplayMode
Dim ObjDirect3Dpp As PresentParameters

' Get the current display mode - when running in windowed mode, it's a must
DispMode = Manager.Adapters( _
            Manager.Adapters.Default.Adapter).CurrentDisplayMode
' Set the presentation parameters to run in windowed mode
ObjDirect3Dpp = New PresentParameters()
ObjDirect3Dpp.Windowed = True
ObjDirect3Dpp.SwapEffect = SwapEffect.Discard
ObjDirect3Dpp.BackBufferFormat = DispMode.Format

' Create the Device - frmDX is a previously created window
objDirect3DDevice = New Device(Manager.Adapters.Default.Adapter, _
    DeviceType.hardware, frmDX.Handle, CreateFlags.SoftwareVertexProcessing, _
    ObjDirect3Dpp)
```

```
' The rendering loop - GameOver is set in the Render procedure when the game ends
Do While Not GameOver
        ' Clear the device, painting it with black
        ObjDirect3DDevice.Clear(ClearFlags.Target, _
                              Color.FromArgb(0, 0, 255), 1.0F, 0)
        ' Start the Scene
        ObjDirect3DDevice.BeginScene()
        ' Render is our drawing procedure
        Render()
        ' End the Scene
        ObjDirect3DDevice.EndScene()
        ' Shows the scene drawn in the screen
        ObjDirect3DDevice.Present()
        ' We must give the application some time to process its events
        Application.DoEvents()
Loop
' Clean-up the house
DispMode = Nothing
ObjDirect3Dpp = Nothing
ObjDirect3DDevice.Dispose()
ObjDirect3DDevice = Nothing
```

That's it. Of course, some mode details are not presented here, the most important one being the error trapping. For instance, in the scene drawing sequence we have three related methods—Begin, End, and Present—that must be executed as a whole; if one of them fails, the others will fail, too. But we'll see the details in the section "The Coding Phase."

If we run this code (see details about setting the correct reference to the managed DirectX type library in the section "The Coding Phase"), all we get is a black window, because we don't know yet what we can use in the Render procedure to draw something. But DirectX will already be up and running, ready for us!

To complete our first program, let's see some basic concepts regarding Direct3D drawing in the next sections.

## 3-D Coordinate Systems and Projections

Even if we have no interest in creating 3-D games, we must understand the basic concepts of a 3-D coordinate system, because everything we do in Direct3D is defined by points and images in a 3-D world. Of course we can ignore the z axis and pretend that we are in a 2-D world—and we'll see how to do this—but the z zeroed value will still be there.

When we are dealing with three Cartesian dimensions, there are two types of coordinate systems: left-handed and right-handed. These names refer to the z-axis position relative to the x and y axis. To determine this position, point the fingers of one hand to the x-axis positive direction and move them in the counterclockwise direction to the y-axis positive position; the z-axis direction will be the direction your thumb points to. Figure 3-2 illustrates this concept.

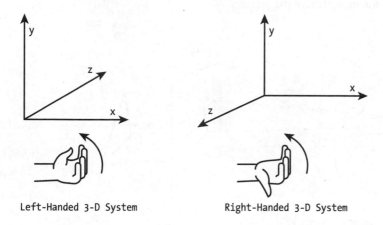

Left-Handed 3-D System          Right-Handed 3-D System

*Figure 3-2. The Cartesian 3-D coordinate systems*

To put it a different way, in the left-handed coordinate system, the z value gets bigger (the positive direction) when we go from the screen to a point away from us (considering that the x axis and the y axis are on the computer screen). The right-handed 3-D system is the opposite: The z values increase toward us from the screen.

Direct3D uses the left-hand coordinate system, which means that positive values for z are visible, and the greater they are for a given object, the farther the object is (and, depending on the projection chosen, the littler it appears on the screen); and negative values are not shown (unless we change our "camera position," which is possible too in Direct3D).

After understanding 3-D coordinate systems, the next step to explore is how they present 3-D objects to our 2-D screen.

Fortunately, all the hard mathematical work is done by DirectX, but we have to know the concept of *projections* and how they apply to DirectX in order to give the basic instructions about how to present the objects on screen.

Direct3D support two different types of projections:

- **Perspective projection:** The most common type of projection, it takes in account the z distance and adjusts the objects accordingly. This projection makes objects appear smaller when far from the screen—the objects get deformed, like in the real world. For example, the borders of a straight road appear to come together in the horizon. Figure 3-3 show a graphical representation of the perspective projection.

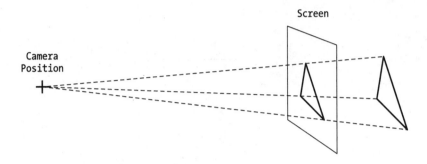

*Figure 3-3. Perspective projection*

- **Orthogonal projection:** In this type of projection, the z component is just ignored, and the objects don't get bigger when closer to the screen or smaller when they are farther away. This projection mostly used for 2-D games or simpler 3-D games. Figure 3-4 presents orthogonal projection.

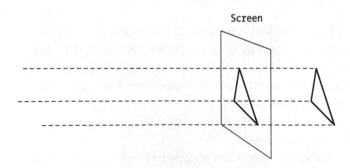

*Figure 3-4. Orthogonal projection*

When defining the projection type, we must choose the type of coordinating system and pass the parameters for the projection, according to its type. Direct3D offers six main functions (besides four others for creating custom coordinates systems) that allow us to specify the projection for our game. These functions return matrices that will be used by Direct3D to calculate the conversion from 3-D coordinates to screen coordinates.

- `Matrix.OrthoRH, Matrix.OrthoLH`: Returns the matrix with the transformations that need to be applied to the object coordinates to define an orthogonal projection (RH stands for right-handed, LH for left-handed). Each function receives the width and the height of the view port (usually, the screen) and the range of z values that will be viewed (points before the first z value and after the last one won't be viewed).

- `Matrix.PerspectiveRH, Matrix.PerspectiveLH`: Returns the transformation matrix for perspective projection, passing the width and height of the viewport and the z distance viewed (first and last points) for right-handed and left-handed coordinate systems.

- `Matrix.PerspectiveFovRH, Matrix.PerspectiveFovLH`: Returns the transformation matrix for perspective projection, passing the angle in radians of our field of view (Fov) and the z distances; for right-handed and left-handed coordinate systems.

Figure 3-5 shows graphically the Fov angle and the z distance viewed (defined by view planes).

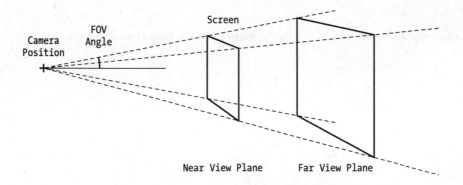

*Figure 3-5. The field of view angle and view planes for perspective projection*

In the next section we'll explore the matrix concept and learn how it helps us to convert coordinates of a 3-D world to screen coordinates, allowing us to easily perform complex operations on our game objects.

## Understanding Matrices and 3-D Transformations

Knowing how to work with transformation matrices is possibly the most important point when dealing with Direct3D. Using matrices, we can perform rotation, scaling, or translation of any object on the 3-D world (or in the 2-D world, if we choose to ignore the z component), and these operations, correctly applied, will help us to define our projection type (as shown in the previous section) or even move the camera to see the same scene from different points.

Let's discuss the use of transformation matrices to do a simple translation, and then extrapolate the idea for more complex operations. Suppose that we want to move a triangle up the y axis, as shown in Figure 3-6.

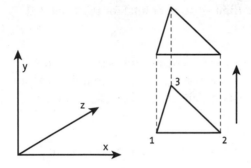

*Figure 3-6. Moving a triangle on the y axis*

Let's assume the triangle vertices are defined by the points shown here.

| VERTEX | X | Y | Z |
| --- | --- | --- | --- |
| 1 | 50 | 10 | 0 |
| 2 | 60 | 10 | 0 |
| 3 | 53 | 25 | 0 |

To translate 40 units over the y-axis positive direction, all we need is to sum 40 to each y position, and we have the new coordinates for the vertices, shown here:

| VERTEX | X | Y | Z |
|---|---|---|---|
| 1 | 50 | 50 | 0 |
| 2 | 60 | 50 | 0 |
| 3 | 53 | 65 | 0 |

The same results can be achieved by representing each vertex as a matrix with one row and four columns, with the vertex coordinates as the first three columns and 1 as the value in the last one, and multiplying this matrix to a special matrix, constructed to produce the translation transformation to the vertex matrix.

Figure 3-7 presents the same operation applied to the first vertex.

$$\begin{matrix} x & y & z \\ [\,50 & 10 & 0 & 1\,] \end{matrix} \times \begin{bmatrix} 1 & 0 & 0 & 0 \\ 0 & 1 & 0 & 0 \\ 0 & 0 & 1 & 0 \\ 0 & 40 & 0 & 1 \end{bmatrix} = \begin{matrix} x' & y' & z' \\ [\,50 & 50 & 0 & 1\,] \end{matrix}$$

*Figure 3-7. Applying a matrix multiplication to a 3-D vertex*

To calculate the resulting matrix, we must take each value in the row of the first matrix and multiply them by each of the values in the corresponding column in the second matrix, and then perform the sum of all results. So, in the previous sample, the calculations are as follows:

$x' = (50 \times 1) + (10 \times 0) + (0 \times 0) + (1 \times 0) = 50$

$y' = (50 \times 0) + (10 \times 1) + (0 \times 0) + (1 \times 40) = 50$

$z' = (50 \times 0) + (10 \times 0) + (0 \times 1) + (1 \times 0) = 0$

We don't want to get into much deeper detail here, but suffice it to say that we can perform translations by putting the desired values for translation over the x, y, and z in the last row of the transformation matrix; perform scaling by replacing the 1s on the diagonal to fractional values (to shrink) or greater values (to expand); and perform rotation around any axis using a combination of sine and cosine values in specific positions in the matrix.

**TIP** *For those who want to know more about the transformation matrices, DirectX SDK help has full coverage of this topic, showing each of the matrices and explaining how to use them.*

Luckily enough, we don't need to understand all these details to use the transformations in our program. All we need to know is the following:

- The transformation matrices can be multiplied by each other without losing information. If we want to translate and rotate an object at the same time, we can simply multiply the translation matrix to the rotation matrix and multiply the result for our vertices, acquiring the desired result.

- The Device object has three special properties: one used to receive the projection matrix (explained in the previous section), <Device>.Transform.Projection; another to indicate the transformations desired in our 3-D world (explained here), <Device>.Transform.World; and the third to specify the camera position (explained in the next section), <Device>.Transform.View.

- The D3DX utility library has functions to create all the transformation matrices for us, functions for matrices multiplication, and a function that returns an identity matrix (a special matrix that returns the vertices without transformations, which is used to clean the old world matrix before updating it). We'll see these functions in the section "The Code Phase."

## Positioning the Camera

As an extra feature when dealing with 3-D coordinate systems, DirectX allows us to position the camera to see the same scene from different points.

The camera position is calculated by some special transformations applied to the object's world coordinates. We can calculate the matrix for these transformations manually, and set it to the <Device>.Transform.View property, or we can use the helper functions Matrix.LookAtLH and Matrix.LookAtRH. These helper functions define the camera position and the direction it's looking to by three points: the 3-D position of the camera, the 3-D position the camera is looking at, and the current "up" direction, usually the y axis.

If we don't define a view (camera) matrix, DirectX will provide a default one for us, but it's an important concept to have in mind. Do you remember the first Prince of Persia game in which, at a given level, the prince drank a special potion and the screen turns upside down? Imagine creating this feature with a single line of code, rotating the view matrix by 180 degrees (multiplying it for a rotation matrix). This scenario shows the benefit of using Direct3D even for 2-D games.

## Drawing Primitives and Texture

We're ready to start working now: We know what adapters and devices are, we understand what display modes are, we know the basic Direct3D program structure, and we know all we need to know (for now) about projections, cameras, and transformations. The stage is all ready for the play. All we need now is to meet the actors: the drawing primitives.

Drawing primitives, or 3-D primitives, are vertex collections that define single 3-D objects. Direct3D uses the simplest polygon—a triangle—as a base to create all other 3-D objects. This is done because a primitive defined with only three points is guaranteed to be in a single plane, and to be convex, and these characteristics are the key to perform the fastest rendering possible.

So, for example, if we want to draw a square on screen, we'll have to use two squares. If we want to create a cube, we'll use 12 triangles (2 for each facet), as shown in Figure 3-8.

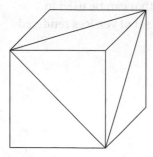

*Figure 3-8. A cube made with triangles*

Along with triangles, Direct3D allows us to define lists of lines and lists of points, which are useful mainly for debugging purposes in that they help us to see the wireframe image for our objects and check the hidden surfaces when we use triangles.

The steps for creating objects in Direct3D are as follows:

1. Define the vertex type.

2. Create a vertex buffer.

3. Fill the buffer with each of the vertices of the object, according to the defined vertex type.

4. Draw the buffer on the device, informing the primitive type.

For now, let's just consider that all the vertices are defined only by x, y, and z coordinates (we'll see more details about this later), so we can concentrate on the drawing primitive types.

Once the vertex buffer is filled, we use the following code lines to draw it on screen, assuming that vertBuffer is a valid VertexBuffer object:

```
ObjDirect3DDevice.SetStreamSource(0, vertBuffer, 0)
ObjDirect3DDevice.DrawPrimitives(<primitive type>, 0, <number of primitives>)
```

A primitive type can be one of the following values of the PrimitiveType enumeration:

- PointList: Each vertex is rendered isolated from the others, so we can see a list of floating points. Not quite useful, even less so now, because since DirectX 8.0 we have a new feature—point sprites—that can be used to create particle system effects. Figure 3-9 presents a set of vertices rendered as a point list.

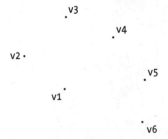

*Figure 3-9. Vertices rendered as a point list*

- LineList: The vertices are rendered in pairs, with lines connecting each pair. This call fails if we fail to pass a vertex buffer with an even number of vertices. Figure 3-10 illustrates the use of a line list primitive type.

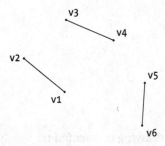

*Figure 3-10. The same vertices rendered as a line list*

- LineStrip: All the vertices in the buffer are rendered as a single polyline. This is useful when debugging, because this primitive type allows us to see a wireframe image of our objects, regardless of the number of vertices. Figure 3-11 presents a line strip primitive type sample.

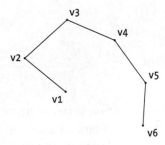

*Figure 3-11. The same vertices rendered as a line strip*

- TriangleList: The vertices are rendered in groups of three, as isolated triangles. This provides us the greatest flexibility when rendering complex scenes, but there's the drawback of having duplicated vertices if we want to draw connected triangles. Figure 3-12 shows the use of the triangle list primitive type to render vertices.

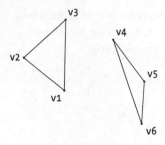

*Figure 3-12. The same vertices rendered as a triangle list*

- `TriangleStrip`: We'll use this primitive type when drawing connected triangles. It's the usual choice for rendering scenes, because it's more efficient, since we don't have to repeat the duplicated vertices. Every new vertex (after the first two) added to the buffer creates a new triangle, using the last two defined vertices. Figure 3-13 presents a triangle strip primitive type example.

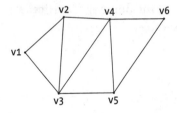

*Figure 3-13. A complex polygon created with a triangle strip*

- `TriangleFan`: In this primitive, all the triangles share a common vertex—the first one in the buffer—and each new vertex added creates a new triangle, using the first vertex and the last defined one. Figure 3-14 illustrates the last of the primitive types, the triangle fan.

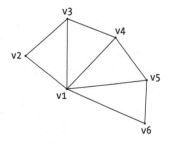

*Figure 3-14. A triangle fan example*

When drawing triangles, we need to take special care about the triangle vertex ordering if we want Direct3D to draw only the front part of a triangle. The feature of hiding the backfaces are called *culling*, and when choosing a culling mode, we must define if we want the front face to be the clockwise-ordered one or the counterclockwise one; so we must draw all triangles using the same ordering for the vertices.

Okay, you're probably thinking, "These primitive types are interesting, but what if I just want to draw a single image, say, a bitmap file on disk, to the screen? Can't I just draw it directly on screen?"

The answer is no. You must create a square (composed with two triangles) and apply the image on it, as a texture. We can even state that a specific color must be treated as transparent, so it appears that we are dealing with nonregular objects. That's what we'll see in the next section.

## Texturing and Coloring with Flexible Vertex Formats

Direct3D gives us the power to choose how we can define the vertices that will compose our drawing primitives, using the so-called flexible vertex formats (FVF).

Before creating a vertex buffer (explained in the previous section), we must specify which kind of information each vertex will hold, creating a custom vertex structure and using it when creating a new VertexBuffer object, as presented in the next code sample:

```
Vbuffer = New VertexBuffer(VertSize, VertNum, Device, Usage, VertexFormat, Pool)
```

The parameters for this code line are as follows:

- VertSize is the size of the custom vertex, in bytes.

- VertNum is the number of vertices we'll want the buffer to hold.

- Device is the Direct3D reference to the current display device.

- Usage defines the purpose of the vertex buffer, allowing Direct3D to perform any extra control it needs. We'll usually use WriteOnly for this, meaning that we are only writing to the buffer and passing it later to the device, and won't read from it. This flag allows Direct3D to choose the best memory allocation for fast writing and rendering.

- VertexFormat is the flexible vertex format used in each vertex, explained a little later.

- Pool provides extra information to Direct3D, defining where the resource must be placed (system memory or managed memory, for example). Usually we'll use the Default enumeration member for this parameter.

The VertexFormat parameter is a combination of flags that will tell Direct3D what information we are using in our vertices, allowing us to include diffuse light or texture information on each vertex. Among the many possible values on the VertexFormat enumeration, the ones we'll be using in this book are as follows:

- Diffuse: We'll include information for a diffuse color (which may be thought of as a diffuse-colored light) in the vertex.

- Position: Our vertex coordinates need transformation (remember the matrices?) from world coordinates to screen coordinates before being displayed. This flag cannot be used with the VertexFormat.Transformed flag.

- Transformed: Our vertices are already in screen coordinates, so we won't need any projection information. This enumeration member can't be combined with the Position one.

- VertexFormat.Texture0 through VertexFormat.Texture8: Our vertices include from 0 to 8 different texture coordinates.

The following code sample shows a complete example, from defining the vertex structure to creating the vertex buffer:

```
' Our Custom vertex format will need to be transformed, and
'  has information about texturing and diffuse colors
Public Const FVF_CUSTOMVERTEX As VertexFormats = VertexFormats.Position Or _
                        VertexFormats.Texture1 or VertexFormats.Diffuse
' We need our vertex buffer to hold 36 vertices
Dim NUM_VERTS = 36
' Here is the vertex structure
Private Structure CUSTOMVERTEX
    Public X As Single
    Public Y As Single
    Public Z As Single
    Public color As Integer
    Public tu As Single
    Public tv As Single
End Structure
```

```
Dim vertBuffer As VertexBuffer
' Create the vertex buffer
vertBuffer = New VertexBuffer(GetType(CUSTOMVERTEX), _
    NUM_VERTS, ObjDirect3DDevice, Usage.WriteOnly, _
    FVF_CUSTOMVERTEX, Pool.Default)
```

**NEW IN .NET**

*The* Type *keyword, used in previous versions of Visual Basic, was upgraded to the* Structure *keyword. The latter is far more flexible, allowing the declarations of functions and different scope specifiers in the members declaration, but still being a value type with all its particularities (classes have similar features to structures, but are reference types and have additional different features and limitations).*

It's important to understand how we can deal with the color and tu/tv (texture) parameters.

The color parameter specifies a color for each vertex. The vertex colors generate gradients between each vertex, as shown in the square in Figure 3-15: The upper-left corner is rendered with blue, the upper-right with red, the lower-left with yellow, and the lower-right with green.

*Figure 3-15. Applying colors to square vertices*

We must specify the colors through their RGB components using the
Color.FromARGB function. The color codes are the same ones defined in the
System.Drawing.Color component. We can't use the old GDI's RGB function to
specify such color, because it is intrinsically different from the new Color.FromARGB
function, and we can have unexpected results, like the blue and red components
being inverted.

Think of the texture position parameters, tu and tv, as the x and y position in
the texture previously loaded that corresponds to the vertex position. All textures
have rectangular shapes, and these values range from (0, 0) for the upper-left
corner of the texture to (1, 1) for the lower-right corner. The texture is applied to
the object according to the values set to all vertices. In Figure 3-16 we see three
vertexes with valid tu and tv values, the texture loaded, and the result rendered by
the device.

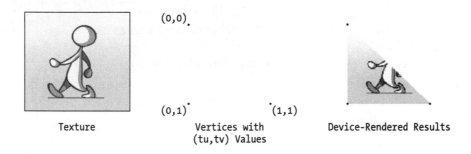

Figure 3-16. *Texture mapping with (tu,tv) pairs of values*

The Device object needs to have the information about which texture it must
use for each call of the DrawPrimitives function (explained in the previous section),
which will receive the vertex buffer with the vertex and texture coordinates. For
this, we must pass a previously loaded texture to the SetTexture method of the
device.

We can load the texture from a file using the FromFile method of the Texture-
Loader helper object, which can receive different parameters depending on the
need of the program. To load opaque textures, it will simply receive the filename
and the device to which the texture will be rendered. When calling the method to
load transparent textures, the functions receive many other parameters, allowing a
greater control over the loaded texture, including a color key that will specify the
transparent color for the texture loaded.

We'll see the details about how to implement texture features on our program
in the next sections. In the following section we'll outline the proposal for the
sample application of this chapter.

# The Application Proposal

Our proposal for this chapter sample is to create a simple application that will help us to understand the basics of DirectX, so we can apply this knowledge to creating games in coming chapters.

To accomplish this, we'll create an application that will test our machines and return the capabilities of the installed hardware and software, and also run some tests that will give us the necessary information on how to

- Create an application that runs in windowed mode.

- Create an application that runs in full-screen mode.

- Create an application that shows a transparent sprite using texture capabilities.

- Create an application that deals with lighting, using different light colors. Although we won't explore this feature extensively in this book, it's quite useful to learn the basics of lighting, so we can create interesting effects in our games.

- Create an application that deals with basic matrix transformations, which will be very useful in our games because they provide a built-in capability to translate (move around the screen), rotate around an axis, and scale any preloaded images to different sizes.

We'll create a separate window for each of the tests listed previously, and all the tests will execute the same drawing procedure—one that will present the walking man textures at full speed on screen in order to give us an idea of how fast our 3-D acceleration board really is.

The walking man drawings used in this chapter were made by Igor Sinkovec, a graphic artist and game programmer (http://maniacco.tripod.com/).

In the next section we'll discuss some extra details about our sample application.

# The Application Project

Our application project will be very straightforward; we can't add too much detail to it for now, because we're focusing on what we can do with Direct3D in this chapter.

The coding phase will be divided into six steps, as described in the following list, each one exploring additional features involved in the Direct3D application:

1.  Create a main window with four list boxes that will show us the machine adapters, the devices for each adapter, the display modes for each device, and the device capabilities. From the main window, present the other windows that will do each of the tests defined in the project proposal. The main window is shown in the Figure 3-17.

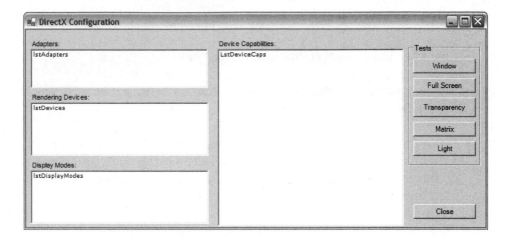

*Figure 3-17. The main window interface*

2.  Create a DirectX windowed test that will use a set of textures to produce the illusion of a walking man. The bitmaps with the walking man images are on the accompanying CD-ROM, within the directory that contains this chapter's sample code.

3.  Adjust the code from the previous step to create a DirectX application that runs in full-screen mode.

4.  Create a new DirectX windowed test, from the test created in step 2, to test the use of transparent textures. For this test we'll create an image with transparent parts that can be moved with the mouse, so we can see that it's really transparent.

5.  From the test created in step 2, create a new test that will exemplify the use of lighting. For this test we'll create a control window that will allow us to change each of the RGB components of the diffuse light colors in each of the figure vertices. Figure 3-18 presents the interface that we'll use to control the light colors.

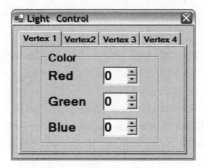

*Figure 3-18. The Light Control window*

6. Our last test will demonstrate the use of matrix transformations on tridimensional figures. For this we'll create a cube and a window that will control the matrix transformations on it. We'll also add an option to make the figure move automatically, shaking around. The matrix transformations control window is shown on Figure 3-19.

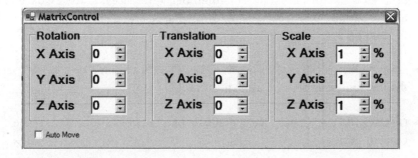

*Figure 3-19. The MatrixControl window*

In the next section we'll start coding our application, starting from the main window code.

## The Coding Phase

Before we start any coding in our project, we need to set a reference to the Direct3D and DX3D components of managed DirectX. To add the references, choose Project × Add Reference, and locate the appropriate components on the list in the .NET components tab. If the components are not in the list, then you possibly don't have the managed DirectX interface installed in your computer. Since this interface is installed with DirectX 9.0, you'll need to install it by downloading the latest version from the Microsoft site.

## First Step: Coding the Main Window

Let's start coding the main window, which will allow us to see our hardware capabilities, and then we can code the tests one by one, from the simpler to the most complex ones.

After creating the main window, as shown in the visual prototype in the project phase, we need to know the functions that list the adapters, devices, display modes supported, and capabilities. A quick look in SDK help shows us these methods and properties of the Manager object:

- Adapters.Count: Returns the number of adapters (3-D boards) in the machine.

- Adapter(n).Information: Returns the adapter characteristics, according to an ordinal adapter number.

- GetDeviceCaps: Returns the device capabilities in a complex structure. The function receives the ordinal number of the adapter and the type of the device (Hardware or Reference). Remember, Reference is software based and always supported; Hardware is hardware based and depends on the boards installed.

- Adapters(n).SupportedDisplayModes: Returns the characteristics of a specific display mode, given its ordinal number.

- CheckDeviceType: Checks if a specific display mode is supported by the current device.

A quick look in the DirectX SDK help will also show us that most of these functions don't return a readable description (which could be used to fill the list), so we'll need to create some functions to return display names where appropriate.

Since all the information between the lists are related (the devices supported may vary for each adapter, and the display modes and device characteristics may vary depending on the device), it's better to force an update of the related list every time a new item is selected on a high-order list. Our program basic structure will be as follows:

```
On the "load" event:
        Load the adapters list
        Select the fist list item, in order to fire the selection changed event
On the adapter list "selected item changed" event:
        Reload the device list
        Select the fist list item, in order to fire the selection changed event
```

```
On the device list "selected item changed" event:
      Reload the display modes list
      Reload the device capabilities list
```

Because we'll be using the Device object all over the form, we can dimension the variable at form level:

```
Dim ObjDirect3DDevice As Device
```

In the Load event, we can call the ListAdapters function:

```
Sub FrmDirectX_Load() Handles MyBase.Load
      ' Fill the Adapters list
      ListAdapters()
End Sub

Sub ListAdapters()
      Dim i As Integer
      Dim AdapterInfo As AdapterDetail
      ' Add each adapter to the lstAdapters list box
      For i = 0 To Manager.Adapters.Count - 1
          AdapterInfo = Manager.Adapters(i).Information
          lstAdapters.Items.Add(AdapterInfo.Description)
      Next i
      ' Select the first availiable index, in order to fire the change event
      lstAdapters.SelectedIndex = 0
End Sub
```

We must remember to add code for releasing the Device object in the Closing event (which replaces the Unload event from the previous versions of Visual Basic):

```
Private Sub FrmDirectX_Closing() Handles MyBase.Closing
      If Not ObjDirect3DDevice Is Nothing Then ObjDirect3DDevice.Dispose()
      ObjDirect3DDevice = Nothing
End Sub
```

If we run our code now, we'll see the first list filled with the adapters' descriptions. The devices list, which must be filled for each adapter chosen, will always have one or two members: the reference rasterizer, which will always be present, and a hardware abstraction layer (HAL) rasterizer, which will be presented only if supported by a 3-D board. To check the presence of hardware acceleration, we can query the device capacities using the previously shown function, and, if there's no error, then we can add the HAL to our list.

The function for filling the devices list and the code for calling it (in the event that handles the selected item change at the adapters list) is shown in the following code sample:

```
Sub lstAdapters_SelectedIndexChanged() Handles _
    lstAdapters.SelectedIndexChanged
        ' Update the devices list every time a new adapter is chosen
        ListDevices(lstAdapters.SelectedIndex)
End Sub


Sub ListDevices(Adapter As Integer)
        On Error Resume Next
        Dim DeviceCaps As Caps
      ' Add each supported device to the lstDevices list box
        lstDevices.Items.Clear()
      ' The Reference Rasterizer will always be supported
        lstDevices.Items.Add("Reference Rasterizer (REF)")

        ' If there's no error when getting the HAL capabilities,
        ' then we have a hardware acceleration board installed
        DeviceCaps = Manager.GetDeviceCaps(Adapter, DeviceType.Hardware)
        If Err.Number = 0 Then
            lstDevices.Items.Add("Hardware Acceleration (HAL)")
        End If
        ' Select the first available index, in order to fire the change event
        lstDevices.SelectedIndex = 0
End Sub
```

The display modes will depend on the adapter and the device chosen, so we can create a function (listDisplayModes) that will receive this information as parameters, and call it on the selection change event of the devices list box:

```
Sub lstDevices_SelectedIndexChanged() Handles lstDevices.SelectedIndexChanged
        ' The first entry in lstDevices is the Reference Rasterizer
        If lstDevices.SelectedIndex = 0 Then
            ListDisplayModes(lstAdapters.SelectedIndex, DeviceType.Reference)
        Else
            ListDisplayModes(lstAdapters.SelectedIndex, DeviceType.Hardware)
        End If
End Sub
```

Listing the display modes is not as straightforward as listing the adapters. First we must check if every mode returned by the adapter is supported by the device, and then we must compose each list item with a combination of various properties that will identify uniquely each display mode:

- Width, Height: The width and height of the screen. If creating a full-screen device, these properties will define the resolution of the screen; when in windowed mode, Direct3D only will manage to create the device without errors if the current display is one of these resolutions.

- Format: The format of the display mode, as explained in the section "Understanding Display Modes."

- RefreshRate: The monitor refresh rate, in MHz, or 0 if the default. Usually we don't have to care about this, but it's possible for a device to support the same resolution with different refresh rates, so it's better to list it in our list box, or we could finish with duplicated entries.

Because the Format property returns a member of the Format enumeration, we can't display it directly in the list box; we must create a "translation" function that will map the valid modes to readable strings.

```
Function DisplayModeName(Format As Format) As String
    Select Case Format
        Case Format.R8G8B8
            DisplayModeName = "R8G8B8"
        Case Format.X8R8G8B8
            DisplayModeName = "X8R8G8B8"
        Case Format.A8R8G8B8
            DisplayModeName = "A8R8G8B8"
        Case Format.R5G6B5
            DisplayModeName = "R5G6B5"
        Case Format.X1R5G5B5
            DisplayModeName = "X1R5G5B5"
    End Select
End Function
```

With this function, we can now complete the Display Modes list box as follows:

```
Sub ListDisplayModes(Adapter As Integer, Renderer As DeviceType)
   Dim DispMode As DisplayMode

   lstDisplayModes.Items.Clear()
   For Each DispMode In Manager.Adapters(Adapter).SupportedDisplayModes
       ' Check to see if the display mode is supported by the device
       If Manager.CheckDeviceType(Adapter, Renderer, _
                DispMode.Format, DispMode.Format, False) Then
       ' Fill the display modes list with the width, height, _
       '  the mode name and the refresh rate
        lstDisplayModes.Items.Add(DispMode.Width & "x" & DispMode.Height & _
            "   ( " & DisplayModeName(DispMode.Format) & " - " & _
           IIf(0, "Adapter Default", DispMode.RefreshRate & "Mhz)"))
       End If
   Next
End Sub
```

Running our program now, we can see the first three list boxes filled with information, as shown in Figure 3-20.

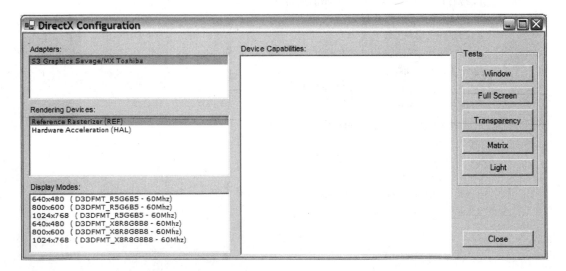

*Figure 3-20. The filled Adapters, Rendering Devices, and Display Modes list boxes*

The last list box, which will list the device capabilities, will be a tougher one to fill. The function GetDeviceCaps returns a complex structure with many dozens of flags, organized in many different enumerations. Since we can't simply list the composed flags, we must create functions to return readable strings for each property. We'll use the descriptions provided in SDK help to create the functions that will list the most important flags for our purposes, but there are some we'll leave aside. If you want to create a comprehensive list, just follow the steps explained here.

The first function we create checks for some simple flags in the Caps structure and adds the appropriate strings to the Device Capabilities list box:

```
Sub listGeneralCaps(DevCaps As Caps, lstCaps As ListBox)
    lstCaps.Items.Add(" -----  General Caps -----------------------")
    If DevCaps.MaxActiveLights = -1 Then
        lstCaps.Items.Add("Maximum Active Lights: Unlimited")
    Else
        lstCaps.Items.Add("Maximum Active Lights: " & _
            DevCaps.MaxActiveLights)
    End If
    If DevCaps.MaxPointSize = 1 Then
        lstCaps.Items.Add("Device does not support point size control")
    Else
        LstCaps.Items.Add("Maximum point primitive size: " & _
            DevCaps.MaxPointSize)
    End If
    lstCaps.Items.Add("Maximum Primitives in each DrawPrimitives call: " & _
            DevCaps.MaxPrimitiveCount)
    lstCaps.Items.Add("Maximum Textures simultaneously bound: " & _
            DevCaps.MaxSimultaneousTextures)
    lstCaps.Items.Add("Maximum Texture aspect ratio: " & _
            DevCaps.MaxTextureAspectRatio)
    lstCaps.Items.Add("Maximum Texture size: " & DevCaps.MaxTextureWidth & _
            "x" & DevCaps.MaxTextureHeight)
    lstCaps.Items.Add("Maximum matrixes blending: " & _
            DevCaps.MaxVertexBlendMatrices)
    lstCaps.Items.Add("Maximum vertex shaders registers: " & _
            DevCaps.MaxVertexShaderConst)
End Sub
```

To help us to show specific device capabilities, we created many other functions with the same basic structure: a simple sequence of if commands, each one testing for a specific flag within the composed flag members. The following code shows an example of such a function, one that lists the flags that compose the Caps member of DriverCaps:

```
Sub listDriverCaps(ByVal DriverCaps As DriverCaps, ByVal lstCaps As ListBox)

    lstCaps.Items.Add(" -----  Driver Caps -----------------------")
    If DriverCaps. SupportsDynamicTextures Then
        lstCaps.Items.Add("The driver support Dynamic Textures")
    End If

    If DriverCaps.CanCalibrateGamma Then
        lstCaps.Items.Add("The driver can automatically adjust the gamma ramp")
    End If

    If DriverCaps. SupportsFullscreenGamma Then
        lstCaps.Items.Add("The driver can do dynamic gamma ramp adjustment" & _
                        " in full-screen mode.")
    End If
End Sub
```

Each if statement in this kind of function tests a specific Boolean value inside the composed flag. In this sample, DriverCaps is a structure with many composed flags, each one being a Boolean value associated with a specific driver feature.

We created similar functions to list the flags for the TextureCaps, RasterCaps, DeviceCaps, and TextureCaps members. Since they present the same structure and the information they add to the list box is basically the one found in SDK help, we won't reproduce them here; for those interested, they can be found in the accompanying CD-ROM.

We can create a special function now that will retrieve the Caps structure for the current device and call the functions created as mentioned previously:

```
Sub ListDeviceCaps(Adapter As Integer,  DeviceType As DeviceType)
    Dim Caps As Caps

    LstDeviceCaps.Items.Clear()
    Caps = Manager.GetDeviceCaps(Adapter, DeviceType)

    ' List some general driver capabilities
    listGeneralCaps(Caps, LstDeviceCaps)
    ' List the device capabilities
```

```
    ListDevCaps(Caps.DeviceCaps, LstDeviceCaps)
    ' List specific driver capabilities
    listDriverCaps(Caps.DriverCaps, LstDeviceCaps)
    ' List rasterizer capabilities
    ListRasterCaps(Caps.RasterCaps, LstDeviceCaps)
    ' List texturization capabilities
    ListTextureCaps(Caps.TextureCaps, LstDeviceCaps)
End Sub
```

We must include a call to this function on the selected item changed event for the Devices list box, so the list gets updated for every new device chosen in the list. Figure 3-21 presents the finished main window of this chapter sample.

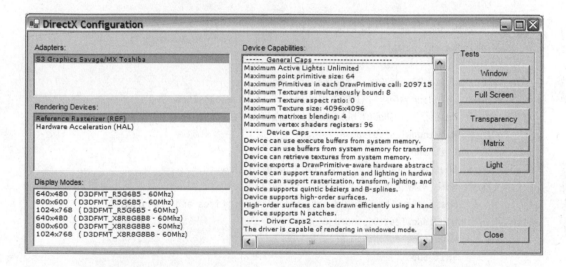

*Figure 3-21. The finished main window*

## Second Step: Coding Our First Windowed Test

This first test is very important, because it will establish the base of all future tests and programs. So we'll make it very simple: Let's just initialize the Direct3D, create the device, draw a simple image, and count the frame rate. In order to allow us to see something happening, let's load an array of images (loaded as textures) and render them one at a time, over a square (composed of two triangles), so we'll see the illusion of a walking guy.

We'll use the basic Direct3D program structure, explained in the "Creating a Simple Direct3D Program" section, dividing the code into two groups:

- In our main window (code in the click event for the corresponding button): the code that simply creates (and destroys) the test window and call to the initialization, finalization, and rendering routines defined in the test window.

- In the test window: all the Direct3D routines—initialization, finalization, and rendering.

The code for the main window, which will be very similar to other tests, is show here:

```
Dim WinWindowTest As New WindowTest()
WinWindowTest.Show()


' Initialize Direct3D and the device object
If Not (WinWindowTest.InitD3D(WinWindowTest.Handle)) Then
        MessageBox.Show("Could not initialize Direct3D.")
        WinWindowTest.Dispose()
        Exit Sub
' Load the textures and create the square to show them
ElseIf Not (WinWindowTest.CreateTextures()) Then
        MessageBox.Show("Could not initialize vertices and textures.")
        WinWindowTest.DisposeD3D()
        WinWindowTest.Dispose()
        Exit Sub
End If


' If we have no errors, then enter the rendering loop
Do While Not WinWindowTest.EndTest
        WinWindowTest.Render()
        ' Frame rate calculation
        WinWindowTest.Text = "Window Test.  Frame rate: " & CalcFrameRate.ToString
        Application.DoEvents()
Loop
' Call the finalization routines and close the window
WinWindowTest.DisposeD3D()
WinWindowTest.Dispose()
```

In the rendering procedure we used a helper function, CalcFrameRate, that we created in order to make our code cleaner. In this function (shown in the next code listing) we are using System.Environment.TickCount to retrieve the current tick of the processor clock (with the precision rate of a millisecond), so we can calculate the frame rate. Note that this function is not very accurate, but since we'll only use frame rate calculations to give us an idea of the speed at which we're drawing the scene, and won't include it in our final games, we think that using it is a valid approach.

```
Public Function CalcFrameRate() As Integer
    Static FrameRate As Integer
    Static LastFrameRate As Integer, LastTick As Integer

    ' Frame rate calculation
    If System.Environment.TickCount - LastTick >= 1000 Then
        LastFrameRate = FrameRate
        FrameRate = 0
        LastTick = System.Environment.TickCount
    End If
    FrameRate += 1
    CalcFrameRate = LastFrameRate
End Function
```

Following the sequence of the code just shown, let's see the initialization routines. The InitD3D procedure will create the Direct3D object, define the presentation parameters for the window creation based on the current display mode, and create the Device object. If you don't understand any part of the following code, refer to the first sections of this chapter for detailed explanations.

Since we'll use the Direct3D object and the Device object on many different functions, let's create them as public variables on the form:

```
Dim ObjDirect3DDevice As Device = Nothing

Function InitD3D( WinHandle As IntPtr) As Boolean
    Dim DispMode As DisplayMode
    Dim ObjDirect3Dpp As PresentParameters

    DispMode = Manager.Adapters(_
                Manager.Adapters.Default.Adapter).CurrentDisplayMode
    ' Define the presentation parameters
    ObjDirect3Dpp = New PresentParameters()
    ObjDirect3Dpp.Windowed = True
    ObjDirect3Dpp.SwapEffect = SwapEffect.Discard
```

```
        ObjDirect3Dpp.BackBufferFormat = DispMode.Format
        ' Try to create the device
        Try
            objDirect3DDevice = New Device(Manager.Adapters.Default.Adapter, _
                DeviceType.Hardware, WinHandle, CreateFlags.SoftwareVertexProcessing, _
                objDirect3Dpp)
            ' Define which type of vertex will be used
            objDirect3DDevice.VertexFormat = fvf_CUSTOMVERTEX
            InitD3D = True
        Catch
            InitD3D = False
        End Try
        ' Dispose the used objects
        DispMode = Nothing
        ObjDirect3Dpp = Nothing
    End Function
```

The most important part in the preceding code is the definition of the presentation parameters, which will rule the device creation. Let's analyze this one line at a time.

In the first line of the code listing, we create the presentation parameters as an object of the PresentParameters type:

```
ObjDirect3Dpp = New PresentParameters()
```

Then we state that we want to run in windowed mode. Since we didn't specify the window size, the device will use the whole client area of the target window (defined by the handle used when creating Device).

```
ObjDirect3Dpp.Windowed = True
```

In the next line, we instruct the device to choose the best memory allocation when doing the screen flips, even if our back buffer got discarded. Note that this option doesn't force the back buffer to be discarded, it just tells the device that we are re-creating the whole scene in the Render procedure, so it doesn't need to preserve the contents of the back buffer when flipping.

```
ObjDirect3Dpp.SwapEffect = SwapEffect.Discard
```

The last line tells the format of our back buffer. Since we are running in windowed mode, it's a must for us to use the current display mode format, because the window will be rendered using the same resolution and colors of the rest of the screen.

```
ObjDirect3Dpp.BackBufferFormat = DispMode.Format
```

The next function, following the main program sequence, is the one that will load the textures from disk and create a square in which to display them. To create such a function, let's first refer to the flexible vertices format (FVF) definition in the "Texturing and Coloring with Flexible Vertex Formats" section. We see that we'll need to create a custom vertex type that will hold texture information in addition to the x, y, and z coordinates. And since we don't want to make any 3-D transformations, let's create the vertex with an extra flag (rhw) that informs the device that the coordinates are already transformed (they are screen coordinates). The definition of our VertexFormat is made using a constant value and creating the corresponding structure:

```
' Simple textured vertices constant and structure
Public Const FVF_CUSTOMVERTEX As VertexFormats = VertexFormats.Transformed Or _
                                    VertexFormats.Texture1

Private Structure CUSTOMVERTEX
        Public X As Single
        Public Y As Single
        Public Z As Single
        Public rhw As Single
        Public tu As Single
        Public tv As Single
End Structure
```

In order to help us fill the VertexFormat structure for each new vertex, it's a good idea to create a helper function that fill the structure members and return the vertex, as show in the following code snippet:

```
Function CreateFlexVertex(X As Single, Y As Single, Z As Single, _
        rhw As Single, tu As Single, tv As Single) As CUSTOMVERTEX
    CreateFlexVertex.X = X
    CreateFlexVertex.Y = Y
    CreateFlexVertex.Z = Z
    CreateFlexVertex.rhw = rhw
    CreateFlexVertex.tu = tu
    CreateFlexVertex.tv = tv
End Function
```

Now we can start thinking about the `CreateTextures` routine. Based on the basic concepts shown earlier, we can create a draft for the function:

1.  Define the array of textures (must be public to the form, since it'll be used in the `Render` procedure).

2.  Create the textures for each array element.

3.  Create and open the vertex buffer.

4.  Define the vertices.

5.  Close the buffer.

The textures we'll be using show a draft of the walking man, and are numbered from walk1.bmp to walk10.bmp, as shown in Figure 3-22.

Figure 3-22. *Walking man textures, from walk1.bmp to walk10.bmp (courtesy of Igor Sinkovec)*

The code for the previous steps is shown next.

**NOTE** *Notice that we created a separate function to generate the vertices, so the code becomes more readable and more easy to expand with different vertices.*

```vb
Dim NUM_VERTS = 4
Dim vertBuffer As VertexBuffer
Dim Textures(10) As Texture

Function CreateTextures() As Boolean
    Dim verts As CUSTOMVERTEX()
    Dim i As Integer

    Try
        ' Load the textures, named from "walk1.bmp" to "walk10.bmp"
        For i = 1 To 10
            Textures(i - 1) = TextureLoader.FromFile(ObjDirect3DDevice, _
                Application.StartupPath + "\..\Walk" & CStr(i) & ".bmp")
        Next

        ' Define the vertex buffer to hold our custom vertices
        vertBuffer = New VertexBuffer(GetType(CustomVertex),_
            NUM_VERTS, ObjDirect3DDevice, Usage.WriteOnly, _
            FVF_CUSTOMVERTEX, Pool.Default)
        ' Locks the memory, which will return the array to be filled
        verts = vertBuffer.Lock(0, 0)
        ' Defines the vertices
        verts = SquareVertices()
        ' Unlock the buffer, which will save our vertex information to the device
        vertBuffer.Unlock()

        Return True
    Catch
        Return False
    End Try
End Function

 Function SquareVertices() As CUSTOMVERTEX()
    Dim vertices As CUSTOMVERTEX()
    ReDim vertices(4)
    ' Create a square, composed of 2 triangles
    vertices(0) = CreateFlexVertex(60, 60, 0, 1, 0, 0)
    vertices(1) = CreateFlexVertex(240, 60, 0, 1, 1, 0)
    vertices(2) = CreateFlexVertex(60, 240, 0, 1, 0, 1)
    vertices(3) = CreateFlexVertex(240, 240, 0, 1, 1, 1)
    SquareVertices = vertices
End Function
```

With all the textures and vertices loaded, all we need now is to code the Render procedure to load one texture a time, and a finalization routine to dispose the used objects. The Render routine follows the structure of the scene starting, ending, and being presented, as shown earlier.

```
Sub Render()
    Static x As Integer = 0

    If (ObjDirect3DDevice Is Nothing) Then Return
     ' Clears the device with blue color
     ObjDirect3DDevice.Clear(ClearFlags.Target, _
                        Color.FromArgb(255, 0, 0, 255), 1.0F, 0)
    ObjDirect3DDevice.BeginScene()

     ' Show one texture a time, in order to create the illusion of a walking guy
    ObjDirect3DDevice.SetTexture(0, Textures(x))
    x += 1
    If x = 10 Then x = 0

     ' Define which vertex buffer should be used
     ObjDirect3DDevice.SetStreamSource(0, vertBuffer, 0)
     ' Draw the vertices of the vertex buffer, rendering them as a
     ' triangle strip, using the given texture
    ObjDirect3DDevice.DrawPrimitives(PrimitiveType.TriangleStrip, _
                        0, NUM_VERTS - 2)
    ObjDirect3DDevice.EndScene()
     ' Present the rendered scene
    ObjDirect3DDevice.Present()
End Sub
```

Note that we don't have any mention of back buffers or screen swapping (flipping) operations here, so why do we care about these in the Device object creation? In fact, everything is done here, but is performed in the background by the device: The back buffer is cleared using the Clear command, it is locked for drawing using the BeginScene method, it's unlocked after we render the scene with the EndScene function, and it is finally flipped to the screen, and maybe discarded, using the Present method.

Our final routine just disposes of all objects created in the previous functions, and it's called by the main program after the main loop is finished and when the window is closing:

```
Sub DisposeD3D()
    Dim i As Integer
    For i = 0 To 9
        If Not (Textures(i) Is Nothing) Then Textures(i).Dispose()
        Textures(i) = Nothing
    Next

    If Not (vertBuffer Is Nothing) Then vertBuffer.Dispose()
    vertBuffer = Nothing

    If Not (ObjDirect3DDevice Is Nothing) Then ObjDirect3DDevice.Dispose()
    ObjDirect3DDevice = Nothing

End Sub
```

This last function ends our sample. After coding a simple escape routine, which will end the form when the Esc key is pressed, we can run our sample and see the results, as presented in Figure 3-23.

```
Public EndTest As Boolean = False
Sub TestWindow_KeyDown(sender As Object, e As KeyEventArgs) _
    Handles MyBase.KeyDown
        If e.KeyCode = Keys.Escape Then
            EndTest = True
        End If
End Sub
```

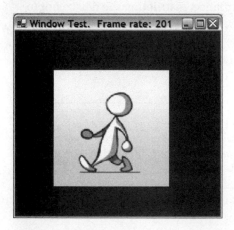

*Figure 3-23. Running our first DirectX program*

## *Third Step: Creating a Full-Screen Sample*

To make our sample run in full-screen mode, all we need to do is change the presentation parameters in the `InitD3D` routine. In order to have all sample codes separated from each other, we'll create a new button in the main window to fire the full-screen mode. Since most of the code will be the same, we can copy all the code from the windowed mode and simply apply the following updates.

Let's analyze the code for setting the presentation parameters, line by line.

The initial lines are the same from the windowed mode; just gather information about the current display mode and create the presentation parameters object:

```
DispMode = Manager.Adapters(Adapter.Default).CurrentDisplayMode
' Define the presentation parameters
ObjDirect3Dpp = New PresentParameters()
```

Following the definition, we set the parameters for creating the back buffer. In our sample, we'll be using the current format, width, and height (we must specify these three parameters); but we could be using any of the formats or resolutions shown in our Display Modes list on the main screen.

```
ObjDirect3Dpp.BackBufferFormat = DispMode.Format
ObjDirect3Dpp.BackBufferWidth = DispMode.Width
ObjDirect3Dpp.BackBufferHeight = DispMode.Height
```

The last line is the same as the one in the windowed mode: Set the flipping operation to the one that has the best performance, instructing the device not to care about preserving the back buffer.

```
ObjDirect3Dpp.SwapEffect = SwapEffect.Discard
```

**NOTE** *Using the* `Discard` *swap effect forces the use of only one back buffer, so we don't need to set the* `BackBufferCount` *property to 1. Another important point is that we don't worry about setting the* `Windowed` *property to false, since running full screen is the default.*

It's enough to make our code run in full-screen mode, but we can make a simple improvement in our SquareVertices function to create a square that covers the entire screen, stretching the walking man textures, to generate a nicer effect. We can gather the screen resolution, using the same method we saw before, with a display mode object. Our final function will be as follows:

```
Private Function SquareVertices() As CUSTOMVERTEX()
    Dim vertices As CUSTOMVERTEX()
    ReDim vertices(4)
    Dim mode As DisplayMode
    mode = Manager.Adapters(Adapter.Default).CurrentDisplayMode

    ' Create a square, composed of 2 triangles, taking all the screen
    vertices(0) = CreateFlexVertex(0, 0, 0, 1, 0, 0)
    vertices(1) = CreateFlexVertex(mode.Width, 0, 0, 1, 1, 0)
    vertices(2) = CreateFlexVertex(0, mode.Height, 0, 1, 0, 1)
    vertices(3) = CreateFlexVertex(mode.Width, mode.Height, 0, 1, 1, 1)
    SquareVertices = vertices
End Function
```

Just run the program now and press the Full Screen button in the main window to see the textures applied to the entire screen, with no visible loss in the frame rate, as presented in Figure 3-24.

*Figure 3-24. Running our DirectX program in full-screen mode*

## *Fourth Step: Using Transparent Textures*

We'll use the same code employed for the windowed mode test as the basis for our transparency test. We'll still have the walking man as a background texture, and will load another texture over it, with a color set to transparent, so we can see the man running behind parts of it.

For this purpose, we created a window drawing and filled the panes and surrounding areas with blue color, as shown in Figure 3-25.

*Figure 3-25. A window, with a flat blue color to be used as a transparent texture.*

We'll follow these steps for including our new transparent texture in the sample:

1.  In the InitD3D routine, let's set the device parameters to indicate that we'll be using transparent textures.

2.  Create a new function that will load the transparent texture.

3.  Create a function to generate a new square in which we'll render the transparent texture.

4.  Change the click button event in the main window to call this function.

5.  Adjust the render procedure to show the transparent texture.

6.  As defined in the game project, we must call the function that creates the square on the MouseMove event of the test window, so we can move the square with the transparent texture to different parts of the window and see the resulting effects.

Let's start with the InitD3D function. All we need to do is to set three new parameters of the device:

```
ObjDirect3DDevice.RenderState.SourceBlend = Blend.SourceAlpha
ObjDirect3DDevice.RenderState.DestinationBlend = Blend.InvSourceAlpha
ObjDirect3DDevice.RenderState.AlphaBlendEnable = True
```

These parameters tell how the rendering must blend together the source and the destination bitmaps to achieve the final transparency effect, and the last one informs the device where we want the blending to occur. The parameters shown in the preceding code must apply to almost all cases, and will be used throughout the rest of this book.

Please note that the blending operation slows performance, so in our real games we'd only set the AlphaBlendEnable property to True just before drawing the transparent textures, and reset it after finish them. Since it's a test, let's just leave it set all the time—performance is not our preoccupation here.

The function for loading the transparent texture is slightly different from the one we saw in the previous samples, as we can see in the next code piece, which needs to be included in the CreateTextures procedure to add transparency support:

```
' We will use blue as the transparent color
Dim ColorKeyVal As Integer = Color.FromArgb(255, 0, 0, 255)

' Load the transparent texture
TranspTexture = TextureLoader.FromFile(objDirect3DDevice, _
          Application.StartupPath & "\..\TranspSample.bmp", _
          64, 64, D3DX.Default, 0, Format.Unknown, Pool.Managed, _
          Filter.Point, Filter.Point, colorKeyVal.ToARGB)
```

Well, okay, this is VERY different. Although we can load an opaque texture specifying only the device and the filename, the overloaded version of the function to load transparent textures will have a lot more features and flexibility (but it'll have worse performance, too). We won't enter into the details about every parameter, since we won't use most of them in this book. All we need to know for now is the following:

- The 64, 64 parameters represent the width and height of the texture being loaded. These must be values supported by the device, usually a power of 2 (16, 32, 64, 128, and so on, with some new boards going up to 4096). These values are automatically calculated in the simpler version of the function.

- The filter parameters presented here are the best performing ones. If you want a little more quality, you can change them from Filter.Point to Filter.Default.

- The ColorKey parameter receives the color that will be transparent. In this case, the alpha component of the color is significant: If you are loading images from file formats that don't support transparency (such as bitmaps), this value will be always 255 (opaque).

The next step is to create a new square to load our transparent texture into. We can copy the functions used in our first sample, and adapt them to receive the x and y coordinates for the texture. Remember, we'll move the texture with the mouse, and the only way to do it (for now, since we haven't discussed transformation matrices yet) is updating the vertex positions, one by one.

```
Dim TranspVertBuffer As VertexBuffer = Nothing
Dim TranspTexture As Texture

Public Function CreateTranspVertices(X As Single, Y As Single) As Boolean
    Dim verts As CUSTOMVERTEX()
    Try
        ' If the vertex buffer was previously created, dispose them
        If Not (TranspVertBuffer Is Nothing) Then TranspVertBuffer.Dispose()

        TranspVertBuffer = New VertexBuffer(GetType(CustomVertex), NUM_VERTS, _
                        objDirect3DDevice, Usage.WriteOnly, _
                        fvf_CUSTOMVERTEX, Pool.Default)
        verts = TranspVertBuffer.Lock(0, 0)
        verts = TranspVertices(X, Y)
        TranspVertBuffer.Unlock()
        Return True
    Catch
        Return False
    End Try
End Function

Function TranspVertices( X As Single,  Y As Single) As CUSTOMVERTEX()
    Dim vertices As CUSTOMVERTEX()
    ReDim vertices(4)

    ' Create a square, composed of 2 triangles.
    ' Our transparent texture is 42 pixels wide and 60 long
    vertices(0) = CreateFlexVertex(X, Y, 0, 1, 0, 0)
    vertices(1) = CreateFlexVertex(X + 42, Y, 0, 1, 1, 0)
    vertices(2) = CreateFlexVertex(X, Y + 60, 0, 1, 0, 1)
    vertices(3) = CreateFlexVertex(X + 42, Y + 60, 0, 1, 1, 1)
    TranspVertices = vertices
End Function
```

To adjust the click event for the button on the main screen, all we need to do is call the preceding function, passing a default position for the transparent window. The full procedure for the Click button is as follows:

```
Dim WinTransparentTest As New TransparentTest()
WinTransparentTest.Show()


' Initialize Direct3D and the device object
If Not (WinTransparentTest.InitD3D(WinTransparentTest.Handle)) Then
    MessageBox.Show("Could not initialize Direct3D.")
    WinTransparentTest.Dispose()
    Exit Sub
' Load the textures and create the square to show them
ElseIf Not (WinTransparentTest.CreateTextures() And _
            WinTransparentTest.CreateTranspVertices(0, 0)) Then
    MessageBox.Show("Could not initialize vertices and textures.")
    WinTransparentTest.DisposeD3D()
    WinTransparentTest.Dispose()
    Exit Sub
End If


' If we have no errors, then enter the rendering loop
Do While Not WinTransparentTest.EndTest
    WinTransparentTest.Render()
    ' Frame rate calculation
    WinTransparentTest.Text = "Transparency Test.  Frame rate: " & _
        CalcFrameRate.ToString
    Application.DoEvents()
Loop
' Call the finalization routines and close the window
WinTransparentTest.DisposeD3D()
WinTransparentTest.Dispose()
```

Adjusting the rendering function is just as easy, since there's no difference in the rendering when displaying a simple texture or a transparent one. We can just add the following lines of code in the Render procedure, just below the lines that draw our walking man:

```
ObjDirect3DDevice.SetTexture(0, TranspTexture)
ObjDirect3DDevice.SetStreamSource(0, TranspVertBuffer, 0)
ObjDirect3DDevice.DrawPrimitives(PrimitiveType.TriangleStrip, 0, NUM_VERTS - 2)
```

Since the background of our transparent bitmap is blue, maybe it's a good idea to change the window background to black, just to create a different look from the previous samples. We can do this by simply adjusting the call to the Clear method of the Device object to

```
ObjDirect3DDevice.Clear(ClearFlags.Target, Color.FromArgb(255, 0, 0, 0), 1.0F, 0)
```

All we need to do now is code the MouseMove event to call CreateTranspVertices. Since we receive the mouse x and y positions as arguments on the event, all we need is this code:

```
Sub TransparentTest_MouseMove(sender as object, e As MouseEventArgs) _
    Handles MyBase.MouseMove
        CreateTranspVertices(e.X, e.Y)
End Sub
```

And that's it. Running our sample will allow us to test our transparent window, moving it with the mouse over the walking man, as shown in Figure 3-26.

*Figure 3-26. Testing the transparent window*

## Fifth Step: Using Colored Lights

We can use the same code we created for testing DirectX in windowed mode to also do our diffuse colored light test.

Although all we need to do to test the use of diffuse light is change the flexible vertex format to support a color value per vertex, and set such values for the vertices, we'll stick to our project and create a light control window in which we can choose the RGB components for the light color on each vertex.

The light control window, shown in Figure 3-18, is composed of four tabs, and each tab has three numeric up-down controls. We named these controls starting with Red1, Green1, Blue1 for the first vertex through to Red4, Green4, Blue4 for the fourth vertex. We'll use the values of each control directly on the color definition for the vertices.

The steps for converting the first sample to implement light control are as follows:

1.  Adjust the flexible vertex format structure and constant used in the vertex buffer creation to accept the color component for each vertex.

2.  Adjust the helper function `CreateFlexVertex` to accept the color parameter.

3.  Adjust the `SquareVertices` function to create the vertices using colors as defined by the numeric up-down controls.

4.  Adjust the click button procedure to create the control window and the test window, and initialize the values of the vertices colors.

5.  Create an event procedure that will update the vertex colors when any color component for any vertex changes.

---

 **NOTE** *The first two steps are very connected; every time we change the structure we'll need to change the constant and our helper function (we'll do it again in the next test, when we'll deal with matrices).*

---

The new code for implementing light control is shown next; we present the updates in bold to illustrate how simple the modifications are:

```
Public Const FVF_CUSTOMVERTEX As VertexFormats = VertexFormats.Transformed _
            Or VertexFormats.Texture1 Or VertexFormats.Diffuse

Private Structure CUSTOMVERTEX
        Public X As Single
        Public Y As Single
        Public Z As Single
        Public rhw As Single
        Public color As Integer
        Public tu As Single
        Public tv As Single
End Structure

Private Function CreateFlexVertex(X As Single, Y As Single, Z As Single, _
    rhw As Single, Color As Integer, tu As Single, tv As Single) _
    As CUSTOMVERTEX
        CreateFlexVertex.X = X
        CreateFlexVertex.Y = Y
        CreateFlexVertex.Z = Z
        CreateFlexVertex.rhw = rhw
        CreateFlexVertex.color = Color
        CreateFlexVertex.tu = tu
        CreateFlexVertex.tv = tv
End Function
```

The `SquareVertices` function will be the same used in the previous samples (except for the full screen one), with the solo update in passing the color parameter for the `CreateFlexVertex` helper function.

To define the color, we'll use the `Color.FromARGB` function we used before (when choosing a blue color for clearing the device).

```
    Private Function SquareVertices() As CUSTOMVERTEX()
        Dim vertices As CUSTOMVERTEX()
        ReDim vertices(4)

        ' Create a square, composed of 2 triangles
        vertices(0) = CreateFlexVertex(60, 60, 0, 1, _
            Color.FromARGB(Red1.Value, Green1.Value, Blue1.Value), 0, 0)
        vertices(1) = CreateFlexVertex(240, 60, 0, 1, _
            Color.FromARGB (Red2.Value, Green2.Value, BLue2.Value), 1, 0)
```

```
        vertices(2) = CreateFlexVertex(60, 240, 0, 1, _
            Color.FromARGB (Red3.Value, Green3.Value, Blue3.Value), 0, 1)
        vertices(3) = CreateFlexVertex(240, 240, 0, 1, _
            Color.FromARGB (Red4.Value, Green4.Value, Blue4.Value), 1, 1)
        SquareVertices = vertices
    End Function
```

The test start procedure, defined in the Click button on the main form, will be very similar to the ones we saw before: It follows the same structure, but creates both test and control windows, and takes special care in initializing the values of all the numeric up-down controls to 255 to fill the vertices with white light, so the walking man image starts with no color distortion (the default value is zero, which would prevent us from seeing anything).

```
Dim WinLightControl As New LightControl()
Dim WinTestLight As New LightTest()

WinLightControl.Show()
WinTestLight.Show()

' Initialize Direct3D and the device object
If Not (WinLightControl.InitD3D(WinTestLight.Handle)) Then
    MessageBox.Show("Could not initialize Direct3D.")
    WinLightControl.Dispose()
    Exit Sub
' Load the textures and create the vertices
ElseIf Not (WinLightControl.CreateTextures()) Then
    MessageBox.Show("Could not initialize the textures and vertices.")
    WinLightControl.DisposeD3D()
    WinLightControl.Dispose()
    Exit Sub
End If

' Start with full white light in all vertices
With WinLightControl
    .Red1.Value = 255 : .Green1.Value = 255 : .Blue1.Value = 255
    .Red2.Value = 255 : .Green2.Value = 255 : .BLue2.Value = 255
    .Red3.Value = 255 : .Green3.Value = 255 : .Blue3.Value = 255
    .Red4.Value = 255 : .Green4.Value = 255 : .Blue4.Value = 255
End With

' Ends the test if ESC is pressed in any of the 2 windows
Do While Not WinLightControl.EndTest And Not WinTestLight.EndTest
```

```
        WinLightControl.Render()
        ' Frame rate calculation
        WinTestLight.Text = "Light Test.  Frame Rate: " & CalcFrameRate.ToString
        Application.DoEvents()
Loop
' Call the finalization routines and close the windows
WinLightControl.DisposeD3D()
WinLightControl.Dispose()
WinTestLight.Dispose()
```

The last step to make our code fully operational is including a call to update the vertex colors every time one vertex color has changed. Since the values of the controls are being read directly in the CreateVertices procedure, we can simply call this procedure on an event that handles changing in all numeric up-down controls:

```
Sub Color_TextChanged(sender As Object, e As EventArgs) Handles _
    Red1.TextChanged, Red2.TextChanged, Red3.TextChanged, Red4.TextChanged, _
    Blue1.TextChanged, BLue2.TextChanged, Blue3.TextChanged, Blue4.TextChanged, _
    Green1.TextChanged, Green2.TextChanged, Green3.TextChanged, Green4.TextChanged

        CreateVertices()
End Sub
```

**NEW IN .NET**

*In previous versions of Visual Basic, when we want to use the same event procedure for different controls, we were forced to give the controls the same name, and it wasn't possible to share event procedures across objects of different types. In Visual Basic .NET, the association of the event procedure with the object is made using the Handles keyword, which can receive different comma-separated controls to handle. This feature ends up with another old problem that occurred in Visual Basic: If you changed the control name after creating the event procedures, they failed to handle the event because the association was made using the event procedure names. In Visual Basic .NET, when we alter any control name, the event procedure name remains the same, but the Handles clause is updated with the new control name.*

Just run our program now, and play a little with the vertex light colors. Figure 3-27 shows a sample color distorted window.

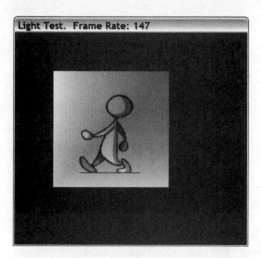

*Figure 3-27. Our old friend walking man in a disco*

# Sixth Step: Testing Matrix Transformations

Adapting our sample to test the matrix transformations, according to what we discussed earlier in this chapter, will be our last and hardest challenge; but if you missed some previous point, this is the perfect way to reinforce the concepts.

Since we're facing a lot of modifications in many procedures, let's see all the code for this sample, starting with the flexible vertex format definition. The FVF definition will be simpler now, because we'll abandon the rhw parameter that indicated in the previous samples that we were working on screen (already transformed) coordinates. In this sample, we'll test all the transformations from world coordinates to screen coordinates.

```
Public Const FVF_CUSTOMVERTEX As VertexFormats = VertexFormats.Position Or _
                                            VertexFormats.Texture1

Dim NUM_VERTS = 36

Private Structure CUSTOMVERTEX
    Public X As Single
    Public Y As Single
    Public Z As Single
    Public tu As Single
    Public tv As Single
End Structure
```

CreateFlexVertex will be simpler:

```
Function CreateFlexVertex(X As Single, Y As Single, Z As Single, _
                tu As Single, tv As Single) As CUSTOMVERTEX
      CreateFlexVertex.X = X
      CreateFlexVertex.Y = Y
      CreateFlexVertex.Z = Z
      CreateFlexVertex.tu = tu
      CreateFlexVertex.tv = tv
End Function
```

Returning to our first example, note that we have an initialization function and a finalization function, which creates the objects we need and destroys them when the window is being closed. Although the DisposeD3D finalization procedure needs no modifications (it just disposes every object), the InitD3D procedure for this sample deserves a closer look, because we have some significant modifications, which appear in bold in the subsequent code:

```
Public Function InitD3D( WinHandle As IntPtr) As Boolean
      Dim DispMode As DisplayMode
      Dim ObjDirect3Dpp As PresentParameters


      DispMode = Manager.Adapters(_
                Manager.Adapters.Default.Adapter).CurrentDisplayMode
      ' Define the presentation parameters
      ObjDirect3Dpp = New PresentParameters()
      ObjDirect3Dpp.Windowed = True
      ObjDirect3Dpp.SwapEffect = SwapEffect.Discard
      ObjDirect3Dpp.BackBufferFormat = DispMode.Format
      ObjDirect3Dpp.EnableAutoDepthStencil = True
      ObjDirect3Dpp.AutoDepthStencilFormat = DepthFormat.D16
      ' Try to create the device
      Try
          objDirect3DDevice = New Device(_
            Manager.Adapters.Default.Adapter, _
            DeviceType.Hardware, WinHandle, _
            CreateFlags.SoftwareVertexProcessing, objDirect3Dpp)
          ' Turn off culling => front and back of the triangles are visible
          ObjDirect3DDevice.RenderState.CullMode = Cull.NONE
          ' Turn off D3D lighting
          ObjDirect3DDevice.RenderState.Lighting = False
          ' Turn on ZBuffer
```

```
        ObjDirect3DDevice.RenderState.ZBufferEnable = TRUE
        ObjDirect3DDevice.VertexFormat = FVF_CUSTOMVERTEX
         ' Set the Projection Matrix to use a orthogonal view
        ObjDirect3DDevice.Transform.Projection = _
                        Matrix.OrthoLH(300, 200, 0, 0)
            InitD3D = True
        Catch
            InitD3D = False
        End Try
        ' Dispose the used objects
        DispMode = Nothing
        ObjDirect3Dpp = Nothing
    End Function
```

Since we're working in a 3-D world now, we need to instruct Direct3D to calculate which drawing primitives are shown and which are not. This is made by setting the EnableAutoDepthStencil member of the presentation parameter to True (yes, we want a depth stencil to be used) and setting the AutoDepthStencilFormat to DepthFormat.D16 (16 bits will be used in the calculation, because this value is the most commonly supported by the current 3-D boards). We'll also need to turn on the z-buffer (another name for depth buffer or depth stencil) calculation for the device.

There are two other important settings here: the one that disables the drawing primitives culling (so the textures will be drawn in the front face) and the one that turns off the lighting for our 3-D world (in other words, the one that tells the device to light everything equally, since we are NOT providing any light in our vertices). A nice test is to comment out each of these lines and see the resulting effects.

The last bold line defines an orthogonal projection matrix to be used when converting the world coordinates to screen ones, with a viewport of 300 pixels wide and 200 pixels tall. This is the simplest projection type, but the z-axis translation will have no effect (we won't see the cube getting smaller when it's far from the screen).

After initializing the objects, we need to start the drawing primitives and load the textures. Based on the CreateSquare function in the last samples, we can create a CreateCube function that will initialize and lock the vertex buffer, call a CubeVertices function that creates all the vertices, and unlock the vertex buffer. There's no difference (except for the name) between the CreateCube and the CreateSquare functions, but let's take a look at the code behind these functions once more to refresh our memories and compose the complete code for this sample:

```
Public Function CreateCube() As Boolean
    Try
        Dim i As Integer

        For i = 1 To 10
            Textures(i - 1) = TextureLoader.FromFile(ObjDirect3DDevice, _
                Application.StartupPath + "\..\Walk" & CStr(i) & ".bmp")
        Next

        vertBuffer = New VertexBuffer(GetType(CustomVertex), NUM_VERTS, _
                        objDirect3DDevice, Usage.WriteOnly, _
                        fvf_CUSTOMVERTEX, Pool.Default)
        ' Lock the vertex buffer (which will return the allocated memory)
        Dim verts As CUSTOMVERTEX() = vertBuffer.Lock(0, 0)
        ' Set the vertices for our cube
        CubeVertices(verts)
        ' Unlocking the buffer commits the data to the array
        vertBuffer.Unlock()
        Return True
    Catch
        Return False
    End Try
End Function
```

The `CubeVertices` function will create each of the vertices of the cube, providing their 3-D coordinates. It's always a good idea to have a paper and a pencil at hand when creating simple 3-D models, so we can draft the figure and understand better how the vertices fit together. Just take a look at Figure 3-28 and compare it to the first lines of the `CubeVertices` function; since the lines that created the other vertices are very similar, we are showing here just the vertices for the first two facets.

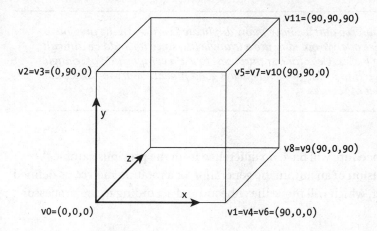

*Figure 3-28. The cube 3-D coordinates for the first two facets*

```
Sub CubeVertices( verts As CUSTOMVERTEX())
    ' 1st facet -----------------------------------------------------
    ' triangle 1
    verts(0) = CreateFlexVertex(0, 0, 0, 0, 0)
    verts(1) = CreateFlexVertex(90, 0, 0, 1, 0)
    verts(2) = CreateFlexVertex(0, 90, 0, 0, 1)
    ' triangle 2
    verts(3) = CreateFlexVertex(0, 90, 0, 0, 1)
    verts(4) = CreateFlexVertex(90, 0, 0, 1, 0)
    verts(5) = CreateFlexVertex(90, 90, 0, 1, 1)
    ' 2nd facet -----------------------------------------------------
    ' triangle 1
    verts(6) = CreateFlexVertex(90, 0, 0, 0, 0)
    verts(7) = CreateFlexVertex(90, 90, 0, 1, 0)
    verts(8) = CreateFlexVertex(90, 0, 90, 0, 1)
    ' triangle 2
    verts(9) = CreateFlexVertex(90, 0, 90, 0, 1)
    verts(10) = CreateFlexVertex(90, 90, 0, 1, 0)
    verts(11) = CreateFlexVertex(90, 90, 90, 1, 1)
. . .
End Sub
```

**TIP** *Observe that we have many duplicated vertices in the previous sample code. We opted to use a triangle list, since it would be difficult (and a lot less clear for our purposes) to use a composition of triangle strips, but in a real game it's always good practice to try to reduce the number of vertices.*

Our render procedure will have no difference from the previous samples, except for the inclusion of an automatic generation of a rotation matrix, as defined in the game project, which will move the cube around according to the processor clock tick:

```
Public Sub Render()
    Static x As Integer = 0
    Dim Tick as integer
    If (ObjDirect3DDevice Is Nothing) Then Return

    ' Move the cube automatically
    If chkAuto.Checked Then
        Tick = Environment.TickCount
        ObjDirect3DDevice.Transform.World = Matrix.RotationAxis(New _
            Vector3(Math.Cos(Tick / 550.0F), 1, _
            Math.Sin(Tick / 550.0F)), Tick / 3000.0F)
    End If

    ObjDirect3DDevice.Clear(ClearFlags.Target Or ClearFlags.ZBuffer, _
            Color.FromARGB (0, 0, 255), 1.0F, 0)
    ObjDirect3DDevice.BeginScene()
    ObjDirect3DDevice.SetTexture(0, Textures(x))
    x += 1
    If x = 10 Then x = 0

    ObjDirect3DDevice.SetStreamSource(0, vertBuffer, 0)
    ObjDirect3DDevice.DrawPrimitives(PrimitiveType.TriangleList, 0, _
        NUM_VERTS / 3)
    ObjDirect3DDevice.EndScene()
    ObjDirect3DDevice.Present()
End Sub
```

Note that the rest of the rendering code is exactly the same as that of the previous samples.

The last part of our test is to update the `Transform.World` matrix device member to the values set in the numeric up-down controls, as defined in our visual prototype in the project phase.

Using the trick we learned in the light sample, we can create a single procedure that will handle the events for all the controls. In order to make our code more understandable, let's create three helper functions that will add the rotation, translation, and scale transformations to the world matrix.

```
Sub Transformations_ValueChanged(sender As Object, e As EventArgs) Handles _
    RotationX.ValueChanged, RotationY.ValueChanged, RotationZ.ValueChanged, _
    TranslationX.ValueChanged, TranslationY.ValueChanged, _
    TranslationZ.ValueChanged, _
    ScaleX.ValueChanged, ScaleY.ValueChanged, ScaleZ.ValueChanged
      If Not ObjDirect3DDevice Is Nothing Then
          ObjDirect3DDevice.Transform.World = Matrix.Identity
          RotationMatrices(RotationX.Value, RotationY.Value, RotationZ.Value)
          TranslationMatrices(TranslationX.Value, TranslationY.Value, _
              TranslationZ.Value)
          ScaleMatrices(ScaleX.Value, ScaleY.Value, ScaleZ.Value)
      End If
End Sub


  ' The following functions create the transformation matrices
  ' for each operation
Sub RotationMatrices(x As Single, y As Single, z As Single)
      ObjDirect3DDevice.Transform.World = _
              Matrix.Multiply(ObjDirect3DDevice.Transform.World, _
              Matrix.RotationX(x * Math.PI / 180))
      ObjDirect3DDevice.Transform.World = _
              Matrix.Multiply(ObjDirect3DDevice.Transform.World, _
              Matrix.RotationY(y * Math.PI / 180))
      ObjDirect3DDevice.Transform.World = _
              Matrix.Multiply(ObjDirect3DDevice.Transform.World, _
              Matrix.RotationZ(z * Math.PI / 180))
End Sub

Sub TranslationMatrices(x As Single, y As Single, z As Single)
      ObjDirect3DDevice.Transform.World = _
              Matrix.Multiply(ObjDirect3DDevice.Transform.World, _
              Matrix.Translation(x, y, z))
End Sub
```

```
Sub ScaleMatrices(x As Single, y As Single, z As Single)
        ObjDirect3DDevice.Transform.World = _
            Matrix.Multiply(ObjDirect3DDevice.Transform.World, _
            Matrix.Scaling(x / 100, y / 100, z / 100))
End Sub
```

The most important part of this code is to remember that we can add transformations by multiplying the matrices (using the `Multiply` method of the `Matrix` object). In the `Transformations_ValueChanged` event procedure, we use the `Matrix.Identity` function to reset any transformations in the `Transform.World` matrix, so we can be sure that any matrix multiplication that occurred in the last call to this function is ignored and doesn't affect the current matrices.

To finish our code and start the test, all we must take care of is to provide good starting values for our matrix transformations; setting the Scale up-down controls with the default value of zero, for example, will simply make our object disappear from screen.

The code for the click event on the button of the main form is as follows:

```
Dim WinMatrixControl As New MatrixControl()
Dim WinMatrixTest As New MatrixTest()
WinMatrixControl.Show()
WinMatrixTest.Show()

' Initialize Direct3D and the device object
If Not (WinMatrixControl.InitD3D(WinMatrixTest.Handle)) Then
        MessageBox.Show("Could not initialize Direct3D.")
        WinMatrixControl.Dispose()
        Exit Sub
' Load the textures and create the cube to show them
ElseIf Not (WinMatrixControl.CreateCube()) Then
        MessageBox.Show("Could not initialize geometry.")
        WinMatrixControl.DisposeD3D()
        WinMatrixControl.Dispose()
        Exit Sub
End If

' Start with a simple rotation, to position the cube more nicely;
'  and with no scale (100% of the original size)
With WinMatrixControl
    .RotationX.Value = 45 : .RotationY.Value = 45 : .RotationZ.Value = 45
    .ScaleX.Value = 100 : .ScaleY.Value = 100 : .ScaleZ.Value = 100
End With
```

```
' Ends the test if ESC is pressed in any of the 2 windows
Do While Not WinMatrixControl.EndTest And Not WinMatrixTest.EndTest
     WinMatrixControl.Render()
     ' Frame rate calculation
     WinMatrixTest.Text = "Matrix Test.  Frame Rate: " & CalcFrameRate.ToString
     Application.DoEvents()
Loop
' Call the finalization routines and close the windows
WinMatrixControl.DisposeD3D()
WinMatrixControl.Dispose()
WinMatrixTest.Dispose()
```

Now we can finally run the test. Modifying the values of numeric up-down controls in the control window will let us see the transformation occurring dynamically; choosing the Auto Move check box will make the cube perform some nice moves automatically on screen. Figure 3-29 shows an example result of this last test.

*Figure 3-29. A moving cube with a walking man in each face*

## Adding the Final Touches

Since this chapter features no games, there's no such thing as "polishing the application." But there's at least one thing we can improve in our samples that will surely be useful in the next chapters: finding a way to create smooth animations.

Although it is very interesting seeing our walking man running at a 400 steps per second, in a real game this kind of behavior will be, at a minimum, strange. So we'd better define a specific frame rate to improve our graphics animation.

Including an `if` command in the loop that calls the `Render` procedure to check the processor clock and just render a new scene at previously defined intervals will suffice to give the desired effect in our test, and maybe even in some basic games. In more sophisticated ones, where different objects can have different animations running at different speeds, the control of what image must be shown at a given time will be the responsibility of each game object.

So let's get into a practical example. Which frame rate would be nice? Well, the best cartoons use a 32 frames per second (fps) rate of animation, but usually 16 frames per second provides a good frame rate. The actual best frame rate must be calculated for each game (or each game object), because different animations require different frame rates. For instance, we can do a walking man with 5, 10, or 20 frames. The more frames, the smoother the final animation will be, and the higher the frame rate must be. For our specific walking man animation, the rate to acquire the best results is only 10 frames per second. So let's use it!

In the following code sample, we define the frame rate for the animation by setting the number of frames with the `DesiredFrameRate` variable.

```
Dim LastTick As Integer, DesiredFrameRate As Integer = 10
. . .
Do While Not WinTransparentTest.EndTest
    ' Force a Frame rate of 10 frames to second on maximum
    If System.Environment.TickCount - LastTick >= 1000 / DesiredFrameRate Then
        WinWindowTest.Render()
        ' Frame rate calculation
        WinWindowTest.Text = "Window Test.  Frame rate: " & _
          CalcFrameRate.ToString
        LastTick = System.Environment.TickCount
    End If
    Application.DoEvents()
Loop
```

The result (a screen drawn at a fixed frame rate, and a man walking at normal speed) is shown in Figure 3-30.

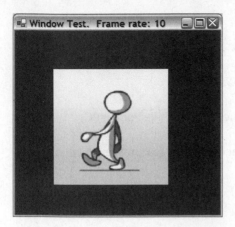

*Figure 3-30. Our walking man, tired of running, now walks at a lazy rate of 10 fps.*

Note that we still continue with the loop running at full speed. In our tests, all the loop does when it's not rendering is process the application events, but we could use an `else` clause with this `if` statement to process any internal calculation only when the screen is not being drawn. The basic idea is shown in the following code:

```
If System.Environment.TickCount - LastTick >= 1000 / DesiredFrameRate Then
        ' Do the game scene rendering
Else
        ' Do the game physics
        ' Calculate collisions
        ' Initialize anything that can help the scene to draw faster
        '  and etc ...
End If
```

## More About DirectX and GDI+

After learning the basics and seeing the power behind the DirectX word, it's time to think how GDI+ and DirectX fit together and how to choose each one (or both) as a basic technology for a game project. Of course there are other technologies, OpenGL (a standard library present in many platforms) being the most well-known one, but we'll stick with DirectX and GDI+ here, as they are more easily available to Visual Basic programmers.

In a general way, we can say that GDI+

- Is a technology to draw 2-D graphics.

- Is the "native" library for working in Windows.

- Is more easily portable to other simpler devices (like Pocket PC).

- Won't use any extended graphics or acceleration features, even when there's a hardware accelerator present.

- Is easy to work with.

And we can say that DirectX

- Is mainly aimed at working with 3-D graphics, but has many features that can be used in 2-D graphics.

- Has special requirements to run games (needs installation).

- Is more easily portable to game consoles—in fact, some of them already work with DirectX as the base library, and usually C/C++ is the language of choice.

- Can use all the power of graphics acceleration devices.

- Needs a little more effort for the starters.

## Summary

In many situations choosing DirectX is a must, such as when we are coding a tridimensional game engine, or when we want to code a fast-paced action game that will need to use hardware acceleration features. But there are other situations in which the decision is not clear. Let's see some examples.

Imagine that you are coding a Sid Meyer's Civilization I clone. Is there really a need to use DirectX? Remember that, although many people have 3-D boards nowadays, not everyone has one, and creating a game that doesn't require such hardware will broaden your game audience. And since a game like this isn't graphics intensive (the graphics are not very sophisticated, and the frame rate is not a problem), it'll be better to center our efforts on creating more sophisticated algorithms, which can run faster and make better gameplay. No gamer likes to wait for the computer to "think" about a better move.

When talking about simpler games, like Minesweeper or Solitaire, there's no need at all to use DirectX. A simpler solution, besides providing the benefits explained in the previous paragraph, will lead to a game that is easier to debug and easier to maintain, maybe resulting in a more sophisticated version.

Even when talking about arcade games, when we deal with games with few animations (Breakout-like games are a good example), we can stay with GDI+ without fear of choosing the wrong platform.

Simply put, GDI+ is great, and not only for card games, and DirectX is really a must to create sophisticated 3-D games. 2-D games will never die, and with some games DirectX will just add complexity without any reward in exchange. So before starting any new game project, think carefully about which platform is the best for your goals.

And let's highlight an important point: We can use both techniques in a game. All we need to do is isolate the GDI+ code from the DirectX one, by not using any GDI+ code between the BeginScene and EndScene methods. The better approach is to create a separate function for any GDI+ code, which will be called after the call to the Render procedure. In fact, in DirectX 7 we could even draw directly to DirectDraw surfaces using GDI commands (and maybe we can still do something like that, accessing some nonsupported feature); but as a rule, using both techniques usually leads to less organized code, so let's just keep this idea in mind for future use, if we need it.

In the rest of the chapters of this book, we'll be dealing mainly with DirectX, but we'll return to GDI+ in the last chapters, when we create a multiplayer version of the .Netterpillars game, and then again when we port our .Nettrix game to run on a Pocket PC.

# CHAPTER 4

# River Pla.Net:
# Tiled Game Fields,
# Scrolling, and
# DirectAudio

IN THIS CHAPTER we'll apply the concepts learned in the previous chapter about Direct3D to implement DirectX gaming classes (such as GameEngine and Sprite), so we'll easily be able to create high-speed graphics games. We'll also introduce basic DirectAudio concepts that will allow us to include sound effects and background music in our games.

We'll also examine the concept of tiled game fields and scrolling in games, and start implementing a clone of Activision's River Raid game, a

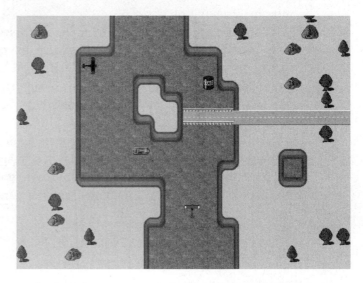

*Figure 4-1. River Pla.Net, a River Raid clone, is this chapter's sample game*

popular title for Atari 2600 and VCS. Our sample game, shown in Figure 4-1, will be finished in the next chapter, where we'll introduce DirectInput and the use of force-feedback joysticks.

Scrolling games and tile-based games have been around since earlier video game consoles and home computers hit the shelves, and we often see games that use both techniques. We'll discuss some interesting points about each in the next sections.

## Scrolling Games

Although the basic concept of scrolling games is very simple, there are many interesting variations we must consider when we start creating a new game. We can define scrolling games as the games in which the background moves in a continuous way. It's a very loose definition, but it'll suffice for our goals here.

Some of the typical choices we must make when coding scrolling games are discussed next.

## Scrolling Direction

All scrolling games are either *vertical scrollers, horizontal scrollers,* or *full scrollers,* meaning that the background on these games scroll in a vertical direction, in a horizontal direction, or in any direction. We'll discuss some variations of these movements in this section.

The most common choice is to implement vertical "up-down" scrollers (as does the sample game for this chapter), where the background moves from the top to the bottom of the screen, and horizontal "right-left" scrollers, where the background moves from right to left. We don't see many scrolling games using the opposite direction schemes because using these directions makes our games seem more natural to players.

Full scrollers are harder to implement and to play, but when made correctly, they can lead to very interesting gameplay. Just imagine a game in which players can move their character in any direction: This might be an interesting feature, but the player could become disorientated, and the game objective would be less clear.

## Parallax Scrolling

*Parallax scrolling* is an ingenious trick that gives players the feeling of being in a 3-D environment, even with flat images.

The basic idea is to create different layers of background objects, each one moving at different speeds. For example, if we are controlling a monkey in a jungle, we can create some bushes and trees that scroll at the same speed as the terrain, trees a little farther off that move a little slower, distant mountains that move very slowly, and maybe a fixed moon in the sky.

This approach creates a more lifelike game, but must be used with care because it can lead to visual clutter and confusion for the player. A good tip is to make distant objects with less vivid colors. This adds to the ambience without distracting the player.

## Player or Engine-Controlled Scrolling

When coding the scrolling for our game, we need to decide whether the background will always be moving (except, perhaps, when facing some end-of-level bosses), if it will move depending solely on the player's input, or if the movement will be a combination of both.

In some scrolling games, the player is always in the same position on the screen (usually the middle), and the background rolls according to the player's movement: When a player moves the joystick to the right, his or her character walks to the right (moving in a fixed position), while the background moves to the left. Many race games use this approach.

Some games use a similar solution: A player walks freely in a restricted area, and when he or she gets near any border, the background starts to move until the player starts walking back toward the center of the screen.

Some other games use a combination of automatic scrolling with player-controlled scrolling; the player controls scrolling right or left, but is always moving from the top to the bottom of the screen.

One last group of games comprises the auto-scrolling ones, such as the sample we'll code in this chapter: The background simply goes on scrolling without player intervention, creating a nonstop action game.

## Choosing the Scrolling Type

Even a topic as simple as choosing the scroll type we should use in our game may lead to extensive discussion. Of course there's a lot more we can do when coding scrolling games; don't be reluctant to try new ideas. For example, we can split the screen and make two areas with different scrolling behaviors, such as in the old arcade game Olympics, where the computer controls a character running in the upper middle of the screen and the player runs in the lower middle; each half-screen scrolls with its own speed.

The most appropriate type of scrolling will vary from game to game, and it will be up to us to make the final choice between code complexity and game playability.

## Technical Tips for Scrolling Implementation

Since there are many ways to implement scrolling—from a "camera" moving over a big image through to the opposite extreme, scrolling based on tiles—there's no universal solution. However, keep in mind the following rules of thumb as design goals:

- Avoid loading images from disk exactly when they are needed. Although it may not be practical to load all images at the start of the game, try to load the images before they're needed; never depend on disk response time, or the game will probably lack smoothness.

- On the other hand, loading every image and creating every vertex buffer for the game when it starts is only practical in small game fields. In bigger games memory can run out in a short time; so balance memory use against the loading speed of the images. A simple technique to avoid memory shortage is dividing the game into levels, and loading the images only for the current level. While the user is distracted with a screen with the current score or a short message, the next level can be loaded.

## Tile-Based Games

A tile is just a small piece of a graphic with a certain property that reveals its status for the game (a background, an enemy, an obstacle, a ladder, etc.). Creating a tiled game field is simply a matter of putting the tiles together in a logical fashion. We can do this by creating a level-map file with a level designer or even with a text editor; our game, when running, translates the tile codes in the file to graphical tiles on screen.

When coding tile-based games, the first question to ask is, Will our tiles be clearly visible, or will we try to hide the repetitive patterns?

There's no correct answer—it just depends on the game.

If we're working with a game that deals with visible blocks or bricks, there's no special trick to use when creating the tiles: We can simply list the tiles we'll use and draw them. Drawing some extra tiles can help the game to look more interesting to the user.

However, using seamless tiles is another matter. The following sections offer some practical tips for when we need seamless tiles.

## Draw the Basic Tile Sets

When creating a new tile set, we first draw the basic tiles for each type of terrain: for example, one tile for water, one tile for grass, one tile for sand, etc. An example of a basic set is show in Figure 4-2.

water.bmp  land.bmp

*Figure 4-2. A basic set of tiles, comprising two terrain types*

With the tiles presented in Figure 4-2 and in other figures in this chapter, we include suggested filenames. Using a logical filenaming scheme for your tiles can help you easily find specific tiles when you need them.

Keeping an eye on our "budget" of memory (how much memory we can use for textures), let's create some simple variations, such as adding different patterns to a sand tile, or some little bushes or small stones to a grass tile.

We should review our basic set, using the game project as a guide, to be sure that we create a tile for every terrain or object we need. Once we are satisfied with our basic set, we can go on to the next step: creating border tiles.

## Create Border Tiles

To create border tiles, we must separate the tiles into groups that will have connections with each other, and then create the borders for the tiles in each group. We must do this because usually some tiles won't need to have borders with some of the others—for example, the tiles that will create internal parts of a building don't need to have any special border with the outside tiles.

Within every group, create the border tiles between each type of terrain. There are basically three types of borders we can create, as shown in Figure 4-3:

- **Border tiles:** With this kind of tile, one terrain type occupies almost all of the area of each tile, leaving just few pixels for the transition to the next terrain.

- **3/4-to-1/4 tiles:** One terrain occupies 3/4 of the tile and another terrain occupies the rest for this tile type. (Think about this texture as cutting a tile in four equal-sized squares and filling three of them with one type of terrain, and one with another.)

- **Half-to-half tiles:** With this kind of tile, each type of terrain occupies half of the tile; the transition between terrain types can be on the vertical, horizontal, or diagonal axis.

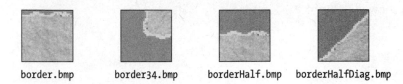

border.bmp        border34.bmp        borderHalf.bmp       borderHalfDiag.bmp

*Figure 4-3. Example of border tiles*

These basic border tiles will suffice to create a continuous-looking terrain, but if we have many of these transition tiles presented to the player on every screen, the set still won't suffice to create an illusion of a nontiled terrain. That's why we need to create extra borders between the most-used terrain types.

## Include Extra Transition Tiles

For those transitions that will be presented most of the time to the player, include some different tiles for each transition and for the basic set, which will be used sparingly to break down the feeling of patterns of repetition. For example, when creating tiles between water and land, include some rocks, a bay, or a larger beach, so you can use them eventually to give more variation to the game visual. Examples of simple variations are shown in Figure 4-4.

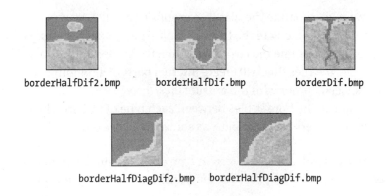

borderHalfDif2.bmp      borderHalfDif.bmp      borderDif.bmp

borderHalfDiagDif2.bmp    borderHalfDiagDif.bmp

*Figure 4-4. Simple variations of border tiles*

To create a better set of tiles, test if the transitions for each tile are seamless in every direction (when we rotate the tiles). An improved game engine can use the same tiles with various rotations to achieve better results. An easy way to do this is to create some tiles with only borders (and a flat color at the middle), and use them as "masks" over other tiles, employing any graphical editor to hide the transitions between the base tiles and the masks. Ensuring that the border pixels are always the same will allow smooth transitions.

In Figure 4-5 we see part of a screen from Sid Meyer's Civilization. Although the terrain looks random at first glance, if we pay a little more attention we can see the same tiles used in different compositions, with great results.

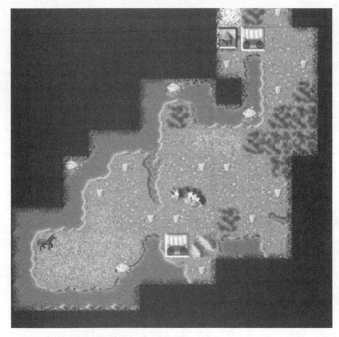

© 2002 Infogrames Interactive, Inc.
All Rights Reserved.
Used With Permission.

*Figure 4-5. Civilization: a successful example of a tile-based game*

## Creating New Game Classes

Looking at the similarities amongst the test programs we did in Chapter 3, we can choose some parts of the code to create DirectX versions for the two basic game classes we created in Chapter 2: a GameEngine class, which will be responsible for initializing, terminating, and managing the device operations, and a Sprite class, which will create some vertices and load the images as textures (transparent or otherwise) from image files.

**NOTE** *We'll try to maintain the class interfaces used in Chapter 2, but since using Direct3D is very different from using GDI+, don't be surprised if we find new ways to do the same things.*

We'll also extend our game class library by creating a GameMusic class according to the basic concepts we'll examine when studying the DirectAudio interface.

## The GameEngine Class

To create the new GameEngine class, we'll use the lessons learned in Chapters 1 and 2 about game engines, plus the Direct3D concepts discussed in Chapter 3. The following sections present the concepts involved in the creation of this class.

### The Class Interface

To include all we learned from the previous chapter, the GameEngine class must have some objects that will store references to Direct3D objects and a reference to the DirectAudio object (which controls the game music and sound effects, as we'll see). Another common theme we can see in the samples of the previous chapter is the use of flexible vertex formats to define figure vertices when creating a device, as well as the use of a background color when clearing the device.

Looking to the game engines from the samples of Chapters 1 and 2, we can again see some common properties, such as the window handle used for drawing, the width and height of the game field, and some flags to control whether the game is over or paused.

Looking again at the samples in Chapter 3, we can see a repetitive pattern in every Direct3D application. This gives us some clues about possible methods to include in our new GameEngine class:

1.  Initialize the various Direct3D objects.

2.  Enter a loop that will call the Render procedure between BeginScene and EndScene methods.

3.  Dispose all Direct3D objects created.

With these ideas in mind, we can imagine three methods that can be called sequentially in a game, as shown in the pseudo-code here:

```
Dim MyGameEngine as clsGameEngine
    ...
    ' Initialize Direct3D and DirectAudio objects
    MyGameEngine.Initialize
    ' Start the game loop, the procedure will only return when the game is over
    MyGameEngine.Run
    ' Dispose the Direct3D and DirectAudio objects
MyGameEngine.Finalize
```

We'll need a fourth method: an empty Render method that will be called from within a loop on the Run method. Each game will create a new class, derived from the generic GameEngine class, that will implement the Render procedure and add any extra features to the Initialize and Finalize methods.

---

 **NOTE** *For more information on flexible vertices and the objects and the methods mentioned in the preceding text, see Chapter 3.*

---

The suggested interface for the GameEngine class is shown in Figure 4-6; when creating new games, we can improve the class as needed.

| GameEngine |
| --- |
| -objDirect3D |
| -objDirect3DDevice |
| -objD3DX |
| -objGameMusic |
| -BackgroundColor |
| -Width |
| -Height |
| -ScreenWinHandle |
| -GameOver |
| -Paused |
| -D3DFVF_CustomVertex |
| -IMAGE_PATH |
| -SOUND_PATH |
| +Initialize() |
| +Render() |
| +Finalize() |
| +Run() |

*Figure 4-6. The GameEngine class interface*

The description of the interface members of the GameEngine class are shown in Table 4-1.

*Table 4-1. Interface Members of the DirectX GameEngine Class*

| TYPE | NAME | DESCRIPTION |
| --- | --- | --- |
| Property | ObjDirect3DDevice | The Device object, used by all graphical operations. |
| Property | BackgroundColor | The color used when clearing the device. |
| Property | Width | The width of the game field. |
| Property | Height | The height of the game field. |
| Property | ScreenWinHandle | The window handle used by all drawing functions. |
| Property | GameOver | If true, the game is over. |
| Property | Paused | If true, the game is paused. This flag and the preceding one store the current game status. Each game uses these flags to end or pause the game. |
| Constant | FVF_CustomVertex | The constant that will define which flexible vertex format we'll be using when creating the device and the vertices of the sprites. |
| Constants | IMAGE_PATH and SOUND_PATH | The relative paths where the images and the sound files are stored. |
| Method | Initialize | The procedure that will initialize Direct3D. |
| Method | Render | The rendering procedure. This procedure will be an empty overrideable function that must be implemented in the derived classes. |
| Method | Finalize | This method will dispose any objects created in the initialize procedure. |
| Method | Run | This method will simply have a BeginScene-EndScene block inside a loop, allowing the game programmer to start the game by calling the Run method. |

The next code listing shows the definition of the GameEngine class, including the proposed properties, methods, and constants:

```
Imports Microsoft.DirectX.Direct3D
Imports Microsoft.DirectX

Public Class clsGameEngine
    Protected Shared objDirect3DDevice As Device = Nothing

    ' Simple textured vertices constant and structure
    Public Const FVF_CUSTOMVERTEX As VertexFormat = VertexFormat.Tex1 Or _
                                            VertexFormat.Xyz

    ' defines the default background color as black
    Public BackgroundColor As Color = Color.FromArgb(255, 0, 0, 0)
    ' Images path, to be used by the child classes
    Protected Const IMAGE_PATH As String = "Images"

    Public Structure CUSTOMVERTEX
        Public X As Single
        Public Y As Single
        Public Z As Single
        Public tu As Single
        Public tv As Single
    End Structure

    Public Width As Integer = 25
    Public Height As Integer = 25

    Private ScreenWinHandle As System.IntPtr

    ' Controls the game end
    Public Shared GameOver As Boolean
    Public Shared Paused As Boolean

    Sub Run()
    Public Overrideable Sub Render()
    Public Function Initialize(Owner As windows.forms.control) As Boolean
    Protected Overrides Sub Finalize()
End Class
```

*The* Imports *clause used in the beginning of the class is a new feature of Visual Basic .NET, and it allows us to use any of the objects of the imported namespace directly, without needing to inform the full object hierarchy. For example, instead of creating a Microsoft.DirectX. Direct3.D .Device object, we can simply use Device in our variable declarations.*

**NEW IN .NET**

Before writing the code for the class methods, let's ensure that we understand the scope modifiers used in the GameEngine class, as explained in the next section.

## Understanding the Scope Modifiers

Now is a good time to look at the scope keywords used before variable and method declarations, and used extensively in the GameEngine class:

- Private: Visible only inside the class

- Protected: Visible only to the class and its derived classes

- Public: Visible to any code outside and inside the class

Other keywords used in this context are

- Shared: Any member declared with this keyword is shared with all the objects created for the class, and can be accessed directly by the class name (we don't need to create objects). Constants are shared by default, even when we don't use the shared keyword.

- Overrideable: This keyword indicates that a class member can be overridden by derived classes. In the preceding sample code, the Render procedure must be an overrideable function, since the code for it will be supplied by the derived classes, although it will be called by the Run method in the base class.

- Overrides: This keyword indicates that the class member is overriding a corresponding member of the base class. For example, to code a working Finalize event for any Visual Basic .NET class, we need to override the base class event Finalize.

- Shadows: When we want to redefine a function in a derived class, we can use this keyword. In this case, we aren't overriding a member from the base class, so when the method is called from the derived class, the method of this class will be called, and when a call is made from the base class, the method of the base class is called.

In the next section we'll examine the code for each method of the GameEngine class.

## Coding the Class Methods

There are no new concepts in these methods, so we can simply copy the code from one of the samples in the previous chapter and organize it as methods of the GameEngine class. As previously explained, we have an Initialize method to do the initialization (as we saw in Chapter 3) for a full-screen application using an orthogonal view. The Finalize method disposes of the objects created, and the Run method has the rendering loop, used in all programs in Chapter 3, that calls the empty Render method for each loop interaction. The Render method will be coded in the derived class, which will include specific features for each game.

```
Sub Run()
    Do While Not GameOver
        If (objDirect3DDevice Is Nothing) Then
            GameOver = True
            Exit Sub
        End If
        objDirect3DDevice.Clear(ClearFlags.Target, BackgroundColor, 1.0F, 0)
        objDirect3DDevice.BeginScene()
        ' Calls the Render sub, which must be implemented on the derived classes
        Render()
        objDirect3DDevice.EndScene()
        Try
            objDirect3DDevice.Present()
        Catch
            ' Some error ocurred, possibly in the Render procedure
        End Try
        Application.DoEvents()
    Loop
End Sub
```

```
Public Overrideable Sub Render()
    ' This sub is specific for each game,
    '    and must be provided by the game engine derived class
End Sub

Public Function Initialize(Owner as Windows.Forms.Control) As Boolean
    Dim WinHandle As IntPtr = Owner.handle
    Dim objDirect3Dpp As PresentParameters
    Initialize = True

    Try
        DispMode = Manager.Adapters(_
                    Manager.Adapters.Default.Adapter).CurrentDisplayMode
        DispMode.Width = 640
        DispMode.Height = 480
        ' Define the presentation parameters
        objDirect3Dpp = New PresentParameters()
        objDirect3Dpp.BackBufferFormat = DispMode.Format
        objDirect3Dpp.BackBufferWidth = DispMode.Width
        objDirect3Dpp.BackBufferHeight = DispMode.Height
        objDirect3Dpp.SwapEffect = SwapEffect.Discard

        objDirect3Dpp.Windowed = True 'False
        ' Create the device
        objDirect3DDevice = New Device(_
            Manager.Adapters.Default.Adapter, _
            DeviceType.Reference, WinHandle, _
            CreateFlags.SoftwareVertexProcessing, objDirect3Dpp)

        ' Tells the device which is the format of our custom vertices
        objDirect3DDevice.VertexFormat = FVF_CUSTOMVERTEX
        ' Turn off culling => front and back of the triangles are visible
        objDirect3DDevice.RenderState.CullMode = Cull.None
        ' Turn off  lighting
        objDirect3DDevice.RenderState.Lighting = False
        ' Turn on alpha blending, for transparent colors in sprites
        objDirect3DDevice.RenderState.SourceBlend = Blend.SourceAlpha
        objDirect3DDevice.RenderState.DestinationBlend = Blend.InvSourceAlpha
        ' The sprite objects must turn on alpha blending only if needed,
        '    using the following line:
        '    objDirect3DDevice.RenderState.AlphaBlendEnable = True
```

```
        ' Set the Projection Matrix to use a orthogonal view
        objDirect3DDevice.Transform.Projection = Matrix.OrthoOffCenterLH(0,_
            DispMode.Width, 0, DispMode.Height, 0.0F, 0.0F)
    Catch de As DirectXException
        MessageBox.Show("Could not initialize Direct3D. Error: " & _
            de.ErrorString, "3D Initialization.", MessageBoxButtons.OK, _
            MessageBoxIcon.Error)
        Initialize = False
    End Try

    ' Dispose the used objects
    DispMode = Nothing
    objDirect3Dpp = Nothing
End Function

Protected Overrides Sub Finalize()
    On Error Resume Next  ' We are leaving, ignore any errors

    If Not (objDirect3DDevice Is Nothing) Then objDirect3DDevice.Dispose()
    objDirect3DDevice = Nothing

    GC.Collect()
    MyBase.Finalize()
End Sub
```

In the initialize procedure, we used a set of common parameters for the device creation; we can change it as needed for each application.

In the next section we'll see the upgraded code for the second game class of our library: the Sprite class.

## The Sprite Class

Here we'll attempt to create a generic Sprite class, which can be improved upon as needed, and can be used to create derived classes that can hold specific properties and methods according to the game being created.

We can use the basic interface for sprites defined in Chapter 2, with the New, Draw, and Load methods, and some simple properties. Looking back at Chapter 3, we can list some suggestions for other interface elements: values for the translation, scaling, and rotation operations in the x and the y axis, and a speed value for both axes (speed is just the counter to be used for the translation in every new frame drawn).

Because a sprite is drawn over a polygon, we'll need a property to store the vertex buffer and a helper function to create the flexible vertices. Because a sprite is a 2-D image, there's no need to store z values for the transformations.

**TIP** *An important point of this new* Sprite *class is that we'll never need to change the vertex coordinates of the sprite to perform any translations or rotations; we can use the matrix transformations as seen in Chapter 3 to do it faster.*

**NOTE** *For more information about flexible vertices, vertex buffers, and matrices, refer to Chapter 3.*

The complete interface for a Direct3D sprite is shown in Figure 4-7.

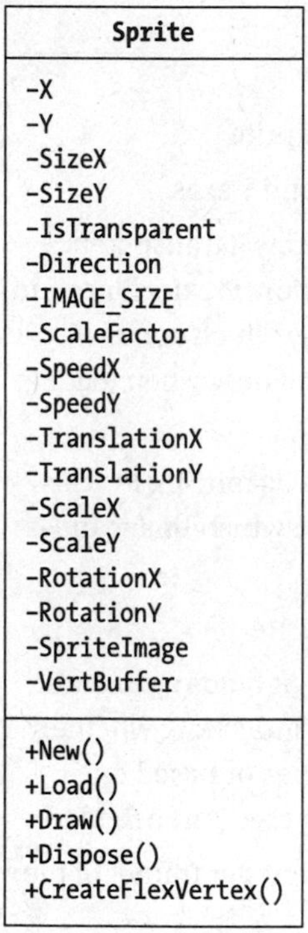

```
┌─────────────────────────┐
│        Sprite           │
├─────────────────────────┤
│ -X                      │
│ -Y                      │
│ -SizeX                  │
│ -SizeY                  │
│ -IsTransparent          │
│ -Direction              │
│ -IMAGE_SIZE             │
│ -ScaleFactor            │
│ -SpeedX                 │
│ -SpeedY                 │
│ -TranslationX           │
│ -TranslationY           │
│ -ScaleX                 │
│ -ScaleY                 │
│ -RotationX              │
│ -RotationY              │
│ -SpriteImage            │
│ -VertBuffer             │
├─────────────────────────┤
│ +New()                  │
│ +Load()                 │
│ +Draw()                 │
│ +Dispose()              │
│ +CreateFlexVertex()     │
└─────────────────────────┘
```

*Figure 4-7. The Sprite class interface*

The Sprite class members are described in Table 4-2.

*Table 4-2. Interface Members for the DirectX Sprite Class*

| TYPE | NAME | DESCRIPTION |
| --- | --- | --- |
| Properties | X and Y | The upper-left position of the sprite. |
| Properties | SizeX and SizeY | The size of the sprite, in the x and y axes. |
| Property | IsTransparent | If true, the Draw function will draw a transparent sprite, loaded in the Load function. We don't need to store a color key property to say which color will be transparent; such a color is used only when loading the textures. |
| Property | Direction | The current direction the sprite is moving in. This property can be used to choose which image must be drawn. |
| Constant | IMAGE_SIZE | The default size for a square sprite. |
| Property | ScaleFactor | Same as the GDI+ Sprite class, it holds a constant used when creating the sprite, indicating whether the x and y values are pixel values or based on IMAGE_SIZE. Useful for creating tiled game fields. |
| Properties | SpeedX and SpeedY | The speed (translation increment per frame) of the sprite on the x and y axes. |
| Properties | TranslationX and TranslationY | The current translation value in each axis, from the initial x,y position. |
| Properties | ScaleX and ScaleY | The scale to be applied to the sprite in each axis. |
| Properties | RotationX and RotationY | The rotation in each axis. |
| Property | SpriteImage | The sprite texture, loaded from an image file. |
| Property | VertBuffer | The vertex buffer with the vertices of the sprite. |
| Method | New | Method for creating a new sprite. |
| Method | Load | Method for loading the image file from disk; it creates the vertices used to draw the image on the screen. |
| Method | Draw | Method that draws the sprite. |
| Method | Dispose | Method that disposes of the texture and the vertex buffer used by the sprite. |
| Method | CreateFlexVertex | Helper method used when creating the sprite vertex buffer. |

The interface code for the Sprite class is shown here:

```
Imports Microsoft.DirectX.Direct3D
Public Class clsSprite
    Inherits clsGameEngine

    Public IsTransparent As Boolean = False
    Public Direction As enDirection

    Public X As Single
    Public Y As Single
    Public SizeX As Single = IMAGE_SIZE
    Public SizeY As Single = IMAGE_SIZE

    Public Const IMAGE_SIZE As Integer = 32
    Public ScaleFactor As enScaleFactor = enScaleFactor.enScaleSprite
    ' speed used in translation
    Public SpeedX As Single = 0
    Public SpeedY As Single = 0

    ' Values used for the operations
    Public TranslationX As Single = 0
    Public TranslationY As Single = 0
    Public ScaleX As Single = 1
    Public ScaleY As Single = 1
    Public RotationX As Single = 0
    Public RotationY As Single = 0

    Protected SpriteImage As Texture
    Protected VertBuffer As VertexBuffer
    Public Enum enScaleFactor
        enScalePixel = 1
        enScaleSprite = IMAGE_SIZE
    End Enum
    Public Enum enDirection
        North = 1
        NorthEast = 2
        East = 3
        SouthEast = 4
        South = 5
        SouthWest = 6
        West = 7
        NorthWest = 8
    End Enum
```

```
      Sub New(...)
      Function Load(...) As Boolean
      Private Function CreateFlexVertex(...) As CUSTOMVERTEX
      Sub Draw()
      Public Sub Dispose()
End Class
```

We must highlight two points in the preceding code: the use of default values for the properties (always use the most common ones), and the use of the inherits clause. The Sprite class will be closely related to the game engine, and it'll need to use some of the game engine properties to work properly, so we must create it as a GameEngine-derived class.

Let's see the code for the methods, starting with the New method. We'll create two overrides for the function: one for creating opaque sprites, and another for creating transparent sprites. The following code sample depicts the difference between these two overrides:

```
Sub New(strImageName As String,  startPoint As POINT, _
      Optional  Scale As enScaleFactor = enScaleFactor.enScaleSprite, _
      Optional  width As Integer = IMAGE_SIZE, _
      Optional  height As Integer = IMAGE_SIZE)
   X = startPoint.x
   Y = startPoint.y
   SizeX = width
   SizeY = height
   ScaleFactor = Scale
   If Not Load(strImageName) Then _
   Err.Raise(vbObjectError + 1, "clsSprite", _
         "Could not create the sprite textures")
End Sub


Sub New( strImageName As String,  colorKey As Integer,  startPoint As POINT, _
      Optional  Scale As enScaleFactor = enScaleFactor.enScaleSprite, _
      Optional  width As Integer = IMAGE_SIZE, _
      Optional  height As Integer = IMAGE_SIZE)
   ' When calling the New procedure with a colorKey,
   '   we want to create a transparent sprite
   IsTransparent = True
   X = startPoint.x
   Y = startPoint.y
   SizeX = width
   SizeY = height
   ScaleFactor = Scale
```

```
    If Not Load(strImageName, colorKey) Then _
        Err.Raise(vbObjectError + 1, "clsSprite", _
                "Could not create the sprite textures")
End Sub
```

The Load procedure will receive an optional colorKey parameter that will be used to load a transparent texture if the IsTransparent property is set to true. Besides loading the texture from an image file, the Load procedure must create the vertex buffer used to show the sprite in the draw procedure, using the CreateFlexVertex helper procedure.

```
' Default colorKey is magenta
Function Load(strImageName As String, _
    Optional colorKey As Integer = &HFFFF00FF) As Boolean
    Dim vertices As CustomVertex()
    Dim i As Integer

    Try
        If IsTransparent Then
            'Load the transparent texture
            SpriteImage = TextureLoader.FromFile(objDirect3DDevice, _
                Application.StartupPath & "\" & IMAGE_PATH & "\" & strImageName, _
                64, 64, D3DX.Default, 0, Format.Unknown, Pool.Managed, _
                Filter.Point, Filter.Point, colorKey)
        Else
            SpriteImage = TextureLoader.FromFile(objDirect3DDevice, _
                Application.StartupPath & "\" & IMAGE_PATH & "\" & strImageName)
        End If

        VertBuffer = New VertexBuffer(GetType(CustomVertex), 4, _
            objDirect3DDevice, Usage.WriteOnly, FVF_CUSTOMVERTEX, Pool.Default)
        vertices = VertBuffer.Lock(0, 0)
        ' CreateFlags a square, composed of 2 triangles in a triangle strip
        vertices(0) = CreateFlexVertex(X * ScaleFactor, Y * ScaleFactor, 1, 0, 1)
        vertices(1) = CreateFlexVertex(X * ScaleFactor + SizeX, _
                                    Y * ScaleFactor, 1, 1, 1)
        vertices(2) = CreateFlexVertex(X * ScaleFactor, _
                                    Y * ScaleFactor + SizeY, 1, 0, 0)
        vertices(3) = CreateFlexVertex(X * ScaleFactor + SizeX, _
                                    Y * ScaleFactor + SizeY, 1, 1, 0)
        ' Release the vertex buffer and commits our vertex data
        VertBuffer.Unlock()
        Return True
```

```
        Catch de As DirectXException
            MessageBox.Show("Could not load image file " & strImageName & _
                ". Error: " & de.ErrorString, "3D Initialization.", _
            MessageBoxButtons.OK, MessageBoxIcon.Error)
            Return False
        End Try
    End Function

    Function CreateFlexVertex( X As Single,  Y As Single,  Z As Single,  _
            tu As Single,  tv As Single) As CUSTOMVERTEX
        CreateFlexVertex.X = X
        CreateFlexVertex.Y = Y
        CreateFlexVertex.Z = Z
        CreateFlexVertex.tu = tu
        CreateFlexVertex.tv = tv
    End Function
```

The Draw method is very straightforward: It simply sets the texture and draws the rectangle defined by the vertex buffer created in the Load procedure, using the concepts shown in the previous chapter.

```
    Sub Draw()
        ' Turn on alpha blending only if the sprite has transparent colors
        If IsTransparent Then
            objDirect3DDevice.RenderState.AlphaBlendEnable = True
        End If
        Try
            objDirect3DDevice.SetTexture(0, SpriteImage)
            objDirect3DDevice.SetStreamSource(0, VertBuffer, 0)
            objDirect3DDevice.DrawPrimitives(PrimitiveType.TriangleStrip, 0, 2)
        Catch de As DirectXException
            MessageBox.Show("Could not draw sprite. Error: " & de.ErrorString, _
                "3D Initialization.", MessageBoxButtons.OK, MessageBoxIcon.Error)
        End Try
        ' Turn off alpha blending  if the sprite has transparent colors
        If IsTransparent Then
            objDirect3DDevice.RenderState.AlphaBlendEnable = False
        End If
    End Sub
```

The last method, `Dispose`, will only dispose of the texture and the vertex buffer created in the `Load` procedure. Calling the `Collect` method of the garbage collector will ensure a faster disposal of memory; and calling the `SupressFinalize` method of this class will prevent errors that can arise if the default finalizer is called before the objects are freed from memory. The `Dispose` method is shown in the next code sample:

```
Public Sub Dispose()
    On Error Resume Next   ' We are leaving, ignore any errors
    SpriteImage.Dispose()
    VertBuffer.Dispose()
    GC.Collect()
    GC.SupressFinalize(Me)
End Sub
```

## DirectAudio Classes

There are two different sets of components for audio input and output: Direct-Music, for background music playback, and DirectSound, for sound effects. These two sets together are sometimes called *DirectAudio*, although they are separate things. DirectMusic doesn't have a managed version, but we can access its features through COM interoperability.

*.NET is kind of an evolution from COM architecture; but we still can use COM objects from .NET programs, and more: The .NET programs generate COM wrappers, so COM-based languages (such as the previous version of Visual Basic) can access .NET components too. To use non-managed DirectX features, we must include in our projects a reference to the VBDX8.DLL.*

**NEW IN .NET**

Besides the components for audio playback, DirectAudio includes Direct-Music Producer, which can be used to create new music based on chord maps, styles, and segments. We'll not enter into any details about DirectMusic Producer here, but if you want to exercise your composing skills, you'll find a lot of relevant material in DirectX SDK.

The main distinction between background music and sound effects is related to the file types used by each one. Sound effect files are MIDI or WAV files that store a single piece of sound that is usually played when a specific action occurs in a game (such as a player getting a bonus or dying). Background music can be produced using a MIDI file playing in a loop, but it's best done with segment (SGT) files. SGT files have a main piece of music and one or more motifs (or waves) that can be played any time, as the program commands, so the music can change subtly from time to time.

---

 **NOTE** *A special music generation program is included with DirectX SDK, and it allows professional musicians to create segment files by connecting the computer to a music device (like a keyboard), or composing the music directly on the computer using instruments from the predefined libraries or even creating new ones. It's beyond the scope of this book to enter into details about the creation of segment files, but those who want to get a deeper knowledge of this subject will find many samples in the DirectMusic help feature on the DirectX SDK.*

---

A lot of theory and technical details are connected to DirectAudio, but we'll stick here to the simplest ways of generating sound for our application.

There aren't many steps we must follow to play sound, but we'll enclose these steps in two classes so every application doesn't need to include these initialization details. To play sounds using managed DirectSound, we need to perform the following four steps:

1. Create the DirectSound device object.

2. Create the DirectSound buffer object.

3. Load the WAV sound file into the buffer.

4. Play the sound using the buffer.

As we can see, only two objects are involved in playing sound through DirectSound:

- `Device`: Responsible for any generic operation regarding the sound device

- `Buffer`: Loads the sound files, sets specific properties, and plays the sounds

When playing files through DirectMusic, we'll have to implement some extra steps and different objects, due to the different nature of the sound files controlled. The steps to play any MIDI or SGT file using DirectMusic are as follows:

1. Create the `Performance` and `Loader` objects.

2. Initialize the `Performance` object.

3. Set the search directory from which the `Loader` object will load the sound files.

4. Load the file with the sound information of a `Segment` object.

5. If the file is an SGT file, download band and wave information for the file to the `Performance` object.

6. Play the sound from the segment object, choosing the audio path to play it in (primary or secondary).

7. If the file is an SGT file, play any included motifs as needed.

From these steps, we can see that there are three main objects we'll need to handle when playing sounds though DirectMusic: `Performance`, `Loader`, and `Segment`. These objects are described in more detail in the following list:

- `Performance`: Responsible for the management of all music playback. This object controls a set of instruments, with their special characteristics, and maps them to specific audio paths. It controls the music tempo, handles messages and events, and sets the music parameters. The performance mixes all sounds from primary and secondary audio paths seamlessly.

- `Loader`: Loads sound files, including instrument data, styles, bands, and collections. When we load a sound file, every related file is loaded too.

- `Segment`: Stores and plays each music piece as it is loaded from the sound file.

With these concepts in mind, we are ready to define the basic audio classes' interface, as shown in Figure 4-8.

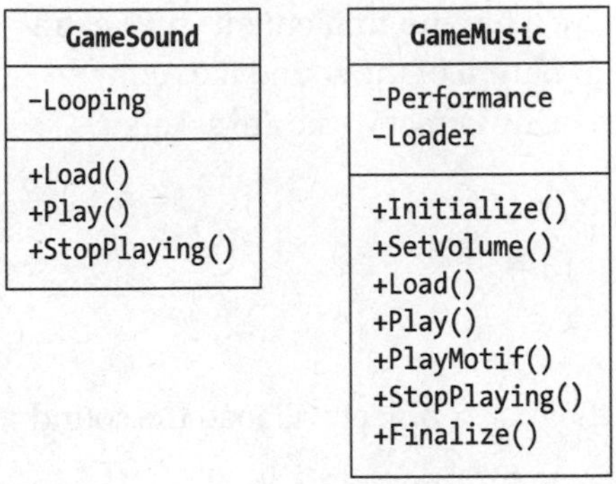

| GameSound |
|---|
| -Looping |
| +Load()<br>+Play()<br>+StopPlaying() |

| GameMusic |
|---|
| -Performance<br>-Loader |
| +Initialize()<br>+SetVolume()<br>+Load()<br>+Play()<br>+PlayMotif()<br>+StopPlaying()<br>+Finalize() |

*Figure 4-8. The audio classes*

We can add new properties and methods as needed when implementing audio management for our games.

In the next sections, we discuss the details for each game audio class.

## The GameSound Class

As we can see in our class definition, to play a sound through managed Direct-Sound, we must load the buffer with the sound file and then play the sound. This way of working gives us two choices for playing multiple sounds in our games:

- Create one single GameSound object and call Load and Play methods for every sound to be played.

- Create a GameSound object for each sound to be played, load each sound once, and call the Play method for the specific object that holds the sound to be played.

For sounds that are constantly playing throughout the game, the second approach is better, because it won't waste time reloading the sounds.

The interface for the class will be as follows:

```
Imports Microsoft.DirectX.DirectSound
Public Class ClsGameSound
    Protected Const SOUND_PATH As String = "Sounds"
    Dim DSoundBuffer As SecondaryBuffer = Nothing
```

```
    Public Looping As Boolean = False
    Private Shared SoundDevice As Device = Nothing
    Sub New(WinHandle As Windows.Forms.Control)
    Function Load(strFileName As String) As Boolean) As Boolean
    Sub StopPlaying()
    Sub Play()
End class
```

In the next sections, we'll look at the code and details for each class method.

## The New Method

On the New method we must initialize the sound device. Since we only need one device initialization for all the sounds we want to play, we must define the device object as shared (as we already did in the class definition), and include code in the New method to initialize the device only if it's not already initialized. The code for this method is presented in the following listing:

```
Sub New(WinHandle As System.Windows.Forms.Control)
    If SoundDevice Is Nothing Then
        SoundDevice = New Device()
        SoundDevice.SetCooperativeLevel(WinHandle, CooperativeLevel.Normal)
    End If
End Sub
```

Besides creating the device, we can see a specific initialization to inform the device of the appropriate cooperative level—in other words, how the sound device object will interact with other applications that may be using the device. The possible values for the SetCoopLevel enumeration follow:

- Normal: Specifies the device be used in a way that allows the smoothest multithreading and multitasking (multiple application) operation. Using this setting will force us to only use the default buffer and output formats, but this will suffice for our samples.

- Priority: Sets a priority level on the device, so we can change buffer and output formats. This member doesn't behave well with other applications trying to share the device, so we must use it only if we don't expect concurrency from other applications.

- Write Only: Specifies that the application plays only on primary buffers. This enumeration member will work only on real hardware devices; if Direct-Sound is emulating the device, the call to SetCooperativeLevel will fail.

Once we've created the device, we can load the sounds into a sound buffer, as described in the next section.

### The Load Method

The Load method will be mainly based on the CreateSoundBufferFromFile function, which requires the following parameters:

```
<Buffer object>.CreateSoundBufferFromFile(FilePath, BufferDescription)
```

The first parameter is the path from which we want to load the sound file. The second is a description of specific properties we'll need for the buffer, from the capabilities we'll have (control volume, frequency, etc.) to how the device must act when playing this buffer, when another application gets the focus. In our sample, we'll only set one flag, GlobalFocus, which tells the device to continue playing the buffer even if other DirectSound applications have the focus.

The full code of the Load function is shown in the following sample:

```
Function Load(strFileName As String) As Boolean
    Try
        Dim Desc As BufferDesc = New BufferDesc()
        Desc.Flags = New BufferCapsFlags() = BufferCapsFlags.GlobalFocus Or _
                        BufferCapsFlags.LocSoftware

        DSoundBuffer = _
        SoundDevice.CreateSoundBufferFromFile(Application.StartupPath & _
                        "\" & SOUND_PATH & "\" & strFileName, Desc)
    Catch de As Exception
        MessageBox.Show("Could not load the sound file. Error: " & de.Message, _
            "Music Initialization", MessageBoxButtons.OK, MessageBoxIcon.Error)
    End Try
    Load = True
End Function
```

In the next section we'll discuss the last two methods of the GameSound class, Play and StopPlaying.

### The Play and StopPlaying Methods

The Play and StopPlaying methods will use the Play and Stop methods belonging to the Buffer object, as shown in the next code listing. Similarly to the CreateSoundBufferFromFile function, the Play method will receive a structure with the playing flags; in our sample we'll use the default settings, and include an extra setting for looping the sound if the Looping property of the class is set.

```
Sub Play()
    Dim PlayFlags As BufferPlayFlags = BufferPlayFlags.Default
    If Looping Then PlayFlags = BufferPlayFlags.Looping

    If Not (DSoundBuffer Is Nothing) Then
        Try
            DSoundBuffer.Play(0, PlayFlags)
        Catch de As Exception
            MessageBox.Show("Error playing sound file. Error: " & de.Message, _
                    MessageBoxButtons.OK, MessageBoxIcon.Error)
        End Try
    End If
End Sub

Sub StopPlaying()
    If Not (DSoundBuffer Is Nothing) Then
        DSoundBuffer.Stop()
        DSoundBuffer.SetCurrentPosition(0)
    End If
End Sub
```

In the next section we'll discuss the second DirectAudio class, GameMusic.

## The GameMusic Class

The basic class interface to access DirectMusic features is shown in the next code listing. The first line imports the library created by Visual Basic as a wrapper to the VBDX8.DLL file, used for COM access to all DirectX features, including DirectMusic.

```
Imports DxVBLibA
Public Class clsGameMusic
    Private Shared DMusicPerf As DirectMusicPerformance8 = Nothing
    Private Shared DMusicLoad As DirectMusicLoader8 = Nothing
    Private DMusicSegment As DirectMusicSegment8 = Nothing

    ' Background music is looped by default
    Public looping As Boolean = True

    ' Default sound files path
    Private Const SOUND_PATH As String = "Sounds"

    Sub SetVolume(intVolume As Integer)
    Function Initialize(WinHandle As IntPtr) As Boolean

    Function Load(strFileName As String, bolLooping As Boolean = True) As Boolean
    Sub Play()
    Function PlayMotif(strMotifName As String) As Boolean
    Sub StopPlaying()
    Protected Overrides Sub Finalize()
End Class
```

In this code sample, we can see that DirectMusic defined the Performance and Loader objects as private so they'll only be accessible to the class. This will prevent us from having to know internal details of the class when playing music from our games.

## The Initialize Method

In the Initialize function, we need to create and initialize the class objects with the most commonly used values. The next code sample shows a possible implementation for this method:

```
Function Initialize(WinHandle As IntPtr) As Boolean
    ' CreateFlags our default objects
    Dim AudioParams As DMUS_AUDIOPARAMS

    DMusicPerf = DX8.DirectMusicPerformanceCreate()
    DMusicLoad = DX8.DirectMusicLoaderCreate()
```

```
Try
    ' Initialize our performance object to use reverb
    DMusicPerf.InitAudio(WinHandle.ToInt32, _
            CONST_DMUS_AUDIO.DMUS_AUDIOF_ALL, AudioParams, , _
            CONST_DMUSIC_STANDARD_AUDIO_PATH.
            DMUS_APATH_SHARED_STEREOPLUSREVERB, 128)
    ' Turn on all auto download
    DMusicPerf.SetMasterAutoDownload(True)
    ' Set our search folder
    DMusicLoad.SetSearchDirectory(Application.StartupPath & "\" & SOUND_PATH)
    Initialize = True
Catch de As Exception
    MessageBox.Show("Could not initialize DirectMusic. Error: " & de.Message, _
        "Music Initialization.", MessageBoxButtons.OK, MessageBoxIcon.Error)
    Initialize = False
End Try
End Function
```

Some of the key functions used in the `Initialize` method deserve a better explanation. Let's start by taking a closer look at the `InitAudio` method and its possible values:

```
<Performance object>.InitAudio(hWnd, Flags, AudioParams, DirectSound, _
                        DefaultPathType, ChannelCount)
```

The first parameter, `HWnd`, receives the window handle. This will usually be the same window used for Direct3D device object creation. If we specify a window handle, we don't need to specify the DirectSound object, so DirectMusic creates a private one for its personal use, making our code simpler.

The second parameter, `Flags`, specifies a member of the `CONST_DMUS_AUDIO` enumeration that will state the requested features for the performance. Although you can specify different values, such as `BUFFERS` to fully support audio path buffers, or `3D` for supporting 3-D sounds, using `ALL`, as in the sample code, will prepare `Performance` to handle any kind of loaded sounds.

The third parameter, `AudioParams`, allow us to specify the desired control parameters for the sound synthesizer, and to be notified of which requests were granted. We can specify details such as the frequency of the sample and the number of voices used; but since we are using only the simplest features from DirectMusic, we'll let all flags remain set to their default values.

The DirectSound object is used when we are employing DirectMusic features to support DirectSound with playing WAV files; since we are dealing with separate classes for each one, we can simply omit this parameter.

The next parameter, `DefaultPathType`, receives a member of the `DMUS_APATH` enumeration, which specifies the default audio path type, as described in the following list:

- `DYNAMIC_3D`: Indicates the audio path will play to a 3-D buffer (the sounds are distributed on the speakers in order to create the illusion of a 3-D environment). For more information on 3-D sounds, refer to the DirectX SDK.

- `DYNAMIC_MONO`: Used for creating an audio path with mono buffering (all music sounds are of equal volume in each speaker).

- `DYNAMIC_STEREO`: Specifies the sounds be played in a stereo environment (the sounds are distributed on the speakers according to how they were recorded—for example, if the percussion instruments were more to the left, the left speaker will have a louder percussion sound).

- `SHARED_STEREOPLUSREVERB`: Indicates the buffer created for the audio path has all the features of the stereo buffer, plus an environmental reverb (echo in music).

The `ChannelCount` parameter specifies the number of performance channels allocated to the audio path. In the code sample, we have 128 performance channels, which means that we can play up to 128 different sounds within the same `Performance` object.

A second function in the preceding sample that deserves a more detailed explanation is `SetMasterAutoDownload`:

```
<Performance object>. SetMasterAutoDownload(value)
```

This method is one of many used to set global parameters for the performance object, passing a single value as a parameter. The following lists a few more of the methods in this category:

- `SetMasterVolume`: Sets the volume, measured in hundreds of decibels, ranging from +20 (amplification) to −200 (attenuation). Values below −100 or above +10 will result in no audible difference, so the useful values are up to 10 times the default volume to 1/100 of it.

- `SetMasterAutoDownload`: Turns on and off automatic loading of instruments when loading the segment files that use them. We'll always want this parameter set to on.

- SetMasterTempo: Represents the "scale factor" for the tempo of the music. The default value is 1, so you can set this to 0.5 and have music playing at half the normal speed, or set this to 2 and double the speed (if you want to hear, say, Lou Reed singing like Madonna). Valid values range from 0.01 to 100.

There are other methods of this type, but these are the ones we'll most commonly want to set. We can create new methods for the GameMusic class to set these parameters, such as a SetVolume method to set the current volume for the performance object, as in the following code sample:

```
Sub SetVolume(intVolume As Integer)
    If Not (DMusicPerf Is Nothing) Then
        Try
            DMusicPerf.SetMasterVolume(intVolume)
        Catch de As Exception
            MessageBox.Show("Could not set the master volume. Error: " & _
                de.Message, MessageBoxButtons.OK, MessageBoxIcon.Error)
        End Try
    End If
End Sub
```

 **NOTE** *As you can imagine, there are complementary methods with the* GetMaster *prefix that are used to retrieve the value of a specific configuration parameter from the* Performance *object. It's beyond the scope of this book to explain every one of them; refer to DirectX SDK help for a comprehensive list.*

The last new function we saw in the sample, SetSearchDirectory, simply informs the Loader object of the directory from which the sound files will be loaded, so we won't need to give the path for every sound loaded.

## The Load Method

The Load method will be mainly based on the LoadSegment function, which receives the file and path from which we want to load the sound file (MIDI or SGT). Since we already gave the search path for the Loader object, we can pass only the filename to the function.

The full code for a first version of the Load function is shown in the following sample:

```
Function Load(strFileName As String, Optional bolLooping As Boolean = True)_
            As Boolean
    ' Backgound music loops by default
    looping = bolLooping

    ' Load the music file
    Try
        DMusicSegment = DMusicLoad.LoadSegment(strFileName)
        ' If it's a segment file, we have some special treatment
        If strFileName.EndsWith(".sgt") Then
            If Not (DMusicSegment Is Nothing) Then '// Download the segment
                DMusicSegment.Download(DMusicPerf.GetDefaultAudioPath)
            End If
        Else
            If strFileName.EndsWith(".mid") Or strFileName.EndsWith(".rmi") Then
                DMusicSegment.SetStandardMidiFile()
            End If
        End If
    Catch de As Exception
        DMusicSegment = Nothing
        MessageBox.Show("Could not load the sound file. Error: " & de.Message, _
                "Music Initialization", MessageBoxButtons.OK, MessageBoxIcon.Error)
        Load = False
        Exit Function
    End Try
    Load = True
End Function
```

**NEW IN .NET**

*In VB .NET, every data type corresponds to a class definition, with its own set of properties and methods, so we can use these methods and properties as we would do with any kind of objects. In the preceding sample code,* EndsWith() *is a method of the string data type, corresponding to the* Right *method in previous versions of Visual Basic, with the only difference being that we don't need to pass the number of characters to check.*

*Another interesting point about the preceding code is the use of the* Try-Catch *block with a specific type of exception. This structured error block, new in Visual Basic .NET, allows the programmer to catch generic errors or errors from a specific set (such as* Exception*).*

**NEW IN .NET**

We can improve the music played from segment files using styles and motifs that are stored in those files by the music author. In the next section we'll examine what these are and how to apply them to our audio class.

## Styles and Motifs

Styles and motifs are intrinsic parts of a segment file, and they allow us to choose from a set of previously created compositions to play at any time during music execution. Each segment file can have one or more styles recorded within it, and every style can have one or more motifs.

A *style* is a collection of instruments and music patterns or *motifs* (sequences of music values for each instrument present in the style). To read a specific style from a music segment, we use the GetStyle method. There are various Get methods in the Segment object, similar to the GetMaster methods present in the Performance object, as we saw before. To retrieve a style, we must pass the style number, from 0 to the number of styles present minus 1. Passing an invalid value will generate an error.

After choosing a specific style, we can retrieve its number of motifs using the GetMotifCount function.

Based on these two functions, we can extend our Load method to retrieve the number of styles and the number of motifs, setting new properties that will allow the game to retrieve the information from the GameMusic class. To do so, we must include the following new properties in the class:

```
Private DMusicStyle As DirectMusicStyle = Nothing
Public MotifCount As Integer = 0
Public StyleCount As Integer = 0
```

And we need to include the following lines in the Load method. Read the following code carefully so you understand the mechanism of reading styles and motifs.

```
    Dim strMotifName As String
    Dim bolLoopStyles As Boolean = True
    Dim bolLoopMotifs As Boolean = True

    Do While (bolLoopStyles)
        ' Count the styles
        Try
            DMusicStyle = DMusicSegment.GetStyle(StyleCount)
            StyleCount += 1
            ' Count the motifs of the style
            bolLoopMotifs = True
            MotifCount += DMusicStyle.GetMotifCount
        Catch
            ' The GetParam will throw an exception if there are no more styles.
            bolLoopStyles = False
        End Try
    Loop
    ' We start counting from zero, so add 1 to have the real Style count value
    StyleCount += 1
```

In the next section we'll discuss the methods for playing and stopping the audio.

## The Play and StopPlaying Methods

Once the styles have been read, we can code the Play and StopPlaying methods, which will use the PlaySegmentEx and StopEx methods belonging to the Performance object, as shown in the following code sample. Both methods receive the segment object (created in the Load method) used to play or stop playing.

```
Sub Play()
    If Not (DMusicSegment Is Nothing) Then
        Try
            If Looping Then
                DMusicSegment.SetRepeats(CONST_DPNWAITTIME.INFINITE)
            Else
                DMusicSegment.SetRepeats(0)
            End If
            DMusicPerf.PlaySegmentEx(DMusicSegment, 0, 0)
        Catch de As Exception
            MessageBox.Show("Error playing music file. Error: " & de.Message, _
                MessageBoxButtons.OK, MessageBoxIcon.Error)
```

```
        End Try
    End If
End Sub

Sub StopPlaying()
    If Not (DMusicSegment Is Nothing) Then
        DMusicPerf.StopEx(DMusicSegment, 0, 0)
    End If
End Sub
```

In the next section, we look at how to play motifs, and create two new methods to add this feature to our GameMusic class.

## Playing Motifs

To finish our GameMusic class, it'll be interesting to have one function to play a motif from the current music segment. We can use such a function to add some subtle variations to our background music, making it a little more exciting. We can simply do this by using the same PlaySegmentEx function. Instead of using the entire sound loaded as a segment object as the first parameter, we'll load the motif from the segment object (using the GetMotif function) and pass the motif as a parameter for that function.

We can create an analogous method that receives a number and plays the associated motif; such a method would be useful if we don't previously know the motif names, but do know how many there are (as calculated in the Load method).

The two overloaded methods are shown in the next listing, and it's up to each game to choose which one best suits its needs.

```
Function PlayMotif(strMotifName As String) As Boolean
    Dim Motif As DirectMusicSegment8
    Try
        ' Get the motif
        Motif = DMusicStyle.GetMotif(strMotifName)
        DMusicPerf.PlaySegmentEx(Motif, _
            CONST_DMUS_SEGF_FLAGS.DMUS_SEGF_DEFAULT Or _
            CONST_DMUS_SEGF_FLAGS.DMUS_SEGF_SECONDARY, 0)
        PlayMotif = True
    Catch
        PlayMotif = False
    End Try
End Function
```

```
Function PlayMotif(intMotifIndex As Integer) As Boolean
        Dim strMotifName As String
        Try
            ' Get the motif
            strMotifName = DMusicStyle.GetMotifName(intMotifIndex)
            ' Call the overloaded method which receives a string
            PlayMotif = PlayMotif(strMotifName)
        Catch
            PlayMotif = False
        End Try
End Function
```

The GetMotifName method, listed in the previous code sample, receives the motif number (ranging from one to GetMotifCount) and returns the motif name (as informed by the composer when creating the segment) as the second parameter. Calling this function with an invalid index will generate an error.

In the next section we'll discuss the final method of our class.

## The Finalize Method

The last class method, Finalize, simply destroys the audio objects, making sure that the Performance object is closed before destroying it, using the CloseDown method.

```
Protected Overrides Sub Finalize()
    ' The object is being destroyed, so ignore any errors
    On Error Resume Next
    MyBase.Finalize()
    'Clean up DMusicSegment
    If Not (DMusicSegment Is Nothing) Then
        DMusicPerf.StopEx(DMusicSegment, 0, 0)
    End If
    DMusicSegment = Nothing
    DMusicStyle = Nothing
    DMusicLoad = Nothing
    If Not (DMusicPerf Is Nothing) Then
        DMusicPerf.CloseDown()
    End If
    DMusicPerf = Nothing
End Sub
```

Now that this class is finished, we have a complete set of classes to help us to include audio capabilities in our games. The most important point to note when using this kind of approach is that when coding a game, we need to be concerned with the game goals, not the less important details such as how to load music or initialize a device.

In the next section we'll discuss the proposal for the sample game used in this chapter and the next, which will allow us to test, in a practical way, our gaming class library.

## The Game Proposal

We are going to do an Activision's River Raid (an old Atari console game) clone, but in this chapter we'll create only half of the game features. Since not everyone will remember the original River Raid game features (or will have ever played it), let's introduce the points we'll want to cover in our first version of the game.

In River Pla.Net the player will control a plane that is flying over a top-to-bottom scrolling river. Even when the player isn't moving the plane, the ground beneath it will be moving. As far as we know, the river goes on forever, so the main goal of the game is to live for as long as possible.

Here are some more details about the game:

- The plane will be controlled by keyboard arrows.

- There will be some obstacles along the river: ships, planes, and bridges. The ships and planes won't move in the first version of the game.

- The plane must always be flying over water; if it flies over land or over an obstacle (bridges, planes, or ships), it will be destroyed.

- To make the level design easier, the game map will be a text file, in which each character will represent a different tile when the game field is created.

- There'll be some gas barrels on the river, which will be collected by the player's plane when it flies over them. In the first version of the game, we won't create a fuel counter.

- After being destroyed, the player's plane will be invincible for a few seconds.

- The game must have background music and different sound effects for each player action: upon being destroyed, when in invincible mode, and while filling the gas tank.

When a team of developers creates a "real" game, the game proposal is normally followed by some drafts showing details about the game (like screen layout and some artwork samples), and must be refined until everyone in the team has a clear understanding of what the game will be. The game proposal goal is to answer the question: *What are we doing?*

Once everyone agrees about the game proposal, it's time to answer the next question we need to ask: *How will we do it?* The game project presents the technical details to answer this question, but both documents aren't static; they can (in fact, they must) be revised every time a new point of view arises and is agreed upon by the game development team. Care must be taken not to include every suggestion, or the planning stage will simply never end.

The last two important questions in a "real" game development are mainly targeted to commercial games (*How long will it take to finish the project? How much will it cost?*), and won't be discussed here.

## The Game Project

Looking back at the project proposal, before starting anything else, we need to decide some higher level details for the game. It's good practice to think about how things will work before writing down any class diagrams or pseudo-code.

In our specific case, maybe the two most important points on the proposal are the following:

- The player will control a plane that is flying over a top-to-bottom scrolling river.

- To make the level design easier, the game map will be a text file, where each character will represent a different tile when creating the game field.

How do we *really* make scrolling games? How can we design a level with Notepad?

In our game, these questions are very much related. First, let's figure out the creation of the game field, and then think about how to do the translation and implementation of the other features described in the game proposal.

## Defining the Game Tiles

River Pla.Net is one of those games that allows us to design the whole game field based on *tiles*. We can create the game field map file with a text editor, using the game program to translate the set of characters in the file to a set of tiles on screen.

Maybe the first thing we must think about when creating a tile-based game is what size our tiles will be. They aren't required to be square ones, but using squares is the best approach, since we can put the tiles together in any direction, without any problems.

To define the number of tiles, we must first decide the resolution for our game. A higher resolution will allow us to use more tiles, if the tiles are a fixed size, or force us to have larger images. Either approach can lead to a reduction in performance because they'll both use more memory than lower resolutions, so let's keep our sample to a 640×480 resolution to make it as fast as possible. With this resolution, if we have square tiles that are 32-pixels wide, we can have 15 tiles for the height and 20 tiles for the width.

Looking at the game proposal, we can list a basic set of tiles to fill the game goals:

- Land

- Water

- Ship

- Enemy plane

- Gas barrel

- Bridge

This reduced set of tiles is probably very close to the one used by the original River Raid, but using just these tiles will result in a very "blocky" game. In Figure 4-9 we see a basic set of tiles.

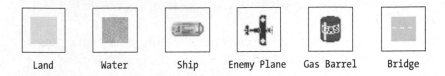

    Land          Water         Ship     Enemy Plane  Gas Barrel    Bridge

*Figure 4-9. A basic set of tiles*

Let's create a game field using any graphical tool (Microsoft's Paint will suffice) to cut and paste the tiles shown in Figure 4-9 so we can see a first "visual prototype" of our game, giving us a better idea about how it'll look. Figure 4-10 shows a screen drawn with these tiles.

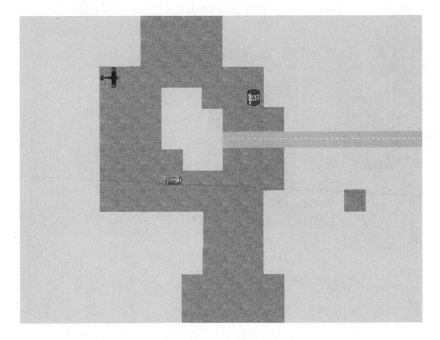

*Figure 4-10. A first screen based on tiles*

As we can see in this first screen, using only this set of tiles will result in a flat block game: All river "curves" are straight, and we can barely see the border between land and water. Creating borders is just a matter of drawing a new set of tiles that can be used to generate an island and a lake, and all river curves can be derived from this set. Figure 4-11 shows such a set of tiles.

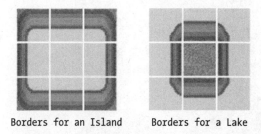

Borders for an Island    Borders for a Lake

*Figure 4-11. The border tiles*

It's important to adopt tile names that will help us to find them easily. For the border tiles, we suggest giving all tiles the "border" prefix and a direction indicator. For example, for the border where the water meets the land to the north, the name would be "borderN", and for a Southwest border the name would be "borderSW". Take a closer look at Figure 4-12 to understand this naming convention and all the border tile names.

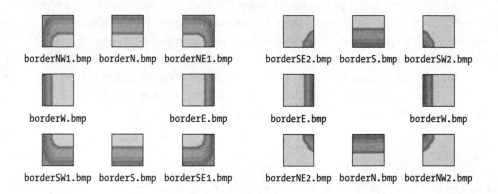

borderNW1.bmp  borderN.bmp  borderNE1.bmp     borderSE2.bmp  borderS.bmp  borderSW2.bmp

borderW.bmp                  borderE.bmp        borderE.bmp                 borderW.bmp

borderSW1.bmp  borderS.bmp  borderSE1.bmp      borderNE2.bmp  borderN.bmp  borderNW2.bmp

*Figure 4-12. The names of the border tiles*

The N, S, W, and E borders are used as island borders and as lake borders by just exchanging positions.

We can remake the screen from Figure 4-10 to add the borders, resulting in the screen shown in Figure 4-13.

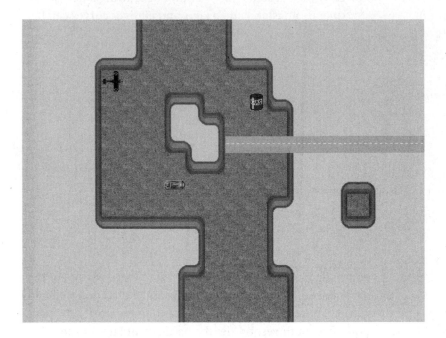

*Figure 4-13. A second screen, based on a larger set of tiles*

Initially it may seem as though these are the only tiles we'll ever need, but just imagine if the plane flies over a straight section of the river, with no bridges or opponents: The player would barely see the scrolling movement—the only tip would be the water movement. So we can add some "final touch" tiles, such as trees and mountains (at least two of each, to give some visual variation), and maybe create a bridge tile different from the road one, to give the game a nicer look and feel. Figure 4-14 shows the "final touch" tiles.

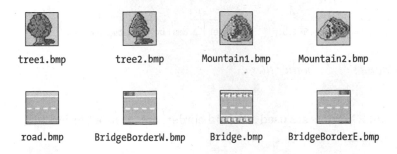

*Figure 4-14. The "final touch" set of tiles*

Creating a bridge with borders forces us to change the road tile and make it thin, and we have to add two new tiles to use when the road is over the river border. Our final screen, using all tiles, is shown in Figure 4-15.

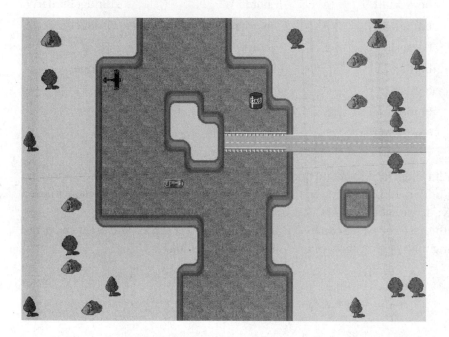

*Figure 4-15. The final screen, using all sets of tiles*

Of course, we can go on creating new tiles. For example, a diagonal border for the river would be interesting, so we can break the "blocky" visual that still persists. We can add different borderlines, with beaches or little bays; and we can add more "final touch" objects, such as houses, buildings, or even animals or people, to arrange around the screen.

The more tiles we include, the more flexibility the level designer will have to create our groundbreaking levels. But for our purpose here, the tiles we've already created will suffice.

Before going to the next topic, we shall define the char codes corresponding to each tile. Doing this at game project phase will allow the level designer to start writing the levels at the same time the programmers start coding. Then again, there's no rule for choosing the chars. A good approach is to choose chars that will give a visual clue about how the level will look; and as for the borders, we can simply choose North as 1 and go on sequentially in a clockwise direction. The characters chosen are shown in Table 4-3.

*Table 4-3. The Tile Codes*

| CODE | TILE | CODE | TILE | CODE | TILE |
|------|------|------|------|------|------|
| 1 | borderN | 9 | borderSW2 | G | Gas |
| 2 | borderNE1 | A | borderW | ( | BridgeBorderW |
| 3 | borderNE2 | B | borderNW1 | ) | BridgeBorderE |
| 4 | borderE | C | borderNW2 | - | Road |
| 5 | borderSE1 | T | Tree | = | Bridge |
| 6 | borderSE2 | M | Mountain | . | Land |
| 7 | borderS | S | Ship | _ | Water |
| 8 | borderSW1 | P | EnemyPlane | -- | -- |

We have decided to create one single char for both types of trees and another one for both mountain types, so the game can randomly choose the image to use and have some subtle visual variations every time it's played.

With these codes, we can look again at our first test screen and create a corresponding map of it, as show in the following code listing:

```
.....4___A......T..
.M...4___A..T...M..
...975___876...M..T
.T.4P_____A......
...4___B2__G86..M.T.
...4___AC2___A....T.
T..4___864===(------
...4___85___A....T.
...4___S____A.976..
..M4_____B3.4_A..
...C11112___A..C13..
..T.....4___A.......
..M....95___86......
....T..4____A....TT
T..M...4____A..T...
.......4____A......
```

## Scrolling Games

When talking about translation, remember that we have already made a scrolling object—our walking-man cube in Chapter 3, when performing translations on it. Since we already have a set of features in Direct3D that allow us to scroll an object without having to move every vertex of it, we can use the same idea here: Simply change the `Transform.World` matrix of the device object to do the translation.

So all we need to do is create the game field and perform small translations on it, for each time frame, to make it scroll. But will we scroll the entire game field? Will moving all the tiles of the game field result in prolonged calculations?

Looking again at the samples in the last chapter, we see that setting the world matrix will only define the transformations to be applied to the vertex buffer when we call the `DrawPrimitivesUP` function; so there's no performance difference when setting the matrix for a scene with a few dozen vertices or for a scene with several thousand.

So what we want to do is to draw the minimum number of vertices possible. Remember, our game field will be defined by a text file. For performance reasons we must load it only once, when starting the game, converting each char in the text file to a tile that will be in a fixed (x,y) position, depending on the position of the char in the map text file. The tiles will be fixed throughout the game, and we'll scroll over them, changing the translation value of the world matrix, to "move the camera" over the game field. Just like a plane moving over a real river, the river is fixed on the ground, and we move over it.

So to minimize the vertices drawn, we can store the current line from the bottom of the screen, and draw the 15 next lines—as mentioned in the previous section, our visual game field will be 20 tiles wide and 15 tiles tall. Since we won't be performing translations on the objects the size of a tile, we'll need to draw an extra line to avoid the top of the screen not being drawn appropriately. It's like being in *The Matrix* (the movie): The world will exist only when we are looking at it.

Another good idea to minimize the number of vertices being drawn is simply remove the Land tile from our set, and draw the other sets over a green background. To make the background green, all we need to do is to use the green color as a parameter of the `Clear` method of the device object.

## The Class Diagram

Since we already have all base classes for the game engine, sprite, game music, and sound, all we need to do is to create derived classes that will supply specific characteristics, according to the game's special needs.

Looking at the game proposal, we can only see two candidates for new classes: `Player` and `Tile`, which will be derived from the `Sprite` class. Of course, we'll need a class derived from the game engine, too (let's call it the `RiverEngine` class), to implement the game code.

After a little brainstorming over the game proposal, we have come up with the class diagram shown in Figure 4-16.

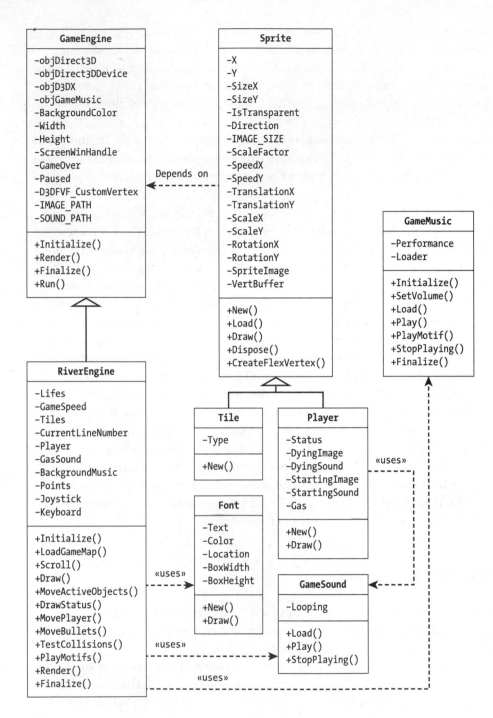

*Figure 4-16. The River Pla.Net game class diagram*

The following tables describe the properties and methods for each of the game classes, starting with the `Tile` class in Table 4-4.

*Table 4-4. The Tile Class*

| TYPE | NAME | DESCRIPTION |
|------|------|-------------|
| Property | Type | A member of an internal enumeration that should store the type of the tile (land, water, enemies, etc.) |
| Method | New | An overloaded method for each `New` method of the `Sprite` class that simply adds an extra parameter for the `Type` property |

Table 4-5 shows the description of the methods and properties for the `Player` class.

*Table 4-5. The Player Class*

| TYPE | NAME | DESCRIPTION |
|------|------|-------------|
| Property | Status | The current status for the player: flying, dying, or starting a new life |
| Property | Gas | The fuel tank value by percentage |
| Property | DyingImage | Image (image file loaded to create textures) to show when the player dies |
| Property | StartingImage | Image to show when the player is in invincible mode (starting a new life) |
| Property | DyingSound | Object that stores the sound to be played when the player dies |
| Property | StartingSound | Object that stores the sound to be played when the player is in invincible mode (starting a new life) |
| Property | GameSound | Object that will initialize the sound components and make them ready to play sounds |
| Method | New | An overloaded method that will load all player images |
| Method | Draw | An overloaded method that will draw the player image based on the current status |

The `RiverEngine` class includes members that are additions to the `GameEngine` class to make it fit our needs. In Table 4-6 we present the descriptions for each class member. As we discussed in earlier chapters, this class interface is a result of many interactions over game project refinements.

*Table 4-6. The RiverEngine class*

| PROPERTY | NAME | DESCRIPTION |
| --- | --- | --- |
| Property | Lifes | Specifies the number of lives of the player. |
| Property | GameSpeed | Indicates the scrolling speed of the game. |
| Property | Tiles | Represents an array with all the tiles of the game. |
| Property | CurrentLineNumber | Specifies the number of the current line at the bottom of the screen. This property is used to control the tiles we should draw. |
| Property | Player | Indicates an object of the Player class. |
| Property | GasSound | Indicates an object of the GameSound class, which will be played when the player passes over a gas barrel. |
| Property | BackgroundMusic | Indicates an object of the GameMusic class, which will play the game's background music. |
| Method | Initialize | Calls the Initialize method of the base class, loads the game map, and creates all game objects (Player, GasSound, and BackgroundMusic). |
| Method | LoadGameMap | Loads the game map text file and populates the Tiles array. |
| Method | Render | Overrides the Render empty method from the base class, and will be called in the game loop (on the Run base class method). All the drawing functions, physics tests, and sound-playing functions should be called from here. |
| Method | Scroll | Scrolls the game field by calculating the game world translation matrix. |
| Method | Draw | Draws the visible tiles of the game field, based on the CurrentLineNumber property and the Height of the screen. |
| Method | MovePlayer | Moves and draws the player, based on the input received from the keyboard. |
| Method | TestCollisions | Tests the collision of the player against the obstacles of the game field. |
| Method | PlayMotifs | Plays the random motifs over the background music to add a little variance to it. |

## The Main Program

This main program will show the splash screen and, after closing it, execute the steps we saw before when presenting the GameEngine class. The pseudo-code for this will be very simple, as shown in the following sample:

```
Create object from RiverPlanet class
Create a window to be the game screen
Show splash screen
Initialize RiverPlanet object
Show the game window
Run the game (execute method RUN from RiverEngine object)
' The Run is a synchronous method, it will return when the game ends
Destroy the RiverEngine object
Dispose the game window
```

And now we are ready to start looking at the code details.


## The Coding Phase

In order to follow a "progressive disclosure" technique, let's do the coding in discrete steps, so we can better test and understand our code. The functionalities of each step will be as follows:

1.  First draft: Code the Tile Class and load the game map and the Draw method to draw the tiles in the Render method.

2.  Second draft: Make the game field scroll.

3.  Third draft: Create the Player class to draw the player's plane, and make it move according to the keyboard input.

4.  Fourth draft: Code the collision detection.

5.  Final version: Play background music and sound effects.

In the next section we start coding the first draft of our game.

## First Draft: Loading and Drawing the Game Field

Our main objective in this first draft is to load the text file and convert it into a graphical game field. For this, we'll code the Tile class, some basic methods of the RiverEngine class, and our main program.

The Tile class, as we saw in the game project phase, will be very simple and will only add a specific Type attribute to the base class Sprite, as shown in the following code sample:

```
Imports Microsoft.DirectX.Direct3D
Public Class ClsTile
    Inherits clsSprite

    Enum enType
        Background = 0
        Water = 1
        Land = 2
        Gas = 3
        Ship = 4
        Plane = 5
        Bridge = 6
    End Enum
    Public Type As enType

    Sub New(strImageName As String, startPoint As POINT, intType As enType)
        MyBase.New(strImageName, startPoint)
        Type = intType
    End Sub

    Sub New(strImageName As String, colorKey As Integer, _
            startPoint As POINT,  intType As enType)
        MyBase.New(strImageName, colorKey, startPoint)
        Type = intType
    End Sub
End Class
```

As for the RiverEngine class, let's define the whole interface and then code only the functions we need at the moment:

```
Imports System.IO
Imports Microsoft.DirectX
Imports Microsoft.DirectX.Direct3D
Public Class ClsRiverEngine
    Inherits clsGameEngine
```

```
Private BackgroundMusic As ClsGameMusic

Public Lifes As Integer = 5463
Public gameSpeed As Integer = 10

' Define the array that will store the reference to the tiles on the game
' field.  Since we don't know its size a priori, we'll REDIM it when reading
' the game map file
Private tiles As ClsTile(,)
Private CurrentLineNumber As Int32 = 0
Public Player As ClsPlayer
Private GasSound As ClsGameSound

Overrides Sub Render()
Sub Scroll()
Sub Draw()
Sub MovePlayer()
Sub PlayMotifs()
Function TestCollision() As Boolean
Public Shadows Function Initialize(Owner as Windows.Forms.Control) As Boolean
Function LoadGameMap() As Boolean
Protected Overrides Sub Finalize()
End Class
```

The `Imports` clause in the header of the class file allows us to include a namespace reference to the current file so we can use its members directly. In the preceding sample code, we import the `System.IO` namespace, which includes classes and enumerations for manipulating files.

---

**NEW IN .NET**

*The fastest way to read and write text files in Visual Basic .NET is to use the* `StreamReader` *and* `StreamWriter` *classes. We'll use the first one, which has some methods dedicated to reading files, including the* `ReadLine` *method, which reads one text line until the new line char (just what we'll need here). The files are opened when creating the object (in the* `New` *method), and closed using the* `Close` *method.*

---

## Coding the LoadGameMap Method

The first problem that comes to mind when we start thinking about how the LoadGameMap function will be implemented is that we read a text file from the first line to the last, but our game field needs to be presented to the player in the reverse order. So, if we open the game map file in Notepad, the last line of the file will be the first one to be drawn at the bottom of the screen, and then we'll draw the next ones over it, to make the game scroll until we reach the first line of the file.

A possible approach to solving this problem is to read the entire file to a string array and then run through this array to create the Tiles array. We'll include a first line in the text file with the number of lines of the array, so we can Redim it accordingly. It's a good idea to create a separate function for translating the chars of each line, so we can isolate the code that is responsible for accessing the file and read lines from the code that will be creating the tiles.

So let's see the code for the LoadGameMap function and the helper function LoadLine:

```
Function LoadGameMap(strGameMapFileName As String) As Boolean
    ' Define the string array that will store the lines read from the map file
    Dim GameMap As String()
    ' Define the streamreader to read the game map file
    Dim GameMapFile As StreamReader
    Dim strLine As String
    Dim i As Int32

    LoadGameMap = True
    Try
        ' Opens the game map text file
        GameMapFile = New StreamReader(Application.StartupPath & "\" & _
                    strGameMapFileName)
        ' reads the first line of the game map, which holds the size of the map
        GameMapSize = Convert.ToInt32(GameMapFile.ReadLine())
        ' Creates the game map array, including tiles and active objects
        ReDim GameMap(GameMapSize)
        ReDim tiles(Width, GameMapSize)

        ' Load the game map array
        For i = 1 To GameMapSize
            GameMap(GameMapSize - i) = GameMapFile.ReadLine()
            ' The game map file ends within the FOR loop
            '   if the game map size read from the file is wrong
```

```
            If GameMap(GameMapSize - i) Is Nothing Then
                MessageBox.Show("Incorrect game map size in " & _
                    strGameMapFileName & _
                    " - Expected size: " & GameMapSize & " / Real Size: " & i, _
                    "Critical error in game map")
                LoadGameMap = False
                Exit Function
            End If
        Next
        ' Checks to see if there are more lines in the game map file
        strLine = GameMapFile.ReadLine()
        If Not (strLine Is Nothing) Then
            ' Informs the user that we missed the last line(s)
            MessageBox.Show("Incorrect game map size in " & strGameMapFileName _
                & " - One or more lines after the " & GameMapSize & _
                "th line were ignored.", "Critical error in game map")
            LoadGameMap = False
            Exit Function
        End If
        GameMapFile.Close()
    Catch
        LoadGameMap = False
        Exit Function
    End Try

    ' Load all the game map lines from the GameMap array into the Tiles array
    For i = 0 To GameMapSize - 1
        If Not LoadLine(GameMap(i)) Then
            LoadGameMap = False
            Exit Function
        End If
    Next
    ' frees the memory used by the game map
    GameMap = Nothing
End Function

Function LoadLine(strLine As String) As Boolean
    Dim x As Integer
    Dim strSpriteFileName As String
    Dim Type As ClsTile.enType
    Static LineNumber As Integer = 0
```

```
LoadLine = True
For x = 0 To Width - 1
    Select Case strLine.Chars(x)
        Case "1"
            strSpriteFileName = "borderN"
            Type = ClsTile.enType.Land
        Case "2"
            strSpriteFileName = "borderNE1"
            Type = ClsTile.enType.Land
        ... < CASES for the other borders > ...
        Case "T"
            If Rnd() * 10 < 5 Then
                strSpriteFileName = "Tree1"
            Else
                strSpriteFileName = "Tree2"
            End If
            Type = ClsTile.enType.Land
        Case "M"
            If Rnd() * 10 < 5 Then
                strSpriteFileName = "Mountain1"
            Else
                strSpriteFileName = "Mountain2"
            End If
            Type = ClsTile.enType.Land
        Case "S"
            strSpriteFileName = "Ship"
            Type = ClsTile.enType.Ship
        Case "P"
            strSpriteFileName = "EnemyPlane"
            Type = ClsTile.enType.Plane
        Case "G"
            strSpriteFileName = "Gas"
            Type = ClsTile.enType.Gas
        Case "("
            strSpriteFileName = "BridgeBorderW"
            Type = ClsTile.enType.Land
        Case ")"
            strSpriteFileName = "BridgeBorderE"
            Type = ClsTile.enType.Land
        Case "-"
            strSpriteFileName = "Road"
            Type = ClsTile.enType.Land
```

```
        Case "="
            strSpriteFileName = "Bridge"
            Type = ClsTile.enType.Bridge
        Case "." ' Green background
            ' Do nothing
            strSpriteFileName = ""
            Type = ClsTile.enType.Background
        Case "_"
            strSpriteFileName = "Water"
            Type = ClsTile.enType.Water
        Case Else
            ' Should never happen
            strSpriteFileName = "InvalidTile"
            Type = ClsTile.enType.Land
    End Select
    Try
        If Type <> ClsTile.enType.Background Then
            tiles(x, LineNumber) = New ClsTile(strSpriteFileName & ".bmp", _
                    New POINT(x, LineNumber), Type)
        Else
            tiles(x, LineNumber) = Nothing
        End If
    Catch e As Exception
        LoadLine = False
        MessageBox.Show("Unpredicted Error when loading game sprites: " & _
                e.Message, "River Pla.Net", MessageBoxButtons.OK, _
                MessageBoxIcon.Stop)
        Exit Function
    End Try
Next
' Increments the line number counter
LineNumber += 1
End Function
```

**NEW IN .NET**

*Visual Basic .NET is far stricter for automatic conversions between data types than the previous versions. To support conversions between types, each data type is treated as a class and has a set of converting methods; but we also have a* Convert *class in the* System *namespace that has many conversion methods, such as the* ToInt32 *method used in the previous code sample.*

As we can see, the LoadGameMap function simply uses the StreamReader methods to run through the text file, just checking the number of lines against the informed game map size (first line). The LoadLine function is just a big Select Case, which will set the image filename to be loaded and the tile type, which will be used to create the Tiles array elements. Each time we call the LoadLine function, we process a full line read from the file and create a new line on the array, composed of a set of 20 tiles (the width of the game field, as expressed in the next code listing). The LineNumber static variable, incremented at the end of the function, controls the number of lines already read to index the Tiles array properly.

As mentioned before, there'll be two types of mountains and trees, so we add a rnd function that will choose one image name or another, with a 50 percent chance for each. Roads, bridge borders, trees, and mountains are all defined as Land tile types, because we don't have any special treatment in code for them.

To allow us to see the map loaded, we have to code the Initialize, Render, and Draw methods, as presented in the next sections.

### Coding the Initialize Method

In the Initialize method, we'll call the LoadGameMap function and the base class Initialize method, which will initialize Direct3D.

```
Private Const GAME_MAP As String = "GameMap.txt"
Public Shadows Function Initialize(Owner As Windows.Forms.Control) _
      As Boolean
    Dim WinHandle As IntPtr = Owner.Handle
    Dim i As Integer
    Randomize()
    Initialize = True

    ' Sets the background color to green
    BackgroundColor = Color.FromArgb(255, 0, 255, 0)
    ' Sets the width and height of the game field
    Width = 20
    Height = 15

    ' Loads the game map (into GameMap array)
    If Not LoadGameMap(GAME_MAP) Then
        Initialize = False
        Exit Function
    End If

    ' If the game map was loaded without errors, start Direct3D
    If Not MyBase.Initialize(WinHandle) Then
        Initialize = False
        Exit Function
    End If
End Function
```

## Coding the Render Method

The Render function will, for now, only call the Draw method. This function will be called from the base class Run method.

```
Public Overrides Sub Render()
    Draw()
End Sub
```

## Coding the Draw Method

The Draw method will be very simple too, because all the complexity for loading textures, initializing Direct3D, and manipulating vertex buffers is in the base classes. All we need to do is call the Draw method for each member of the Tiles array, starting from the line prior to the current line (which must have a default value of 1) and going through the height of the screen plus 1, so that we'll draw only the visible tiles, with a little margin to avoid any problems.

```
Public Sub Draw()
    Dim x As Integer, y As Integer
    Dim LineCount As Integer = 0

    ' Draw the game field
    y = CurrentLineNumber - 1

    ' We will draw a line below the current line number and a line above
    '    the last line on screen (CurrentLineNumber + Height)
    Do While LineCount < Height + 2
        For x = 0 To Width - 1
            If Not (tiles(x, y) Is Nothing) Then
                tiles(x, y).Draw()
            End If
        Next
        LineCount += 1
        y += 1
    Loop
End Sub
```

The last thing we must do is code the main procedure.

We'll be following the guidelines of the pseudo-code written in the game project, and adding a splash screen (just a screen with a nondynamic image) that will close when the player presses any key, as shown in the following code:

```
Sub frmSplash_KeyDown(sender As Object, e As KeyEventArgs) Handles MyBase.KeyDown
    Me.Dispose()
End Sub
```

The intro screen is shown in Figure 4-17.

*Figure 4-17. The game splash screen*

The final code for the main program is as follows:

```
Public RiverPlanet As ClsRiverEngine

Sub main()
    Dim winGameWindow As New GameWindow()
    Dim winSplash As New frmSplash()

    winSplash.ShowDialog()

    RiverPlanet = New ClsRiverEngine()
```

```
    If Not RiverPlanet.Initialize(winGameWindow) Then
        MessageBox.Show("Error initializing the game", "Critical Error", _
            MessageBoxButtons.OK, MessageBoxIcon.Stop)
        Exit Sub
    End If
    winGameWindow.Show()
    ' The run procedure will return only when the game is over
    RiverPlanet.Run()

    ' Destroying the object calls the finalize method
    RiverPlanet = Nothing
    winGameWindow.Close()
End Sub
```

We can run our game now, and see the resulting screen, which is exactly the same as our visual prototype, shown in Figure 4-15.

In the next section we'll implement the scrolling of our game field.

## Second Draft: Scrolling

To see our game field scrolling, all we need to do is to add code to the Scroll method and call it on the Render procedure before calling the Draw method.

The new Render method will be as follows:

```
Public Overrides Sub Render()
    Scroll()
    Draw()
End Sub
```

To appropriately control the scrolling, the Scroll function must store Matrix as a static variable that will maintain the current translation to be applied to the Transform.World matrix of the objDirect3DDevice, created in the base class. To implement the translation, we must use the concept we learned in Chapter 3: Multiplying matrices has the same effect as adding the transformations of each one.

Since the base GameEngine class uses an orthogonal view of the textures, everything is automatically translated to pixel coordinates, so we can control the current line number by simply counting the number of pixels translated and, when the sum of pixels exceeds the tile size (the clsSprite.IMAGE_SIZE constant), add 1 to the current line property.

To avoid our game running at full (and unplayable) speed, we must control the frame rate using the technique we learned in Chapter 3 to control the walking man's speed: We store the system time using System.Environment.TickCount and only do the scroll processing when a given time has passed.

Taking all this into consideration, we can code a fully working scroll routine. Spend some time analyzing the following code to make sure you understand the basic concept here, which will be used later to move the player's plane.

```
Public Sub Scroll()
    Static ScrollMatrix As Matrix = Matrix.Identity
    Static LastTick As Integer
    Static PixelCount As Integer

    ' Force a Frame rate of 'GameSpeed' frames to second on maximum
    If System.Environment.TickCount - LastTick >= 1000 / gameSpeed Then
        LastTick = System.Environment.TickCount
        ' Scrolls the game field (translation on the Y axis)
        '  since the Y axis increases when going up on the screen,
        '  we use a negative transation value to make the tiles scroll down
        ScrollMatrix = _
                Matrix.Multiply(ScrollMatrix, _
                Matrix.Translation(0, -gameSpeed, 0))

        ' updates the current line number, used to control the screen drawing
        PixelCount = PixelCount + gameSpeed
        If PixelCount > clsSprite.IMAGE_SIZE Then
            CurrentLineNumber += 1
            PixelCount -= clsSprite.IMAGE_SIZE
        End If
    End If
    objDirect3DDevice.Transform.World = ScrollMatrix
End Sub
```

A set of scrolling images is shown in Figure 4-18.

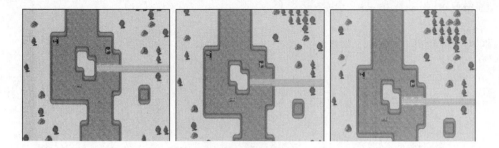

*Figure 4-18. Testing the scrolling game field*

In the next section we'll code the player's plane, including the controls for using the keyboard.

## Third Draft: Coding the Player

To add a player to our scrolling game field, we'll need to follow four steps:

1.  Code the Player class.

2.  Code the keyboard event of the game window to gather the player's input and set the appropriate values for doing the translations (moving) the player's plane.

3.  Code the MovePlayer method of the RiverEngine class.

4.  Call the MovePlayer method from within the Render procedure.

We won't code the collision detection now, but we can already include the images for dying and starting a new life in the Player class, as defined in the game project and shown in the next sample.

```
Imports Microsoft.DirectX.Direct3D

Public Class ClsPlayer
    Inherits clsSprite
    Public Status As enPlayerStatus
    Enum enPlayerStatus
        Flying = 0
        Dying = 1
        Starting = 2
        Shooting = 3
    End Enum

    Protected DyingImage As Direct3DTexture8
    Protected StartingImage As Direct3DTexture8
    Private DyingSound As ClsGameSound
    Private StartingSound As ClsGameSound

    Public Gas As Single = 100

    Sub New()
    Shadows Sub Draw()
End Class
```

The images for the player's plane are shown in Figure 4-19.

Plane.bmp        StartingPlane.bmp    DyingPlane.bmp

*Figure 4-19. Images used for the player's plane*

## Coding the New Method

In the New method, we'll have to initialize the game variables. Calling the Load method of the base class, we can load the default Image property for the Player class, and we'll have to add special code for loading the DyingImage and StartingImage properties. We can simply copy and paste the code from the previously defined Sprite class, which loads a file to a texture.

```
Sub New()
    Dim colorKey As Integer

    colorKey = Color.FromArgb(255, 255, 0, 255)
    IsTransparent = True
    X = 0 : Y = 0
    If Not Load("plane.bmp", colorKey.ToArgb) Then _
        Err.Raise(vbObjectError + 1, "clsPlayer", _
                "Could not create the player textures")
    Try
        DyingImage(i - 1) = TextureLoader.FromFile(objDirect3DDevice, _
                    Application.StartupPath & "\" & IMAGE_PATH & _
                    "\dyingPlane" & i & ".bmp", _
                    64, 64, D3DX.Default, 0, Format.Unknown, Pool.Managed, _
                    Filter.Point, Filter.Point, colorKey.ToArgb)
        StartingImage(i - 1) = TextureLoader.FromFile(objDirect3DDevice, _
                    Application.StartupPath & "\" & IMAGE_PATH & _
                    "\startingPlane" & i & ".bmp", _
                    64, 64, D3DX.Default, 0, Format.Unknown, Pool.Managed, _
                    Filter.Point, Filter.Point, colorKey.ToArgb)
    Catch
        MsgBox("Could not create the player textures", MsgBoxStyle.Critical)
    End Try
End Sub
```

In the next section we'll code the Draw method, which will enable us to see on screen the images loaded by the New method.

## Coding the Draw Method

As for the Draw method, we'll have to shadow the base property Draw, including a select Case that will choose which image must be drawn based on the current player status. This player status must be set to Dying by the game engine when a collision occurs or when the plane runs out of fuel.

We'll need to control the time for displaying the images for dying and starting a new life on screen; for this we'll employ the same technique we have used before for controlling the frame rate (getting the current clock tick and controlling the milliseconds for each image).

The next code sample shows our Draw procedure, including a Gas property that is decremented as the plane flies. If we run out of gas, the player status will be automatically set to Dying.

```
Shadows Sub Draw()
    Static LastTick As Integer = 0
        ' Turn on alpha blending only if the sprite has transparent colors
        If IsTransparent Then
            objDirect3DDevice.RenderState.AlphaBlendEnable = True
        End If


        Select Case Status
            Case enPlayerStatus.Flying
                objDirect3DDevice.SetTexture(0, SpriteImage)
                objDirect3DDevice.SetStreamSource(0, VertBuffer, 0)
                objDirect3DDevice.DrawPrimitives(PrimitiveType.TriangleStrip, 0, 2)
                ' when flying, subtracts the gas counter every half second
                If System.Environment.TickCount - LastTick >= 500 Then
                    LastTick = System.Environment.TickCount
                    Gas -= 0.5
                    ' if the tank is empty, destroy the plane
                    If Gas < 0 Then
                        Status = enPlayerStatus.Dying
                    End If
                End If
                LastTick = System.Environment.TickCount
            Case enPlayerStatus.Dying
                DyingSound.Play()
                objDirect3DDevice.SetTexture(0, DyingImage)
                objDirect3DDevice.SetStreamSource(0, VertBuffer, 0)
                objDirect3DDevice.DrawPrimitives(PrimitiveType.TriangleStrip, 0, 2)
                ' start a new life after 2 seconds
                If System.Environment.TickCount - LastTick >= 3000 Then
                    LastTick = System.Environment.TickCount
                    Status = enPlayerStatus.Starting
                End If
            Case enPlayerStatus.Starting
                objDirect3DDevice.SetTexture(0, StartingImage)
                objDirect3DDevice.SetStreamSource(0, VertBuffer, 0)
                objDirect3DDevice.DrawPrimitives(PrimitiveType.TriangleStrip, 0, 2)
                ' restore the flying status after 3 seconds
                If System.Environment.TickCount - LastTick >= 3000 Then
                    Status = enPlayerStatus.Flying
                End If
        End Select
```

```
' Turn off alpha blending  if the sprite has transparent colors
If IsTransparent Then
    objDirect3DDevice.RenderState.AlphaBlendEnable = False
End If
End Sub
```

That's all for the `Player` class. Now we want to create the player object on the `GameEngine` class, and code the `MovePlayer` method, which will move the player across the screen, as described in the next sections.

## Creating the Player Object

We'll create the player object inside the `Initialize` method of the `GameEngine` class. Since the `New` method of the `Player` class takes no parameters, all we need to do is create the object and check if this has been done correctly.

```
Player = New ClsPlayer()
If Player Is Nothing Then
    Initialize = False
    Exit Function
End If
```

In the next section we'll include the code for the `GameEngine` class that will call the `Draw` method of the `Player` class, allowing us to see the player's plane on the screen and move it.

## Coding the MovePlayer Method

Before coding the keyboard control and the `MovePlayer` procedure, let's take a step back and review the concepts for applying transformations to objects.

As we were reminded when coding the scrolling feature of the game, to perform transformations on an object defined by its vertices stored in the vertex buffer, all we need to do is set the `Transform.World` property of the device object.

But what if we want to apply different transformations to a certain object? In our specific case, we want the game field to scroll and the player's plane to move according to the keys pressed by the player.

In such a case, all we need to do is to set different world matrices for each object according to the effect we want to have. For this example, we'll loop through the following steps:

1. Set the world matrix to perform the translation to implement the scrolling.

2. Draw the tiles.

3. Set the world matrix to perform the translation, according to the keys pressed, to implement the player's movements (overwriting the previous world matrix).

4. Draw the player.

As we did in the Scroll procedure, to control the player we'll use a static Matrix to store the player's movements. Looking at the New procedure shown previously, we can see that the player coordinates were set to (0,0); and although the vertices will all stay in the position in which they were first created, we'll see the player's plane moving if we set the correct translations.

The value for the translations to be applied in each direction will be set at the KeyDown event of the game window, by simply setting the SpeedX or SpeedY properties (defined in the base class Sprite) to the current game speed using negative values where appropriate.

```
Sub GameWindow_KeyDown(sender As Object, e As KeyEventArgs) _
                                      Handles MyBase.KeyDown
    Select Case e.KeyCode
        Case Keys.Right
            RiverPlanet.Player.SpeedX = RiverPlanet.gameSpeed
        Case Keys.Left
            RiverPlanet.Player.SpeedX = -RiverPlanet.gameSpeed
        Case Keys.Up
            RiverPlanet.Player.SpeedY = RiverPlanet.gameSpeed
        Case Keys.Down
            RiverPlanet.Player.SpeedY = -RiverPlanet.gameSpeed
    End Select
End Sub
```

The MovePlayer method will follow the basic structure of the Scroll method, but it'll use the properties set for the player in the preceding code to build the translation matrix.

```
Public Sub MovePlayer()
    ' Initializes the player position in the middle of screen (x-axis)
    '    and 3 tiles up (y-axis)
    Static PlayerMatrix As MATRIX = Matrix.Translation( _
            10 * clsSprite.IMAGE_SIZE, 3 * clsSprite.IMAGE_SIZE, 0)

    If Player.Status = Player.enPlayerStatus.Flying Or _
       Player.Status = Player.enPlayerStatus.Starting Then
        ' Draw the player sprite, moving acording to the arrow keys pressed
        If Player.SpeedX <> 0 Or Player.SpeedY <> 0 Then
            PlayerMatrix = Matrix.Multiply(PlayerMatrix, _
                Matrix.Translation(Player.SpeedX, Player.SpeedY, 0))
        End If
        ' Reset the speed of the sprite to prevent the plane from moving
        '  after the player releases the arrow keys
        RiverPlanet.Player.SpeedX = 0
        RiverPlanet.Player.SpeedY = 0
    End If
    objDirect3DDevice.Transform.World = PlayerMatrix
    Player.Draw()
End Sub
```

All we need to do now is include a call to the MovePlayer method in the Render procedure, and we are ready to test our plane by moving it around the screen. By this stage, our game designer should have developed a larger game field, so we can fly around over whole new backgrounds, as shown in Figure 4-20.

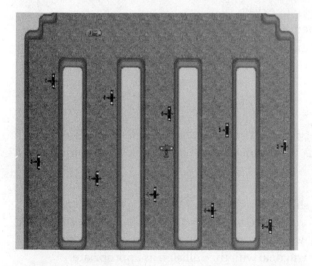

*Figure 4-20. Our plane flying over trouble waters*

If you were to test this game at this point, one thing you'd discover is that you can drive your plane off the screen. Although you can come back later, it's not a good game practice. So we'd better include some testing on our movement procedure to avoid this, just after the line in which we set the PlayerMatrix variable, inside the if command:

```
'    the m41 element represents the translation on the X axis
If PlayerMatrix.m41 < clsSprite.IMAGE_SIZE Then _
    PlayerMatrix.m41 = clsSprite.IMAGE_SIZE
If PlayerMatrix.m41 > (Width - 1) * clsSprite.IMAGE_SIZE Then _
    PlayerMatrix.m41 = (Width - 1) * clsSprite.IMAGE_SIZE

'    the m42 element represents the translation on the Y axis
If PlayerMatrix.m42 < clsSprite.IMAGE_SIZE Then _
    PlayerMatrix.m42 = clsSprite.IMAGE_SIZE
If PlayerMatrix.m42 > (Height - 1) * clsSprite.IMAGE_SIZE Then _
    PlayerMatrix.m42 = (Height - 1) * clsSprite.IMAGE_SIZE
```

We can now control the plane within the screen limits.

In next section we'll code the collision detection functions, so the first version of our game will be almost finished.

## Fourth Draft: Collision Detection

The collision detection in our game will be fairly simple: We'll use an algorithm that will provide approximate results to make the code simpler. Although it's not very accurate, it'll suffice for fair game play.

The basic idea here is to check the current player position, convert it to (x,y) coordinates of the Tiles array, and then check the tile array element we are over, to see if we are colliding. There'll be three types of collisions:

- If we are over water, we aren't colliding.

- If we are over a gas barrel, we aren't colliding, but we'll need to destroy the gas barrel tile, fill our tank with some gas, and create a new tile (with water) to replace the gas tile.

- If we are over a bridge, a ship, or a plane, we are colliding.

The TestCollision method will return a Boolean indicating if we are colliding or not, so the Render procedure will deal with the collision as appropriate.

One last point before looking at the code for this procedure: As mentioned in the previous draft, when coding the player's movements, the player vertices will always be at the original positions they were created; what we'll do is change the world matrix to see the player in different positions. So, to allow the `TestCollision` procedure to get the current player position, we'll need to update the X and Y properties of the player as he or she moves. All we need to do is to add the next lines of code to the `MovePlayer` method, just before the lines in which we set the `PlayerMatrix` transformation matrix:

```
' Updates the player location (used in collision detection)
  Player.X = PlayerMatrix.m41
  Player.Y = PlayerMatrix.m42
```

The complete code for the `TestCollision` procedure is shown in the following sample:

```
Private Function TestCollision() As Boolean
    Dim x As Integer, y As Integer
    Dim i As Integer


    x = Player.X / 32
    y = (Player.Y + 16) / 32 + CurrentLineNumber

    ' If we are over water or over a gas barrel, we are not colliding
    If Not (tiles(x, y) Is Nothing) Then
        If tiles(x, y).Type = ClsTile.enType.Water Then
            TestCollision = False
        ElseIf tiles(x, y).Type = ClsTile.enType.Gas Then
            ' Remove the gas barrel from screen
            tiles(x, y).Dispose()
            tiles(x, y) = New ClsTile("water.bmp", _
                New POINT(x, y), ClsTile.enType.Water)
            TestCollision = False
            Player.Gas = Player.Gas + 30
            If Player.Gas > 100 Then Player.Gas = 100
        Else
            ' If we collide with a ship or a plane, destroy it...
            If tiles(x, y).Type = ClsTile.enType.Plane Or _
                tiles(x, y).Type = ClsTile.enType.Ship Or _
                tiles(x, y).Type = ClsTile.enType.Bridge Then
                tiles(x, y).Dispose()
                tiles(x, y) = New ClsTile("water.bmp", _
                    New POINT(x, y), ClsTile.enType.Water)
```

```
                End If
                TestCollision = True
            End If
    Else
                TestCollision = True
    End If
End Function
```

The code for the Render procedure will have to deal with the results of the TestCollision procedure, changing the player status and removing one life from the game's Lifes property, as shown in the following code sample:

```
Public Overrides Sub Render()
    ' Scrolls the game field and moves the player
    Scroll()
    Draw()
    MovePlayer()

    ' Only tests for collision if flying
    If Player.Status = Player.enPlayerStatus.Flying Then
        ' If there's a collision, set player status to dying
        If TestCollision() Then
            Player.Status = Player.enPlayerStatus.Dying
            Lifes -= 1
            If Lifes = 0 Then
                GameOver = True
            End If
        End If
    End If
End Sub
```

We can now run the game's new version, flying more carefully because now we are flying at lower altitude, as shown in Figure 4-21.

*Figure 4-21. The plane now collides with any solid obstacles—in this case, a bridge*

## Final Version: Music and Sound Effects

Since our base sound manipulation library is coded, the task of including sounds in our application is very simple. All we need to do is to create the sound objects and call them as appropriate. Since we want to play some motifs randomly over the background music, we'll code the PlayMotifs method, as defined in the game project, to do so.

The BackgroundMusic object and the GasSound object must be created in the Initialize method of the RiverEngine class, so they'll be accessible to all other methods. As for the background music, we can start playing it right after the object creation; it'll be looping until the game end.

```
' Start the background music
BackgroundMusic = New ClsGameMusic()
BackgroundMusic.Initialize(WinHandle)
If Not BackgroundMusic.Load("boidsd.sgt") Then
    MessageBox.Show("Error loading background music", "River Pla.Net")
End If
BackgroundMusic.Play()

' Initializes the gas filling sound effect
GasSound = New ClsGameSound(Owner)
If Not GasSound.Load("FillGas.wav") Then
    MessageBox.Show("Error loading Gas sound effect", "River Pla.Net")
End If
```

As for the player game effects, we need to add the object creation to the New procedure of the Player class:

```
' Initializes the sound effects
DyingSound = New ClsGameSound(Owner)
If Not DyingSound.Load("explosion.wav") Then
    MessageBox.Show("Error loading explosion sound effect", "River Pla.Net")
End If
StartingSound = New ClsGameSound(Owner)     If Not
StartingSound.Load("init.wav") Then
    MessageBox.Show("Error loading starting sound effect", "River Pla.Net")
End If
```

Once we have created the sound objects, all we need to do is call the Play method of each object where appropriate.

- In the TestCollision procedure, when the player collides with a gas barrel, we'll play the "gas bonus" sound.

```
GasSound.Play()
```

- In the Draw method of the Player class, we'll play the "dying" sound every time the player has a status of Dying.

```
DyingSound.Play()
```

- In this same method, we'll play the "starting a new life" sound every time the player has a status of Starting.

```
StartingSound.Play()
```

This will suffice to add music and sound effects to our game. And to add that little bit extra, for subtle variations in the background music from time to time, we'll code the PlayMotifs function. This function will be called with every frame that's drawn on the Render method, so we'll include two random choices: first, choosing a random time (let's say, between 5 and 15 seconds) to wait for the next motif to play, and choosing a random motif to play, using the PlayMotif method of our GameSound class and passing an index between zero and the value of the MotifCount property, as shown in the next code sample:

```
Sub PlayMotifs()
    Dim MotifIndex As Integer
    Static LastTick As Integer
    Static Interval As Integer

    ' Plays a random motif every 5 to 15 seconds
    If System.Environment.TickCount - LastTick >= Interval Then
        LastTick = System.Environment.TickCount
        ' Gets a new random interval (in miliseconds) to play the next motif
        Interval = (Rnd() * 10 + 5) * 1000
        MotifIndex = Rnd() * BackgroundMusic.MotifCount
        BackgroundMusic.PlayMotif(MotifIndex)
    End If
End Sub
```

And that's all for this chapter. The game is up to the standard described in the game project. But there are a lot of improvements we can make, as shown in the next section and in the next game version, in Chapter 5, when we'll introduce DirectInput and joystick control.

## Adding the Final Touches

We'll code a second version of our game in the next chapter, with many improvements, but there is already some upgrading we can do right now, as shown in the next sections.

## *Including Player Animations*

A good improvement would be to include some player animations for dying and starting a new life.

Animations are only a set of images that are presented, one at a time, using specific time intervals. To define an animation, we should take into account the total time we'll have to play the animation and the number of frames we want to display.

For the total time for each animation, we can simply check the duration of each sound effect: about 1 second for the explosion sound, and about 2 seconds for the sound of starting a new life.

To create an interesting explosion animation, we'll need as many images as possible. Figure 4-22 shows a minimal set for an explosion animation.

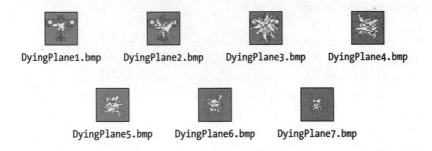

DyingPlane1.bmp    DyingPlane2.bmp    DyingPlane3.bmp    DyingPlane4.bmp

DyingPlane5.bmp    DyingPlane6.bmp    DyingPlane7.bmp

*Figure 4-22. Explosion images for dying animation*

Since we have seven images, we can calculate the desired interval between each image: about 0.15 seconds.

Figure 4-23 shows a second set of images that will be used to give the player a visual clue that the plane is invincible when starting a new life.

StartingPlane1.bmp    StartingPlane2.bmp    StartingPlane3.bmp    StartingPlane4.bmp

*Figure 4-23. Flashing planes for starting a new life animation*

In this case, we can use a different approach: Let's simply show the images from the first to the fourth, and then from the fourth down to the first, so the animation will appear to be flashing to the player.

To implement the animations, we'll need to change the Player class as follows:

- Change the DyingImage and the StartingImage properties from variables to arrays.

- Adjust the New method to dimension the arrays to the appropriated values.

- On the New method, load each of the images to the corresponding array position.

- On the Draw method, include the code for displaying the images one at a time, taking into account the specified interval between images.

The modifications of the `Player` class are shown in the following code listing:

```
Protected DyingImage() As Direct3DTexture8
Protected StartingImage() As Direct3DTexture8
Sub New()
    ReDim DyingImage(7)
    ReDim StartingImage(4)
    Dim colorKey As Integer
    Dim i As Integer

    colorKey = Color.fromARGB(255, 255, 0, 255)
    . . .
    Try
        For i = 1 To 7
            DyingImage(i - 1) = TextureLoader.FromFile(objDirect3DDevice, _
                        Application.StartupPath & "\" & IMAGE_PATH & _
                        "\dyingPlane" & i & ".bmp", _
                        64, 64, D3DX.Default, 0, Format.Unknown, Pool.Managed, _
                        Filter.Point, Filter.Point, colorKey.ToArgb)
        Next
        For i = 1 To 4
            StartingImage(i - 1) = TextureLoader.FromFile(objDirect3DDevice, _
                         Application.StartupPath & "\" & IMAGE_PATH & _
                         "\startingPlane" & i & ".bmp", _
                         64, 64, D3DX.Default, 0, Format.Unknown, Pool.Managed, _
                         Filter.Point, Filter.Point, colorKey.ToArgb)
        Next
    Catch
        MsgBox("Could not create the player textures", MsgBoxStyle.Critical)
    End Try
    . . .
End Sub

Shadows Sub Draw()
    Static CountAnim As Integer = 0
    Static LastTick As Integer = 0
    Static IncAnim As Integer = 1
    . . .
    Select Case Status
        Case enPlayerStatus.Flying
            . . .
        Case enPlayerStatus.Dying
            If CountAnim = 0 Then
                DyingSound.Play()
```

```
                    End If
                    ' Each frame will be shown for .15 seconds,
                    '   the 7 frames of the explosion in about 1 second
                    If System.Environment.TickCount - LastTick >= 150 Then
                        LastTick = System.Environment.TickCount
                        CountAnim += 1
                    End If
                    objDirect3DDevice.SetTexture(0, DyingImage( _
                            IIf(CountAnim - 1 < 0, 0, CountAnim - 1)))
                    objDirect3DDevice.SetStreamSource(0, VertBuffer, 0)
                    objDirect3DDevice.DrawPrimitives(PrimitiveType.TriangleStrip, 0, 2)
                    ' The dying animation is 7 frames long
                    If CountAnim = 6 Then
                        CountAnim = 0
                        Status = enPlayerStatus.Starting
                    End If
                Case enPlayerStatus.Starting
                    If CountAnim = 0 Then
                        StartingSound.Play()
                    End If
                    objDirect3DDevice.SetTexture(0, StartingImage(CountAnim))
                    objDirect3DDevice.SetStreamSource(0, VertBuffer, 0)
                    objDirect3DDevice.DrawPrimitives(PrimitiveType.TriangleStrip, 0, 2)
                    ' The starting animation is 4 frames long,
                    '    and must run in a reverse loop
                    If CountAnim = 3 Then IncAnim = -1
                    If CountAnim = 0 Then IncAnim = 1

                    ' Each frame will show a different frame of the animation
                    CountAnim += IncAnim

                    ' restore the flying status after 4 seconds
                    If System.Environment.TickCount - LastTick >= 4000 Then
                        CountAnim = 0
                        Status = enPlayerStatus.Flying
                        ' We have a new plane, fill the tank!
                        Gas = 100
                    End If
            End Select
        . . .
    End Sub
```

## Implementing a Neverending Game Map

So we managed to define a map with several hundreds of tiles. And what happens when the user reaches the end of the game map?

Since we'll have no ending screen, we can use a little trick to make our game field infinite in length.

Adding some code to reset the scroll translation matrix to the beginning of the game map when we reach the end will make the player loop forever on our game. To allow a smooth transition, we can copy the first 15 lines of the game to the end of the game map, so when we return to the beginning the player won't notice a difference.

We can add an extra degree of playability to our game by including the concept of different phases: Every time the player reaches the end of the map, we can increase the game speed, so that even though he or she starts the same game field, the game increases in difficulty.

To do this we'll need to change the code for the Scroll method, including a new test within the if command that increments the current line number counter, to reset the scroll matrix and increase the game speed (using a new constant, gameSpeedIncrease), as shown in the next code lines:

```
Private gameSpeedIncrease As Single = 1.3
. . .
' If we ended our game map, start it all over again, but with increasing speed
If CurrentLineNumber + Height = GameMapSize Then
    gameSpeed = gameSpeedIncrease * gameSpeed
    ' The maximum gameSpeed will be the size of a tile per frame
    If gameSpeed > 32 Then gameSpeed = clsSprite.IMAGE_SIZE
    ScrollMatrix = Matrix.Identity
    CurrentLineNumber = 0
End If
```

In the next chapter we'll see some more improvements when we code the second version of River Pla.Net.

## Improving the Performance

Taking our sample game as an example, we can see that we are spending a lot of time drawing each tile by itself. Looking at the Draw method of the Tile class, we can see that for every tile we are calling three functions:

```
objDirect3DDevice.SetTexture(0, SpriteImage)
objDirect3DDevice.SetStreamSource(0, VertBuffer, 0)
objDirect3DDevice.DrawPrimitives(PrimitiveType.TriangleStrip, 0, 2)
```

In commercial games we'll usually want a higher frame rate, so we need to set aside the simplicity and use higher performance algorithms.

A simple way to speed up the game is to group equal tiles together, in a big vertex buffer, so we could call these three functions only once for each texture. Since the DrawPrimitives function can receive the first vertex to draw and the number of primitives (triangle strips, in our case), all we need do is store a vertex number in the Tile class, so we can pick the first tile and the last tile of each type on screen and calculate the values for the DrawPrimitives function.

Since our main goal here is to introduce the gaming concepts, we didn't spend time on optimizations; in the next chapter we'll include extra features in our game, such as joystick control, but the game engine will remain basically the same.

## Summary

In this chapter, we managed to use the Direct3D concepts discussed in the previous chapter to create an interesting new game, River Pla.Net. Among the many new points learned are the following:

- An introduction to DirectAudio library, including the basic concepts about music and sound reproduction through the DirectSound and DirectMusic interfaces.

- The creation of a new game library, including two graphic classes (Sprite and GameEngine) and two audio classes (GameSound and GameMusic).

- How to employ some advanced object-oriented concepts in programming, like the use of overrideable functions.

- The introduction of two new game concepts, tile-based game fields and scrolling games, and a practical example of their use.

In the next chapter, we'll include some enhancements in our game, introducing two new concepts indispensable in every game: input device control with DirectInput, including the use of force feedback in joysticks, and the practice of writing text on the device context screen used by Direct3D.

# CHAPTER 5

# River Pla.Net II: DirectInput and Writing Text to Screen

IN THIS CHAPTER, we'll improve the Activision River Raid clone, River Pla.Net, by including some extra features, such as proper input device controls and force-feedback joystick control (see Figure 5-1).

The implementation of appropriate handling for input devices is crucial to guarantee a smooth, playable game and to get the user's attention. In this chapter, we'll examine the DirectInput set of components, which deals with collecting player input from various devices and returning feedback when the peripherals have a purpose for this.

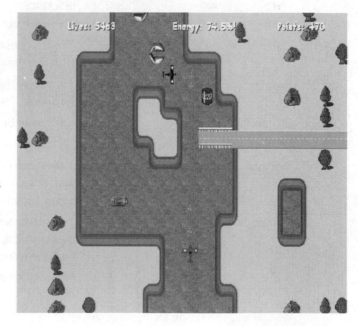

Figure 5-1. River Pla.Net II, this chapter's sample game

We'll also extend the use of matrices for moving objects, as we saw in the last chapter, to implement moving enemies and bullets.

Another new technique we'll discuss in this chapter is how to write text directly to a given position of our device.

We'll apply all the concepts explained in the next sections in the second version of our game.

# The GameFont Class

Writing text on screen isn't difficult, but we can make it even simpler by creating a specific class to handle text output to the current device.

Since we'll have to access the device object created in the GameEngine class, we should derive our new GameFont class from it, so the device object will always be encapsulated and hidden from our eyes when we are creating new games.

The GameFont class will be very simple, with only five properties and two methods, as shown in Table 5-1.

*Table 5-1. The GameFont Class Members*

| TYPE | NAME | DESCRIPTION |
|---|---|---|
| Property | Font | The D3DFont object used for writing on screen. |
| Property | Location | The (x,y) point from the top-left position from which to draw the font. |
| Properties | BoxWidth and BoxHeight | The size of the box that will contain the text to be drawn. |
| Property | Text | The text to be drawn. |
| Property | Color | The color used for the text. |
| Method | New | The class constructor, which will receive the text, position on screen, and font characteristics. |
| Method | Draw | As with the New method, creating some overloaded functions with different parameters will give us the flexibility necessary to cover each game's needs. |

Here is the code for the class interface:

```
Public Class ClsGameFont
    Inherits clsGameEngine

    Public D3DFont As Font
    Private BoxWidth As Integer, BoxHeight As Integer
    Public Location As Point
    Public Text As String
    ' Default color: Yellow color
    Public Color As Integer = Color.FromARGB(255, 255, 255, 0)
```

```
    Sub New(strName As String, intSize As Integer, _
            strText As String,  startPosition As Point)
    Public Sub Draw()
End Class
```

The DirectX Font data type, used to define the D3DFont object, has the usual parameters we would expect for font objects: size, font name, style (italic, bold, etc.), and others. To create this object, we'll use a regular system Font object, setting its properties and then passing the handle of such an object to the creator of the DirectX Font.

Once created, we'll use three simple methods of the Font object to draw the font:

- **Begin**: Informs the device that we are going to write something on screen

- **Draw**: Receives the text to be drawn, the text color, the containing box, and the text alignment to be used, and does the writing

- **End**: Informs the device we have finished writing

We need to use a block with these three commands for every piece of text we want to write at a minimum, since we can effectively have many Draw calls between Begin and End. These commands will be encapsulated inside the Draw method of our GameFont class.

In the next sections we'll see the code for the GameFont's New and Draw methods.

## Coding the New Method

The New method is very straightforward; we simply create the Font object according to the parameters received, create the DirectX Font, and set some of the class properties.

```
    Sub New(strName As String, intSize As Integer, _
            strText As String, startPosition As Point)
        Dim SystemFont As System.Drawing.Font
        SystemFont = New System.Drawing.Font(strName, intSize, _
                    FontStyle.Bold, GraphicsUnit.Pixel)
        ' Creates the Font object
        D3DFont = D3DX.CreateFont(objDirect3DDevice, SystemFont)
```

```
        ' Sets the class properties
        ' Usually the width of a char is less than the height so using the height
        '  will provide us with a reasonable approach
        BoxWidth = SystemFont.Height * strText.Length
        BoxHeight = SystemFont.Height
        Location = startPosition
        Text = strText
        SystemFont.Dispose()
    End Sub
```

In the next section, we'll look at the Draw method implementation.

## Coding the Draw Method

The Draw method, as we expect, will draw specific text, using the chosen font, on the screen.

We can think of a dozen possible overloads for the Draw method, receiving one or more of the following parameters: the text color, the text position, any of the font style properties, etc. However, we're going to create only three overloads: one with no parameters (which will use the default values when creating the font), one that will receive the text to be drawn, and one that will receive the text and position on screen. If we think other overloads will be useful in future games, we can add these one at a time, as they are needed.

The next code listing presents these three overloads:

```
Public Sub Draw()
    D3DFont.Begin()
        D3DFont.DrawText(Text, New Rectangle(Location.X, _
            Location.Y, BoxHeight, BoxWidth), 0, Color)
    D3DFont.End()
End Sub

Public Sub Draw( Text As String)
    D3DFont.Begin()
        D3DFont.DrawText(Text, New Rectangle (Location.X, _
            Location.Y, BoxHeight, BoxWidth), 0, Color)
    D3DFont.End()
End Sub
```

```
Public Sub Draw( Text As String,  Location As POINT)
    D3DFont.Begin()
        D3DFont.DrawText(Text, New Rectangle (Location.X, _
            Location.Y, BoxHeight, BoxWidth), 0, Color)
    D3DFont.End()
End Sub
```

In the next sections we'll discuss the classes employed for gathering user input through the keyboard, mouse, or joystick.

## The Game Input Classes

DirectX provides a specific set of objects to handle input from the various input devices. These objects are flexible enough to allow the game to use any advanced game device. This set of objects is called *DirectInput*.

DirectInput basically deals with three different input devices: keyboard, mouse, and joystick—everything that is neither a mouse nor a keyboard (for example, game pads and steering wheels) is grouped into this last type.

---

 **NOTE**  *It makes sense that DirectInput is used for controlling joysticks, but why use it as the handler for the mouse and keyboard, instead of using the default windows handler? There are two main reasons for this: speed and control. DirectInput gives much greater control over the data gathered from the device, so you can include in your program exactly what you want to; and as for the speed, maybe a simple example may clarify this point: If you use DirectInput to gather input from the keyboard, a simple "Hello" entered by the user would appear as "HHHHHHHHHHHeeeeeeeeeeellllllllllloooooooooooo". Got it?*

---

Although we can include the device state polling in the main game loop, this isn't a good practice, since we want a loop that will result in a very tight device state, and is as independent from the other game routines as possible.

To accomplish this goal, we'll use a different thread to pool the devices, creating one extra thread for each device type. We present the threads concept in the next section.

## Threading Basic Concepts

We won't go into great detail about threads here, since we'll see them in a future chapter, but you have to know enough about them to understand the code in this section.

**NEW IN .NET**

*With .NET, Visual Basic finally has true multithreading. A thread can be thought of as a unit of execution inside our program (or process). We usually have only one thread per program, which means that we'll have only one code sequence (defined by an instruction pointer of the operating system) being executed at any one time. Creating additional threads, we can have two or more instruction pointers for our program, which means parallel execution of different code sequences.*

To create a thread, all we need to do is create an object of the Thread class, which receives a function address as the constructor parameter, and call its Start method to begin thread execution, as shown in the following lines of code:

```
Dim NewThread as Thread
   NewThread = New Thread(AddressOf Me.MyFirstThread)
   InputThread.Start()
. . .
Sub MyFirstThread ()
   ' Do something
End Sub
```

When dealing with threads, we can encounter some problems, usually called *race conditions*, when two threads of the same process try to update the same variable or structure. This can lead to corruption of structures and losing values of variables.

To avoid this, we must use the Synclock method, which forces a given block of code to be thread safe. This prevents two threads from executing the same block at the same time.

In the next section, we'll see how we can use threads with DirectInput to gather user data.

## DirectInput Basics

Getting back to DirectInput, the basic routine to initialize and get data from input devices is very simple, and can be expressed in the following steps:

1. Initialize DirectInput.

2. Create the input device object, according to the input device desired.

3. Set the data format to be read from the device object.

4. Set the cooperative level for the device (how our application will interact with other applications, in regard to the input device).

5. Enter a loop (in an extra thread) that will check if the application can access the input device and get the data from it.

Most of the code is the same for any device, but since the data structures are very unique, let's create three classes for handling the input: Mouse, Keyboard, and Joystick.

In order to provide a higher-level interface for the game engine, we'll create specific events for each class, which will translate the input device data into more meaningful information, as stated here:

- Keyboard class: Keypress event

- Mouse class: MouseMove, MouseUp, and MouseDown events

- Joystick class: JoystickMove and JoystickButtonPressed events

In the following sections, we'll discuss the details of each input class and the corresponding code.

## Defining the Input Classes

All the classes we'll define to encapsulate the features of DirectInput will have similar structures: Each of them must have two properties to store the InputObject, a reference to the input device, and a method that runs in a separated thread and is used to pool the device.

The InputObject is a reference to the main DirectInput object, which allows us to perform generic DirectInput operations, such as creating a reference to the input device in order to control and get information about a specific device.

Since a thread is also an object, each of the classes must also have another property to store a Thread object and events to send the data gathered from the device to the main application.

In Figure 5-2, we can see the class interfaces for all the input classes. Let's take the Mouse class as an example to illustrate the flow of a typical program that uses DirectInput.

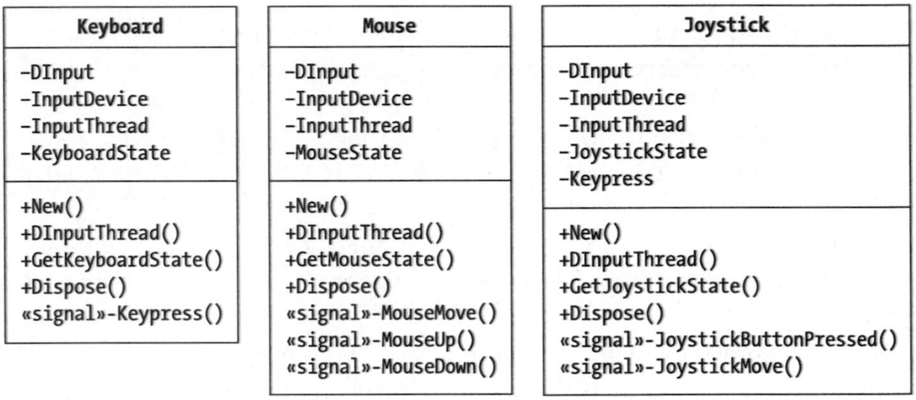

| Keyboard |
| --- |
| -DInput<br>-InputDevice<br>-InputThread<br>-KeyboardState |
| +New()<br>+DInputThread()<br>+GetKeyboardState()<br>+Dispose()<br>«signal»-Keypress() |

| Mouse |
| --- |
| -DInput<br>-InputDevice<br>-InputThread<br>-MouseState |
| +New()<br>+DInputThread()<br>+GetMouseState()<br>+Dispose()<br>«signal»-MouseMove()<br>«signal»-MouseUp()<br>«signal»-MouseDown() |

| Joystick |
| --- |
| -DInput<br>-InputDevice<br>-InputThread<br>-JoystickState<br>-Keypress |
| +New()<br>+DInputThread()<br>+GetJoystickState()<br>+Dispose()<br>«signal»-JoystickButtonPressed()<br>«signal»-JoystickMove() |

*Figure 5-2. The input classes*

When the program creates a new Mouse object, the New method will get a reference to the mouse device and create a new thread that will run the DInputThread method. The reference to this thread is stored in the InputThread variable.

The `DInputThread` method will have a never-ending loop that keeps polling the device for data, and every time it gathers some data from the device, it'll call the `GetMouseState` method. This last method will then analyze the data gathered from the mouse and generate the proper event for the application.

The `Dispose` method will simply free all used resources.

This same steps will be followed by each class that manages a device, in an analogous way. The class interfaces for the input classes are shown in the diagram in Figure 5-2.

As you see, most of the properties and methods of the input classes are the same, regardless of the device type. All classes will have a reference to `InputObject` and to a device, and all classes will rely on looping inside a thread to pool the device.

Table 5-2 lists the properties and methods that are common for every input device, so if we understand how these properties and methods work together, we'll understand all input devices. If you have any doubts about this topic, go back and review the mouse example earlier in this section.

*Table 5-2. Members of the Common Game Input Classes*

| TYPE | NAME | DESCRIPTION |
| --- | --- | --- |
| Property | InputDevice | Reference to the input device that will be used to perform operations over the device and to gather data. |
| Property | InputThread | Thread object that will have the loop used to pool the input device. |
| Method | New | Method that will initialize the basic objects and start the polling thread. |
| Method | DInputThread | Method with the loop for gathering data from the input device. |
| Method | Dispose | Finalizer that will destroy appropriately the objects created in the New method. |

Each of the input device control classes will have extra members, according to the type of the device being read. For example, the `Mouse` class will have events to inform the application about mouse movements and button clicks, whereas the `Keyboard` class will only generate events when keys are pressed.

The Keyboard class will have the extra elements shown in Table 5-3.

*Table 5-3. Members of the Keyboard Class*

| TYPE | NAME | DESCRIPTION |
| --- | --- | --- |
| Property | KeyboardState | KeyboardState structure that will be filled by calling the GetCurrentKeyboardState method of the InputDevice object |
| Event | Keypress | Event generated by the class to inform the game engine of the code of the keys pressed |
| Method | GetKeyboardState | Method that will translate the code from the KeyboardState array into values of the System.Windows.Forms.Keys enumeration and generate the Keypress event |

The Mouse class will also have some extra elements, which are described in Table 5-4.

*Table 5-4. Members of the Mouse Class*

| TYPE | NAME | DESCRIPTION |
| --- | --- | --- |
| Property | MouseState | MouseState structure that will be filled by calling the CurrentMouseState method of the InputDevice object. This structure holds data from three mouse buttons and a three-coordinate system in which the z axis is usually associated with the mouse wheel. |
| Event | MouseMove | Event generated by the class to inform the game engine about mouse movements. |
| Events | MouseDown and MouseUp | Events generated by the class to inform the game engine when a given button is pressed and when it's released. |
| Method | GetMouseState | Method that will translate the code from the MouseState structure and generate the mouse events. |

The Joystick class will have the extra members listed in Table 5-5.

*Table 5-5. Members of the Joystick Class*

| TYPE | NAME | DESCRIPTION |
|---|---|---|
| Property | JoystickState | JoyState structure that will be filled by calling the CurrentJoyState method of the InputDevice object. This structure holds up to 31 buttons, point-of-view (POV) coordinates, three axes for rotation, three axes for the three-coordinate system, and two extra axes as a slider object, whose semantics will depend on the input device type. In our Joystick class, let's reduce our scope to the buttons and the x and y coordinates. |
| Event | JoystickMove | Event generated by the class to inform the game engine about joystick movements. |
| Event | JoystickButtonPressed | Events generated by the class to inform the game engine when a given button is pressed. |
| Method | GetJoystickState | Method that will translate the code from the JoystickState structure and generate the joystick events. |

Next, we'll code the input classes for each device type.

## Creating the Mouse and Keyboard Initialization Code

The Keyboard class interface is shown in the next code listing; the interface for the mouse devices is very similar, with a few differences discussed later.

```
Imports Microsoft.DirectX.DirectInput
Imports Microsoft.DirectX
Imports System.Threading

Public Class ClsKeyboard
    Inherits clsGameEngine
    ' General use properties and enumerations
    Private InputDevice As Device = Nothing
    Private InputThread As Thread = Nothing
```

```
    ' Keyboard properties and events
    Public Shared keyboardState As keyboardState
    Public Event Keypress(Keycode As Keys)

    Public Sub New(Parent As Window.Control.Forms)
    Public Sub DInputThread()
    Public Sub GetKeyboardState()
    Public Sub Dispose() Implements System.IDisposable.Dispose
End Class
```

The New method will follow the same basic structure for every device, as shown in the next code snippet:

```
Public Sub New(ByVal Parent As Window.Control.Forms)
    ' Create the device and set the data format
    Try  'Ignore errors for now
        InputDevice = New Device(SystemGuid.Keyboard)
        InputDevice.SetDataFormat(DeviceDataFormat.Keyboard)
        ' Set the cooperative level for the device.
        InputDevice.SetCooperativeLevel(Parent, _
            CooperativeLevelFlags.Exclusive Or _
            CooperativeLevelFlags.Foreground)
    Catch
    End Try

    ' Create the thread that the app will use
    ' to get state information from the device.
    InputThread = New Thread(AddressOf Me.DInputThread)
    ' Name it something so we can see in the output
    ' window when it has exited.
    InputThread.Name = "DInputThread"
    InputThread.Start()
End Sub
```

The direct input methods used in the previous code deserve additional explanation.

The first method is the DirectInput object constructor, which receives a handle from the current application instance and creates the higher level object for input handling.

The Device's New method creates a new DirectInput Device object, according to the identifier received. There are two identifier constants for the keyboard (SystemGuid.Keyboard) and the mouse (SystemGuid.Mouse), which will define the device type we'll be gathering data from. For the joystick, we'll have code that is a little more complex, and it will be shown in the next section.

The next method, SetDataFormat, simply informs the newly created Input-Device object what the expected data format to be read from the input device is, according to the DeviceDataFormat enumeration. The possible values are Joystick, Keyboard, and Mouse. The joystick and mouse have alternative structures with extra attributes, used if our input device has features in addition to those supported by the basic structures. For example, there are three more members with regard to the joystick data formats: Joystick2, frameJoystick, and frameJoystick2; refer to the SDK documentation to see what the provided data structure is for each member of the enumeration.

The last DirectInput function seen in the New method is the SetCooperativeLevel, which determines how the instance of the device will interact with other instances created by our application and by other applications. This method receives as parameters the window handle to which the device is attached and a combination of CooperativeLevelFlags enumeration members, which can be any of the following:

- **Background**: Our application can gather data from the input device at any time, even if the application window is in the background (it's not the active window).

- **Foreground**: Our application will only gather data from the input device when it's in the foreground (when it's the system active window).

- **Exclusive**: The application requires exclusive access to the input device; that means other applications can't require this type of access (they receive an error if they try to), but other applications can require nonexclusive use. If our application uses the exclusive mode, the menus and window buttons won't work.

- **NonExclusive**: The application requires nonexclusive access to the input device.

- **NoWinKey**: This disables the use of the Microsoft Windows logo key. When in exclusive mode, this key is disabled by default.

We'll use a combination of the Foreground plus the Exclusive enumeration members for all devices. This works pretty well for full-screen applications, and the mouse cursor isn't shown, so we can draw our own mouse pointers.

The last three lines of the New procedure deal with the creation of the new thread (associating it with the DInputThread function), giving a name to this thread (only meaningful for debugging), and starting the new thread.

When we call the Start method, the function specified in the Thread constructor is called once. If we need a one-time action, like playing a sound, this is okay. But to implement polling, we'll code this function with a loop that will keep the thread running until the game is over. Since our class is derived from the GameEngine class, we can control such a loop with the shared property GameOver. The thread function is discussed in the section "Polling the Devices."

## Creating the Joystick Initialization Code

Coding for joystick devices is far more complex than for keyboards and mice, since we'll have a large variety of devices that will be handled as joysticks. A drawback to this flexibility is more complex initialization and data-processing routines.

To initialize the joystick, we'll need to discover the specific GUID to be passed to the Device function, which will vary depending on the devices attached to the computer. To recover this GUID, we'll need to call the GetDevices method on a for-each loop, which will run once for each attached joystick device, and then get the specific GUID for the current joystick.

The following code shows the New method for the Joystick class, which is analogous to the ones used for the mouse and keyboard, except for calling GetDevices and setting specific joystick properties, as discussed later.

```
Public Sub New(ByVal Parent As Window.Control.Forms)
    Try 'Ignore errors for now
        For Each DevInstance In Manager.GetDevices(DeviceType.Joystick, _
                EnumDevicesFlags.ForceFeeback Or EnumDevicesFlags.AttachedOnly)
            ' Simply pick the first joystick available
            InputDeviceInstance = DevInstance
        Next
        InputDevice = New Device(InputDeviceInstance.InstanceGuid)

        InputDevice.SetDataFormat(DeviceDataFormat.Joystick)
        ' Set the cooperative level for the device.
        InputDevice.SetCooperativeLevel(Parent,_
                CooperativeLevelFlags.Exclusive Or _
                CooperativeLevelFlags.Foreground)
        ' ----- Set the joystick properties
        ' Set the DeadZone for each axis
        InputDevice.Properties.SetDeadZone(ParameterHow.ByOffset, _
```

```
            JoystickOffset.X, 1000)
        InputDevice.Properties.SetDeadZone(ParameterHow.ByOffset, _
            JoystickOffset.Y, 1000)
        ' Set the Joystick range
        Dim Axis As DeviceObjectInstance
        For Each Axis In InputDevice.Objects
            If (Axis.ObjectId And CInt(DeviceObjectTypeFlags.Axis)) <> 0 Then
                ' Set the range for the axis.
                InputDevice.Properties.SetRange(ParameterHow.ById, _
                    Axis.ObjectId, New InputRange(0, +10000))
            End If
        Next
    Catch
    End Try

    ' Create the thread that the app will use
    ' to get state information from the device.
    InputThread = New Thread(AddressOf Me.DInputThread)
    ' Name it something so we can see in the output
    ' window when it has exited.
    InputThread.Name = "DInputThread"
    InputThread.Start()
End Sub
```

In the previous code listing, we are using the Properties object of the input device to set specific properties associated to joysticks. This object can be used to cover a wide range of properties and have many specific methods, each one corresponding to a specific joystick characteristic or property.

In our sample code, we are setting two properties: one defining the range to be used by the joystick, and one defining the so-called dead zone.

By setting the joystick range from 0 to 10,000, we are saying that the centered joystick will have the values (0,0) for the (x,y) coordinate pair, and when the joystick is totally pulled to one direction, this direction will have the value 10,000.

The dead zone setting informs DirectInput about the responsiveness we want for our joystick. Setting the dead zone for 1000 in each axis, as we did in our sample, will result in our game only being informed of a joystick movement if it's 1/10 or greater than the total distance from the center to the movement limit. If we didn't set a dead zone, our game may become unplayable, since the slightest movement of the joystick would be significant in the game.

In the next section we see how to code the thread function, which will be used for polling the devices.

## Polling the Devices

As we saw earlier in the section "Defining the Input Classes," the initialization code for each device must start a new thread, which will be responsible for gathering data from the device in a continuous loop.

On the polling loop, shown later in this section, we'll go through the following steps:

1. Poll the device to check if we have access to it (using the Poll method of the InputDevice object).

2. If we don't have access, try to acquire it (using the Acquire method of the InputDevice object).

3. If we can't acquire the device, we simply don't try to gather any data. This isn't necessarily an error: Since we specified we need Foreground access, if our window isn't the active one, we won't be able to acquire the device.

4. If we do acquire the device, get data from the device using the Current<*device*>State set of methods of the InputDevice object (GetCurrentKeyboardState, CurrentMouseState, and CurrentJoyState), which returns as a parameter the data in the format specified by the SetDataFormat function, used in the New method.

5. Call the specific method for each device that will generate the events (as stated in the class diagram, GetKeyboardState, GetMouseState, and GetJoystickState).

The data formats for each device type will be defined as follows:

```
Public Shared KeyboardState As KeyboardState
Public Shared MouseState As MOUSESTATE
Public Shared JoystickState As JOYSTATE
```

We'll see some of the attributes of these structures in the functions that process the input device data to generate the class events.

The remainder of the code, shown here, is just thread synchronization and error trapping, to make the method less error prone. The following code listing shows the polling thread for the keyboard:

```vb
Public Sub DInputThread()
    Dim CanReadDevice As Boolean = False

    ' Make sure there is a valid device.
    If (Not InputDevice Is Nothing) Then
        While (Not GameOver)
            Try
                ' check if we can get the device state.
                InputDevice.Poll()
            Catch ex As InputException
                ' Check to see if either the app needs to acquire the device, or
                ' if the app lost the input device to another process.
                If TypeOf ex Is NotAcquiredException Or _
                    TypeOf ex Is InputLostException Then
                    Try
                        ' Acquire the device.
                        InputDevice.Acquire()
                        CanReadDevice = True
                    Catch ex2 As InputException
                        If TypeOf ex Is OtherApplicationHasPriorityException Then
                            Throw New Exception("Unknown error occcurred. " & _
                                "This app won't be able to process device info.")
                        End If
                        ' Failed to aquire the device. This can happen when
                        ' the app doesn't have focus.
                        CanReadDevice = False
                    End Try
                End If
            End Try
            If (CanReadDevice = True) Then
                ' Lock the class so it can't overwrite
                ' the input device State structure during a race condition.
                SyncLock (Me)
                    ' Get the state of the device
                    Try
                        InputDevice.GetCurrentKeyboardState
                        ' Call the function in the other thread
                        ' that generates keyboard events.
                        Me.GetKeyboardState()
                        ' Catch any exceptions. None will be handled here,
                        ' any device re-aquisition will be handled above.
                    Catch ex As InputException
                    End Try
```

```
            End SyncLock
        End If
    End While
  End If
End Sub
```

The methods that will process the data acquired with Current<*device*>State are unique, because they will be totally related to the data structures read; we'll see every method in detail in the coming sections.

The last common method for our input device classes is Dispose, shown here, which will release the resources used and free the objects created in the class:

```
Public Sub Dispose() Implements System.IDisposable.Dispose
    ' Unacquire and destroy all Dinput objects.
    InputDevice.Unacquire()
    InputDevice.Dispose()
End Sub
```

We'll see now the specific details about processing the data gathered from each input device, starting with the keyboard, in the next section.

## Processing the Keyboard Input

In the GetKeyBoardState method, we'll have to translate the KeyboardState byte array into keycodes from the Keys enumeration. When a key is pressed, its corresponding array element returns with the seventh bit (128, or 80 in hexadecimal notation) set; so all we have to do is to loop through all elements in the array and check the bits of each element. Since the array position has no relation at all with the ASCII values or any other character table (they just start with 1 for the Esc key, and go on sequentially left to right and then up to down), we'll have to create a Select Case command to translate it into keycodes, as shown in the subsequent code:

```
Public Sub GetKeyboardState()
    Dim i As Integer = 0
    Dim keyCode As System.Windows.Forms.Keys

    SyncLock (Me)
        ' Get the keys pressed from the keyboard
        For i = 0 To keyboardState.Length - 1
            If (keyboardState(i) And &H80) <> 0 Then
                Select Case i
                    Case 208
                        keyCode = Keys.Down
                    Case 203
                        keyCode = Keys.Left
                    Case 205
                        keyCode = Keys.Right
                    Case 200
                        keyCode = Keys.Up
                    Case 57
                        keyCode = Keys.Space
                    Case 128
                        keyCode = Keys.Escape
                End Select
                RaiseEvent Keypress(keyCode)
            End If
        Next
    End SyncLock
End Sub
```

To know the exact code for each key, we'll have to do some tests. For example, we can include an else clause in the select case statement shown previously and include a message box that displays the value of i.

**NOTE** *Of course, we don't have to loop through the entire array if all we want to check is six keys, as shown in the previous listing; we can test only the elements we need, ignoring any other keys.*

Note that if we are capturing the keyboard, our window won't respond to any commands, including Alt-F4 to close, so we'd better include an escape sequence for users to cancel the game if they want to. Let's use the letter "Q" and inform the user of this exit key on the opening screen, as shown in the next code snippet and in Figure 5-3.

```
Public Sub GetKeyboardState()
      Dim i As Integer = 0
      Dim keyCode As System.Windows.Forms.Keys

      SyncLock (Me)
            ' Get the keys pressed from the keyboard
            If (KeyboardState(208) And &H80) <> 0 Then
                keyCode = Keys.Down
            ElseIf (KeyboardState(203) And &H80) <> 0 Then
                keyCode = Keys.Left
            ElseIf (KeyboardState(205) And &H80) <> 0 Then
                keyCode = Keys.Right
            ElseIf (KeyboardState(200) And &H80) <> 0 Then
                keyCode = Keys.Up
            ElseIf (KeyboardState(57) And &H80) <> 0 Then
                keyCode = Keys.Space
            ElseIf (KeyboardState(1) And &H80) <> 0 Then
                keyCode = Keys.Escape
            ElseIf (KeyboardState(16) And &H80) <> 0 Then
                keyCode = Keys.Q
            End If
            RaiseEvent Keypress(keyCode)
      End SyncLock
End Sub
```

*Figure 5-3. The game intro screen must notify the user of the keys used in the game.*

Next, we'll see the mouse handling routine.

## Processing the Mouse input

The GetMouseState method will read the MouseState structure and convert its information into workable events. This structure is very simple, with an array that returns the state of three mouse buttons, and three attributes returning the coordinates of the mouse on each of the 3-D axes.

Since the structure returned just has the current information, we'll have to store the last state of each button so we can instigate the MouseDown and MouseUp events only once, when the button state changes.

As for the MouseMove event, it must be generated by every mouse movement. We need to be careful to check if the axis attributes have real values (sometimes they can be zeroed). Since the mouse coordinates will be closely related to the screen resolution, we must check the GameEngine class for the screen resolution, and only generate a mouse movement event within the current resolution. We'll have to calculate the mouse position on screen based on the mouse data read from the device, as shown in the next code listing, because the device only returns the variation in each axis from the previous position, and not an absolute position.

Here is the final code for this method:

```
Public Sub GetMouseState()
    Dim buttons() As Byte = MouseState.GetMouseButtons()
    Static LastButtonState(3) As Integer
    ' Lock the UI class so it can't overwrite
    ' the MouseState structure during a race condition.
    SyncLock (Me)
    ' Update the mouse position if the mouse moved
        If (0 <> (MouseState.X Or MouseState.Y)) Then
            X += MouseState.X : Y += MouseState.Y
            If X < 0 Then X = 0
            If Y < 0 Then Y = 0
            If X > clsGameEngine.Width Then X = clsGameEngine.Width
            If Y > clsGameEngine.Height Then Y = clsGameEngine.Height
            RaiseEvent MouseMove(X, Y)
        End If


' Generates the events according to the button pressed
' Button 0 = Right button
        If (Buttons(0) <> LastButtonState(0)) Then
            If Buttons(0) <> 0 Then
                RaiseEvent MouseDown(X, Y, enButton.Right)
            Else
                RaiseEvent MouseUp(X, Y, enButton.Right)
            End If
            LastButtonState(0) = Buttons(0)
        End If
        ' Button 1 = Left button
        If (Buttons(1) <> LastButtonState(1)) Then
            If Buttons(1) <> 0 Then
                RaiseEvent MouseDown(X, Y, enButton.Left)
            Else
                RaiseEvent MouseUp(X, Y, enButton.Left)
            End If
            LastButtonState(1) = Buttons(1)
        End If
        ' Button 3 = middle or function button
        If (Buttons(2) <> LastButtonState(2)) Then
            If Buttons(2) <> 0 Then
                RaiseEvent MouseDown(X, Y, enButton.Other)
            Else
                RaiseEvent MouseUp(X, Y, enButton.Other)
```

```
        End If
        LastButtonState(2) = Buttons(2)
      End If
    End SyncLock
End Sub
```

Now we'll see details about processing the input data gathered from joystick devices.

## Processing the Joystick Input

The last input device method, GetJoystickState, will deal with the JoyState structure. As mentioned before, this structure has many attributes that will be filled according to the joystick type.

In order to guarantee that our class will work even with the simplest joystick-type peripheral, we'll keep it as simple as possible; but some processing will still be needed. We'll generate the JoystickPressed event according to the Buttons array, simply by passing the button index to the application; and, for the JoystickMove event, we'll pass the (x,y) coordinates and, to help the applications to create simpler code, the joystick direction, according to the enDirection enumeration defined in the GameEngine class. To calculate this direction, we have to check the X and Y joystick data members; each of these will range from 0 to 10,000, according to the values depicted in Figure 5-4.

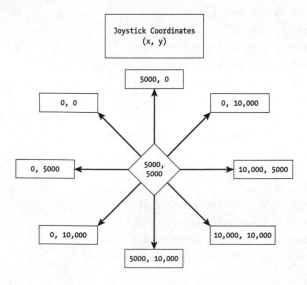

*Figure 5-4. The values for the X and Y joystick members for each joystick position*

If the application requires greater precision, it can use the joystick coordinates directly passed as a parameter to this event. The following code listing shows the full code for the GetJoystickState method:

```
Public Sub GetJoystickState()
    Dim direction As enDirection = clsGameEngine.enDirection.None

    ' Lock the UI class so it can't overwrite
    ' the JoystickState structure during a race condition.
    SyncLock (Me)
        Dim B As Byte, buttonNumber As Integer
        ' There's a lot of extra information coming from the joystick devices,
        ' but we'll deal here only with buttons and simple 2-D movement
        buttonNumber = 0
        For Each B In JoystickState.GetButtons
            buttonNumber += 1
            If (B <> 0) Then
                RaiseEvent JoystickButtonPressed(buttonNumber)
            End If
        Next
        ' Calculates the direction of the movement
        '     Center position is 5000, 5000
        '     X goes from 0 to 10000, left to right
        '     Y goes from 0 to 10000, top to down
        '     We'll ignore movements < 1000 from the center
        Select Case JoystickState.X
            Case Is < 4000  ' X is to the west (left)
                Select Case JoystickState.Y
                    Case Is < 4000  ' Y is to the North (top)
                        direction = clsGameEngine.enDirection.NorthWest
                    Case Is > 6000  ' Y is to the south (down)
                        direction = clsGameEngine.enDirection.SouthWest
                    Case Else       ' Y is centered
                        direction = clsGameEngine.enDirection.West
                End Select
            Case Is > 6000  ' X is to the east (right)
                Select Case JoystickState.Y
                    Case Is < 4000  ' Y is to the North (top)
                        direction = clsGameEngine.enDirection.NorthEast
                    Case Is > 6000  ' Y is to the south (down)
                        direction = clsGameEngine.enDirection.SouthEast
                    Case Else       ' Y is centered
                        direction = clsGameEngine.enDirection.East
```

```
                End Select
            Case Else        ' X is centered
            Select Case JoystickState.Y
                Case Is < 4000  ' Y is to the North (top)
                    direction = clsGameEngine.enDirection.North
                Case Is > 6000  ' Y is to the south (down)
                    direction = clsGameEngine.enDirection.South
                Case Else        ' Y is centered
                    direction = clsGameEngine.enDirection.None
            End Select
        End Select

        If direction <> clsGameEngine.enDirection.None Then
            RaiseEvent JoystickMove(JoystickState.X, JoystickState.Y, direction)
        End If


    End SyncLock
End Sub
```

Now that we have all of our classes in code, we can begin the new version of the River Pla.Net game, starting with the game proposal.


# The Game Proposal

Our goal in this chapter's game is to improve the sample from the previous chapter, River Pla.Net, to include some extra features, such as force-feedback joystick control.

The following are the features we'll add:

- The plane will be controlled by the joystick.

- The ships and planes will move in order to make the game tougher and increase the need for a high-quality game input device.

- The player's plane will shoot when the user presses the fire button of the joystick. There'll be a maximum of 16 bullets on screen, and the bullets can destroy planes, ships, and bridges.

- We want to give users a visual feedback about how well they are doing; so we'll include a status line with the total points achieved (they earn points for flying and destroying enemies), the amount of fuel in the fuel tank, and the number of lives they have left.

- As an extra feature, we can create new obstacles in the river: steel arrows that will throw the player's plane to the side the arrow is pointing to. When the plane hits such an arrow, the joystick must give force feedback to the user, in order to provide a clue that the plane is being moved against his or her will.

In the next section we'll examine in more detail these new features before entering the code phase.

## The Game Project

Although our project goal in this chapter is simply to improve a previously created game, we can't neglect to create the game project. However, it'll be a little simpler. We'll basically add some properties and methods to the classes created in the last chapter, with only two new classes: the GameFont class and the GameInput class, described in the previous sections.

Let's see what additional features our classes must implement in order to reach each of the goals defined in the game proposal.

### Controlling the Plane with the Joystick

The RiverEngine class must create a Joystick object and change the control from the Keypress event of the GameWindow form to the JoystickMove event generated by this class. Since some functions will remain on the keyboard, such as the pause feature and the exit feature, we'll have to create a Keyboard class as well, and include its event handler.

### Including Moving Ships and Planes

We have already seen how to move objects independently in the last chapter: The plane moves according to the arrow keys, and the game field scrolls. All we have to do is to extend this concept, moving the planes and ships down (scrolling with the game field) and left to right. Reflecting on this point, it should be noted that we can't move the plane and ship tiles, or we'll create holes in our game field; so we must find a different approach. For example, we can create a second array of active objects that holds only the active objects, and another one that holds the game field. We'll have two layers of objects, so we'll need an additional method (let's call it MoveActiveObjects) that must be called after the Scroll and Draw methods so the active objects may appear over the game field.

## Making Our Plane Shoot

Following the ideas expressed previously, we'll create an extra array (with 16 elements) to hold the bullets, and an extra method, MoveBullets, to move the bullets. Of course, even though the TestCollision method may continue with the same interface, the code will have to be deeply modified to consider the collision of the plane and the bullets with the moving objects.

## Adding a Status Line

We can create a simple function, DrawStatus, that will present on screen the Gas and Lives properties, and a newly created Points property that may be incremented in the Scroll and the TestCollision methods from GameEngine.

## Adding Support for Force-Feedback Joysticks

As presented in the section "the Game Proposal," support for force-feedback joysticks in our game will be treated as an extra feature, so we'll implement it in "Adding the Final Touches" at the end of this chapter.

## Defining the Class Diagram

Our final class diagram will include the classes defined in the previous chapter and the methods and properties suggested previously, as shown in Figure 5-5.

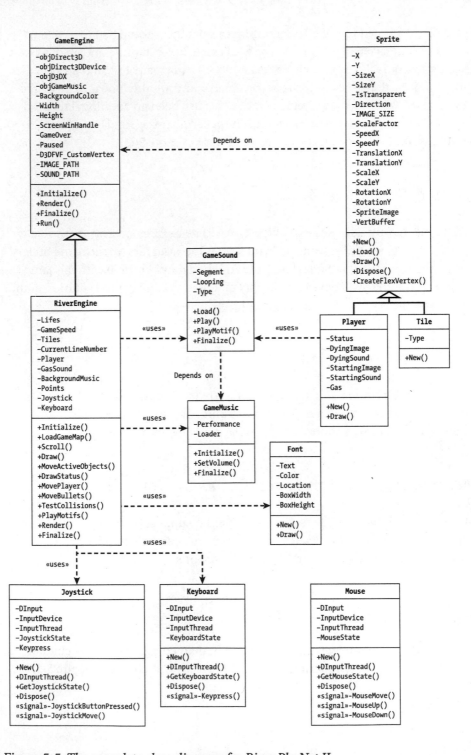

*Figure 5-5. The complete class diagram for River Pla.Net II*

## The Coding Phase

As in the previous chapter, let's define the steps we'll take in completing the final version:

1. First draft: Include DirectInput joystick and keyboard support.

2. Second draft: Implement moving enemies.

3. Third draft: Include the shooting feature.

4. Final version: Draw the game status on screen.

## *First Draft: Including DirectInput for the Joystick and Keyboard*

Including DirectInput to add support for joysticks and keyboards is very simple: We just need to define the objects we have previously created, and code the events for them.

When declaring the objects private to the RiverEngine class, we mustn't forget to use the WithEvents keyword to allow our objects to work with events.

```
Private Shared WithEvents Joystick As ClsJoystick
Private Shared WithEvents Keyboard As ClsKeyboard
```

In the initialize procedure, we'll create these objects, passing the window reference as a parameter as follows:

```
' Initializes the input devices
Joystick = New ClsJoystick(Owner)
Keyboard = New ClsKeyboard(Owner)
```

And then we'll code the events. The Keypress event will be almost an exact copy of the code that was previously used in the Keypress event of the GameWindow form, including just one extra line for the Q key to quit the game.

```
Private Shared Sub KeyPress(KeyCode As Keys) Handles Keyboard.Keypress
    Select Case KeyCode
        Case Keys.Right
            Player.SpeedX = gameSpeed
            Paused = False
        Case Keys.Left
            Player.SpeedX = -gameSpeed
            Paused = False
        Case Keys.Up
            Player.SpeedY = gameSpeed
            Paused = False
        Case Keys.Down
            Player.SpeedY = -gameSpeed
            Paused = False
        Case Keys.Escape
            'GameOver = True
            Paused = Not Paused
        Case Keys.Q
            GameOver = True
    End Select
End Sub
```

As for the joystick, we'll have to add code for two new events: moving the plane in JoystickMove, and firing in JoystickButtonPressed. First we'll code only the former event; we'll include the code in the latter event when we code the shooting feature.

```
Private Shared Sub JoystickMove(x As Integer, y As Integer, _
                    direction As enDirection) Handles Joystick.JoystickMove
    Select Case direction
        Case clsGameEngine.enDirection.West
            Player.SpeedX = gameSpeed
            Paused = False
        Case clsGameEngine.enDirection.East
            Player.SpeedX = -gameSpeed
            Paused = False
        Case clsGameEngine.enDirection.North
            Player.SpeedY = gameSpeed
            Paused = False
        Case clsGameEngine.enDirection.South
            Player.SpeedY = -gameSpeed
            Paused = False
        Case clsGameEngine.enDirection.NorthWest
```

```
            Player.SpeedX = gameSpeed
            Player.SpeedY = gameSpeed
            Paused = False
        Case clsGameEngine.enDirection.NorthEast
            Player.SpeedX = -gameSpeed
            Player.SpeedY = gameSpeed
            Paused = False
        Case clsGameEngine.enDirection.SouthWest
            Player.SpeedX = gameSpeed
            Player.SpeedY = -gameSpeed
            Paused = False
        Case clsGameEngine.enDirection.SouthEast
            Player.SpeedX = -gameSpeed
            Player.SpeedY = -gameSpeed
            Paused = False
    End Select
End Sub
```

As we saw in the last chapter, once we have created basic classes to handle DirectX complexity, it becomes very easy for any program to use these classes. And as we create more games, we can improve our base classes to gain more control or more performance, using any new tricks we learn.

Running our program now, we'll see that even with the keyboard our control over the plane is better, and we can also use any joystick device we choose to control it.

## Second Draft: Implementing Moving Enemies

As we said in the game project, we'll "promote" our enemies from tiles to active objects.

### Loading the Active Objects

After creating an array to hold these objects (identical to the tiles array), we'll need to change the LoadGameMap and LoadLine procedures to load both the Tiles array and the ActiveObjects array, as shown in the next piece of code:

```vb
Private tiles As ClsTile(,)
Private ActiveObjects As ClsTile(,)


Function LoadGameMap(ByVal strGameMapFileName As String) As Boolean
. . .
    ReDim tiles(Width, GameMapSize)
    ReDim ActiveObjects(Width, GameMapSize)
. . .
    ' Load all the game map lines from the GameMap
    '  into the Tiles array and the ActiveObjects Array
    For i = 0 To GameMapSize - 1
        If Not LoadLine(GameMap(i)) Then
            LoadGameMap = False
            Exit Function
        End If
    Next
. . .
End Function

Function LoadLine(ByVal strLine As String) As Boolean
    Dim x As Integer
    Dim strSpriteFileName As String
    Dim Type As ClsTile.enType
    Static LineNumber As Integer = 0

    LoadLine = True
    For x = 0 To Width - 1
        Select Case strLine.Chars(x)
            Case "1"
                strSpriteFileName = "borderN"
                Type = ClsTile.enType.Land
            Case "2"
                strSpriteFileName = "borderNE1"
                Type = ClsTile.enType.Land
. . . (all other tiles...)
            Case "." ' Green background
                ' Do nothing
                strSpriteFileName = ""
                Type = ClsTile.enType.Background
            Case "_"
                strSpriteFileName = "water"
                Type = ClsTile.enType.Water
```

```
            Case Else
                ' Should never happen
                strSpriteFileName = "InvalidTile"
                Type = ClsTile.enType.Land
        End Select
        Try
            Select Case Type
                Case ClsTile.enType.Background
                    tiles(x, LineNumber) = Nothing
                    ActiveObjects(x, LineNumber) = Nothing
                Case ClsTile.enType.Water To ClsTile.enType.Land
                    tiles(x, LineNumber) = New ClsTile(strSpriteFileName & _
                                    ".bmp", New POINT(x, LineNumber), Type)
                    ActiveObjects(x, LineNumber) = Nothing
                Case Else 'Active objects must be created over water
                    tiles(x, LineNumber) = New ClsTile("water.bmp", _
                            New POINT(x, LineNumber), ClsTile.enType.Water)
                    ActiveObjects(x, LineNumber) = New ClsTile(strSpriteFileName_
                            & ".bmp", Color.FromARGB(255, 255, 0, 255), _
                            New POINT(x, LineNumber), Type)
                    ActiveObjects(x, LineNumber).SpeedX = gameSpeed
            End Select
        Catch e As Exception
            LoadLine = False
            MessageBox.Show("Unpredicted Error when loading game sprites: " & _
                        e.Message, "River Pla.Net", MessageBoxButtons.OK, _
                        MessageBoxIcon.Stop)
            Exit Function
        End Try
    Next
    ' Increments the line number counter
    LineNumber += 1
End Function
```

The code just shown is exactly the same as that seen in the last chapter, with the single difference that here we included an extra check on the object type, at the end of the Select Case statement: If the current tile isn't background, land, or water (or, in other words, if it's a ship, a bridge, a gas barrel, or a plane), then we'll create a water tile in the Tiles array (active objects must always be created over water, to simplify our code) and add a new object to the ActiveObjects array. In all other cases, the ActiveObjects array will be filled with nulls.

> **TIP** *This approach will simplify our treatment of collisions, too. If the player collides with an active object, we can simply destroy the object in the array, so it won't be drawn anymore. In the previous chapter, we needed to destroy the object and create a new water tile in the position previously occupied by the object.*

## Moving the Planes and Ships on Screen

If we now run our code, we'll see everything looking just like the version in the last chapter, but without the enemies, bridges, and gas barrels. Only the tiles are being drawn.

We'll have to code a new method, MoveActiveObjects, that will move and draw the elements from the ActiveObjects array. This method will present no new concepts, but it will stretch your knowledge of transformation matrices. Let's look at it step by step, so that we can get the most out of the concepts being used.

A quick way to start is to copy the code from the Scroll and Draw methods and adapt it to draw our active objects, scrolling with the same speed as the tiles but not yet moving. Since the scrolling has already been applied to the Transform.World matrix, we can use this by simply calling the MoveActiveObjects before the Scroll and Draw procedures:

```
Public Sub MoveActiveObjects()
    Dim x As Integer, y As Integer
    Dim LineCount As Integer = 0

    ' Draw the game field
    y = CurrentLineNumber - 1
    If y < 0 Then y = GameMapSize
    ' We will move the objects a line below the current line number and a line
    '   above the last line on screen (CurrentLineNumber + Height)
    Do While LineCount < Height + 2
        For x = 0 To Width - 1
            If Not (ActiveObjects(x, y) Is Nothing) Then
                ActiveObjects(x, y).Draw()
            End If
        Next
        LineCount += 1
        y += 1
        If y > GameMapSize Then y = 0
    Loop
End Sub
```

If we run our game now, we'll be able to see the active objects back on the screen. To make these objects (ships and planes) move, all we have to do is to produce a new transformation matrix, including a translation in the x axis, to the world matrix. Since every object will have to set its own world matrix with its own particular transformations, we'll need to add two new Matrix variables to the procedure: one for holding the initial world matrix (with the scroll information), and another to be used by the objects when applying the transformations. Note that to add transformations, we can simply multiply the transformation matrices, which can be done using the helper function Matrix.Multiply.

The new code for the procedure is as follows:

```
Public Sub MoveActiveObjects()
    Dim x As Integer, y As Integer
    Dim LineCount As Integer = 0
    ' Stores the current World Matrix (with the scrolling calculation)
    Dim WorldMatrix As Matrix = objDirect3DDevice.Transform.World
    Dim ObjectMatrix As Matrix


    ' Draw the game field
    y = CurrentLineNumber - 1
    If y < 0 Then y = GameMapSize
    ' We will move the objects a line below the current line number and a line
    '   above the last line on screen (CurrentLineNumber + Height)
    Do While LineCount < Height + 2
        For x = 0 To Width - 1
            ObjectMatrix = WorldMatrix
            If Not (ActiveObjects(x, y) Is Nothing) Then
                if ActiveObjects(x, y).Type = ClsTile.enType.Plane or _
                    ActiveObjects(x, y).Type = ClsTile.enType.Ship then
                        ObjectMatrix = Matrix.Multiply(ObjectMatrix, _
                            Matrix.Translation( _
                            ActiveObjects(x, y).TranslationX, 0, 0))
                        ' update the location - used for collision detection
                        ActiveObjects(x, y).X += (ActiveObjects(x, y).SpeedX / 32)
                        ' update the translation value
                        ActiveObjects(x, y).TranslationX += _
                            ActiveObjects(x, y).SpeedX
                End if
                objDirect3DDevice.Transform.World = ObjectMatrix
                ActiveObjects(x, y).Draw()
            End If
        Next
        LineCount += 1
```

```
            y += 1
            If y > GameMapSize Then y = 0
        Loop
    End Sub
```

If we ran our code now, we'd immediately notice two mistakes: The ships and planes are moving on screen, but they are only going from right to left, and the ships don't stop when they reach the banks. We'll have to add some code to make the planes go back (or enter again from the left side of the screen), and to make the ships stay over water, going back when they reach the margin. To simplify our code, let's make the enemy plane enter again from the left-hand side of the screen, so we won't need different images for it (one for flying east, and another for flying west).

Since we'll have different tests for planes and ships, we'll need to include a second if statement that will check if the plane goes beyond the screen's width and update its position to be at the beginning of the screen; and check the nearby tiles (in the Tiles array) to invert the ship speed if it gets close to a margin. To see our ships and planes moving on screen, just add the following code in the right place in the MoveActiveObjects procedure:

```
If ActiveObjects(x, y).Type = ClsTile.enType.Plane Then
    ' Ensures that the translation will not take the enemy plane out of the screen
    If ActiveObjects(x, y).X * 32 > (Width * 32) Then
        ActiveObjects(x, y).X -= CInt(ActiveObjects(x, y).X)
        ' update the translation value
        ActiveObjects(x, y).TranslationX = -(Width * clsSprite.IMAGE_SIZE - _
            ActiveObjects(x, y).TranslationX)
    End If
Else 'ActiveObjects(x, y).Type = ClsTile.enType.Ship
    ' Ensures that the translation will not take the enemy ship over land
    If tiles(ActiveObjects(x, y).X + 1, y).Type = ClsTile.enType.Land Then
        ActiveObjects(x, y).SpeedX = -gameSpeed
    End If
    If tiles(ActiveObjects(x, y).X - 1, y).Type = ClsTile.enType.Land Then
        ActiveObjects(x, y).SpeedX = gameSpeed
    End If
End If
```

## Coding the Collision Detection

Everything now looks okay, but our plane still doesn't collide with the moving enemies. The code we did for the TestCollision method in the previous chapter just checks the Tiles array for any tile that isn't water, so at this stage we only collide with the margins.

The new version of this function becomes more sophisticated, including three different tests:

1.  Test for collision with the margins, in the Tiles array.

2.  Test for collision with active nonmoving objects (bridges and gas barrels), taking the appropriated actions (fill the tank if it's a barrel, crash the plane if it's a bridge).

3.  Test for collision with the active moving objects in the current line. We'll use the bounding box algorithm for testing this collision, simplified here because we only need to check the x coordinates—the y coordinates have already been checked, because we are testing the objects in the current player's line.

The final code for the collision detection procedure is shown here:

```
Private Function TestCollision() As Boolean
    Dim x As Integer, y As Integer
    Dim i As Integer, j As Integer

    x = Player.X / 32
    y = (Player.Y + 16) / 32 + CurrentLineNumber

    ' 1. Test the tiles: If we are over water, we are not colliding
    If Not (tiles(x, y) Is Nothing) Then
        If tiles(x, y).Type = ClsTile.enType.Water Then
            TestCollision = False
        Else
            TestCollision = True
        End If
    Else
        TestCollision = True
    End If
```

```
' 2. Test nonmoving active objects: bridges and gas barrels
If Not (ActiveObjects(x, y) Is Nothing) Then
    ' If we are over a gas barrel, fill the gas tank
    If ActiveObjects(x, y).Type = ClsTile.enType.Gas Then
        TestCollision = False
        Player.Gas = Player.Gas + 30
        If Player.Gas > 100 Then Player.Gas = 100
        GasSound.Play()
        ' If we are over a bridge, we are colliding
    ElseIf ActiveObjects(x, y).Type = ClsTile.enType.Bridge Then
        TestCollision = True
    End If
    ActiveObjects(x, y).Dispose()
    ActiveObjects(x, y) = Nothing
End If


' 3. Test collision against moving Active objects on the current line
For i = 1 To Width
    If Not (ActiveObjects(i, y) Is Nothing) Then
        If ActiveObjects(i, y).Type = ClsTile.enType.Plane Or _
            ActiveObjects(i, y).Type = ClsTile.enType.Ship Then
            ' checks collision using the bounding box algorithm; simplified _
            ' because y is already checked against the current line number
            If ActiveObjects(i, y).X * 32 > Player.X And _
              ActiveObjects(i, y).X * 32 < Player.X + 32 Then
                ActiveObjects(i, y).Dispose()
                ActiveObjects(i, y) = Nothing
                TestCollision = True
            End If
        End If
    End If
Next
End Function
```

If you remember the bounding box algorithm, explained in Chapter 1, it'll be easier to understand the collision-checking if statement in the previous code. Of course, the use of approximations for the current line and each object's coordinates will lead to an inaccurate result, but we can always return at a later date and improve the code. Everything is organized so that if we want to alter this algorithm, all we'll need to change is this function.

Figure 5-6 shows a screen with some moving planes. Notice the plane at the far left of the screen: It's flying over land. Although every active object is being created over water, planes don't have any limitations except to keep looping in the game window.

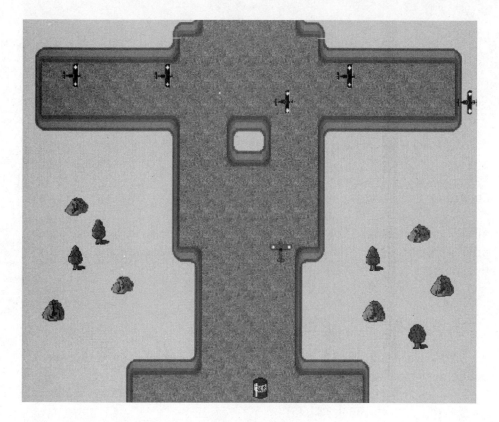

*Figure 5-6. Flying enemy planes in our way*

## Third Draft: Including the Shooting Feature

To include a shooting feature in a game requires a series of steps, even in a simple 2-D game like ours. We'll have to do the following:

1. Create some kind of structure to hold the bullets. Since we already have the Sprite class, which stores information such as the image and the current position, we can use an array (with 16 elements, as stated in the game proposal).

2. Add some code to the input device handlers to inform the player that he or she must shoot.

3. Add code to the player's movement routine to handle the information gathered from the device and create the bullets.

4.  Add a procedure for moving the bullets.

5.  Add code to this procedure to check for collision with obstacles, which may vary from game to game. In our case, the bullet will only be destroyed when it leaves the window (at the top), or if hits a plane or a ship (river borders, for example, won't be an obstacle).

We'll see details of each step in the following sections.

## Creating the Bullets Array

All shooting handling will be done in the RiverEngine class, so we'll have to create a private property to store the bullets. Also creating a constant, which defines the total number of bullets, will help us to easily modify this value if we want to:

```
Private Bullets As clsSprite()
Private Const TOTAL_BULLETS As Integer = 16
```

We'll have to define the array size in the Initialize event of the class, simply by adding the following line:

```
ReDim Bullets(TOTAL_BULLETS)
```

## Handling Data from the Input Devices

Before including any code for the event handlers of the input devices, we have to have a way to tell the player he or she must shoot. For this, we can extend the enStatus enumeration of the Player class to include a "shooting" status:

```
Enum enPlayerStatus
    Flying = 0
    Dying = 1
    Starting = 2
    Shooting = 3
End Enum
```

Now, all we have to do is add the code in the Keypress event for the keyboard, and create the JoystickButtonPressed event. In order to test if our code is okay up to this point, we can include a message box to see the result when we fire.

```
Private Shared Sub KeyPress(KeyCode As Keys) Handles Keyboard.Keypress
    Select Case KeyCode
        Case Keys.Right
            Player.SpeedX = gameSpeed
            Paused = False
            . . . (other key codes)
        Case Keys.Space
            ' Just shoot if we are neither dying nor starting a new life
            If Player.Status = ClsPlayer.enPlayerStatus.Flying Then
                Player.Status = ClsPlayer.enPlayerStatus.Shooting
                MessageBox.show("BANG!")
            End If
    End Select
End Sub

Private Shared Sub JoystickButtonPressed(Button As Integer) _
                          Handles Joystick.JoystickButtonPressed
    ' Shoot with any joystick button
    ' Just shoot if we are neither dying nor starting a new life
    If Player.Status = ClsPlayer.enPlayerStatus.Flying Then
        Player.Status = ClsPlayer.enPlayerStatus.Shooting
        MessageBox.show("BANG!")
    End If
End Sub
```

In Figure 5-7, we see our first shot. Don't forget to remove the MessageBox lines before going on to the next step!!

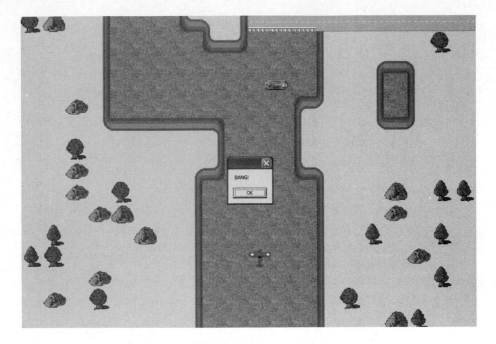

*Figure 5-7. A message box indicates the first user shot.*

## Making the Player Shoot

To make the player shoot, we'll add code to the MovePlayer method. This method was coded in the previous chapter and, until now, simply moves the player if any of the "speed" properties are nonzero. The speed properties are set, as we saw before, when the player moves the joystick or presses the navigation keys on the keyboard. The movement code is presented in the previous chapter, so we won't revisit it here.

To make the player shoot, we'll create a new sprite with the bullet image, set its speed to some value greater than the current gameSpeed (to avoid any strange behavior), and then code the procedure that will move the bullets and check for collision.

Since we'll have a limited array of bullet objects, before creating the bullet we'll have to loop through this array and check if there are any free elements. If not, all of the array positions are set, so we'll create a new bullet sprite just in front of the player's plane and set its speed, as shown in the next code sample:

```
Public Sub MovePlayer()
    Dim i As Integer
. . .
' If the player is shooting, create a bullet and reset the status to flying
If Player.Status = Player.enPlayerStatus.Shooting Then
    Player.Status = Player.enPlayerStatus.Flying
    ' Look for an empty position on the bullets array
    i = 0
    Do Until Bullets(i) Is Nothing
        If i = TOTAL_BULLETS - 1 Then
            Exit Do
        End If
        i += 1
    Loop
    ' If not all the array positions have bullets, create a new one
    If Bullets(i) Is Nothing Then
        Bullets(i) = New clsSprite("bullet.bmp", _
                        Color.FromARGB(255, 255, 0, 255), _
                        New POINT(Player.X + clsSprite.IMAGE_SIZE / 2 - 4, _
                        Player.Y + clsSprite.IMAGE_SIZE - 4), _
                        ClsSprite.enScaleFactor.enScalePixel, 9, 9)
        Bullets(i).SpeedY = gameSpeed * 1.5
    End If
End If
. . .
End Sub
```

In the next section, we'll code the movement of the bullets we have just created.

## Moving the Bullets

Once the bullets have been created, we'll have to move them to the top of the game field, using the same approach as before with transformation matrices.

The bullets' movements will be totally independent of the scrolling, so we'll reset the world matrix with a simple translation using the bullet speed, set in the MovePlayer method (as we saw in the previous item).

In the next code sample, we'll go through the following steps:

1. For each bullet in the bullets array, check if the bullet object is set.

2. If so, create the translation matrix, based on the current TranslationY property of the bullet object.

3. Increment the TranslationY property with the current bullet speed, so the bullet will go further with every call of the method.

4. Also increment the y position, so we'll always have an up-to-date x,y position of the bullet (and we'll use this later to calculate the collisions).

5. If the bullet goes off the screen, destroy it (freeing the array element, so it can be used for another shot).

6. If the bullet isn't off the screen, set the world matrix and draw it.

```
Private Sub MoveBullets()
    Dim i As Integer
    Dim BulletMatrix As Matrix

    For i = 0 To TOTAL_BULLETS - 1
        '--- 1. Move the bullets
        If Not Bullets(i) Is Nothing Then
            ' Creates the bullet translation matrix using the position plus the
            '  speed of the bullet
            BulletMatrix = Matrix.Translation(0, _
                          Bullets(i).TranslationY, 0)
            ' Updates the bullet location (used on collision detection)
            Bullets(i).Y += Bullets(i).SpeedYq
            Bullets(i).TranslationY += Bullets(i).SpeedY
            ' If the bullet get out of the screen, destroy it
            '    the m42 element represents the translation on the Y axis
            If BulletMatrix.m42 > (Height - 1) * clsSprite.IMAGE_SIZE Then
                Bullets(i).Dispose()
                Bullets(i) = Nothing
            Else
                objDirect3DDevice.Transform.World = BulletMatrix
                Bullets(i).Draw()
            End If
        End If
    Next
End Sub
```

We'll have to set the world matrix for every bullet, because although all bullets may have the same speed, they'll have different translation values.

If we run the game now, we'd be able to see the bullets being fired from the plane to the screen top, but they would still have no effect on the enemies because we have yet to code the collision detection algorithm.

## Implement the Bullets' Collision Detection

Since we'll have to test the collision for each bullet, we can include the following code inside the first if statement of the MoveBullets method, inside the for statement.

Basically, we'll ignore the background (the Tiles array) and check for collisions with elements from the ActiveObjects array (specifically, bridges, planes, and ships, as fuel barrels won't be destroyed). And since there are two types of objects—static and moving ones—we'll have to test the current bullet position against the current x,y position of the objects, and not simply against the ActiveObjects array coordinates.

```
Dim j As Integer
Dim y As Integer
'--- 2. Test the collision for the bullets with the active objects
If Not Bullets(i) Is Nothing Then
' Convert the bullet position into indexes for the ActiveObjects array
    y = (Bullets(i).Y + 5) / 32 + CurrentLineNumber
    If y < GameMapSize Then
        ' loop through the ActiveObjects array
        For j = 1 To Width
            ' Test the objects (planes, ships or bridges) for the current line (y)
            If Not (ActiveObjects(j, y) Is Nothing) Then
                If ActiveObjects(j, y).Type = ClsTile.enType.Plane Or _
                    ActiveObjects(j, y).Type = ClsTile.enType.Ship Or _
                    ActiveObjects(j, y).Type = ClsTile.enType.Bridge Then
                    ' checks collision using the bounding box algorithm;
                    ' simplified here because y is already checked against the
                    ' current line number
                    If Bullets(i).X > ActiveObjects(j, y).X * IMAGE_SIZE _
                    And Bullets(i).X < (ActiveObjects(j, y).X + 1) * IMAGE_SIZE_
                    Then
                        'Player gets 200 points per enemy destroyed
                        Points += 200
                        ' If colliding, destroy the bullet and the active object
                        ActiveObjects(j, y).Dispose()
```

```
                        ActiveObjects(j, y) = Nothing
                        Bullets(i).Dispose()
                        Bullets(i) = Nothing
                        ' Plays the Explosion sound effect
                        ExplosionSound.Play()
                        Exit For
                    End If
                End If
            End If
        Next
    End If
End If
```

As far as the game physics is concerned, we're finished. Our game can now be played, and although it won't be a huge hit in today's market, it's still very playable and fun, too. Figure 5-8 shows our new game screen.

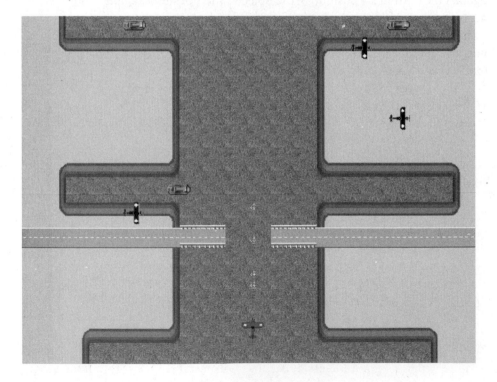

*Figure 5-8. Shooting and destroying enemies*

## Final Version: Drawing the Game Status on Screen

One last thing our game must have is a display for the player's current status. There are a lot of ways you can do this, and usually the graphical ones are the best: little planes at one edge of the screen to represent the number of lives left, a solid bar that gets smaller the further you fly to indicate fuel consumption, and so on. For our purposes (to test the Font class), all we need to do is to add some status text.

To use the Font class, at first we need to define the font variables and create the font objects. The variables will be defined as properties of the GameEngine class, and the Initialize method of this class is the most appropriate place to carry out the object creation, as shown in the next code sample:

```
' Status text
Private LivesText As ClsGameFont
Private GasText As ClsGameFont
Private PointsText As ClsGameFont

Function Initialize(Owner As Windows.Forms.Control) As Boolean
    ...
    ' Initializes the game text fields
    LivesText = New ClsGameFont("Comic Sans MS", 16, "Lives: " & _
            Lives.ToString, New POINT(100, 10))
    GasText = New ClsGameFont("Comic Sans MS", 16, "Energy: " & _
            Player.Gas.ToString, New POINT(300, 10))
    PointsText = New ClsGameFont("Comic Sans MS", 16, "Points: " & _
            Points.ToString, New POINT(500, 10))
...
End Function
```

To write the status text on the screen, we'll create a DrawStatus method, which will simply set the text color and call the Draw method to show the values of the Lives, Points, and Gas properties.

In order to make the status text easier to see against any kind of background, we'll use a little trick and include a dark gray shadow with the text to make it more readable. All we need to do is to write the same text twice, moving the text a pixel to the left and down when drawing the shadow, as shown in the following code example:

```
Sub DrawStatus()
    ' Draw the dark gray shadow
    LivesText.Color = Color.FromARGB(255, 50, 50, 50)
    GasText.Color = Color.FromARGB(255, 50, 50, 50)
    PointsText.Color = Color.FromARGB(255, 50, 50, 50)
    LivesText.Draw("Lives: " & Lives.ToString, New POINT(101, 11))
    GasText.Draw("Energy: " & Player.Gas.ToString & "%!", New POINT(301, 11))
    PointsText.Draw("Points: " & Points.ToString, New POINT(501, 11))

    ' Draw the yellow text
    LivesText.Color = Color.FromARGB(255, 255, 255, 0)
    GasText.Color = Color.FromARGB(255, 255, 255, 0)
    PointsText.Color = Color.FromARGB(255, 255, 255, 0)
    LivesText.Draw("Lives: " & Lives.ToString, New POINT(100, 10))
    GasText.Draw("Energy: " & Player.Gas.ToString & "%!", New POINT(300, 10))
    PointsText.Draw("Points: " & Points.ToString, New POINT(500, 10))
End Sub
```

If we want to include a border around all the text borders, we can use a similar trick, drawing the same text four times: one pixel to the left, one pixel down, one pixel to the right, and a pixel up. This will create a complete border. Depending on the character size, you can try moving two pixels instead of one; experiment to see which result is best for each type of game.

Figure 5-9 shows the game screen with the status text at the top.

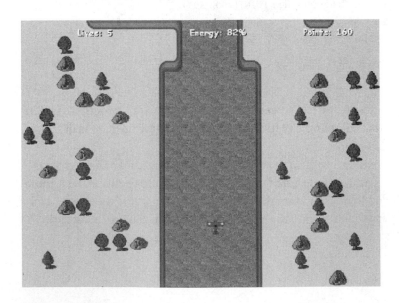

*Figure 5-9. Score, fuel, and lives-left information, finally!*

Including this status text ends our coding phase. In the next section, we'll add some final details to our game that will make it even more interesting.

# Adding the Final Touches

When coding a game, a lot of ideas come to mind about how to make it better. As we stated before, although it's not always possible to implement all the new suggestions that arise, we must write them down for later use. Maybe a suggestion will be implemented in a future version of the game, or even in other related games.

As for our game, we'll implement two new features—a "game pause" key, and support for force-feedback joysticks. In addition, you might want to consider other extra features for your version of the game, such as building a high scores table, implementing animation for when the enemy explodes, and improving the collision detection algorithm to produce more accurate results.

## *Including a Pause Feature*

We included a pause feature to our sample games in Chapters 1 and 2, but these are very simple games compared to River Pla.Net. In this game, we'll have to take into account many things, like ignoring the input from DirectInput and stopping the music and the scrolling, as well as enemy and bullet movements.

We can start coding our pause feature by changing the DrawStatus method, in order to display a "Game Paused" message if the game is paused. To do this, we'll have to include the next lines in the method:

```
Dim PauseText As ClsGameFont
PauseText = New ClsGameFont("Comic Sans MS", 20, _
            "Game Paused - Move or Shoot to Continue ", New POINT(100, 220))
If Paused Then
    PauseText.Color = Color.FromARGB(255, 255, 255, 0)
    PauseText.Draw()
End If
```

To avoid re-creating a font object every time we are in pause mode, we can define the PauseText variable as a class property, and initialize it in the Initialize method.

As for the music, we must know when the paused status has changed so that we call the StopPlaying and Play methods only once. The following code listing must be included in the RiverEngine's PlayMotifs method:

```
Static OldState As Boolean = Paused

' If the states changes, stop or start the background music
If OldState <> Paused Then
    If Paused Then
        BackgroundMusic.StopPlaying()
    Else
        BackgroundMusic.Play()
    End If
    OldState = Paused
End If
```

As for all the movement methods (MovePlayer, MoveBullets, MoveActiveObjects, and Scroll), we can't simply enclose all the method lines in a big if statement to avoid them from being called when the game is paused. We must apply the current transformations for the movements, but not change the translation values.

For example, for the MovePlayer method, we must apply the current translation to the player plane and redraw it for every frame in the same position. In other words, all we need to do is not increment the translation values on every call of the method.

All the movement methods must follow this same rule of thumb. The next code listing shows the MovePlayer method as an example; the code for the other methods is given completely on the accompanying CD-ROM.

```
Public Sub MovePlayer()
    Dim i As Integer
    ' Initializes the player position in the middle of screen (x-axis)
    ' and 3 tiles up (y-axis)
        Static PlayerMatrix As Matrix = Matrix.Translation(_
                10 * clsSprite.IMAGE_SIZE, 3 * clsSprite.IMAGE_SIZE, 0)

        If Not Paused Then
            ' ... Player position updating code
        End If
        objDirect3DDevice.Transform.World = PlayerMatrix
        Player.Draw()
    End Sub
```

The screen showing the game pause method is given in Figure 5-10.

*Figure 5-10. Paused game screen*

Next we'll learn how to add force-feedback effects when controlling our game with a joystick.

## Adding Support for Force-Feedback Joysticks

When dealing with joysticks, an interesting feature is to include force-feedback control in our games, so the user can enjoy a more interactive experience.

When creating force effects, there are two basic approaches: loading the effects from a previously created effect file, or creating the effect from scratch for our program.

The effect files are created with the Force Editor, a tool that comes with the DirectX SDK for creating and testing force-feedback files. It saves the effects into files, and we'll load them later with the CreateEffectFromFile function. This is the easier way to deal with effects, allowing us to include sophisticated force effects without a lot of programming.

We'll see here how to create a simple force effect in our program, including a new method in the Joystick class to generate movement in the joystick according to a direction passed as a parameter.

When creating an effect, we can define the following properties:

- **Magnitude**: The strength of the force to be applied generated by the joystick, ranging from 0 (no force) to 10,000 (maximum force for the device), growing linearly.

- **Direction**: The direction from which the force comes. The default behavior is to use polar coordinates, where the direction is measure by hundreds of degrees from the north direction (the negative y axis); but this can be changed to use Cartesian coordinates. For example, while the left direction is represented by x = -1, y = 0 in Cartesian coordinates, it will be represented by degrees = 27,000 in polar coordinates.

- **Duration**: The amount of time the effect lasts in microseconds.

We can also specify if the effect will be a ramp force or periodic effect. A *ramp force* is a steady rising or decreasing force with a minimum and a maximum magnitude. A *periodic effect* will repeat the force effect at specific time intervals.

To create a new effect in our code, we must set the parameters of an Effect data structure and call the CreateEffect function. The object returned by the function will be a reference to the feedback effect and can be triggered by calling the Start method.

The next code listing shows a function to be included in our Joystick class, which will generate a simple effect that pulls the joystick away from the center, according to the direction specified as a parameter.

```
Sub ForceEffect(ByVal Direction As enDirection)
    Dim EffectData As New Effect()
    Dim effDirection(1) As Integer
    Dim effAxes(1) As Integer

    With EffectData
        ' We are using the default value for these members
        '.StartDelay = 0
        '.TriggerRepeatInterval = DI.Infinite
        '.UsesEnvelope = False
        '.SamplePeriod = 0

        ' Set the effect type and flags that will control the effect
        .EffType = EffectType.ConstantForce
        .Flags = EffectFlags.Cartesian Or EffectFlags.ObjectOffsets
        ' Set the magnitude and the gain
        .Constant.Magnitude = DI.NominalMax
        .Gain = DI.NominalMax
```

```
    ' Set the duration (in microseconds).  For infinite time use DI.Infinite;
    .Duration = 100000   ' One tenth of a second
    ' Set the trigger button - No trigger button
    .TriggerButton = Button.NoTrigger
    ' Set the axes we will be working on
    effAxes(0) = JoystickOffset.X
    effAxes(1) = JoystickOffset.Y
    .SetAxes(effAxes)
    ' Finally, set the direction
    Select Case Direction
        Case clsGameEngine.enDirection.South
            effDirection(0) = 0
            effDirection(1) = -2
        Case clsGameEngine.enDirection.SouthWest
            effDirection(0) = 1
            effDirection(1) = -1
        Case clsGameEngine.enDirection.west
            effDirection(0) = 2
            effDirection(1) = 0
        Case clsGameEngine.enDirection.NorthWest
            effDirection(0) = 1
            effDirection(1) = 1
        Case clsGameEngine.enDirection.North
            effDirection(0) = 0
            effDirection(1) = 2
        Case clsGameEngine.enDirection.NorthEast
            effDirection(0) = -1
            effDirection(1) = 1
        Case clsGameEngine.enDirection.East
            effDirection(0) = -2
            effDirection(1) = 0
        Case clsGameEngine.enDirection.SouthEast
            effDirection(0) = -1
            effDirection(1) = -1
    End Select
    .SetDirection (effDirection)
End With

If Not DIEffect Is Nothing Then
    Call DIEffect.Unload()
End If
DIEffect = New EffectObject(ForceFeedbackGuid.ConstantForce, _
             EffectData, InputDevice)
DIEffect.Start(1)


End Sub
```

In the previous code sample, we only set the minimum number of parameters needed to create the required effect. Duration, Axis, and Constant.Magnitude are the ones used to set the basic effect characteristics discussed previously. The Gain and TriggerButton members should be set for all effects, since the default values of 0 aren't suitable. Setting Gain to 0 will scale down our force to zero, while 10,000 (the value we used) will apply no scale over the Magnitude value. TriggerButton specifies the joystick button number that will trigger the effect (useful, for example, if we want our effect to be triggered and move our joystick back every time we shoot a gun); the default value of zero will associate the effect with the first joystick button.

**TIP** *The Effect data structure has many other parameters that allow us to create very complex force effects, including members to control periodic effects, ramp forces, and constant force feedback. Refer to the SDK help files for a complete description of each of the structure's members.*

To make us able to test the newly created force effect feature, we must define when the effect will be fired. Since our goal here is simply to test the effects, let's create a new obstacle that will shake our plane a little and move it left or right. The new obstacles will be floating arrows over the river and are shown in Figure 5-11.

*Figure 5-11. New force-feedback obstacles appearing on screen*

Of course we'll need to make three adjustments to our game code: Create the new type of tiles in the `Tiles` class, include the lines to load the new tile types in the initialization of the `RiverEngine` class, and include the code for generating the effect in the `TestCollision` method of the `RiverEngine` class.

The new enumeration of the `Tiles` class will be as follows:

```
Enum enType
    Background = 0
    Water = 1
    ArrowWest = 2
    ArrowEast = 3
    Land = 4
    Gas = 5
    Ship = 6
    Plane = 7
    Bridge = 8
End Enum
```

The lines to be included in the `LoadGameLine` function are variations of the current code, as shown in the next code listing:

```
Case "<"
    strSpriteFileName = "ArrowLeft"
    Type = ClsTile.enType.ArrowWest
Case ">"
    strSpriteFileName = "ArrowRight"
    Type = ClsTile.enType.ArrowEast
```

The next code listing shows the lines we must include in the `TestCollision` method to test the collision:

```
' Test collision against force feedback obstacles
If Not (ActiveObjects(x, y) Is Nothing) Then
    ' Generate force effects according to the force feedback obstacle we hit,
    '    moving the player to the same direction of the arrow
    If ActiveObjects(x, y).Type = ClsTile.enType.ArrowEast Then
        Joystick.ForceEffect(clsGameEngine.enDirection.East)
        Player.SpeedX = clsSprite.IMAGE_SIZE
        TestCollision = False
    ElseIf ActiveObjects(x, y).Type = ClsTile.enType.ArrowWest Then
        Joystick.ForceEffect(clsGameEngine.enDirection.West)
        Player.SpeedX = -clsSprite.IMAGE_SIZE
        TestCollision = False
    End If
End If
```

We can now change our game map to include as many force-feedback obstacles as we want. Feel free to use a lot of them together to see the final effect on the game's playability.

Some additional improvements to our game would be including force-feedback effects when shooting and dying, and using the newly learned text output features to create a high scores screen. We leave this for you to do as an exercise on your own.

## Summary

In this chapter, we finished the River Pla.Net game, including extra features to support different input devices and to add user feedback about the game's current status on screen.

The points covered in this chapter include the following:

- Introduction to DirectInput and the basic concepts regarding gathering input from different input devices

- Presenting text output on the screen device, a much-needed feature to present game information to the player

- Adding three classes to our game classes library, used to control the different input devices and send feedback to the events controlled by the use of the game

- Adding one more class to our game library to control the display of text on screen

- Adding simple force-feedback effects to our games to explore new horizons in our games

In the next chapter, we'll introduce the DirectShow set of components, used to include streaming media support in our games (such as playing video files or MP3 music files), while examining basic gaming concepts about creating adventure games. We'll also look at how to code data access in .NET using ADO.NET.

## CHAPTER 6

# Magic KindergarteN.: Adventure Games, ADO.NET, and DirectShow

IN THIS CHAPTER we'll use some of the game classes created in the previous chapters, which will allow us to easily create a new kind of game—an adventure game—with only a few adjustments, as shown in Figure 6-1. This will also allow us to concentrate our efforts on creating new classes for this specific kind game. We'll create classes to manage the adventure game cursor and the player, and to load screens and objects, among other things.

*Figure 6-1. Magic KindergarteN., this chapter's sample game*

We'll also explore basic DirectShow concepts, which will allow us to play streaming media—for example, MP3 sound files or MPEG video files—as well as learn how to access data for our games using ADO.NET.

Before discussing any of these topics, we'll first look at the history of adventure games.

## Adventure Games

We don't know for sure when the term *adventure game* originated, but we can assume that the first person to use it was a role-playing game (RPG) fan, since the RPGs first became popular in the United States almost at the same time as the first Z80 computers hit the shelves.

The following sections present a short history of adventure games.

## Text-Based Adventures

The earlier adventure games didn't have any graphical element and were just interactive stories that you read through computer output and controlled by typing commands on a keyboard.

The very first adventures ran on mainframes (some well known titles were Adventure and Star Trek) whose dumb terminals didn't have any graphical capabilities. Sometime later they appeared on the first personal computers, but the video capabilities on these first desktops were very limited, with only block graphics or no graphics at all.

Even with these extremely limited graphics capabilities, we could find some adventure games that showed very simple graphics, sometimes built up with characters, but these graphics were used only as illustrations like those in books.

Most of these earlier adventure games took place in castles, caves, or labyrinths, just like the first board RPGs. Since then, both genres of game have evolved quite a bit, in different ways but always with many things in common. Since the first computer-based versions of some famous board RPGs appeared, such as Dungeon and Dragons, the border between computer RPGs and adventures has become fuzzy. Sometimes it's difficult to tell exactly the genre of some games, because adventures have also come to incorporate many RPG elements through the years.

One main difference between an RPG and an adventure game is the focus of the game. The main focus of an RPG is the player's character, who evolves as the player undertakes specific quests until the player is able to achieve the final goal, which is usually saving the world from some kind of danger. In adventures, we could say that the focus is more on the puzzles and the story than on the player, because the player character doesn't evolve or earn "experience points" as he or she solves the puzzles—the player just keeps solving the problems until the game is over. In adventures we usually see more text and more variation in the stories, and in RPGs we usually have more action than in adventures, but, as we said before, the border is sometimes fuzzy.

Examples of earlier adventures are Castle Elsinore and The Phantom's Revenge, from Temple Software. In these games, the normal game flow was something like this:

1.  The computer tells the user his or her current position and describes any game characters and what the player is carrying (the inventory).

2.  The player types the action he or she wants the computer to do.

3.  The computer parses the typed phrase and, hopefully, does something. Many times, all the player gets as a response is "I don't understand what you are saying."

If you're like us, you probably still remember the first adventure game you played, and the specific scene when the computer gave such a good answer that you became an instant fan of this type of game. However, you might also have become frustrated with the lack of useful responses. The input/output of such a game is shown in the following snippet. Try to imagine it on a black monochrome screen (such as a Hercules monitor, one of the most common ones when these early text-based adventure games were being played), which only displays 80 characters across and 25 rows down, with squared, glowing green characters and a blinking cursor. The capitalized phrases are the player's.

```
You are in a dark room.
You are carrying a glass of water.
> TURN ON LIGHT
The light is turned on.
You are in a big room. There is a sword on the floor.
There are doors to the north and the west.
You are carrying a glass of water.
> GET SWORD
You get the sword.
You are in a big room. There is a sword on the floor.
There are doors to the north and the west.
You are carrying a glass of water and a sword.
> GO WEST
You enter a small room. There is a flower here.
The flower is begging for water.
You are carrying a glass of water and a sword.
> WATER FLOWER
I don't understand "Water flower"
> GIVE WATER TO THE FLOWER
I don't understand "Give water to the flower"
> USE GLASS WITH WATER ON FLOWER
I don't understand "Use glass with water on flower"
> KILL FLOWER
Don't be ridiculous!
```

And that's it. This sort of treatment inspired one of your authors to write his first adventure game, Deep Cave. This adventure never hit the shelves, but was a good starting point to help him understand what is behind a game project.

The first graphical adventure game appeared shortly after that, as we'll discuss in the next section.

## Graphical Adventures

The first graphical adventure games offered little improvement over the text-based ones: They simply exchanged the room description with a static graphic, usually without colors. Still, these games were an important step forward because they allowed players to really see the differences from one room to another, as well as move through the game without needing to draw a map on a piece of paper to see where they were going and where they had been. There were many games with this primary interface, like The Hobbit and Inca Adventure, but just a few became widely recognized.

A big improvement occurred when Sierra launched its Leisure Suit Larry in the Land of the Lounge Lizards game. This was possibly the first adventure game to become a blockbuster, and it had many sequels.

"Larry," as the game was called by its fans, arrived before the mouse became widely used, so it still suffered from the interpretation problems of text-based adventure games: Sometimes the game simply didn't understand the command the user was typing. But it was packed full of humor, and the player character was finally seen on screen and actually moved and did actions as commanded. All of this was done using then cutting-edge 4-color enhanced graphics adapter (EGA) graphics.

Figure 6-2 shows a screen from the first of the Leisure Suit Larry series.

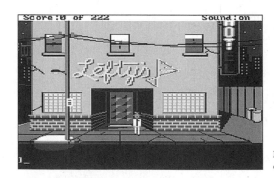

Leisure Suit Larry is a trademark
of Sierra Entertainment, Inc.

*Figure 6-2. Leisure Suit Larry in the Land of the Lounge Lizards*

Although games like this one usually had a help screen describing all verbs handled by the game, there was still room for improvement. The growing use of the mouse with PCs signaled the beginning of a new adventure game generation.

## Point-and-Click Adventures

The advent of the mouse greatly improved the usability of the adventures. Leisure Suit Larry had many sequels, and new series arose: King's Quest, Police Quest, Space Quest, Monkey Island, and many others.

Almost all of the first mouse-enabled adventure games had interfaces with some common points, which were improved upon in subsequent versions of each game: a main screen, a verb list, and an inventory. The *main screen* is where the actions take place and where the player must click objects to act upon them. A *verb list* is where the player chooses the current action by clicking a verb. An *inventory* is a list of the objects carried by the player. The last important component of an adventure is the dialog between the player-controlled character and the game characters. In a mouse-enabled adventure game, the dialog choices usually pops up somewhere on screen to allow the player to choose the phrases when talking to the nonplayer characters.

A good example of this kind of adventure is LucasArts Entertainment's The Secret of Monkey Island, which attracted a legion of new fans to this game genre. A screen shot of this game is shown in Figure 6-3.

© 1990 LucasArts Entertainment Company LLC.

*Figure 6-3. The Secret of Monkey Island*

As we can see in Figure 6-3, the inventory is just a list of names of objects (on the bottom-right side), and 12 different verbs (Open, Close, Push, Pull, Use, Walk to, etc.) from which to choose on the bottom-left side.

With each new version, the adventures gained simpler interfaces: fewer verbs, more tips on which objects can be used in the game (the *active objects*), improved gameplay and graphics. The genre then received a new description: *point-and-click* adventure games.

Eventually, the verbs were replaced by different mouse pointers, with each pointer representing one type of action, of which there were usually no more than five—for example, an eye icon for examining items, a hand for getting objects, a wrench for using objects, a pair of legs for walking, and a mouth for eating and talking.

LucasArts' Sam and Max Hit the Road reached even higher levels of abstraction, where even phrases in a dialog were not presented to the player to choose from. Only graphical tips for the phrases appeared on screen: The player would select a question mark to ask a question, an exclamation mark to explain something, a duck to chat, and sometimes a face to talk about a specific game character and an object icon when the player needs to talk about such an object in the game. Adventure game fans didn't like this kind of totally wordless interface, and later games returned to the previous formula. Figure 6-4 presents a typical Sam and Max Hit the Road screen.

© 1994 LucasArts Entertainment Company LLC.

*Figure 6-4. Sam and Max Hit the Road*

As we can see from this figure, the user interface has been reduced to a single box in the bottom-right corner of the screen for accessing the inventory. The mouse cursor changes to represent the verbs and icons to control the dialog, which appears only when the player starts a conversation. A typical example of icon dialogs is shown in Figure 6-5.

© 1994 LucasArts Entertainment Company LLC.

*Figure 6-5. Sam and Max Hit the Road dialog icons*

In the next section, we'll summarize the most important points to keep in mind when coding an adventure game.

# Technical Tips for Coding Adventure Games

As we've discussed previously, before writing the first line of code in any game, it's very important to generate a project in which we describe the game goals, details about the gameplay, design, etc. But when coding an adventure game, this kind of work is even more important.

Possibly the most critical item we must take into account when planning an adventure is the story. Of course the interface must be user friendly, or users may abandon the game before they've had enough time to understand the story, but the story is what will keep the user playing until the end of the game and produce enough interest to justify sequel games.

Many factors contribute to create a good story: the story flow, a good ending, deep characters with strong personality, well-thought-through and logical puzzles (neither too easy, nor too hard), and good dialogs. Making a good adventure game is a challenge that can be compared to making a good movie.

Here's a summary of the ten steps necessary to creating an adventure game. Of course this is not an exhaustive list, but it'll help you when creating your first adventure. After that, you'll be able to incorporate the extra steps you think are necessary, according to your own experience.

1. Define the main focus of your story: comedy, drama, terror, or what?

2. Define the game's goal: Will the player save the world? Will he or she defeat an enemy? Will the player find a treasure?

3. Choose the genre of graphics you'll use: Will they be realistic, cartoonish, or surreal? Defining the graphics genre early on will help your artistic team to start thinking about different possibilities when the next steps are discussed.

4. Write the game flow: How will the story go from beginning to end?

5. Describe game characters: Which characters will be presented? Which ones will be there to give playing tips? Which ones will only add color to the surroundings? Which will be friendly and which will be hostile? For each important character, you must define the character's background: What is his or her main motivation? What are his or her most important characteristics?

6. Specify the screens or rooms: What will be the game locations that the player will move across? Basically, we must read the game story and create "shots," breaking it into discrete pieces, one for each location.

7.  Create the puzzles and objects: These objects are usually very closely related. Logical puzzles are the key to a good adventure. You know that a specific adventure fails when you see the user is stuck, trying each object in the inventory with all objects on screen to find a solution. This is very common, and the game developer must create a balance between logical puzzles and easy ones to make the game more appealing.

8.  Write the game dialogs: It's in these dialogs that the player will discover the background of each of the characters. In some games a player might run into a muscly, angry-faced character and, upon talking to him, discover that in fact he is a friendly guy. This kind of surprise makes the game more interesting. Good dialog requires the development team to write different dialog paths in order to give the player a flexible approach when talking to the characters. Also, in some games the dialogs are part of the puzzles: You can solve a puzzle only by choosing the right words when speaking.

9.  Define a table describing the result for each action over each active object and character, and a table describing which objects will act with others: It's important not only to define the actions that will help with the game solution, but also extra actions that will add fun to the game's story.

10. Add the final touches: Think about *cut-scenes* (short movies used on introduction and between different game phases) that go deeper into the characters' backgrounds and the story flow. Create extra puzzles and characters. Define some *easter eggs* (hidden actions or screens that will only appear when the player does some specific action). Decide whether the game will have cheats or not, like secret codes to give extra power to the player character, or specific keyboard sequences that allow the player to go to the next the game level.

---

 **NOTE** *One important thing to remember when writing your games is that it's almost impossible to define ALL of your game details at the planning stage. When coding, new ideas will arise about how to increase character appeal, or new puzzles and extra features to be created; so it's up to you to create the perfect balance between planning too much and planning too little. An extreme in either category will usually lead to disaster.*

---

Another important point to stress is that the planning documents (scripts, storyboards, technical projects, spreadsheets, etc.) are not static, but living, and they get updated with more details and corrections as the project evolves.

On the technical side, you must think about the game interface: Will your game follow some interface pattern common to other games, or will you create something totally new? Where on screen will dialogs take place (below or above characters' heads, within balloons, etc.)? How can the user distinguish between background objects and active objects—with status text tips, highlights, or mouse pointer changes? Which actions will the game deal with? Will the mouse pointer change to reflect different action verbs chosen by the player? How many objects can be carried by the player? How will the player access these objects—through a game inventory?

## ADO.NET and Data Access in Games

It's not our goal in this section to discuss everything about data access or about ADO.NET; we'll only see the basic information we need to create a simple program that reads data from a given data source, and then use these concepts later in the chapter. We also won't see any details about how to update data or making searches on a database.

Game development teams usually choose to create their own data structures, not only for in-memory handling but also to store information on disk using their homemade data access routines. This approach is especially valuable when coding games of high graphical intensity, when you need to achieve the best performance results possible in every aspect of the game. But in other games (like most adventures), we don't think this is imperative, because extra time is spent writing data access routines instead of improving other aspects of the game.

---

 **TIP** *Using simple data access methods—such as reading text files or using premade data access routines, like ADO.NET—will also give your game extra appeal to international audiences: The easier the game is to translate (we are not talking about real localization, just translation), the better.*

*A good example of this is the first game of Sid Meyer's Civilization series: Much of the game's text was in text files and you could find, some time after the game was released, translated files (French, Portuguese, etc.) for this game on fan sites throughout the Internet.*

---

In the gaming world, ADO.NET can be used to read configuration files written with XML, read game data, and even save game files. Although writing your own read and save routines will always provide faster code, it is important to balance speed with the effort it takes to write your customized routines for each type of data access used in each new game.

ADO.NET has better XML integration (it can read and write XML files easily), better support to work with disconnected data (ideal for accessing remote data), better performance, and good integration with the .NET Framework, allowing you to navigate and retrieve data using arrays and collections, for example, thereby making the programs easier to write and maintain.

 **NOTE** *If you don't understand or don't care about XML and disconnected data, all you need to know is that ADO.NET is an evolution of the previous ADO library, and that it's faster and easier to use.*

ADO.NET offers two basic ways to manipulate data from a data source: using a DataSet, which allows us to read, navigate, and update data in the database, or reading the data directly from the database using a DataReader.

Choosing the object to access data is a matter of balancing flexibility against speed: DataSets are in-memory database representations that maintain synchronization with the database through a DataAdapter object and allow the program to update and navigate freely through the data read. With the DataReader object, the program can only read the data in a sequential way, but it is a lot faster.

On any of these approaches, our program must use a Connection object to make a link with the database, and a Command object to perform a data-retrieving operation. Usually the operations of opening a connection and executing a command consume a lot of time, so we must plan carefully how many times we'll open the connection and issue new commands.

Here is an explanation of the main ADO.NET objects:

- The Connection object handles the connection to the data source and controls the database transactions.

- The Command object represents a command to be executed upon a data source and includes explicit functionality such as the ExecuteNonQuery method for commands that do not return arguments, and the ExecuteScalar method for queries that return a single value rather than an argument set.

- The `DataSet` and `DataReader` objects are in-memory representations of a data source. The former provides a dynamic connection to the database, helping you update the data as necessary, and also provides some methods to read relational data as an XML hierarchy and transform it using XSL and XPath. The latter of these provides less functionality and fast read-only serial access to data, in a disconnected manner.

- The last object, `DataAdapter`, provides a bridge between the `DataSet` and the data source, hiding any specific details about the source from the `DataSet` and handling updates on the data sent back to the data source.

Visual Studio help is filled with explanations and simple examples, so we won't include additional details about ADO.NET; but we will instead provide the basic information to help us understand the data access code used in this chapter's sample game, Magic KindergarteN.

---

 **TIP** *If you want to learn more about .Net, refer to William R. Vaughn's book,* ADO.NET and ADO Examples and Best Practices for Visual Basic Programmers, *which is one of the best sources on the subject.*

---

Since we only need to read data sequentially, our program will follow three steps:

1. Create a `Connection` object and connect to the data source.

2. Create a `Command` object to execute a command—such as `Select * from ActiveObjects`, or, in common language, "read all information in the Active Objects table."

3. Create a `DataReader` to retrieve the result of the command and write the data into our game internal structures.

The following listing shows a complete sample of code for retrieving data from the Northwind.mdb database, the sample database that comes with Microsoft Access and Visual Studio, including the error trapping code:

```
Dim StrCategories as string = "Categories: "
Dim Conn As OleDbConnection
Dim Cmd As OleDbCommand
Dim DataReader As OleDbDataReader
Try
    ' Open the connection with the database
    ' (it must be in the application directory)
    Conn = New OleDbConnection( _
```

```
            "Provider=Microsoft.Jet.OLEDB.4.0;Data Source=" & _
            Application.StartupPath & "\NorthWind.mdb")
        Conn.Open()
        ' Create and execute the command that will retrieve the data
        Cmd = Conn.CreateCommand()
        Cmd.CommandText = "SELECT CategoryName from Categories"
        ' Fill the DataReader with the command data
        DataReader = Cmd.ExecuteReader()
        ' Display all category names in a message box
        Do While DataReader.Read()
            If (DataReader.IsDBNull(0)) Then
                StrCategories = StrCategories & _
                    "-" & DataReader.GetString(0)
            End If
        Loop
        MessageBox.Show(strCategories, "NorthWind Categories")

    Catch e As Exception
        MessageBox.Show("Unpredicted error when loading data: " & e.Message, _
            "Error", MessageBoxButtons.OK, MessageBoxIcon.Error)
    Finally
        ' Close the DataReader and free the command
        DataReader.Close()
        Cmd.Dispose()
    Conn.Close()
    End Try
```

In the next section we'll explore DirectShow, the object library that provides access to streaming media.

## Introducing DirectShow

DirectShow is the set of components within the DirectX architecture that enables capture, editing, and playback of multimedia streams.

The full set of features of DirectShow is very wide, but in the first version of managed DirectShow—for use inside the .NET Framework—we only have access to basic playback capabilities for streaming media, which can help us a lot if all we need is to play sound files like MP3 and WAV and video files such as MPEG, ASF, and AVI. As with all other DirectX components, DirectShow will take advantage of any video or audio acceleration hardware to improve its performance.

Since we don't have access to many features of DirectShow with this first managed version, it'll suffice for us to have a simple class, with a New method, where we'll perform the initialization, a Play method to start playing the streaming media, and a StopVideo method to stop playing any streaming media.

**NOTE** *We can't name the stop method "Stop" because this is a reserved word for Visual Basic.*

To implement these basic methods we'll add a reference to the AudioVideo-Playback interface of DirectX. This interface has only two objects, Video and Audio, which will enable the program to play a video or an audio file. These objects are very simple, with a basic set of methods and properties that help the program to perform streaming media playing operations and check state data. These objects don't support any events, which would be useful to inform the application about the state of any playing operation.

In our constructor (the New method) we must receive the control used as a video window, according to the parameters expected by the Video object constructor. The Play method must receive the name of the file to play; all other methods will not require any parameters.

Our Video class interface is described in the following piece of code:

```
Imports Microsoft.DirectX.AudioVideoPlayback
Public Class clsVideo
    Public VideoSize As Size
    Private VideoWindow As Windows.Forms.Control
    Public IsPlaying as boolean

    ' The class methods
    Public Sub New(ByVal WndVideo as Windows.Forms.Control)
    Public Sub Play(ByVal strFileName As String)
    Public Sub StopVideo()
    Public Sub PauseVideo()
End Class
```

After we implement this class, all we need to do to play a video is to create an object of this class, passing a reference to a window or form control, and then call the Play method for each file we wish to play.

Let's now look at and comment on the code for each method, to uncover some details about the DirectShow AudioVideoPlayback library. The following code sample shows the constructor of our class:

```
Public Sub New(ByVal WndVideo As Windows.Forms.Control)
    ' Stores the video window control and size for later use
    VideoWindow = WndVideo
    VideoSize = VideoWindow.Size
End Sub
```

As we can see, all we do in this first method is store the parameters in class properties. All the playing file work is done in the Play method, as we show in the subsequent code sample:

```
Public Sub Play(ByVal strFileName As String)
    ' Store the path to the file.
    strFileName = Application.StartupPath & "\" & VIDEOS_PATH & "\" & strFileName
    DxVideo = Nothing
    ' Set the control used as a owner to play the videos
    DxVideo = New Video(strFileName)
    DxVideo.Owner = VideoWindow

    ' Start playing
    DxVideo.Play()

    ' We must set the video window size again, because
    '  playing a video resizes the windows to the video's
    '  default size
    VideoWindow.Size = VideoSize
End Sub
```

The StopVideo method is also very simple; all we need to do is call the Stop method of the Video object, as presented in the following code sample:

```
Public Sub StopVideo()
    ' If there's no media running, there might be errors.
    '  -> We'll just ignore them
    Try
        DxVideo.Stop()
    Catch
    End Try
End Sub
```

The PauseVideo method follows the same structure as the previous code sample, using the Pause method of the Video object.

The last element of our class is the IsPlaying property. We can calculate it comparing the video's current position with its duration, as we do in the next code example: If they are equal, it means that the video is over.

```
Public ReadOnly Property IsPlaying() As Boolean
    Get
        Try
            If DxVideo.CurrentPosition = DxVideo.Duration Then
                IsPlaying = False
            Else
                IsPlaying = True
            End If
        Catch
            ' Ignore error if DxVideo is not initialized
        End Try
    End Get
End Property
```

Once this class is finished, we can play a video with three lines of code, as shown in the following code:

```
Public Video As clsVideo
Video = New clsVideo(picVideo)
Video.Play("MySampleVideo.AVI")
```

In the next section, we'll discuss the proposal for the sample game of this chapter and the next, including the concepts discussed in the previous sections.

## The Game Proposal

In this chapter, we'll create a very simple adventure game named Magic KindergarteN.

While our adventure is simple, it must still address some of the most common problems encountered when coding a complex adventure:

- Choosing verbs, or actions, with the mouse pointer (right button changes the mouse pointer icon). We'll use the verbs Walk to, Use, Talk, Take, and Examine.

- Controlling an inventory to show the objects carried by the player.

- Using objects from the inventory with other objects on screen.

- Controlling the dialog between the player's character and nonplayer characters.

- Controlling the navigation within the game (walking from one screen to another).

Initially, our adventure will be much like a book, because we'll use only static images as we build the game in this chapter. In the next chapter, we'll discuss basic animation and incorporate simple animation into our game.

As for the dialogs, we'll implement them only in the next chapter, when presenting the basics about the Speech API.

The game storyline for our game will be as follows:

*The main character in our game will be a little boy, a magician's son, who is studying basic tricks in a magic kindergarten. Natanael (that's his name) arrives one day at school and finds no one there, just a big television that can play some movies and a magic book. Looking around, he finds a mud monster. It turns out to be Natanael's teacher, Fiona. Fiona was trying some metamorphosis tricks when she lost her magic wand. She asks Natanael to find it for her.*

*Natanael looks around and can't find the wand, but he does find a magic mushroom, which is able to make him small. When he turns small, he manages to enter a mouse hole inside the school, where he can find the wand, and then help his teacher to get back to her normal form.*

Based on this storyline, we'll now create the screens, dialogs, active objects, and tables that describe the results of each action over each object.

## The Game Project

Our project will be divided into three main sections: defining the game screens and the flow between these screens; defining what characters will be present, and what will be the result of each action on each character; and defining the results of these actions on all other active objects in our game. Besides these sections, which will help us to define how we'll implement the storyline described in the game proposal, we'll include in our project some technical sections to define the game interface elements, the class diagram, and the database that will store the game data.

After we write all the sections in the game project, we'll have enough detail to start coding our game. Since it's very important that the whole team shares the same vision of what the game will be, it's good practice to include as many visual feedback elements in the project phase as possible. This is usually done by including early drafts of screens, characters, and objects, but in our case we'll show the final drawings, since they've already been done. All the drawings for this game (except for the table and the TV used to test DirectShow) were made by Waldivar Cesar (http://wace.cosmo.com.br), a Brazilian graphical artist.

As for the technical side, we'll create a class diagram depicting the classes we'll use in the coding phase, including the classes we created in the previous chapters, and highlighting the new classes to be created.

## Creating Game Screens

We'll use the storyline described in the section "The Game Proposal" to determine the screens needed for our game.

We must imagine the story as a comic book, with as few scenes as possible, to define our screens. This technique is also used when defining the cut-scenes in many games, and is usually called *storyboarding*.

Let's read our little story again and start creating the game screens and composing the presentation text used in each screen, which will be displayed every time the player enters each screen.

*The main character in our game will be a little boy, a magician's son, who is studying basic tricks in a magic kindergarten. Natanael (that's his name) arrives one day at school and finds no one there, just a big television that can play some movies and a magic book.*

The first sentence describes the player's character, while the second one describes the first location: a school. Figure 6-6 shows the first game screen.

*Figure 6-6. The magic kindergarten school*

To adapt the story to presentation text, we must use shorter sentences, since the player will be reading them on screen. And since we won't implement dialogs with the game characters in this first version, we'll substitute the dialog with fixed sentences on each screen. One possible approach to the text of this screen is as follows:

> *Natanael arrives on his first day at magic kindergarten, but he doesn't find anyone waiting for him there.*

> *"Where's my teacher?" he thinks.*

Looking back at the first sentence, we can see that, in fact, it describes two locations: one depicting an outside view of the school (*he arrives . . .*), and another representing the inside of it ( *. . . there*). Figure 6-7 shows the inside view of the school.

*Figure 6-7. The magic kindergarten schoolroom*

We include a table inside the school because we need to use DirectShow somewhere in this game, so we'll create a TV on the table that can play some movies for us. There must be a mouse hole somewhere, too (an active object, to be added later), as we read in the story. The presentation text will be as follows:

*Inside the kindergarten school, there's a huge table with a TV on it. There's a mouse hole in the wall.*

Of course, the player will have already seen the TV and the mouse hole on screen, but including these items in the text will give hints to the player about which visual cues are the important objects on screen.

Getting back to our story, let's see the next sentences:

*Looking around, he finds a mud monster. It turns out to be Natanael's teacher, Fiona. Fiona was trying some metamorphosis tricks when she lost her magic rod. She asks Natanael to find it for her.*

In the previous text, we can see a description of a second game character, a nonplayer character called Fiona. Write this down on a piece of paper; we'll be detailing the game characters in the next section.

Following the idea of thinking about the story as a comic book, we see that we can't place the Fiona character in any of the first screens designed for the game, because the first part of the story states that the player didn't find anyone at the school (outside and inside). We'll need a third screen, some location in which to put our nonplayer character. This can be a forest clearing near the school, as shown in Figure 6-8.

*Figure 6-8. A clearing in the forest*

The presentation text for this screen will be as follows:

*Entering the forest, Natanael meets a mud monster.*

*Natanael, please help me! Says the monster.*

*I'm Fiona, your teacher! I was practicing my mutation magic when I lost my magic wand. Can you find it for me?*

Continuing with our story, we have this text:

*Natanael looks around and can't find the wand, but he does find a magic mushroom that is able to make him small.*

We could simply include a mushroom (it will be one of the game's active objects) on the same screen as Fiona's character, but that would be too easy. It's not our goal here to create a great adventure, with many clever puzzles, but let's at least add an extra screen so the player will need to do some more walking before finding the mushroom. The next screen, illustrating another part of the forest, is depicted in Figure 6-9.

*Figure 6-9. Another part the forest—the mushroom clearing*

This screen will have the following presentation text:

*Natanael finds another clearing in the forest, with an old tree and an owl. In the middle of the clearing, there's a strange mushroom.*

The last sentence of our story suggests still another screen, as we can see in the following text:

*When he gets small, he manages to enter a mouse hole inside the school, where he can find the wand, and then help his teacher to get back to her normal form.*

The wand is found inside the mouse hole, so we'll need an inside view of the mouse hole. We must remember later to include an active object representing the mouse hole inside the school. Figure 6-10 shows the last of our game screens.

*Figure 6-10. Inside the mouse hole*

We can describe this screen as follows:

*Natanael finds the magic wand. It's inside the mouse hole. Hopefully, there are no mice here right now, so all he needs to do is take the wand and give it to Fiona.*

In Figure 6-11 we show the flow between the screens, and give a number to each one to help us identify them later on in the project.

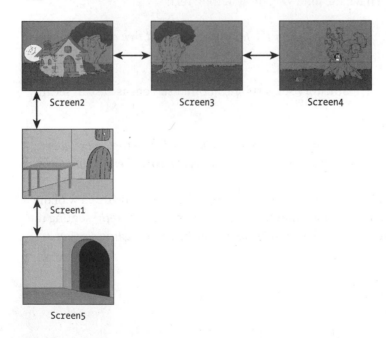

*Figure 6-11. The game flow between screens*

In the diagram presented in Figure 6-11, we can see the screens ordered as the game flows; for example, when the player walks to the right from Screen2, he or she will go to Screen3. The story begins when Natanael arrives at the school, so our game will begin on Screen2. From this screen, this character can walk into the school (Screen1) or away to the forest (Screen3).

In the next section we'll see the details of the game characters.

## Drawing Game Characters

As we saw in the previous sections, our game will consist of two main characters: the player, Natanael, and his teacher, Fiona.

Before drawing anything, we must create a profile for each character so our team of artists can understand exactly what we want. So let's look at a short briefing of each character and then see the artistic result:

- **Natanael:** He's a young boy, about five years old. Although his parents are magicians, he is a regular boy, and dresses like one. (No hats here!) He lives in a house near school, in a forest, and walks to kindergarten everyday, where he is learning the first magical tricks a magician must learn. Figure 6-12 shows the graphical artist's view of our character.

*Figure 6-12. Natanael, the player's character*

- **Fiona:** Fiona is Natanael's teacher at the magic kindergarten. She is an old woman, and dresses like a fairy, but for most of our game flow she is a monster composed only of mud (no clothes). She is a very kind person, and this must be clear from looking at her, and she also gets a little confused from time to time (as we can guess based on her losing her magic wand). Figure 6-13 shows Fiona's character as a mud monster, and Figure 6-14 shows her in her human form.

*Figure 6-13. Fiona, the player's teacher, as a mud monster*

*Figure 6-14. Fiona back to human form*

A question that arises for many developers when starting to code games is, Why must we describe character profiles? What's the point, after all, in saying that a character is a "very kind person," or that he "gets a little confused"?

Although such profiles may not appear to have a direct impact on the game, they are very important, even for fast-paced action games, because they allow the team to understand the images we are trying to put across to the player. These profiles help the artist to understand what we want, and create more realistic or more cartoonlike characters; and they also help the coders to think about new jokes, puzzles, or action sequences that fit the character's personality.

In a real game, at this point the team must start thinking about extra characters that will add some color to the scenery, making the game more interesting. Since our objective is to keep the game very simple, we won't add other characters, but we'll suggest some in the "Adding the Final Touches" section, so you can think about new game sequences.

To finish our characters' descriptions, we must define the result of each action over each of the characters. Regarding the player's character, Natanael, in our game, he will not be an active object. This means that we can't try to take him, or examine him, or execute any other action on him. As for Fiona, the following tables present the result of each verb the player issues over her, starting with Fiona as a monster, presented in Table 6-1.

*Table 6-1. Result of Each Action on Fiona as Mud Monster*

| ACTION | EXECUTE? | DISPLAY TEXT |
| --- | --- | --- |
| Examine | Yes | Ech! It's a mud monster! |
| Take | No | I don't want to put my hands on this dirty thing! |
| Walk to | No | I'd rather not. I would get stuck in the mud. |
| Use | No | I can't use a monster! |

Table 6-2 shows the results of the same actions when performed over Fiona's character when transformed back to human.

*Table 6-2. Result of Each Action on Fiona in Human Form*

| ACTION | EXECUTE? | DISPLAY TEXT |
| --- | --- | --- |
| Examine | Yes | My teacher is cured! |
| Take | No | I can't take her. |
| Walk to | No | I can't walk to her. I'm already here. |
| Use | No | I can't use my teacher. |

In the next section, we'll discuss these same actions for each of the active objects in the game.

## Active Objects

An *active object* is any element on screen that the player can act upon—for example, the television in the kindergarten and the magic mushroom. In this class we'll have some extra elements: invisible objects that will mark the transition from one screen to another, so the player can "walk" to the next screen.

Reading the storyline for our game again and looking at the screen definitions, we can create a list of the basic active objects, including the screen transitions (see Table 6-3). In a real adventure, such a list can take dozens of pages, and gets updated as the game project evolves and new ideas arise.

*Table 6-3. The Active Objects List, with Verbs Results*

| SCREEN | OBJECT | ACTION | EXECUTE? | DISPLAY TEXT |
|---|---|---|---|---|
| 1 | Magic book | Examine | Yes | It's my teacher's magic book. |
| | | Take | No | I'd rather not. I don't want to be transformed into a frog. |
| | | Walk to | No | Walk into a book? I'm still in the kindergarten! |
| | | Use | No | No, thanks. I could mess things up. |
| | Television | Examine | Yes | Wow, it's a huge TV! How can I turn it on? |
| | | Take | No | The TV is too heavy to carry. |
| | | Walk to | No | I still haven't learned the magic for walking into a TV, yet. |
| | | Use | Yes | What happens if I press these buttons? |
| | Door | Examine | Yes | This door leads to outside the school. |
| | | Take | No | I can't take it. It's bolted to the wall. |
| | | Walk to | Yes | OK, I'll go outside. |
| | | Use | No | It's already unlocked. |
| | Mouse hole | Examine | Yes | I can see the magic wand in there, but I can't take it! |
| | | Take | No | I can't take a hole! |
| | | Walk to (when big) | No | I'm too big to fit in there! |
| | | Walk to (when small) | Yes | Now I can go in there! |
| | | Use | No | I can't use a hole! |

*Table 6-3. The Active Objects List, with Verbs Results (continued)*

| SCREEN | OBJECT | ACTION | EXECUTE? | DISPLAY TEXT |
| --- | --- | --- | --- | --- |
| 2 | Door | Examine | Yes | It's my school's entrance door. |
| | | Take | No | Are you kidding? Take a door? |
| | | Walk to | Yes | OK, let's go in! |
| | | Use | No | There's nothing to do here. It's unlocked. |
| | Path to forest | Éxamine | Yes | If I walk this way, I'll reach the forest. |
| | | Take | No | I can't take a path! |
| | | Walk to | Yes | Let's go to the forest! |
| | | Use | No | I can't use a path! |
| 3 | Exit to school | Examine | Yes | If I walk this way, I'll go back to my school. |
| | | Take | No | I can't take a path, I must walk on it! |
| | | Walk to | Yes | It's time to get back to school. |
| | | Use | No | I can't use a path, I must walk on it! |
| | Exit to forest | Examine | Yes | That's the path to the deep forest. |
| | | Take | No | I can't take this. |
| | | Walk to | Yes | OK, it's far from school, but I'll go there! |
| | | Use | No | I can't use this. |
| 4 | Exit to monster clearing | Examine | Yes | I must walk this way to get back to the forest. |
| | | Take | No | I can't take a path! |
| | | Walk to | Yes | Let's get back to the forest! |
| | | Use | No | I can't use a path! |
| | Mushroom | Examine | Yes | It's a big and weird mushroom. |
| | | Take | No | It's stuck to the forest ground. |
| | | Walk to | No | I can't walk to it |
| | | Use | Yes | I ate a piece of it . . . Oh, my, I feel SO strange . . . |

*Table 6-3. The Active Objects List, with Verbs Results (continued)*

| SCREEN | OBJECT | ACTION | EXECUTE? | DISPLAY TEXT |
|---|---|---|---|---|
| 5 | Magic wand | Examine | Yes | It's my teacher's magic wand! |
| | | Take | Yes | I'll take it and give it to my teacher! |
| | | Walk to | No | I can't walk over a magic wand! |
| | | Use | No | I must use it ON something. |
| | | Use (with teacher) | Yes | Wow! I managed to transform the monster back to my teacher! |
| | | Use (with any other) | No | I can't use the magic wand on THIS! |
| | Mouse hole | Examine | Yes | I must walk this way to get out of here. |
| | | Take | No | I can't take a hole! |
| | | Walk to | Yes | OK, it's time to get out of here. |
| | | Use | No | I can't use a hole! |

Table 6-3 summarizes everything we need to know about the game active objects, and with it we have enough planning information to start our game. But on the technical side, before coding we'd better define a draft of the user interface elements. These are the game classes, including some previously created classes we'll use and new ones we must create, as well as other details, like defining the entity-relationship data model for our project so we can have better control over the development phase.

The user interface elements are described in the next section.

## User Interface Elements Draft

Before writing the game classes, it's always good practice to draw some sketches of the user interface elements. This usually serves as a guide to the game classes' creation.

Figure 6-15 shows a first draft of the game user interface elements.

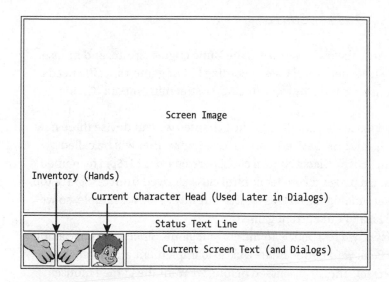

*Figure 6-15. Game user interface elements, first draft*

As shown in Figure 6-15, our user interface will be very simple: Almost all of the screen will show the current screen image. We'll have a status text line and an area reserved for displaying the current screen text (sufficient to display 4 lines of about 60 characters each). A character's head will represent the current character in a dialog (used only in the next version of the game, in the next chapter), and our inventory is represented by the image of two hands, upon which the objects currently carried will be shown.

Another interface element, not expressed in Figure 6-15, is the mouse pointer. In our game, we'll have four action verbs (walk, take, examine, and use), which will be active according to the current mouse pointer. The possible mouse pointers, including one extra pointer for a "wait" state, are displayed in Figure 6-16.

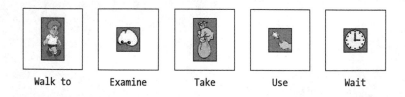

*Figure 6-16. Mouse pointer icons for each action*

The mouse pointers must cycle when the user presses the right button on the mouse.

In the next section we discuss the suggested class diagram for our game.

## Creating the Class Diagram

In our project we'll use the base classes for the game engine, sprite, and mouse control, and then create derived classes according to our game's specific needs. We'll also create a new class to control DirectShow streaming media playing features.

Using the experience we gained in the last chapter, we can devise three new classes: a game control class, derived from clsGameEngine, that will be called clsKinderEngine; an active objects control class, derived from clsSprite, named clsActiveObject; and a player character control class, derived from clsSprite too, named clsAdvPlayer. Analogous classes exist in our River Pla.Net sample, so we just transpose the idea to our current game.

Two other classes will be specific to the current game. Since we'll have a non-continuous game field, we'd better create a class to implement any details at screen level (clsScreen); and, as discussed before, we want the game's mouse pointer to have custom images that can be replaced according to the action to be performed. So we'll create a class named clsAdvPointer to handle this.

The next sections describe the main properties and methods for each of the game classes, starting with the game engine class. In real game projects, these first drafts of the properties and methods are the result of a brainstorming session between the game team members, and other interface elements may be included in the classes as the project evolves; but here we will just present the results of such efforts.

### The Game Engine Class

The game engine class (clsKinderEngine) interface is presented in Table 6-4. We present here a brief explanation of the class members; we'll look at them in more detail in the section "The Coding Phase."

*Table 6-4. The Game Engine Class*

| TYPE | NAME | DESCRIPTION |
| --- | --- | --- |
| Property | TalkingHead | Indictates the current character head, to be shown on screen |
| Property | LeftHand | Represents the left hand (first inventory slot) |
| Property | LeftHandObject | Represents the object carried by the left hand |
| Property | RightHand | Represents the right hand (second inventory slot) |
| Property | RightHandObject | Represents the object carried by the right hand |
| Property | TextBackground | Specifies the text background to be displayed on screen |
| Property | Text | Indicates the current screen text (array with four elements) |
| Property | StatusText | Indicates the status text |
| Property | CurrentScreen | Specifies the current screen object |
| Property | Pointer | Indicates the mouse pointer |
| Property | Player | Represents the player's character |
| Property | Video | Represents the Video class object to play videos on the TV |
| Property | Mouse | Indicates the DirectInput class that controls the mouse |
| Method | Initialize | Initializes all objects and properties |
| Method | TestCollision | Checks for collision to update the status text |
| Method | Render | Draws the screen |
| Method | MouseDown | Changes the mouse pointer, executes the action (Do . . .) methods |
| Method | MouseMove | Moves the mouse pointer and calls the TestCollision method |
| Method | DoExamine | Executes the Examine action on an object |
| Method | DoTake | Executes the Take action on an object |
| Method | DoWalk | Executes the Walk to action on an object |
| Method | DoUseAlone | Executes the Use action on an object |
| Method | DoUseWith | Uses one object in the inventory with another object on screen |
| Method | PlayTVChannel | Calls DirectShow playing features |

Although we are usually tempted to not include much detail in our project, the game engine class includes a lot of properties and methods. By spending some extra time thinking about which details we'll need in our code to implement all features planned, we'll save ourselves a lot of effort later, and ultimately we'll have a better game made in less time. Take a little time to carefully read each of the properties and methods in the preceding table, in order to guarantee that you understand what we'll do in our sample.

## The Active Object Class

Table 6-5 shows the description of the methods and properties for the active object (clsActiveObject) class, which is more straightforward than the clsKinderEngine class. It includes only the properties directly associated with the actions that can be executed over the object.

*Table 6-5. The Active Object Class*

| TYPE | NAME | DESCRIPTION |
| --- | --- | --- |
| Property | Name | Represents the name of the active object |
| Property | CanTake | Specifies if the player can take the object |
| Property | CanWalk | Specifies if the player can walk to the object |
| Property | CanUseWithOther | Specifies if the player can use the object with another object |
| Property | CanUseAlone | Specifies if the player can use the object (alone) |
| Property | ExamineText | Indicates the text to be displayed when executing the Examine action |
| Property | TakeText | Indicates the text to be displayed when executing the Take action |
| Property | WalkText | Indicates the text to be displayed when executing the Walk to action |
| Property | UseWithOtherText | Indicates the text to be displayed when using the object with another object |
| Property | UseAloneText | Indicates the text to be displayed when executing the Use action |
| Method | New | Does the class initialization, loading the object data from a database |

Since the game's active objects are derived from our basic Sprite class, defined in Chapter 4, all the properties and methods of the base class will be present, too: Width, Height, Draw, etc.

## The AdvPlayer Class

The next class to be described is the class that will control the adventure player, clsAdvPlayer. This class will be very simple. Besides the elements of the base class, we'll only need an extra property to determine if the player is in a normal state or reduced, and a new Draw method that will draw the player accordingly.

The screen control class will also be very simple, and it'll be named clsScreen. Since it will be derived from the clsSprite class, all we need to do is to create an array to hold all the screen's active objects, and specific New and Draw methods that will load the active objects when the screen is created and draw the active objects on the screen.

The last of our game classes, as mention before, will be the game pointer class, clsAdvPointer, which will store each of the possible action icons and the associated text for the verbs. Table 6-6 shows the first draft for the properties and methods of this class.

*Table 6-6. The Adventure Pointer Class*

| TYPE | NAME | DESCRIPTION |
|------|------|-------------|
| Property | Status | Indicates the current action verb/pointer status |
| Property | WalkIcon | Specifies the image to draw for the Walk to action |
| Property | ExamineIcon | Specifies the image to draw for the Examine action |
| Property | TakeIcon | Specifies the image to draw for the Take action |
| Property | UseIcon | Specifies the image to draw for the Use action |
| Property | WaitIcon | Specifies the image to draw when in wait state |
| Property | Object1Icon | Specifies the image to draw when carrying one object in the left hand |
| Property | Object2Icon | Specifies the image to draw when carrying one object in the right hand |
| Property | WalkText | Indicates the Walk to action text |
| Property | ExamineText | Indicates the Examine action text |
| Property | TakeText | Indicates the Take action text |
| Property | UseText | Indicates the Use action text |
| Method | Draw | Draws the pointer according to the current status |
| Method | NextStatus | Cycles the pointer status |

We suggested the creation of properties to hold the action text to make a possible translation easier: All user interface strings will be located in tables in a Microsoft Access database that will be read when loading each object.

Figure 6-17 shows the final class diagrams, depicting the classes described in this section plus the base classes we'll use.

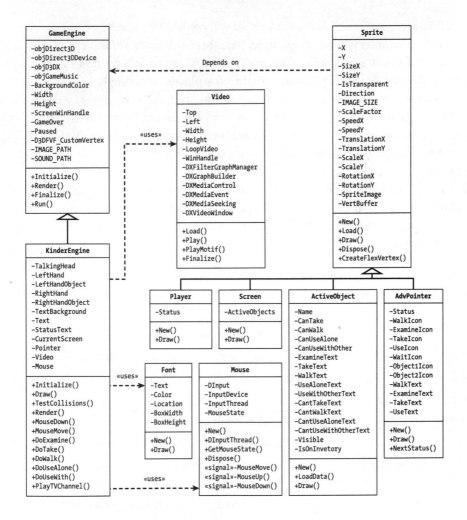

*Figure 6-17. Magic KindergarteN. class diagram*

In the next section we'll define the data model for our game, according to the properties of the game classes.

## Creating the Game's Data Model

We'll create a simple Microsoft Access database to store all the game data. Microsoft Access has the advantage of being very easy to use and also being portable—you can simply copy the .mdb file from one place to another to move your data.

Since we are planning to put all the game strings in this data file, we must create a new table to hold the game pointer verbs (with just one record with the verbs used for the current language), and tables for screen text, screen number, and active objects data. The Screen table is the one that glues everything together, as we can see from Figure 6-18.

*Figure 6-18. Magic KindergarteN. data model*

The Active Object table in Figure 6-18 holds all the class properties, as described in the previous section, plus some extra information we'll explain in the next sections. For example, we create some extra properties to control the use of one object with another, and create pairs of texts for each verb: the text to display when you can't execute the verb, and the text to display when you can.

In the next section we'll discuss the game's main program flow, finalizing the game project phase.

## *Planning the Main Program Flow*

The main program for our game will be analogous to the main program we saw in the previous chapter, although the games are completely different. The pseudo-code for it will be very simple, as shown in the following sample:

```
Create a window to be the game screen
Create an object from KinderEngine class
Create the splash screen
Show the splash screen
Initialize KinderEngine object
Show the game window
Close the splash screen
Run the game (execute method RUN from KinderEngine object)
' The Run is a syncronous method, it will return when the game ends
Destroy the KinderEngine object
Dispose the game window
```

Comparing this sample code with the sample code from Chapter 4, you'll notice that there are very few differences between them; in fact, we can say that almost all games will follow this basic structure.

In the next section we'll show the main parts of our adventure game.

## The Coding Phase

Even a simple adventure like this involves hundreds of lines of code, and we can get lost in the tiny details if we try to look at all of them here. Instead, we'll take a look at the game's main routines, to understand what is being done, and we'll leave some details aside. To see the complete sample code, refer to the accompanying CD-ROM.

We'll divide our coding phase into discrete steps, so we can focus on specific features to understand every main aspect of the game, and easily reuse the techniques shown in other games:

1.  First draft: Code the screen and active objects data loading.

2.  Second draft: Code the mouse pointer cycling (action verbs) and status text updating.

3.  Third draft: Code the mouse pointer actions.

4.  Final version: Code the player and the inventory.

Our main purpose in dividing the program into well-controlled steps is to establish milestones, where we can check the game coding process and the overall code quality. This is a very common approach, and this quality practice can be reinforced by creating day builds of the program and following the paradigm, "You must always have an executable version."

In the next section we'll use ADO.NET to load data for the screens and objects.

## First Draft: Loading the Game Data

Our main objective in this first step is to load information from the game database and transform it into the game objects—screens and active objects. After loading the data, we'll code the basic game routines to display the objects on screen.

Let's start coding the Initialize method of the KinderEngine class, so we'll have a better idea about how the New method of the Screen class must work to get things running.

Since we want to load all the data for the screens at startup, a possible pseudo-code for the Initialize method is shown in the next listing:

```
From Screen1 to Screen5
     Create the screen object
     Load the screen data
     Load the Active Objects for the screen
Create the font objects that will display the screen text for the current screen
Set the current screen to Screen2     ' as planned in the game flow diagram
```

The font objects mentioned in the previous code listing are the same objects we created in the preceding chapter to display text on screen.

The next listing shows the code for the `Initialize` method of the `KinderEngine` class. One important point to remember is that this class is derived from `clsGameEngine`, the generic game engine class created earlier in this book. We'll need to call the base class `Initialize` method in order to properly initialize the Direct3D components. Two other important functions we must code are the `Render` method, which will actually put the drawings of our game on screen and is called by the loop inside the `Run` method of `clsGameEngine` class, and the `Finalize` method, if we want to add any specific finalization code.

```
Public Shared Text() As ClsGameFont
Private Shared Screen() As ClsScreen
Private Shared CurrentScreen As ClsScreen
...
Public Shadows Function Initialize(owner As Windows.Forms.Control) As Boolean
    Dim WinHandle As IntPtr = owner.Handle
    Dim i As Integer
    ReDim Text(3)
    ReDim Screen(5)

    Initialize = True
    ' Start Direct3D, with a full screen 800x600 resolution
    If Not MyBase.Initialize(WinHandle, True, 800, 600) Then
        Initialize = False
        Exit Function
    End If

    ' Load the screens
    For i = 0 To 4
        Screen(i) = New ClsScreen()
        If Not Screen(i).LoadData(i + 1, 0) Then
            Initialize = False
            Exit Function
        End If
    Next

    ' Initialize the game text fields
    For i = 0 To 3
        Text(i) = New ClsGameFont("Microsoft Sans Serif", 14, Space(120), _
            New POINT(236, 525 + i * 18))
    Next
```

```
    ' Set the startup screen
    CurrentScreen = Screen(1)
    ' Update the text strings with the current screen text
    UpdateScreenText()
End Function

Shared Sub UpdateScreenText()
    Dim i As Integer
    For i = 0 To 3
        Text(i).Text = CurrentScreen.Text(i)
    Next
End Sub
```

As we can see in this code listing, it would appear to be better to create a separate method, LoadData, to load each screen data (based on the screen number), so we can retrieve easily any error and abort the program. Another point that deserves a special mention is the creation of the Font objects: the position of the text on screen, given by the Point parameter, was calculated via a trial-and-error algorithm; we simply keep changing these numbers until we have positioned the text as we wish to.

If we create the clsScreen class now with empty methods, we can already run our code and test it. Besides the New and Draw methods, mentioned in the class diagram, we must define the LoadData method, which will load the screen data based on the screen number and three extra properties: the Text string array, which will hold the screen text; the ScreenNumber, which will store the screen identification number; and the ActiveObjectsNumber, which will express the quantity of active objects on the current screen.

---

 **TIP** *Once again, why did some methods and properties not appear in the class diagram? As we have said in previous chapters, in a real-world game project we must try to create the best project possible, with enough details that will guarantee quality code; but we must take care to maintain a proper balance and not get into an "analysis-paralysis" hole, and never finish the project. So we are using the same paradigm here, at a simpler level: We define in our class diagrams only the obvious properties and methods, and discover new ones when coding, because we then see, as in a real project, new details that were not clear when planning.*

---

The next code listing shows the Screen class interface:

```
Imports Microsoft.DirectX.Direct3D
Imports Microsoft.DirectX

Public Class ClsScreen
    Inherits clsSprite
    Public ActiveObjectsNumber As Integer = 0
    Public ActiveObjects() As clsActiveObject
    Public ScreenNumber As Integer

    ' The four text lines for the current screen.
    ' Each line can have up to 60 chars
    Public Text() As String

    Sub New()
    Shadows Sub Draw()
    Function LoadData(ByVal intScreenNumber As Integer, ByVal screenStatus As
End Class
```

We are able to run our program now, and see the splash screen as shown in Figure 6-19.

*Figure 6-19. The game splash screen*

After the screen is loaded, the video goes blank, because we haven't included any code in the Render method to draw anything yet. And of course, there's nothing to be shown until we code the screen class.

The most important method in the screen class is LoadData, which will open the database and load the screen data (in our case, only the screen text) and then load all active objects for the current screen. We can do this last step by calling a LoadData method on the ActiveObject class, passing the appropriate parameters. For example, we can pass the screen number and the object number; or we can open the database and access the Active Objects table in the screen LoadData method, and then pass the record to the ActiveObject class to read the object data. This last approach is better, since we can reuse the opened connection to the database and generate faster code.

The next listing shows the LoadData code. Some lines have been suppressed for clarity—such as the error handling routines. As we can see, the data access code is very similar to the one we saw when presenting ADO.NET, which can be divided into these three steps:

1. Open the connection.

2. Create a command and read the screen text (from the ScreenText table).

3. Create a command and read the ActiveObjects data (from the Active Objects table).

After this last step, we create the active objects, passing the DataReader object as a parameter to the New method. We'll code the ActiveObject class using this sequence. Refer to the code comments to find out the purpose of each code line.

```
Function LoadData(intScreenNumber As Integer, screenStatus As Integer) As Boolean
    Dim i As Integer
    LoadData = True
    ScreenNumber = intScreenNumber
    ReDim Text(3) ' Redim the array erases any previous contents

    ' Load the data for the current screen from the database
    Dim StrConnection as string = _
        "Provider=Microsoft.Jet.OLEDB.4.0;Data Source=" _
        & Application.StartupPath & "\Data\KinderData.mdb"
    Dim Conn As OleDbConnection
    Dim Cmd As OleDbCommand
    Dim DataReader As OleDbDataReader
```

```
' Load the current screen image, using the Load method of the base class
If Not Load("screen" & screenNumber & ".bmp") Then
    MessageBox.Show("Error loading the screen image", _
        "KindergarteN. Error", MessageBoxButtons.OK, MessageBoxIcon.Error)
    LoadData = False
End If


' Open the connection with the database
Conn = New OleDbConnection(StrConnection)
Conn.Open()
' Create and execute the command which will retrieve the screen text
Cmd = Conn.CreateCommand()
Cmd.CommandText = "SELECT text from ScreenText where ScreenNumber = " & _
                ScreenNumber & " order by TextNumber"
DataReader = Cmd.ExecuteReader()
' Load the screen text from the database
i = 0
Do While DataReader.Read()
    If (DataReader.IsDBNull(0)) Then
        Text(i) = " "
    Else
        Text(i) = DataReader.GetString(0)
    End If
    i += 1
Loop
' Close the DataReader and free the command
DataReader.Close()
Cmd.Dispose()


' We'll have 5 objects at maximum on each screen
ReDim ActiveObjects(5)
' Create and execute the command to retrieve the active objects data
Cmd = Conn.CreateCommand()
Cmd.CommandText = _
    "SELECT * from ActiveObject where ScreenNumber = " & ScreenNumber
DataReader = Cmd.ExecuteReader()
' Load each of the objects
Do While DataReader.Read()
    ActiveObjects(ActiveObjectsNumber) = New clsActiveObject(DataReader)
    ActiveObjectsNumber += 1
Loop
' Close the DataReader and free the command
DataReader.Close()
```

```
        Cmd.Dispose()
        ' Close the connection with the database
        Conn.Close()
End Function
```

If we comment the active object lines in the previous procedure and run our program, all we'll see is the current screen, without objects or any interface elements. So, before running our program, we'll code the active object class. The class interface, shown in the next code listing, is a direct representation of the class diagram and the data model of our project, although some extra properties will be included when we code the inventory handling.

```
Public Class clsActiveObject
    Inherits clsSprite

    Public Name As String
    Public CanTake As Boolean
    Public CanWalk As Boolean
    Public CanUseWithOther As Boolean
    Public CanUseAlone As Boolean
    Public CanTalk As Boolean

    ' Text to show when doing each action
    Public ExamineText As String
    Public TakeText As String
    Public WalkText As String
    Public UseWithOtherText As String
    Public UseAloneText As String

    ' Text to show when each action can't be done
    Public CantTakeText As String
    Public CantWalkText As String
    Public CantUseAloneText As String
    Public CantUseWithOtherText As String

    ' Is the object visible?
    Public Visible As Boolean = True

    ' Icon to be shown in the inventory, if the object is taken
    Public Icon As clsActiveObject = Nothing

    Public Sub New(ByVal DataReader As OleDbDataReader)
    Public Sub LoadData(ByVal DataReader As OleDbDataReader)

End Class
```

We create a LoadData method in order to give our code a little more flexibility. With this approach we can, for example, create an overloaded New method that would receive the object number or name, open the connection to the database, and call the LoadData method, passing the appropriated DataReader, and thus being able to create objects not tied to a specific screen.

In our New method we'll simply call the base class New method, which will effectively create the sprite to be drawn, and then call our LoadData method.

The parameters expected by the base class (clsSprite) include the image name, the transparent color, the x and y starting position for the sprite, the width and height of the sprite, and the scale factor to be applied when doing matrix transformations on it. The code to call this method using the values from the DataReader received as a parameter is shown in the following code lines:

```
MyBase.New(DataReader.GetString(2), Color.FromArgb(255, 255, 0, 255), _
    New POINT(DataReader.GetInt32(3), DataReader.GetInt32(4)), _
    clsSprite.enScaleFactor.enScalePixel, _
    DataReader.GetInt32(5), DataReader.GetInt32(6))
```

As we can see, it's pretty difficult to read this code, since the data is accessed from the DataReader according to the absolute position of the field within the record. That's the fastest way to access data, but the code becomes unreadable. To minimize this problem and improve the readability of our code, we'll create an enumeration that will list the DataReader fields, as shown in the next listing:

```
' This enum is just to make the data reading code clearer
Private Enum Fields
    Name = 2
    X = 3
    Y = 4
    Width = 5
    Height = 6
    CanTake = 7
    CanWalk = 8
    CanTalk = 9
    CanUseWithOther = 10
    CanUseAlone = 11
    ExamineText = 12
    TakeText = 13
    WalkText = 14
    UseAloneText = 15
    UseWithOtherText = 16
    NoTakeText = 17
    NoWalkText = 18
```

```
            NoUseAloneText = 19
            NoUseWithOtherText = 20
            Visible = 21
            ImageName = 22
End Enum
```

Using the enumeration we have just created, the new version of the constructor for the `ActiveObject` class is shown in the next listing:

```
Public Sub New(ByVal DataReader As OleDbDataReader)
    ' Create the image, calling the base class constructor
    MyBase.New(DataReader.GetString(Fields.ImageName), _
        Color.FromArgb(255, 255, 0, 255), _
        New POINT(DataReader.GetInt32(Fields.X), _
        DataReader.GetInt32(Fields.Y)), clsSprite.enScaleFactor.enScalePixel, _
        DataReader.GetInt32(Fields.Width), DataReader.GetInt32(Fields.Height))
    LoadData(DataReader)
End Sub
```

The `LoadData` method will simply fill the object properties using the data read from the record received as a parameter, as shown in the next code listing:

```
Public Sub LoadData(ByVal DataReader As OleDbDataReader)
    Icon = New clsActiveObject(DataReader.GetString(Fields.ImageName), _
        Color.FromArgb(255, 255, 0, 255), _
        New POINT(8, 8), clsSprite.enScaleFactor.enScalePixel, 64, 64)

    Name = DataReader.GetString(Fields.Name)
    Icon.Name = Name
    Visible = DataReader.GetBoolean(Fields.Visible)

    CanTake = DataReader.GetBoolean(Fields.CanTake)
    CanWalk = DataReader.GetBoolean(Fields.CanWalk)
    CanUseAlone = DataReader.GetBoolean(Fields.CanUseAlone)
    CanUseWithOther = DataReader.GetBoolean(Fields.CanUseWithOther)
    CanTalk = DataReader.GetBoolean(Fields.CanTalk)

    ' Text to show when doing each action
    ExamineText = DataReader.GetString(Fields.ExamineText)
    TakeText = DataReader.GetString(Fields.TakeText)
    WalkText = DataReader.GetString(Fields.WalkText)
    UseAloneText = DataReader.GetString(Fields.UseAloneText)
    UseWithOtherText = DataReader.GetString(Fields.UseWithOtherText)
```

```
' Text to show when each action can't be done
CantTakeText = DataReader.GetString(Fields.NoTakeText)
CantWalkText = DataReader.GetString(Fields.NoWalkText)
CantUseAloneText = DataReader.GetString(Fields.NoUseAloneText)
CantUseWithOtherText = DataReader.GetString(Fields.NoUseWithOtherText)
End Sub
```

In the previous code listing, notice the parameters of the object icon creation: The object icon is a new active object, with the same image as the current object, but with the dimensions 64×64 pixels. The initial position of this icon is (8,8) on screen, which is in the bottom left of the screen. This initial position will allow us to draw the icon directly over the right side of the inventory, and with a little translation on the x axis, draw it over the left side of the inventory. We'll see more details on this when talking about inventory control later in the chapter.

We do not need to code a Draw method for the ActiveObject class, since the base class one will suffice.

Before we can finally see the results of our code on screen, we have to code the Draw method of the screen class (which will draw the screen and call the Draw method of each of the screen active objects) and the Render method of the KinderEngine class (which will simply call the screen Draw method). The following code listing shows these two methods:

```
Shadows Sub Draw()
    Dim i As Integer
    ' Draw the screen background
    MyBase.Draw()
    ' Draw all the active objects
    For i = 0 To ActiveObjectsNumber-1
        If Not ActiveObjects(i) Is Nothing Then
            If ActiveObjects(i).Visible Then
                ActiveObjects(i).Draw()
            End If
        End If
    Next
End Sub
. . .
    Public Overrides Sub Render()
        CurrentScreen.Draw()
    End Sub
```

Running our sample now, we can see the current screen and any active objects it has. In order to see a screen with visible active objects (the invisible objects, like the exits on each screen, are not shown, as indicated in the previous code sample), we'll change the `Initialize` method of the `KinderEngine` class, just for the moment, to set the current screen to `Screen1`, replacing the `CurrentScreen = Screen(1)` command with `CurrentScreen = Screen(0)`. The result is shown in Figure 6-20, where we can see the screen and three active objects: the television and the magic book on the table, plus the mouse hole behind the table.

*Figure 6-20. The kindergarten indoors, including active objects*

The other screen elements, as depicted in earlier in Figure 6-15, are just sprites that can be created by including the following lines in the `Initialize` method:

```
' Load the screen elements (hands, head and text background)
RightHand = New clsSprite("RightHand.Bmp", New POINT(4, 4), _
        clsSprite.enScaleFactor.enScalePixel, 72, 72)
LeftHand = New clsSprite("LeftHand.Bmp", New POINT(80, 4), _
        clsSprite.enScaleFactor.enScalePixel, 72, 72)
TalkingHead = New clsSprite("NatanaelFace.Bmp", New POINT(156, 4), _
        clsSprite.enScaleFactor.enScalePixel, 72, 72)
TextBackground = New clsSprite("TextBackground.Bmp", New POINT(232, 4), _
        clsSprite.enScaleFactor.enScalePixel, 564, 72)
```

After including the code for drawing these sprites in our `Render` method, we'll be able to see all interface elements on screen. The final touch is to create a procedure to display the screen text in the `Text()` font array we created earlier, as shown in the next listing:

```
Sub DrawText()
    Dim i As Integer
    For i = 0 To 3
        Text(i).Draw()
    Next
End Sub
```

Figure 6-21 shows the final interface for the Magic KindergarteN. adventure.

*Figure 6-21. The Magic KindergarteN. interface elements in place*

In the next section we'll create the last interface element for our game, the mouse pointer.

## Second Draft: Coding the Mouse Pointer

The last user interface element is the mouse pointer, which will represent a specific action verb to be applied to an active object when clicking.

Although simple, the coding for the mouse pointer must take into account the following requirements:

• One object must display different images according to the current status, so the basic Sprite methods will not suffice.

- The pointer must move according to the mouse movement, so we'll need to code the mouseMove event of the clsMouse class (created in the previous chapter) to update the object's position on screen.

- Every time the pointer passes over an active object, we'll need to update the status text on screen; so we'll need to code a collision detection algorithm in the game engine class.

- When the user clicks an active object, we'll need to handle this event, checking the current mouse status and running the appropriate action.

Since we are including all game strings in the database, to make the translation easier, we'll need to read the verbs from the database, too, and include some private properties to store the verbs to be used in the game, plus one extra property to store the "with" word, employed to compose the status text on screen when the player is using an object in the inventory with another on the current screen. To allow the game engine to easily retrieve the verb for the current pointer, we'll need an extra property, PointerText, that must be updated every time the current status changes.

The next code listing shows the interface for the adventure pointer class:

```
Public Class clsAdvPointer
    Inherits clsSprite

    Public PointerText As String = "Examine "
    Private pStatus As enStatus = enStatus.Examine

    ' These properties will hold each of the pointer icons
    Private WalkIcon As Direct3DTexture8
    Private ExamineIcon As Direct3DTexture8
    Private TakeIcon As Direct3DTexture8
    Private UseIcon As Direct3DTexture8
    Private WaitIcon As Direct3DTexture8

    ' Set default values for english verbs
    Private WalkText As String = "Walk to "
    Private ExamineText As String = "Examine "
    Private TakeText As String = "Take "
    Private TalkText As String = "Talk "
    Private UseText As String = "Use "
    Private WithText As String = " With "
```

```
      Enum enStatus
          Walk = 0
          Examine = 1
          Take = 2
          Use = 3
          Wait = 4
      End Enum

      Public Sub New()
      Shadows Function Load(strImageName, colorKey) As Direct3DTexture8
      Function CreateVertexBuffer() As Boolean
      Sub ReadVerbs()
      Sub NextStatus()
      Shadows Sub Draw()
  End Class
```

The Sprite New method creates a single vertex buffer for a single image. Since we'll use a single buffer with many images, we'll have to create new methods for the whole texture creation process.

We can copy the methods from the Sprite class and adapt them to create a Load method that does not create a vertex buffer, so we can load many different textures onto the verb icon and include a separate method to create a solo vertex buffer. The code for the New, Load, and CreateVertexBuffer methods is shown in the following listing:

```
Public Sub New()
    IsTransparent = True
    X = 0
    Y = 0
    Width = 32
    Height = 64
    ScaleFactor = clsSprite.enScaleFactor.enScalePixel

    ExamineIcon = Load("IconExamine.Bmp", _
                    Color.FromArgb(255, 255, 0, 255).ToArgb)
    TakeIcon = Load("IconTake.Bmp", Color.FromArgb(255, 255, 0, 255).ToArgb)
    WalkIcon = Load("IconWalk.Bmp", Color.FromArgb(255, 255, 0, 255).ToArgb)
    UseIcon = Load("IconUse.Bmp", Color.FromArgb(255, 255, 0, 255).ToArgb)
    WaitIcon = Load("IconWait.Bmp", Color.FromArgb(255, 255, 0, 255).ToArgb)
    CreateVertexBuffer()
End Sub
```

```
Shadows Function Load(strImageName As String, _
                      Optional colorKey As Integer = &HFFFFOOFF) As Texture
    Try
        Load = TextureLoader.FromFile(objDirect3DDevice, _
            Application.StartupPath & "\" & IMAGE_PATH & "\" & strImageName)
    Catch de As DirectXException
        MessageBox.Show("Could not load image file " & strImageName & ". _
            Error: " & de.ErrorString, "3D Initialization - AdvPointer.", _
            MessageBoxButtons.OK, MessageBoxIcon.Error)
        Return Nothing
    End Try
End Function


Function CreateVertexBuffer() As Boolean
    Dim vertices As CustomVertex()
    Dim VertexType As CustomVertex

    Try
        VertBuffer = New VertexBuffer(VertexType.GetType, 4, objDirect3DDevice, _
                        Usage.WriteOnly, FVF_CUSTOMVERTEX, Pool.Default)
        vertices = VertBuffer.Lock(0, 0)
        ' Create a square, composed of 2 triangles in a triangle strip
        vertices(0) = CreateFlexVertex(X * ScaleFactor, _
                                    Y * ScaleFactor, 1, 0, 1)
        vertices(1) = CreateFlexVertex(X * ScaleFactor + Width, _
                                    Y * ScaleFactor, 1, 1, 1)
        vertices(2) = CreateFlexVertex(X * ScaleFactor, _
                                    Y * ScaleFactor + Height, 1, 0, 0)
        vertices(3) = CreateFlexVertex(X * ScaleFactor + Width, _
                                    Y * ScaleFactor + Height, 1, 1, 0)
        ' Release the vertex buffer and commit our vertex data
        VertBuffer.Unlock()

        Return True
    Catch de As DirectXException
        MessageBox.Show("Could not create vertex buffer for AdvPointer. Error: " _
& de.ErrorString, "3D Initialization.", MessageBoxButtons.OK,
MessageBoxIcon.Error)
        Return False
    End Try

End Function
```

The functions used to load the texture and to create the vertex buffer, and further explanations on how to use them, are presented in Chapter 3.

Once the textures for the pointer are loaded, we need to code the Draw procedure, the NextStatus procedure (to cycle between the possible statuses), and the ReadVerbs procedure. This will set the text values for each verb so we can see the results on screen.

In the Draw method, shown in the next listing, we apply the current translation information to the world matrix, choose the texture to be used, and draw our vertex buffer, resetting the world matrix after that. (If we don't do this last step, everything on screen will move with the mouse pointer!) Refer to Chapter 3 if you're still unclear about matrix transformations and how to use them.

```
Shadows Sub Draw()
    ' If the sprite has a speed, increment the translation
    If (SpeedX + SpeedY) > 0 Then
        TranslationX += SpeedX
        TranslationY += SpeedY
    End If

    ' If there's a scale to be applied, apply it...
    If (ScaleX + ScaleY) > 0 Then
        objDirect3DDevice.Transform.World = _
            Matrix.Multiply(objDirect3DDevice.Transform.World, _
            Matrix.Scaling(ScaleX, ScaleY, 0))
    End If

    ' If there's a translation to be applied, apply it...
    If (pTranslationX + pTranslationY) > 0 Then
        objDirect3DDevice.Transform.World = _
            Matrix.Multiply(objDirect3DDevice.Transform.World, _
            Matrix.Translation(pTranslationX, pTranslationY, 0))
    End If

    ' If there's a rotation to be applied, apply it...
    If (RotationX + RotationY) > 0 Then
        objDirect3DDevice.Transform.World = _
            Matrix.Multiply(objDirect3DDevice.Transform.World, _
            Matrix.Scaling(RotationX, RotationY, 0))
    End If
```

```
    ' Turn on alpha blending, since sprite has transparent colors
    objDirect3DDevice.RenderState.AlphaBlendEnable = True
    Select Case pStatus
        Case enStatus.Examine
            objDirect3DDevice.SetTexture(0, ExamineIcon)
        Case enStatus.Take
            objDirect3DDevice.SetTexture(0, TakeIcon)
        Case enStatus.Use
            objDirect3DDevice.SetTexture(0, UseIcon)
        Case enStatus.Walk
            objDirect3DDevice.SetTexture(0, WalkIcon)
        Case enStatus.Wait
            objDirect3DDevice.SetTexture(0, WaitIcon)
    End Select
    objDirect3DDevice.SetStreamSource(0, VertBuffer)
    objDirect3DDevice.DrawPrimitives(PrimitiveType.TriangleStrip, 0, 2)
    ' Turn off alpha blending
    objDirect3DDevice.RenderState.AlphaBlendEnable = False
    ' Reset the world matrix
    objDirect3DDevice.Transform.World = Matrix.Identity
End Sub
```

The mouse cycling method will just increment the current status property, resetting the status counter to the first status after the last one, as shown in the next listing:

```
Sub NextStatus()
    Status += 1
    ' we can go through all the mouse states, except wait
    If Status = enStatus.Wait Then
        Status = 0  ' restart
    End If
End Sub
```

To ensure that every time we change the Status property the PointerText property will remain synchronized, even if the game engine changes it without using the NextStatus method, we must define Status as a property procedure, and code the Set procedure to update the PointerText procedure according to the current Status being set. The code for the property procedure is shown in the following listing:

```
' This property is defined as a property procedure, and
'  it uses the enumeration above as property types
Property Status() As enStatus
    Get
        Status = pStatus
    End Get
    Set(ByVal Value As enStatus)
        pStatus = Value
        ' We could have done this with an array, but this way the code is clearer
        Select Case pStatus
            Case enStatus.Examine
                PointerText = ExamineText
            Case enStatus.Take
                PointerText = TakeText
            Case enStatus.Use
                PointerText = UseText
            Case enStatus.Walk
                PointerText = WalkText
        End Select
    End Set
End Property
```

The last method of this class, ReadVerbs, will only load the verbs from the database, using the same ADO.NET objects and methods we have already seen. If the database contains English verbs, the values will be the same as the default values, but you can translate them in the database if you want to play the games in other languages. The code for the method is on the sample CD-ROM that accompanies this book, with the full code for the game inside the Chapter 6 directory.

We need to include a call for the drawing method of the Render procedure of the game engine class—Pointer.Draw() will suffice for displaying the game pointer on screen. If we run our game now, we'll be able to see the mouse pointer in the bottom left of the screen, but it isn't working yet, since we haven't written the code for moving and cycling it.

Creating one object of the clsMouse class (which wraps DirectInput, as shown in the previous chapter), we can make our pointer move and act as expected, just by coding the mouse events in the KinderEngine class.

We can now see how easy coding games becomes when using our base classes. In this example, we'll initialize DirectInput with just one line—when creating the mouse object in the Initialize method of the game engine class.

```
Mouse = New ClsMouse(Owner)
```

We can control the movement of our pointer by simply adding two lines to the MouseMove event of the Mouse object, and do the action verb cycling by adding one line to the MouseUp event, as shown in the next listing:

```
Sub Mouse_MouseMove(X As Integer, Y As Integer) Handles Mouse.MouseMove
    Pointer.TranslationX = X
    Pointer.TranslationY = clsGameEngine.Height - Y
End Sub
Sub Mouse_MouseUp(X As Integer, Y As Integer, _
            Button As KindergarteN.ClsMouse.enButton) Handles Mouse.MouseUp
    If Button = ClsMouse.enButton.Left Then Pointer.NextStatus()
End Sub
```

Since the y axis value is counted from the bottom up, as explained in Chapter 3, we must subtract it from the height of the screen to calculate the proper translation value for this axis.

We can now run our program and move our pointer on the screen, and cycle the actions by clicking the left mouse button. Figure 6-22 shows the screen with the mouse moving over it.

*Figure 6-22. Moving the pointer with the Examine verb*

In the next section we'll add the code to the KinderEngine class to update the status line when moving over an active object, as well as the code to effectively execute the actions when clicking them, including playing the video using DirectShow.

## Third Draft: Coding the Mouse Pointer Actions

There are two main points we must take into account when coding the mouse pointer actions: First, we must update the status text every time the mouse passes over an active object, regardless of its visibility; and second, we must code the click event to trigger the appropriate action, according to the current pointer status and the clicked object.

For these two actions we'll have a collision testing procedure that must check the current pointer against all active objects on screen. Returning the active object will allow the calling procedure to take the appropriate action in each case. The next code listing shows the TestCollision procedure, which uses the bounding box algorithm (discussed earlier in this book) to calculate the collision and return, if any, the colliding object:

```
' Test for collision with the pointer, update the status line
'    and return the colliding object
Private Sub TestCollision(ByRef ClickedObject As clsActiveObject)
    Dim i As Integer
    ClickedObject = Nothing
    For i = 0 To CurrentScreen.ActiveObjectsNumber - 1
        If Not CurrentScreen.ActiveObjects(i) Is Nothing Then
            If Pointer.CenterX > CurrentScreen.ActiveObjects(i).X And _
                Pointer.CenterX < CurrentScreen.ActiveObjects(i).X + _
                CurrentScreen.ActiveObjects(i).Width Then
                    If Pointer.CenterY > CurrentScreen.ActiveObjects(i).Y And _
                        Pointer.CenterY < CurrentScreen.ActiveObjects(i).Y + _
                        CurrentScreen.ActiveObjects(i).Height Then
                            ClickedObject = CurrentScreen.ActiveObjects(i)
                    End If
            End If
        End If
    Next
End Sub
```

We'll use this procedure in the Render method to check for collision every time the screen is being drawn, and use the resulting information to update the status text, which can be created by including the following code line in the Initialize method of the KinderEngine class:

```
StatusText = New ClsGameFont("Microsoft Sans Serif", 14, _
            Space(135), New POINT(4, 508))
```

In the Render method, we should retrieve the current game pointer action verb—the PointerText property—and concatenate the object name to it, when there's an object under the mouse pointer. Thus, when we move the mouse pointer in Examine status over an object, let's say a magic book, the status line will display "Examine magic book". This will give the player the clue he or she needs to figure out which objects on screen are active ones.

```
' The TestCollision procedure returns the object that
'  is colliding with the mouse - if there's any
TestCollision(ClickedObject)

' Updates the status line text
StatusText.Text = ""
StatusText.Text = StatusText.Text & Pointer.PointerText
If Not ClickedObject Is Nothing Then
        StatusText.Text = StatusText.Text & ClickedObject.Name
End If
' Centers the status text on screen (a line can show 135 characters)
StatusText.Text = Space((135 - Len(StatusText.Text)) / 2) & StatusText.Text
StatusText.Draw()
```

If we run our program now, we can move the pointer over the first screen and check the two active objects—the entrance to the school and the exit to the forest.

To code the actions, we must update the MouseUp event, now including code for pressing the right mouse button. The code, shown in the next listing, will call the TestCollision procedure and, if there is any active object under the game pointer when the button is pressed, call the appropriate procedure to process the action:

```
Sub Mouse_MouseUp(X As Integer, Y As Integer, _
        Button As KindergarteN.ClsMouse.enButton) Handles Mouse.MouseUp
    Dim clickedObject As clsActiveObject
    If Button = ClsMouse.enButton.Left Then
        Pointer.NextStatus()
    Else
        TestCollision(clickedObject)
        If Not clickedObject Is Nothing Then
            Select Case Pointer.Status
                Case clsAdvPointer.enStatus.Examine
                    DoExamine(clickedObject)
                Case clsAdvPointer.enStatus.Take
                    DoTake(clickedObject)
                Case clsAdvPointer.enStatus.Use
```

```
                    DoUseAlone(clickedObject)
                Case clsAdvPointer.enStatus.Walk
                    DoWalk(clickedObject)
            End Select
        End If
    End If
End Sub
```

Each of the preceding procedures is unique: The DoWalk procedure, in our game, will not make the player really walk, but will change the current screen; the DoUseAlone procedure will process special actions associated with the Use verb—for example, turning on a television; the DoExamine will show the description of each object (stored in the ActiveObject class); and the DoTake procedure will store objects in the inventory, if they can be carried.

Every time the player executes an action upon an object, text is displayed in the text box on the screen—reinforcing the reaction of the player when executing the action, or giving the proper excuses for not executing it. We'll create a helper function, Say, to display text in this box. The DoExamine method will simply call this procedure, as shown in the next code listing, but the other methods will do a lot more.

```
Sub Say(strText1 As String, Optional strText2 As String = "", _
        Optional strText3 As String = "", Optional strText4 As String = "")
    Text(0).Text = strText1
    Text(1).Text = strText2
    Text(2).Text = strText3
    Text(3).Text = strText4
End Sub

Sub DoExamine(ByVal clickedObject As clsActiveObject)
    Say(clickedObject.ExamineText)
End Sub
```

The DoWalk method will be responsible for the navigation between screens. To implement this, we must know exactly which object was clicked, and then execute four steps:

1. Check the CanWalk flag on the clicked object. If the player can't walk to the object, simply display the CantWalkText property on screen, using the Say method. If the player can walk to the object, check the object name (according to the name stored in the database) and execute the next steps.

2. Update the `CurrentScreen` variable, so the next execution of the `Render` method will draw the new screen.

3. Update the displayed text on the current screen.

4. Update the player position, if the player must appear in a different screen position. We'll talk more about the player in the next section of this chapter.

At this point, we must refer to our storyline and class diagram and check if there are any special conditions when walking from one place to another. In our game, such special conditions will occur only when walking to the mouse hole: The player can indeed walk to the mouse hole, but only if he or she has become small, as a result of eating the magic mushroom. So we must check the player status property (refer to the class diagram and to the next section), and, if the player is small, grant access to the hole; if not, just display the `CantWalkText` property (in this case, "I'm too big to fit in there!").

---

 **NOTE** *One extra point that we can't forget is to restore the "Big" status of the player when entering the hole, since the player must appear big when inside the hole, and restore the "Small" status when walking outside the hole again.*

---

The next code sample shows part of the `DoWalk` method:

```
Sub DoWalk(ByVal clickedObject As clsActiveObject)
    If clickedObject.CanWalk Then
        Say(clickedObject.WalkText)
        ' If we can walk, load the next screen
        '  (show the wait Pointer icon)
        Pointer.Status = clsAdvPointer.enStatus.Wait
        Select Case clickedObject.Name
            Case "kindergarten door"
                CurrentScreen = Screen(0)
                UpdateScreenText()
                '  Set the player position on the new screen
                Player.X = 525
                Player.Y = 0
            Case "door"
                CurrentScreen = Screen(1)
```

```
                    UpdateScreenText()
                    '  Set the player position on the new screen
                    Player.X = 300
                    Player.Y = 0

    . . .

            Case "mouse hole"
                If Player.status = clsAdvPlayer.enStatus.Small Then
                    CurrentScreen = Screen(4)
                    Player.status = clsAdvPlayer.enStatus.Big
                    UpdateScreenText()
                    '  Set the player position on the new screen
                    Player.X = 325
                    Player.Y = 0
                Else
                    Say(clickedObject.CantWalkText)
                End If
            Case "exit"    ' Going out the mouse hole
                CurrentScreen = Screen(1)
                UpdateScreenText()
                Player.status = clsAdvPlayer.enStatus.Small
                '  Set the player position on the new screen
                Player.X = 50
                Player.Y = 0
        End Select
        ' Restore the previous mouse pointer
        Pointer.Status = clsAdvPointer.enStatus.Walk
    Else
        Say(clickedObject.CantWalkText)
    End If
End Sub
```

The next method to explore, DoUseAlone, will have a structure similar to the one in the previous listing: It must check if the object can be used, and if so use it accordingly. But the actions to be executed will be unique, depending on each object clicked in a game: You can unlock a door, eat a meal, or turn on a sound system. In our game, we'll have only two objects that can be used with the mouse pointer: the TV, which will play video files, and the magic mushroom, which will make the player shrink and grow.

The next code sample presents the code for doing these actions:

```
Sub DoUseAlone(ByVal clickedObject As clsActiveObject)
    If clickedObject.CanUseAlone Then
        Say(clickedObject.UseAloneText)
        Select Case clickedObject.Name
            Case "television"
                If Not Video.IsPlaying Then
                    ' Turn on the TV
                    PlayTVChannel()
                End If
            Case "mushroom"
                ' Using the magic mushroom changes the player size
                If Player.status = clsAdvPlayer.enStatus.Small Then
                    Player.status = clsAdvPlayer.enStatus.Big
                Else
                    Player.status = clsAdvPlayer.enStatus.Small
                End If
        End Select
    Else
        Say(clickedObject.CantUseAloneText)
    End If
End Sub
```

The PlayTVChannel procedure, called when using the television, will employ DirectShow to play four different videos on the TV, cycling each time the TV is clicked. Since video play is asynchronously controlled by DirectShow, we must stop drawing the screen in order to display video without flickering.

To do this, we'll check the IsPlaying property and stop everything else when a video is playing, by including proper code in the game to prevent the Render procedure from being called, the pointer from processing the mouse events, and a new video from playing—as we can already see in the previous code listing. The complete code is on the CD-ROM for this book.

In order to use DirectShow, we must create the Video object in the Initialize method of the KinderEngine class before calling the Play method, as shown in the next piece of code. PicVideo is a pictureBox control that will be used to play the video inside the television image on screen, and that will be passed as a new parameter to the Initialize method.

```
Public Video As clsVideo

Shadows Function Initialize(ByVal owner As Windows.Forms.Control, _
        WndVideo as Windows.Forms.Control) As Boolean
  . . .
  ' Create the Video Object
  '  The Video Position must be over the TV bitmap
  Video = New clsVideo(VideoWindow)
  . . .
End Sub

Sub PlayTVChannel()
    Static Channel As Integer = 1
    Channel += 1
    If Channel > 4 Then Channel = 1

    Select Case Channel
        Case 1
            Video.Play("SlapMont.AVI")
        Case 2
            Video.Play("VideoFX.AVI")
        Case 3
            Video.Play("Pyramids.Avi")
        Case 4
            Video.Play("skiing.Avi")
    End Select
End Sub
```

Figure 6-23 presents the use of DirectShow in our game, while testing the Use verb on the kindergarten television.

*Figure 6-23. The mouse pointer triggers an action—turn on the TV.*

All the videos we use in this program were created by Jasmine Multimedia, and are royalty free. The television cycles through the videos shown in the following list:

- **Skiing:** This video clip is from the SPORTS IN MOTION CD-ROM.

- **Video Effects:** This is a sample of the video clips available on Video Special Effects—Volumes I & II CD-ROMs.

- **Egyptian Pyramids:** This video clip comes from the Famous Places CD-ROM.

- **Slapstick Montage:** This video clip is from Amazing Movies CD-ROM.

In the next section we'll discuss the DoTake method, which will add objects to the inventory, and one extra method we'll need to create, DoUseWith, which will be called when using two objects together (one from the inventory, another from the current screen).

# Final Version: Coding the Player and the Inventory

In this section we'll finalize our game, including the code for drawing the player and all operations related to inventory handling, such as taking the objects, drawing the objects in our inventory, and using them with other objects on screen.

Since our player character for this game will be very simple (only a fixed sprite on screen), all we have to do is to include the action for scaling the character when its status is "Small", creating a new Draw procedure. The next code listing displays the most important lines of the clsAdvPlayer class:

```
Enum enStatus
    Big = 0
    Small = 1
End Enum
Public status As enStatus = enStatus.Big

Shadows Sub Draw()
    If status = enStatus.Small Then
        ScaleX = 0.2
        ScaleY = 0.2
        ' When we scale the image, the axis is scaled too, so we must:
        '    1) move the object to (0,0), scale it and move it back
        '                    - OR -
        '    2) apply a new translation to balance the scaling
        '    We use 2) here, because we don't need a generic routine
        TranslationX = X + 75
        TranslationY = Y + 75
    Else
        ScaleX = 1
        ScaleY = 1
        TranslationX = X
        TranslationY = Y
    End If
    MyBase.Draw()
End Sub
```

To draw the player on screen, all we need to do is to add the following line to the Render procedure:

```
Player.Draw()
```

Figure 6-24 shows a screen with the player character.

*Figure 6-24. The player is finally shown on screen—in this case, inside the mouse hole.*

As for the inventory control, since we have only two slots to carry objects (the right hand and the left hand), we can choose a simpler way to control it: Instead of creating functions to pick an object from the inventory and then using this object on other objects, we'll simply add new actions to our mouse pointer, showing icons of the inventory objects. Once we have added a new action to the game pointer, we can use a procedure similar to the one we saw in the last section to execute the other actions.

To implement this solution, first we'll need to adjust our `clsAdvPointer` class to use two more statuses, which will present the objects being carried, if any. The code for creating the new statuses and the updated cyclical routine is presented in the next listing:

```
Enum enStatus
    Walk = 0
    Examine = 1
    Take = 2
    Use = 3
    Object1 = 4
    Object2 = 5
    Wait = 6
End Enum
```

```
Public Object1 As clsActiveObject = Nothing
Public Object2 As clsActiveObject = Nothing

Sub NextStatus()
    Status += 1
    ' Only stay on status Object1 and Object2 if we are carrying objects
    If Status = enStatus.Object1 And Object1 Is Nothing Then
        Status += 1
    End If
    If Status = enStatus.Object2 And Object2 Is Nothing Then
        Status += 1
    End If
    ' We can go through all the mouse states, except wait
    If Status = enStatus.Wait Then
        Status = 0  ' restart
    End If
End Sub
```

We'll need to update the status property procedure to update the `PointerText` property accordingly, and also add new lines to the `Draw` method to draw the icon of the object in the inventory, as displayed in the next piece of code:

```
Sub Draw()
...
    Case enStatus.Object1
        objDirect3DDevice.SetTexture(0, Object1.Icon.SpriteImage)
    Case enStatus.Object2
        objDirect3DDevice.SetTexture(0, Object2.Icon.SpriteImage)
...
End sub
```

In order to display our objects in the inventory, we'll need to create two extra active objects—`RightHandObject` and `LeftHandObject`—that will store the images to be displayed in the inventory. The real object of the inventory will be stored in the mouse pointer, so we can access it easily when needed.

When the player executes the Take action on an object that can be picked up, we must update the mouse pointer class and that of the object. We'll always try to carry the object in the right hand. If it is occupied, we'll use the left hand. If the left hand is also occupied, then we'll display the `CantTakeText` property. The full code for the `DoTake` method is presented in the next code listing. It is executed when the player clicks an active object with the Take mouse pointer.

```
Sub DoTake(ByVal clickedObject As clsActiveObject)
    If clickedObject.CanTake Then
        ' If the right hand is empty, store the object in it
        If RightHandObject Is Nothing Then
            ' Set the right hand object to the icon of the object we took
            ' All object icons are created by default over the right hand,
            ' so the Render procedure will draw the object icon over this hand
            RightHandObject = clickedObject.Icon
            ' Set the pointer of the mouse to the object we took
            Pointer.Object1 = clickedObject
            ' The object will be invisible, since we take it
            clickedObject.Visible = False
            clickedObject.IsOnInventory = True
        ' If the left hand is empty, store the object in it
        ElseIf LeftHandObject Is Nothing Then
            ' Set the left hand object to the icon of the object we took
            ' so the Render procedure will draw the object over the hand
            LeftHandObject = clickedObject.Icon
            ' All object icons are created by default over the right hand,
            ' so we must translate the icon to make it appear over the left hand
            clickedObject.Icon.TranslationX = 84
            ' Set the pointer of the mouse to the object we took
            Pointer.Object2 = clickedObject
            ' The object will be invisible, since we take it
            clickedObject.Visible = False
            clickedObject.IsOnInventory = True
        Else
            Say(clickedObject.CantTakeText)
        End If
        Say(clickedObject.TakeText)
    Else
        Say(clickedObject.CantTakeText)
    End If
End Sub
```

As we can see in the previous listing, in the RightHandObject and LeftHandObject active objects we store only the icon of the object we are taking, so it can be drawn in the inventory. Referring to the previous sections, remember that the icon for every object is already created with the appropriated size and in the correct position to be displayed in the right hand. To display it in the left hand all we have to do is perform a simple translation on the x axis (that's why we set clickedObject.Icon.TranslationX to 84).

The full object is stored in the game pointer class for later use, and we set two flags with the object on screen. The first one is to make the object invisible, and the second one is to inform the player that the object is in the inventory. This last flag will be used repeatedly in the program. For example, in the collision detection routine, it is used to inform a procedure that this object should be ignored.

The comments in the previous code listing should make it clear what each line is supposed to do.

To draw the objects in the inventory (over the corresponding hand), we must include some extra lines in the Render procedure, as displayed in the next listing:

```
' If we are carrying any objects, draw them in the inventory
If Not RightHandObject Is Nothing Then
    RightHandObject.Draw()
End If
If Not LeftHandObject Is Nothing Then
    LeftHandObject.Draw()
End If
```

The last part of our inventory handling routine is the creation of a special procedure—DoUseWith—to be called every time the user clicks an object icon over another object.

Although we could create specific code for every object action in this procedure, our experience tells us that most occurrences of using one object upon another can be reduced to a few simple questions:

- Will Object 1 (the carried object) be destroyed after using it with Object 2?

- Will Object 2 be destroyed after the action?

- Will a new object be created?

These questions will allow us to address situations like the following:

- **Using a glass with water and a flower:** Destroy the glass with water, don't destroy the flower, and create a new object—a glass without water (so it will look like we have watered the flower).

- **Using paper on a waste basket:** Destroy the paper, don't destroy the basket, and don't create any objects.

- **Using a magic wand on a mud monster:** Don't destroy the wand, destroy the mud monster, and create a new object—a teacher.

With a little imagination, we can use this approach to generically address many diverse situations. In our game, we created new properties in the clsActiveObject class and in the database, so we can handle these situations, as shown in the next code listing. The DoUseWith function, as with the analogous procedures show earlier in this chapter, must be called from the MouseUp event handling procedure, and will pass as parameters the clicked object, the mouse pointer object, and a Boolean value informing the procedure whether the object on the mouse pointer was in the right hand or the left, in the inventory.

```
Sub DoUseWith(Object1 As clsActiveObject, _
            clickedObject As clsActiveObject, RightHand As Boolean)
    Dim i As Integer

    ' Checks if the clicked object is the one object1 can be used with
    If Object1.UsesWith.ObjectName = clickedObject.Name Then
        Say(Object1.UseWithOtherText)
        ' If we are expected to create a new object, then create it
        If Object1.UsesWith.CreateObjectAfterUse <> "" Then
            ' Create the new object on the screen
            CurrentScreen.ActiveObjects(CurrentScreen.ActiveObjectsNumber) = New _
                clsActiveObject(Object1.UsesWith.CreateObjectAfterUse)
            CurrentScreen.ActiveObjectsNumber += 1
        End If
        ' If we must destroy the other object after using it, destroy it
        If Object1.UsesWith.DestroyOtherAfterUse Then
            For i = 0 To CurrentScreen.ActiveObjectsNumber - 1
                If Not CurrentScreen.ActiveObjects(i) Is Nothing Then
                    If CurrentScreen.ActiveObjects(i).Name = _
                            clickedObject.Name Then
                        CurrentScreen.ActiveObjects(i) = Nothing
                        clickedObject = Nothing
                        Exit For
                    End If
                End If
            Next
        End If
        ' If we are expected to be destroyed after used,
        ' then destroy the object from the inventory
        If Object1.UsesWith.DestroyMeAfterUse Then
            Pointer.NextStatus()
            ' Destroy the object on the mouse pointer
            Object1 = Nothing
            ' Reset the object drawing on the inventory
```

```
            If RightHand Then
                RightHandObject = Nothing
            Else
                LeftHandObject = Nothing
            End If
        End If
    Else
        Say(Object1.CantUseWithOtherText)
    End If
End Sub
```

In Figure 6-25 we can see the player getting the magic wand: It disappears from the screen and is displayed over the right hand, in the inventory section of the screen.

*Figure 6-25. The player gets the wand, which is then stored in the inventory (right hand).*

Now our game is complete. If we take the magic wand, a new icon will appear as our mouse pointer (a magic wand), and we can use it on the mud monster to return the character's teacher back to her normal self. Figure 6-26 shows the last screen of the game, when the mission is completed.

*Figure 6-26. The game ending: Fiona is a nice witch again!*

That's all for this chapter's sample game. We just finished our first adventure game, while creating a library of classes that can be used to build other analogous games as well.

## Adding the Final Touches

In the next chapter we'll add some extra features to our game, such as including a dialog control to make the player character able to communicate with other characters in the game, and introduce Speech API and animation concepts so we can make our character talk—and see his lips moving!

As for this chapter's final touches, a simple suggestion is a more complex storyline using more complex puzzles, with more situations, and more characters to improve the game.

Based on the same basic principles, here's a possible extended story, along with some new images drawn by Waldivar Cesar:

*The main character in our game will be a little boy, a magician's son, who is studying basic tricks in a magic kindergarten.*

*Natanael (that's his name) arrives one day at school and finds his pal, Michael, outside the school (see Figure 6-27). Michael tells him that there's no one at school, and his father told him to stay here and wait for Fiona, their teacher.*

Figure 6-27. Michael, a supporting character and Natanael's friend

Natanael enters the school and finds no one there, just a big television that can play some movies, a magic book, and a box on the table. There is also a bucket on the floor (see Figure 6-28). He examines the magic book, and a page of the book falls on the floor. Natanael picks up the page. He looks at the page and sees that it's a magic potion for shrinking people, using a mushroom and water from a waterfall.

Figure 6-28. New objects: a box and a bucket

Exiting from the school, Natanael decides to go into the forest to see if he finds anyone. He finds a mud monster near a tree that has a big hole in it. The monster tells him that, in fact, it is Natanael's teacher, Fiona. Fiona was trying some metamorphosis tricks when she lost her magic wand, and she asks Natanael to find it for her.

Natanael goes back to school and sees the magic wand inside a mouse hole, but he can't get it. He then remembers the shrinking potion.

*Going deeper into the forest, Natanael finds a place with many mushrooms. When he tries to get a mushroom, a dwarf appears and says that he can't get a mushroom unless he brings something in exchange (see Figure 6-29). The dwarf tells him that he wants a feather from an owl so that he can do some magic.*

*Figure 6-29. The dwarf, king of the mushrooms*

*Going back to where the mud monster is, Natanael examines the hole in the tree, and finds an owl. When he tries to take the owl, all he gets is a feather, which he gives to the dwarf. He receives a mushroom in exchange. Walking away from the forest, he finds a waterfall, but he has nothing to put the water in (see Figure 6-30).*

*Figure 6-30. A waterfall in the forest*

*Natanael goes to school and puts the mushroom in the bucket. He takes the bucket and goes back to the waterfall. Using the bucket at the waterfall, Natanael fills the bucket, which contains the mushroom, with water from the waterfall, making it a shrinking potion. He throws away (automatically) the magic page, since he doesn't need it anymore.*

*Natanael drinks the potion and becomes small. He goes to school, and, when entering the mouse hole, he finds a mouse that doesn't let him take the wand (see Figure 6-31).*

*Figure 6-31. An armed mouse*

*Natanael comes out of the mouse hole and uses the potion again, and grows. Looking at the box on the table, he opens it and finds some cheese. He uses the potion once again, and enters the mouse hole with the cheese. When he gives the cheese to the mouse, it becomes occupied with eating the cheese, allowing Natanael to escape with the wand.*

*Natanael uses the wand on the mud monster, and helps his teacher to get back to her normal form.*

The images presented in this section are on the accompanying CD-ROM, so you can play with them and extend the game, creating your storyline and puzzles as needed. We'll use some elements of this new storyline in the next chapter.

## Summary

In this chapter, we reused our basic game classes, `clsGameEngine` and `clsSprite`, created in Chapter 4, to construct a game of a totally different genre—an adventure game. Although very simple, this chapter sample helps you to understand the points you must take into account when creating adventures. We also discussed the following:

- Some of the history of adventure games, including concepts associated with the creation of games of this genre

- The managed DirectShow component library, and the basic concepts of streaming media reproduction

- The creation of a new game class that handles the playing of streaming media

- Introduction of data access concepts in Visual Basic .NET, with the use of ADO.NET objects

In the next chapter, we'll create a new version of our game, including dialog handling—an essential part of any adventure game. We'll also be exploring notions about the animation of characters and looking at the Speech API, which will enable our games to talk to us—and, eventually, to make them understand what we are saying to them.

## CHAPTER 7

# Magic KindergarteN. II: Animation Techniques and Speech API

IN THIS CHAPTER, we'll extend the adventure game created in the previous chapter to add dialog between the player's character and game characters (see Figure 7-1). With these dialogs, we can extend the game puzzles and add one extra level of interaction to our game.

We'll use this feature to introduce two new concepts: animation in games and the use of Speech API, which performs text-to-speech conversion and voice recognition. As usual, we'll create a

*Figure 7-1. Magic KindergarteN. II, this chapter's sample game*

new game class to allow us to easily control the speech generation. Also as usual, we won't get too deep into these concepts, only going through enough information to enable us to create the sample game and do initial steps in speech generation and use of animation in games.

We'll begin with a look at some animation concepts that any game programmer must keep in mind when designing a game. All of the drawings in this section are by the Slovenian game developer, cartoonist, and graphical artist Igor Sinkovec, unless otherwise stated.

## Character Animation in Games

You might be thinking, "Well, I'm a programmer, I don't need to worry about character animations. That's the job of the graphical artist, right?" Wrong!

Even if you were born with no drawing skills at all, and even if you aren't planning to draw anything in your games, knowing some basic animation concepts will help you to better understand your team of artists and improve your communication with these team members.

On the other hand, if you are a lone programmer, and you'll need to create your own art, these little tips may help you to create simple graphics with a professional touch.

We don't include a full drawing course nor an advanced animation course. Many excellent books on these topics are available to anyone who wants to master them; our goal here is just to introduce some concepts that any serious gamer must know in order to create better game animations.

In the following sections we present some character animation tips, exemplifying four of the most important animation concepts: cycling, squashing and stretching, anticipation, and posture.

## Animating Cycling Movements

One cannot talk about animation in games without mentioning *cycling*. First, this is because many of the animations will be cycles executed in response to a player action, and second, we cannot create a game like we would a TV cartoon—there are limits we must respect about the size and quantity of the animations. The most obvious example of a cycling movement is a walking character: Every time the player moves the input device in a different direction, the player character is shown to be walking by cycling through the animation (usually, a single step) many times.

The main characteristic of an animation cycle is that the last position in the cycle is the same as the first one. A typical game has many cycling animations: a jump (which starts and ends with the player character standing), a shooting sequence, and so on. Because each game character must usually return to its initial position after an animation—in order to repeat or start a different animation—we can see that most, if not all, of the animations used in games are cycles.

Each image that composes an animation is called a *frame*, and the most important ones are usually called *key frames*. A simple walking animation in a TV cartoon takes 12 frames on average, but in a game we can work with less ambitious numbers, depending mainly on the size of the character on screen and the level of detail required. Figure 7-2 presents an animated walking cycle with 10 frames.

*Figure 7-2. A simple walking cycle, with 10 frames*

In games with small characters, we can usually cope with fewer frames. A cycle with 6 frames is okay if we don't need a realistic look and feel, and even cycles with 4 frames can work, if they're done particularly well.

Earlier games had walking cycles with 3 or even 2 frames, but we would only recommend this be used today for games that are aiming for a "retro" look and feel. Figure 7-3 shows the same walking animation cycle presented earlier, but this time with only 4 frames.

*Figure 7-3. A simple walking cycle, with 4 frames*

Now, how can a programmer apply this idea in his or her games? The best advice, if you're not an artist, is to find an artist to join your team. You can always do some rough sketches, however, to at least have an approximation of how your animation would work when testing your game before applying the final artwork. Because we can barely draw two parallel lines, we always have a sample at hand when beginning to draw, and we suggest you do the same. If you collect enough samples, you'll be able to create your own characters by simply adapting the ideas from those samples.

In Figure 7-4, we show one of author's own sketches, based on Igor's sample walking man. It's no Renoir, but it sufficed for the first animation tests on a game we were working on, some years ago.

Figure 7-4. A 5-frames zombie boy animation cycle

---

 **NOTE** *Keep in mind the cycling concept, because we'll be using it throughout the next section, which will explain other animation concepts, starting with the idea of squashing and stretching characters when animating.*

---

## Animating Squashing and Stretching Motions

Although *squash and stretch* sounds like the name of a second-rate cartoon, it's actually a very important concept—one that will give your game a much more professional look.

The idea behind squashing and stretching characters is that game characters represent (somewhat) real things, and as such, they are smooth and flexible. Usually a character squashes when it is pressed by gravity, when it finishes a jump, or when an anvil drops on it. A character stretches when something pulls it, such as gravity, if it starts falling, or if a rope is tied around its neck.

Forgetting to incorporate these concepts in your animations will make your characters look like hard metal balls when they bounce against any obstacles. Compare the images in Figures 7-5 and 7-6 to see an example of this.

Figure 7-5. A squashing and stretching bouncing ball

*Figure 7-6. The same bouncing movement, without squash and stretch*

We must use this same idea when animating characters, especially in jumping sequences and when hitting (or being hit by) an obstacle. Figure 7-7 shows the same concept used for a jumping rabbit character.

*Figure 7-7. A squashing and stretching jumping rabbit*

Although we can create a jump by just moving a character up and down, including squashing and stretching will make that character much more lifelike. Looking at Figure 7-7, we can see that it's hard to imagine creating a jumping character without using these concepts. Nevertheless, forgetting them is more common than you would think. For example, Mario and Luigi in the first Mario Brothers games jumped like bricks.

**TIP** *Including flexible parts with or on our characters—such as a tail, a feather on a hat, or the ears of our rabbit—that can be moved to emphasize the effects of momentum and gravity on the drawings can strengthen the illusion of movement.*

Looking again at Figure 7-7, we can see that the last position is almost the same as the sixth one, except for some minor details. If we simply copy the first five positions, in reverse order, after the current last one, we'll have a complete jumping cycle that can be used along with any other animation.

In Figure 7-8 we have tried to create a jumping rabbit using Igor's drawings, but without squashing and stretching. The result is not very realistic, as you can see.

*Figure 7-8. Without squashing and stretching, the jumping rabbit looks like a statue.*

In the next section we discuss anticipation, an animation concept that works closely with squashing and stretching to help us improve the movement of our game characters.

## Animating Anticipation

*Anticipation* is an animation concept based on observation of real movements. Although it sounds like an obvious concept, even today we see many commercial games that fail to include anticipation in their characters' animation.

The basic idea is simple: Before starting any movement, a character will always do a "preparation" movement, usually in the opposite direction. For example, if the character is sitting down, before it stands up it will lower its head and shoulders a little, just like we would. If the character is going to run to the left, it will first gain momentum by moving a foot to the right.

The most common example of anticipation is crouching before and after jumping, as we have already seen with the jumping rabbit in Figure 7-7. If we don't use anticipation when creating a jump, the result will be as unrealistic as the jumping rabbit in Figure 7-8. Any doubts? Just take a look at Figure 7-9, where we see the jumping rabbit without the anticipation frames.

*Figure 7-9. A jumping rabbit without anticipation*

Next we'll discuss another very important and widely overlooked animation concept: the use of correct character posture.

## Animating Posture to Reveal Emotions

The use of posture in our characters is directly associated with the characters' emotions. Basically, posture constitutes the "corporal language" used to express an emotion. Body language is universal—we needn't explain anything else in a game if we use this animation trick.

Although using different character postures is not necessary in every game (its most commonly used when creating adventure games), we must understand posture basics in order to guide character animations for all games, if we want to add an extra feeling of reality. Will a particular character be a happy, sad, or pompous person? Will that character get angry any time?

Each emotion will be associated with a bodily posture, and the best part is that it's easier than it seems to convey these emotions using postures; this subject has been considered by a great number of people previously, and we now have a complete guide available in most animation books.

Figure 7-10 shows two frames from walking animations for a happy (or proud of itself) character and for a sad one.

*Figure 7-10. A happy and a sad character—which is which?*

Postures will reflect directly animation velocity too: A happy character will walk at normal pace, a sad character will usually walk a little slower, a creeping character will walk very slowly, and a character in a hurry, well, it'd usually run. If we extend the concept of character postures, we can encompass under the category "postures" different walking speeds: walking, running, running real fast, and so on. Figure 7-11 shows a sample of a running character.

*Figure 7-11. A game character in a hurry*

In the next section, we'll look at some technical tips and lots of examples to help you in animating your games.

## Technical Tips

Now that you understand some basic animation concepts, let's discuss some tips and guidelines for using them in your games. We'll start with the idea of animating parts of an image.

### Animating Parts of an Image

Animating only parts of an image, rather than animating the full drawing, can lead to poor animation. Nothing is worse than a static guy whose mouth opens and closes when he talks, without any additional movement. However, knowing how to animate only specific parts of an image helps us create animations faster, and for those of us who aren't the next Monet, it may even improve the animation quality, as we'll see in the next paragraphs.

Let's start with the example of the walking man animation cycle, shown earlier in Figure 7-2. If we look at this in detail, we see that the same image can be used for the head and the body; we'd only need to move it up and down as the character walks. Figure 7-12 shows the same character, divided into three different animations: body and head, arms, and legs.

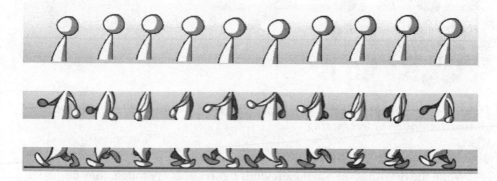

*Figure 7-12. The walking cycle, divided into three different animations*

Although skilled graphical artists don't need to use such a trick, it will help the rest of us a lot, since we'll have no problem trying to repeat the same head and body; that must look the same regardless of the setting.

For games with simple graphics, this tip will work wonderfully. Figure 7-13 shows the different body parts for a sketchy Viking character from an old game of ours.

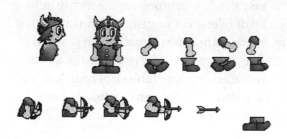

*Figure 7-13. Animations of different body parts for creating game animation cycles*

Figure 7-14 shows the character's final animation, based on the body parts shown in Figure 7-13.

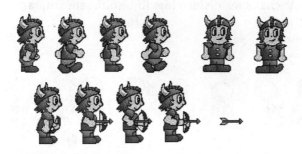

*Figure 7-14. A simple walking cycle, with 4 frames, a shooting animation, and a simple animation of feet moving*

While the drawings seen in the previous figures are very rough, they do demonstrate the point of creating animation using body parts.

As mentioned at the start of this section, one part of the body that deserves special attention is the mouth. If our character must speak during the game, we may wish to make his mouth move accordingly, and that's what we'll discuss in the next section.

## Animating the Mouth

To provide a realistic animation of our characters when speaking is one of the most challenging tasks in a game. The easy part is synchronizing the mouth animations with the sound of the voice; a lot of references (usually cartoon animation books) are available that will help you in associating the correct mouth position with each syllable. The hard bit is including the gestures that reinforce the words, since every character must make gestures when speaking (unless, of course, it is a mummy or something like that). There are also books that explain how to create mouth animations in 3-D characters, so we can improve the gestures by moving the head accordingly.

Here we'll only deal with the easy part, synchronizing mouth movement with sound, as this will suffice for this chapter's game and also act as an introduction to the subject for those who wish to study it further.

There are various ways of creating mouth animations, ranging from simpler ones (with 4 mouth positions for the vowels and 5 mouth positions for groups of consonants) to very complex ones (with more than 20 different mouth positions).

Figure 7-15 shows a variation of the mouth positions used by Disney in its earlier movies (such as *Snow White and the Seven Dwarfs*), which is ample for any game featuring speaking characters.

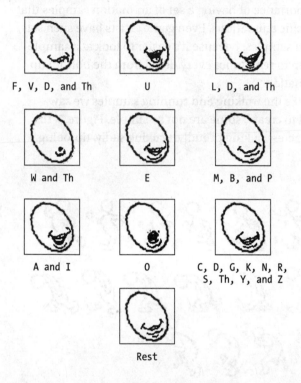

F, V, D, and Th            U            L, D, and Th

W and Th            E            M, B, and P

A and I            O            C, D, G, K, N, R,
                                        S, Th, Y, and Z

Rest

*Figure 7-15. The mouth positions with their associated sounds*

**NOTE** *Of course, the images in Figure 7-15 show the mouths for a specific head position; if the character is looking in any different direction (up, down, or wherever) we'll need new drawings, but those in Figure 7-15 are a very good starting point.*

Talking about starting points, in the next section we'll discuss animation guides, the starting point for any game animation.

## Compiling Animation Guides

As any good game programmer has his or her own set of game programming libraries, we can't forget the importance of having a set of animation samples that will help us to create game-specific animations. Even game artists have such sets, sometimes rising to hundreds of samples, because it's easier to look at a sample and create a new animation than to remember every detail from the bottom up every time you need a new animation.

While simple animations (like the walking and running samples we saw before) are very straightforward to create, some are not so simple. Figure 7-16 shows a simple guide for a character walking proudly, walking sadly, tiptoeing, and jumping.

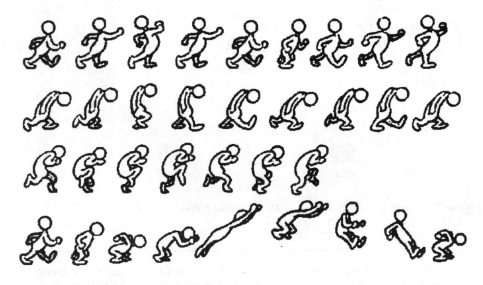

*Figure 7-16. A sample of an animation guide with some walking movements*

To be comprehensive, we must include in our animation guides every animation we can get our hands on: birds flying, four-legged animals moving, and characters using different kinds of objects, like the cyclist in Figure 7-17.

*Figure 7-17. An animation guide for bike-riding characters*

 **NOTE** *It's not in the scope of this book to include every animation guide from our personal libraries, mostly because many of them are samples from different copyrighted commercial games. However, we suggest the same approach: While you can't use copyrighted graphics from other games in your own games, as long as you have bought the games you can copy some animations (any screen capture utility will help with this) to your personal library, so they can serve as a basis for your own original graphics.*

Next we'll introduce the Speech API, the function set responsible for voice generation and recognition.

## Introducing Speech API

*Application programming interfaces* (APIs) are present all over the Windows environment, offering high-level interfaces that allow applications to access device features. By "device," we mean not only physical devices, such as joysticks or graphics acceleration boards, but also logical devices, like the ODBC or OLE DB devices for data access, or the focus of this section, the interface for speech engines.

Speech engines are special drivers that control speech recognition and/or speech generation (based on text). You can buy the speech generation/recognition drivers, as data access drivers, from various providers, but the Speech API (SAPI) hides the specific details from each driver, allowing any application to use a simple set of functions to access every driver. To have access to the Speech API, we must install Microsoft's Speech SDK, which, besides installing the API, installs basic engines for voice recognition and generation. You can download the Microsoft Speech SDK for free from the Microsoft Web site, at `http://msdn.microsoft.com/downloads/default.asp?URL=/downloads/sample.asp?url=/MSDN-FILES/027/000/781/msdncompositedoc.xml`, or simply by searching for the keywords "Speech SDK" at `http://msdn.microsoft.com/downloads`.

Figure 7-18 depicts the relationship between an application and SAPI, also showing the speech drivers and their connection with SAPI.

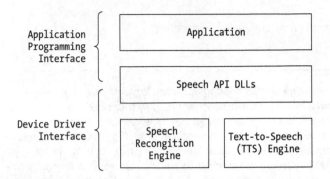

*Figure 7-18. The relationship between applications and speech engines*

As shown in Figure 7-18, the Speech API provides access to two types of engines, text-to-speech (TTS) systems (to convert text strings and files into spoken audio) and voice recognition devices (which do the opposite, converting human voice into strings and files). To ease access from Visual Basic and other COM applications, Microsoft developed a COM interface to access various functions from the API, which can be done by setting a reference to the SpeechLib DLL, installed with the speech SDK. A managed version has yet to be released at the time of writing this book, so we'll use the COM interface in this chapter.

In the next sections we'll discuss the two basic engines provided by the Speech API, and then create a class to handle voice generation for our applications.

## API for Speech Recognition

A game that speaks is a common thing, but a game that can understand what you are saying is a true novelty.

Discussing speech recognition in any great depth is beyond the scope of this book, but in this section we'll explain the basic concepts of recognizers and how they work, and then you can study the topic further in another book dedicated to the subject.

All the complexity of speech recognition is handled by the speech engine and accessed by a simple COM interface to the SAPI functions. The main objects used for speech recognition are spInProcRecoContext, which handles a recognizer with full control and speed, and spSharedRecoContext, which shares a recognizer with other applications. Both objects have specific properties, methods, and events to help the programmer when creating a voice recognition application based on previously requested speech recognition events.

After creating the recognition context object and setting the events that will be handled, a speech application must create, load, and activate the recognition grammar method, ISpRecoGrammar. We can do this by calling the CreateGrammar method of the recognition context object, calling LoadDictation or LoadCmdxxx (to load a dictation utterance grammar or a command and control word grammar) from the grammar object, and finally calling SetDictationState or SetRuleState (depending on whether the program loaded a dictation or a command and control word grammar) to activate the grammar and start voice recognition.

The application will then receive events with the results of the speech recognized, translated into text.

In the next section we'll discuss the voice generation engines in enough detail to allow us to create a voice generation application.

## API for Converting Text to Speech

To control text-to-speech (TTS) devices, after setting the proper reference to the SpeechLib reference, all we need to do is to create an spVoice object and call the Speak method to generate the speech from text data. The complexity of the speech generation is so well hidden from the application that we can create a "Hello World" speaking application with only three lines, as shown in the next code sample:

```
Dim voice As SpeechLib.SpVoice
Set voice = New SpeechLib.SpVoice
voice.Speak "Hello World", SpeechLib.SpeechVoiceSpeakFlags.SVSFlagsAsync
```

The Speak method can be called synchronously (the call of the method will only return after all the voice generation is done) or asynchronously (the method returns immediately, and the program continues to run while the voice is being generated), according to the second parameter passed to it. In the preceding code sample, we are using the default voice, but we can choose the voice to be used according to the voices installed on our computer; the GetVoices method allows us to list all the voices if we want to.

The spVoice object also has some properties, methods, and events that will help us with controlling some of the speaking characteristics (like choosing the synthetic voice, the volume, or the speaking speed). We can also get feedback about what is being spoken with events that occur at every word end, at every viseme, or at custom bookmarks from the application. *Visemes* are mouth animations associated with the various speaking sounds, or, as the Speech API help states, "viseme is a unit of speech that is detected in a spoken phrase."

The core event we must handle to synchronize our mouth animations with the text being spoken is the Viseme event, which receives the following parameters:

```
SpVoice.Viseme(StreamNumber As Long, StreamPosition As Variant, _
    Duration As Long, NextVisemeId As SpeechVisemeType, _
    Feature As SpeechVisemeFeature, CurrentVisemeId As SpeechVisemeType)
```

The parameters in the preceding code function as follows:

- **StreamNumber** is a unique number associated with the stream used to generate the voice (useful when the same spVoice object is generating more than one voice at the same time).

- **StreamPosition** is the character position where the viseme begins within the input stream.

- **Duration** is how much time the viseme will take to be spoken.

- **NextVisemeId** and CurrentVisemeType identify the next viseme and the current one, based on the SpeechVisemeType enumeration, which will help us to choose the proper mouth animation.

- **Feature** indicates the emphasis or stress of the viseme, being one of three possible values from the SpeechVisemeFeature enumeration: SVF_None (no stress or emphasis), SVF_Stressed (the viseme is stressed compared to other visemes within the current word), or SVF_Emphasis (the current word has an emphasis in comparison to other words in the phrase).

The next code listing shows all possible values of the SpeechLib.SpeechVisemeType enumeration; each comment represents the corresponding sound for each value. Comparing the sounds of this enumeration with the mouth positions we learned about at the beginning of this chapter, we see that there is no perfect match; but, as mentioned before, there are a lot of mouth positions used to create speaking animations; here we're only choosing the simplest ones that provide good results.

```
Enum SpeechVisemeType
    SVP_0 = 0          'silence
    SVP_1 = 1          'ae ax ah
    SVP_2 = 2          'aa
    SVP_3 = 3          'ao
    SVP_4 = 4          'ey eh uh
    SVP_5 = 5          'er
    SVP_6 = 6          'y iy ih ix
    SVP_7 = 7          'w uw
    SVP_8 = 8          'ow
    SVP_9 = 9          'aw
    SVP_10 = 10        'oy
    SVP_11 = 11        'ay
    SVP_12 = 12        'h
    SVP_13 = 13        'r
    SVP_14 = 14        'l
    SVP_15 = 15        's z
    SVP_16 = 16        'sh ch jh zh
    SVP_17 = 17        'th dh
    SVP_18 = 18        'f v
    SVP_19 = 19        'd t n
    SVP_20 = 20        'k g ng
    SVP_21 = 21        'p b m
End Enum
```

Now we are ready to create a class that will generate speech based on text strings and generate events for calling applications that will allow us to create the mouth animations.

## Creating a Speech Generation Game Class

To add extra functionality to our speech generation class, besides the speech generation and events we saw in the previous section, we'll create a method that translates the viseme codes into actual player images, chosen among predefined mouth positions stored as images.

To generate these images, we'll simply apply the mouth positions we saw in Figure 7-15 to our character's head. Since the speaking head won't move (it's shown in a square at the bottom of the screen), we won't have to deal with more complex problems, like making the mouth move while the character is walking, or adding gestures that reinforce the speaking animation.

Figure 7-19 presents the mouth animation we'll use in our game, drawn by the Brazilian graphical artist Waldivar Cesar.

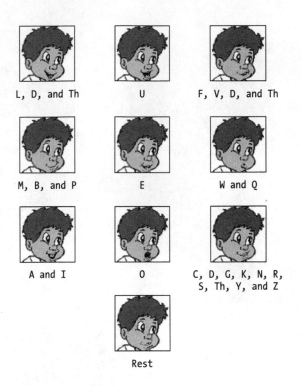

L, D, and Th          U          F, V, D, and Th

M, B, and P          E          W and Q

A and I          O          C, D, G, K, N, R, S, Th, Y, and Z

Rest

*Figure 7-19. Different mouth animations for Natanael, our game character*

Besides a method to load such images and the event to handle the visemes, we'll add extra events for each event generated by the spVoice object (for future use, if we want to use this class in other projects) and methods to speak, stop speaking, and pause voice generation.

Table 7-1 shows the interface elements of the PlayerVoice class, which will wrap up the calls to the Speech API.

*Table 7-1. PlayerVoice Class Interface Members*

| TYPE | NAME | DESCRIPTION |
|------|------|-------------|
| Property | Voice | Represents the spVoice object from Speech API (private). |
| Property | CurrentMouthType | Indicates a Sprite object that holds the image for the mouth type to be drawn. |
| Properties | NatanaelMouthxxx | Represent Sprite objects that store each of the possible mouth positions. |
| Method | New | Constitutes the class constructor, which initializes the spVoice object, chooses which voice will be spoken, and loads the mouth images. |
| Method | LoadMouthImages | Loads the sprite mouth animations. |
| Method | ListVoiceNames | Generates the VoiceName event, sending strings with each of the voice names (useful if an application wants to display a list to the user). |
| Method | Voice_Viseme | Serves as handler for the Viseme event of the spVoice method, sets the CurrentMouthType property, and generates the NewMouthType event. |
| Method | Speak | Receives a string and generates the speech. |
| Method | PauseSpeak | Pauses any speech that is running at the same time as another. |
| Method | ResumeSpeak | Resumes paused speaking. |
| Method | StopSpeak | Stops speaking. |
| Methods | Voice_xxx | Applies to all methods starting with "Voice_", which serve as handlers for the events generated by the spVoice object. We created the interfaces to make our class more complete, but only the Voice_Viseme method has actual code. |
| Event | VoiceName | Runs once for each voice installed on the machine, and passes to the application a string with the voice name; this event is generated by the VoiceName method. |
| Event | NewMouthType | Runs every time a new mouth position occurs when speaking; this event is generated by the Voice_Viseme method. |

The final class interface, including the specific parameters for the spVoice event handlers, is shown in the next code listing:

```
Imports SpeechLib
Imports Microsoft.DirectX.Direct3D

Public Class clsPlayerVoice
    ' Speech API object interface
    Private WithEvents Voice As SpVoice

    ' We'll have two events: one to list the existing voices,
    '  and another that will be fired every time the mouth format changes
    Public Event VoiceName(VoiceName As String)
    Public Event NewMouthType(CurrentMouthImage As clsSprite)

    Public CurrentMouthType As clsSprite

    Private NatanaelMouthFVD As clsSprite
    Private NatanaelMouthU As clsSprite
    Private NatanaelMouthLDTh As clsSprite
    Private NatanaelMouthWQ As clsSprite
    Private NatanaelMouthE As clsSprite
    Private NatanaelMouthMPB As clsSprite
    Private NatanaelMouthAI As clsSprite
    Private NatanaelMouthO As clsSprite
    Private NatanaelMouthCDG As clsSprite
    Private NatanaelMouthRest As clsSprite
    Private NatanaelMouthSilence As clsSprite

    Private Sub LoadMouthImages()
    Private Sub Voice_Viseme(StreamNum As Integer, StreamPos As Object, _
            Duration As Integer, VisemeType As SpeechVisemeType, _
            Feature As SpeechVisemeFeature, VisemeId As SpeechVisemeType) _
            Handles Voice.Viseme
    Sub New(strVoiceName As String)
    Sub ListVoiceNames()
    Sub PauseSpeak()
    Sub ResumeSpeak()
    Sub StopSpeak()
    Sub Speak(strTextToSpeak As String)
    Private Sub Voice_EndStream(StreamNum As Integer, StreamPos As Object) _
            Handles Voice.EndStream
```

```
    Private Sub Voice_StartStream(StreamNum As Integer, StreamPos As Object) _
        Handles Voice.StartStream
    Private Sub Voice_VoiceChange(StreamNum As Integer, StreamPos As Object, _
        Token As SpObjectToken) Handles Voice.VoiceChange
    Private Sub Voice_Word(StreamNum As Integer, StreamPos As Object, _
        Pos As Integer, Length As Integer) Handles Voice.Word
End Class
```

We are now ready to code the class methods.

## Coding the New and LoadMouthImages Methods

Let's start looking at the code from the New and LoadMouthImages methods, where we'll initialize the spVoice object and the sprites with the mouth animations.

```
Sub New(strVoiceName As String)
    ' Create the voice object
    Try
        Voice = New SpVoice()
    Catch ex As Exception
        MessageBox.Show("Could not initialize Speech API. Error: " & _
            ex.Message, "SAPI Initialization.", MessageBoxButtons.OK, _
            MessageBoxIcon.Error)
    End Try

    ' Change the voice to the selected one
    Try
        Voice.Voice = Voice.GetVoices("Name = " & strVoiceName).Item(0)
    Catch
        ' If we can't find the named voice, simply pick the first one
        Voice.Voice = Voice.GetVoices().Item(0)
    Finally
        ' Load the images for the mouth positions
        LoadMouthImages()
    End Try
End Sub

Private Sub LoadMouthImages()
Try
    NatanaelMouthFVD = New clsSprite("NatanaelMouthFVD.Bmp", _
        New Point(156, 4), clsSprite.enScaleFactor.enScalePixel, 72, 72)
```

```
        NatanaelMouthU = New clsSprite("NatanaelMouthU.Bmp", _
            New Point(156, 4), clsSprite.enScaleFactor.enScalePixel, 72, 72)
        NatanaelMouthLDTh = New clsSprite("NatanaelMouthLDTh.Bmp", _
            New Point(156, 4), clsSprite.enScaleFactor.enScalePixel, 72, 72)
        NatanaelMouthWQ = New clsSprite("NatanaelMouthWQ.Bmp", _
            New Point(156, 4), clsSprite.enScaleFactor.enScalePixel, 72, 72)
        NatanaelMouthE = New clsSprite("NatanaelMouthE.Bmp", _
            New Point(156, 4), clsSprite.enScaleFactor.enScalePixel, 72, 72)
        NatanaelMouthMPB = New clsSprite("NatanaelMouthMPB.Bmp", _
            New Point(156, 4), clsSprite.enScaleFactor.enScalePixel, 72, 72)
        NatanaelMouthAI = New clsSprite("NatanaelMouthAI.Bmp", _
            New Point(156, 4), clsSprite.enScaleFactor.enScalePixel, 72, 72)
        NatanaelMouthO = New clsSprite("NatanaelMouthO.Bmp", _
            New Point(156, 4), clsSprite.enScaleFactor.enScalePixel, 72, 72)
        NatanaelMouthCDG = New clsSprite("NatanaelMouthCDG.Bmp", _
            New Point(156, 4), clsSprite.enScaleFactor.enScalePixel, 72, 72)
        NatanaelMouthRest = New clsSprite("NatanaelMouthRest.Bmp", _
            New Point(156, 4), clsSprite.enScaleFactor.enScalePixel, 72, 72)
        NatanaelMouthSilence = New clsSprite("NatanaelMouthSilence.Bmp", _
            New Point(156, 4), clsSprite.enScaleFactor.enScalePixel, 72, 72)
    Catch
        MsgBox(Err.Description & ":" & Err.Number, MsgBoxStyle.OKOnly,_
            "Error when loading mouth images")
    End Try
End Sub
```

The only novelty in this sample code is the use of the GetVoices() collection of the Voice object to choose a specific voice, according to the voice name, passed as an argument to the New method. The sprite initialization is the same one we've been using since Chapter 4. (After all, that's the beautiful part of object orientation—improve the code and reuse it!)

## Coding the ListVoiceNames Method

Our New method presumes that the application knows the names of the voices installed on the computer. To provide a way for the application to get such a listing, we've added two members to our class: the ListVoiceNames method and the VoiceName event. When the application calls this method, an event is triggered for each voice installed on the computer. The code for these two members is presented in the next listing:

```
Public Event VoiceName(VoiceName As String)

Sub ListVoiceNames()
    ' Return all the voice names through the VoiceName event
    Dim Token As ISpeechObjectToken

    For Each Token In Voice.GetVoices
        RaiseEvent VoiceName(Token.GetDescription())
    Next Token
End Sub
```

## Coding the Speech Generation Methods

Once the application knows which voice it wants to use and has created the Player-Voice object, it'll use the methods to play, pause, resume, and stop voice generation as needed. The code for these methods is very simple, and it's shown in the next code listing:

```
Sub PauseSpeak()
    Voice.Pause()
End Sub

Sub ResumeSpeak()
    Voice.Resume()
End Sub

Sub StopSpeak()
    ' Cancel current speech and clear internal buffers
    Voice.Speak(vbNullString, SpeechVoiceSpeakFlags.SVSFPurgeBeforeSpeak)
End Sub

Sub Speak(strTextToSpeak As String)
    Voice.Speak(strTextToSpeak, DefaultSpeakFlags)
End Sub
```

The `Speak` method of the `spVoice` object receives two parameters: the string containing the text to be spoken, and a flag that will tell us how to generate the voice. We created a constant with the default behavior we want: Generate the voice asynchronously and purge any previous voice being generated if we call the `Speak` method again. The constant definition is shown in the next code fragment:

```
' Speak flags is a combination of bit flags
Private DefaultSpeakFlags As SpeechVoiceSpeakFlags = _
SpeechVoiceSpeakFlags.SVSFlagsAsync Or SpeechVoiceSpeakFlags.SVSFPurgeBeforeSpeak
```

When we call the `Speak` method, the voice will then be generated and our application will start receiving events from the `Voice` object. The most important of these events is the `Viseme` event, which is called every time a new sound is started. In this event, we set the `CurrentMouthType` sprite to the corresponding mouth position loaded previously and generate the `NewMouthType` event to inform the game that the new mouth position must be drawn on screen.

## Coding the Viseme Event Handler

In the next code sample we present the `Viseme` event. Look at the comments in each of the branches of the `Case` statement to see the relationship between the constants generated by the Speech API and the mouth positions previously created.

```
Private Sub Voice_Viseme(StreamNum As Integer, StreamPos As Object, _
 Duration As Integer, VisemeType As SpeechVisemeType,_
 Feature As SpeechVisemeFeature, VisemeId As SpeechVisemeType) _
Handles Voice.Viseme
    Static PreviousMouthType As SpeechVisemeType = SpeechVisemeType.SVP_0
    ' Show different mouth positions according to the viseme
    Select Case VisemeId
        Case SpeechVisemeType.SVP_0        'silence
            CurrentMouthType = NatanaelMouthSilence
        Case SpeechVisemeType.SVP_3, _
            SpeechVisemeType.SVP_10    'ao 'oy
            CurrentMouthType = NatanaelMouthO
        Case SpeechVisemeType.SVP_4        'ey eh uh
            CurrentMouthType = NatanaelMouthU
        Case SpeechVisemeType.SVP_7        'w uw
            CurrentMouthType = NatanaelMouthWQ
        Case SpeechVisemeType.SVP_1, _
            SpeechVisemeType.SVP_2, _
```

```
            SpeechVisemeType.SVP_8, _
            SpeechVisemeType.SVP_9              'ae ax ah 'aa 'ow 'aw
            CurrentMouthType = NatanaelMouthAI
        Case SpeechVisemeType.SVP_11         'ay
            CurrentMouthType = NatanaelMouthE
        Case SpeechVisemeType.SVP_14, _
            SpeechVisemeType.SVP_17          'th dh 'l
            CurrentMouthType = NatanaelMouthLDTh
        Case SpeechVisemeType.SVP_13, _
            SpeechVisemeType.SVP_15, _
            SpeechVisemeType.SVP_16, _
            SpeechVisemeType.SVP_20              'r 's z 'sh ch jh zh 'k g ng
            CurrentMouthType = NatanaelMouthCDG
        Case SpeechVisemeType.SVP_18, _
            SpeechVisemeType.SVP_19          'f v 'd t n
            CurrentMouthType = NatanaelMouthFVD
        Case SpeechVisemeType.SVP_21         'p b m
            CurrentMouthType = NatanaelMouthMPB
        Case Else
            ' SpeechVisemeType.SVP_6,              'y iy ih ix
            ' SpeechVisemeType.SVP_12         'h
            CurrentMouthType = NatanaelMouthRest
    End Select

    If PreviousMouthType <> VisemeId Then
        PreviousMouthType = VisemeId
        RaiseEvent NewMouthType(CurrentMouthType)
    End If
End Sub
```

## Finishing the Speech Generation Class

As for the remaining methods of the PlayerVoice class, which handle the spVoice events, we need to code only the EndStream and the EndWord events to reset the mouth animation to the Silence position when the engine stops generating the voice. The other methods will be empty, to be coded if we need other features in other voice generation applications.

The next code piece shows the remaining methods of the `PlayerVoice` class:

```
Sub Voice_EndStream(StreamNum As Integer, _
                    StreamPos As Object) Handles Voice.EndStream
    ' Reset the mouth to silence position
    CurrentMouthType = NatanaelMouthSilence
    RaiseEvent NewMouthType(CurrentMouthType)
End Sub

Private Sub Voice_StartStream(StreamNum As Integer,_
  StreamPos As Object) Handles Voice.StartStream
    ' Include here any code needed before character starts speaking
End Sub

Private Sub Voice_VoiceChange(StreamNum As Integer,_
  StreamPos As Object, Token As SpObjectToken) Handles Voice.VoiceChange
    ' Include here any code needed when the voice changes
End Sub

Private Sub Voice_Word(StreamNum As Integer, StreamPos As Object,_
  Pos As Integer, Length As Integer) Handles Voice.Word
        ' Include here any code needed when a new word is to be spoken
End Sub
```

In the next section we discuss the proposal for the sample game of this chapter, including the concepts discussed in the previous sections.

## The Game Proposal

For this project we'll extend the Magic KindergarteN. adventure game, including dialogs among the player's character and the game characters and adding the `PlayerVoice` class we discussed in the previous section to make our character really speak.

We won't change the storyline we saw in the previous chapter, we'll just add dialogs between Natanael and the mud monster, and add an extra character, a mouse, that will prevent Natanael from getting the magic wand unless he gives something to the mouse—maybe the big cheese on the table?

All drawings use in this game were created by Waldivar Cesar (http://wace.cosmo.com.br), a Brazilian graphical artist, unless otherwise stated.

In the next section we'll discuss the dialogs and what we'll need to add to our game to implement them.

# The Game Project

Our game project will only describe the updates we must make to the previous chapter's project, plus the dialogs that now must be created between the characters.

We have excluded the television and included a cheese in its place to add an extra puzzle players must solve before getting the rod.

## Screens

We won't make changes to the screens created in the previous chapter; but we'll need to remove the dialogs used in the forest clearing from the screen presentation text, as the dialogs will now be performed when the player applies the Talk action.

The new text for this screen could be something like this:

*Entering the forest, Natanael meets a mud monster. It seems to be a friendly monster.*

All other screen text may remain the same.

In the next section we'll see the modifications to the game characters.

## Characters

The game characters Natanael and Fiona (the mud monster) will remain unchanged; but we'll include a new character, a mouse that lives in the mouse hole.

The profile and the image for the new character will be as follows:

- **Mouse:** This character is a human-like mouse, named Sidney, that lives in the hole inside the magic kindergarten (see Figure 7-20). He's not a magic mouse, though. He isn't very friendly, and doesn't like visitors inside his hole; but he will get out of the way of the magic wand if he receives something in exchange.

*Figure 7-20. Sidney, the not-so-friendly mouse*

Table 7-2 describes the result of each action on Sidney.

*Table 7-2. Result of Each Action on Sidney the Mouse*

| ACTION | EXECUTE? | DISPLAY TEXT |
|---|---|---|
| Examine | Yes | It's a HUGE, armed mouse! |
| Take | No | I can't take him! |
| Walk to | No | He won't let me walk this way. |
| Use | No | I don't want to fight! |
| Talk | Yes | |

We'll also need to update the mud monster's actions to allow Natanael to start a conversation with it, while making sure all other objects don't talk. If the player character tries to talk to any nontalking object, we'll simply show the text "I can't talk with this" on screen.

Now we'll discuss the updates of the game's active objects.

## Active Objects

The active objects remain the same, except for the television, which will be replaced by a cheese. Table 7-3 shows the results of each action on the cheese.

*Table 7-3. Results of Each Action on the Cheese*

| SCREEN | OBJECT | ACTION | EXECUTE? | DISPLAY TEXT |
|---|---|---|---|---|
| 1 | cheese | Examine | Yes | It's a big cheese. |
| | | Take | Yes | I'll take it, it may be useful. |
| | | Walk to | No | I can't walk into a cheese! |
| | | Use | No | No, thanks, I'm not hungry! |
| | | Use with | Yes (with mouse) | The mouse is gone! I hope he enjoys the cheese! |

In the next section we'll discuss dialog creation and describe the dialogs for each game character.

## Dialogs

The dialogs are an essential part of any adventure game; they are one of the main contributors to the ambience of a game, so special care must be taken when writing them to avoid jargon and create dialogs that represent the personality of each character.

In a real game, besides many dialog paths we'll have many possible dialogs with each character, depending on the current status of the player. For example, a dialog with a pirate may be different if you have a sword or not in your inventory. Also, some dialog paths may be different according to whether you have talked with a specific character before—for example, you won't introduce yourself every time you start a new conversation.

In our game we'll create a simple dialog that doesn't change in any situation, but this should be enough to give anyone the first steps for creating a more complex dialog structure, if needed. More sophisticated games will have different dialog paths associated with each game character, depending on specific conditions; for example, if your character is driving and a policeman asks for that character's license, we will have different dialog paths with the policeman depending on whether the character is carrying a license or not.

Basically, we'll create "answer blocks" for each game character. Each of these blocks will be composed of a question to be chosen by the player, the answer provided by the character, and the next block to be displayed. When starting to talk with a character, we'll present the questions from block number 0, and a next block with a special value (let's say -1) will end a dialog.

For example, let's analyze answer block number 0 for the mud monster, presented in Table 7-4.

*Table 7-4. Mud Monster Answer Block 0*

| QUESTION NUMBER | QUESTION | ANSWER | NEXT ANSWER BLOCK |
|---|---|---|---|
| 0 | Hello, my name is Natanael. Who are you? | Hi Natanael! I'm Fiona, your magic teacher! | 1 |
| 1 | Ahem . . . Excuse me? | Yes? Oh, it's you, Natanael!! I'm your teacher, Fiona! | 1 |
| 2 | Ouch! A mud monster?? Where are you from? | Natanael!! I'm your magic teacher, Fiona! Respect me! | 1 |
| 3 | Never Mind. Bye. | Bloop! | −1 |

As we can see in this table, we have possible initial questions to ask the mud monster, numbered from 0 to 3. The first three present the answer of the mud monster and then go to answer block number 1. The last one interrupts the dialog (next block number equals -1), so after the answer the dialog is over.

Table 7-5 presents the full dialog paths for the mud monster, whereas Table 7-6 presents the dialogs for Sidney the mouse.

*Table 7-5. Mud Monster Dialogs*

| ANSWER BLOCK | ANSWER SEQUENCE | QUESTION | ANSWER | NEXT ANSWER BLOCK |
|---|---|---|---|---|
| 0 | 0 | Hello, my name is Natanael. Who are you? | Hi Natanael! I'm Fiona, your magic teacher! | 1 |
| 0 | 1 | Ahem . . . Excuse me? | Yes? Oh, it's you, Natanael!! I'm your teacher, Fiona! | 1 |
| 0 | 2 | Ouch! A mud monster?? Where are you from? | Natanael!! I'm your magic teacher, Fiona! Respect me! | 1 |
| 0 | 3 | Never Mind. Bye. | Bloop! | −1 |
| 1 | 0 | Fiona? Is it really you? What happened to you? | I became a mud monster when practicing a new magic trick. | 2 |
| 1 | 1 | No, I can't believe you! How can I be sure? | Oh, please, just believe me! I need your help! | 2 |
| 1 | 2 | Wow, that's great! Can you teach me how to become a mud monster? | Natanael, it's not time for fun! Can you help me? | 2 |
| 1 | 3 | OK, and I'm Ronald Reagan. Bye! | Bye! | −1 |
| 2 | 0 | And how can I help you? | Please find my magic wand and bring it to me! | 3 |
| 2 | 1 | I think I can help you later. Bye! | OK. But if you find my magic wand, please bring it to me! | −1 |
| 3 | 0 | OK, I'll look for it! Bye! | Thank you very much! Bye! | −1 |

*Table 7-6. Sidney the Mouse Dialogs*

| ANSWER BLOCK | ANSWER SEQUENCE | QUESTION | ANSWER | NEXT ANSWER BLOCK |
|---|---|---|---|---|
| 0 | 0 | Hello, my name is Natanael. Who are you? | Humph! My name is Sidney. What do you want here? | 1 |
| 0 | 1 | Ahem . . . Excuse me? | No. What do you want? | 1 |
| 0 | 2 | Get away from here! I want this magic wand! | This is my hole! YOU get away from here!! Bye!! | −1 |
| 0 | 3 | Never Mind. Bye. | So long! | −1 |
| 1 | 0 | Would you please give me that magic wand? | Of course not! But I can exchange it for something else . . . | 2 |
| 1 | 1 | I want that magic wand. | Did I hear a "please"? | 1 |
| 1 | 2 | Get away from here! I want this magic wand! | No way! YOU'RE the one who must get out of here! Bye! | −1 |
| 1 | 3 | Never mind. See you! | Bye! | −1 |
| 2 | 0 | What do you want for the magic wand? | Just give me anything I can eat and I'll go away! Bye! | −1 |
| 2 | 1 | No, I don't have anything for you! Just give me this magic wand! | No way! Get away and find something to trade! Bye! | −1 |
| 2 | 2 | No way. Bye! | OK, bye! If you have something for me, get back here! | −1 |

Once we've defined how the dialog structure will work, a nonprogrammer member of the team can easily create a table with possible dialog paths—preferably, someone deeply integrated with the story so that he or she can relate the correct character personality in each dialog.

Now let's move on to the changes to the technical side of the game.

## User Interface Elements

Our game interface will remain the same, but we must define how dialogs will take place.

Dialogs will occur in four steps:

1. The game shows the questions from the current answer block, presenting a button to the left of each question.

2. The player chooses a specific question by clicking the corresponding button.

3. The game presents the question chosen by the player, the answer from the character, and a button to continue.

4. The player presses the Continue button, and then the game chooses the new answer block and goes back to step 1, or ends the dialog if the answer block number is -1.

This description will suffice for you or your team's programmer to add the code needed to control the dialog. In the next section we'll see the class diagram for the new version of the game.

## The Class Diagram

We'll use the same classes expressed in the previous chapter, with the exception of the Video class, which will be removed because our television was exchanged for a cheese.

We'll also add an extra class—the PlayerVoice class, presented earlier in this chapter—to handle the interaction with the Speech API. To test speech generation, we'll implement a new dialog feature in our game, so each object in the game will have two extra members: the CanTalk property, which states whether the object can talk, and a AnswerBlock() property array, to store answer blocks, which will be structured to support all data needed in a dialog.

Figure 7-21 shows the new class diagram, including the updates discussed.

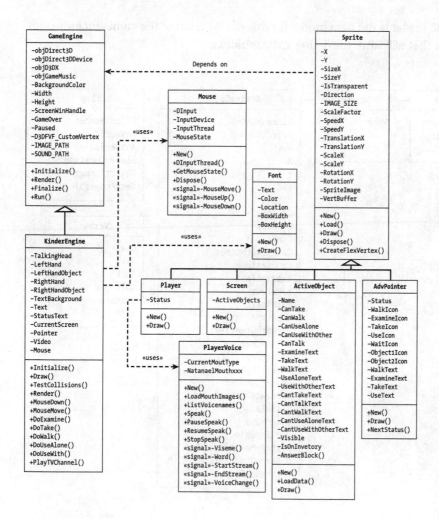

*Figure 7-21. Magic KindergarteN. II class diagram*

We'll now show the new data model for our game, generated according to the properties of the game classes.

## The Game's Data Model

Figure 7-22 presents the data model for this new version of the game, including an extra table that will store the dialog answer blocks.

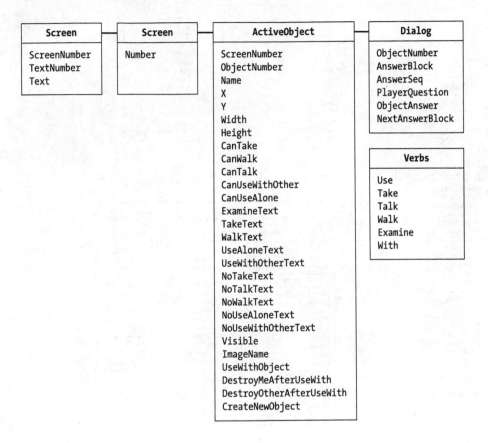

| Screen | Screen | ActiveObject | Dialog |
|---|---|---|---|
| ScreenNumber<br>TextNumber<br>Text | Number | ScreenNumber<br>ObjectNumber<br>Name<br>X<br>Y<br>Width<br>Height<br>CanTake<br>CanWalk<br>CanTalk<br>CanUseWithOther<br>CanUseAlone<br>ExamineText<br>TakeText<br>WalkText<br>UseAloneText<br>UseWithOtherText<br>NoTakeText<br>NoTalkText<br>NoWalkText<br>NoUseAloneText<br>NoUseWithOtherText<br>Visible<br>ImageName<br>UseWithObject<br>DestroyMeAfterUseWith<br>DestroyOtherAfterUseWith<br>CreateNewObject | ObjectNumber<br>AnswerBlock<br>AnswerSeq<br>PlayerQuestion<br>ObjectAnswer<br>NextAnswerBlock |

| Verbs |
|---|
| Use<br>Take<br>Talk<br>Walk<br>Examine<br>With |

*Figure 7-22. Magic KindergarteN. II data model*

**NOTE** *Our game code will have specific updates to control the dialog flow, but most of the code will remain unchanged.*

In the next section we'll see what's new in the coding of Magic KindergarteN. version II.

# The Coding Phase

Again, we have divided our coding phase into discrete steps, so we can focus on specific features to see what's being done in this update. The steps in this chapter are simpler than the ones in the previous chapter, since the main code has already been done. We've divided the coding phase into three steps:

1.  First draft: Adapt the ActiveObject class to handle dialog data, add the extra verb to the mouse pointer (at the AdvPointer class), and code the cheese puzzle.

2.  Second draft: Include code for implementing dialogs with the game characters.

3.  Final version: Add mouth animation and speech generation to the player character.

Now let's finish our ActiveObject class by including new properties and ADO.NET code to load data.

## First Draft: Updating the ActiveObject and the AdvPointer Classes, and Coding the Cheese Puzzle

In this first step all we need to do is create new properties for the ActiveObject class and add code to load the dialog data from the game database.

### Adding Dialog Support to Active Objects

At first, we must create a structure to store the answer blocks. An active object will have an array of answer blocks, where each element will hold a complete block, comprised of one to four questions, one to four answers, and other fields as described earlier in this chapter. The code definition for the AnswerBlock structure and array is shown in the next code piece:

```
Structure stAnswerBlock
    Dim QuestionNumber As Integer
    Dim PlayerQuestion() As String
    Dim ObjectAnswer() As String
    Dim NextAnswerBlock() As Integer
End Structure

Public AnswerBlock() As stAnswerBlock
```

We'll load the answer blocks in the LoadData method, created in the previous chapter. The next code sample presents only the new lines of this method:

```
Public Sub LoadData(DataReader As OleDbDataReader)
    Dim answerBlockCount As Integer = -1
    Dim PreviousAnswerBlock As Integer = -1
    Dim StrConnection = "Provider=Microsoft.Jet.OLEDB.4.0;Data Source=" & _
                        Application.StartupPath & "\Data\KinderData.mdb"
    Dim Conn As OleDbConnection
    Dim CmdDialog As OleDbCommand
    Dim DataReaderDialog As OleDbDataReader
    Dim AnswerSeq As Integer
...
    CanTalk = DataReader.GetBoolean(Fields.CanTalk)
    CantTalkText = DataReader.GetString(Fields.NoTalkText)

    ' Load the Dialog - Use a fixed size of 4, since we don't know previously _
          the size of the answer block
    Conn = New OleDbConnection(StrConnection)
    Conn.Open()
    CmdDialog = Conn.CreateCommand()

    ' Read all dialogs for the current object number
    CmdDialog.CommandText = "SELECT * from Dialog where ObjectNumber = " & _
                        DataReader.GetInt32(1) & _
                        " order by AnswerBlock, answerSeq"

    DataReaderDialog = CmdDialog.ExecuteReader
    Do While DataReaderDialog.Read()
        ' Create the answer blocks if there's any dialog for the current object
        If answerBlockCount = -1 Then
            ReDim AnswerBlock(4)
        End If

        If DataReaderDialog.GetInt32(_
                DialogFields.AnswerBlock)>PreviousAnswerBlock Then
            answerBlockCount = _
                DataReaderDialog.GetInt32(DialogFields.AnswerBlock)
            PreviousAnswerBlock = answerBlockCount
            ReDim AnswerBlock(answerBlockCount).PlayerQuestion(4)
            ReDim AnswerBlock(answerBlockCount).ObjectAnswer(4)
            ReDim AnswerBlock(answerBlockCount).NextAnswerBlock(4)
        End If
```

```
AnswerSeq = DataReaderDialog.GetInt32(DialogFields.AnswerSeq)
AnswerBlock(answerBlockCount).QuestionNumber += 1
AnswerBlock(answerBlockCount).PlayerQuestion(AnswerSeq) = _
        DataReaderDialog.GetString(DialogFields.PlayerQuestion)
AnswerBlock(answerBlockCount).ObjectAnswer(AnswerSeq) = _
        DataReaderDialog.GetString(DialogFields.ObjectAnswer)
AnswerBlock(answerBlockCount).NextAnswerBlock(AnswerSeq) = _
        DataReaderDialog.GetInt32(DialogFields.NextAnswerBlock)
    Loop
End Sub
```

**NOTE** *Because we didn't need to modify any of the class interfaces, we won't need to update the code that is creating the active objects; the program is ready to run, but at the moment there is no visible difference.*

## Creating the Mouse Pointer for the Talk Action

To update the mouse pointer, we'll have to add an extra verb to the AdvPointer class; we'll do this by simply copying a line of the code into all methods that deal with the various pointers and adapt it to reflect the change. For example, we'll need to create a new sprite, TalkIcon, to store the new mouse pointer, and add an extra line in the new procedure:

```
TalkIcon = Load("IconTalk.Bmp", Color.FromArgb(255, 255, 0, 255))
```

Similarly, we'll need to create a new string property, TalkText, to store the verb used for talking (remember, it could be "falar", if we are translating it to Portuguese), and add one extra line to load the verb string from the database in the ReadVerbs procedure:

```
TalkText = DataReader.GetString(2)
```

Finally, we'll need to create a new member of the enStatus enumeration to represent the status of the Talk action, and include one extra case clause in the Draw method:

```
Case enStatus.Talk
        objDirect3DDevice.SetTexture(0, TalkIcon)
```

Since these changes are very simple, we'll not reproduce the complete code of the class here; its logic remains the same—we just included one extra state for the mouse pointer. The dialog icon is shown in Figure 7-23.

*Figure 7-23. The dialog mouse pointer*

### Coding the Cheese Puzzle

The last small update we'll do is to include code to implement the cheese puzzle: If the mouse is in our way, we can't take the magic wand. If we give the cheese to Stanley, the mouse will go away, and we can then take the wand.

Since the database data will only say if a specific object (in this case, the magic wand) simply can or can't be taken, we'll need an extra variable to control this specific feature in the DoTake method: We'll create a Boolean variable that is false by default, and is set to true only if the cheese is given to the mouse.

The updates to implement the cheese puzzle are described in the next code listings, starting with the code for the DoTake method: Add one extra test to see if the MouseIsHere variable is set, and if so, we can't take the magic wand.

```
' Status variables to control the puzzle solving
'    - as for now, only to control if the mouse in the way
Private MouseIsHere As Boolean = True

Sub DoTake(clickedObject As clsActiveObject)
    If clickedObject.CanTake Then
        ' If it is the magic wand, we only can take it if there's no mouse
        '  in the way
        If clickedObject.Name = "magic rod" And _
            MouseIsHere Then
            Say(clickedObject.CantTakeText)
        Else
        ...
End Sub
```

Then we'll need to add some lines of code to the DoUseWith method to reset this variable: one extra test to see if we can use something with the mouse (only the cheese can be used with the mouse), and if so, set MouseIsHere to false.

```
Sub DoUseWith(Object1 As clsActiveObject, clickedObject As clsActiveObject, _
                    RightHand As Boolean)
      If Object1.UsesWith.ObjectName = clickedObject.Name Then
          ' If we are using the cheese with the mouse,_
 solve the puzzle by setting the variable
          If Object1.UsesWith.ObjectName = "mouse" Then
              MouseIsHere = False
          End If
          ...
End Sub
```

This kind of code, which adds one variable to control a game state, may not appear to be obvious straight away. In fact, it's not, but there's no other way to deal with special situations in the game. We'll create a generic class that will handle most of the situations, and eventually we'll need to create a "state" class that will store the control variables for all special cases.

To include all state variables in a class will help us with controlling these exceptions, but since here we have only one special case, we implement the control in a variable. The use of classes to control these situations also has an added attraction: It gets easier to implement a saved game feature that stores the current player status.

Figure 7-24 presents our first test on this version of the game, when we are just about to give the cheese to the mouse.

*Figure 7-24. There's nothing like cheese to get a mouse out of the way.*

In the next section, we'll code the dialog logic, and then we'll see the new data we are loading into the active objects.

## Second Draft: Coding the Dialogs

If we review the code from the MouseUp event from the previous chapter, we'll see that we have a simple Select Case statement that executes the corresponding functions that will do the real work for each verb action. Our dialog will start the same way: If the player clicks an active object with the Talk mouse pointer, we'll call the DoTalk method, which will start the dialog control.

The next code listing presents the updated version of the MouseUp event of the KinderEngine class:

```
Sub Mouse_MouseUp(X As Integer, Y As Integer, Button As ClsMouse.enButton) _
                Handles Mouse.MouseUp
    Dim clickedObject As clsActiveObject

    If Button = ClsMouse.enButton.Left And GameStatus = enGameStatus.Normal Then
        Cursor.NextStatus()
    Else
        TestCollision(clickedObject)
        If Not clickedObject Is Nothing Then
            Select Case Cursor.Status
                Case clsAdvCursor.enStatus.Examine
                        DoExamine(clickedObject)
                Case clsAdvCursor.enStatus.Take
                        DoTake(clickedObject)
                Case clsAdvCursor.enStatus.Use
                        DoUseAlone(clickedObject)
                Case clsAdvCursor.enStatus.Walk
                        DoWalk(clickedObject)
                Case clsAdvCursor.enStatus.Talk
                        DoTalk(clickedObject, 0)
                Case clsAdvCursor.enStatus.Object1
                        DoUseWith(Cursor.Object1, clickedObject, True)
                Case clsAdvCursor.enStatus.Object2
                        DoUseWith(Cursor.Object2, clickedObject, False)
            End Select
        End If
    End If
End Sub
```

The `DoTalk` method will execute the first of the four steps in a dialog control, as we saw previously in this chapter; it'll receive the number of the answer block to present on screen. Since we'll always start with block number 0, we zero the second argument when calling it to start a dialog.

## Presenting the Dialog Choices on Screen

Before entering the code of `DoTalk` and the other helper methods, let's review the four steps of a dialog:

1. The game shows the questions from the current answer block, with a button at the left side of each question.

2. The player chooses a specific question by clicking the corresponding button.

3. The game presents the question chosen by the player, the answer from the character, and a button to continue

4. The player presses the Continue button, and the game then chooses the new answer block and goes back to step 1, or ends the dialog if the answer block number is -1.

To implement these steps, we'll code the following methods in the `KinderEngine` class:

- **DoTalk**: If we can talk with the object, this method presents the questions and buttons on screen and stores the object we are trying to talk to in a variable so we can use it later in other methods.

- **DoSimpleClick**: This method will handle the player's click of a specific question button and present the corresponding answer on screen, implementing steps 2 and 3. It'll also check if the button clicked is the Continue button and, if so, call the `DoTalk` method again and pass the next answer block as a parameter, or call the `EndDialog` method to end the dialog.

- **EndDialog**: This method cleans up the code and displays the screen presentation text again, resetting the game from dialog mode to normal mode.

Besides creating these methods, we'll also need to make some updates to many other methods. For instance, to implement the DoTalk method as discussed, we'll need to add extra class members (the buttons) and add code to the Initialize and Draw methods to create and draw the buttons on screen (four buttons for dialog answers, one extra "continue" button), when they are visible. We'll also need an extra class member to store the current object we are talking to.

Therefore, to implement the DoTalk method, the updates to the KinderEngine class are shown in the subsequent code fragment:

```
' Dialog control buttons
Private DlgButton() As clsActiveObject
' The Object we are talking to
Private DlgObject As clsActiveObject
' Dialog control helper variables
Private CurrentAnswerBlock As Integer
Private NextAnswerBlock As Integer

Function Initialize(Owner as Windows.Forms.Control) As Boolean
    Redim DlgButton(4)

        ...

    ' Initialize the game text fields and buttons
    For i = 0 To 3
        Text(i) = New ClsGameFont("Microsoft Sans Serif", 14, Space(120), _
                    New Point(252, 525 + i * 18))
        ' Load the dialog control buttons
        DlgButton(i) = New clsActiveObject("button.bmp",_
            New Point(232, 5 + i * 18), _
          clsSprite.enScaleFactor.enScalePixel, 16, 16)
        DlgButton(i).Name = "Dialog " & (3 - i).ToString
        DlgButton(i).Visible = False
    Next
    ' Initialize the button for controlling the dialog
    DlgButton(4) = New clsActiveObject("button.bmp", New Point(232, 5),       _
        clsSprite.enScaleFactor.enScalePixel, 16, 16)
    DlgButton(4).Name = "Continue"
    DlgButton(4).Visible = False
End Function

Public Sub Draw()
    Dim i As Integer
...

    ' Draw the dialog buttons (will be drawn only if visible)
    For i = 0 To 4
```

```
        DlgButton(i).draw()
    Next
End Sub


Sub DoTalk(clickedObject As clsActiveObject, AnswerBlock As Integer)
    Dim i As Integer
    If clickedObject.CanTalk Then
        DlgObject = clickedObject
        CurrentAnswerBlock = AnswerBlock
        For i = 0 To DlgObject.AnswerBlock(0).QuestionNumber - 1
            Text(i).Text = _
                DlgObject.AnswerBlock(CurrentAnswerBlock).PlayerQuestion(i)
            DlgButton(i).Visible = True
        Next
    Else
        Say(clickedObject.CantTalkText)
    End If
End Sub
```

As we can see in the preceding code, the DoTalk procedure will check whether the object can talk, and if so, update the screen text with the questions read from the answer block depending on which number is received as a parameter. The procedure also sets the visible property of the question buttons to true, so the next call to the Draw method will show the updated text and buttons. In the Draw method, we don't need to test for the visible property, since this test is already done inside the Sprite class—when a sprite is not visible, it simply won't draw its image automatically.

As you can see, the buttons have been named "Dialog 0" to "Dialog 3" and "Continue". These names are important because we'll need them to check which button has been pressed in the DoSimpleClick method.

## Letting the Player Choose the Character's Speech

The next method to implement, DoSimpleClick, will process the click of any of the buttons and will also involve modifying other points of the KinderEngine class, such as the TestCollision method, which will need to include one special treatment for clicking the objects. We need to do this update because the buttons aren't related to a specific screen, and the code we created for the TestCollision method only tests the active objects on the current screen.

Having two sets of objects when calculating the collision detection raises an interesting question: What happens if the player, in the middle of a dialog, clicks another object on screen, executing another action or even starting a new dialog?

The answer is simple: We can't let the player start any other action when in conversation with a character. In order to know whether the player character is talking or not, we'll include a new control, the game state, which will basically allow the player to click the objects on screen only if not in dialog mode.

To create this state, we'll need to define a new enumeration and create a variable that will store the current game status, as shown in the next code listing:

```
' Control the game status - normal or dialog
Enum enGameStatus
    Normal = 0
    Dialog = 1
End Enum
Public Shared GameStatus As enGameStatus = enGameStatus.Normal
```

We'll also need to create a new state in the advPointer class, an arrow pointer, which will be used when in dialog mode. The changes to this class are simple and follow the same pattern discussed previously to include the dialog icon. Figure 7-25 presents the icon used for the arrow pointer.

*Figure 7-25. The arrow mouse pointer*

In the DoTalk procedure, we'll need to add two extra lines when showing the dialog buttons to set the proper game state and mouse pointer.

```
        GameStatus = enGameStatus.Dialog
        Pointer.Status = clsAdvPointer.enStatus.Arrow
```

This variable will be reset only in the EndDialog method, when the dialog ends, and must be checked in the MouseUp event so the mouse state isn't changed when the left button is pressed, and the DoSimpleClick method is called if the right button is pressed. We'll also need to add code in the Render method to refrain from updating the status line, even if the mouse pointer moves over a button—the button's name is not to be visible to the player! The code to be included in these functions is as follows:

```
Sub Mouse_MouseUp(X As Integer, Y As Integer, Button As ClsMouse.enButton) _
        Handles Mouse.MouseUp
    Dim clickedObject As clsActiveObject

    If Button = ClsMouse.enButton.Left And GameStatus = enGameStatus.Normal Then
        Pointer.NextStatus()
    Else
        TestCollision(clickedObject)
        If Not clickedObject Is Nothing Then
            Select Case Pointer.Status
                Case clsAdvPointer.enStatus.Examine
                    DoExamine(clickedObject)
                ...
                Case clsAdvPointer.enStatus.Arrow
                    DoSimpleClick(clickedObject)
            End Select
        End If
    End If
    ...

End Sub

Sub Render()
...
    ' Updates the status line only if we are not in Dialog mode
    If GameStatus = ClsKinderEngine.enGameStatus.Normal Then
        StatusText.Text = StatusText.Text & Pointer.PointerText
        If Not ClickedObject Is Nothing Then
            StatusText.Text = StatusText.Text & ClickedObject.Name
        End If
    End If
End Sub
```

Now we are finally ready to update the TestCollision method to test the buttons, when in dialog mode, so we can have the right "clicked object" variable in the MouseUp event. The next code listing shows the full code for TestCollision so that we can compare the collision algorithm for the buttons (first if clause) with the algorithm for the active objects (the else clause). As we can see, they are almost the same; the only difference is that in the first case we are checking the mouse pointer coordinates against the DlgButton array, and in the second, we are checking the CurrentScreen.ActiveObjects array.

```
Private Sub TestCollision(ByRef ClickedObject As clsActiveObject)
    Dim i As Integer
    ClickedObject = Nothing

    If GameStatus = ClsKinderEngine.enGameStatus.Dialog Then
        ' Test the collision with the dialog buttons
        For i = 0 To 4
            With DlgButton(i)
            If Pointer.X >.X And _
                Pointer.X <.X + .Width Then
                    ' We increment the Y position since the coordinates are inverted
                    '   (Y equals 0 on the lower part of the image)
                    If Pointer.Y + Pointer.PointerHeight > .Y And _
                        Pointer.Y + Pointer.PointerHeight < .Y + .Height Then
                        If .Visible Then
                            ClickedObject = DlgButton(i)
                        End If
                    End If
            End If
            End With
        Next
    Else
        ' Test the collision with the active objects on the screen
        For i = 0 To CurrentScreen.ActiveObjectsNumber - 1
            If Not CurrentScreen.ActiveObjects(i) Is Nothing Then
                With CurrentScreen.ActiveObjects(i)
                    If Not .IsOnInventory Then
                        ' If the Pointer is an arrow, _
                        '   the hot spot is the upper left corner,
                        '   otherwise it is the center
                        ' Test the colision with the active objects
                        If Pointer.CenterX >.X And _
                            Pointer.CenterX <.X + .Width Then
                            If Pointer.CenterY > .Y And _
                                Pointer.CenterY <_.Y + .Height Then
                                ClickedObject=CurrentScreen.ActiveObjects(i)
                            End If
                        End If
                    End If
                End With
            End If
        Next
    End If
End Sub
```

At this time, you are probably thinking that there are just too many details to consider and maybe even to allow us to maintain a complete view of what we are trying to do. Just keep one thing in mind: When you are coding your own game, on your own or with a team, you'll probably forget some of these details.

### Reviewing the Code Written up to This Point

We can't avoid forgetting small details when coding, but after coding a game we must pass it through a complete set of tests that will try to discover all bugs and strange behaviors. For instance, if we didn't included the code to avoid the status text update, the status text would present the object names (no verbs, since the arrow has no associated text) when our arrow pointer moves over them. So we must try to think about every possible eventuality, and correct the problems for the ones that we didn't think about.

Anyway, let's review what we have done up to now to implement the dialog feature in our game:

- We created a game state that will tell us if we are in dialog mode or in normal mode.

- We created four (invisible) buttons on the left-hand side of each text line on screen in the game initialization.

- We updated the mouse pointer class to include two new icons: the dialog icon (to start a dialog) and the arrow icon (to choose a question when in conversation). We have also updated the `MouseUp` event to handle clicks with these two new pointers, calling the `DoTalk` and the `DoSimpleClick` methods, respectively.

- When the user clicks one active object with the dialog icon, we call the `DoTalk` method, which will check whether the object can talk, and if so, set the proper variables, including the game state to `Dialog` and the mouse pointer to `Arrow`. The `DoTalk` method will also present the dialog phrases on screen and set the `visible` property of the buttons to true.

- We updated the `Draw` method to show the buttons, and the `TestCollision` method to test the collision of the mouse pointer with the buttons, since this was only calculating a collision with the active objects associated with the current screen.

- We also added a test to the `Render` method to avoid updating the status line text when we click the buttons or move over them.

- When in dialog mode, with the arrow icon pointer, if the player clicks one of the buttons, the MouseUp event will call the DoSimpleClick method, which will handle the next steps of the dialog flow.

As we saw before, when we code the DoTalk procedure, all we do is make the dialog response buttons visible, set the proper game status, and make the corresponding adjustments to some of the KinderEngine class procedures.

Now, it's up to the player to click the buttons so the DoSimpleClick event will run and we can present the chosen question, the corresponding response, and the Continue button, which will end the dialog or call the DoTalk procedure again with the new answer block number as a parameter.

Analyze the code for the DoSimpleClick, shown in the following listing, and refer to the dialog control steps we presented before to understand exactly what is being done. The code is extensively commented to improve its readability.

```
Sub DoSimpleClick(clickedObject As clsActiveObject)
    Dim i As Integer
    Dim DialogNumber As Integer

    Select Case clickedObject.Name
        Case "Dialog 0", "Dialog 1", "Dialog 2", "Dialog 3"
            DialogNumber = Right(clickedObject.Name, 1)
            ' Set the number of the next answer block, which will be handled
            '     when the player presses the "continue" button
            With DlgObject.AnswerBlock(CurrentAnswerBlock)
                NextAnswerBlock = .NextAnswerBlock(DialogNumber)
                ' Show the question chosen by the  player_
                '    in the first line on the screen
                Text(0).Text = .PlayerQuestion(DialogNumber)
                ' Show the character's answer on the second line on the screen
                Text(1).Text = .ObjectAnswer(DialogNumber)
            End With
            ' The third line is blank
            Text(2).Text = ""
            ' Show the text "continue" on the forth line.
            ' The "continue" button always appear on _
            '    the left side of the forth line
            Text(3).Text = "< Continue >"
            ' Hide the question buttons
            For i = 0 To 3
                DlgButton(i).Visible = False
            Next
            ' Show the "continue" button
```

```
            DlgButton(4).Visible = True
      Case "Continue"
            ' If the next answer block number is -1, we'll end the dialog
            If NextAnswerBlock = -1 Then
                  EndDialog()
            Else
                  ' Else, go back to the DoTalk method to _
                  ' show the next answer block phrases
                  DoTalk(DlgObject, NextAnswerBlock)
            End If
   End Select
End Sub
```

Let's take a closer look at one line of code to try to understand it better:

```
Text(0).Text = _
      DlgObject.AnswerBlock(CurrentAnswerBlock).PlayerQuestion(DialogNumber)
```

In the chosen line, we are setting the first text line on the screen (Text(0).Text) to the phrase chosen by the player. The player's choice is passed to the DoSimpleClick method as the DialogNumber parameter; and the DlgObject is a variable set in the DoTalk method to hold a reference to the object that was clicked to start a dialog. In order to make it clearer, let's try to translate the assignment in the previous code to plain English. It would read something like this:

"Assign the first sentence on the screen to the question chosen by the player (PlayerQuestion(DialogNumber)) from the set of possible question-answer options, that is, the current answer block (AnswerBlock(CurrentAnswerBlock)). This answer block was read from the character on screen for which we are establishing a conversation (DlgObject)."

It's quite a long sentence, but not totally incomprehensible.

## Finishing a Dialog

The last helper method to control the dialog is EndDialog, which will reset all that was done in the DoTalk method to allow the game to return to normal mode without any problems. The code for the EndDialog method is shown in the next listing:

```
Sub EndDialog()
    Dim i As Integer
    ' Reset all dialog variables
    NextAnswerBlock = 0
    CurrentAnswerBlock = 0
    For i = 0 To 4
        DlgButton(i).Visible = False
    Next
    DlgObject = Nothing
    GameStatus = enGameStatus.Normal
    'Show the current screen text
    ShowScreenText()
End Sub
```

We are now finally ready to test our dialog routines. Figure 7-26 shows the result of clicking the mud monster with the dialog icon pointer.

*Figure 7-26. Talking to the mud monster*

Figure 7-27 shows the second screen in a dialog: the question we chose, the answer of the monster, and the Continue button.

*Figure 7-27. Getting an answer from the mud monster*

In the next section, we'll include the code in the KinderEngine class to generate a voice and update the mouth positions when Natanael is speaking.

## Final Version: Including Voice Generation

Since we have already coded the PlayerVoice class, including voice generation in any game will be very simple—just a matter of including three lines: the object definition, the object creation, and a call to the Speak method.

In our game, these steps will be done in the KinderEngine class by calling the Speak method inside the DoSimpleClick procedure, so the player will only hear Natanael speaking when he or she chooses a question to ask a game character.

The following code listing presents all the updates we must do to generate voices in our game. We choose the "LH Michael" voice, which is installed with the Speech API SDK, because it appears to be the most appropriate for Natanael. If the player's computer doesn't have this voice, the code in the New method will use the computer's default voice.

```
Private WithEvents PlayerVoice As clsPlayerVoice

Function Initialize(Owner as Windows.Forms.Control) As Boolean
...
        ' Initialize the player's voice object
        PlayerVoice = New clsPlayerVoice("LH Michael")
...
End Function

Sub DoSimpleClick(ByVal clickedObject As clsActiveObject)
        Dim i As Integer
        Dim DialogNumber As Integer

        Select Case clickedObject.Name
            Case "Dialog 0", "Dialog 1", "Dialog 2", "Dialog 3"
                DialogNumber = Right(clickedObject.Name, 1)
                With DlgObject.AnswerBlock(CurrentAnswerBlock)
                    NextAnswerBlock = NextAnswerBlock(DialogNumber)
                    ' Show the question chosen by the  player_
                    '  in the first line on the screen
                    Text(0).Text = .PlayerQuestion(DialogNumber)
                    ' Speak player text
                    PlayerVoice.Speak(.PlayerQuestion(DialogNumber))
...
End Sub
```

To include the mouth animations in our game is even simpler, since we coded the PlayerVoice with specific images for our game: All we need to do is update the screen image with the image received as a parameter in the NewMouthType event, since this event is generated every time a new mouth position is needed. The following listing shows the event code that will make our character's mouth move:

```
Sub PlayerVoice_NewMouthType(CurrentMouthImage As clsSprite) _
                                            Handles PlayerVoice.NewMouthType
        TalkingHead.SpriteImage = CurrentMouthImage.SpriteImage
End Sub
```

If we want to use this class in other games, we can update the images inside it, or, even better, store the animations outside the class so that they will be easy to access from other classes. In this game, we chose to include the mouth animations in the PlayerVoice class in order to have most of the speaking-related code inside a single program module, thereby making the explanations clearer.

Figure 7-28 shows Natanael's mouth moving whilst he speaks to Sidney the mouse.

*Figure 7-28. Natanael's mouth moves as he talks—as expected.*

That's all for this game! In the next section, we'll present some ideas on how we could improve our game to make it even better.

## Adding the Final Touches

Improving an adventure game is mostly a question of improving the puzzles and storyline, as we discussed in the previous chapter. Of course, astonishing graphics and animations will help a lot with first impressions—which is really important. But without a good storyline and puzzles, the game will never be a hit.

After the storyline, the next steps of a team to improve this game could be the following:

- **Including full animation of the game:** Using the animation guides, a first step could be to make Natanael walk on screen from one place to another. After that, specific animations could be created to represent every action, for every game character.

- **Including an opening sequence and an ending sequence:** Including some full-screen drawings, or if possible an animation to start and end the game, has become an essential part of every adventure.

- **Including voices for all characters:** Since the speech SDK offers some different voices, male and female, it'd be very interesting to update the "talking head" graphic with the faces of each character, including different voices and specific mouth animations for each one.

As we can see, that's a lot to do before we can call the game created in these last two chapters an adventure game, but the most important concepts of adventure creation are presented here; all we need now is some talented graphical artists, storyline writers, and sound effect producers—most of the programming logic is complete.

## Summary

In this chapter, we improved the Magic KindergarteN. adventure game created in the previous chapter by including the last main important feature of an adventure that we hadn't coded before: the dialog control between the player's character and the game's characters.

We also discussed the following:

- Basic concepts about drawing effective animated graphics, including how to associate mouth animations with speech.

- The Speech API, which lets us generate voice from text and generate text when recognizing voice input. We implemented voice generation in a new game class for our library.

- We used all these concepts, including mouth animation, in our dialogs when the player character is speaking.

In the next chapter, we'll introduce the last of the DirectX component set members, DirectPlay, which will help us to create network games, and use it to build a new version of the .Netterpillars game, the sample game created in Chapter 2.

CHAPTER 8

# .Netterpillars II: Multiplayer Games and DirectPlay

IN THIS CHAPTER, we'll improve the .Netterpillars game created in Chapter 2 to include multiplayer features (see Figure 8-1). We'll create two new options: Host a Death Match and Join a Death Match, which will respectively set up a DirectPlay session to receive connections from other computers and connect to a DirectPlay session on a remote computer, allowing two players to compete against one another across the network.

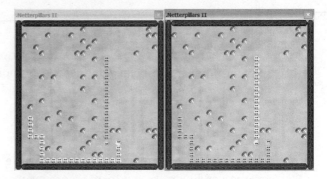

Figure 8-1.
*.Netterpillars II, this chapter's sample game*

In the coming sections, we'll discuss the main challenges we face when creating multiplayer games, and then introduce DirectPlay, the set of components on DirectX that allow us to easily add connectivity to our games.

## Introducing Multiplayer Games

All articles and books in which you'll read about multiplayer games (also known as *network-enabled games* or simply *networked games*) agree on one thing: Coding multiplayer games is really hard. Once you code your first multiplayer game, you'll discover why this is. This type of game is so hard to code because there are just too many extra problems to deal with—challenges that stem from creating a program with different and sometimes independent parts that must work together seamlessly.

Your program will receive messages from the host or other players, send messages back to them, process the player input, and perform the physics and artificial intelligence calculations, all while not letting the screen freeze between each frame drawn. This is the worst thing that can happen in a multiplayer game.

Fortunately, DirectPlay can help you with solving some of the problems you'll come across, like controlling the message flow between players and host to guarantee that no message is lost and all messages arrive in the same order they were sent. Nevertheless, there will still be some problems to solve.

Before discussing the details of DirectPlay, let's look at some basic concepts about networked games and some of the most common problems faced when coding such games, in the next sections.

## Choosing the Connection Type

The most common types of connections between players we must think about when coding multiplayer games are peer-to-peer and client-server connections.

### Peer-to-Peer Connections

In peer-to-peer connections, every player is aware of every other player in the game, sending messages to and receiving messages from all players, as illustrated in Figure 8-2.

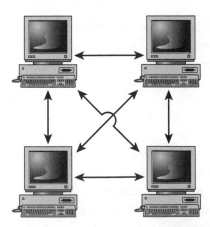

Figure 8-2. Peer-to-peer connections

The most obvious benefit of using this network organization is that we don't need a dedicated server to play the game, so players within a group can play it within their own local area network (LAN), or even through the Internet, as long as they know the addresses of the other members of the group.

In this type of connection, one of the players acts as a host, so all the new players will connect to his or her system, but once connected the messages will flow directly from one player to all the others.

The main problem we face when coding peer-to-peer games is that we can't afford to have too many players in the same game session, since the number of messages will increase exponentially with every new player that joins. For instance, in Figure 8-2 we have four players, so every time a player needs to update his or her status (e.g., move), we'll have three messages. Since we have four players, during each turn of a player we'll exchange 12 messages ($4 \times 3 = 12$). Making the same calculations with a five-player game increases this figure to 30 messages per turn ($6 \times 5 = 30$); and in a six-player game, it reaches 56 messages ($7 \times 6 = 56$).

Usually, having more than ten players in the same game session isn't suggested, because every message can take dozens of bytes, and we'll consume the bandwidth available in our network very quickly. But it's still possible, as long as we deal with very small messages. The most famous example of a game that uses this approach is LucasArt's X-Wing versus Tie Fighter, which runs peer-to-peer across the Internet. The game developer team manages to reduce the messages to (in most cases) only the players' input, so the game on every player's machine calculates everything else from this input.

## Client-Server Connections

The second most common game network topology is the client-server connection. In this kind of network, all players connect to a dedicated host system. This system processes the messages and does the synchronization of all players, sending messages back to each of them, as presented in Figure 8-3.

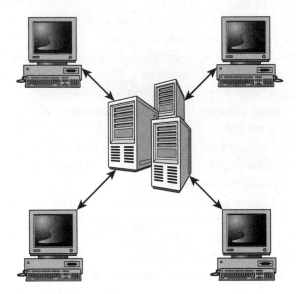

*Figure 8-3. Client-server connection*

Client-server games consume a lot less bandwidth per player, which allows us to send more data to the players (and maybe create a more complex game); on the other hand, the player depends on having a host to connect to (so he or she can't usually play on a private LAN).

When coding client-server games, we must decide which actions will take place on the host, and which actions will take place on the client machines. Is it better to put all the game physics and intelligence on the players' machines, using a host just as a forwarder of messages? Or is it better to include all the game code on the host, leaving just the input gathering and rendering code to the players?

There is no right answer to this question, but the optimum would probably be somewhere between the two. When making our decision, we'll have to take into account how many players we'll have connected to the host, and how much it will cost the host processor to perform each activity (for all players). We'll also have to consider the cost of each player's machine doing its own calculations, and what impact passing results between the host and players will have on the bandwidth. Even when a specific operation could be better done by the host, we may decide to run it on the clients if passing the results of the operation to the players' machines will use a large amount of the available bandwidth.

## Other Options

Besides these two types of topologies, we have other types of network organization. Some are useful in game development, others aren't. For example, in a ring topology, each player sends messages to one specific player, creating a ring that will eventually return to the first player in the sequence, as shown in Figure 8-4.

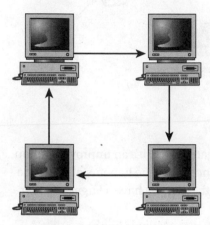

*Figure 8-4. Ring network topology*

This network organization is usually not practical for games, since the first player in the sequence would have to wait for the message to go around to every other player before it gets back to him or her, which can easily lead to unacceptable waiting times.

Another example of a different approach is using network groups. Each group of players will exchange messages only with the other players in his or her group, and the host (or a specific player, if it's a peer-to-peer game) will exchange information with other groups, where needed. The group organization must be designed so that the number of messages passed within the group is as small as possible. Figure 8-5 illustrates a game network topology based on groups.

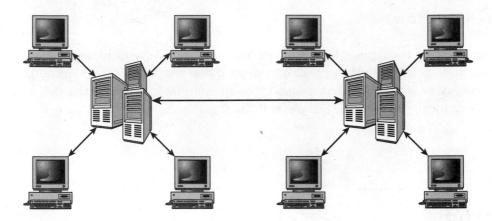

*Figure 8-5. A group-based network topology*

This approach is very common in network games, and it's an improvement on the client-server and peer-to-peer topologies, since it has the benefits of each one while also allowing us to consume less bandwidth when we have a larger number of players.

There are also other network technologies that can help us improve our games; broadcasting is possibly the most important one. Usually, to send a message to all players in a game, we'll send a message to each one, consuming extra bandwidth as the number of players grows. With broadcasting, when we need to send the same message to different players, all we have to do is to add extra destination addresses to our message, and it'll be routed to all of the destinations, just like an e-mail, which can be sent to different people without us having to worry about copying it. The problem is that not all networks support broadcasting.

Fortunately, DirectPlay will use the network resources available, hiding the internal complexities from us. So, if the network supports broadcast, DirectPlay will use it; if not, it'll simply send a single message to each player.

## Making Choices: Decisions Surrounding a Network Game Project

There are many decisions to make when planning a network game. In the following sections, we'll discuss some choices we must make when producing our network game project.

## Choosing Between Turn-Based and Real-Time Games

This is probably one of the first decisions when thinking about multiplayer games, and the one that will have the most impact on our game project.

In turn-based games, each player will think about his or her move, do the proper action, and then pass the control to the next player. Although the first type of game that comes to mind is board games like chess or Monopoly, there are very sophisticated action games based on turns, such as the X-COM series, where players move each soldier (using his energy to walk or fire), and then the aliens move, using the same rules.

Choosing this approach will save us a lot of headaches when trying to deal with the latency between our game messages, especially when running across the Internet, but may lead to a less than optimal gameplay if the project isn't very well written or the game doesn't run well in turns.

**TIP** *Never choose this approach if you have many players (say, more than three or four, depending on the game pace), because if each player needs to wait more than a couple of minutes to move again, the game will rapidly become uninteresting—except, of course, if the players actually expect a delay, like in a chess match. A practical idea is letting the players communicate with each other (by voice or by typing a message), even when it isn't their turn, so that you can improve the interaction between players and make the waiting less boring.*

Creating continuous action multiplayer games, such as Doom or Quake, is very challenging, mainly because we must transfer a certain amount of data (which we have to attempt to minimize) within very tight time frames, which unfortunately depends on the response time of something beyond our control—the network. At the same time, we need to make sure that all players have synchronized information, especially in fast-paced action games where players are fighting against each other.

One possible approach is to send all of the data updates to each of the players, so that we can ensure that everyone has the most recent events on their machines. However, this approach will obviously consume the entire bandwidth available with even a few players, even on an intranet.

In the other extreme, we can carefully calculate exactly which information should be sent to each player, and then send the minimum data needed. For instance, if another player is behind us or in another part of the labyrinth, we can't see him or her, so we don't need to receive information from him or her. But this kind of approach will consume most of the CPU's capacity on the players' machines by calculating the data to send, leaving fewer cycles to calculate the game physics and draw the graphics.

Then again, the best approach is to find a balance according to our game requirements. There is no right answer; just minimize the data while trying not to expend too much processing time on this minimization, and always keep in mind that the game will be run on slower machines and may facing unpredictably bad network response times.

In the next section, we'll discuss another point we must think about when coding a multiplayer game: whether to make it context-based or not.

## Choosing Between Constant World or Context-Based

Peer-to-peer games are inherently context based, since we don't have a server to host a world even when no players are connected. Client-server games, on the other hand, may or may not have constant conditions.

Games like Multitude's FireTeam provide some arenas in which players can connect and play together, but once the game ends, the server won't maintain any information about the previous game—except, maybe, for statistical data in some games.

Other games allow players to control one or many characters and interact with a preexisting world on the server that includes, besides its own physics, other characters that may be controlled by the computer or other players. Once a player disconnects from the host, his or her character data is saved somewhere while the world continues its normal existence. A good example of this kind of game is Ultima Online, which creates a large world where players can interact and improve their own character's skills.

 **TIP** *The experimental game Terrarium, from the GotDotNet site (http://www.gotdotnet.com/terrarium), is also an example of a game based in a continuous world. In this game, the players create animals or plants by using a wizard or coding from the ground up. Then players release their creations into the game environment to see the result of natural selection among all other "life beings" on the host. It's a game for programmers, and it's really worth a look.*

Possibly the most difficult challenge we face when creating games with constant worlds is doing our best to avoid cheating. There are many hackers who will attempt to break into a game server, especially if there is a fee to connect to it, and there is no 100 percent foolproof method of preventing them from doing this. We must therefore define recovery routines to return the game to a playable state, and backup and restore procedures for when there is no dynamic recovery possible.

This and other technical and economical problems will arise in every multi-player game, and continuous worlds add some extra issues to our ever-growing list.

In the next section, we'll list technical tips that may help us when creating this kind of project.

## Technical Tips

In this section, we look at some technical tips we must keep in mind when coding a multiplayer game. Although this list isn't exhaustive, we have asked the opinion of many game developers about the most common problems to make sure we touch on the important points.

### *Plan the Game Carefully Before Starting*

If creating a good project is important to every game, when talking about multi-player games a detailed project is a must. Since we'll have different programs, or at least different parts of the same program, interacting through the network, we must define every single message that will be exchanged and every way in which the programs will process them.

It's crucial to the success of the game that we define *where* and *when* each process will occur, in order to guarantee that each player is synchronized. Programmers tend to forget these details, since in stand-alone programs everything occurs directly after the command is processed. In multiplayer games this isn't the case. For example, in a real-time game, one player may be shooting at another player's character and, almost at the same time, the other player's character may be moving out of the firing range of the first player. If all processing occurs locally on each player's machine, the first player will see a successful hit, just after his or her shot. Meanwhile, the message with the shot information won't reach the other player's machine, the remote player having jumped out of the way, so the remote player will see the shot missing his or her character.

So devising an algorithm that will guarantee synchronization is as important as not using a lot of bandwidth. Considering that we may face very bad response times when running across the Internet, this is very challenging.

## Always Code from the Ground Up

Every programming team that has ever tried to adapt a stand-alone game to run multiplayer will agree with this tip: It's far better to code everything from the ground up than to try to simply adjust the stand-alone game's code. Even in a simple program, such as this chapter's sample game, we'll face situations that could be done better if the whole game was created from scratch.

So, if you ever try to write a multiplayer game on your own at home, remember this tip and you'll be okay.

As mentioned, we are creating a multiplayer version of the .Netterpillars game in this chapter, which we originally created as a stand-alone game in Chapter 2. Although we have planned the game to be multiplayer, and although the game is very simple, we'll probably see some bits that would've been better served by starting with the multiplayer version.

## Define Carefully the Message Types and Sizes

Bandwidth is a rare and expensive thing, so use it sparingly.

After defining all messages that our programs will exchange, in the project phase, we must go back and draw the complete flow of a typical game cycle (the game's main loop), so we'll be able to see if we are forgetting anything important. We must create this flow for at least two to three players, plus the host, if any exists, since there are some situations that will occur with three players that won't occur with two.

After being sure that we aren't forgetting anything, we must go back and recheck every message to see if we are using the minimum space possible for each message, especially those that will be exchanged most frequently. For example, a single bit can be used as a flag, so a byte can comprise up to eight flags; and a byte takes 256 different values, so if our values are within this range, we can use the *byte* data type instead of the *int16* one, which will take 2 bytes.

A final word on this: Be sure that you know the real size of the data types you are using. An integer, for example, usually takes up 4 bytes, but in old 16-bit operating systems, it took 2 bytes, and in 64-bit machines it takes 8 bytes. Another interesting item of note involves strings: They *do not* occupy the same amount of bytes as the number of characters. They have extra internal control bytes that help to define, for example, their length; and if we are talking about Unicode strings, the strings will use 2 bytes per character.

**NOTE** *ANSI strings are the default for most Western countries, but this doesn't suffice for writing every character in Eastern countries, such as the characters in the Japanese and Chinese languages, since we have only 256 possible characters in ANSI. UNICODE is the default for such countries, and in this case every character could be one of up to 65,536 different values, enough for any language. So if you are reading this book somewhere in Asia, please be sure to use arrays of bytes instead of strings, unless you want to send text in local characters only.*

## Hide the Latency from the Player

Latency is the single worst enemy of every multiplayer game programming team. And, what is worse, we can't simply provide a solution. It's not a bug, it's a fact of life, so we must learn to live with it.

Since we never know for sure how much time we'll need to receive the next message, we can use some tricks to distract the player while he or she waits. For example, if our game is similar to Ensemble Studios' Age of Empires, the player can give orders to game characters, but the characters will only move after the client machine receives information from the host that the command has been received. We can make our characters say "Yes, Master!" (this sounds very innovative . . . ) just after the command is issued, so the player has the impression that the result is immediate, although it will really occur (hopefully) a number of milliseconds later.

This same idea can be used with animations instead of sounds. The game character can start a little animation, like picking up some object or moving his head around as if looking for a way to start the command. This kind of trick is very effective.

Another thing we can do when facing extra long waiting times for the next message is let our program continue the action based on the last input, maybe at a lower rate. For example, if we know the speed and the direction of the other players' starships in a space battle game, we can suppose that they are still moving in the same direction, and move them a little using this supposition. But as soon as the new message arrives, we must check and correct all the positions of the other players. This can be very challenging, even for experienced programmers, and can lead to problems in the game, like a spaceship "jumping" from one place to another. Such a problem can be solved with a smoothing trick, adjusting the position in more than one game cycle, but this trick will add extra complexity to our game.

The important thing about latency is that while it'll probably always be a problem, players did not, do not, and will not ever understand latency. So your team will have to expend some hours on this topic during the game's project stage, if you are planning to do a serious multiplayer game.

## Include Artificial Intelligence in Your Multiplayer Game

Many players don't like to play games with other players, or simply don't have the money or the time to do so. Most of the games that only run over a network are a failure, so be careful if you want to follow this approach.

We'll give a simple example: Just imagine if games like Doom or Quake were only multiplayer. What is a single player, without a network card, meant to do in them? Run around the corridors and rooms with no opposition? These games would definitely not be as successful if they didn't have intelligent computer-controlled characters to play against. And we must remember that having computer-controlled characters is useful even in network games.

## Create a Community for Your Game

Every game should have a community, and in multiplayer games, this is a must. Creating a site where players can enter and interact brings many benefits to our game: The site helps to create a group of loyal players who will always play the game and help the game team by providing fast feedback if anything goes wrong with the game, quickly fixing the problem and informing other users.

The site can also add extra value to our games, because we can include game statistics, records, and add-ons to it, and it can help us to create our own statistics, if there are special zones (for example, the add-ons download area) that are only accessible by players who register their games.

## Prevent Players from Cheating

You'll be surprised to know how determined hackers are when they want to be. It's hard to avoid cheating, but we must at least try to discourage it, since nothing is worse for the players than to feel cheated. And believe us, they will blame you, not the cheater.

The bare minimum we must do is to check each message received on the client and on the server (if we have one) to see if it's valid. We must not try to encrypt or include checking codes on our messages, because even if such security measures are good for preventing cheating, they'll consume a lot of bandwidth and CPU cycles to decrypt and check. Instead, we must try to imagine the simplest checks we can do that will gain the best results. For example, we want to check whether the current player position and ammunition received in a message are compatible with the previous ones, so a player can't "teleport" or enter in "god mode" (all guns and ammo) by simply manipulating his or her messages.

## Test, Test, Test!

Multiplayer games have extra sources of errors, and sometimes these errors are harder to find and fix, so starting testing from the very beginning is a real must.

The first test we must do is with message delivery. In theory, TCP (the protocol used by DirectPlay) will guarantee that the messages always arrive at the destination, and always arrive in the same order in which they were sent, but doing our own test to check this will help with creating statistical information about the latency times and exposing bottlenecks on the network. The same test can show bottlenecks in our game, when it's nearly done.

Hackers and curious programmers that want to "explore" the game messages may try to send modified messages just "to see what happens," so we must never use a message's contents before checking if the message is valid. We've seen some game servers go down because of a single message with invalid values, due to no checking and weak error trapping on the host program, so we must be careful.

Another scary statistic has to do with multiplayer game reliability. Just imagine that we have created a game that has an uptime of 99.9 percent, which means that our game can run on the average for 23 hours and 59 minutes without crashing, or a minute out on each day.

If we have ten players in our game, they won't crash at the same time, so we can divide 24 hours by 10 and see that every 2 hours and 24 minutes we'll have a crash. If our program is good enough, the other players can continue playing, but it will be very frustrating for all of the players if they are playing in team, because from time to time a player will simply disappear from the team.

And we are only talking about the players. If we consider the host, and the errors that can arise from errors on the client machines, it gets even worse. So our tip is simply this: Test, test, test. And after that, test all over again.

## Include Different Threads

This is a simple but important tip. Having a specific thread dedicated to message sending and receiving and another thread or threads to deal with game physics and artificial intelligence will give us more flexibility to hide the latency and get the most from our hardware.

A simple example of using different threads, called DataRelay, can be found in the DirectX SDK: A thread receives messages and pushes them into a queue (a simple message array inside the program), while another thread keeps removing the messages from this queue. Understanding this program's details is a good step to being able to create multithreaded multiplayer games.

### Create a Balanced Game

While in a stand-alone game a player can win 100 percent of the time if he or she plays hard enough, in multiplayer games two players with the same skills, playing as hard as they can, will win 50 percent of the matches on the average.

Although it looks like a simple thing, finding the proper balance in multiplayer games can be a very tricky challenge. There can be no "golden path," no way that ensures the victory of any one player. The game levels must be balanced so that there's no place in the game field that provides a large tactical advantage, and there aren't any guns or tricks that allow a player to remain at an advantage to the others.

Another important detail is to provide some mechanism that will allow the player to indicate his or her skill level, or to choose a group with the same skill to play against, so that newbies will have a fair chance to play as well as experts.

The game community can help the game team a lot with the task of finding and fixing any unbalanced aspects of the game, so creating beta testing groups before releasing the final version of a game will help with correcting such problems, while at the same time creating a group of loyal users even before the game hit the shelves.

### Never Trust the Internet!

The Internet is untrustworthy, and unfortunately we can't fix it.

While we can expect times from 20 to 150 milliseconds (ms) on a good intranet (with an average of about 100 ms), over the Internet we can expect a very bad average time to deliver a message, about 500 ms. Another problem is that messages can take 1, 5, and even 20 seconds to arrive, and some messages simply never arrive.

DirectPlay uses the TCP protocol to send messages, which ensures message delivery and arrival order. However, this can be a problem on the Internet, because if a message gets lost along the way, when the next message arrives the remote computer will ask for the lost one. This is why we sometimes face such bad delivery times.

Most multiplayer games rely on User Datagram Protocol (UDP), a simpler protocol that guarantees neither message delivery nor arrival order. In this case, the program controls the order (usually, a simple counter on the messages allow the remote machine to check the order) and packets lost, which sometimes can simply be forgotten, if the next message gives enough information to "reconstruct" the lost message on the remote machine.

It's a good idea to start by creating simpler TCP-based games, which give us enough knowledge to create games that are more advanced later. And that's what we'll do in this chapter—create a simple DirectPlay class to deal with message handling as shown in the next section.

## Introducing DirectPlay

DirectPlay is a set of functions and components within the DirectX architecture that enables the creation of multiplayer game hosts (which other players can connect to), handles the connection between players and the host, and includes many extra features, such as built-in support for Network Address Translation (NAT) and firewall traversal, and also support for voice communications.

DirectPlay also supports group creation (through CreateGroup and related methods), which allows game developers to use broadcasting if the network supports it without any extra lines of code. Broadcasting, as mentioned earlier in this chapter, is the network support to send one single message to different destinations, saving bandwidth and CPU cycles.

**NOTE** *It's not our goal here to explore every single feature available with DirectPlay; instead we'll create a simple class to illustrate the basic features needed to implement simple multiplayer games.*

Although coding a complete multiplayer game may be challenging, the basic steps for creating a multiplayer host to which players can connect are very simple. The game host can be a player, in a peer-to-peer game, or a server machine, if we are using the client-server approach. There are four steps to create a host:

1. Choose the service provider and store its address.

2. Create a session, defining its unique identifier and name.

3. If the host is a player, set the player name.

4. Create the multiplayer game host.

Similarly, we can resume the creation of a game client in five simple steps, which will be valid for both peer-to-peer and client-server games.

1. Choose the service provider and store its address.

2. Choose the host to connect to.

3. Choose the session to join.

4. Set the player information.

5. Join the session.

Before presenting any code, let's look at each of the objects that are implicitly or explicitly described in the previous lists.

## Understanding Service Providers

The first step with the client-server approach is choosing which service provider we'll use in our game. The service provider is the registered "network service type" we can use to communicate with other computers. The most common service providers are the TCP-IP provider, the modem provider, and the serial provider. Unless you plan to provide some serial cable or connect directly via modem, we suggest you use the TCP-IP provider. In a real game, we can fix this option in the code, or let the player choose the connection type with a special configuration program, since it's not common to deal with different service providers in the same game. In DirectPlay, the object used to manage service providers is called `ServiceProvider`.

Each service provider has a unique address that the game will use in order to access this service provider. DirectPlay offers a specific object to store and perform any operations with this address, the `Address` object.

## Understanding Sessions

The next important concept regarding multiplayer games is the session. A *session* is a group of players that will be exchanging messages among themselves, using a host or not. A host computer can control one or more sessions, so after choosing the host, the clients must choose the session. This approach is especially useful if we are planning to offer different sessions for users of different abilities. The object in DirectPlay used to control sessions is called `ApplicationDescription`.

When creating a session, the host must give its name, which will be presented to the clients when they ask for the session name on the host, and a unique identifier that will be used by the computers to define this particular session. This unique identifier is a GUID, or Global Unique Identifier, used by Windows to uniquely define each installed application.

The client computers on a client-server game or all the computers in a peer-to-peer game must identify themselves as players to the host, setting the player data through a DirectPlay's Player object. The player data is usually only the player name, but the Player object allows us to add some status information too, if we need to.

## Understanding Hosts

Another important concept mentioned in the preceding steps is the host. The host computer is the one responsible for storing the sessions and controlling the users connecting to each session. The Host method of the Peer object is used to create a host, and can be used to implement client-server games, where the host machine also controls the message flow between all players, and to create peer-to-peer games, where the host is also a player and doesn't have any influence on the exchange of messages.

The Peer object, as we'll see, is the most important object in a DirectPlay game, since it will create the host and connect to the host, and also provides methods to send data and events and receive data from other players. We can understand the Peer as the object that represents a specific machine, server, or client, in a multiplayer game, and almost all the important operations in DirectPlay depend on this object.

DirectPlay also offers a specific object to create clients that can access massive multiplayer games in lobbies, the Lobby object. Lobby servers are specific applications located on a remote host (usually on the Internet) that offers, besides the host facilities described previously, other features like chat rooms, game statistics, game merchandizing, etc. Since DirectPlay doesn't offer any support for lobby server creation, we won't go into any details about the Lobby object in this book.

In the next section, we'll explore the objects and concepts involved in making DirectPlay-based games by creating the NetworkGame wrapper class, which will simplify the use of network features in our games.

## Defining the NetworkGame Class

Since most of the operations we'll perform on a server, like sending and receiving data, setting player information, and choosing the service provider, will also occur on a client program, there's no point in creating two different classes for accessing DirectPlay features. We'll create a single class, the interface for which is shown in Figure 8-6, including comments in the code to make it clear which part is specific to the host and which is used only by the client.

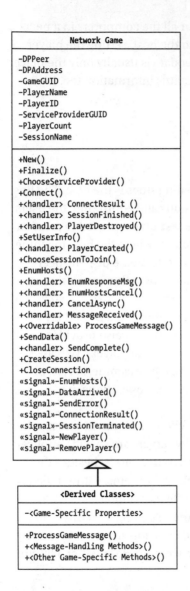

```
                    Network Game
    ─────────────────────────────────────
    -DPPeer
    -DPAddress
    -GameGUID
    -PlayerName
    -PlayerID
    -ServiceProviderGUID
    -PlayerCount
    -SessionName
    ─────────────────────────────────────
    +New()
    +Finalize()
    +ChooseServiceProvider()
    +Connect()
    +<handler> ConnectResult ()
    +<handler> SessionFinished()
    +<handler> PlayerDestroyed()
    +SetUserInfo()
    +<handler> PlayerCreated()
    +ChooseSessionToJoin()
    +EnumHosts()
    +<handler> EnumResponseMsg()
    +<handler> EnumHostsCancel()
    +<handler> CancelAsync()
    +<handler> MessageReceived()
    +<Overridable> ProcessGameMessage()
    +SendData()
    +<handler> SendComplete()
    +CreateSession()
    +CloseConnection
    «signal»-EnumHosts()
    «signal»-DataArrived()
    «signal»-SendError()
    «signal»-ConnectionResult()
    «signal»-SessionTerminated()
    «signal»-NewPlayer()
    «signal»-RemovePlayer()
    ─────────────────────────────────────
```

```
                  <Derived Classes>
    ─────────────────────────────────────
    -<Game-Specific Properties>
    ─────────────────────────────────────
    +ProcessGameMessage()
    +<Message-Handling Methods>()
    +<Other Game-Specific Methods>()
```

*Figure 8-6. The NetworkGame class implements access to the DirectPlay features.*

As we can see in Figure 8-6, the `NetworkGame` class won't implement any processing of the message data; this handling will be done by derived classes, which will include code for the `ProcessGameMessage` method.

DirectPlay also uses a lot of events and event handlers to control connections and messages, as presented in Figure 8-6. We'll discuss each of them when discussing the details of the `NetworkGame` class.

The class interface derived from the previous class diagram is presented in the next code listing:

```
Imports Microsoft.DirectX.DirectPlay

Public Class ClsNetworkGame
    ' The main DirectPlay object
    Public WithEvents DPPeer As Peer = Nothing
    ' The Address object used to create and locate hosts
    Public DPAddress As Address = Nothing
    ' The unique identifier for our game - a random number
    Protected GameGuid As Guid = New Guid(7530573, 15564, 7321, _
                                2, 15, 7, 9, 13, 11, 6, 5)


    ' Player Properties
    Public PlayerName As String
    Public PlayerID As Integer
    Public PlayerCount As Integer = 1 ' Start Counting the local player

    ' The session name
    Public SessionName As String

    ' Event used to enumerate hosts to connect
    Public Event EnumHost(AppDesc As ApplicationDescription, _
                        host As Address, device As Address)

    ' Events used to handle message transfering
    Public Event DataArrived(strData As String)
    Public Event SendError(errCode As ResultCode)

    ' Events used to handle connections
    Public Event ConnectionResult(connected As Boolean, errcode As ResultCode)
    Public Event SessionTerminated(msg As TerminateSessionMessage)

    ' Events used to handle Players
    Public Event NewPlayer(Name As String, ID As Integer)
    Public Event RemovePlayer(PlayerId As Integer)
```

```
Public Sub New()
' -----------------------------------------------------------
' Functions to help choose the Service Provider
' -----------------------------------------------------------
Public Function ChooseServiceProvider() As Boolean
Public Sub SetServiceProviderGUID(SPGUID As Guid)


' -----------------------------------------------------------
' Functions that handle connections
' -----------------------------------------------------------
Public Function Connect(AppDesc As ApplicationDescription, _
            host As Address, device As Address) As Boolean
Private Sub ConnectResult(sender As Object, _
            dpMsg As ConnectCompleteEventArgs) _
            Handles DPPeer.ConnectComplete
Private Sub SessionFinished(sender As Object, _
            dpMsg As SessionTerminatedEventArgs) _
            Handles DPPeer.SessionTerminated


' -----------------------------------------------------------
' Functions that handle player creation and destruction
' -----------------------------------------------------------
Private Sub PlayerDestroyed(sender As Object, _
            dpMsg As PlayerDestroyedEventArgs) _
            Handles DPPeer.PlayerDestroyed


Public Sub SetUserInfo(Optional strPlayerName As String = "")
Private Sub PlayerCreated(sender As Object, _
            dpMsg As PlayerCreatedEventArgs) _
            Handles DPPeer.PlayerCreated
' -----------------------------------------------------------
' Functions used to enumerate the hosts to the client,
'  Helping to choose the session to join
' -----------------------------------------------------------
Public Function ChooseSessionToJoin() As Boolean
Public Sub EnumHosts()
Private Sub EnumResponseMsg(sender As Object, _
            dpMsg As FindHostResponseEventArgs) _
            Handles DPPeer.FindHostResponse
Public Sub EnumHostsCancel()
Private Sub CancelAsync(sender As Object, _
            dpMsg As AsyncOperationCompleteEventArgs) _
            Handles DPPeer.AsyncOperationComplete
```

```
        Protected Overrides Sub Finalize()
        ' ----------------------------------------------------------
        '  Functions that will read a data packet when it arrives
        ' ----------------------------------------------------------
        Private Sub MessageReceived(sender As Object, _
                    dpMsg As ReceiveEventArgs) _
                    Handles DPPeer.Receive
        Protected Overridable Sub ProcessGameMessage(message As NetworkPacket)

        ' ----------------------------------------------------------
        '  Functions that will send a data packet to the target server
        ' ----------------------------------------------------------
        Private Sub SendComplete(sender As Object, _
                    dpMsg As SendCompleteEventArgs) _
                    Handles DPPeer.SendComplete
        Protected Sub SendData(message As NetworkPacket)
        ' ----------------------------------------------------------
        '  Functions used on the host to create a session.
        '   If a name is not provided, we'll display a dialog
        '   to prompt for it
        ' ----------------------------------------------------------
        Public Function CreateSession() As Boolean
        Public Function CreateSession(strSessionName As String) As Boolean
        Public Sub CloseConnection()
End Class
```

It's quite a long class, but, referring to the class diagram in Figure 8-6, note that most of the methods are event handlers, and the most important ones match exactly the simple steps given earlier in this chapter to follow when creating DirectPlay games.

Our methods are divided in to logical groups, surrounded by comments in the previous code listing. The only exception is the New procedure, which isn't related to any specific operation. In this method, we'll just create the Peer object, which will be used by many other methods, as shown in the following piece of code:

```
Public Sub New()
    ' Create the main directplay object
    DPPeer = New Peer()
End Sub
```

In the next sections we'll discuss the coding of those methods.

## Coding the Service Provider Methods

For both client and server, the very first job is to choose the network service provider. Since there may be many service providers, and each one is identified by a unique GUID, we must list the service providers for the player to let him or her choose the desired one.

To do this, we'll create a simple window, with a list box and two buttons (OK and Cancel), so all we need to do in the code for the ChooseServiceProvider method is present our window, as shown in the next code listing:

```
Public Function ChooseServiceProvider() As Boolean
    Dim winChooseProvider As frmServiceProviders
    ChooseServiceProvider = True

    ' The DialogBox will call the SetServiceProviderGUID to set
    '  the chosen service provider
    winChooseProvider = New frmServiceProviders()
    If winChooseProvider.ShowDialog() <> DialogResult.OK Then
        ChooseServiceProvider = False
    End If
End Function
```

We will write the code for listing and choosing the service provider in the frmServiceProviders window, but since we'll need our class to store information about which service provider is chosen, we'll code the SetServiceProvider method to receive the GUID and create an Address object pointing to the specified service provider, as presented in the following code snippet:

```
' This function will be called by the ChooseServiceProvider method
Public Sub SetServiceProviderGUID(SPGUID As Guid)
    ' Create a new address object with this service provider
    DPAddress = New Address()
    'Set the address's service provider (this will be the device address)
    DPAddress.ServiceProvider = SPGUID
End Sub
```

The SetServiceProvider method gives us the flexibility to set the GUID in the window or in any other code in the program that uses this class; so if we create a more sophisticated program, we can store the service provider in the registry and only present the window in the setup or under a configuration menu.

Now let's see the code for the window.

This window will have to present a list of all service providers registered on the system, which can be done by calling the GetServiceProviders method of the DPPeer object (created in the New method). This window is a separate part of our project, so we'll have to pass a reference to the current NetworkGame object from it so that it'll be able to list the service providers. The next code portion presents the customization we'll need to make to the New method of the window to receive this object and store it in a local variable for later use:

```
Dim WithEvents objGameClient As ClsNetworkGame

Public Sub New(GameClient As ClsNetworkGame)
    MyBase.New()
    objGameClient = GameClient
    'This call is required by the Windows Form Designer.
    InitializeComponent()
End Sub
```

Of course, we'll need to adjust our ChooseServiceProvider method by adding a reference to the current object when calling the constructor of the window. The new line in this method will be as follows:

```
    winChooseProvider = New frmServiceProviders(Me)
```

Once we make the Peer object accessible to the window, we can code the Load event to add the items to the service providers list, as presented in the next code listing:

```
Sub frmServiceProviders_Load(sender As Object, e As EventArgs) _
                                        Handles MyBase.Load
    Dim i As Integer
    Dim dpPeerSPInfo As ServiceProviderInformation()

    'Fill up our list box with the service providers
    dpPeerSPInfo = objGameClient.DPPeer.GetServiceProviders(False)
    For i = 0 To dpPeerSPInfo.Length - 1
        lstServiceProviders.Items.Add(dpPeerSPInfo(i))
    Next
End Sub
```

As we can see from the previous listing, the GetServiceProviders method of the Peer object returns a list of ServiceProviderInformation objects that have the name GUID, and flags for each service provider. Since this type of object implements the ToString method, it can be converted to strings and used by the list box.

**NEW IN .NET**

*In Visual Basic .NET, we can add any type of object as an item of a list box, as long as it implements the ToString method. This new feature is very useful, since we can build our own complex structures and classes and present them directly to the user. In the previous version, we had to create a separate array to store the objects, and search the array for a specific item.*

In Figure 8-7, we can see the window that allows us to choose the service provider already listing the available service providers.

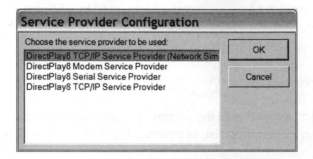

*Figure 8-7. The Service Provider window*

To complete our window, the code for the Cancel button will simply close the window, setting the appropriated result, and the code for the OK button will call the SetServiceProviderGuid of the NetworkGame class and then close, as we can see in the following code sample:

```
Sub btnCancel_Click(sender As Object, e As EventArgs) Handles btnCancel.Click
    DialogResult = DialogResult.Cancel
End Sub

Sub btnOK_Click(sender As Object, e As EventArgs) Handles btnOK.Click
    Try
        objGameClient.SetServiceProviderGUID(lstServiceProviders.SelectedItem.guid)
    Catch
```

```
        MessageBox.Show("Please select a service provider before clicking OK.", _
            "No Service Provider", MessageBoxButtons.OK, _
            MessageBoxIcon.Information)
        Return
    End Try
    DialogResult = DialogResult.OK
End Sub
```

If we want to add registry support to our window, making it store in the registry the last service provider chosen and select it when the window is open next time, we can use the registry access objects present in the Microsoft.Win32 namespace.

To do this, we'll need to add an "Imports" clause in the window, and store the value chosen by adding extra code to the OK button, as shown in the next code sample:

```
Imports Microsoft.Win32

Sub btnOK_Click(sender As Object, e As EventArgs) Handles btnOK.Click
...
    ' Create a registry key with the service provider GUID
    Dim RegKey As RegistryKey = _
        Registry.CurrentUser.CreateSubKey("Software\\Games\\NetterpillarsII")
    If Not (RegKey Is Nothing) Then
        RegKey.SetValue("GameGuid", lstServiceProviders.SelectedItem.guid())
        RegKey.Close()
    End If
```

We'll also need to include extra code in the Load method to read the value in the registry if the window has previously been used. The lines to be inserted open the registry keys and select the corresponding service provider from the window list, and are presented in the following listing:

```
Sub frmServiceProviders_Load(sender As Object, e As EventArgs) _
                                            Handles MyBase.Load
...
    'Get the default Service Provider from the registry if it exists
    Dim RegKey As RegistryKey = _
            Registry.CurrentUser.OpenSubKey(_
            "Software\\Games\\NetterpillarsII")
    If Not (RegKey Is Nothing) Then
        Try
            Dim DefaultGuid As Guid = RegKey.GetValue("ServiceProviderGUID", 0)
```

```
            For i = 0 To lstServiceProviders.Items.Count - 1
                If lstServiceProviders.Items(i).GUID.Equals(DefaultGuid) Then
                    lstServiceProviders.SelectedIndex = i
                End If
            Next
            RegKey.Close()
        Catch
            lstServiceProviders.SelectedIndex = 0
        End Try
    Else
        lstServiceProviders.SelectedIndex = 0
    End If
End Sub
```

In the next section, we'll write the code for creating game sessions and joining them.

## Coding the Session Methods

Although we are coding a single class, for the sessions there'll be specific methods executed by the host and others used by the client. We'll discuss these methods in separated sections so that we won't confuse the two.

### Creating and Destroying Sessions

To create a session in DirectPlay, we simply call the Host method of the Peer object, passing the appropriated parameters, which enables us to receive connections from other computers.

The Host method will receive two parameters: an ApplicationDescription object, which will give the game GUID and the session name, and the Address object, which points to the service provider to be used:

```
Public Function CreateSession(strSessionName As String) As Boolean
    Try
        ' Create the application description object
        Dim AppDesc As New ApplicationDescription()
```

```
        AppDesc.GuidApplication = GameGuid
        AppDesc.SessionName = strSessionName
        ' No special flags
        AppDesc.Flags = 0
        'Host a game on DPAddress as described by AppDesc
        DPPeer.Host(AppDesc, DPAddress)
        CreateSession = True
    Catch e As DirectPlayException
        MessageBox.Show("Error when creating a session: " & e.ErrorString & _
            " - " & e.ErrorString, "clsGameServer.CreateSession")
        CreateSession = False
    End Try
End Function
```

We must follow here a rule of thumb for any program: Close what you opened. So we'll add code for the CloseConnection method, which can be called if the program wants to explicitly close the connection to other computers.

```
Public Sub CloseConnection()
    DPPeer.Dispose()
End Sub
```

These two methods will be used only by the Host, and they are all we need to create and destroy game sessions. Since many games will need a configuration screen to receive the session name from the player, we can add an extra Create-Session method that receives no parameter and presents a window that will ask for the session name.

The code for such an overloaded method is given in the next code section:

```
Public Function CreateSession() As Boolean
    Dim WinCreateSession As frmCreateSession
    CreateSession = True

    WinCreateSession = New frmCreateSession(Me)
    If WinCreateSession.ShowDialog() <> DialogResult.OK Then
        CreateSession = False
    End If
End Function
```

The window that will receive the session name contains only a text box and two buttons, as shown in Figure 8-8.

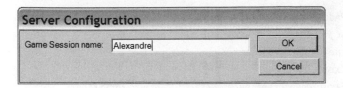

*Figure 8-8. Entering a session name in the Server Configuration window*

We'll add code in this window to receive the NetworkGame object and store the previous session name in the registry, as shown in the Service Provider window. We'll also call the CreateSession method in the NetworkGame object to effectively create the session. The full code for this window is shown in the following listing:

```
Private objGameClient As ClsNetworkGame

Public Sub New(GameClient As ClsNetworkGame)
    MyBase.New()

    'This call is required by the Windows Form Designer.
    InitializeComponent()
    objGameClient = GameClient

    'Get the default session from the registry if it exists
    Dim RegKey As RegistryKey = _
            Registry.CurrentUser.OpenSubKey(_
            "Software\\Games\\NetterpillarsII")
    If Not (RegKey Is Nothing) Then
        txtSession.Text = RegKey.GetValue("DirectPlaySessionName", Nothing)
        RegKey.Close()
    End If
End Sub

Sub btnOK_Click(sender As Object, e As EventArgs) Handles btnOK.Click
    If ((txtSession.Text = Nothing) Or (txtSession.Text = "")) Then
        MessageBox.Show(Me, "Please enter a session name before clicking OK.", _
            "No sessionname", MessageBoxButtons.OK, MessageBoxIcon.Information)
        Return
    End If
```

```
    ' Save the session name to the registry as a new default
    Dim RegKey As RegistryKey = _
            Registry.CurrentUser.CreateSubKey(_
            "Software\\Games\\NetterpillarsII")
    If Not (RegKey Is Nothing) Then
        RegKey.SetValue("DirectPlaySessionName", txtSession.Text)
        RegKey.Close()
    End If
    If objGameClient.CreateSession(txtSession.Text) Then
        Me.DialogResult = DialogResult.OK
    Else
        Me.DialogResult = DialogResult.Cancel
    End If
End Sub
```

In the next section, we'll present the code that will run on the client side used to list all sessions on a specific host.

## Listing Existing Sessions on a Remote Computer

To connect to a session on a host involves knowing the server name and the session name and GUID we want to connect to, since all these pieces of information when used together uniquely define a session. We'll also need to get the player name as an input so we can pass it to the host when connecting.

Our ChooseSessionToJoin method will be very similar to the ChooseServiceProvider one; it will only create a window that prompts for the user name and presents a list of available sessions in a given host, as presented in the next code listing:

```
Public Function ChooseSessionToJoin() As Boolean
    Dim WinJoin As frmJoin
    ChooseSessionToJoin = True

    WinJoin = New frmJoin(Me)
    If WinJoin.ShowDialog() <> DialogResult.OK Then
        ChooseSessionToJoin = False
    End If
End Function
```

As in the `ChooseServiceProvider` method, we'll also pass the current object as a parameter to the window, which will be stored in a variable to be used in the window. However, as we'll see, connecting to a remote session takes a lot more effort than simply choosing a service provider.

Figure 8-9 presents the window interface that will allow us to choose the session on the remote computer.

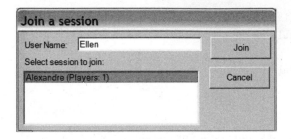

*Figure 8-9. Join a session window*

The first problem in this window arises from the transitory nature of the sessions. We can't simply list all the sessions in a host when the window loads, because while the user types his or her name or reads the available session names, the remote computer may already have closed some of them. We can work around this problem by inserting a timer in the window and including code for refreshing the list to remove items that are no longer valid, while inserting new ones.

Looking back at the `GameNetwork` class definition, we'll see that there is already a method that will list the hosts and sessions, called `EnumHosts`, so we can call it in the `Load` event of the form and in the `Tick` event of the timer.

The `EnumHosts` method of our class will use the `FindHosts` method of the `Peer` class to loop through the sessions running on a specific host.

**TIP** *The* `FindHosts` *method enumerates sessions in a host, not hosts in a network, despite its name.*

The FindHosts method will receive the ApplicationDescription with information about the application we are looking for, including its unique identifier, the Address that points to the service provider, and a handle that will be used to control the operation—which is asynchronous by default. The method also receives the Address of the host, which is optional, and an enumeration value. Through this value we can set some method execution directives, forcing the method to run synchronously, to not use broadcasting if it's available, and to ask for extra information if needed (for example, the host name if it's not provided).

FindHosts won't produce any visible results when called; we must code another function to handle the FindHostResponse event of the Peer object, which will be called once for each session present on the remote computer. To allow our NetworkGame class to pass information to the calling application, in this case the window shown in Figure 8-9, we'll run an event on our handler function.

Let's look at all of these pieces one by one, starting with the EnumHosts method, which will set the appropriate parameters and call the FindHosts method.

```
Private EnumHostsAsyncHandle as integer

Public Sub EnumHosts()
    Dim desc As ApplicationDescription = New ApplicationDescription()
    ' Get the current game GUID from the class property
    desc.GuidApplication = GameGuid

    'Try to enum the game hosts
    Try
        DPPeer.FindHosts(desc, Nothing, DPAddress, Nothing, Timeout.Infinite, _
            0, Timeout.Infinite, EnumHostsAsyncHandle, _
            FindHostsFlags.OkToQueryForAddressing)
    Catch e As DirectPlayException
        MessageBox.Show("Error when looking for hosts: " & e.ErrorString)
    End Try
End Sub
```

When we call the FindHosts method, it will present a window to the user asking for the host name, because we don't provide a specific host name. There's no way of customizing this window, which is shown in Figure 8-10. However, we can create our own window and pass the host name as the second parameter of the FindHosts method, which is receiving Nothing in the previous code listing.

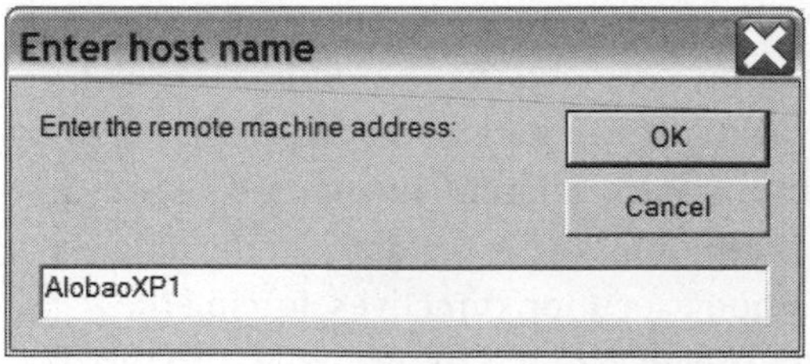

*Figure 8-10. The* FindHosts *method asking for the host name*

In the following code sample, we see the event's definition (as shown in the class definition, earlier in this chapter) and the code for the EnumResponseMsg method. This method is the handler of the FindHostResponse event, which will be triggered by DirectPlay when we call FindHosts.

```
' Event used to enumerate hosts to connect
Public Event EnumHost(AppDesc As ApplicationDescription, _
                   sender As Address, device As Address)

Sub EnumResponseMsg(sender As Object, dpMsg As FindHostResponseEventArgs) _
                                        Handles DPPeer.FindHostResponse
    ' Generate an event to
    RaiseEvent EnumHost(dpMsg.Message.ApplicationDescription, _
       dpMsg.Message.AddressSender, dpMsg.Message.AddressDevice)
End Sub
```

With these two methods, we'll be able to call EnumHosts from the window and receive events with the session data so we can update our list box; but three extra methods are needed to allow proper control of the asynchronous session listing.

We'll need one method to allow the main program to cancel the enumeration if it needs to, and another method to receive the result of the asynchronous operation when it's completed. Finally, we must explicitly cancel the asynchronous operation if the NetworkGame object has been destroyed to avoid errors that can arise if DirectPlay sends an event and the calling object is no longer valid.

The code for these methods is shown in the next listing:

```
Public Sub EnumHostsCancel()
    If (EnumHostsAsyncHandle <> 0) Then
        DPPeer.CancelAsyncOperation(EnumHostsAsyncHandle)
    End If
End Sub
```

```
Private Sub AsyncComplete(sender As Object, _
        dpMsg As AsyncOperationCompleteEventArgs) Handles _
        DPPeer.AsyncOperationComplete
    If (dpMsg.Message.AsyncOperationHandle = EnumHostsAsyncHandle) Then
        EnumHostsAsyncHandle = 0
    End If
End Sub


Protected Overrides Sub Finalize()
    MyBase.Finalize()
    If (EnumHostsAsyncHandle <> 0) Then
        DPPeer.CancelAsyncOperation(EnumHostsAsyncHandle)
    End If
End Sub
```

With all these methods in place, we can now go to the window we created to list the sessions and start adding code to the Load event and the Tick event of the timer, and coding the handler of the NetworkGame object that will update the list box in the window.

The simplest code that will allow us to list the sessions as shown in Figure 8-9 is given in the following code sample:

```
Sub form_Load(sender As Object, e As EventArgs) Handles MyBase.Load
    'Enum the game hosts
    lstSession.Items.Clear
    objGameClient.EnumHosts()
End Sub


Sub ListHosts(AppDesc As ApplicationDescription, _
        sender As Address, device As Address) Handles objGameClient.EnumHost
    lstSession.Items.Add(SessionInfo)
End Sub


Sub tmrUpdateConnections_Tick(sender As System.Object, _
            e As System.EventArgs) Handles tmrUpdateConnections.Tick
    'Enum the game hosts
    lstSession.Items.Clear
    objGameClient.EnumHosts()
End Sub
```

Although very simple, this code isn't effective, since the list box is cleared on each tick of the timer, creating a "flashing" effect for the player; the items are removed and included again at every timer cycle, making it impossible for the player to select a specific session from the list. We need to store some extra information in the list box to determine when a specific item is included, so that it's only removed after a specific time-out (say, 2 seconds).

The main problem with this approach is that we are storing only the session names in the list box, whereas we'll need the host address and the device address (received as parameters by the ListHosts method), in addition to the inclusion time value, to allow us to connect to a remote session.

We'll need to improve our routines to store all the information we need in the list box. We don't need to create an object for this—we can use a simple structure, as defined in the next code sample:

```
Private Structure stSessionInfo
    Public LastEnumTime As Integer
    Public AppDesc As ApplicationDescription
    Public host As Address
    Public device As Address

    Public Overrides Function ToString() As String
        If AppDesc.MaxPlayers > 0 Then
            Return AppDesc.SessionName & " (Players: " & _
                AppDesc.CurrentPlayers & "/" & AppDesc.MaxPlayers & ")"
        Else
            Return AppDesc.SessionName & " (Players: " & _
                AppDesc.CurrentPlayers & ")"
        End If
    End Function 'ToString
End Structure
```

In this structure, the ToString method is mandatory, or we'll get an error when trying to include the object in the list box. The list box always looks for this conversion method to find out what to show the user.

The new version of the ListHosts method that will store all values in the list box is shown in the next listing:

```
Sub ListHosts(AppDesc As ApplicationDescription, _
        host As Address, device As Address) Handles objGameClient.EnumHost
    Dim Found As Boolean = False
    Dim i As Integer
    Dim SessionInfo As stSessionInfo = New stSessionInfo()
```

```
With SessionInfo
    .AppDesc = AppDesc
    .device = device
    .host = host
    .LastEnumTime = Environment.TickCount
End With

'Check the list of items first and see if this one already exists
For i = 0 To lstSession.Items.Count - 1
    If SessionInfo.AppDesc.GuidInstance.Equals( _
            lstSession.Items(i).AppDesc.GuidInstance) Then
        lstSession.Items(i) = SessionInfo
        Found = True
    End If
Next

'If the item is not on the list, add it
If Not Found Then
    lstSession.Items.Add(SessionInfo)
End If
End Sub
```

In the previous code sample, we checked for repeated items before including any values in the list, since now we won't clear the items from the list every time we want to enumerate the sessions.

The Tick event of the timer will also need to be updated to check for timed-out items and remove them from the list, as we can see in the following code listing:

```
Sub tmrUpdateConnections_Tick(sender As System.Object, _
            e As System.EventArgs) Handles tmrUpdateConnections.Tick
    Dim i As Integer
    ' Remove any timed-out sessions
    For i = 0 To lstSession.Items.Count - 1
        'Check to see if this session has expired (every 2 seconds)
        If (Environment.TickCount - lstSession.Items(i).LastEnumTime > 2000) Then
            lstSession.Items.RemoveAt(i)
            Exit For
        End If
    Next
    'Enum the game hosts
    objGameClient.EnumHosts()
End Sub
```

Since we are now removing only the timed-out items and including only extra sessions in the list, we can set the timer to do updates at shorter time intervals—for example, every 500 ms (although we should keep it at every second or two if we are using the Internet).

In the next section, we'll see how to connect to a remote session using the data collected when we listed all sessions on a host.

## Connecting to a Remote Session

Once we have the remote host address, the address of the device, and the `ApplicationDescription` that uniquely defines a remote session, we can connect to the host by calling the `Connect` method of the `Peer` object, as we can see in the next code snippet:

```
Public Function Connect(AppDesc As ApplicationDescription, _
    host As Address, device As Address) As Boolean
    DPPeer.Connect(AppDesc, host, device, Nothing, _
        ConnectFlags.OkToQueryForAddressing)
End Function
```

The `Peer` object will trigger an event to the application saying that the connection has been completed. Since our `NetworkGame` class is encapsulating the features from DirectPlay, we'll also trigger an event to the main program so that it will know that the connection has been completed. Besides the connection result code, we'll send a Boolean value indicating the connection result (true for connected, false for error) so the application can easily check if it's connected or not.

The following code sample presents the event definition and the handler for the `ConnectComplete` event of the `Peer` object:

```
Public Event ConnectionResult(connected As Boolean, errcode As ResultCode)

Private Sub ConnectResult(sender As Object, _
        dpMsg As ConnectCompleteEventArgs) Handles DPPeer.ConnectComplete
    If (dpMsg.Message.ResultCode = 0) Then
        RaiseEvent ConnectionResult(True, dpMsg.Message.ResultCode)
    Else
        RaiseEvent ConnectionResult(False, dpMsg.Message.ResultCode)
    End If
End Sub
```

The last thing we must do to complete the coding that deals with connections is to write the event handler for the `SessionTerminated` event of the `Peer` object so we can inform the main application that the session has been terminated, which usually happens when we face a network problem or the remote computer has disconnected.

```
Public Event SessionTerminated(msg As TerminateSessionMessage)

Private Sub SessionFinished(sender As Object, _
        dpMsg As SessionTerminatedEventArgs) Handles DPPeer.SessionTerminated
    ' Well, this session is being terminated, let the user know
    RaiseEvent SessionTerminated(dpMsg.Message)
End Sub
```

In the next section, we'll see the code that will enable us to access the features in DirectPlay to manage players.

## Managing Players

There are three operations we must code to equip our `NetworkGame` class with basic user management capabilities: `SetUserInfo`, which will enable the program to give the local player's name; `PlayerCreated`, which will trigger events in the main application to inform the host that a new player has connected to a given session; and `PlayerDestroyed`, which will be called when a player has disconnected.

The next code listing presents the first of these methods, which will call the `SetPeerInformation` method of the `Peer` object to set the player data. This same method can be used to set information about the server and groups, if we need it to.

```
Public Sub SetUserInfo(Optional strPlayerName As String = "")
    If strPlayerName <> "" Then
        PlayerName = strPlayerName
    End If
    PlayerInfo.Name = PlayerName
    DPPeer.SetPeerInformation(PlayerInfo, SyncFlags.PeerInformation)
End Sub
```

The following listing presents the code for the event handlers that will manage the player events sent by the `Peer` object. We'll also use these methods to update the `PlayerCount` property, which will store the number of players in the current session.

```
Public PlayerCount As Integer = 1 ' Start Counting the local player

' Events used to handle Players
Public Event NewPlayer(Name As String, ID As Integer)
Public Event RemovePlayer(PlayerId As Integer)

Private Sub PlayerDestroyed(sender As Object, _
     dpMsg As PlayerDestroyedEventArgs) Handles DPPeer.PlayerDestroyed
    ' Send an event informing that the player is out from our session
    RaiseEvent RemovePlayer(dpMsg.Message.PlayerID)
    ' Update our number of players
    PlayerCount -= 1
End Sub

Private Sub PlayerCreated(sender As Object, _
     dpMsg As PlayerCreatedEventArgs) Handles DPPeer.PlayerCreated
    ' Get the PlayerInfo and store it
    Dim dpPlayerInfo As PlayerInformation
    dpPlayerInfo = DPPeer.GetPeerInformation(dpMsg.Message.PlayerID)

    If Not dpPlayerInfo.Local Then
        ' This isn't me, send an event with this player data
        RaiseEvent NewPlayer(dpPlayerInfo.Name, dpMsg.Message.PlayerID)
        ' Update our number of players
        PlayerCount += 1
    Else
        ' Store our player ID number
        PlayerID = dpMsg.Message.PlayerID
    End If
End Sub
```

We are now able to create and list hosts, create a session and connect to a remote one, and manage players in our NetworkGame class. All we need to do now to complete our class is to code the message handling routines, which we do in the next section.

## Handling Messages

Both the host and the clients will have to include code for methods to send messages and to handle received messages.

To send messages is simply a matter of calling the SendTo method of the Peer object. This method receives a network packet with the message content to send, the chosen timeout, and the ID of the remote player. We can send messages to all other players by specifying zero as the remote player ID. The last parameter in this method lets us specify the message characteristics, like the priority or whether the message will loop back to the sender or not. The flags used in the following code sample will suffice for any simple game:

```
Protected Sub SendData(message As NetworkPacket)
    ' timeout 200 ms
    ' Server ID = 0 send messages to everyone
    DPPeer.SendTo(0, message, 200, SendFlags.NoLoopback Or SendFlags.NoCopy)
End Sub
```

DirectPlay gives the result of the send operation by firing the `SendComplete` event of the `Peer` object. We can handle this event and generate an error event for the application if anything goes wrong, as presented in the next code listing:

```
Public Event SendError(errCode As ResultCode)

Private Sub SendComplete(sender As Object, _
        dpMsg As SendCompleteEventArgs) Handles DPPeer.SendComplete
    ' Send an error event if we couldn't send the packet
    If dpMsg.Message.ResultCode <> 0 Then
        RaiseEvent SendError(dpMsg.Message.ResultCode)
    End If
End Sub
```

As for the arriving messages, we won't include any special treatment in the `NetworkGame` class, since every game must define its own set of messages. We'll instead include the code for an overridable function that receives a network packet, and that will effectively be coded in the derived classes, as presented in the following code sample:

```
Private Sub MessageReceived(sender As Object, _
        dpMsg As ReceiveEventArgs) Handles DPPeer.Receive
    ProcessGameMessage(dpMsg.Message.ReceiveData)
End Sub

Protected Overridable Sub ProcessGameMessage(message As NetworkPacket)
    ' This function must be coded by the derived classes
    ' that will handle the message received according to
    ' the game needs
End Sub
```

This concept of creating an overridable function isn't new; we used it when creating the GameEngine class in Chapters 4 through 7. This special function type allows us to define in the base class a function that is coded by the derived classes but called by methods in the base class.

In the next section, we take a look at a simple example that will help us to put all the concepts we have seen here together.

## Testing the NetworkGame Class

In this section, we'll create a very simple example that will help us understand and test the NetworkGame class.

We'll create a window with three buttons and two text boxes that allows us to create a host, connect to a host, and send messages between client and server. Figure 8-11 presents the window we'll use in the sample.

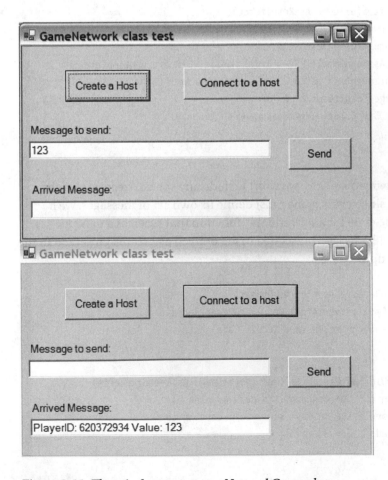

*Figure 8-11. The window to test our NetworkGame class*

The first step to using our `NetworkGame` class is to include this class in our project, as well as the windows that are used by it when choosing service providers, sessions, and setting the session name.

The next step is to create a class to handle the game-specific messages derived from the `NetworkGame` class. In our example, we'll create a simple class that sends a message composed of two numbers, the player ID and a message code, which will be entered by the user.

The following code presents a full listing of the `NetworkGameTest` class, used in our sample:

```
Inherits ClsNetworkGame

Private Structure GameMsg
    Public PlayerId As Integer
    Public MessageCode As Integer
End Structure

Public Event MessageArrived(PlayerID As Integer, MessageCode As Integer)


' -----------------------------------------------------------------
' The next function processes the arrived messages
' -----------------------------------------------------------------
Protected Overrides Sub ProcessGameMessage(Message As NetworkPacket)
    Dim Msg As GameMsg
    Msg = CType(Message.Read(GetType(GameMsg)), GameMsg)

    RaiseEvent MessageArrived(Msg.PlayerId, Msg.MessageCode)
End Sub

Public Sub SendMessage(message As Integer)
    Dim Msg As GameMsg
    Dim gameMsgPacket As New NetworkPacket()

    ' Fill the message fields
    Msg.MessageCode = message
    Msg.PlayerId = Me.PlayerID
    ' Put the message on a packet and send it
    gameMsgPacket.Write(Msg)
    SendData(gameMsgPacket)
End Sub
```

As we can see, all we need to include in the derived class is the code for dealing with the game-specific messages. All other features will be obtained from the base class.

In the example window, we'll need to define an object from our class using the WithEvents clause, so we can handle the MessageArrived event, defined in the previous code sample.

```
Public WithEvents NetworkGameTest As clsNetworkGameTest
```

The code for the Create Host button will simply call the ChooseServiceProvider and the CreateSession methods, and the class will present any necessary windows to gather user information, so we can create our host with only two lines of code.

Of course, our program will usually include some error checking to display messages to the user if anything goes wrong. The next code listing presents the full code for the Create Host button:

```
Sub cmdHost_Click(sender As Object, e As EventArgs) Handles cmdHost.Click
    NetworkGameTest = New clsNetworkGameTest()
    ' Choose the service provider
    If Not NetworkGameTest.ChooseServiceProvider() Then
        MessageBox.Show("Error when choosing tyhe service provider")
        Me.Close()
    Else
        ' Create the session
        If Not NetworkGameTest.CreateSession() Then
            MessageBox.Show("Error when creating a session")
            Me.Close()
        Else
            ' Enable the send button
            cmdSend.Enabled = True
        End If
    End If
End Sub
```

The Connect to Host button will be very similar: By calling the ChooseServiceProvider and ChooseSessionToJoin methods, we are able to connect to the remote host, as presented in the next code sample:

```
Sub cmdConnect_Click(sender As Object, e As EventArgs) Handles cmdConnect.Click
    NetworkGameTest = New clsNetworkGameTest()
    ' Choose the service provider
    If Not NetworkGameTest.ChooseServiceProvider() Then
        MessageBox.Show("Error when choosing tyhe service provider")
```

```
        Me.Close()
    Else
        If Not NetworkGameTest.ChooseSessionToJoin() Then
            MessageBox.Show("Error when connecting to a session")
            Me.Close()
        Else
            ' Enable the send button
            cmdSend.Enabled = True
        End If
    End If
End Sub
```

With two extra lines of code, we'll be able to send and receive messages from the remote player. The next listing presents the final lines of our simple example:

```
Sub cmdSend_Click(sender As Object, e As EventArgs) Handles cmdSend.Click
    NetworkGameTest.SendMessage(CInt(txtSendMessage.Text))
End Sub

Sub NetworkGameTest_MessageArrived(PlayerID As Integer, MessageCode As Integer) _
                              Handles NetworkGameTest.MessageArrived
    txtArrivedMessage.Text = "PlayerID: " & PlayerID & " Value: " & MessageCode
End Sub
```

The full code for this sample is on the accompanying CD-ROM. It's the project named NetworkGameTest inside the Chapter 8 directory.

In the next section, we'll discuss the proposal for the sample game of this chapter, where we exercise the concepts discussed in the previous sections.

## The Game Proposal

As we've said, we're going to create a multiplayer version of the .Netterpillars game, built in Chapter 2.

It's not typically a good approach to convert a game from single player to multiplayer. However, although we didn't say this in Chapter 2, the game is already designed to be multiplayer. Even so, if we analyze the code phase in detail, we'll see that some things could be done better if we had decided to make a multiplayer version of the game from scratch.

In the multiplayer version, we'll have two extra options: Host a Death Match, which will prompt the player for the session name and enable his or her machine to receive remote connections, and Join a Death Match, which will enable the player to connect to a remote player machine.

A death match will be a special type of game in which two players can play one another, in a medium-sized game field, with a fixed number of mushrooms. In this case, there won't be any configurations for the number of players, the game field size, or the quantity of mushrooms.

The criteria for ending this game will also be different from the stand-alone version: The game will only end when a player dies, even if the players have eaten all the mushrooms.

Besides this additional feature, we'll add a specific screen at the game's end that will display the name of the winner and the length of each player's netter-pillar.

Refer back to the game proposal in Chapter 2 to review all the details from the first version of the game, which will still be valid in this chapter sample.

In the next section we'll discuss some technical details about our game.

## The Game Project

We'll follow the same project created in Chapter 2, adding the class diagram we saw in the section "Introducing DirectPlay" earlier in this chapter.

To complete the project for our multiplayer game, all we need to do is clearly define the message flow between the server and the client, and to define each type of message we'll use in our game.

Table 8-1 presents all the game messages with details.

*Table 8-1. .Netterpillars II Messages*

| MESSAGE | ORIGIN | DESTINATION | MEANING | DATA |
| --- | --- | --- | --- | --- |
| SyncGameField | Server | Client | Synchronize the mushroom positions. | Array with mushroom positions |
| OkToStartGame | Client | Server | Inform the server that the game field is synchronized. | N/A |
| NetterDirection | Both | Both | Send the local player input to the remote machine. | Direction of the movement |
| EndDeathMatch | Both | Both | Inform the remote player that the local player is dead. | ID of the dead player |

The EndDeathMatch message may seem unnecessary: Because the game fields are synchronized, the remote player will already know that the local player is dead when he or she hits a wall. Nevertheless, it's useful when a local player quits, because one player can wait forever for the next message if we don't inform him or her that the other player is leaving the game.

In the next steps, we describe the game's basic flow, including the message exchange between server and client:

1.  The server creates a session and creates a game field, populating it with mushrooms.

2.  The client connects to the session, and creates an empty game field.

3.  The server receives the information from DirectPlay that a remote player has connected.

4.  The server sends an array with the position of all mushrooms to the client (SyncGameField message).

5.  The client populates its game field with the mushrooms in the same position as the mushrooms on the game field of the server.

6.  The client informs the server that it has finished the synchronization (OkToStartGame message).

7.  The server gets the input from the local player and sends it to the client (NetterDirection message).

8.  The client receives the information about the remote player's movements, and gets the input from the local player.

9.  The client updates the netterpillar positions in the game field, and sends the local player's movement information to the server.

10. The host receives the information about the remote player's movements, and updates the netterpillar positions in the game field.

11. Steps 7 through 10 repeat until a player is dead.

12. When a player is dead (client or server), the local machine sends the EndDeathMatch message to the remote machine.

13. Both machines end the game at the same time.

**TIP** *Review these steps until you are sure you understand exactly what we'll do in the coding phase.*

One last point we must explore before entering the code phase is redefining the main program workflow, which changed with the inclusion of multiplayer features. Figure 8-12 presents the previous flow, used in Chapter 2 for the standalone version of the game.

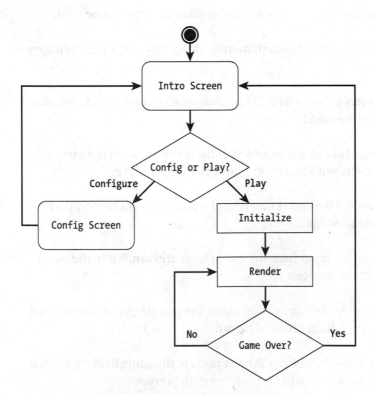

*Figure 8-12. The main program workflow for the stand-alone version of .Netterpillars*

Our aim is to include the multiplayer options without modifying the main program workflow, so we could use most of the code from the previous version without making any huge adjustments. Figure 8-13 presents the proposed workflow for the main program of .Netterpillars II.

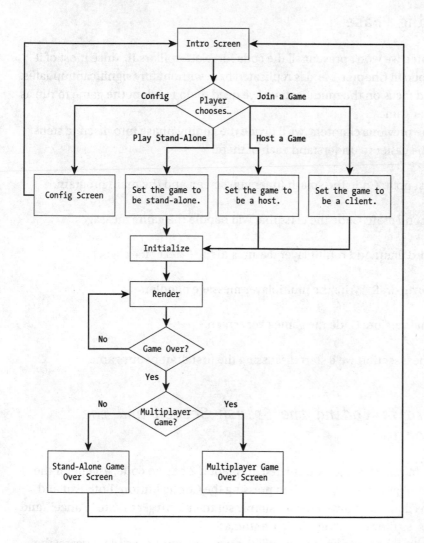

Figure 8-13. The main program workflow for the multiplayer version of .Netterpillars

As we can see, apart from the inclusion of the extra options to the introduction screen, all we did was include a different game over screen.

In the next section, we'll code this chapter's sample game.

## The Coding Phase

In this chapter, we won't present all the code for .Netterpillars II, since most of it was developed in Chapter 2 and is replicated here without any significant updates. We'll instead focus on the modifications we need to do to adapt the game to run as a multiplayer game.

As in the previous chapters, we'll divide the coding phase into discrete steps so that it'll be easier to understand each of them:

1. First draft: Code the splash (opening) screen and the main program.

2. Second draft: Code the class that will handle the game messages.

3. Third draft: Add multiplayer features to the GameEngine class.

4. Fourth draft: Write the multiplayer message handlers.

5. Final version: Code the game over screen.

In the next section we'll start discussing the first draft of our game.

### First Draft: Coding the Splash Screen and the Main Program

Recall that the splash screen we created in Chapter 2 has no code, except for the call to the configuration screen when pressing the Config button. Both Exit and Play buttons don't have any code; we simply set their DialogResult to "Cancel" and "OK" values, so they close the window automatically.

We'll follow the same approach with the new buttons we need to create: the Host a Death Match button and the Join a Death Match button. Since there are no appropriate values to represent this type of result, we'll simply set their DialogResult property to Yes and No. This could be any other value, as long as it's different from those already used; the main program will deal with the various dialog return values.

Figure 8-14 presents the new splash screen, including the two additional buttons and a slightly different background image.

*Figure 8-14. .Netterpillars II splash screen*

In the main routine, we'll have only two updates: setting the game network type (host, client, or none) according to the result of the splash screen, and presenting the proper game over screen according to the network type.

To store the game network type, we'll create a new enumeration and a new property in the GameEngine class, as presented in the next code sample:

```
'Update to NetWork Gaming: New enum to control network types
    Public Enum enNetWorkGame
        No = 0
        Host = 1
        Client = 2
    End Enum
'Update to NetWork Game: variable to store the network gaming type
    Public NetWorkType As enNetWorkGame
```

The next code listing shows the updated main procedure. The updates are marked with comments in the code; if you have any doubts about any other part of the procedure, refer to Chapter 2 for a full explanation of this routine.

```
Sub main()
    Dim WinSplash As frmSplash
    Dim WinGameField As frmGameField
    Dim WinGameOver As New frmGameOver()
    Dim WinDeathMathGameOver As New FrmDeathMatchGameOver()
    Dim LastTick As Integer, DesiredFrameRate As Single = 10
    Dim SplashResult As DialogResult
    ' Create the game engine object
    objGameEngine = New clsGameEngine()
    WinSplash = New frmSplash()


    ' Loop until the user selects "Exit" on the main screen
    Do While True
        ' Update to network gaming: handle different results
        '    from the opening screen:
        '       DialogResult.Cancel = Close game
        '       DialogResult.OK = Start a new standalone game
        '       DialogResult.Yes = Host a death match game
        '       DialogResult.No = Join a death match game
        SplashResult = WinSplash.ShowDialog()
        Select Case SplashResult
            Case DialogResult.OK
                objGameEngine.NetWorkType = clsGameEngine.enNetWorkGame.No
            Case DialogResult.Yes
                objGameEngine.NetWorkType = clsGameEngine.enNetWorkGame.Host
            Case DialogResult.No
                objGameEngine.NetWorkType = clsGameEngine.enNetWorkGame.Client
            Case DialogResult.Cancel
                Exit Do
        End Select

        WinGameField = New frmGameField()
        WinGameField.Show()
        Application.DoEvents()
        'Creates a copy of the background image to allow erasing the sprites
        objGameEngine.BackgroundImage = WinGameField.PicGameField.Image.Clone
        objGameEngine.CreateGameField(WinGameField.PicGameField.Handle)
```

```
        Do While Not objGameEngine.GameOver
            If Not objGameEngine.Paused Then
                ' Force a Frame rate of 10 frames per second on maximum
                If System.Environment.TickCount - LastTick >= _
                    1000 / DesiredFrameRate Then
                    MoveComputerCharacters()
                    objGameEngine.Render()
                    LastTick = System.Environment.TickCount
                End If
            End If
            Application.DoEvents()
        Loop
        ' Close the current connection, if it's open
        Try
            objGameEngine.GameClient.CloseConnection()
        Catch
            ' Ignore any errors
        End Try
        ' Update to Network game: different game over screens
        If objGameEngine.NetWorkType = clsGameEngine.enNetWorkGame.No Then
            WinGameOver.ShowDialog()
        Else
            WinDeathMathGameOver.ShowDialog()
        End If
        WinGameField.Dispose()
    Loop
    objGameEngine = Nothing
    WinSplash.Dispose()
    WinGameOver.Dispose()
End Sub
```

In the next section, we'll code the NetworkNetterpillars class, the class derived from the GameNetwork class that will handle our game-specific messages.

## Second Draft: Coding the NetworkNetterpillars Class

As we discussed earlier in this chapter when coding the GameNetwork class, each game has its own set of messages, so every game that wants to use this class must code its own derived class, which must code the ProcessMessage method to manage its messages. In our case, we'll create a class named NetworkNetterpillars.

Referring to our game project, we'll see that we planned four different messages for this game: SyncGameField, OkToStartGame, NetterDirection, and EndDeathMatch.

For each of these messages to really encapsulate the networking details from our program, we'll have to create methods to send messages to the remote player and to process the incoming messages.

Both methods from each message will heavily depend on the message format, so the first step to coding our class must be to code the message structures.

We'll create an enumeration to define the message type. Following the guide given in Table 8-1, in the game project we'll create a specific structure for each message, plus a generic structure used to read the message type.

The next code presents the enumeration plus the structures for each message:

```
Private Enum gameMessageType
    SyncGameField = 0 'Message containing one array to sync the game field
    OkToStartGame = 1 'Message to start the game
    NetterDirection = 2
    EndDeathMatch = 3
End Enum
' -----------------------------------------------------------------
' We need to create one specific structure to read each message type;
'   plus one structure that will be used for reading the message type code.
' -----------------------------------------------------------------
' Structure used only for reading the message type
Private Structure GameMsg_Generic
    Public Type As gameMessageType 'What type of packet is this?
    Public PlayerId As Integer    ' Who sent this message?
End Structure


' Structure used only for informing the direction of the next
'   movement of the Netterpillar
Private Structure GameMsg_NetterDirection
    Public Type As gameMessageType 'What type of packet is this?
    Public PlayerId As Integer    ' Who sent this message?
    Public Direction As Byte
End Structure


' Structure used only for informing about the end of the Death Match
Private Structure GameMsg_EndDeathMatch
    Public Type As gameMessageType 'What type of packet is this?
    Public PlayerId As Integer    ' Who sent this message?
    Public PlayerKilled As Byte
End Structure
```

In the previous code sample, we used the generic message structure to send any messages that only need to include the message code (such as the OkToStartGame message). We'll also use the generic message type to send messages that can't fit into a structure, such as messages that have strings or arrays (for example, the SyncGameField message).

Let's start looking at the logic of sending the messages to the remote player.

## Creating the Methods That Send Messages

Looking back at the GameNetwork class, we can see that we already have a function that will send generic data through the network: the SendData method. This method receives a NetworkPacket variable as a parameter.

---

 **NOTE** *A* NetworkPacket *is similar to a common stream used to write files, with the only difference being that it's defined by DirectPlay with the specific purpose of sending a packet of data through the network.*

---

To code specific functions to send data, we need to create a method that receives the data that will be sent as a parameter, create the structure, fill it with the proper data, write it to a network packet using the Write method, and finally send the packet using the base class SendData method.

The next code sample shows the method created to send the netterpillar's direction to the remote player:

```
Public Sub SendNetterDirection(Direction As Byte)
    Dim Msg As GameMsg_NetterDirection
    Dim gameMsgPacket As New NetworkPacket()

    ' Fill the message fields
    Msg.Type = gameMessageType.NetterDirection
    Msg.PlayerId = PlayerID
    Msg.Direction = Direction

    ' Put the message in a packet and send it
    gameMsgPacket.Write(Msg)
    SendData(gameMsgPacket)
End Sub
```

The methods to send OkToStartGame and EndDeathMatch will follow the same structure as this, and will be called SendOkToStartGame and SendEndDeathMatch. The code for these methods is included on the accompanying CD-ROM, along with the full code for this chapter's sample game.

The method to send the SyncGameField message has a little peculiarity that we must look at carefully: We can't use the Write method of the NetworkPacket to write a structure that has strings or arrays as members, since DirectPlay can't compute a valid size for the structure. This happens because strings can have any extension, and arrays can be redimensioned by the program, so the message size can't be calculated.

To work around this problem, we'll use the generic message structure to write the player ID and the message type, and use the Write method to write the array after the message basic structure on the packet. The full code for the SendSyncGameField method is presented in the following listing:

```
Public Sub SendSyncGameField(ArrMushrooms(,) As Byte)
    Dim Msg As GameMsg_Generic
    Dim gameMsgPacket As New NetworkPacket()

    ' Fill the message fields
    Msg.PlayerId = PlayerID
    Msg.Type = gameMessageType.SyncGameField
    ' Put the message on a packet and send it
    gameMsgPacket.Write(Msg)
    gameMsgPacket.Write(ArrMushrooms)
    ' The previous code line corresponds to the following code piece:
    'Dim i As Integer
    'For i = 0 To 74
    '    ' Write the bytes for the X,Y position for each mushroom
    '    gameMsgPacket.Write(ArrMushrooms(i, 0))
    '    gameMsgPacket.Write(ArrMushrooms(i, 1))
    'Next
    SendData(gameMsgPacket)
End Sub
```

## Creating the Methods That Receive Messages

To process the game messages received from the remote player, we'll override ProcessMessage from the base class and include a Select Case command that will call a specific function to process each type of message. Each of these functions will read the message data and send an event to the game, so we'll also have to create four events—one for each message type. One extra method will be necessary to read the message type from the incoming network packet.

The next code listing shows the events declaration, the ProcessMessage, and the ReadMessageType method used for reading the message type.

```
Public Event SyncGameField( playerId As Integer,  ArrMushrooms(,) As Byte)
Public Event StartDeathMatch()
Public Event EndDeathMatch( PlayerKilled As Integer)
Public Event NetterDirection( playerId As Integer,  Direction As Integer)

Overrides Sub ProcessGameMessage(Message As NetworkPacket)
    Select Case ReadMessageType(Message)
        Case gameMessageType.SyncGameField
            ' Call the function that will process the SyncGameField message
            ProcessSyncGameField(Message)
        Case gameMessageType.OkToStartGame
            ProcessStartDeathMatch(Message)
        Case gameMessageType.NetterDirection
            ' Call the function that will process the NetterDirection message
            ProcessNetterDirection(Message)
        Case gameMessageType.EndDeathMatch
            ' Call the function that will process the NetterMovement message
            ProcessGameOver(Message)
    End Select
End Sub

Function ReadMessageType(Message As NetworkPacket) As gameMessageType
    Dim Msg As GameMsg_Generic
    ' We'll always reset the packet, so we don't need to
    '   care if it was read before calling the current function
    Message.Position = 0

    Msg = CType(Message.Read(GetType(GameMsg_Generic)), GameMsg_Generic)
    Return Msg.Type
End Function
```

All Process . . . methods are analogous to the ReadMessageType method, with the only difference being that they will be raising a method-specific event by the end of each method. The ProcessSyncGameField method will be the only slightly different one, reading the array sent byte by byte instead of using a specific structure for it, due to the problems with array deliverance that we have already talked about.

The code for `ProcessSyncGameField` method is given in the following listing:

```
Sub ProcessSyncGameField(ByVal Message As NetworkPacket)
    Dim Msg As GameMsg_Generic
    Dim i As Integer
    Dim ArrMushrooms(75, 2) As Byte

    ' We'll always reset the packet, so we don't need to
    '   care if it was read before calling the current function
    Message.Position = 0

    Msg = CType(Message.Read(GetType(GameMsg_Generic)), _
                GameMsg_Generic)
    For i = 0 To 74
        ' Write the bytes for the X,Y position for each mushroom
        ArrMushrooms(i, 0) = Message.Read(GetType(Byte))
        ArrMushrooms(i, 1) = Message.Read(GetType(Byte))
    Next
    RaiseEvent SyncGameField(Msg.PlayerId, ArrMushrooms)
End Sub
```

In the next section, we'll discuss the updates we need to make to the `GameEngine` class to include multiplayer features in our game.

## Third Draft: Adding Multiplayer Features to the Game Engine

The next step to make our game multiplayer is updating our `CreateGameField` method of the `GameEngine` class to initialize DirectPlay.

We'll also need to initialize any new variables used by this version of the game, such as the byte array with the mushroom positions that will be sent by the `SyncGameField` message.

One last adjustment refers to adding a new property to the `Netterpillar` class, `IsRemote`, which will control the drawing of the netterpillars (the remote player character is green, while the local one is yellow). To set this property, we'll add an extra parameter to the `Netterpillar` New method.

## Updating the CreateGameField Class

In the next code listing we present the updates made to the CreateGameField method. Look for the "Update to network game" comments to see where extra code was added; the full code for this procedure, including extra comments, is available on the CD-ROM that accompanies this book.

```
Sub CreateGameField(ByVal WinHandle As System.IntPtr)
    ReDim arrGameField(width, height)
. . .

    ' Create the Netterpillars for standalone game
    Select Case NetterpillarNumber
        Case 1
            objNetterpillars(0) = New clsNetterpillar(Int(Me.width / 2), _
                Int(Me.height) / 2, clsSprite.enDirection.South, False, False)
            Player1 = objNetterpillars(0)
        Case 2
            ' Update to network game: Inform which netterpillar is remote
            '   if we are client on a deathmatch game,
            '   we will control the second Netterpillar
            ' OBS: The last two parameters of the New method set the properties
            '   IsComputer and IsRemote of the Netterpillar, respectively
            Select Case NetWorkType
                Case enNetWorkGame.Client
                    objNetterpillars(0) = New clsNetterpillar(Int(Me.width/3), _
                        Int(Me.height) / 2, clsSprite.enDirection.South, _
                        False, True)
                    objNetterpillars(1) = New clsNetterpillar(Int(Me.width/3)*2,_
                        Int(Me.height) / 2, clsSprite.enDirection.North, _
                        False, False)
                    Player1 = objNetterpillars(1)
                Case enNetWorkGame.Host
                    objNetterpillars(0) = New clsNetterpillar(Int(Me.width/3),_
                        Int(Me.height) / 2, clsSprite.enDirection.South, _
                        False, False)
                    objNetterpillars(1) = New clsNetterpillar(Int(Me.width/3)*2,_
                        Int(Me.height) / 2, clsSprite.enDirection.North, _
                        False, True)
                    Player1 = objNetterpillars(0)
                Case enNetWorkGame.No
                    objNetterpillars(0) = New clsNetterpillar(Int(Me.width/3),_
                        Int(Me.height) / 2, clsSprite.enDirection.South, _
```

```
                            False, False)
                objNetterpillars(1) = New clsNetterpillar(Int(Me.width/3)*2,_
                    Int(Me.height) / 2, clsSprite.enDirection.North, _
                    True, False)
                Player1 = objNetterpillars(0)
        End Select
...
    End Select


...


'Update to NetWork Game: If we are client on a death match,
'  do not create the mushrooms, they will be created by the host
If NetWorkType <> enNetWorkGame.Client Then
    ' Create the mushrooms
    objMushrooms = New clsMushroom()
    For i = 0 To MushroomNumber - 1
        ' Check to seek if we are not creating the mushrooms
        '    over other objects
        Do
            x = Int(Rnd(1) * (Me.width - 2)) + 1
            y = Int(Rnd(1) * (Me.height - 2)) + 1
        Loop While arrGameField(x, y) <> enGameObjects.Empty
        arrGameField(x, y) = enGameObjects.Mushroom

        'Update to NetWork Game: Create an array with the mushrooms positions
        If NetWorkType <> enNetWorkGame.No Then
            arrMushrooms(i, 0) = x : arrMushrooms(i, 1) = y
        End If
    Next
    Redraw()
End If


'Update to NetWork Game: Create our DirectPlay client object
If NetWorkType <> enNetWorkGame.No Then
    GameClient = New clsNetworkNetterpillars()
    ' Choose the service provider
    If Not GameClient.ChooseServiceProvider() Then
        GameOver = True
        Return
    End If
    If NetWorkType = enNetWorkGame.Host Then
        ' Create the session
```

```
            If Not GameClient.CreateSession() Then
                GameOver = True
                Return
            End If
        Else 'NetWorkGame = enNetWorkGame.Client
            ' Join a session
            If Not GameClient.ChooseSessionToJoin() Then
                GameOver = True
                Return
            End If
        End If
        Redraw()
    End If
End Sub
```

There's nothing essentially new to us in the previous sample code, since we have already seen the details of the DirectPlay initialization when we created the NetworkGame class.

As for the netterpillar creation in the code, the only difference is setting the IsRemote property properly, according to the current network type. For stand-alone games, no player is remote; for a host game, the first netterpillar is local and the second one is remote; and for a client game, the first netterpillar is remote and the second one is local. We also set the Player1 variable to the locally controlled netterpillar, since the local player controls the netterpillar through this variable.

## Updating the Render Method

We'll also need to update the Render procedure to reflect the changes for multi-player games. This method will be core to the game synchronization, and we'll depend heavily on the guarantee that TCP delivers all messages, and that they will be delivered in the same order they were sent.

We'll also not include any special treatment to hide the latency. Let's suppose this game will run on a local network, and forget about this problem to make the code simpler.

Even with all these assumptions, the code may appear a little confusing to you if you've never written a network-enabled application, so we include loads of comments in the code, and we'll see what happens, step by step.

Before looking at the code, let's remember the four steps (previously steps 7 to 10) we planned in the game project with regards to keeping the game fields synchronized between players:

1.  The server gets the input from the local player and sends it to the client (NetterDirection message).

2.  The client receives the information about the remote player movement, and obtains the input from the local player.

3.  The client updates the netterpillar positions in the game field, and sends their positions to the server.

4.  The host receives the information about the remote player's movements, and updates the netterpillar positions in the game field.

We can summarize these steps in a single statement: Both client and server will only move after receiving the input from the local player and the direction of the movement from the remote player. The input from the local player is sent only once to the remote player, to avoid synchronization problems, like moving in a certain direction twice on one machine and once on another.

We can control this easily with a pair of variables: a static local variable in the Render method that will be set when we send our position, and a private class variable that will be set when we receive the direction from the remote player. Both variables will be reset when we move the netterpillars.

In the next code sample, we present the updates to the Render procedure that implement the multiplayer features in our game. Refer to the comments in the code to see how we are implementing the synchronization control.

```
Sub Render()
    Dim i As Integer
    Static DirectionSent As Boolean = True

    ' Update to network game: maintain the game field drawn
    Redraw()
    ' Update to network game: only move in network mode
    ' if we send and receive the new directions
    If NetWorkType <> enNetWorkGame.No Then
        ' Update to network game: send the player movement to the oponent
        If Not DirectionSent Then
            DirectionSent = True
            Player1.Direction = Player1.Direction
            If NetWorkType = enNetWorkGame.Host Then
                GameClient.SendNetterDirection(Player1.Direction)
            End If
        End If
        ' If we didn't receive the remote player movement, exit the function
```

```
        If Not DirectionArrived Then
            Return
        Else
            ' Update to NetWork game: The game won't run until the next
            ' direction from the remote player arrives; and we will send our
            ' new direction to him only once
            DirectionSent = False
            DirectionArrived = False
            If NetWorkType = enNetWorkGame.Host Then
                ' Move the Netterpillars when we receive the remote player
                '   direction
                MoveNetterpillars()
            Else  'Client
                GameClient.SendNetterDirection(Player1.Direction)
                ' Move the Netterpillars
                MoveNetterpillars()
            End If
        End If
    Else
        ' Move the Netterpillars
        MoveNetterpillars()
    End If
...
    ' Update to network game: game over when the first player dies
    If NetWorkType <> enNetWorkGame.No Then
        For i = 0 To NetterpillarNumber - 1
            If objNetterpillars(i).IsDead Then
                GameOver = True
            End If
        Next
    Else
        ' On standalone game, GameOver if all Netterpillars die
        GameOver = True
        For i = 0 To NetterpillarNumber - 1
            If Not objNetterpillars(i).IsDead Then
                GameOver = False
            End If
        Next
        ' If all mushrooms got eaten - Game Over
        If MushroomNumber = 0 Then
            GameOver = True
        End If
    End If
```

```
' Game over will happen if the player dies or closes the game window
If gameOver Then
    If NetWorkType = enNetWorkGame.Client Then
        GameClient.SendEndDeathMatch(1)
    ElseIf NetWorkType = enNetWorkGame.Host Then
        GameClient.SendEndDeathMatch(0)
    End If
End If
...
End Sub
```

Besides the synchronization, in the previous code listing we are also setting the new criteria for game over (the death match ends as soon as one player dies, not when the last netterpillar dies). We send the EndDeathMatch message to the remote player when the game is over, which will occur if the local player dies or closes the game field window.

In the next section, we present the message handlers for our game, the last step required before being able to play our game through the network.

## Fourth Draft: Writing the Multiplayer Message Handlers

In this section, we'll put together everything that we have done in the previous sections, so we can see how the game will work across the network.

Let's look at the messages exchanged by both players in sequence, according to the time they occur in a common game. Refer to the steps described in the game project if you have any doubts about this sequence. All events that handle these messages are defined in the NetworkNetterpillar class or in its base class. The GameClient is the object from the class we defined in the GameEngine class.

The first message received in a game is the NewPlayer message, received on the host when a new player connects to a session. This message is defined in the NetworkGame class, and reflects directly the message received by the Peer object.

When the host receives this message, it will send the array with the mushroom positions (created in the CreateGameField method) to the client, using the SendSyncGameField method of the NetworkNetterpillar class, as we can see in the next code sample:

```
Sub GameClient_NewPlayer(Name As String, ID As Integer) _
                                Handles GameClient.NewPlayer
    ' If we are the host, send mushroom positions to the client
    If GameClient.PlayerID <> ID And NetWorkType = enNetWorkGame.Host Then
        ' Store the remote player name
        GameClient.SendSyncGameField(arrMushrooms)
    End If
End Sub
```

When the host sends the SyncGameField message, the event that processes this message is triggered on the client machine. This machine reads the messages and creates all the mushrooms in the game field, and then sends the OkToStartGame message back to the host, as we can see in the next code sample:

```
Sub GameClient_SyncGameField(playerId As Integer, ArrMushrooms(,) As Byte) _
                                Handles GameClient.SyncGameField

    Dim i As Integer
    Dim x As Integer, y As Integer

    If GameClient.PlayerID <> playerId Then
        ' Create the mushrooms
        objMushrooms = New clsMushroom()
        For i = 0 To 74
            arrGameField(ArrMushrooms(i, 0), ArrMushrooms(i, 1)) = _
                enGameObjects.Mushroom
        Next
    End If
    GameClient.SendOkToStartGame()
End Sub
```

The host will then receive the OkToStartGame message and send the current local player direction to the remote player. This will start the "loop" of message exchanges between server and client, where each of them will pass its direction to the remote player and receive a direction from him or her.

```
Sub GameClient_StartDeathMatch() Handles GameClient.StartDeathMatch
    If NetWorkType = enNetWorkGame.Host Then
        GameClient.SendNetterDirection(Player1.Direction)
    End If
End Sub
```

The client will receive the direction from the host, update the correct netter-pillar direction, and simply set the `DirectionArrived` variable to True. This variable, as we have just seen in the previous section, will indicate that the local machine has already received the remote player movement, and can go on to update the screen in the `Render` method.

```
Sub GameClient_NetterDirection(playerId As Integer, Direction As Integer) _
        Handles GameClient.NetterDirection
    If NetWorkType = enNetWorkGame.Client Then
        ' If we are the client, update the 1st netterpillar
        '   (the host controlled one)
        objNetterpillars(0).Direction = Direction
    Else ' NetWorkType = enNetWorkGame.Host
        ' If we are the host, update the 2nd netterpillar
        '   (the client controlled one)
        objNetterpillars(1).Direction = Direction
    End If
    ' The game can go running
    DirectionArrived = True
End Sub
```

In the `Render` method, as we saw in the previous section, the local player will send his or her direction to the remote player, continuing in this loop until one of the players dies. When a player dies or closes the game window, the `EndDeathMatch` message is sent by the `Render` method, which will be handled by the remote player's client simply by setting the remote player character to dead, as we can see in the next bit of code:

```
Sub GameClient_EndDeathMatch(PlayerKilled As Integer) _
    Handles GameClient.EndDeathMatch
    ' Kill the netterpillar that died in the remote game
    objNetterpillars(PlayerKilled).IsDead = True
End Sub
```

One final message can be received by any of the players when the connection with the remote player is broken. In this case, all we do is present an error message to the local player, as shown in the next listing:

```
Sub GameClient_SessionTerminated(msg As TerminateSessionMessage) _
        Handles GameClient.SessionTerminated
    If Not GameOver Then
        MessageBox.Show("Connection with oponnent was terminated." & _
        ControlChars.CrLf & "We can't continue playing.")
        GameOver = True
    End If
End Sub
```

We are now able to run our program and see the results. If we want to test it on a single machine, this is still possible, but we need to lower the frame rate (thus resulting in slower netterpillars on screen) because we'll need to control both local and remote players.

Figure 8-15 presents our first .Netterpillars II test, showing the netterpillars moving in sequence on the screens for the local and remote player.

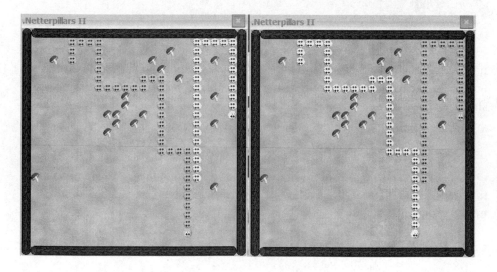

*Figure 8-15. Running a death match in .Netterpillars II*

In the next section, we'll finish our program, including a specific screen for the end of the death match game.

## Final Version: Coding the Game Over Screen

Our goal for the game over screen in a death match is to present the local and remote player's names, showing which one is the winner. We can also use the code from the previous game over screen to include the length of a player's netterpillar on screen.

The first thing we must do is to create a new property in the NetworkNetterpillar class to store the remote player name.

```
Public RemotePlayerName As String
```

We'll need to set this property properly. On the host, we'll receive the remote player's name in the NewPlayer event, coded in the previous section; so all we need to do is store the name in the newly created property, including the next code line in that event handler:

```
GameClient.RemotePlayerName = Name
```

As for the client, we'll assume that the remote player's name is the session name on the remote computer so we can store the remote player's name at the end of the CreateGameField method, just after connecting to a remote session, as shown in the next line of code:

```
GameClient.RemotePlayerName = GameClient.SessionName
```

Now that we have the names of the local and remote players, all we need to do is code the Load event of the death match game over screen, as presented in the next code listing:

```
Sub FrmDeathMatchGameOver_Load(sender As Object, e As EventArgs) _
              Handles MyBase.Load
   ' write the name of the winner
   '  Remember, objNetterpillars(0) is always the host
   If objGameEngine.objNetterpillars(0) Is Nothing Or _
      objGameEngine.objNetterpillars(0).IsDead Then
        If objGameEngine.NetWorkType = clsGameEngine.enNetWorkGame.Host Then
            LblWinnerName.Text = objGameEngine.GameClient.RemotePlayerName
        Else
            LblWinnerName.Text = objGameEngine.GameClient.PlayerName
        End If
```

```
    Else
        If objGameEngine.NetWorkType = clsGameEngine.enNetWorkGame.Host Then
            LblWinnerName.Text = objGameEngine.GameClient.PlayerName
        Else
            LblWinnerName.Text = objGameEngine.GameClient.SessionName
        End If
    End If

    ' Write the players name
    If objGameEngine.NetWorkType = clsGameEngine.enNetWorkGame.Host Then
        LblPlayer1.Text = objGameEngine.GameClient.PlayerName
        LblPlayer2.Text = objGameEngine.GameClient.RemotePlayerName
    Else
        LblPlayer1.Text = objGameEngine.GameClient.SessionName
        LblPlayer2.Text = objGameEngine.GameClient.PlayerName
    End If
    'write the players length
    LblPlayer1Length.Text = objGameEngine.objNetterpillars(0).NetterBodyLength
    LblPlayer2Length.Text = objGameEngine.objNetterpillars(1).NetterBodyLength
End Sub
```

Running our game again, we can now see the game over screen for a death match, as shown in Figure 8-16.

*Figure 8-16. The game over screen for a death match*

In the next section, we'll discuss some suggestions on how to improve our game.

## Adding One Final Touch

There's a lot of opportunity for improvement in our game. For example, we could create customized screens for network configuration. We could also have a specific place to configure the network options, and buttons to start the game, so the player would not have to give network details, such as the provider or the remote machine name, every time he or she wants to start a new game.

The main goal for this chapter is to present the features of DirectPlay in the simplest possible way, so some usability aspects such as easy network configuration were neglected.

Therefore, as a final touch, all we'll do is create a smoother game start, and leave all the other improvements as an exercise for you to do on your own time. Enjoy!

## *Smoothing the Game Start*

Playing our own games is surely the best way to find weaknesses in them. In the case of this chapter's sample game, one thing that really annoys us is the way the game starts, with the netterpillars running at full speed. Sometimes we didn't have time to think before we died!

So, we'll address this issue by including a netterpillar acceleration at the beginning of the game: The game characters will start to move slowly, and then increase their speed until they reach full velocity.

This can be done in a very simple way. In the Main subroutine, we'll set the DesiredFrameRate variable to 2 (2 frames per second), and we'll increment it slowly (let's say 0.2 frames per second) until it reaches our current frame rate of 10, as shown in the next code listing:

```
Sub main()
    ...
    ' Reset the frame rate, to do the initial acceleration
    DesiredFrameRate = 2
    Do While Not objGameEngine.GameOver
        If Not objGameEngine.Paused Then
            ' Force a Frame rate of 10 frames to second on maximum
            If Environment.TickCount - LastTick >= 1000 / DesiredFrameRate Then
                ' Increase the DesiredFrameRate from 2 to 10 when
                '    starting the game, so the player can see the
                '    netterpillar speed increasing
                If DesiredFrameRate < 10 Then DesiredFrameRate += 0.2
                MoveComputerCharacters()
```

```
            objGameEngine.Render()
            LastTick = System.Environment.TickCount
        End If
    End If
    Application.DoEvents()
Loop
...
End Sub
```

With this simple trick, our game will have a smooth start. Play it again and you'll see the difference!

That's all for this chapter's sample game. In the next section, we'll recap the main points we have discussed.

## Summary

In this chapter we went back to the sample game created in Chapter 2 and added multiplayer features to it using DirectPlay.

This chapter's sample was a simple one, but it was definitely hard enough to show the problems and challenges we face when coding multiplayer games.

Among the points discussed were the following:

- Details about how to create multiplayer games and choices we must make when thinking about coding such games

- The use of managed DirectPlay to connect computers

- The creation of a new game class that handles the connection between remote computers and the delivering and receiving of messages.

In the next chapter, we'll go back to the basics and create a very simple game in order to reinforce the single most important thing in game creation: enjoying the programming. At the same time, we'll explore new concepts that may help us in building other games, such as multithreading, creating windows with different shapes, and accessing nonmanaged code from the underlying Windows API.

# D-iNfEcT: Multithreading, Nonrectangular Windows, and Access to Nonmanaged Code

IN THIS CHAPTER, we'll go back to basics by creating a very simple game with a few dozen lines of code to reinforce the ideas you have encountered in this book: Creating games can be simple, and, most of all, it can be fun.

We'll create an original game, called D-iNfEcT (see Figure 9-1), which uses some simple concepts that haven't been covered in previous chapters but that may help us add some extra spice to our game projects. We'll see some more details about multi-threading, discover how to

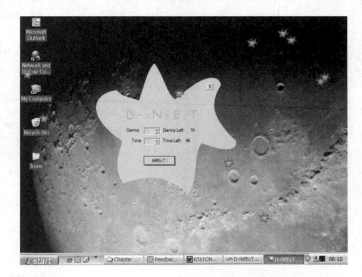

*Figure 9-1. D-iNfEcT, this chapter's sample game*

create nonrectangular windows, and you'll learn how you can access nonmanaged code—and why you would want to do such a thing.

# Multithreading

Visual Basic .NET opened up whole new horizons for Visual Basic programmers, and probably one of the most exciting of its latest features is its multithread capabilities.

To understand what a thread is, first you must understand what a process is. Microsoft's MSDN library (http://www.msdn.microsoft.com/) defines a *process* as a "single instance of a running application. Each process has at least a primary thread, which executes code within the process. You can also create additional threads in a process, limited only by RAM." In other words, a process is an EXE file held in memory, and a thread is what executes the program code.

As for a *thread*, MSDN library states that "a thread executes code in a process. Each thread has a stack, where the linker sets the stack size of all threads created in a process. Each process has a primary thread and can have as many additional threads as permitted by available RAM. Threads within a process share the address space of the process. A thread also has associated registers such as the instruction pointer. These associated registers are known as the context." In less technical terms, we can say that a thread is a "unit of execution" inside a process, comprising an instruction pointer (which tells which instruction will be executed next) and some context data associated with it.

A better way to really understand these concepts is by studying a graphical depiction of the relationship between processes and threads, as shown in Figure 9-2.

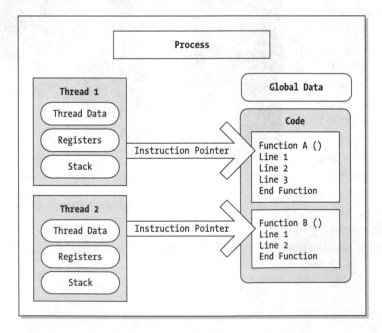

*Figure 9-2. Processes and threads*

If a process has only the primary thread, it's called *single-threaded*. If it has more than one thread, it's called *multithreaded*.

---

*Visual Basic .NET allows you to create multithreaded applications through the declaration of a* Thread *object, which is associated with a function. When the function ends, the thread is destroyed. We control the execution of the thread with the methods* Start, Stop, Suspend, Sleep(time), Resume, *and* Abort.

**NEW IN .NET**

---

## Creating Multiple Threads in a Program

The following code sample shows a simple program that creates two extra threads besides the primary one, which is automatically created for every program.

```
Imports System.Threading
Private secondThread As Thread
Private ThirdThread As Thread

Sub Main()
    secondThread = New Thread(AddressOf ThreadCode)
    secondThread.Name = "Second Thread"
    secondThread.Start()

    ThirdThread = New Thread(AddressOf ThreadCode)
    ThirdThread.Name = "Third Thread"
    ThirdThread.Start()
End Sub

Public Sub ThreadCode()
    Do while MessageBox.Show( "Do you wish to end this thread?", _
                "Calling from inside " & Thread.CurrentThread.Name, _
                MessageBoxButtons.YesNo, MessageBoxIcon.Question) = vbNo
    loop
End Sub
```

With multithreading, we can make our program run different pieces of code at the same time. We have already used this feature to pool the input devices in Chapter 5, but we can do a lot more. For example, since we can create functions that can keep running calculations even while we draw the screen, we can create more complex AI code to take into account more variables and achieve more interesting results, or we can improve our collision detection algorithms to produce more accurate results.

Of course, we can't go on creating new threads forever. Although we can create a few hundred threads in the same program, there is a practical limit to the number of threads we can include, just as there is a practical maximum to the number of programs we can run on Windows before it becomes too slow to use.

## Avoiding Errors in Multithreaded Programs

When our programs gain multiple threads, we must be particularly careful about the so-called critical sections of our code: The code from different threads may access program data at the same time, generating unexpected results. Just to give a simple example, consider the following situations regarding the use of a global counter from two threads of the same process.

The first sequence refers to normal processing, with no errors:

1.   Thread 1 reads the counter. Its value is 10.

2.   Thread 1 increments the counter (counter's new value: 11).

3.   Thread 1 saves the value (value saved: 11).

4.   Thread 2 reads the counter. Its value is 11.

5.   Thread 2 increments the counter (counter's new value: 12).

6.   Thread 2 saves the value (value saved: 12).

The previous situation occurs when the threads execute sequentially; but since we have multiple instruction pointers, there's no guarantee that the processing will happen this way. The next steps represent another valid operation sequence, which leads to an incorrect result:

1.   Thread 1 reads the counter. Its value is 10.

2.   Thread 1 increments the counter (counter's new value: 11).

3.   Thread 2 reads the counter. Its value is 10.

4.   Thread 1 saves the value (value saved: 11).

5. Thread 2 increments the counter (counter's new value: 11).

6. Thread 2 saves the value (value saved: 11).

This kind of error can be disastrous when we are accessing non–thread-safe resources from our application, and can lead to instability in the program. To avoid these problems, VB .NET offers a new construct, SyncLock(), that helps with protecting critical sections and data.

**NEW IN .NET**

*The* SyncLock()/End SyncLock *block in Visual Basic .NET informs the program that any data inside the statements must only be accessed one thread at a time. The* SyncLock() *method receives as a parameter a reference type (usually a class, but this also can be a module, an array, an interface, or a delegate), and prevents the thread from executing the block until it has an exclusive lock on the object referenced by this parameter. For example,* SyncLock(me) *blocks the current object.*

This code sample shows how a global variable can be protected from problems that occur due to concurrent threading:

```
Imports System.Threading
Private MyGlobalVar as integer = 0
Private secondThread As Thread
Private ThirdThread As Thread

Sub Main()
    secondThread = New Thread(AddressOf SecondThreadCode)
    secondThread.Name = "Second Thread"
    secondThread.Start()

    ThirdThread = New Thread(AddressOf ThirdThreadCode)
    ThirdThread.Name = "Third Thread"
    ThirdThread.Start()
End Sub
Public Sub SecondThreadCode()
    Synclock(me)
        MyGlobalVar += _
        inputbox ("Enter the value to sum to the global variable", _
                Thread.CurrentThread.Name  )
    End Synclock
End Sub
```

```
Public Sub ThirdThreadCode()
    Synclock(me)
            MyGlobalVar += _
            inputbox ("Enter the value to sum to the global variable", _
                    Thread.CurrentThread.Name )
    End Synclock
End Sub
```

In the preceding sample code, we protect the global variable from being over-written by concurrent threads, but what if we wanted to know the final value of the variable, after the two threads had ended? The `Join` method of the threads will help us when waiting for a thread to end, enabling our programs to do any syn-chronization that's possible.

**TIP** *The* `<Thread>`.`Join` *method forces the caller thread to go to sleep until the destination thread ends.*

Adding the next lines to the end of the `Main` procedure in the previous code sample forces our main program to wait for both threads to end before con-tinuing, so the message box presents the correct final value of the global variable. Remember that the threads run asynchronously (just like separate programs), so if we simply include the message box, without calling the `Join` method, it would be presented as soon as the threads were created, showing a zeroed variable.

```
Secondthread.join()
Thirdthread.join()
MessageBox.show("Final value of the global variable: " & _
        MyGlobalVar.ToString)
```

In the next section, we'll discuss how to create nonrectangular windows, which are a nice touch when making splash or configuration screens for our games.

## Creating Nonrectangular Windows

Creating nonrectangular windows can help us to come up with customized window shapes that may improve the visual appearance of our game. Perhaps the most common example of a program that uses this resource is Windows Media Player, in which each skin we choose implies in a different window shape.

To change a window's shape, all we need to do is to set the Region to a previously created graphics path. We talked about graphics paths when introducing GDI+ in Chapter 1, and used them to draw gradient-filled squares for our first sample game, but here's a brief recap: Graphics paths represent series of connected lines and curves, and are used by functions that draw, fill, or clip a specific region of the window. We can create graphics paths by adding lines, open or closed curves, Bezier curves, arcs, rectangles, and other geometric shapes.

To illustrate this concept, let's create a graphics path composed of two rectangles and then set the region property of the window to this graphics path, creating a cross-shaped window. First, open a new project in Visual Studio and create a window with two labels, which will be used as a visual clue in design mode to the window's final shape. Figure 9-3 shows the design mode window.

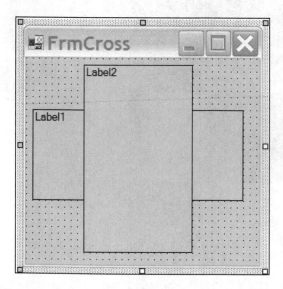

*Figure 9-3. A window with two labels forming a cross shape*

All we need to do now is to include in the Load event of the window the code to set the Region property to the path composed of the two rectangles, as shown in the following code listing:

```
Private Sub FrmCross_Load(sender As System.Object, e As System.EventArgs) _
                Handles MyBase.Load
    'Shape the window to make it look like a cross
    Dim GraphicsPath As New Drawing2D.GraphicsPath()

    GraphicsPath.AddRectangle(New Rectangle(Label1.Location, Label1.Size))
    GraphicsPath.AddRectangle(New Rectangle(Label2.Location, Label2.Size))

    Me.Region = New Region(GraphicsPath)
End Sub
```

Running our program, the result is a little surprising. Figure 9-4 shows the result.

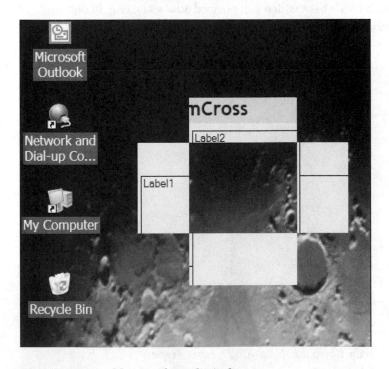

*Figure 9-4. An odd cross-shaped window*

As we can see in Figure 9-4, there are still some details to learn about graphics paths.

The first lesson is that the graphics path will receive window coordinates, with the (0,0) point located the upper-left corner of the title bar. The labels, on the other hand, have client coordinates, and in this case the (0,0) point is in the upper-left corner of the client area. The *client area* is the region "inside" the window, without the title bar and the window borders, whereas the *window area* is the complete window area, including the area of the borders and the title bar. That's why the title bar appears as part of our cross window in Figure 9-4: The coordinates weren't translated from client to window coordinates, so the cross appears shifted to the top-left of the window.

To solve this problem, the easiest thing to do is simply remove the form border by setting its FormBorderStyle property to None. With this setting, the window is presented without borders and title area, so the client area will match the window area.

The second strange thing we see in Figure 9-4 is that there's a hollow region in the middle of the labels. This happens because the application can fill and clip the internal region of the graphics paths in two modes: alternate (the default) or winding.

The *alternate mode* uses a simple algorithm to determine if a point in the window is inside or outside a path. It creates a line from the point to another point that is outside the graphics path. If the point crosses an odd number of graphics path segments, the point is inside the window; if it crosses an even number of segments, it's outside the window. This algorithm works well if we have convex paths or we want to create a window with hollow regions, but it doesn't work if we simply want to add shapes to create the window border, as we did in our example.

The *winding mode* basically takes a starting point on the path and goes on adding segments to the path, using a simple algorithm at each path intersection to decide if the segment is inside or outside the path. In other words, we can say that this mode looks for the outermost border of the figures added to create a path.

Adding the following line to our code will change the fill mode property of the graphics path:

```
GraphicsPath.FillMode = Drawing.Drawing2D.FillMode.Winding
```

If we run our program again now, we can see the expected result, shown in Figure 9-5.

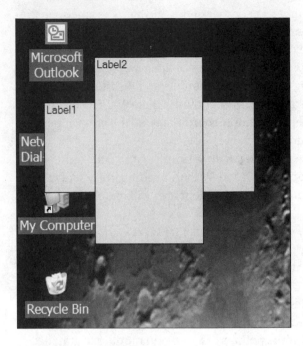

*Figure 9-5. A cross-shaped window*

In the next section, we'll discuss how to access nonmanaged code from our .NET applications.

## Accessing Nonmanaged Code

The .NET framework, as it is now, is a hybrid set of classes: Some classes are entirely managed code, and some are .NET wrappers to access the operating system or extended library features that still do the work behind the scenes. Sometime in the next few years, we'll have operating systems that will be more stable, reliable, and secure because they'll be fully .NET enabled; but for now we need to find a way of making the old and the new work together.

Sometimes our games may need to access a feature from the operating system that isn't mapped to a wrapper class. For instance, some members of WinMM.DLL, which is responsible for multimedia control in windows, have no wrappers in .NET.

Visual Basic, since its earlier versions, always had a way to call the Windows APIs directly, and Visual Basic .NET is no exception. Although calling such functions will mark your code as unsecure (since it'll be stepping out of the sandbox that .NET creates around programs so they don't mess up others), sometimes you may want to do this, at least until the final managed operating system is released.

To use external API functions from our program, we must declare them before calling them. In Visual Basic .NET there are two ways to doing this. To demonstrate these, let's use the function that plays a sound file through the default sound system on a machine, the sndPlaySoundA function, in our samples.

The "classic" way is to declare the function and its parameters, and return values using the Declare statement, as shown in the next code snippet:

```
Declare Function sndPlaySoundA Lib "winmm.dll" (lpszSoundName As String, _
                                       uFlags As Integer) As Integer
```

Visual Basic .NET introduces a new way to perform this declaration, using a declarative attribute that tells the application that the function is implemented as an export from a nonmanaged function that resides in a DLL outside .NET. This is the preferred way of performing a declaration. Its syntax is equivalent to that of a classical function definition, but it must be left empty, as shown in the following code:

```
<DllImport("winmm.dll")> Function sndPlaySoundA(lpszSoundName As String, _
                                       uFlags As Integer) As Integer
    ' If you declare it this way you will need to keep the function empty.
    '    (But either way will work).
End Function
```

---

**NEW IN .NET**

*Such use of attributes is very common in Visual Basic .NET, and they are beneficial for many things, like "signing" your program by including attributes with the author name; including any extra info for external and internal use (like ODBC data source names); and even help making your code more secure against viruses, since there are special attributes you can use to specify which facilities from the operating system your program can and can't use.*

---

**NOTE** *It's beyond the scope of our book to go any further with the topic of declarative attributes, but it's a new and interesting feature that is present in Visual Basic .NET. For further information, refer to the Visual Studio help files.*

To use the sndPlaySoundA function, we can call it directly, as we would any common function. In this specific case, there are also some constants used by the function we'll declare if we want to make our code clearer. The next code listing shows a complete sample of code to play a WAV file:

```
<DllImport("winmm.dll")> Function sndPlaySoundA(lpszSoundName As String, _
                                       uFlags As Integer) As Integer
    ' If you declare it this way you will need to keep the function empty.
    ' (But either way it will work).
End Function

Const SND_SYNC = &H0
Const SND_ASYNC = &H1
Const SND_NODEFAULT = &H2
Const SND_LOOP = &H8
Const SND_NOSTOP = &H10
Const SND_PURGE = &H40

Public Sub Main()
    Dim strSoundFile As String = "C:\temp\MySound.Wav"
    sndPlaySoundA(strSoundFile, SND_ASYNC Or SND_NODEFAULT)
End Sub
```

Next we'll discuss the proposal for the sample game used in this chapter, which will include the features discussed in the previous sections.

## The Game Proposal

The basic idea behind this chapter's sample game is creating a task to clean up the player's computer from a (kind of) virus attack.

The game will be composed of a main window, which will have an irregular shape to mimic some kind of bacterium or germ (viruses are harder to draw), with options to choose the time for the game and the number of germ children, and a button to start the game.

Once started, the game will generate new threads (one for each germ) that will move across the screen in an erratic way. The player will have to catch all of them before the specified time is up by clicking each one with the mouse pointer. When the time is up, we display a message box telling the player that the computer is irreversibly sick; if the player catches all the bacteria, we'll display a congratulations message.

Although the game concept is very simple, the game can be very addictive, as you'll see. In the next section, we'll discuss some extra details about the game project.

## The Game Project

This game will be so simple that we won't need to use any of the previously created game classes; we'll simply add code to a couple of window events. We'll have two windows—the startup window and the child germ window.

Table 9-1 presents the logic for the main window events.

*Table 9-1. Logic for the Main Window Events*

| EVENT | ACTION |
|---|---|
| Load | Change the shape of the window. |
| Start button click | Create as many threads as chosen by the user on screen, and activate a timer to count the time left to the end of the game. |
| Close button click | Close all threads and the main window. |
| Every second | When the game is running, decrease the Time Left label on screen. If time's up, display the game over message. |

Table 9-2 describes the actions for each germ window event.

*Table 9-2. Logic for the Germ Window Events*

| EVENT | ACTION |
| --- | --- |
| Load | Change the shape of the window. |
| Click on the form | Close the form, decrease the number of active germs on the main window, and play a sound using the unmanaged function described earlier in this chapter. |
| Every 0.1 seconds | Choose a direction and move the window. |

The last thing we must do before moving on to the coding phase is to draw the germ form on a piece of paper, so we can use it later to create the germ. Figure 9-6 shows a graphic representation of the germ, with the highlighted control points needed to draw a Bezier curve (which will be used to create our graphic's path).

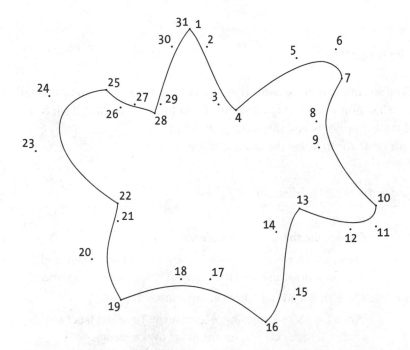

*Figure 9-6. The germ form that will serve as a model for our window shape*

As we can see in Figure 9-6, to draw figures using Bezier curves may be a little tricky: The whole image is a composition of smaller curves, and each of those curves is defined by exactly four points: the starting and the ending points, which the curve passes through, and two "attraction points," which attract the curve but don't force the curve to pass through themselves. The curve tool on Microsoft's Paint works in the same way. So, if we push the intermediate points in opposite directions, we'll have an S-shaped curve like the one defined by points 13 to 16 in Figure 9-6; if we push them in the same direction, we can create simple curves, like the one created using points 4 to 7. Since we are drawing a closed curve, the last point of the last curve must be on the same coordinates as the first point of the sequence (that's why numbers 1 and 31 are at the same point of Figure 9-6).

Drawing the figure and marking the points on a piece of square paper, we can get the correct coordinate values for each point, which gives us enough information to create the Bezier curves for our program in the coding phase.

Our project is as simple as that. Let's get coding!

## The Coding Phase

We'll divide the coding phase into three steps, one for each of the features we saw earlier in this chapter, as expressed in the following list:

1.  First draft: Create the game main window.

2.  Second draft: Code the threads.

3.  Final version: Add final touches and include access to nonmanaged code.

## First Draft: Creating the Game Main Window

Let's start by creating the function to change the window shape. Since we'll need to change the shape of both the main window and the child windows, we'll create a function that will fill an array with the points we'll use to change the shape of the window; this function will receive an integer value that will be used to scale the points accordingly—so the same function can be used to generate the points for the main window and the smaller child windows.

The following code listing shows this function, which can be included in a separate module of our project:

```
Public Function BezierPoints(intSize As Single) As Point()
 Dim ArrPoints As Point() = { _
  New Point(intSize * 54, 4 * intSize), New Point(intSize * 60, 10 * intSize), _
  New Point(intSize * 64, 30 * intSize), New Point(intSize * 70, 32 * intSize),_
  New Point(intSize * 91, 14 * intSize), New Point(intSize * 105, 11 * intSize),_
  New Point(intSize * 107, 21 *intSize), New Point(intSize * 98, 36 * intSize),_
  New Point(intSize * 99, 45 * intSize), New Point(intSize * 119, 65 * intSize),_
  New Point(intSize * 119, 72 *intSize), New Point(intSize * 110, 73 *intSize),_
  New Point(intSize * 92, 66 * intSize),  New Point(intSize * 84, 74 * intSize),_
  New Point(intSize * 90, 97 * intSize), New Point(intSize * 80, 105 * intSize),_
  New Point(intSize * 61, 90 * intSize), New Point(intSize * 51, 90 * intSize), _
  New Point(intSize * 30, 97 * intSize), New Point(intSize * 20, 83 * intSize), _
  New Point(intSize * 29, 70 * intSize), New Point(intSize * 29, 64 * intSize), _
  New Point(intSize * 0, 46 * intSize), New Point(intSize * 5, 27 * intSize), _
  New Point(intSize * 25, 25 * intSize), New Point(intSize * 30, 31 * intSize), _
  New Point(intSize * 35, 30 * intSize), New Point(intSize * 42, 33 * intSize), _
  New Point(intSize * 44, 30 * intSize), New Point(intSize * 48, 10 * intSize), _
  New Point(intSize * 54, 4 * intSize)}
 BezierPoints = ArrPoints
End Function
```

In order to test this code, we can create a form and set the Region property of the window to the graphics path created from a Bezier curve that has the points described in the previous code listing. We can simply add the next code listing to the Load event of a new form to test our Bezier curve:

```
Dim GraphicsPath As New Drawing2D.GraphicsPath()
' Create a window with the scale of 4
GraphicsPath.AddBeziers(BezierPoints(4))
Window.Region = New Region(GraphicsPath)
```

We include the preceding lines in a procedure so we can call it from the main and the child windows without needing to replicate code. Such a function will receive the window and the germ scale as parameters.

Set the background color of the form to green and run the project. You should see results similar to what appears in Figure 9-7.

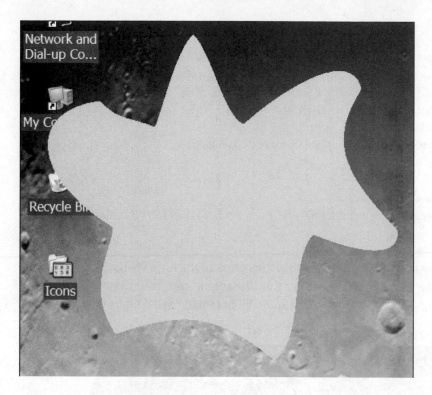

*Figure 9-7. A germ-shaped window*

We can now use some tricks we discussed for graphics in Chapter 1 to create a function that will, besides changing the window shape, add a border and fill the window with varying shades of green. We'll make this last feature optional (controlled by a parameter), so we can turn the fill off if we want.

The code for this function, which receives three parameters (the window handle, the scaling factor, and a Boolean value) to turn the filling on or off is shown in the following code listing:

```
Sub PaintGerm(WindowHandle As IntPtr, GermSize As Single, Fill As Boolean)
    Dim GraphicsPath As New Drawing2D.GraphicsPath()
    Dim GameGraphics As Graphics
    Dim brushSquare As Drawing2D.PathGradientBrush

    ' Create the path that will be used when drawing
    GraphicsPath.AddBeziers(BezierPoints(GermSize))

    ' Get the Graphics object of the background picture
    GameGraphics = Graphics.FromHwnd(WindowHandle)
```

```
If Fill Then
    ' Create the gradient brush which will draw the germ
    ' Note: There's one center color and an array of border colors
    brushSquare = New Drawing2D.PathGradientBrush(GraphicsPath)
    brushSquare.CenterColor = Color.LightGreen
    brushSquare.SurroundColors = New Color() {Color.DarkGreen}
    ' Finally fill the germ
    GameGraphics.FillPath(brushSquare, GraphicsPath)
End If

    ' Draw the germ border
    GameGraphics.DrawBeziers(New Pen(Color.Green, 6), BezierPoints(GermSize))
End Sub
```

We must call this function in the Paint event of the form we have just created so that the window is updated every time the system runs this event. We can see the result of calling this function with the fill parameter set in Figure 9-8.

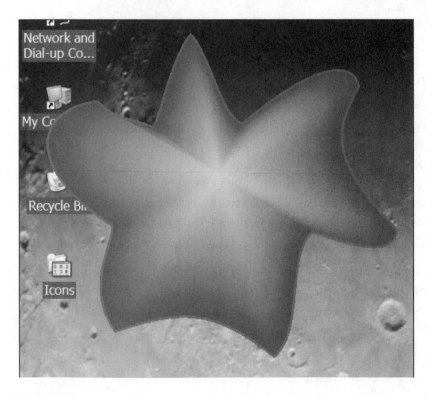

*Figure 9-8. A gradient-filled, germ-shaped window with borders*

Since our window is the right shape, we can go to the next step: creating the controls and putting them in the window in the right place (that's the tough part). We'll create two up-down controls to let the player choose the number of germs to catch and the duration of the game in seconds, as well as labels to display the remaining time and number of germs. We'll also add a bitmap bearing the game name in the middle of the window, a button to start the game, and a button to close the window.

Place all the window controls so they appear in the locations shown in Figure 9-9. It may take you a couple of attempts before you manage to position all the window controls properly.

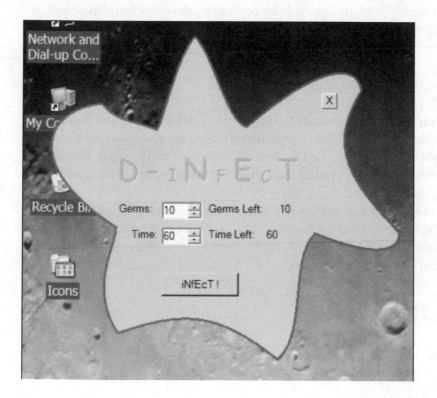

*Figure 9-9. The final interface for the main window*

You may also have to turn off the gradient shading, as we did, because it might not look right with your images and labels.

To synchronize the values of the up-down controls with the labels that will control the remaining time and germs, we'll add two lines in the ValueChanged event of this controls, as depicted in the subsequent code listing:

```
Sub NumTime_ValueChanged(sender As System.Object, e As System.EventArgs) _
            Handles NumTime.ValueChanged
        lblTimeLeft.Text = NumTime.Value
End Sub

Sub NumGerms_ValueChanged(sender As System.Object,  e As System.EventArgs) _
            Handles NumGerms.ValueChanged
        lblGermsLeft.Text = NumGerms.Value
End Sub
```

With this last step, we've completed the coding of the main window interface. In the next section, we'll include code for controlling the threads and the creation of the child windows.

## Second Draft: Coding the Threads

When coding the threads, we must be careful when creating them and destroying them. In order to have a reference to each new thread created, we'll define an array of Thread objects that can be used to abort all of the threads, if needed. This array must be declared as a form variable so that it can be used when creating and destroying the threads.

To create the threads, we'll need to define a function that will be passed as an argument to the New method of the Thread object. For now, our thread will be a function that will simply create and display a second form (the child form), so the thread is finished when the form is closed. The code for creating the threads is as follows:

```
Private GemThread As Thread()

Private Sub cmdGO_Click(sender As System.Object, e As System.EventArgs) _
            Handles cmdGO.Click
    Dim i As Integer
    ReDim GemThread(NumGerms.Value)
    ' Create as many germs as defined by the user on the main window
    For i = 0 To NumGerms.Value - 1
        GemThread(i) = New Thread(AddressOf NewGerm)
        GemThread(i).Name = "Germ " & (i + 1)
        GemThread(i).Start()
    Next
    ' Enable the timer that will count down the time
    TmrTime.Enabled = True
End Sub
```

```
Public Sub NewGerm()
    Dim f As New FrmGerm()
    ' Show the window
    f.ShowDialog()
    ' If we get here, the window was closed - so the germ was caught
End Sub
```

If we run our program now, we'll see that we can create as many windows as defined in the germs number control box in the main dialog box, but they still won't look like germs, nor will they close when we close the main window.

First, let's deal with the question of closing, so we can conclude the thread handling in the main window. The next code listing shows a function that aborts all the threads, ignoring any errors that may arise if the thread is already closed; the call to this function appears in the Closing event of the main window. We also show the code for the close button—just a call to the Close method of the form.

```
Sub KillGerms()
    Dim i As Integer

    For i = 0 To NumGerms.Value - 1
        Try
                GemThread(i).Abort()
        Catch
                ' Ignore errors if thread doesn't exists
        End Try
    Next
End Sub

Private Sub cmdClose_Click(sender As System.Object, e As System.EventArgs) _
            Handles cmdClose.Click
    Me.Close()
End Sub

Private Sub frmStart_Closing(sender As Object, e As CancelEventArgs) _
        Handles MyBase.Closing
    KillGerms()
End Sub
```

Placing the call to KillGerms in the Closing event will force the application to always close all child threads before leaving; regardless of the way the main form is closed—when the user clicks the close button, when he or she presses ALT+F4, or when he or she uses any other way of closing it.

We must now create the code in the child form to change the window shape (by calling the ChangeWindowShape function in the Load event), define a startup position for the window, paint the germ (by simply calling PaintGerm in the Paint event), and finally close the window if the player clicks it. For now, let's not include any code to move the germs on screen, so we can easily click them and test our code.

The implementation of these modifications is shown in the next piece of code. Remember that we must set the form border property to None, or else the picture we'll see won't be what we were expecting.

```
Sub Form_Load(sender AsObject, e As EventArgs) Handles MyBase.Load
    Dim x As Integer
    Dim y As Integer
    ' Change the window shape to the bezier germ-like curve
    ChangeWindowShape(Me, 0.3)

    ' choose a random position on the screen
    Randomize()
    x = Rnd() * Screen.PrimaryScreen.WorkingArea.Width
    y = Rnd() * Screen.PrimaryScreen.WorkingArea.Height
    Me.Location = New Point(x, y)
End Sub


Sub Form_Click(sender As Object, e As EventArgs) Handles MyBase.Click
        ' If the form was clicked, the germ was caught
        Me.Close()
End Sub


Sub FrmGerm_Paint(sender As Object,  e As PaintEventArgs) Handles MyBase.Paint
    PaintGerm(Me.Handle, 0.3, True)
End Sub
```

If we run our program now, we'll be able to click the game start button (in this case, the iNfEcT! button) and see lots of newly generated germs all over the screen. We can kill each of them by clicking them—not very challenging, since they are stationary. Figure 9-10 displays a screen showing all germs—our first test of the multithreaded program.

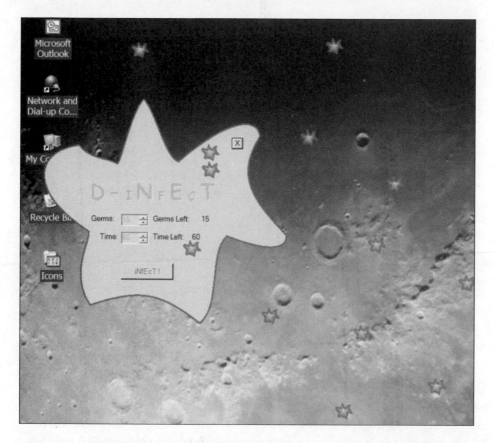

*Figure 9-10. The main germ window, reproducing . . .*

In the next section, we'll code the final touches for our game—such as making the child germs move and including a call to the nonmanaged API function that plays a sound every time a germ is caught.

## Final Version: Final Touches and Access to Nonmanaged Code

There are just a few details we must code to finish our simple game, including the movement of the child windows, and checking the game over conditions.

To make our child windows move, we can simply create a timer and add a constant value to the x and y coordinates on every timer tick. In the next code sample, we show the code to move the window, checking the screen resolution limits to change direction to avoid the germ going off the edge of the screen.

```
Const randomness As Single = 0.05
Sub Timer1_Elapsed(sender As Object, e As ElapsedEventArgs) Handles Timer.Elapsed
    Dim x As Integer = Me.Location.X
    Dim y As Integer = Me.Location.Y
    Static incX As Integer = 10, incY As Integer = 10

    If Rnd(1) < randomness Then incX = -incX
    If Rnd(1) < randomness Then incY = -incY

    If x + incX > Screen.PrimaryScreen.WorkingArea.Width Then incX = -incX
    If y + incY > Screen.PrimaryScreen.WorkingArea.Height Then incY = -incY
    If x + incX < 0 Then incX = -incX
    If y + incY < 0 Then incY = -incY

    x += incX
    y += incY

    Me.Location = New Point(x, y)
End Sub
```

To help us test various types of random behavior when choosing a new direction, in the previous code sample we define a constant, randomness, which can be changed to give the germs a more erratic or more constant behavior. Since our timer is triggering the elapsed event every 0.1 seconds, using values higher than 0.05 (5 percent) will lead to such erratic movements that the player will hardly be able to catch any germs. Try different values and decide for yourself which is the best randomness factor!

Running our code now, we can see the germs moving and can play at catching them, but the game still doesn't terminate (except for when we press the close button), so we must now code the game over conditions.

For this game, we'll have two different ending conditions: The player catches all the germs, so he or she wins and the game is over; or the time runs out before the player has caught all the germs, and he or she loses the game.

To control the time, we'll need to add a timer control on the main form, set its interval to 1 second, and add code to decrement the label that states the time remaining every time the event is run. If the label reaches zero, then we must end the game. The next code listing shows the code for the Tick event of the main window timer:

```
Sub TmrTime_Tick(sender As Object, e As EventArgs) Handles TmrTime.Tick
    ' decrement the time counter
    lblTimeLeft.Text -= 1
    ' Check to see if time's up
    If lblTimeLeft.Text = 0 Then
        ' abort all active threads
        TmrTime.Enabled = False
        KillGerms()
        MsgBox("Your computer cannot be cured anymore!", _
                MsgBoxStyle.Critical, "Time's up!")
    End If
End Sub
```

To control the number of active germs, we can add extra code to our NewGerm function, which handles the germ window creation, to decrement the remaining germs label and perform the corresponding action when the last germ is caught. The full code for the function is presented in the next code sample:

```
Public Sub NewGerm()
    Dim f As New FrmGerm()
    ' Show the window modally
    f.ShowDialog()
    ' If we get here, the window was closed - so the germ was caught
    SyncLock (Me)
        ' Decrement the number of live germs
        lblGermsLeft.Text -= 1
        ' check to see if we were the last germ
        If lblGermsLeft.Text = 0 Then
                MessageBox.Show("You saved your computer!! The virus is gone!", _
                    "Congratulations!", MessageBoxButtons.OK, _
                    MessageBoxIcon.Exclamation)
                TmrTime.Enabled = False
        End If
    End SyncLock
End Sub
```

Refer to the previous code sample to see the use of the SyncLock/End SyncLock block to prevent any problems when accessing the main window objects, which are external to the child threads and therefore work like global variables.

For an extra touch, in the child window we'll play a sound every time a germ is caught, using the sndPlaySoundA function, and call it in the Closing event of the child window.

The full code to call the DLL function, including a wrapper function to perform the calls, is presented in the next code fragment:

```
Declare Function sndPlaySoundA Lib "winmm.dll" (lpszSoundName As String, _
                                       uFlags As Integer) As Integer
'or
' <DllImport("winmm.dll")> Function sndPlaySoundA(lpszSoundName As String, _
'                                       uFlags As Integer) As Integer
' If you declare it in this way you will need to keep the function empty.
' (But either way it will work.)
'End Function

Const SND_SYNC = &H0
Const SND_ASYNC = &H1
Const SND_NODEFAULT = &H2
Const SND_LOOP = &H8
Const SND_NOSTOP = &H10
Const SND_PURGE = &H40

Public Sub PlaySound(strSoundFile As String)
    sndPlaySoundA(strSoundFile, SND_ASYNC Or SND_NODEFAULT)
End Sub
```

That's all for this chapter's sample game, except for some little improvements that we'll discuss in the next section. As we said before, this chapter's sample is an example on how simple, yet fun, a game can be.

## Adding the Final Touches

As with the .Nettrix sample, there is little room for improvement in a game with such simple concepts; but, as always, we can try to make it better with some small enhancements, as described in the following sections.

## Improving the Interface

In our game, as it is now, the main window controls remain enabled while the game is running. What if the player clicks the game start button again and again? This will result in many uncontrolled threads being run on the computer, possibly consuming the whole CPU because of their excessive numbers. So we'd better disable all controls, replacing the various settings of the Enabled property of the timer we saw in the previous code listings with calls to the function presented in the next code piece, EnableInterface:

```
Sub EnableInterface(Enable As Boolean)
    TmrTime.Enabled = Not Enable
    NumGerms.Enabled = Enable
    NumTime.Enabled = Enable
    cmdGO.Enabled = Enable
End Sub
```

## Adding Further Improvements

What else can we do to improve the game? Here are some suggestions to inspire you to play a little with the game code. Feel free to try your own ideas!

- We can create different shapes for the germs, and cycle between the shapes every half second, or every Tick event of the timer from the child windows. Be careful—some graphics boards can make the screen flash if we do this too often, with too many windows.

- We can change the color of the germs every clock tick, using different degrees of green (or another color), to create the illusion that the germs are glowing.

- We can create new ways of playing. For example, we could create a kill-or-get-killed game where there's no time limit, but every germ can generate another germ after 30 seconds; the game ends if we catch them all or if the germs reach epidemic proportions and there are 20 of them on the screen at once.

As we can see, even a simple game can benefit from new ideas, and exercising our minds looking for such ideas will only make us better game developers!

## Summary

In this chapter, we did a back-to-basics game, to remind us that a game doesn't need to be complex to be fun.

We also learned some new concepts about Visual Basic .NET, including the following:

- What threads are, how to control them, and how to create multithreaded programs

- How to improve our game by creating nonrectangular windows

- How to access nonmanaged code, which will be useful until all operating systems are constructed using .NET libraries

With this chapter, we conclude the main part of our book. We hope that it was as much fun and instructive for you to read as it was for us to write.

To give you some ideas about the next steps you can take in the game developing world, we present appendices written by from some famous names in the game developing industry. Find out what these authors say about what you must consider if you want to get serious about game programming.

Good luck with your games!

# Porting .Nettrix to Pocket PC

IN THIS BONUS CHAPTER, we'll go back to our first sample game, .Nettrix, and update it to make it run on a Pocket PC (see Figure 1). There'll be no new features, except for a few adjustments to the interface to make it playable on a Pocket PC and an update on the score counting.

Before starting the migration of our game, let's talk a little more about creating programs for mobile devices in the next section.

## Programming for Mobile Devices

The .NET framework opens whole new horizons to all programmers, and especially to game pro-grammers, with its property of running the same code across different devices running different operating systems.

In this first version, .NET is, most of the time, a simple wrapper to the operating system functions, which are still present running everything in the

*Figure 1.*
*.Nettrix II, running on a Pocket PC*

background; but Microsoft and other companies are already working on operating systems based on the .NET Framework, so we can expect the compatibility to grow over the next few years.

**NOTE** *Of course, this compatibility will never be 100 percent, since every device has its own characteristics, with its own strengths and weaknesses; but it's really great to be able to write our program for a PC and make it run on a Pocket PC, with just a few adjustments!*

## Creating Smart Device Applications in .NET

In versions of Visual Studio prior to .NET, if we wanted to create a program to run on a mobile device such as the Pocket PC, we had to use a specific version of the compiler, and there was no compromise from the operating system in providing compatible functions. Therefore, porting a program was sometimes a matter of erasing and rewriting everything.

This porting problem was especially true when dealing with graphical functions. Even simple programs sometimes needed adjustments before running on a different device.

Visual Studio .NET 2003 (code-named Everett) already has built-in support for the .NET Compact Framework, with the corresponding assemblies and project templates to support project-targeting mobile devices. The new project templates are named Smart Device Application and ASP.NET Mobile Application, and they allow us to create applications to be used on either Pocket PC– or Windows CE–based devices. Figure 2 shows the New Solution dialog box of Visual Studio, highlighting the Smart Device Application item.

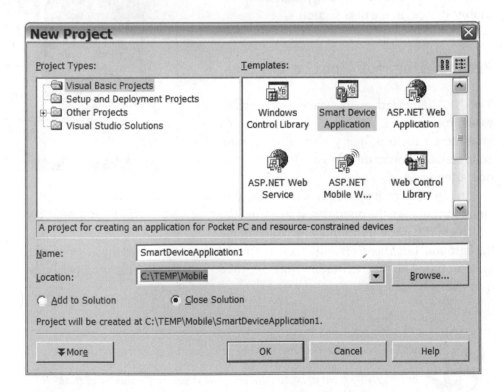

*Figure 2. One of the new Visual Studio .NET 2003 application types*

## Choosing the Platform and Project Type

Once we have created a new smart device application, Visual Studio .NET presents a new dialog box that lets us choose the target platform (Windows CE or Pocket PC) and listing the project types available to the platform, as shown in Figure 3.

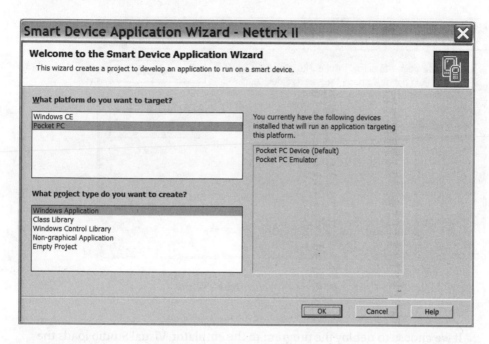

*Figure 3. Choosing the platform and the project type*

For each target platform, the Smart Device Application Wizard presents the available devices the application can be deployed to. In Figure 3, we can see to the right of the target platform list window that there are two possible target devices: a physical Pocket PC (we used a Compaq iPaq for the purposes of this chapter) and a Pocket PC emulator, which is installed along with the Visual Studio .NET 2003.

## Deploying Your Program to an Emulator

Once the project is created, we can see that we have new menu options: On the Tools menu, there now appears a Connect to Device option, and under the Build menu appears the Deploy option.

After creating a program, we can click the Start button in the Visual Studio toolbar just like we would in any project targeting regular PCs. Visual Studio then builds the program with the proper libraries according to the platform we choose, and opens a dialog box that allows us to choose the target device for the application, as presented in Figure 4.

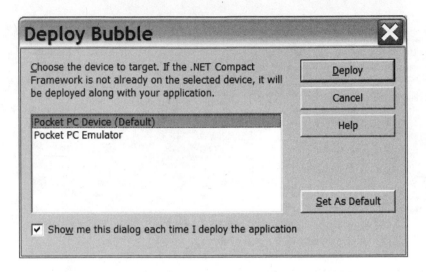

*Figure 4. Choosing the target device for our application*

If we choose to deploy the program to the emulator, Visual Studio loads the emulator before starting to deploy. The emulator is an exact copy of the Pocket PC system, including all programs (yes, it comes with Solitaire, too), right down to the emulator *skins*, which are bitmaps with active buttons. This emulator allows us to test our application in the exact same way we would with a real device without having to own a real device.

Figure 5 presents the first screen of the emulator, when it's opened for the first time. We have already seen an emulator with a skin in Figure 1; but for practical reasons we use the emulator without a skin throughout this chapter.

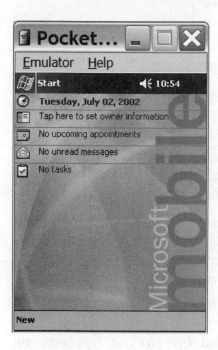

*Figure 5. The Pocket PC emulator*

Once the emulator is loaded or the device is connected, Visual Studio .NET deploys not only the application we created, but also any necessary libraries to make our program run on the desired device. The application is deployed to the \Windows directory on the device, and Visual Studio automatically runs it, and it even allows us to debug the application.

**TIP** *One last word about the emulator: When we close the emulator window, it presents us with a dialog box that allows us to save the emulator state (thus preserving the deployed files) or simply shut down the program, losing all changes since the last time we saved the state. For small projects, you'll probably want to simply shut down the emulator, since the deployment of the .NET Compact Framework doesn't takes too long; but if you are working with a large project that has many extra files (like video or image files, or even many different applications), you'll probably want to save the emulator state so you won't need to redeploy all project files every time you start working with the project.*

Figure 6 presents the closing dialog box of the emulator.

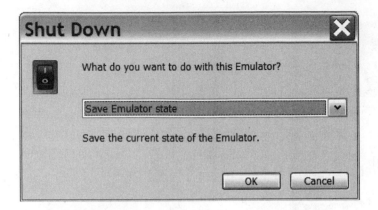

*Figure 6. Choosing the target device to run our application*

## Running Desktop PC Programs and Operating Systems on Mobile Devices

You'll be able to run any simple desktop PC program with very few adjustments on this type of project, and some programs actually won't need any updates, just a new compilation and, of course, replacement of form interface controls with the corresponding ones for the smart device project.

As for the graphical functions, of course, GDI+ is not completely present in the mobile device, but many of its functions are there and use the same interfaces, so porting graphical applications is simpler than in previous versions of Visual Studio.

And as for DirectX, only DirectPlay for Pocket PC is available, and can be downloaded from `http://msdn.microsoft.com/directx` by following the DirectX Downloads link and selecting DirectPlay for PocketPC.

The Window CE operating system runs on many different devices, from pocket computers to automobiles, so the support for various DirectX technologies is built in when the device manufacturers create their operating system. Depending on the device, different DirectX technologies can be supported, if any. DirectX technologies for Windows CE can't be downloaded and then added to an operating system as in the Windows desktop world: Just as there is no one Windows CE operating system, there is no one level of DirectX support.

Windows CE .NET, the newer version of the operating system, has the ability to support DirectDraw, DirectSound, and DirectShow, depending on the device. More information about multimedia on Windows CE can be found at `http://msdn.microsoft.com/library/en-us/wcemain4/htm/ _cmoriMultimediaTechnologies.asp`.

Since there are different versions of DirectX for Windows CE and Pocket PC, our DirectX programs won't be portable across these platforms with a simple recompilation; and there's no .NET interface for DirectX on mobile devices, so we'll need to access DirectX directly, using Visual C++ for mobile devices.

Another important point to make regarding DirectX on mobile devices is that since the operating systems are designed for the capabilities and limitations of embedded systems, the DirectX implementations running over them tend to be pared down from the desktop offerings (this is especially true of Direct3D). So, don't expect to create a full-speed Doom IV for a Pocket PC or Windows CE.

Now let's move on to discuss the proposal for this chapter's sample game, .Nettrix II.

## The Game Proposal

Our main objective is to do the minimum number of updates while preserving the performance of the new device.

We'll also do an interface update: including navigation buttons on the interface so that the player can play it by tapping the screen.

In the next section, we'll discuss some extra details in the game project.

## The Game Project

There's no need for a full project for this game, because we already did one in Chapter 1. So all we'll do as a project and also as an introduction to creating mobile device programs is to make a new project—.Nettrix II—and to define the basic interface to meet the needs of our game proposal. Let's say that this interface is a "visual prototype" of the game.

Figure 7 presents our visual prototype, including the desired navigation buttons. For the sake of simplicity, we set the text of each button to <, >, /\, and \/ for right, left, up, and down directions, in that order.

*Figure 7. Our game interface, updated for Pocket PCs*

Now we can live out the dream of every unorganized programmer: to start coding without a real project! A brief word about this: Sometime ago a guy told one of us that this is called "Zen game programming," referring to the Zen philosophy we've all already heard about in dozens of movies. ("Don't plan to reach the target, BE the target," and other things like that.) But remember, we already did a project in Chapter 1, that's why we don't need one here!

Before entering the code phase, let's look at Figure 8, which shows the .Nettrix class diagram we came up with in Chapter 1.

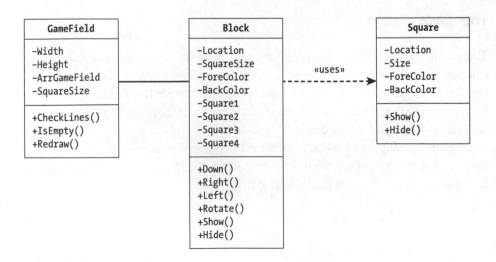

*Figure 8. .Nettrix class diagram*

To refresh your memory, let's take a quick look at the details of this diagram. The Square class draws and erases a square on the screen; the Block class draws, erases, and moves four squares to form a basic .Nettrix block with different shapes; and the GameEngine class has some general-use functions, such as the collision detection support array and the basic functions to deal with this array. Besides these classes, we implemented the game logic directly in the main form events: The game variables are initialized in the Load event, the game loop is in the Tick event of a timer, and the input handling routine is in the KeyPress event.

In the coding phase, we'll discuss the necessary modifications to update our code to run on the Pocket PC.

## The Coding Phase

Although this is our first game targeting a mobile device, porting a game is so simple that we'll do everything in one simple step (hence, no first draft, second draft, and so on).

First, we'll copy the code from Chapter 1, build it, and see which errors occur and fix them. Then we'll perform any updates to the game needed to make it run, if it doesn't run after removing the build errors, and include the code for the new interface elements.

## Adapting the Code to Build for a Pocket PC Target

Copying the code from Chapter 1 into our project and compiling it will present us with some compatibility issues, but they should be fairly easy for us to fix. Once we have done this, there'll probably be tougher problems to solve for functions and methods that preserve the same interface but do not behave the same.

Our first build presents us with only three errors: two when building the program and one when running it.

The first one is the MessageBox parameters, which are different on the Pocket PC version. The last parameter (the default button) is mandatory, and we also have to modify the icon name, since the Stop icon corresponds to the Hand icon (the older name used on the desktop platform) in the Pocket PC. So we need to change our "game over" message box line as follows:

```
MessageBox.Show("GAME OVER", ".NetTrix", MessageBoxButtons.OK, _
                MessageBoxIcon.Hand, MessageBoxDefaultButton.Button1)
```

This error illustrates perfectly the first kind of error we would expect to find when porting games to mobile devices: Some functions take slightly different parameters, and some of the overrides (or different ways to call the same functions) are missing. These are the easier problems to solve, since all we have to do is to make simple adjustments, such as completing the extra parameters or correcting the parameter values.

**NOTE** *An interesting detail is that* MessageBoxIcon.Hand *does work on desktop PCs, so this update is only needed because we weren't targeting both platforms at the beginning of the project in Chapter 1.*

The second update refers to the Activated event for the form, which doesn't exist on the Pocket PC. The new event name is GotFocus, so all we need to do is replace the Handles clause of the event with the following:

```
Sub FrmNetTrix_Activated(sender As Object, e As EventArgs) _
    Handles MyBase.GotFocus
```

This error is a good example of the second type of problem we face when porting our games to mobile devices: Some functions, methods, and events are missing or correspond to different ones. This kind of error may be somewhat difficult to fix, since we must look for the relevant method, event, or function and, if there's no exact match, sometimes have to rewrite part of the program.

We'll come across another error of the same type in the Square class: The Graphics object for the Pocket PC is far simpler than the one for desktop computers, and it doesn't support the DrawPath method used to draw a gradient square. In this case, we'll need to rewrite the whole Draw method of this class to make it simply draw a square with a solid border.

The code for this update is presented later in the chapter, in the section "Updating the Square Class."

After fixing these three compilation errors, our program will run on the Pocket PC, but it'll abort as soon as we click the Start button, with a "Null Reference" error.

The Visual Studio .Net online documentation indicates that in this version of the .NET Compact Framework we need to explicitly create bitmaps for the picture boxes in code. To fix this problem, we need to add two extra lines to the form initialization:

```
PicBackground.Image = New Bitmap(PicBackground.Width, PicBackground.Height)
PicNextBlock.Image = New Bitmap(PicNextBlock.Width, PicNextBlock.Height)
```

Since we are working with a beta version, this behavior may change in the final release. However, it illustrates very well the third variety of error we can find when moving programs to other platforms, such as mobile devices: The program generates a runtime error because something (a function, method, or event) doesn't behave as expected.

This class of errors is a little more difficult than the previous ones to fix, since the error can occur in a different place from where it is generated. In our sample, we get an error inside the Square class the first time we try to create a Graphics object to draw on the screen; but the error is raised over the call stack until the Click event on the Start button. So we could get confused when debugging the code, until we set breakpoints and do a step-by-step debugging.

Once we have fixed this error, our program should run without errors. But when we click the Start button, we'll see that the blocks are falling slower than expected.

This error exemplifies the last and toughest error category we'll encounter when porting our programs: Everything works fine, but something doesn't behave as expected. Or, in other words, there are no errors, but our program doesn't work as planned.

Experienced programmers probably have a good idea about what is happening in our program: The program is working fine, the timer is okay, the collision detection code is facing no problems, and the game over tests are functioning as expected, but the screen drawing on a Pocket PC is simply slower than on a desktop PC.

So let's try fixing the problem.

If we run through our program, we see that we are creating the Graphics object inside the Show and Hide methods of the Square class. That's no big deal when running in a desktop PC, but when we run on a mobile device, we need to improve this code to make it faster. This can be done by creating a Graphics object for each pictureBox when initializing the game, and then passing this object to the drawing functions.

In the next sections, we'll look at the required updates to each of the game classes and the main form to improve the game speed.

## Updating the GameEngine Class

Most of the updates will occur in the GameEngine class; we'll have to add some extra properties and methods and make adjustments to the Block and Square classes:

- We need to include a Graphics object for each pictureBox on the form.

- We need a method to initialize these new properties to their proper values.

- We also need to create a Clear method to erase the pictureBoxes.

After we have implemented these modifications, we need to adapt the game's main loop (remember, in this game the "loop" is the code inside the Tick event of the timer) to clear the back buffers and to refresh them, and make the adjustments to the base classes (Block and Square) to deal with the new logic.

The updates to the GameEngine class are shown in the following code listing:

```
' Update to Pocket PC - Create rectangles to store the screen position
Public Shared rectBackground As Rectangle
Public Shared rectNextBlock As Rectangle

' Update to Pocket PC - New Global Graphics objects
Public Shared GraphBackground As Graphics
Public Shared GraphNextBlock As Graphics

' Update to Pocket PC : New method to clear the game field and the next block
' images, instead of using the Invalidate method of a pictureBox
Public Shared Sub Clear()
    ' Since we are working in a solid background, we can just draw a solid
    '    rectangle in order to "clear" the game field
    GraphBackground.FillRectangle(New SolidBrush(backcolor), rectBackground)
    ' Clear the "next block" image
    GraphNextBlock.FillRectangle(New SolidBrush(backcolor), rectNextBlock)
End Sub

' Update to Pocket PC : New method Create graphics objects that will
'    be used throughout the application
Public Shared Sub Initialize(frmSource As Form, PicBackground As PictureBox, _
                        PicNextBlock As PictureBox)
    ' Set the game field backcolor
    backcolor = Color.Black
```

```
        ' Update to Pocket PC - Create rectangles to help on drawing to screen
        rectBackground = New Rectangle(0, 0, _
                                    PicBackground.Width, PicBackground.Height)
        rectNextBlock = New Rectangle(0, 0, _
                                    PicNextBlock.Width, PicNextBlock.Height)

        ' Update to Pocket PC: Create Graphics to draw on the back buffers
        GraphBackground = Graphics.FromImage(PicBackground.Image)
        GraphNextBlock = Graphics.FromImage(PicNextBlock.Image)
End Sub
```

In the next section, we'll discuss the modifications needed to update the Square and Block classes.

## Updating the Square Class

The Square class will need two updates: changes to the interface of the Draw and Hide methods so they will receive the Graphics object to use instead of a handle of the pictureBox; and rewrites to the Draw method to draw a solid square instead of a gradient-filled one, since the Pocket PC version of the Graphics object doesn't support this feature.

The final version of the code, presented in the next listing, is far simpler than the corresponding one for the desktop version of the game. Refer to Chapter 1 to compare both implementations.

```
Public Class ClsSquare
    Public location As Point
    Public size As size
    Public forecolor As Color
    Public backcolor As Color

    ' Update: There's no graphics path on pocket PC
    ' So we draw a solid rectangle with a border
    Public Sub Show(Graph As Graphics)
        ' Draw the square
        Graph.FillRectangle(New Drawing.SolidBrush(backcolor), _
                        location.X, location.Y, _
                        size.Width, size.Height)
        ' Draw the square border
        Graph.DrawRectangle(New Pen(forecolor), _
                        location.X, location.Y, _
                        size.Width - 1, size.Height - 1)
    End Sub
```

```
    Public Sub Hide(Graph As Graphics)
        Dim rectSquare As Rectangle
        ' Since we are working in a solid background, we can just draw a solid
        ' rectangle in order to "hide" the current square
        rectSquare = New Rectangle(location.X, location.Y, _
                                    size.Width, size.Height)
        Graph.FillRectangle(New SolidBrush(ClsGameField.backcolor), rectSquare)
    End Sub

    Public Sub New(InitialSize As size, InitialBackcolor As Color, _
                    InitialForecolor As Color)
        size = InitialSize
        backcolor = InitialBackcolor
        forecolor = InitialForecolor
    End Sub
End Class
```

In the next section, we'll present the modifications we need to make to the Block class.

## Updating the Block Class

The block class has more than 300 lines of code, including eight methods, two enumerations, and a bunch of properties. Since everything is well organized, all we need to update is the two methods that draw and hide a block, so they will receive a Graphics object as a parameter and use this object when calling the corresponding methods of the Square class. The following code listing presents the new code for these methods:

```
' Draw each square of the block on the game field
Public Sub Show(Graph As Graphics)
    ' Update to Pocket PC: Show method now receives a graphics object
    square1.Show(Graph)
    square2.Show(Graph)
    square3.Show(Graph)
    square4.Show(Graph)
End Sub

' Hide each square of the block on the game field
Public Sub Hide(Graph As Graphics)
    ' Update to Pocket PC: Hide method now receives a graphics object
    square1.Hide(Graph)
```

```
    square2.Hide(Graph)
    square3.Hide(Graph)
    square4.Hide(Graph)
End Sub
```

Besides these modifications, we need to change the calls for these methods inside the Rotate, Down, Left, and Right methods, passing the Graphics object from the GameField class, as illustrated in the next code line:

```
Show(ClsGameField.GraphBackground)
```

With these simple updates, the porting of our Block class is complete. Note that the entire collision detection algorithm (implemented in the Down, Left, and Right methods) and the complicated logic in the Rotate method doesn't need to be updated.

In the next section we'll discuss the updates needed to the main game form.

## Updating the Game Form

After updating the game classes, we'll need to modify the game form to adapt to these updates.

We'll need to update the form Load event, the Click event of the Start button, and the Tick event of the timer. Besides these changes, we'll have to add code for the extra interface buttons we created for the Pocket PC version.

Let's look at each of these updates in detail.

Starting with the form's Load event, we need to include a call to the Initialize method of the GameEngine class so the back buffers will be created as well as the Graphics objects for them and for the form, as presented in the next piece of code:

```
' Update to Pocket PC: The initialize function will create the
'    buffers and Graphics objects used to draw on the screen
ClsGameField.Initialize(Me, PicBackground, PicNextBlock)
```

To update the Start button code, we'll need to replace the call to the Invalidate method of the pictureBoxes on the form (which was used to clean the screen when starting a new game) to a call to the Clear method of the GameEngine class, which explicitly cleans the images by drawing a black rectangle on them.

We'll also have to update the call to the Show method of the blocks to use the correct parameters, and call the Invalidate method of the pictureBoxes that will commit the drawings to screen.

The final code for the Click event of the Start button is presented in the following code listing:

```
Sub CmdStart_Click(sender As Object, e As EventArgs) Handles cmdStart.Click
    TmrGameClock.Enabled = True
    cmdStart.Enabled = False
    LblScoreValue.Text = 0

    ' Clean the collisions control array
    ClsGameField.Reset()
    ' Clean the game field
    ' Update to Pocket PC: we must draw the blank screen, instead of simply
    '   invalidating a picture box image
    ClsGameField.Clear()

    ' Create and show the current and next blocks
    CurrentBlock = New clsBlock(New Point(ClsGameField.SquareSize * 6, 50))
    CurrentBlock.Show(ClsGameField.GraphBackground)
    NextBlock = New clsBlock(New Point(20, 10))
    NextBlock.Show(ClsGameField.GraphNextBlock)

    ' Refresh everything (updating the screen)
    PicBackground.Invalidate()
    PicNextBlock.Invalidate()
End Sub
```

In the Tick event of the timer, we'll do the same updates as we did in the preceding listing: Replace the call to the pictureBox Invalidate method to a call to the new GameEngine Clear method and update any calls to the Show and Hide methods of the Block class to pass the correct parameters.

The full code of the Tick event is presented in the following code segment. The updates in the code are marked with the comment "Update to Pocket PC":

```
Sub tmrGameClock_Tick(sender As Object, e As EventArgs) Handles TmrGameClock.Tick
    Static stillProcessing As Boolean = False
    Dim ErasedLines As Integer

    Try
        ' Prevent the code from running if the previous tick
        '   is still being processed
        If stillProcessing Then Exit Sub
        stillProcessing = True
```

```vb
        ' Control the block falling
        If Not CurrentBlock.Down() Then
            ' Test for game over
            If CurrentBlock.Top = 0 Then
                TmrGameClock.Enabled = False
                cmdStart.Enabled = True
                ' Update to Pocket PC  - Different parameters
                '    on the MessageBox Show Method
                MessageBox.Show("GAME OVER", ".NetTrix", _
                    MessageBoxButtons.OK, MessageBoxIcon.Hand, _
                    MessageBoxDefaultButton.Button1)
                stillProcessing = False
                Exit Sub
            End If
            ' Increase the score using the number of deleted lines, if any
            ErasedLines = ClsGameField.CheckLines()
            LblScoreValue.Text += 100 * ErasedLines
            ' Clear the game field
            If ErasedLines > 0 Then
                ' Update to Pocket PC  - Clear method
                ClsGameField.Clear()
                ClsGameField.Redraw()
            End If
            ' Release the current block from memory
            CurrentBlock = Nothing
            ' Create the new current block
            CurrentBlock = New clsBlock(New Point(ClsGameField.SquareSize * 6, _
                                    0), NextBlock.BlockType)
            CurrentBlock.Show(ClsGameField.GraphBackground)
            ' Release the next block from memory
            NextBlock.Hide(ClsGameField.GraphNextBlock)
            NextBlock = Nothing
            ' Create the new next block
            NextBlock = New clsBlock(New Point(20, 10))
            NextBlock.Show(ClsGameField.GraphNextBlock)
        End If
        ' Update to Pocket PC  - use of invalidate to redraw the screen
        ' Refresh the screen
        PicBackground.Invalidate()

        stillProcessing = False
    Catch ex As Exception
        MessageBox.Show(ex.Message)
    End Try
End Sub
```

In Figure 9, we can see the result of the updates: The game is already ready to play.

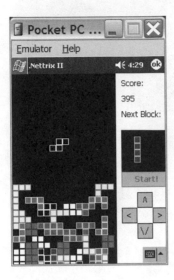

*Figure 9. With just a few updates, here is .Nettrix II.*

The final update to our code is to include the event handlers for the new buttons we have created, named cmdUp, cmdDown, cmdLeft, and cmdRight. The code for these buttons is very straightforward—just call the corresponding methods of the currentBlock variable as we did with the KeyPress event (coded in Chapter 1, and used without any updates in this version of the game).

The next code listing shows the code for the four buttons:

```
Sub cmdUp_Click(sender As Object, e As EventArgs) Handles cmdUp.Click
    CurrentBlock.Rotate()
End Sub

Sub cmdDown_Click(sender As Object, e As EventArgs) Handles cmdDown.Click
    CurrentBlock.Down()
End Sub

Sub cmdRight_Click(sender As Object, e As EventArgs) Handles cmdRight.Click
    CurrentBlock.Right()
End Sub

Sub cmdLeft_Click(sender As Object, e As EventArgs) Handles cmdLeft.Click
    CurrentBlock.Left()
End Sub
```

The KeyPress event, as we said before, won't need any updates. We can leave it on the form so that players can eventually play with the navigation keys when using a keyboard attached to the mobile device.

Now we can run our game and play .Nettrix II on the emulator or on a real device, as depicted in Figure 10.

*Figure 10. Our game is working well, and we have reached "Game Over."*

This is all we need to do to create a mobile version of our game. In the next section we'll look at some fine-tuning.

## Adding the Final Touches

Given the sample game's simplicity, there is little room for improvement in this chapter, but we can always add some extra touches to our games to improve playability.

In this chapter's sample game, after playing a few dozen times, we feel that using the Pocket PC buttons interface is not as simple as using a keyboard, since on a keyboard we can use more than one finger at once on the navigation keys to control the blocks.

We can't solve this issue, but we can increase the game rewards so players will feel more comfortable with the scoring, even if they don't manage to clear many lines. To do this, we'll improve the score counting to add 5 points to the score for each block dropped. Referring back to Chapter 1, recall that the game score only increased when a line is filled (up to 100 points per line); including these extra rewards will make the game more addictive.

In the code, all we need to do is to include one more line of code inside the If block of the Tick event that tests for collisions, as presented in the following code snippet:

```
If Not CurrentBlock.Down() Then
    ' Increase 5 points on the score for each block drop
    lblScoreValue.Text += 5
    . . .
```

And that's all for this chapter's sample game!

## Summary

In this bonus chapter, we presented a simple example that shows how to port a GDI+-based game to another platform—in this case, a Pocket PC.

Although this chapter doesn't go through all the possible issues you can face when porting a game, it provides at least a good example of each of the error classes we discussed:

- Compilation errors due to modifications in the function or event interfaces

- Compilation errors due to missing functions and events in the target platform

- Runtime errors due to differences in the behavior of compatible functions or object initialization

- Program malfunctioning in which there are no visible errors, but the program doesn't work as expected due to slightly different behavior in compatible functions

One of the most interesting details about this migration is that once we have migrated the code to Pocket PC, we can copy all the code back to the desktop .Nettrix project, and it will run without any modifications. After the updates, the code becomes 100 percent compatible between the two platforms—and, since the Pocket PC version was optimized, copying it back will lead to a better .Nettrix game for the desktop, too, with faster code and drawing routines.

# APPENDIX A

# The State of PC Gaming

IN THIS APPENDIX we have an article by Paul Sullivan that gives a clear and critical view of the game industry and where it is going. This article is a must for anyone interested in creating games. The article was first published in 2001 at the FiringSquad site (http://firingsquad.gamers.com), and is reproduced here with the permission of the author.

## The Current State of PC Gaming

### Introduction

When you walk into your favorite computer or electronics store, what kind of physical setup do you see in the PC gaming section? Most likely, you will see rows of largish boxes with all sorts of eye-catching colors and titles just sitting there, mockingly begging you to throw your money at them.

The promotional information on those boxes promise all kinds of ground-breaking fun that certainly "redefines the genre," and some even sport quotes from industry heavies praising the devastating awesomeness that the game brings to the table. Potential buyers are bombarded by all of this promotional hype not only on the boxes, but in the popular gaming magazines and web sites as well.

As you step back to ponder and start to pay even closer attention, you begin to realize some fundamental truths. Many of the games that make it onto the shelves are backed by huge publishing companies. Many of these companies buy tons of advertising to promote their new releases in an effort to make the public aware of them.

In fact, the more you think about it, the more you realize that modern day game production and promotion is starting to look like the Hollywood movie industry. Promotion is less about the actual plot and the gameplay and more about creating buzz around the product by highlighting certain features, like the graphics engine or the big name development talent working on the title.

Remember American McGee's Alice? When the industry started hearing about it, it was all about a well-known story, Alice in Wonderland, being twisted to fit the vision of one of the biggest names in the industry: American McGee. He was one of the id luminaries behind the Doom and Quake franchises and was well regarded by fans of those series. Much of the early hype seemed to focus on just how cool Alice could look when it was made using the incredible Quake III Arena engine, which fellow Doomer John Carmack created. Imagine the minds of two Doom alumni brought together on a new engine with a new concept.

Only when you started digging deeper did you find elements of the story and the gameplay. Much to his credit, American McGee fought mega publisher Electronic Arts on the idea of putting his name in the title of the game. From the press reports, it looked like he was more interested in focusing on the game itself and not on the personalities involved. He also seemed to make it clear that he wanted to use the Q3A engine not because it was hyped up in the press, but because it was powerful and flexible enough to help him realize his vision for the look of the game itself. His intentions seemed honorable and true to the gamers he hoped to serve.

## Compromises in Development

### Ads, Reviews, Super Bowl Spots

Unfortunately, when the big marketing engine revs up, it is sometimes very hard to bring it back down to idle. In the end, the game was finally released and viewed by the public. When you took a good crack at playing the title, you could see so much potential in the game itself, but somehow it felt like it was not quite finished and lacked some of the magical visionary polish that you had anticipated. The graphics were at times stunning, but somewhat inconsistent. Some of the textures looked incredible, while others looked bland. Some of the levels were truly inspired, while others seemed like nothing more than a fairly complex jump puzzle that seemed to end earlier than it should. Some felt that the $50 they spent was a bit much for what they got.

To this day, American McGee should be applauded for his drive to get this work in the hands of gamers, but some may always remember it in a "what could have been" type of way. Impressions were that somewhere along the way, the big guns stepped in and started to push the marketing angle more than the actual quality of the gameplay experience.

EA eventually pressured McGee to put his name on the title, even though he still fought the idea for the reasons stated earlier. They seemed to be more worried about getting the product out the door as fast as they could with as much marketing buzz as possible and less interested in releasing the title when the game would actually be finished according to McGee's original vision and attention to detail.

© 2000 Electronic Arts Inc.

*Figure A-1. Alice*

© 2000 Electronic Arts Inc.

*Figure A-2. Scary? Maybe . . . Big? Yeah.*

## What Does Everyone Want?

Unfortunately, for developers all over the world, it seems that in today's computer gaming market you have to make some sacrifices to get your product made. Development is becoming increasing complex, and thus prohibitively expensive, and you need big backers with very deep pockets to get the product completed. In order to keep those backers happy, you may have to give up some of your creative control and scale back your vision, which means in the end, your product may not be all that you wanted it to be.

Thinking about all of this seems to evoke some basic questions: What do gamers want and expect, and what do publishers want and expect? The rest of this article looks at the gaming market from a variety of perspectives in an effort to see what actually happens out there and perhaps find some answers to those questions.

# The Consumer World

## *The Consumer Side: Value and Gameplay*

Gamers can be a fickle lot, but in spite of that fact, there are some fundamental truths that seem to exist. Gamers like value and gamers like good gameplay. Many of them don't care how flashy a title might be—if it costs too much and doesn't deliver the goods, they will avoid it like the plague.

Most consumers want a game that they can get into without too much hassle. They want a game that plays in a way that they are familiar with and make sense to them. They want to be able to sit down, open the game and start having fun without worrying about DirectX or OpenGL, without worrying about installing extra video codecs, reconfiguring their hardware or upgrading drivers.

Even so, consumers realize that sometimes you cannot have everything you want. They feel that if these game developers are going to force them to jump through all of these hoops, those developers had better make sure that the product ends up giving gamers one heck of a ride for the money. The problem is, many finished products don't even come close.

## *When the Move to 3D Goes Wrong*

Let's look at a few simple examples. Remember Earthworm Jim? This simple and fun 2D scroller was incredibly popular on the PC and spawned follow-up versions that also did well. But then, somebody on the development side had this brilliant idea that they needed to respond to the exciting new trend of 3D environments. I mean, if people were going nuts over Quake and Unreal, they would go crazy to have Earthworm Jim in 3D right? Wrong. Earthworm Jim 3D was an unmitigated disaster. The price was not too high so people went ahead and gave it a try, but word of mouth quickly killed any chance it had to be a real hit. Gameplay was too different and too hard compared to the simple but highly effective 2D world that Jim had previously inhabited.

The same thing happened with Lode Runner and Lemmings when they tried to go 3D. People simply decided that the games were too different and too hard to get used to (at least in comparison to their satisfyingly simple predecessors), so even though they were not very expensive, they were shunned. The Lemmings folks came back with a hybrid product that worked pretty well, one in which you were still in a 2D environment that looked 3D, but by then the damage had been done.

What had the developers done wrong? They forgot that it is all about the gameplay. Just because a title is inexpensive does not mean it will be a hit. Well, who did it right then? The folks that made Frogger 3D and Frogger 2: Swampy's Revenge. They took advantage of the nostalgia angle to get their foot in the door and even though the first Frogger 3D was a buggy mess, people fell all over it. Why? Because it played like they expected it to play, even though it was in 3D. It was about hopping back and forth, side to side, dodging the bad guys. You had a view that was only slightly modified from a strict top-down look, and that meant people could control it pretty easily. For Joe Schmoe, Swampy's Revenge added some very cool visual effects and incredible colors and 3D shapes, but preserved the gameplay that made it a video game classic.

## High- and Low-End Consumers

### Battle of the Titans

Why did Unreal Tournament outduel Quake 3 Arena in sales and customer satisfaction? Many speculate that the reason was because the focus in Q3A was more on the graphics and the engine than the actual gameplay. Even though Unreal Tournament had an older, arguably less-capable engine, flat textures and odd colored lighting, it gave you more bang for your buck in terms of gameplay. Capture the Flag, Domination, Assault—it was just more fun to play for many people. It had more gameplay modes and weapons that were more balanced and better thought out.

Yes, Quake 3 Arena had incredible model and animation, introduced shaders and texture modifiers, and insanely high-polygon curved surfaces, but for many, it was just plain old Deathmatch. If it had not been for the massive hype and extreme devotion of the hardcore audience of Quake fans, it would not have sold nearly as well as it did. id software had built a lot of goodwill with their earlier efforts and people expected that anything they produced would be among the best. Unreal Tournament on the other hand had the legacy of a buggy first release but unanimously made up for it with a focus on different gameplay, did quite well because of it. Eventually, word of mouth is what made UT outsell Q3A, and that is a lesson that developers should pay attention to.

Quake® is a trademark of Id Software.

*Figure A-3. Q3A had the graphics . . .*

©1999 - 2001 Epic Games Inc.

*Figure A-4. UT had the gameplay modes*

## And Then the Flipside . . .

Another question developers should ask themselves is, "Why do consumers buy these inexpensive retreads like Deer Hunter and Who Wants To Be A Millionaire?" They don't have fancy cutting edge graphics and killer sound engines, but people are snapping them up like crazy. The answers are pretty simple.

First, they are almost always less than $30, which seems to be the magic number for consumers. They feel a whole lot better about dishing out $29 than $39–$49. It seems to be a psychological barrier. Even though many consumers can afford more than $20 or $30, they are out of their comfort zone past that point. It is harder for them to justify mentally. Why do people drive 50 extra miles to save 10 cents a gallon on gas?

Second, they offer up heaps of "good old fashioned" fun. They are easy to play and easy to enjoy, and that is really what computer games are supposed to be about. Entertainment is the focus on these titles, and that is one of the reasons they sell so well.

Above all, these titles are marketed perfectly to their demographic. Deer Hunter is sold at every Walmart, and while computers may be popping up in more homes than ever, most of them could not be considered state of the art. A fully 3D, realistic Deer Hunter would not have sold nearly as well due to the system requirements alone, and as popular as the show is, nobody wants a 3D Regis with full surround sound.

The bottom line is that so many gamers out there like to buy things they can play in a fun, predictable manner. They seldom have the time or energy to invest in a new gaming paradigm. Why do you think that classics like Space Invaders and Asteroids still sell well? They don't want to shell out $50 for a pretty game that is hard to play and not much fun to boot.

## Planet Industry

### *The Industry Side: Originality vs. Practicality*

The industry side is a hard one to figure out. Small gaming companies seem to be the closest to the actual PC gaming community, but have a hard time getting their products to market. Why? It takes some serious dollars to obtain shelf space in the computer super stores. It takes even more money to buy advertising to get your product noticed. It is like the small mom and pop store going up against Walmart. Chances are that unless you have a top-notch product and some seriously good word of mouth, consumers are going to go for the cheaper or better-advertised products every time. Why? See the part about being fickle in the earlier section.

So what is the industry supposed to do? They are faced with two primary options: Push the envelope and bring out new games based on new technology and ideas or play it safe and take the practical approach by releasing games based on established franchises and technologies. Either way they go, it seems that they get criticized.

If you take a look at the games on the shelves, you will see a lot of sequels. Quake 3 Arena, Sim City 3000, Caesar III, Chessmaster 8000 and many, many more. Some of these introduce new technology, like Q3A, but most focus on expanding an existing hit concept into another iteration. Chessmaster 8000 focused on smoother graphics, more chess sets, improved AI (artificial intelligence) and internet gaming. Sim City 3000 increased resolution, added more features and tightened up the user interface. This practical approach is very sound in terms the business—if it ain't broke, don't fix it.

## Take It Slow and Steady

Some games already have an established history and identity, so you can build upon that and save the extra money of creating a totally new brand. If you stick close to the same formula, you have a better chance that you will not alienate fans of the earlier releases. You can spend your time and resources addressing the concerns that players expressed with the previous games to bring them more of what they already love. You can ride this franchise to help build the bottom line, and at the same time please the gamers you worked so hard to cultivate in the first place. You not only release sequels, but expansion packs as well, to help wring even more out of the same audience. As long as the gamers are happy and the stockholders are happy, nobody's getting hurt, right?

But sometimes you have the chance to push the envelope and possibly come up with the next big thing. Franchises don't last forever, and new ideas are crucial to keeping the bottom line strong. This is a much riskier strategy, however, because it is hard to tell what gamers are willing to do when it comes to making a purchase. Take a look at a few recent titles for instance.

Clive Barker's Undying was by all accounts an incredibly good game. It used the Unreal engine very well, had a great story, impressive sound and visuals. It had a big name smack on the box and a fair amount of promotion. How could it possibly go wrong? Feedback seems to indicate that the game was just too hard to play for some, and for others who were weaned on Quake, it was too slow and involved. You have a company pushing hard to make a quality game, and they are rebuffed by their own customers.

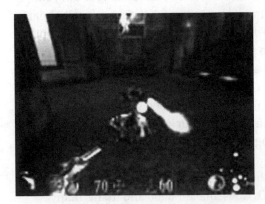

© 2000 Electronic Arts Inc.

*Figure A-5. Undying had graphics . . .*

© 2000 Electronic Arts Inc.

*Figure A-6. And refreshing gameplay*

## ReTread Lightly

### Take 2, 3, 4 . . .

Not every game can be a home run, but what happened here is that the developers took their eye off the ball. Pretty cut-scenes and a creepy atmosphere are not enough to satisfy this MTV generation. They are used to 3D shooters with fast and furious gameplay and simple objectives. Maybe it is not fair that this game was pigeonholed into the 3D shooter genre, but consumers do not always have the energy to bother discerning between shades of gray. A 3D shooter is supposed to play like a 3D shooter. Who wants to have to reload a pistol every 6 shots and actually think about using the tools at hand to get the results you want? After all, that is what RPG's (role playing games) are for, right?

Diablo caught the industry by storm. So did Myst. Both sold well and continue to do so. Why bother taking chances when you can just go with the flow. When other games were focused on interactive 3D worlds and very high resolutions, these games stuck to the basics and made tons of money while keeping fans happy. Diablo was easy to play, did not require a ton of complex inventory controls and had simple objectives. Myst had great looking 2D pictures, a very simple interface and fun puzzles. Neither had a particularly deep and meaningful story, but that was really not needed. What mattered is that once people got into the game, they had fun playing it.

### Who Did It Well?

Diablo had a hugely successful add-on pack that convinced the industry to keep doing more of the same. They worked for years on Diablo 2 and when it came out it was a HUGE smash. Did it have an incredible new high-resolution 3D engine?

No. Did it have groundbreaking new levels? No. What did it have? More of the same—and that is all gamers really wanted. Sure, they made adjustments, but on balance, Diablo 2 is a lot like the original. Online play is improved and the world may be a bit more complex, but not that much. Certainly not enough to alienate players. Blizzard asked gamers what they wanted, and they listened to the answers. It worked out great for everyone. The Myst franchise did the same thing. Riven was a smash, and the new Myst III is selling like crazy. Some formulas just work.

Perhaps the single largest example of this "retread" idea is the Tomb Raider series. Critics decry it as unoriginal, but gamers keep on forking out the cash for the new releases because they liked what the first one had to offer. It is so popular it has even become a major motion picture. The old adage "Keep it Simple Stupid" sure seems to apply here. Eidos kept cranking out tweaked versions until the franchise ran out of steam, and made millions in the process. Well, that's great for Eidos, but not quite so for the early adopters who are looking for the "next big thing."

Take the case of the famous and talented John Carmack, engine developer at id software. He is one of the best advocates for pushing technology forward that the industry has ever seen. But he has gotten a great deal of criticism for focusing more on the technology than on the gameplay. Most people agree that Quake 3 Arena is a technological marvel, but many critics point out that the game itself is uninspired and unoriginal. His work on Doom 3 will likely be some of the best code ever written for a gaming engine. But already people are starting to decry the system requirements. If they are not able to run at 100 frames per second in their hardcore shooter, they just are not happy at all. From the industry side, it sure looks that you are damned if you do and damned if you don't.

So how are you supposed to know what the smart move is? That is where good old facts and data come into play.

## Analyzing Market Trends

### The Technical Side: Facts, Data, and Commentary

This is an opinion piece, but it is also based on good old facts and data. The web was scoured to find as much raw data as was needed to back it up. Data companies have charged between $4500 and $7000 for single data reports in the past, and as a result, custom reports have not been readily available.

The selected sampling of data gave a good idea of what PC gamers have purchased in the past. The data came from the largest gatherer around: NPD Intellect (formerly PC Data). The hard work they have done to provide gaming sites with sales data has been invaluable to many sites and print publications.

To start things out we looked at the data from 1998. Instead of capturing a one week sales period, the decision was made to use an entire year to create a firm foundation to build upon.

The 10 best-selling PC games of 1998 (full year) were:

1. Starcraft

2. Deer Hunter

3. Deer Hunter 2

4. Myst

5. Big Game Hunter

6. Titanic: Adventure Out of Time

7. Lego Island

8. Frogger

9. Riven: The Sequel to Myst

10. Unreal

Starcraft was an RTS made by the same company as the incredibly popular Warcraft II (and was also berated at the time for not moving to 3D graphics). Deer Hunter and Deer Hunter 2 were both low cost, simple games that were fun to play. Myst was a 2D puzzle game with great graphics that the whole family could play. Big Game Hunter was along the lines of the Deer Hunter franchise and was also in the low-cost arena. Titanic was here due to the hype of the movie more than anything else. Lego Island was a popular low-cost family game, as was the Frogger remake. Riven was the well-received sequel to Myst and Unreal was a more colorful version of the ubiquitous first person shooter that focused more on single player than anything else. Unreal was buggy, but people liked it because it pushed things along in the single player arena when most other 3D games were leaning heavily towards multiplayer deathmatch.

With a full year of data as a base, looking at weekly sales data seemed the logical choice. This weekly look focused attention on trends or promotions and also showed which titles had a long lasting life to them. Star Wars Episode 1 was released in movie theaters during this time, for instance.

The 10 best-selling PC games for the week of May 16–22, 1999:

1.  Star Wars Episode 1

2.  Star Wars Episode 1 Racer

3.  Baldur's Gate: Tales of Sword Coast

4.  Total Annihilation

5.  Big Game Hunter 2

6.  Sim City 3000

7.  Baldur's Gate

8.  Civilization: Call To Power

9.  Roller Coaster Tycoon

10.  Half Life

As the data showed, trends were starting to become readily apparent. As with Titanic, the games with movie tie-ins did well. Baldur's Gate and its expansion pack were hot, as were the sequels Big Game Hunter 2 and Sim City 3000. Known quantities sold well, but the last spot showed a new entry, Valve's Half Life, which took some serious chances by adding a story and some atmosphere to the first person shooter genre. Roller Coaster Tycoon was another sim-style game that was familiar to gamers and did not push beyond their comfort level.

# The Data Explained

## *Has Anything Changed?*

We moved ahead to the new millennium to see what changed. Another trend showed itself here, with the explosive popularity of the Regis Philbin vehicle Who Wants To Be A Millionaire. This ABC show captured the minds of viewers, but just how well will did it hold up?

The 10 best-selling PC games for the week of May 14–20, 2000:

1. Who Wants To Be A Millionaire: 2nd Edition

2. The Sims

3. Roller Coaster Tycoon

4. Age of Empires II: Age of Kings

5. Who Wants To Be A Millionaire

6. EverQuest: Ruins of Kunark

7. Starcraft

8. Roller Coaster Tycoon: Corkscrew Follies

9. SimCity 3000 Unlimited

10. Sim Mania Pack

Millionaire was a tie-in to the very hot TV show and a game concept that people were familiar with. SimCity 3000 Unlimited was a spruced up refresh of the SimCity 3000 game, which was in itself a sequel to SimCity and SimCity 2000. Roller Coaster Tycoon was back, as was its add-on pack, which was repeated with the Sims franchise. Familiar names and concepts were clearly obvious.

Our last weekly grab was from last month. Some titles faded, others remained. It was hard to piece it all together at times, but luckily we had even more data from the same source.

The 10 best-selling PC games for the week of July 15–21, 2001:

1.  Diablo II: Lord of Destruction

2.  Flight Simulator 2000

3.  The Sims

4.  The Sims: House Party

5.  Diablo II

6.  Roller Coaster Tycoon

7.  The Sims: Livin' Large

8.  Mech Commander 2

9.  Age of Empires II: Age of Kings

10. Tribes 2

As you can see, the Sims franchise was going very strong, as was Diablo II and the expansion pack. Sequels were the norm here, that was for sure. Even though Roller Coaster Tycoon was not really a sequel, it was a sim genre game, and again, one that people were comfortable with.

To give you some overall perspective, we took a look at the best-selling PC games in history, all of those years included.

The 10 best-selling PC games of all time were:

1.  Myst

2.  Roller Coaster Tycoon

3.  The Sims

4.  Flight Simulator

5.  Who Wants To Be A Millionaire

6.  Riven: The Sequel to Myst

7.  Age of Empires II: Age of Kings

8. Monopoly

9. Lego Island

10. Diablo

Franchises absolutely dominated the charts. Monopoly sold very well, another game that people were familiar with. Lego Island was a similar happening, and both were low-cost family titles. The list was somewhat surprising in that it mixed genres and old school verses new school ideas, but nobody could doubt the effectiveness of these titles.

From the data collected, there were some obvious patterns. Even though a few A+ titles made it into the mix, consistently it was the basics that most consumers were willing to pay for. Value was important, which was obvious by the inclusion of lower cost, lower technology titles. But if the data was extrapolated a bit more, it could be seen that familiarity was very important to consumers. Groundbreaking games like System Shock and Thief were not among the best sellers, while unsophisticated but well-understood titles like Monopoly and Lego Island were. Riven was little more than a retread, but it was still the sixth best-selling game of all time. Who Wants To Be A Millionaire was a surprising entry—a trend with legs.

With the exception of the tie-ins to movies and TV, most of the games people purchased were the ones that they knew and were comfortable with. Monopoly was fun to play and a game that consumers grew up with. Diablo was certainly not the most hardcore RPG around, but again, it was fun and easy to play. "God" type games were a big hit as well. People have historically liked to build and tinker with worlds of their own, and as the Reality TV trend has shown, many consumers have been long-term voyeurs at heart. Based upon all of this research, if you had represented a big gaming company and needed to show a profit, what kind of games would you have produced?

# Conclusion and Suggestions

## Final Thoughts from an Avid Gamer

If you're a gamer, you need to vote with your wallet and express your opinions. Buy the good games and write letters (yes, actual letters) to developers telling them exactly what you liked, and what you want. Let them know that you want more than just another number tacked onto the end of the title, or more colors and textures pasted over the same game. In short, take the time to get involved. On the flip side, if you are a developer, you need to listen to your customers. Encourage them to contact you and share their ideas. Ask for their feedback and suggestions. After all, these are the people who are going to be spending their hard-earned dollars on your product. As with any relationship, if you want it to work you have to put some serious effort into communicating with each other.

Remember back in the day when shareware was such a hot concept? Four or five guys would work on a game, and during development they would release playable snippets that could be downloaded from bulletin boards and played for free by the masses. These unwashed, caffeine-hopped college students would play these low resolution tidbits for hours and give the programmers some feedback on what they liked and what they didn't. The developers would take these comments, make some changes and release more snippets. The cycle would continue until they could release Episode 1 of the mighty adventure as shareware. If you liked what you saw, you ordered and paid for Episodes 2 and 3. It was a total win-win situation for everyone involved. It was a collaborative effort that helped make huge companies out of id and Epic and many others.

As it stands now, big companies spend years developing a game and only after it is done do they bother releasing the demo. How are you supposed to get and incorporate useful feedback from your audience if you don't include them in the process? Why wait until after the game is finished and the demo is out? If it turns out the game is bad, all that money may have been wasted. If you had bothered to communicate with your audience beforehand, you could have made changes and tweaks during development so that the game ended up being the type of release that gamers are willing to spend their money on. By waiting until the game is finished, you are stuck with the end result, unable to take a step back and rework it.

On the other hand, responsibility lies with gamers too. You want good games? Let the developers know what you like and by all means, pay for the games that deserve to be paid for. Don't keep pirating titles and hope that these developers will be able to stay in business. It is not fair to anybody. Don't let apathy take over either. If you are passionate about your games, put your money where your mouth is and start kicking out the cash. Lick some stamps and mail some letters to the developers and tell them why you felt that game was worth the money. Conversely, if you are let down, let them know why and give your suggestions on how you would have done things differently.

If developers and gamers work together as a team and keep the lines of communication open, we are all sure to end up winners in the long run.

# Motivations in Games

THIS APPENDIX FEATURES an article by Sarbasst Hassanpour, UI/game designer at MindArk (developer of the upcoming Project-Entropia), discussing one of the most important things to know when developing a game: how to keep a player interested in your game. The article was first published in 2001, at the GameDev.Net Web site (http://www.gamedev.net), and is reproduced here with the permission of the author.

## Motivations in Games

Hi everyone. I'll try to bring forward some of the elements that bind people to a game for hours and days. These elements can be used to create a game or application that motivates the user to use/play it. Think of it, an educational game that the kids at school will enjoy and learn from, or of course a game of games!

Now this is not the almighty recipe for creating the captivating game of the year, but some of these elements are often overlooked. And that's a shame.

The elements are:

- Reward

- Competition and comparison with others

- Anticipation

- Participant-ship

- Tempo

- The Grand Ending

## Reward

There are many different levels of rewarding, and they are related to one another. If you achieve the right balance of rewarding, depending on your game goal and type, you will succeed in capturing the player. Now that, my friend, is a bold statement.

Let's look at this as some rules within a specific time span, say between two character levels, or between the first upgrade and the second.

First the different aspects, and then some more comments on each.

- The player needs to be rewarded often and in small portions.

- The player needs to be rewarded with a greater reward that is expected and the time of the reward is **known**.

- The player needs to be rewarded with a greater reward that is expected but the time of the reward is **unknown**.

### Smaller and Often

If the smaller rewards are useful in some way they will not become routine and needless. If you give the player a healing, it is useful to the powerful and novice. But if you reward with a great flashy effect, it will lose its strength along the way. You are quite safe if you make the small rewards lead to a greater reward, e.g., money, experience for leveling, points for extra life, and so on.

### Greater and Known Occurrence

This is something the player will anticipate and strive to achieve. She can see the goal as she progresses towards it. There could be many known goals. There is nothing wrong with giving away a lot of goals to give the player the thrill of imagining what to do and how to get to them, as well as dreaming of different combinations and so on. But remember, once you give away a greater reward the smaller rewards will mean a little less.

Example: The leveling of a character or skill tree and descriptions of skills and their cost.

Example: The different items the player could buy if he had the cash.

## Greater and Unknown Occurrence

When the player has a chance of getting a greater reward and it could come anytime, the anticipation is always there, and in the times of gloom there is always a hope of getting some reward. This hope can save the day many a time. Remember though, the player needs to know about the rewards and expect them, but their trigger could be anytime within the rules.

Example: Every time you defeat a spaceship you could get an "ancient artifact."

Example: Every trader could have a "crystal sword," but the chances are very low.

Example: If you kill an orc, you might find a "steel claw" if you are lucky.

## The Relations Between the Rewards

Ah, the most interesting part! One should first focus on the goal and type of the game. Is it to be replayed a lot of times or more like "play it, have an experience, and then put it on the shelf"? Should the same game (not replaying it) be able to be played a long time?

If the player becomes too powerful due to the rewards, the game will have a climax, and then the game cannot beat what it has previously given the player. Thus the game will have reached its designed content limit. Designed content limit is not the same as the game limit. The player could play a lot of quests and content in general, but it's more like a walk in the park, and the next "level" of rewarding is not as important, or even unreasonably far away.

A very potent and time-cheap design method is to give the player a difficulty option or adapt the game by changing some colors and increasing the difficulty.

Never ever "steal" a greater reward given to the player, not even to make the game more exciting and/or harder. The frustration is exceptionally high, and the relationship (trust) between the player and the game will be crippled. If you decide to "steal" a greater reward, be sure to explain why the game did it.

Example: Never take a level from a character as a punishment or special event. If you do, tell the player why.

Always reward smart playing and creativity by the player. Sometimes the reward is automatic since it was probably the right way to play the game. As you all know, the right way to play a game doesn't necessarily mean the way the designer intended the game to be played. The majority of players are like water: They always find the natural way of flowing down the mountain. But what I'm talking about here is some designed content.

Example: If the player clicks on the well in the middle of the village, he doesn't have to purchase new water skins.

## Competition and Comparison

- If the player can be acknowledged by others, he will be motivated to continue and strive to perfection. This acknowledgement could be in the game or outside. Of course this is not applicable to everyone but to surprisingly many of us.

- Remember the example of rewarding with a flashy effect? Well, if the other players see the effect, and the player knows others can see it, it will have its strength every time the player is rewarded by it (that is, if others see it at that given time).

- If the player feels (is reminded) that she is getting better at the game, the motivation factor is increased also.

## Anticipation

Small, frequent hints about what is to come build anticipation and provide a very good way of building motivation. The important thing about anticipation is the trust between the player and the game. The player needs to be rewarded a few times to come to trust the game. Then a positive spiral is created and the player and the game will steadily climb to a memorable experience. Alas, beware, once the player is betrayed by the game, the relation has to be created all over again.

An example: The player has previously helped a village and the reward was a unique item and a nice story revelation. Before that he helped a little kid find his lost dog, and the reward was a very funny story and some very tasty candy. Now the player trusts the game.

If you give him a hint of some event, or a quest or whatever, the player will anticipate the ending and strive to achieve it. Also some hints here and there of the grand content of the game will lead to an ever present, underlying anticipation.

The hardest part is to reuse the material used for the anticipation.

Never, ever send a player on a quest/task without designing the harvest of her labors.

## Participant-ship

If the player feels that he is a part of the world and that he is affecting the course of events, the motivation to continue is greatly increased. Here we give the imagination of the player a chance to be one with the game world. The UI (user interface) is one of the important parts of this. If the UI is out of line, it will interfere with the "becoming one with the game" part.

A good example is when you are watching a movie and you are enthralled by it, and a friend asks you something. Now it will take you some time to get into the movie again. Think of a UI that shatters the flow of the game on every turn.

In addition, the player should not be hindered from using his abilities. For instance, if the player is very good at a fast 3D shooter with a really high speed, he will find himself limited when playing another 3D shooter which is slow. The problem in this example is hard to get around. Often the target group is chosen and the issue is solved. Still there are some given standards, and one should think twice before aiming lower than these standards, especially with a sequel.

## Tempo

The music, the environmental feel, and the action or tranquility of the game is the tempo. The important part is to change between fast/exciting and slow/relaxing. Otherwise each will lose its strength. The contrast is actually vital to uphold each extreme's meaning.

Even by itself the tempo can be very powerful in capturing the player for hours.

There is a lot to be learned from the movies industry. Did you know the best way to describe silence is to have a distant and small sound that reminds one of the silence? This could be something like a crow, a creaking door, and so on.

If you put the player in a very intense environment where she has to put her senses and skill to the test, you will need to give her some time in a calm and tranquil environment afterward so that she can rest. Also, the contrast will make her feel the intense environment fully (once it starts again).

## The Grand Ending

If the ending is very good the player will have a solid anticipation when she is playing your next game. Not only that, the ending is one of the things people tend to remember long after they have played the game. This is the final reward and the meaning of the game. This is where the meaning of the hours played will be revealed.

The ending is a very important part and actually often overlooked. One good method is to design the ending early in the development.

## Complex UI

If the players are motivated enough, you could have the most complex UI ever created. Now, I'm not saying that a complex UI design is the best way to go, but often a more simple design is used when a more complex one would be better.

A UI that is mastered by the player should not hinder his abilities to interact with the game. This means some slow method to achieve something will have to adapt to the skill of the player, providing a faster method later on. In the end the UI is almost "invisible."

An example: To choose a weapon the novice player will probably use a menu and see the actual weapons and so forth. But the expert will use the keyboard to do the same action. The keyboard is the final level of UI to achieve this purchasing of weapons.

Another one: A very advanced navigation system might require five frustrating hours to master, but in the end the gameplay will benefit from the rich environmental feeling, especially if navigation is a major part of the game (such as in space games).

The optimal approach is to provide the player a set of interfaces for different levels of mastery. The hard part is to make these sets work together and resemble each other, since the player might master one aspect of the interface (e.g., navigation) and not the rest. This sounds harder than it really is. All you have to do is to provide an alternative, faster way, even if it demands more from the player.

That's my silver coin.

Good Luck Champions!

—Sarbasst Hassanpour

# APPENDIX C

# How Do I Make Games?

In this appendix we have an article written by Geoff Howland that goes through the logical steps to becoming a better game programmer and other issues. The article was first published on 2001, on the Lupine Games site (http://www.lupinegames.com), and is reproduced here with the permission of the author.

## How Do I Make Games?—A Path to Game Development

When I talk to people looking to get into game development some of the first things I often hear fall along the lines of, "How do I make games?" or "I want to make a game like Quake/Everquest/Starcraft and . . ." The first is just way out of the realm of answerability, as there are too many aspects to possibly go into, and each of those components can be infinitely complex.

The second, however, falls into just being unrealistic in expectations. Starcraft, Everquest and Quake were all made by *teams* of professionals who had budgets usually million dollar plus. More importantly though, all of these games were made by people with a lot of experience at making games. They did not just decide to make games and turned out mega-hit games, they started out small and worked their way up. This is the point that anyone who is interested in getting into game development needs to understand and repeat, repeat, repeat until it becomes such a part of your mindset that you couldn't possibly understand life without this self evident, universal truth.

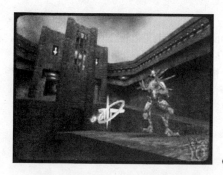

Quake® is a trademark of Id Software.

*Figure C-1. A screen shot from Quake 3: Arena*

Until you understand that all skills in game development are learned by experience, (meaning to start *very* small and working your way up) you will be absolutely doomed to never finish your projects. Even the infinitesimal number of teams that do manage to finish a non-trivial project before they have made any smaller ones have to learn incrementally, it just takes them many times longer than if they had started out with smaller projects.

## So Where Do I Start?

Tetris.
Tetris is the perfect game to begin your journey on the path to becoming an able bodied game developer. Why? Because Tetris contains the all the elements found in every game, and can be done with just about the least amount of work. Also, you don't have to be an artist to make a good looking Tetris game. Anyone who can draw a block, which is everyone with a paint program, can make a commercial quality version of Tetris.

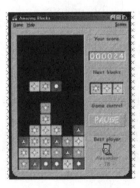

*Figure C-2. A tetris clone—Amazing Blocks*

This is another one of the big benefits of starting with Tetris. Not only can you make a fully functioning game that is fun and addictive, but it looks basically just as good as any commercial version done of it. Blocks are blocks no matter who draws them, and tetraminos (the shapes used in Tetris) are all just a collection of four blocks.

Tetris has all the individual components that ALL games share in common. It has a game loop (the process of repeating over and over until the game is quit). The game loop reads in input, processes the input, updates the elements of the game (the falling tetraminos), and checks for victory/loss conditions.

Every single game you will *ever* make does all of these things, so learning the process and actually implementing it is extremely important. After you have completed this the first time, it will give you an insight into how hard it will be and how long it may take on future games. Without having done this *all the way*, at least once, you will never fully have a proper grasp of each of the elements. When you have larger projects, there will be more unknowns that you can't judge for in complexity and time. If you don't even fully understand the entire process because you have failed to DO it, you will likely be helpless to create schedules or estimate times properly and will most likely not succeed at the endeavor.

Something I need to mention is that when you make your Tetris game, you can't call it "Tetris." Tetris is a trademark of the Tetris Company, which is owned by Alexey Pajitnov, the creator of Tetris. It is his exclusive right to use the name Tetris, and I believe they may have won a lawsuit saying that you cannot make a falling blocks game with the syllable "tris," as it is obviously playing off the popularity of the of the name Tetris.

However, this means nothing to you if you call your game "The Sky is Falling," or anything without a "tris" in it, as they do NOT own the gameplay, interface, or idea of falling blocks. If you hear anything differently from anyone, tell them you can't own ideas, and if you require further proof you can look up information on this subject at the USPTO (http://www.uspto.gov/).

## What's Next?

After you have totally, completely, absolutely finished your version Tetris, you are ready for your next challenge: Breakout.

Breakout is also a similar game, but it adds in much more advanced collision detection than was necessary in Tetris. You will also need to add some simple deflection physics of the ball rebounding off different portions of the paddle and the blocks.

Level layout also becomes an issue in Breakout, and in order to have more than one level you will need to come up with a way to save the maps. This deals with another component found in all larger games, which is saving and loading resources and switching levels.

After you finish your Breakout masterpiece you should move on to making Pac-Man. Pac-Man is an evolutionary step because it adds in the element of enemy artificial intelligence (AI). You may not have been aware of this, but in the original Pac-Man the four different ghosts had different goals to try to defeat you as a team. The aggressor would try to follow the shortest path to you, making you directly avoid him. The interceptor would try to go to a junction that was closest to where you would have to move to avoid the aggressor. A second interceptor would try to stay more towards the middle and try to cut you off from using the tunnel through the sides. The last ghost would sort of wander aimlessly about, which often kept him staying in a section you needed to finish the map.

This kind of detailed AI was quite advanced for games of that time, and should give you a good challenge for your first game with enemy AI.

Pac-Man also increases the complexity of maps, and adds a good deal more flexibility for using sounds, as sound was certainly a crucial element to the success of Pac-Man. (After all, what would Pac-Man be without some sort of "wakka-wakka" sound?)

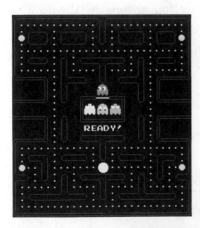

© 1980 Namco Ltd., All Rights Reserved.
Courtesy of Namco Holding Corp.

*Figure C-3. Pac-Man screen shot*

The last game I suggest you should create is a side scroller, such as Super Mario Brothers, where you can jump on multiple platforms, shoot, duck and interact with enemies. As there is added art involved in this game, I would suggest looking into using SpriteLib for some free and easy to use artwork, which is available at http://www.arifeldman.com/free/spritelib.html.

Side scrollers introduce the possibility of added enemy AI complexity through the use of enemy bosses which have patterns you must learn to beat, as well an added screen complexity. Now you must make a screen that is capable of scrolling in at least two directions, if not four, and deal with screen clipping, which can have a bit of a learning curve. You must also work on the physics of any jumping, bouncing of the character or shooting projectiles.

There will additionally need to be a lot more enemies than before, and you will need to keep track of their current game state (alive/dead, active/inactive), by whether they are on the screen or have already been dealt with. The level complexity and map/character storage complexity will have also increased and you will most certainly need to make a level editor at this point.

The level editor should be capable of placing tiles, scrolling through tiles, scrolling over the map, choosing tiles as brushes, cycling through the brushes, cutting and pasting, an undo, and placing enemies. If you decide to skip writing any of these, you will most likely feel sorry about it, and if you have an artist or level designer, they will probably not be very happy with you either (how would YOU feel if you had to go through someone's text files containing a bunch of numbers and commas to edit a level?). I would also suggest making back ups of previously saved maps, as it is often easier to just back things up by versions, than redrawing them.

Finally, the side scroller has a real victory condition! When you get to the end of the side scroller, you have actually GONE somewhere, so you can add on a story to progress through the game as well (and don't forget some sort of fireworks on the screen for the end of a level, so that the player has a sense of accomplishment and a REAL show of fireworks for beating the game . . . merely putting the words "You Have Won!" on the screen when a player has spent endless hours trying to beat your game is anti-climatic).

## Get Out the Polish . . .

Finishing a game does not merely mean you get it to a point where it is playable, and then move on—this is not a finished game. A finished game will have an opening screen, a closing screen, menu options (if applicable, at least instructions on how to play and start), introduction screens to playing, reward screens and a score board (where applicable).

If you couldn't put your game in an 80's arcade game and not be able to tell it doesn't belong just by the modes it goes through (minus the attract mode or demo mode), then your game is not finished.

© 1980 Namco Ltd., All Rights Reserved.
Courtesy of Namco Holding Corp.

*Figure C-4. Galaga—everything explained at a glance*

There is a big difference between a game that is "bare bones", and a game you have put all the finishing touches on. This difference will be a matter of a couple of days to two weeks (depending on the size of the game). It will get increasingly (sometimes exponentially) more involved as you move from Tetris to Breakout and so on.

The result, though, will be very important, both in terms of your understanding game development, and your own pride in your work and satisfaction/fulfillment. (Accomplishment does wonders for self-esteem!)

It's not easy to show people your game and have to constantly tell them to overlook different things and feel the same as if they picked it up and had no problems moving through it and everything was well presented and complete feeling. Other game developers are a bit more forgiving, since they know the process.

Most importantly though, you will learn all the details that go into really finishing a game. If you stop at just working gameplay, you will still miss out on the details of wrapping things up, which will leave a blank spot in your mind when trying to plan larger projects in the future.

# But, These Games Are Stupid!

Actually, these games clearly show the basis for ALL games' gameplay. Throw a fancy 3D interface over a shooter and it's still a shooter. You could create the same game in a 2D overhead view and the gameplay would be coded exactly the same.

Is it stupid to be able to make a game with EXACTLY the same controls, responses and enemies as Quake? If you remove the 3D interface, and look at what is really happening from a directly overhead view, does it still seem as out of reach?

Even so, this is not a beginning project. There are too many elements that need to be developed and refined for a first project, so I strongly urge you to follow the order of games I suggest to gradually build up your understanding of game development. (When you learned how to swim, did you IMMEDIATELY start out with a high dive into the deep water? NO! You start in the shallow end, you learn to dog paddle, and progress from there.)

© 1998 - 2000 Midway Games West Inc.

*Figure C-5. Gauntlet*

One thing that you need to clarify to yourself before starting anything, is what you want out of it. Do you want to make games, or just duplicate the technology in Quake? If all you are interested in is the technology, then skip all the games stuff and get started on graphics technology.

If you are really interested in making games, then you need to separate your desire to create the next cutting edge, hard core game, and focus on building your ability to do so. The best way to do that is through actually making and (more importantly) *finishing* games, which is what following this path (or a similar one) will give you experience in.

## Be Proud of Your Games!

You don't hear people in college embarrassed about being in college because they don't have a job yet. You are learning, and making even a simple game is hard, especially if you want it done WELL. This is shown clearly by all the people who have NOT made even simple games but talk about it constantly. Once you have finished a game, consider yourself to have more of a track record than anyone who has not finished a game even if their idea sounds phenomenal and like it's up there with the latest cutting edge games. If you can't play it, it's not a game.

When you have a finished product you can show, you need to accept that for what it is, not what it isn't or compare it to people with 5+ years of experience and million dollar budgets who work on games full time.

## I Made My Game, Now Where's My Ferrari?

Sorry, one game, two games, five games probably won't cut it. Last year there were 3,500 games released on the PC, and only a few handfuls made back a large portion of cash. Most of those that did weren't made by small groups who were self-funded, they were funded by large publishers and probably had multi-million dollar budgets, and definitely near or well over million dollar advertising campaigns. This isn't a world you can't join though; it just takes a good deal of time and experience and track record of making quality games, that hopefully sell well, to give publishers confidence in your team, so that they will entrust you with this kind of financial responsibility.

*Figure C-6. Where's my Ferrari?*

However, there is more to making a living of games than the multi-million dollar budgets and I strongly suggest you take a look at the other things as well. There is nothing bad or embarrassing about making budget games; they can be just as or more fun than the high budget commercial games, and it is a lot easier to get publisher to trust you with smaller budgets. On top of that, you don't have to spend *years* working on the same project, and if it doesn't go over well, you don't have to feel as much loss with it.

Just have an understanding of what you really want out of making games and then concentrate on making that come true.

# APPENDIX D

# Guidelines for Developing Successful Games

THE TEXT IN this appendix was first presented by Bruce Shelley as a speech at the United States' Game Developers Conference in 2001, and shows the vision of one of the most successful team of game developers, Ensemble Studios (responsible for the blockbuster Age of the Empires), about some points you must keep in mind when thinking about developing commercial games.

## Guidelines for Developing Successful Games

### Introduction

The title for this presentation includes two words that need defining at the start. I use the word "guidelines" in the sense of suggestions or check boxes, but not as a recipe. I use "successful" here to mean the commercial success of a game: sales and profits.

The goal of this presentation is to suggest policies, methods, and features that can lead to commercial success. The more of these guidelines that you follow or incorporate into your development, the greater the probability of success from the resulting game.

The sources of these guidelines are many, but mostly they come from practical experience. That includes my personal 20 years making and playing games of one sort or another, lengthy discussions with colleagues at Ensemble Studios, discussions with friends in the industry, and discussions with other colleagues in the past, most notably Sid Meier. Many of the thoughts presented here I first heard spelled out in one form or another from him.

Before beginning, I have two caveats. First, the guidelines I present today are applicable mainly to empty map games and strategy games. The emphasis would be different for story-based, linear games. Second, this presentation was made with PC games in mind, although many of the guidelines would be appropriate for console games as well.

## Reach for a Broad Audience

When you set out to develop a PC game, the potential market is everyone on Earth who owns a PC. Once you begin making decisions about your game (gory, sci-fi, RTS, shooter) you begin losing potential customers who are not interested in your topic, genre, or style. Commercially successful games hold on to significant share of that market because they choose a topic, genre, and style that connect with a broad audience. The acceptance of the PC into more world communities, different age groups, and by women means that games do not need to be targeted, and perhaps should not be targeted, solely to the traditional gaming audience of young males.

Games that have been strong traditionally with the hard-core (young male) audience, must remain attractive to that group, but expanding the appeal can bring in the much larger casual audience. In these cases we need the hard core to approve the game and spread word of their approval to the market. This increases awareness within the casual market where the bulk of sales probably reside.

Achieving broad appeal requires that some aspects or game options appeal to the hard core while others, possibly the same or possibly different, appeal to the casual gamer. Know how the game will appeal to the different market segments and why each will like it. This differentiation often requires both single and multi-player game options.

Strive to be the best game in your genre and about your topic. The best games make the bulk of the profits, while the mediocre games suffer.

The rest of this presentation deals with what to do or include in a game in order to entertain a large audience. That usually means creating something that is commercial art, not fine art. The best games entertain by engaging the player's mind, not by providing titillation (which wears off quickly).

## Differentiate and Innovate, Don't Imitate

The majority of the gameplay ideas in any game come from other games. It is natural to be inspired by successful games and practical to borrow from them when creating games of your own. To be successful, however, new games must be clearly differentiated from the competition and innovative as well. Games that imitate without differentiation and innovation are considered clones. Clones are usually commercial failures.

Any new game will have competition in the form of games very like it in topic, style, or genre. To succeed the new game must match or exceed the competition in those areas where their game excels. The new games must also exceed the competition where it is weak. Identify important features and components that the competition is executing poorly or not at all. These are your opportunities. They are the principal ways that your game can be differentiated and distinguished in the market place. Examples of elements in Age of Empires I that were opportunities because few if any of the competing were executing them (or doing them well) include historical theme, organic units, random maps, non-cheating AI, levels of difficulty, multiple victory conditions, historical notes, and stunning animations. Including all of these elements differentiated the Age of Empires games. Executing these elements well helped establish the reputation of Ensemble Studios as masters of the real-time strategy genre. Analyzing the strengths and weaknesses of potential competitors in other genres will reveal where the competition is strong, where it is weak, and where are your opportunities.

## Prototype Early

Prototype all important systems and technologies as a proof of concept as early as possible. Prototyping is very useful from a technology standpoint, but it is critical for testing gameplay. Designers are largely guessing until their games can be played. There are always surprises when a game is first played, and not all are good ones. Prototyping for gameplay testing is especially useful for strategy and other empty map games that do not depend on pre-planned or linear story lines.

## Design by Playing

Once a playable prototype has been created, play every day, make adjustments based on testing, create new versions quickly, and evolve the game through this process. Rely on your instincts as gamers for guidance for what is working and not working. Larger test groups create more valuable testing feedback and create games of wider appeal. Test for both hard-core and casual gameplay. Everyone at Ensemble Studios is asked to test our current projects at least once per week and provide feedback.

The downside of this process is that it is difficult to predict and often costly. It does, however, lead ultimately to creating a fun game.

## Interesting Decisions = Fun

Presenting the player with interesting and well-paced decisions is the rocket science of game design. Players have fun when they are interested in the decisions they are making, when they are kept absorbed by the pacing of the required decisions, and when they feel a sense of reward and accomplishment as good decisions are made. When the required decisions are too often trivial or random, fun sags. You risk boring the player and driving him/her out of the game. The Age of Empires games demonstrated that our customers consider automating trivial activities (queues, waypoints) a positive improvement.

Good pacing can heighten interest in decision making. Real time games have an inherent advantage versus turn-based games because the continual ticking of the game clock adds a sense of desperation. If the player has many reasonable decisions to deal with but time to make only a few, everything being considered becomes much more interesting.

When considering a new feature for a game, apply the interesting decisions test. Is this new element or twist going to add an interesting decision to what the player is doing? If the answer is not a strong "yes," leave it out.

## Provide a Great First 15 Minutes of Easily Accessible Play

A player must be actively engaged by a new game within 15 minutes of starting play or we risk losing that player forever. There are three keys to getting a new player into a game: (1) an interesting starting situation; (2) minimal barriers to entry (interface, back-story); and (3) giving the player only a few decisions to make immediately but growing that number exponentially (this is the inverted pyramid of decision making). Get the player into the game quickly and easily so that he or she is absorbed and having fun without frustration. When done properly, the player gets into the game successfully and significant time may pass before he or she is aware of it.

Games that necessarily require a lot of pre-play work from the player because of special controls, character introductions, or story background must create tutorials or other clever ways to educate the player while providing entertainment. In-game tutorials are the best. Games that require uninteresting pre-play work or retard entry with frustrating interfaces are likely to fail.

## The Player Should Have the Fun, Not the Designer, Programmer, or Computer

Although this principle seems obvious, many games fail because the wrong entity has most of the fun. That can be the designer who allowed feature creep to overrun the product or a designer who did a brilliant analysis and installed an amazing single path to victory that no one else could find. The producer can direct great graphics and cinematics to suck up the budget, making all the artists happy, but leaving little time for inserting actual game play. If a player finds himself waiting too often while the computer grinds through some brilliant calculations, maybe the computer is having more fun than the player is.

Game development should focus on creating entertainment for players by engaging their minds. Everything the team does in development and the machine does in operation is directed toward that goal. All code, game features, art pieces, sound effects, music scores, and computer operations should enhance entertainment. An exception to this rule may be elements included for marketing considerations, such as opening cinematics.

Two additional points to keep in mind:

1. The player should be the hero or heroine.

2. In single play, the player should sweat but win in the end.

## Create Epic Games That Can Launch/Extend a Franchise

The greater the newness of a game (genre, topic, artistic style, technology, developer, publisher) the more difficult it is to get shelf space, media coverage, a web following, and customer awareness, all of which relate directly to commercial success. Creating a great franchise makes those tasks much easier and makes it possible to increase the customer base for each succeeding product. Choose genres and topics that can capture the imagination of the market and the media, and thereby establish a new epic series of forthcoming related games. Publishers want franchises and are more willing to invest in them.

## Set Production Values High

While great gameplay is the key to creating great games, graphics, sound effects, and music have very important supporting roles. Graphics and sound effects are key elements in the game interface. Graphics must be attractive, enticing, and inspire inquisitiveness. Graphics and sound effects should convey information quickly with minimum player effort. Acting together, these three elements set the mood of the game and help the player forget that he or she is playing a game. Graphics and sound have important ancillary roles in helping to market the game.

High production values for graphics, sound effects, and music enhance the player's experience and contribute to the game's overall cachet of quality. Low quality elements among others of high quality stand out like off-key notes, greatly diminishing the overall impact of the product. A high standard of quality in production values enhances the reputation of the game, the developer, and the publisher.

## Interface Goals: Intuitive, Easy to Use, and Minimize Frustration

The interface often gets treated as an afterthought because it rarely has the ability to create a sensation for the player as gameplay features, graphics, sound effects, and music can do. No one gets excited about how a game drops down menus or presents buttons. While the interface has little chance to dramatically enhance a game, there is a great risk, however, that poor interface design can do real harm. Keep in mind that capturing the player's imagination with great gameplay, visuals, and sound is only part of the battle. Giving the player access to all of these cool things easily without frustration is the other half. A confusing, difficult, and frustrating interface can ruin a game. Players encountering these problems in their first play session may easily lose interest and give up.

Minimize the layers of an interface (menus within menus) and control options (being able to play the Age of Empires games using only a mouse is a good thing). Provide an interesting and absorbing tutorial when learning controls and operations can be daunting, or if the player must learn quite a bit before beginning play.

## Provide Multiple Gaming Experiences Within the Box

To help reach a broad audience, include a variety of game types and adjustable game parameters that combine in different ways to create a range of quite different gaming experiences, all within the same game. Examples of different gaming experiences with the Age of Empires games are multiplayer death matches, single player campaigns, random map games, cooperative play games, king of the hill games, and wonder races. Victory conditions, map types, and level of difficulty settings are examples of parameters that can be adjusted to create different gaming experiences. Multiple options in each dimension (variable parameter) create a volume of different game types.

We want the smartest kid in junior high school (a hard-core gamer) telling his or her friends that our game is his or her favorite right now. When those friends buy our game, they probably won't be able to complete with the star, but by adjusting those parameters they can still find a type of game that suits them and have fun. The average kids and the smart kids can both enjoy our game, although they play quite different parts of it.

When we provide a variety of gaming experiences within the single box, we increase the number of people who can buy our game and be happy with it. Each of these successful customers becomes in turn a potential evangelist.

## Player Investments

Some of the most successful games ever require the player to invest in the experience of play by building empires, character statistics, or city infrastructures. Players enjoy creating things within a game, taking possession of their creations, molding them to their personal taste, and using them to further their game goals. Examples of games requiring player investment include Sim City (city infrastructure), Diablo (character statistics), and Age of Kings (empire and technology). Building, defending, and using in-game investments create a strong bond between the player and the game.

## Facilitate Consumer Content

Player's enjoy creating additional content for their favorite games, whether it is new planes for Flight Simulator, skins for their favorite shooter, or scenarios for Age of Kings. They get a chance to be a game designer, make the game/add-on they want but that does not exist, and see their own work running on-screen. Players get a chance to be game designers. Consumer content lengthens the working life of a game and helps increase awareness of it in the marketplace.

## Replayability

It is better to create a game that can be played over and over, rather than one that is usually played only once. Providing replayability increases consumer satisfaction and the perceived value of the game. The AOE games provide replayability through randomly generated worlds, variety of maps, variety of game types, and multiple civilizations to be played.

## Story

The story of a game (or narrative or plot) is the experience of playing it through the series of events that extend from start to completion (victory condition). A great game story keeps the player engaged, intrigued and playing, increasing satisfaction. The story a game tells depends on the topic and victory condition, plus the hurdles the player must overcome to reach victory (completion). A great story uses plot twists, reversal of fortune, and other ploys to keep the player interested. Adventure games require the designer write the story and the player act it out. RTS games usually provide no story, but instead an empty map, like an empty page, on which the players write the story themselves as they play.

## Quality vs. Budget and Schedule

An extraordinary game that ships late makes its money in the long run, and has positive effects on customer satisfaction, the franchise, and developer/publisher reputations. A mediocre game that ships on time is a disaster (financial, brand, reputation).

Game development is more an art than a science, and therefore difficult to predict. Developers must demonstrate that a project is making good progress toward a goal. Publishers must assess that progress. There is no reasonable justification for major compromises in the quality of a product. Make a great game or kill it early. One of the values of early prototyping is that it can reveal that a game is not going to work early in the process.

## Gameplay vs. Realism or History

We are in the entertainment business, not simulation or education. Our priority is to create fun, engaging gameplay. Realism and historical information are resources or props we use to add interest, story, and character to the problems we are posing for the player. That is not to say that realism and historic fact have no importance. They are just not the highest priority. Any education that follows from playing our games is a very positive, though secondary, benefit. This is a great marketing point and adds to the reputation of the developer and publisher.

## Polish the Game

Budget time at the end of a project to polish the game, bring all elements to a high production value standard, and add the little touches. Test rigorously to insure balance (where appropriate), to insure there is no single optimal winning strategy (or unit, or spell, etc.), and to eliminate any potentially fatal gameplay flaws. When the game reaches the customer, we want them to feel that every aspect of the game was well planned and executed. Polish tells our customers that we took the time and made the effort to craft an extraordinary product.

Polishing a game increases customer satisfaction, enhances the reputation of the developer and publisher, and builds fan loyalty. Lack of polish has a negative effect in all of these areas, working against the goals of everyone involved in development. There is no acceptable excuse for not polishing a game. If you cannot afford to polish, you are in the wrong business or your team was inadequate (too small or unskilled). Nearly done is not an acceptable standard for going gold.

# Index

# W

WAV files, 234
Web sites
 artificial intelligence resources, 79
 DirectPlay for Pocket PC, 580
 DirectX, 143
 FiringSquad, 595
 game communities and, 488
 GameDev.Net, 611
 GotDotNet, 484
 Lupine Games, 617
 Speech SDK, 435
 USPTO, 619
Who Wants To Be A Millionaire? games, 600,
 607, 608, 609
winding fill mode, 555–56
window area, 555
windowed mode, 167, 168, 177–85
windows
 creating Graphics objects from handles for,
 6
 Direct3D main, 170–77
 DirectX and, 149–50 (*see also* DirectX)
 forms and, 109
 game field (*see* game fields)
 main, 97, 168 (*see also* main windows)
 nonrectangular, 553–56
 redrawing, 66
 server configuration, 503–4
 test, for NetworkGame class, 516–19
Windows
 GDI+, 1–4
 logo key, 303
 Windows CE and mobile devices, 576–77,
 580–81
WithEvents keyword, 319
women, 628
world, constant, 484–85
world matrix transformation, 257
wrapper classes, 556
write-only properties, 126
writing text to screens, 292–95, 337–39

# X

X8R8G8B8 format, 150
XML files, ADO.NET, 356
X1R5G5B5 format, 150
X-Wing versus Tie Fighter game, 479

# Z

z axis, 153
zoning
 with arrays of bits, 20–21, 54–56
 with bits, 18–20
 collision detection and, 17

# About Apress

Apress, located in Berkeley, CA, is a fast-growing, innovative publishing company devoted to meeting the needs of existing and potential programming professionals. Simply put, the "A" in Apress stands for *The Author's Press™*. Apress' unique approach to publishing grew out of conversations between its founders, Gary Cornell and Dan Appleman, authors of numerous best-selling, highly regarded books for programming professionals. In 1998 they set out to create a publishing company that emphasized quality above all else. Gary and Dan's vision has resulted in the publication of over 70 titles by leading software professionals, all of which have *The Expert's Voice™*.

# Do You Have What It Takes to Write for Apress?

Apress is rapidly expanding its publishing program. If you can write and you refuse to compromise on the quality of your work, if you believe in doing more than rehashing existing documentation, and if you're looking for opportunities and rewards that go far beyond those offered by traditional publishing houses, we want to hear from you!

Consider these innovations that we offer all of our authors:

- **Top royalties with *no* hidden switch statements**
  Authors typically receive only half of their normal royalty rate on foreign sales. In contrast, Apress' royalty rate remains the same for both foreign and domestic sales.

- **Sharing the wealth**
  Most publishers keep authors on the same pay scale even after costs have been met. At Apress author royalties dramatically increase the more books are sold.

- **Serious treatment of the technical review process**
  Each Apress book is reviewed by a technical expert(s) whose remuneration depends in part on the success of the book since he or she too receives royalties.

Moreover, through a partnership with Springer-Verlag, New York, Inc., one of the world's major publishing houses, Apress has significant venture capital and distribution power behind it. Thus, we have the resources to produce the highest quality books *and* market them aggressively.

If you fit the model of the Apress author who can write a book that provides *What The Professional Needs To Know™*, then please contact us for more information:

editorial@apress.com

apress™

# License Agreement (Single-User Products)

THIS IS A LEGAL AGREEMENT BETWEEN YOU, THE END USER, AND APRESS. BY OPENING THE SEALED DISK PACKAGE, YOU ARE AGREEING TO BE BOUND BY THE TERMS OF THIS AGREEMENT. IF YOU DO NOT AGREE TO THE TERMS OF THIS AGREEMENT, PROMPTLY RETURN THE UNOPENED DISK PACKAGE AND THE ACCOMPANYING ITEMS (INCLUDING WRITTEN MATERIALS AND BINDERS AND OTHER CONTAINERS) TO THE PLACE YOU OBTAINED THEM FOR A FULL REFUND.

## *APRESS SOFTWARE LICENSE*

1.  GRANT OF LICENSE. Apress grants you the right to use one copy of this enclosed Apress software program (the "SOFTWARE") on a single terminal connected to a single computer (e.g., with a single CPU). You may not network the SOFTWARE or otherwise use it on more than one computer or computer terminal at the same time.

2.  COPYRIGHTS. The SOFTWARE copyright is owned by Apress, with portions owned by Microsoft Corporation, and is protected by United States copyright laws and international treaty provisions. The SOFTWARE contains a licensed software program, the use of which is governed by an English language break-the-seal end user license agreement inside the licensed software program. You must treat the SOFTWARE like any other copyrighted material (e.g., a book or musical recording) except that you may either (a) make one copy of the SOFTWARE solely for backup or archival purposes, or (b) transfer the SOFTWARE to a single hard disk, provided you keep the original solely for backup or archival purposes. You may not copy the written material accompanying the SOFTWARE.

3.  OTHER RESTRICTIONS. You may not rent or lease the SOFTWARE, but you may transfer the SOFTWARE and accompanying written materials on a permanent basis provided you retain no copies and the recipient agrees to the terms of this Agreement. You may not reverse engineer, decompile, or disassemble the SOFTWARE. If SOFTWARE is an update, any transfer must include the update and all prior versions. Distributors, dealers, or other resellers are prohibited from altering or opening the licensed SOFTWARE package.

4.  By breaking the seal on the disc package, you agree to the terms and conditions printed in the Apress License Agreement. If you do not agree with the terms, simply return this book with the still-sealed CD package to the place of purchase for a refund.

## DISCLAIMER OF WARRANTY

NO WARRANTIES. Apress disclaims all warranties, either express or implied, including, but not limited to, implied warranties of merchantability and fitness for a particular purpose, with respect to the SOFTWARE and the accompanying written materials. The software and any related documentation is provided "as is." You may have other rights, which vary from state to state.

NO LIABILITIES FOR CONSEQUENTIAL DAMAGES. In no event shall be liable for any damages whatsoever (including, without limitation, damages from loss of business profits, business interruption, loss of business information, or other pecuniary loss) arising out of the use or inability to use this Apress product, even if Apress has been advised of the possibility of such damages. Because some states do not allow the exclusion or limitation of liability for consequential or incidental damages, the above limitation may not apply to you.

## U.S. GOVERNMENT RESTRICTED RIGHTS

The SOFTWARE and documentation are provided with RESTRICTED RIGHTS. Use, duplication, or disclosure by the Government is subject to restriction as set forth in subparagraph (c) (1) (ii) of The Rights in Technical Data and Computer Software clause at 52.227-7013. Contractor/manufacturer is Apress, 2560 Ninth Street, Suite 219, Berkeley, California, 94710.

This Agreement is governed by the laws of the State of California. Should you have any questions concerning this Agreement, or if you wish to contact Apress for any reason, please write to Apress, 2560 Ninth Street, Suite 219, Berkeley, California, 94710.